TURNING POINT
1968

BOOKS BY IRWIN UNGER

The Vulnerable Years: The United States, 1896–1917
The Movement: A History of the American New Left
The Greenback Era

TURNING POINT
1968

Irwin Unger and Debi Unger

CHARLES SCRIBNER'S SONS · NEW YORK

To our friends
Dolores and Bob, Sandy and David,
Olive and Ari, Trina and Jerry.
With affection.

Copyright © 1988 by Irwin Unger and Debi Unger

All rights reserved. No part of this book may be reproduced or
transmitted in any form or by any means, electronic or mechanical,
including photocopying, recording, or by an information storage and
retrieval system, without permission in writing from the Publisher.

Charles Scribner's Sons
Macmillan Publishing Company
866 Third Avenue, New York, NY 10022
Collier Macmillan Canada, Inc.

Library of Congress Cataloging-in-Publication Data
Unger, Irwin.
  Turning point: 1968.
  Bibliography: p.
  Includes index.
  1. United States—History—1961–1969. 2. United
States—Social conditions—1960–1980. I. Unger, Debi.
II. Title.
E846.U53 1988   973.923   88-6447
  ISBN 0-684-18696-9

Macmillan books are available at special discounts for bulk purchases for sales
promotions, premiums, fund-raising, or educational use. For details, contact:
Special Sales Director
Macmillan Publishing Company
866 Third Avenue
New York, NY 10022

10 9 8 7 6 5 4 3 2 1

Designed by Jack Meserole

PRINTED IN THE UNITED STATES OF AMERICA

Contents

Acknowledgments

Like all authors we are indebted to many people and institutions. Our knowledge of 1968 gained immeasurably from research on the American New Left that took us to many libraries around the country. We invariably were treated with kindness and would especially like to thank for their help the staffs at the State Historical Society of Wisconsin, the Bancroft Library of the University of California at Berkeley, the library of the Hoover Institution at Stanford University, the Labadie Library at the University of Michigan, the Kent State University Library, the New York Public Library, the Peace Collection at Swarthmore College, the Lyndon Baines Johnson Library at Austin, the Library of Congress, and the Elmer Bobst Library at New York University, especially its Tamiment division.

Some of these gracious people, and others, deserve individual mention. We would particularly like to thank Dorothy Swanson of the Bobst Library's Tamiment division; we are also grateful to Demetrios James Mihailidis of the Elmer Bobst newspaper and periodicals division. At the Asbury Park Public Library, adjacent to our summer base, we always found Suzanne York and Ruth Bell sources of helpful advice and information. Rose Ehrlich of the Mercantile Library in Manhattan was generous with her time.

These days authors rely on the services of people with skills in the visual fields. We appreciate the photocopying help of Bill Marbit of Readers. Ted Slate of *Newsweek* went to considerable trouble to procure prints for us from the magazine; Scott Jahn of Bettmann Archive and Ann Schneider of Archives also helped us in selecting pictures.

Authors require aid in still other ways. We wish to thank our editors Laurie Schieffelin and Robert Stewart at Scribners for their advice and suggestions. Erika Goldman helped guide the book speedily through the production process. Linda Horkitz was the efficient and careful copyeditor; Tony Davis handled production editing.

We are also grateful to friends and colleagues for encouragement and advice. Gerry McCauley was not only our agent, but also a friend in need. Professor Robert Sobel of Hofstra University made several key suggestions for chapter one; Professor David Burner of SUNY at Stony Brook read the whole manuscript carefully and applied to it his knowledge of recent American history and his unusual editorial skills. Professor Paul Goodman of the University of California at Davis offered us generous hospitality when we were on the West Coast and often discussed with us, at times with passion, some of the issues considered in *Turning Point*. None of these scholars, friends, or librarians should be held responsible for our opinions. Indeed, several emphatically demurred from them. Yet even when we disagreed we always learned and they have our gratitude.

NOTE TO READERS

The quotations footnoted in the text that follows are, with few exceptions, the actual words of contemporaries, rather than those of the authors of the works cited.

Prologue

NINETEEN SIXTY-SEVEN had not been a good year. The college quadrangles had reverberated with the clamor of angry, rebellious students. In the squalid Casbahs of the festering cities, young blacks had burned, smashed, grabbed, and hurled provocation at Whitey. Abroad, ninety-four hundred American young men had died in the rice paddies and jungles of Vietnam. The nation's political life was in disarray, with the majority party, the mighty Democrats, in full-tilt revolt against their own president. As the professional pundits considered the old year from the perspective of late December, they agreed that it had not been one of the nation's choicest. "Nineteen sixty-seven had a bad press," wrote James Reston of *The New York Times*, "and even the obit writers weren't sorry to see it go."[1]

The soothsayers who flourish each December expected little better in the year ahead. Dr. Thomas Tomlinson of the Office of Economic Opportunity predicted another round of ghetto riots during the summer. Nothing foreseeable could prevent recurrences "until the well of available cities runs dry."[2] *Newsweek* columnist Kenneth Crawford saw the twelve months ahead as "a vintage year for wormwood and gall." "If our institutions and basic freedoms come through . . . intact . . . there will be cause for self-congratulation."[3]

Nineteen sixty-eight would be even more calamitous than the pessimists anticipated. Even the sedate *New York Times* could not avoid full eight-column headlines twenty times during the year.

The headlines came in clusters. The first were on April 1 and 2 following President Lyndon Johnson's surprise announcement that he would not run for reelection in the fall. The second came a day or two later when a demented bigot, probably in the pay of right-wing fanatics, shot Dr. Martin Luther King, Jr., and set off a chain of riots in a hundred black ghettos around the country. June brought the third batch, when an Arab nationalist killed Senator Robert Kennedy following his victory in the California Democratic presidential primary.

It was an explosive year. Of the remaining dozen or more eight-column *Times* headlines, only a handful—two concerning the space program and several announcing the fall presidential election results—failed to proclaim some extraordinary individual or collective act of violence.

But the edge-to-edge *Times* banners did not do justice to the powerful jolts the nation experienced in that unquiet year. Many of the most disturbing events unfolded in installments that individually did not rate such sensational headline attention. The January *Times* carried lead stories on draft-card burning and the indictments of Dr. Benjamin Spock and the Reverend William Sloane Coffin on the charge of conspiracy to encourage draft evasion. On January 31 through February 3 the North Vietnamese–Vietcong Tet offensive against the Americans and South Vietnamese preempted much of the paper's front-page space. March brought news of maneuvering between Robert Kennedy and Eugene McCarthy for leadership of the antiwar, dump-Johnson movement. The spring, as usual, was the season of student discontent. In April Students for a Democratic Society (SDS) shut down Columbia University, while abroad their German equivalents went on a two-week rampage in the Federal Republic. May brought the student explosion at Nanterre and the Sorbonne in France that almost brought the Fourth Republic to its knees. The August "police riot" at the Chicago Democratic convention seemed to confirm every apocalyptic warning of left and right alike about the direction of the American Republic. And so it went: in 1968 the Western world, as Americans had experienced it for almost a quarter of a century, seemed on the verge of disintegration.

It was more than a matter of events. Behind the violent and disruptive deeds were fierce, divisive words. This was the year when Eldridge Cleaver, the Black Panther "minister of information," told a white reporter: "America will be painted red. Dead bodies will litter the streets. . . ."[4] It was also the year when George Wallace, the segregationist former governor of Alabama, announced that when he became president he would run over any antiwar demonstrator who lay down in front of his car. Just a few months earlier, author Susan Sontag had called "the white race . . . the cancer of human history."[5]

Yet it was not just ferocious and tumultuous; it was also a year that changed America. In that twelve-month span the country pivoted. Old forces and currents lost their forward momentum and began to reverse; new ones appeared. Nineteen sixty-eight was a turning point that marked the beginning of our own dubious age of privatism and social confusion.

It was the year that the liberal consensus of the early sixties fell apart and was replaced by rancorous resistance to further social change.

In 1964 Lyndon Johnson had won election as president in his own right by the largest popular majority in American history against a candidate who threatened to subvert the new, liberal postwar social and political order. His victory coincided with an economic boom of unprecedented proportions. What followed was the Great Society, a campaign to disseminate the benefits of postwar affluence and upgrade the quality of American life.

For almost three years following the 1964 election, the Johnson coalition of old-line New Deal Democrats, civil rights advocates, and liberal intellectuals succeeded in writing into law more social legislation than at any time in our history. Then, in 1968, the economic skies darkened. America, the Free World's economic pacesetter for a generation, began to falter. Under the powerful strains of changes that it had itself helped to midwife, the liberal coalition fell apart. Reform stopped.

Almost every part of the coalition disarticulated in that

calamitous year. Polarization became the order of the day. In the civil rights movement, Black Power had already driven whites from the Student Nonviolent Coordinating Committee and the Congress of Racial Equality, two of the cutting-edge forces of the civil rights drive. In 1968 black separatism would further cleave the liberal coalition by driving a wedge in New York between Jews and blacks, former close allies in the movement to end discrimination.

Black Power would also shatter the fragile alliances that held the black civil rights forces themselves together. Roy Wilkins of the National Association for the Advancement of Colored People would denounce it; so would Whitney Young of the National Urban League. Martin Luther King would seek to contain it by moving to the left. In December 1967 King would announce that the Southern Christian Leadership Conference was planning a Poor People's Campaign, a massive and prolonged civil disobedience demonstration in Washington for the spring and summer, to call attention to job and housing discrimination and income inequality. King did not live to see his plans fulfilled. He was shot in April, and in the riots that followed forty-six people died—all but five black—and a hundred cities went up in flame. Twenty-one thousand federal troops and thirty-four thousand national guardsmen would have to be called in to quell the violence.

Under the leadership of King's lieutenant, the Reverend Ralph Abernathy, the Poor People's Campaign set out in April by mule train for Washington to dramatize the plight of the ghetto poor. The campaign was a dismal failure. Heavy rains inundated the camp site and drenched spirits as well as clothes and bodies. Some of the residents were black street youths who attacked reporters, stole property, and staged wild, all-night parties. The number of protesters soon declined to five hundred, and after their permit expired in June almost all drifted away. The Southern Christian Leadership Conference, King's creation and chief vehicle, was now virtually dead. The typical black leader of the next few years would be a rifle-carrying black revolutionist shooting it out with the police or an angry black spokesman disrupting white church services on Sunday demanding "reparations" for three hundred years of black oppression. A tiny minority of what journalist Tom Wolfe would call the "radical chic" would support the Panthers and the militants, but many liberal Americans would conclude that there was little if anything that they could do about satisfying the *enragés*.

Nineteen sixty-eight would also witness the collapse of the Democratic hegemony that had prevailed since the 1930s. The right of the party, the white South and the Northern backlash, would be carried off by Governor George Wallace of Alabama, the apostle of "never" in the racial realm. The "New Politics" left, comprising men and women disgusted with the war and determined to continue and expand the Great Society, would rally around Eugene McCarthy and Robert Kennedy. Its chances of victory would be cruelly thwarted by Kennedy's assassination.

Party division would produce humiliating defeat in the fall. In March Lyndon Johnson, anticipating repudiation in the primaries and hoping to expedite Vietnam peace talks, would unexpectedly renounce a full second term. With Kennedy's death and Johnson's withdrawal the nomination of Vice-President Hubert Humphrey at Chicago in August became a foregone conclusion.

But then all the furies of the sixties' insurgency descended on the Democrats at Chicago and helped guarantee victory for Richard Nixon in the fall. The peace movement, the "counterculture," the New Politics forces, the New Left, challenged and provoked Mayor Daley's forces of law and order. The raging antagonists turned the week of the convention into a nightmare vision of apocalypse. Outside the Hilton, the major convention hotel, police and demonstrators stoned, gassed, and beat one another, while horrified bystanders, reporters, and hotel guests looked on. Thousands of angry voters remembered the lurid scenes in November and got even by voting Republican.

In 1968 division—and excess—began the quick demise of the New Left. The founding generation of Students for a Democratic Society, the key organization of the sixties' New Left, were the children of middle-class white America, young men and women for whom society's failings no longer seemed primarily want or poverty but alienation, repression, coercion, powerlessness.

In 1968 the founders and their immediate successors were

thrown on the defensive by a band of invaders allied with the Red Chinese Progressive Labor party. Already impatient of "participatory democracy" and certain their society was hopelessly depraved and unsalvageable without revolution, the young men and women began to use Marxist–Leninist jargon—"class analysis," "imperialism," "vanguard party"—and read Mao Tse-tung, Che Guevara, and Frantz Fanon. They soon lost interest in "relevant" courses or Dow Chemical recruiters or university "war complicity." The real issue was the survival of the benighted capitalist world.

In December 1968, at Ann Arbor, the mainstream leaders surrendered SDS's founding vision and embraced the Marxist "labor metaphysic." A year later, calling themselves the Weathermen, they would close the SDS Chicago office and go underground to plant bombs.

Change did not all go in one direction. It was not all breakup, disruption, collapse, defeat. There were also victories and even new beginnings.

Nineteen sixty-eight was the year when men and women who rejected patriarchy, instinctual prudence, heterosexual exclusiveness, and traditional gender roles came to the surface. Such people had long lived defensively within the social interstices of America. In 1968 they loudly and proudly announced their presence and declared that they intended to be heard in the public realm.

The peak year of the counterculture, as the instinctual rebels were called, was 1967 when Haight-Ashbury in San Francisco and the East Village in New York abruptly blossomed as psychedelic oases where young people could indulge their liberated preferences with a minimum of hassle. The 1967 Summer of Love ended with cosmic letdown followed by ugly incidents of murder and mass flight.

But the exodus from the hippie ghettos only scattered the counterculture seed. During 1968 hippies descended in clouds on the cool, foggy mountains of northern California to create rural communes; they popped up in the New Mexico and Arizona desert where they established "tribes" in imitation of the Native American peoples; they fled to the Vermont mountains, long considered the East's own Arcadia; they alighted on low-rent city neighborhoods and even suburbs.

Nineteen sixty-eight was the year when a new brand of militant feminism, "women's liberation," became an assertive movement.

The liberationists sprang from soil prepared by the new feminism of mid-decade whose apostle was Betty Friedan. Friedan's 1963 book, *The Feminine Mystique,* undermined the fifties' cult of child-centered female domesticity and had led to the formation of the National Organization of Women (NOW) in 1966.

NOW was the NAACP of feminism—liberal, ameliorative, and middle-class. The new liberationist movement, the precipitate of male-female resentments within the New Left, placed the plight of women in the center of the historical stage. The exploitation and domination of one-half of the human race by the other, liberationists said, was the prototype and ultimate source of all oppression. Men were the enemy, whether white or black, worker or capitalist, left or right. Unless destroyed, "patriarchy" would survive capitalism and women would continue to be oppressed.

In September 1968 a group called New York Radical Women burst into the public's consciousness by disrupting the Miss America Contest at Atlantic City. The intellectual and ideological content of the demonstration was lost, and the public absorbed instead an impression of sour-faced, unfeminine "bra-burners." Here was yet another atrocity to raise the hackles of traditional Americans and make them wonder if the nation was not irredeemable. But here too was a momentous repositioning of men and women in the eternal battle of the sexes. The effects would last far beyond the sixties.

In nineteen sixty-eight the Vietnam War peaked and began its slow demise. As the year began, the undeclared war was already three years old, and for months administration officials and the military had been proclaiming victory imminent. Then, on January 30, at the feast of Tet, the Lunar New Year, the Vietcong Communist guerrillas struck all the major South Vietnamese cities in a series of attacks that caught the Americans by surprise. The enemy took ferocious losses and were beaten back, but the Tet offensive destroyed the illusion of impending victory and heartened the peace forces.

In February General William C. Westmoreland asked for an additional 206,000 troops for Vietnam, a request that set off a major debate within the Johnson administration. The outcome was a pivotal decision by the "Wise Men," the foreign policy elite who had constructed the postwar anti-Soviet containment policy, to stop the escalation and gradually to shift the burden of the fighting and dying to the South Vietnamese themselves. Days later, Lyndon Johnson, faced by serious challenges to his leadership by the antiwar groups in his own party and determined to start fruitful peace talks with the North Vietnamese, renounced a second full term for president in the same speech in which he announced a bombing halt in Vietnam and a new peace initiative. The war would last for five more years, but with each passing month the number of Americans risking their lives in the jungles and the swamps of Vietnam would decline.

Nineteen sixty-eight was the year liberalism destroyed itself; but viewed another way, it is also the year when traditional America began the long reconquest that culminated in the election of Ronald Reagan.

The political ground was prepared by a path-breaking new theory authored by a Republican congressional aide, Kevin Price Phillips, a twenty-eight-year-old Harvard Law School graduate from New York's multiethnic, blue-collar Bronx. Phillips believed that two great social forces were changing the country in ways that would inevitably end the reign of liberalism: movement out of the northeast quarter to what he called the Sunbelt; and movement out of the central cities to the suburbs. Both these migrations would weaken the Democrats and strengthen the Republicans. But the Republican gain was only potential. The party had to harvest the ripe ears by recognizing the resentments these refugees carried with them: against the chic liberals of the silk-stocking inner-city districts and the acre-plot suburbs who allied themselves with the underclass against the solid working people; against the big government that zapped their paychecks with high taxes; against the scabrous long-haired freaks who mocked decent values; against the flag- and draft card–burners who hated America; against the arrogant radical students who were ungrateful for their advantages; against the black rioters and looters who were destroying the cities. If the Republican party sent these people the message that it would hold the wreckers and knockers and mockers in line, then it could become the party of the "emerging majority."

Phillips's analysis would suffuse the presidential campaign of Richard Nixon. Yet Nixon's nomination at the 1968 Republican convention in Miami was not a victory for the most conservative wing of the party represented by Ronald Reagan, the governor of California. The Goldwater debacle of 1964 was too recent for that. Nixon stood in the party's center where he could capture the backlash voters without frightening the party's moderates or the centrist independents as the Arizona senator had done four years before. But Nixon knew that his fate depended on an arrangement with the conservative white South, and he clinched the nomination by an understanding with southern Republicans that he would respect their views on race, social disorder, the collapse of morals, and preserving America's military strength. The "southern strategy" marked the end of a century of a Democratic "solid South."

Despite the new backlash currents, despite the resentment of Chicago, Nixon only squeaked through. In the end the Wallace campaign faltered and the liberals were able to regroup behind Humphrey to narrow Nixon's daunting early lead in the polls. On November 5 Humphrey fell only five hundred thousand popular votes behind the winner and received two-thirds as many votes in the electoral college. Yet these results are misleading. Nixon and Wallace together won almost 57 percent of the total popular vote. The outcome, says political reporter and historian Theodore White, was in fact "a landslide," an emphatic repudiation of the Johnson administration, a telling plebiscite against the whole liberal thrust of the early and middle sixties.[6] Twenty-eight percent of the Democrats who had endorsed LBJ in 1964 abandoned his party and his ideology four years later.

Nothing else during the year serves as such an obvious symbol for the decade's climacteric as the Nixon–Agnew victory. Yet as we have noted, there were other signs and portents: the abandonment by SDS of its student focus, foreshadowing the organization's breakup; the exhaustion of the rage and energies that lay behind the ghetto riots and the end of the annual "long, hot summers"; the collapse of the civil rights movement after the death of Martin Luther King; the decline of hippiedom following the dispersion from Haight-Ashbury and the East Village; and the degrading of the counterculture into commercial freak-chic. In many cases the currents of the decade still had some months to play themselves out. In one or two cases—the new feminism, for example—the year was a starting point, not a conclusion. But if any single year can be called a historical pivot, it was 1968.

What followed was a dozen years of uncertainty and drift. But the drift was rightward—with a four-year false political detour under President Jimmy Carter owing to the accident of Watergate. In 1980, with the election of Ronald Reagan, the uncertainty ended. Those forces that had begun to rally in 1968 were finally in the saddle. Here was the true culmination of that momentous year, 1968.

1

The Poor Are Always with You

As USUAL Lyndon and Lady Bird Johnson spent the Christmas holidays at the LBJ Ranch in the Texas hill country near Austin. There the president could relax—take off his business suit and low shoes and put on Texas gear: tooled-leather boots, open-necked khaki shirt, five-gallon hat. He could also squeeze in some deer hunting or rock climbing and visit with friends and hill country relatives. Lyndon Johnson was land proud and often conducted guided tours of his four hundred acres on the banks of the Padernales. Visitors would find themselves hurtling along the back roads of the ranch at sixty miles an hour with the president of the United States at the wheel of his cream-colored Lincoln pointing out his improvements and the beauties of the countryside.

The last day of 1967 was a Sunday, and the Johnsons attended Roman Catholic mass at St. Francis Xavier Church near Stonewall. The president had visited the Vatican during his recent trip around the world, and he brought Pastor Winibald Schneider a message from the pope. As Johnson left, Father Schneider thanked him for coming and for conveying the Holy Father's greeting.

Johnson usually managed to squeeze in some business during the holidays. The 1967 Christmas–New Year's season was especially busy. All through the week officials had shuttled down from Washington, their four-engined Jetstars landing on the ranch runway and roaring up close to the two-story white frame house. The most important visitor was Treasury Secretary Henry Fowler, who arrived with his staff on December 27 after a stopover in Little Rock to lunch with Wilbur Mills, the powerful head of the House Ways and Means Committee. The secretary and his aides spent long hours at the ranch with the president conferring about the boiling international monetary crisis.

On New Year's Day Johnson held a press conference for a half dozen reporters from the major dailies, the press services, and the TV networks. He had an important announcement. He would ask for sweeping changes in U.S. economic relations with other nations, he said. The United States was running a serious deficit in its balance of international payments, and the Treasury's gold supply was under siege. He would recommend a ceiling on American corporate investments abroad and ask for restrictions on how much U.S. tourists could spend in their travels; fewer American civilians would be allowed to work at American bases overseas, and American military outlays in North Atlantic Treaty Organization countries would be reined in.

This was important news. Since the end of World War II goods, capital, and people had moved freely across national boundaries as never before. The open economic frontiers had sparked extraordinary economic growth. By 1967 the whole Western world had reached a level of affluence and stability beyond anyone's dreams. But the world's greatest wealth-producing engine, the gargantuan American economy, was beginning to overheat. By year's end the postwar monetary system, the rails on which the engine had moved, would begin to wobble. Before the new year was out the sense of well-being that had been built up over two decades would falter and with it would go the domestic fruit of postwar prosperity, the Great Society.

Prosperity had been the centerpiece of American life during the entire post–World War II era. There had been a brief downturn in 1945–47 while factories converted from arms to civilian goods and millions of servicemen returned to offices and production lines. The massive expenditures for guns, planes, ships, and tanks to fight the "police action" in Korea had ended another slump in 1949. Another recession came in 1954 and still another in 1959. Yet in the two decades that followed World War II, each year saw higher output and incomes; only in 1954 did gross national product actually drop and then by barely 1 percent. And growth was not achieved at the cost of price stability. Price rises between 1947 and 1967 had averaged only 2 percent a year. Fast growth and low inflation! Truly it was a marvelous time. As the economist Martin Feldstein would write: "The first two decades of the postwar period were a time of unsurpassed economic prosperity, stability, and optimism."[1]

Good times, like other successes, claim many fathers. One was the simple rebound from the Great Depression and wartime austerity. During the immediate postwar period consumers took war bonds and cash out of their safe-deposit boxes and bought the cars, the houses, and the appliances that they had done without, many for ten years or more, since the 1929 stock-market crash. For millions of returning veterans peace meant marrying, settling down, and incurring the expenses of new households: homes, furniture, linens, cribs. For others it meant outlays for books and tuition subsidized by the GI Bill. Postwar private spending provided a powerful lift for the economy that offset the decline of government outlays for war.

American postwar prosperity was also fueled by world devastation. Only the United States, among the industrial powers, had increased its output during the war. In 1945, and for a decade after, it alone could provide the grain, the cotton, the steel, the machinery that could keep Europeans and Asians alive and help them restore their shattered cities and factories, worn-out railroads and highways, wrecked power stations. After 1945 a mighty flood of goods made and grown in America poured across the oceans to help rebuild war-ravaged economies and lives.

But revived world trade was as much the result of conscious planning as war devastation and other impersonal forces. In 1944, at Bretton Woods, New Hampshire, in the closing months of the Axis collapse, the allied nations had laid the foundation for the new postwar economic order. The countries meeting at the stately White Mountain resort established the International Bank for Reconstruction and Development to help postwar rebuilding, and created the International Monetary Fund (IMF) to place the world economy on a new basis.

Forty-four countries sent representatives to the Bretton Woods Conference, but only two really counted: Britain, long the leader in international finance; and the United States, the new Western superpower. The chief American representative was Harry Dexter White, a senior Treasury official later to be accused of Communist sympathies; the British delegation was led by John Maynard Keynes, Britain's most distinguished economist and the father of a modern revolution in economic thought. Both men were determined to prevent a return to the policies of economic self-sufficiency and beggar-thy-neighbor that frightened nations had adopted to save their economic necks during the grim days of the Great Depression. These policies had only prolonged the collective suffering and the world chaos and insecurity that had fostered the great war just now sputtering to an end.

In its Articles of Agreement, the IMF pledged to promote international cooperation and international trade and to ensure world economic stability. Never again would any country be tempted to erect tariff barriers or to impose exchange controls in order to protect itself against supposed economic adversaries and by so doing export its economic troubles.

The goals of a freer world economic order were to be achieved by a new international monetary standard. Any country that bought more from its trading partners than it sold could borrow either gold or American dollars from the IMF to make up the deficit. In this way it could easily offset any short-term trade shortfall; there would be no need to impose protective trade restrictions that would clog the channels of international commerce.

A vital part of the new system was a new "gold exchange" standard. This was not identical with the old pre-depression gold standard. No one envisioned restoring those satisfying "eagles" and sovereigns and gold francs that our parents could heft and jangle in their pockets. But the world's gold stock—valued at thirty-five American dollars an ounce—would nevertheless once again become a reference point for international currencies and international trade. Each nation's currency would be tied to gold by law, with each franc, pound, yen, or whatever being exchangeable on demand for a fixed amount of gold. Since gold would be the common backing for all, each currency would have a stable value relative to all the others.

The American dollar would play a special role in this system. The IMF's capital was made up of sums deposited by each member nation in either gold or American dollars. Since the United States promised to exchange an ounce of gold for every thirty-five dollars submitted, and for this purpose maintained a multibillion-dollar "gold cover," the American dollar, the currency of the most powerful economy in the world, became a kind of paper gold that people around the world were willing to accept for almost any transaction. In the immediate postwar period, billions of American dollars would go into the reserves of foreign banks and into the safes and mattresses of foreign private citizens.

The Bretton Woods system, combined with the tariff-lowering 1947 General Agreement on Tariffs and Trade, not only carried the devastated countries of Europe and Asia through their immediate postwar crises, they helped to stimulate an international trade boom of unprecedented proportions. Though Europe regained its economic health by the early fifties and ceased to need major infusions of American goods, foreign trade roared ahead. Between 1950 and 1965 America's international commerce leaped from $20 billion to $50 billion. Even allowing for inflation, this was a spectacular advance.

Pent-up consumer demand and bounding exports stimulated the fifties' economy; sixties' prosperity also owed much to federal fiscal policies. In part this was yet another legacy of Maynard Keynes.

Keynes was a Cambridge *Wunderkind* and charter member of the Bloomsbury set, that brilliant collection of English intellectuals, writers, eccentrics, and academics that included Virginia Woolf, Clive Bell, Lytton Strachey, Duncan Grant, and occasionally Bertrand Russell. He had first made his mark in 1919 with *The Economic Consequences of the Peace,* a caustic indictment of the

Versailles Treaty as a prescription for economic disaster. In 1936, with the world economy congealed into the greatest depression of modern times, he wrote his breakthrough masterpiece, *The General Theory of Employment, Interest, and Money.*

Keynes tried to answer two major questions that defied the analytic power of traditional economic theory: what caused such a giant breakdown, and what could be done to end it? The answer to the first, he said, was that rich societies saved too much and that these savings were drained from the income stream. The result was insufficient demand. Savings were normally offset by private business investment in plant and equipment, but when the investment impulse failed, total demand dropped off, unsold inventories piled up, and businessmen cut their labor force. The downturn would then feed on itself. Jobless men and women had no choice but to reduce their spending. Demand for consumer goods now dropped still further, impelling businessmen to cut investment and their work force once again to stave off bankruptcy. Down, down, down, the grim spiral would go. When it finally bottomed out, society would find itself in an abyss, paying an enormous price in lost wealth and human despair.

Keynes and his disciples sought to save the capitalist order by repairing its chief defect. The wild roller-coaster rides of booms and busts were not ordained, the Keynesians said. The way out was for government to maintain a high level of demand when normal forces flagged. It could do so in two ways. Since it need not worry about profits, even in bad times when private business had hunkered down and slashed investment, it could pump money into the anemic income stream by expenditures on roads, bridges, schools, post offices, and dams. Such a policy not only would provide jobs and income but would also improve the nation's public facilities. The government should not pay for these facilities out of taxes, however; that would merely reduce private demand, offsetting the increase in public spending. Instead, they should be financed by borrowing, that is, through deficit spending.

Keynesian rules allowed another way to restore consumer confidence and encourage demand: cut taxes, giving the public more money to spend. With cash in their pockets, people would buy cars, houses, washing machines, and all the other emblems of a mass-consumption society. This approach assigned the gains of higher income to private use; each person would decide how to spend the tax money he or she had saved. There would be no direct improvement of public facilities.

By the mid-1950s the Keynesian system had conquered academic economics. In a few university backwaters there was still some disciples of Adam Smith and David Ricardo, but most were over fifty; as yet the followers of Milton Friedman of the University of Chicago, an economist who favored "monetary" over "fiscal" policy, were a small, isolated minority. Government was still resistant to the new ideas, however, especially during the Eisenhower years. The general himself knew little of economics and was strongly influenced by the business community, where the old ideas of balanced budgets and self-righting business cycles persisted.

The election of John F. Kennedy in 1960 brought to the White House a young man determined to break out of his predecessor's mold. Kennedy probably knew little more than Ike about formal economics, but he enjoyed stylish ideas and was determined to make his own mark. He was scarcely an enemy of the business community. He once told a business audience bluntly: "Far from being natural enemies, government and business are necessary allies."* He chose Douglas Dillon, a Harvard-educated Republican investment banker, as secretary of the treasury to reassure the business community that even the Democrats respected capitalism.

Yet he also was attracted to the "new economics" of government activism preached by the Keynesians and chose as head of his Council of Economic Advisers (CEA) Professor Walter Heller of the University of Minnesota, one of the new breed. Heller completed Kennedy's imperfect economic education and profoundly affected the economy's course during the 1960s.

Heller was a "conservative" Keynesian willing to accept tax cutting, instead of added spending, as the way to stimulate the sluggish economy. He and his supporters saw themselves as realists. Congress, they argued, would accept unbalanced budgets if brought about by lower taxes that directly increased John Q.

Public's take-home pay. It would not accept deficits if these meant such remote boons as better highways or more forest-ranger stations. Opposed to Heller were the Keynesian spenders, led by the craggy and lofty Harvard economist John Kenneth Galbraith. These experts wanted to shift the income stream from private to public goods. In 1958 Galbraith had written *The Affluent Society,* a best-seller demonstrating that an otherwise prosperous society had shamefully neglected its roads, parks, streets, and public buildings. For far too long, they held, the nation had tolerated public squalor amid private luxury, and the balance had to be redressed. The spenders saw themselves as heirs of the New Deal tradition; their foes perceived them as visionaries if not in fact quasi-socialists.

Under Kennedy and Johnson the right-wing Keynesians won out. Kennedy had won in 1960 in part because the economy was in a slump and the voters believed his promise to "get the country moving again." Recovery began soon after, but its pace was slow. In 1963 Kennedy sent Congress a bill that proposed to cut personal income taxes by over $11 billion and to reduce corporate tax rates from 52 to 47 percent. To prepare the way he had toured the country delivering vest-pocket Keynesian lectures to businessmen and college audiences describing how full employment and faster growth would follow deliberately engineered federal deficits.

The bill was soon caught in a cross fire. From the far right, the anti-Keynesian followers of Milton Friedman announced that federal deficits would absorb savings needed by private investors. From the left, Galbraith and his liberal academic and trade union allies thundered that it was a gift to the rich. Kennedy's school-masterish talks—and the promised 5 percent reduction in corporate taxes—had impressed businessmen, however, and the tax-cut bill sailed through the lower house. Then came the tragedy at Dallas as the president and his beautiful wife passed in an open limousine through ranks of cheering citizens. All legislative action stopped while the nation underwent the catharsis of mourning a young hero's death; not until February 26, 1964, did Lyndon Johnson sign the Tax Reduction Act, lopping 20 percent off the nation's tax bill.

The consequences were spectacular. The economy, already beginning to move, now zoomed. GNP for 1965 leapt to $618 billion, $9 billion more than the Council of Economic Advisers had predicted; unemployment, already low by 1980s' standards, sank to the "full employment" level of 4.1 percent. Real GNP growth rates during the early and middle 1960s shot far ahead of the previous decade, averaging a full percentage point higher most years. The surge was durable. By mid-1968 the financial analysts were trumpeting the "eighth year of [the] longest up-trend in history."[3]

The stock market heralded the results. The postwar bull market had begun in mid-1949 with the Dow Jones industrial average at 161. Ten years later the Dow had reached 685 despite the recessions of the Eisenhower years. But then it had stalled, and in 1960 there "was a mood of Armageddon on Wall Street."[4] Nineteen sixty-two was the worst year for speculators since 1931. Then, even before the tax bill was signed, came the turnaround. In the forty-three months following June 1962 the Dow Jones leaped 460 points, an advance that surpassed proportionately even the fabled bull market of the 1920s. The five years following the 1964 tax cut would be the best in Wall Street's history until our own remarkable day.

The end of 1965 marked Keynes's apotheosis. *Time* magazine in its final issue for the year placed Keynes's donnish face on its cover. The inside story was titled "We Are All Keynesians Now."[5]

Bounding prosperity provided the material means for broadcasting the benefits of postwar affluence. Never before had middle-class Americans felt so confident of their own continued well-being; never before could they afford so readily to consider the plight of others. The New Deal in some ways had been a redistributive movement. It presumed that the American economy had reached a "mature" phase and would not grow further. Logically then, the only way to make the poor richer was to make the rich poorer. It was this belief, perhaps, that made the affluent such intransigent enemies of President Roosevelt and his economic programs. But the War on Poverty occurred at a time of buoyant economic growth. There was no need now to play Robin Hood, take from the rich to give to the poor. Americans could have the best of both worlds: they could have easy consciences and fatter wallets at the same time. It was a rare moment indeed in social evolution!

But as the philosophers say, though a necessary condition, prosperity was not a sufficient one. It permitted generous social welfare spending programs; it did not mandate them.

Experts disagree over the forces that actually incited the nation to action against privation during the 1960s. The liberal economist Lester Thurow believes the War on Poverty was another cold-war artifact: the Johnson administration had to raise the productivity of the poor if the United States was to "stay ahead of the Russians."[6] Political radicals, who often dismiss liberal reform as "social control" to keep the poor in line, suggest an even less generous interpretation. According to social activists Frances Fox Piven and Richard Cloward, Johnson and the Democrats had to buy off militant black leaders to keep the ghettos from exploding and to retain black political support. "Recent federal reforms," they wrote in 1966, "have been impelled in part by widespread unrest in the ghetto and instances of more aggressive Negro demands."[7]

Both these explanations are ideological. Both deny generosity and attribute a degree of contrivance and clarity of thought to "the system" that it rarely possesses. Neither accepts the messiness of human motives—even those of capitalists and their liberal political allies.

Kennedy and Johnson were not indifferent to ghetto riots; they were undoubtedly oversensitive to Soviet rivalry. Yet there is no evidence that, as motives for the crusade against poverty, these were fundamental considerations with either man. If any single force can be held responsible, it was middle-class guilt, a historical energizer much underrated by scholars.

Social guilt was hard to avoid in the early 1960s. Evidence was by then rapidly accumulating that the rising postwar economic tide had not lifted all ships. In 1957 Robert Lampman of the University of Wisconsin had shown that 20 percent of American families were living below the "poverty line." Two years later a

University of Michigan study claimed that another 10 percent were right on the line itself. Then, in 1962, came Michael Harrington's *The Other America,* a smoothly written polemic against the nation's neglect of the forty to fifty million citizens who were poor. "Tens of millions of Americans," Harrington proclaimed, "are at this very moment maimed in body and spirit, existing at levels beneath those necessary for human decency. . . ." These people were not starving, but they were hungry and "without adequate housing and education and medical care."[8]

Harrington was a socialist and the book can be seen as a socialist tract. But it pricked the conscience of thousands of educated middle-class Americans who had assumed that only racial minorities and the elderly had failed to benefit from the postwar boom. One reader of the Harrington book was John F. Kennedy, and it left its mark.

The young president was a complicated mixture of the self-serving and the generous, the insensitive and the caring, the hedonistic and the cerebral, the ambitious and the conscientious. In recent years his reputation has suffered from revelations of his family's opportunism and his own sexual adventurism. But the pendulum has swung back too far from the days after November 1963 when martyrdom cast its autumnal glow over his administration and the nation remembered his White House as a Camelot fairyland.

Kennedy was capable of compassion and of concern for the good opinion of history. At the end of 1962 he was looking for new worlds to conquer, and soon after reading Harrington he told Walter Heller, his chief economic adviser, "I want to go beyond the things that have already been accomplished. . . . Give me facts and figures on the things we still have to do. For example, what about the poverty problem in the United States?"[9]

JFK's remaining months produced few concrete results. Heller asked two other members of the Council of Economic Advisers, Robert Lampman of Wisconsin, the author of the 1957 poverty study, and William Capron of Stanford, to look into the matter for him. The two professors held a series of Saturday-morning seminars with federal officials from the Commerce and

Labor departments, hoping to find out what practical steps might be taken to help the poor. But the bureaucrats had little information on poverty and few interesting ideas about how to deal with it, and the sessions came to little.

Undeterred, Theodore Sorensen, JFK's aide and speech writer, asked the CEA in September 1963 to appoint a task force to draw up an antipoverty program. As before, no one seemed to know what to do. In mid-November Heller reported this back to the president. Kennedy was annoyed at the slow progress, but ordered his adviser to get a program ready for presentation to Congress in January. With only six weeks left to come up with some scheme, Heller turned to Lyndon Johnson for help. The vice-president could supply enthusiasm but little else.

Then the task force discovered David Hackett, a school chum and an aide to Attorney General Robert Kennedy, John's younger brother. Since 1961 Hackett had been working for his boss on the problem of juvenile delinquency, one of the few social issues that had disturbed 1950s' middle-class equanimity. In 1961 Hacket got himself appointed executive director of a new President's Committee on Juvenile Delinquency and used this post as a base to attack the problem of teenage crime. As his chief adviser he chose Lloyd Ohlin, the forty-four-year-old research director of the Columbia School of Social Work.

Ohlin would leave a vivid imprint on the poverty program. A sociologist trained at the University of Chicago, he was strongly influenced by the "Chicago School" view that criminal behavior was a rational response to the slum environment. Delinquency could be reduced, not by case-worker advice and guidance, but by giving slum dwellers some sense of control over their communities and their lives and slum kids new opportunities to achieve status, self-respect, and a decent income within the legal system.

This vision in part derived from years of experimentation in slum neighborhoods by university faculty and independent reformers. Among the latter was Saul Alinsky, a former sociologist turned radical activist. In the 1930s Alinsky had evolved a self-help approach to poverty and inequality and had gone to live in a Chicago slum neighborhood where he tutored the poor on how to improve their lives. In 1963–64 he was still an antipoverty activist, heading the Industrial Areas Foundation dedicated to self-help organizing among the poor. Alinsky was respected by the sociology professors, and his experiences had confirmed a profound distrust of the welfare professionals among the Chicago School.

In 1959 Ohlin and his Columbia colleague, Richard Cloward, established Mobilization for Youth (MFY) in a predominantly black and Puerto Rican Manhattan neighborhood to try their theories out. Before they were very far along, Hackett brought Ohlin to Washington to take charge of a new federal program to fund local community anti–teenage crime efforts. Ohlin stayed in Washington for only one year, but by the time he left he had transmitted to Hackett and his friend, the attorney general, his enthusiasm for the Mobilization for Youth plan that Cloward had developed for New York's Lower East Side: teenage public service jobs, centralized neighborhood centers to dispense welfare services, and agencies run by slum dwellers themselves to provide neighborhood input and to create a sense of community autonomy.

Over the next two years Hackett, Ohlin, Robert Kennedy, and other enthusiasts established small antidelinquency programs on the New York model in cities across the country, using federal funds scraped up from here and there. Increasingly, these programs came to emphasize "community competence," the creation of grass-roots leadership cadres that could challenge the elected officials at city hall in the community's interest. The plan set Hackett and Ohlin on an inevitable collision course with elected officials that would help wreck the War on Poverty.

Hackett took the community-participation theories of Ohlin and his colleagues and planted them in the heart of the anti-poverty program. In a thirty-nine page memo to Heller of early November 1963 he proposed a set of task forces to study the problem of poverty—in the cities, on the Indian reservations, among Mexican Americans, in Alaska. After extensive field work to see how the problems appeared to the victims themselves, they would select a group of communities for federally supported demonstration projects where local solutions would be tried out. Only after this lengthy process had been completed would the government launch an all-out campaign against want and deprivation.

The assassination in Dallas failed to stop the poverty program's forward momentum. On December 20 Heller submitted to Sorensen a "Community Action Program" proposal calling for five urban and five rural demonstration projects to test various antipoverty approaches, all headed by a cabinet-level committee to provide overall direction. During Christmas week 1963 Heller and Kermit Gordon, U.S. budget director, flew to the LBJ Ranch to sell the new proposal to President Lyndon Johnson.

Kennedy knew poverty only by rumor and through books; LBJ, born in the thin-soiled Texas hill country to a father more talented in human relations than practical affairs, had at times lived it and had seen it all around him in Texas when he was growing up in the 1930s. As a young schoolteacher in Cotulla, Texas, he had taught tattered and hungry Mexican American children who lived in dirt hovels. As an official of the New Deal National Youth Administration he had honed his political skills in a job that brought him in constant touch with the poor and unemployed.

Besides his empathies, he was also driven by ambition. Lyndon Baines Johnson was determined to leave his mark as the most dedicated champion of the common man and the greatest benefactor of the nation since his youthful hero, Franklin Delano Roosevelt. At the ranch, he listened patiently to Heller and Gordon but was not impressed. What sort of piss-ant idea was this? He wanted something "big and bold" that would "hit the whole nation with real impact."[10] No, the proposal must be sharply upgraded. Every community that applied should be given its own community action program with the federal government paying the bill. The poverty task force should start again and prepare a measure along these lines. What had begun as a preliminary had been transformed by LBJ's Texas-size thinking into the main event itself.

On January 8, in his first State of the Union Address, Johnson proclaimed that his administration "today, here and now, declares unconditional war on poverty in America."[11] Two weeks later he released some of the details of his antipoverty campaign including the community action idea. Soon after, he took responsibility for preparing an antipoverty bill from the task force and gave it to Peace Corps administrator Sargent Shriver, JFK's brother-in-law, one of the few Kennedy clansmen he liked.

Shriver was a square-jawed lawyer and businessman who had managed Joseph Kennedy's Merchandise Mart in Chicago and then married Eunice Kennedy, the boss's daughter. A man of action indifferent to ideology, he understood the difficulty of bypassing elected officials and traditional channels and getting local bodies to work together. When told about the community action scheme, he responded bluntly: "It'll never fly."[12] But he did not eliminate the program entirely. Instead, he placed it second, behind a Job Corps, a domestic version of the Peace Corps, that would take inner-city youths and train them in basic skills so that they could compete successfully in the job market.

Over the next few weeks Shriver interviewed sociologists, criminologists, and public officials and wrangled with the new-minted poverty experts over the bill's details. Hackett and Shriver did not get along, and the attorney general's old chum soon ceased to play a direct role in the discussions. But his spirit remained in the form of "Hackett's guerrillas," his community action allies and associates. The chief guerrilla was Richard Boone, another Chicago School sociologist, a former associate of Alinsky and a man considered a "Mau Mau" on the subject of community involvement.[13] Boone and his allies championed the "maximum feasible participation" of the poor in community programs and repeated the phrase so often that Adam Yarmolinsky, a Shriver associate, at one point could stand it no longer. "You have used that phrase four or five times now," he exclaimed. "Yes, I know," Boone responded. "How many times do I have to use it before it becomes part of the program?"[14] In the end the fatal phrase was written into the community action section of the bill submitted to Congress.

On March 16, 1964, the administration transmitted the Economic Opportunity Act to the House. Robert Kennedy, still the attorney general, testified in its favor. The law would remedy the poor's "sense of helplessness and futility," much of which came from "the feeling of powerlessness to affect . . . [big-city] organizations."[15] On August 20 the president signed the bill into law in a White House ceremony in which he used seventy-two pens, a mark of the measure's perceived importance.

The law established an Office of Economic Opportunity (OEO) as the overseer of a dozen new programs designed to end poverty in a generation. Under Title I, written by Daniel Moynihan, the puckish assistant secretary of labor, these included the Job Corps, a Neighborhood Youth Corps, a College Work-Study program, and other employment and training programs for the unskilled poor. Title II, the work of Richard Boone, established the Community Action Program (CAP) to handle programs to be originated, and to some extent administered, by local community bodies, Community Action Agencies (CAAs), these to be formed in as yet unspecified ways. Other "titles" of the bill were a Migrant Farm Workers program, a Rural Loan program, a Small Business Development Center, a VISTA (Volunteers in Service to America), a domestic equivalent to the much-praised Peace Corps. Eventually the War on Poverty also included Head Start, to give poor children a leg up on the educational ladder; a high school dropout employment program; a provision for neighborhood health centers; Upward Bound, to help minority students attend college; a legal services program for the poor; and a small business incentive program aimed at minorities. As expected, Johnson appointed Shriver head of the OEO, and for the next four years he remained on the front line of the fiercest domestic struggle waged during the Johnson presidency.

The War on Poverty was only the first element in a broad program to make American life richer, fairer, juster, and more enlightened, a program that the president would call the Great Society. Johnson first used the phrase in 1964 at the University of Michigan's annual commencement at Ann Arbor where, on a warm May day, wearing a black academic cap and gown, he told eighty thousand graduates and guests of his dreams for America's future. The nation had the opportunity, the president said, "to move not only toward the rich society and the powerful society but upward to the Great Society." This Great Society of course demanded an end to poverty and racial injustice. But it was more than this. It was also a society where "leisure is a welcome chance to build and reflect," where "the city of man serves not only the needs of the body and the demands of commerce, but the desire for beauty and the hunger for community," where "man can renew contact with nature." The president did not give specifics, but he did lay out a process. He was going to create working groups to hold conferences and conduct studies, he said, and from these we "will begin to set our course toward the Great Society."[16]

LBJ's landslide victory over Barry Goldwater that November seemed a sweeping mandate for change. His 60 percent plus vote, he claimed, raised the Great Society above partisanship. He was now the spokesman for a "consensus" of the American people who had collectively enlisted in a massive movement for social reform.

The president was essentially right. Seldom had any president or set of presidential policies received such an overwhelming vote of confidence. Yet with all the talk of a great national consensus, Johnson remained uneasy. The judgment of history was still not certain, greatness was not yet assured. And time was short. LBJ feared that his reserve of goodwill and support would quickly be drained off by each measure Congress enacted. He had won a sixteen-million-vote majority over Goldwater, he privately told his congressional liaison staff in January 1965, because his Republican opponent "had simply scared hell" out of the voters.[17] Since November, as part of the inevitable rebound effect, he had already lost three million of that sixteen, and after a struggle with Congress this number would further erode. It was essential to move quickly before the well ran dry.

In 1965 the president submitted sixty-three separate legislative proposals to Congress. These were prepared by seventeen task forces manned mostly by academics. Though Lyndon Johnson distrusted professors, he had no alternative but to tap the reservoir of trained intelligence available in the colleges and universities.

Of course he did not get all he asked Congress for, but the

year saw a deluge of social legislation unequaled in all previous American history. In April came the Elementary and Secondary School Act, appropriating $1.3 billion to school districts with a high proportion of needy children. LBJ signed the bill in the one-room schoolhouse where he had learned his letters fifty years before with "Miss Kate" Loney, his first teacher, by his side. At the end of July Congress passed the Medicare bill, filling a large gap in the New Deal–Fair Deal welfare system by providing health insurance for the retired. On July 30 the president flew to Independence, Missouri, to sign the law in the presence of ex-President Harry Truman, the man, he later wrote, who "had started it all so many years before."[18] Harry and Bess Truman received the first two Medicare cards.

During the rest of 1965 and into 1966 the legislative mill continued to grind out installments of the Great Society: in August the Housing and Urban Development Act, to provide rent supplements to low-income families; in October the Higher Education Act, creating the first federal scholarships for college students; the following September a new minimum wage of $1.60 an hour for thirty million workers; in November the Clean Waters Restoration Act, for constructing sewage treatment plants to clean up the nation's drinking and recreational water; that same month the Model Cities and Metropolitan Area Redevelopment Act, to rehabilitate the slums. Eric Goldman, the Princeton history professor who served as the White House intellectual-in-residence, later recalled: "The legislation rolled through the House and Senate in such profusion and so methodically that you seemed part of some vast, overpowering machinery, oiled to purr."[19]

The president did not rely only on his lopsided 295 to 140 congressional majority to get his programs through. Johnson's strength of will and persuasive powers were legendary. George Wallace, the segregationist governor of Alabama, once came to the White House to discuss the impasse with the federal government over the civil rights demonstrations in Selma, Alabama, and after three hours with LBJ fled for fear that if he had stayed any longer "he'd have had me coming out *for* civil rights."[20]

The president's success derived not just from the notorious Johnson "treatment": the powerful grip on the subject's lapel or arm, the wheedling, exhorting, pleading, and threatening cornpone voice, the intimidating massive physical presence. Johnson was also a virtuoso of the legislative process. His long years as Senate minority and majority leader had created incomparable connections on "the Hill" and taught him how to get laws passed. Unlike most of his successors, he had not built his career around alienation from the federal government. He was a Washington "insider," indeed the quintessential insider, who functioned more like a European prime minister, the czar of the legislature, than an American president, the head of a separate and generally competing government branch.

Johnson knew how to trade favors for cooperation, but he did not rely on crude bribery. If you paid for each vote, you would start a bidding war that would kill you in the end. A congressman helpful on a single bill might be invited to a state dinner or get a personal phone call from the Oval Office, but the more substantial rewards—roads, bridges, dams, appointments, pardons—came only after a consistent pattern of votes. Loyalty, not just cooperation, was the price of important, career-enhancing preferment.

The War on Poverty and the Great Society were examples of what the English philosopher Alfred North Whitehead called "a certain extravagance of objectives" that afflict "vigorous societies."[21] Clearly, they were immoderately oversold as a solution to society's age-old ills of squalor, privation, and insecurity. Yet they achieved a portion of their ends. The Great Society programs tailored primarily for the middle class—aid to college students, national foundations for the arts and the humanities, Medicare and expanded Social Security benefits, conservation and environmental protection, for example—did in fact improve the overall quality of American life or at least helped check its deterioration. But even the War on Poverty had its clear and direct successes. Head Start took thousands of very young slum children out of culturally deprived homes and introduced them to school and the three Rs early in life, before nonliterate, antiacademic attitudes had hardened. Investigators would find that the program permanently raised IQs and reading scores and reduced the incidence of dropping-out and falling-behind. The Legal Services Program, administered by CAP, brought two thousand lawyers to slum neighborhoods and provided help for thousands of poor people forced to negotiate the labyrinthine turns of the welfare system or desperate to avoid the toils of the criminal law.

In the end, of course, poverty programs did not cure the misery and hopelessness of the ghettos and slum enclaves. The poor we still have with us. But the programs had a wide range of indirect benefits that are difficult to quantify but equally difficult to deny.

One class of poverty program beneficiaries, ironically, was the white middle class. VISTA, for example, transported thousands of idealistic young men and women from the college campuses, the law offices, the farms, the hospitals, and the professional schools to the city slums, the Appalachian valleys, and the Indian reservations where they found outlets for their enthusiasm, skills, and compassion. VISTA one-year volunteers lived in the community on minimal pay of fifty dollars a month. They taught basic reading and writing skills, got people jobs, helped them with medical problems, started credit unions, created recreation programs, and brought the poor in touch with legal help. In all, during the program's first four years, about thirteen thousand young men and women served as VISTA workers.

Though VISTA did not make a serious dent in the misery and despair of the nation's underclass, it often brought deep satisfaction to the volunteers themselves. Judy Lewis, a VISTA volunteer from Coral Gables, Florida, with a B.A. from Michigan in American Studies, spent her year in black-Hispanic East Harlem, New York, intervening for the local people in disputes with landlords, helping to establish a food-buying cooperative, finding support for a summer recreation program to give local children something to do when school was out. She lived on East 118th Street, in the crumbling neighborhood she ministered to, and came to admire the people who in turn came to love her. When someone asked her why she did not return to school and earn a social work degree, she replied: "Money's not important to me. I've been trained for this job and I like it. The more I get involved, the more people around here think of me as their neighbor. . . . I feel at home here."[22] We do not know what finally happened to Judy Lewis, but her VISTA experience was clearly a socially valuable rite of passage from middle-class adolescence to middle-class womanhood.

The social work professionals benefited in more material ways. Hundreds of graduates of the nation's schools of social work were drawn into the poverty programs. For a time social work became a valuable professional option to thousands of bright young men and women. As a writer for *Fortune* remarked in August 1965, "Whatever it may do for the poor, the war on poverty is the best thing that's happened to social workers since the New Deal was established." There was now "a gigantic sellers' market" for social workers, welfare administrators, and "consultants" on welfare problems.[23]

Critics would denounce the War on Poverty as a feeding trough for the white middle class. But the jobs, the salaries, the benefits would spill over onto those upwardly mobile hustlers and strivers who waited in the ghettos for the first hint of encouragement and opportunity to appear.

Federal jobs with OEO were exceptionally well paid by ghetto standards, and they were good, keep-your-hands-clean jobs as teachers' aides, consumer protection aides, health service assistants, neighborhood organizers—not the gritty, sweaty ones the ghetto economy usually provided. Local black leaders could seldom resist treating the War on Poverty as a giant pork barrel for their people, the biggest on record. Conservative critics found the black feeding trough even more deplorable than the white, as if blacks must be more upright or were less deserving. As early as August 1965 Republican Senator Everett Dirksen of Illinois called the OEO the "greatest boondoggle since bread and circuses in the days of the ancient Roman Empire, when the republic fell."[24]

Dirksen may have remembered ancient Rome, but he had conveniently forgotten the rest of history. Patronage is as old as politics and in America has been woven tightly into the very fabric of democratic life. Government jobs have always been used to reward political supporters and pay off political debts. At the lower levels the jobs have often gone to new arrivals in the cities—Irish, Slavs, Jews, Italians. In many big northern cities to this day—as folk wisdom attests—the police are Irish, sanitation workers heavily Italian, and schoolteachers disproportionately Jewish. Here, with the advent of the War on Poverty, was a new opportunity to pay off favors. Why not a black War on Poverty bureaucracy? Everyone else had gotten "pieces of the action," why not—finally—black Americans too?

One great advantage of this scheme was that all the poverty jobs were new; the new patronage holders need not displace anyone else. Upwardly mobile blacks would find niches for themselves without seriously penalizing other groups. The benefits of this arrangement would become brilliantly clear when the poverty war ended. Then, black ambition would not be satisfied so easily. The result, affirmative action—preferential treatment for blacks and other victims of discrimination—would create enormous social tensions and resentments and a decade of group conflict.

Success or failure, within a year the War on Poverty, the Great Society centerpiece, had become badly frayed. Part of the problem was a deep conceptual fault that ran right through it. The war, as we have seen, attempted to merge old-fashioned welfare state liberalism that dated back to the Progressives and the New Deal with the Chicago School view of community competence. In the first, poverty's victims profited best from programs developed and dispensed by public officials and the federal bureaucracy. Local agencies might help by delivering the services efficiently, but that was the extent of their function. In the other, the poor were to be encouraged to develop and administer the programs that they themselves favored. The purpose here was not merely efficient administration but to make the poor aware of their rights and their own competence. The first appealed especially to the old Democratic politicians who saw visions of jobs, contracts, and patronage. The second appealed to the liberal academics and the social scientists who yearned to test Chicago School social theories. It would, of course, also appeal to the poor themselves.

Within the two positions, well hidden at first, lurked a fundamental left-right tension over the direction in which America should go. These positions correlated roughly with two different

views of the causes of poverty. The conservatives believed that
poverty was culturally derived. The poor belonged to a separate
"culture of poverty" that was self-perpetuating. They were used
to failure and had never developed the mechanisms to cope with
it. They lacked the foresight to plan for the future and the steady
habits that were needed for getting ahead in American society.
Their values were different. They insisted on immediate gratifi-
cation. The persistance of pockets and islands of poverty at a time
when the country was close to full employment seemed to confirm
the arguments of the culture-of-poverty theorists. How could
such handicapped people decide for themselves what would end
the vicious cycle that victimized them? As Anne Roberts, staff
director of New York City's antipoverty board, said, "You can't go
to a street corner with a pad and pencil and tell the poor to
write you a poverty program. They wouldn't know how."[25]

The liberal-left view held that poverty resulted from serious
inadequacies in the American system. The poor were the victims
of discrimination—racial or class. Either because they *were* poor,
or because they were black or brown, they lacked power to
influence their fate. It was untrue that their values were harmful.
The poor did have different values, but they were not pathologi-
cal. In fact, they were often superior to those of the middle class,
and must be respected. Another version of the attack on
the culture-of-poverty idea insisted that the poor prized the
same things that everyone else did. As the black sociologist Lee
Rainwater would later write: "The alternative value system of the
lower class seems to exist more in the minds of middle-class
romantics . . . than in the wishes of the lower-class people
themselves."[26]

The culture-of-poverty idea easily slipped over into the concept that the poor were to blame for their failures. This view
comforted the successful and excused the inadequacies of "the
system." It justified programs primarily devoted to retraining and
reconditioning the poor, making them over into middle-class
people with ingrained habits of punctuality, foresight, and
perseverance. It was essentially moderate and reformist and
certainly represented the views of Johnson himself and most of
the American public. The opposing view easily mutated into an

apology for the poor and a concerted assault on the system. Poverty was not an accident of American society; it was inherent. In the end a solution would require the redistribution of national income. As the intellectual climate grew more radical, this dissenting mood would become a powerful disruptive force within the War on Poverty programs themselves. It would divide radicals from moderates and pit the poor against the elected authorities in militant confrontations that would offend conservatives, moderates, and even many liberals, and would undermine public support for the entire antipoverty program.

The battleground for these opposing positions was the Community Action Agencies within the Community Action Program. But we should not exaggerate the adversary role of the CAAs. Many programs were controlled from the outset directly by Office of Economic Opportunity officials. In other cases, despite the mandated "maximum feasible participation" of the poor, the CAAs were little more than rubber stamps for federal or local officials, and were run entirely on the old principle that a benevolent bureaucracy knows best.

From the outset, however, the community-competence position had caught the eye of black activists. One of the first black leaders to see the OEO's political potential was Congressman Adam Clayton Powell of New York, the head of the House Labor and Education Committee. The suave, articulate Powell was an ordained minister, the pastor of Harlem's most prestigious black congregation, the Abyssinian Baptist Church. Minister or no, Powell was a flamboyant character with an eye for the dollar, the ladies, and the main chance. But he was also a "race man," a black man who put the interests of his people high on his agenda and could be counted on to see that their rights were respected. As the poverty bill wended its way through Congress in early 1964, Powell made his committee's hearings into a forum where black leaders from New York, Chicago, Detroit, Los Angeles, and other cities could air the ghettos' complaints against the local welfare authorities and the city halls. Powell himself made headlines when he denounced white welfare officials for their patronizing attitude toward the poor and their insensitivity to their needs. The publicity of the Powell committee sent a signal through many black communities: be alerted, power and influence, not to speak of money and jobs, were about to descend from Washington.

However powerful the incentive, only a small number of Community Action Programs were ever run entirely by local community people. These were generally programs actually initiated by local voluntary associations as provided under Title II. But whoever ran the show, the results of local programs were not always happy. Where government officials reigned, red tape, community suspicion, federal-local battles over turf, conflicting ideologies, and incompatible interests all impeded success.

A typical case was Oakland, California, where the Economic Development Administration (EDA) of the Department of Commerce had mounted a major ghetto employment project in 1966 with over $23 million of federal funds. In this case social pacification was in fact a major goal. A decaying city with a festering black ghetto, Oakland was ripe for riot and seemed salvageable only by restoring hope and purpose to the hundreds of unemployed young men who had provided the tinder for the city conflagrations of the recent past. An explosion might be avoided if enough money could be pumped into the city to create two thousand jobs in the minority, largely black, community.

Everything seemed to go wrong. First the project's federal directors, on their initial reconnaissance of the city, failed to pay their respects to the mayor on the grounds that such a visit would identify them with the "establishment." Then the head of the EDA resigned because he foresaw serious federal funding cutbacks: "Vietnam was eating everything up," he said.[27] Next, serious engineering problems on the construction projects developed, followed by the discovery that the costs of the projects had been underestimated. Jurisdictional disputes in Washington and between the EDA and the ghetto community held up the job training programs. Meanwhile, the white mayor and the militant black community leaders clashed over who should control ghetto-oriented programs.

By early 1969 the program was clearly a failure. True, Oakland had not exploded in flames like Watts, Detroit, or Cleveland, but it was hard to see how the Economic Development

Administration program could have contributed anything to the pacification. As a *Los Angeles Times* article of mid-March 1969 noted, the program had created a total of twenty new jobs, a hundred times fewer than had been projected by its supporters!

Yet the record of the community-controlled programs was even more controversial. Many of the patronage jobs were little more than well paid sinecures. But cushy jobs were only part of it. The other half was plain old-fashioned graft. Money was gushing from the federal pipe and many local people saw no reason why they should not fill their buckets. In Trenton, one elected CAA member reported how he held up the renting of a neighborhood-center building because he felt that "somebody was gettin' a nice rakeoff on rentin' that old department store, and I figured I might as well get somethin' out of it too."[28]

Another source of trouble was that community action benefits went disproportionately to blacks and Hispanics. Over 70 percent of those Americans called "poor" were white, yet most of the OEO's funds went to the big-city racial ghettos. In Detroit, according to one observer of the local poverty program, there was "almost complete failure to establish rapport with or provide services for a sizable poor white population."[29] Patronage benefits too, at the lower administrative levels, were disproportionately targeted to racial minorities. One 1966 study of nine cities showed that while almost 90 percent of the cities' labor force was white, 80 percent of the OEO's nonprofessional aides were black.

Militancy was even more damaging than waste, favoritism, and corruption. In fact it was the militancy of many of the community action organizers that ultimately demolished the CAP, the OEO, and the War on Poverty itself.

Even before the OEO Community Action Programs were created, community groups in some cities had begun to confront the established city governments and official bureaucracies. In New York, Richard Cloward's Mobilization for Youth, the slum-youth juvenile delinquency program where it all began, encouraged school boycotts, rent strikes, and other extralegal challenges to the institutions that regulated slum life. One of MFY's community projects was MOM, an organization that claimed to represent Puerto Rican mothers. In 1964 MOM ferociously attacked the local school principal, accusing him of racism and neglect of his pupils. If he was not fired and the school's programs changed, they declared, they would withdraw their children and boycott the school. The Public School 140 principal was Irving Rosenbloom, who, like so many other members of the New York Board of Education bureaucracy, was Jewish, and the attack soon took on ugly anti-Semitic overtones.

In Newark too community action programs clashed head on with the liberal establishment. Newark's OEO had been preceded by the Newark Community Union Project (NCUP) run by Carl Wittman and Tom Hayden of the radical Students for a Democratic Society. The NCUP was part of SDS's Economic Research and Action Project (ERAP) program, a "back to the people" project financed by money donated by the United Automobile Workers in mid-1963.

In the summer of 1964 the Newark SDSers rented a house in the Newark black ghetto and fanned out into the neighborhood to help create "an interracial movement of the poor." At first the liberal officials at city hall and moderate community leaders affiliated with Americans for Democratic Action (ADA), the National Association for the Advancement of Colored People (NAACP), the Congress of Racial Equality (CORE), and other organizations had welcomed the students. But the honeymoon did not last. From their house-headquarters on Peshine Street, Hayden, Wittman, and their friends were soon hard at work fomenting rent strikes, attacking welfare practices, and picketing city hall. Before many months had passed the liberals had come to see the Newark ERAP project as a major threat. As Newark City Councilman Lee Bernstein explained in early 1965, at first he had worked with the SDSers, but he now believed that their efforts were "harmful to the city" and "potentially very dangerous." They did not want to cooperate with their liberal well-wishers, he explained; "They just want to create incidents."[30]

Despite the NCUP's local notoriety, Frank Mankiewicz, a Shriver associate in the OEO, called Hayden to Washington to share his experiences with officials of the poverty program, and later several ERAPers became paid consultants of the OEO's VISTA program.

Mankiewicz belonged to an emerging circle of left-leaning idealists within the OEO, young men "full of hope and ideas,"[31] who carried the community-competence idea to an extreme. The poor should be trained to take on the "establishment" and seize for themselves a share of the power and income of the middle class. Richard Boone was one of this group. So was William Haddad, former associate director of the Peace Corps, appointed by Shriver as OEO inspector general, the officer charged with overseeing the organization's subordinate divisions. According to one historian of the War on Poverty, Haddad used "his powers ferociously and in favor of his own theories, which were along the lines of organizing communities against the 'local establishments.' "[32]

With such men in charge it is not surprising that in some cities the CAPs were taken over by radicals. In Syracuse, for example, black militants gained control of the Community Development Association, the local OEO community action agency. The militants ousted the white leadership and placed a black activist in charge who promptly announced that "no ends are accomplished without the use of force. . . ." Under his direction the Community Development Association attacked Mayor William F. Walsh and sought to defeat him for reelection in 1965. They launched demonstrations against city hall and then used poverty funds to bail out people who were arrested. When the mayor protested this use of federal money, OEO officials told him that it was perfectly legal.

Despite the early problems, for a time the OEO was Johnson's pet. During the summer of 1965 the president told his department heads at a cabinet meeting where Shriver was present: "You save money on your programs," and, pointing to the OEO head, "You-all give it to him."[33]

But the experience of Syracuse and a dozen other cities soon began to erode the president's faith and affection. Even where they did not become tools of confrontation-minded activists, CAAs often offended local officials, many of them good, and even liberal, Democrats. It is easy to see that the problem was usually jurisdiction or perhaps, more bluntly, power. The mayors resented having to deal with interest blocs created by federal action and antagonistic to their own authority. They opposed control by such groups of funds that they felt belonged properly in their hands. As early as May 1965, with the War on Poverty barely a year old, the U.S. Conference of Mayors was narrowly averted from adopting a resolution attacking the OEO for "creating tensions" and failing "to recognize the legal and moral responsibilities of local officials who are accountable to the taxpayers for expenditures of local funds."[34]

The War on Poverty's first big crisis came that September when the mayors conferred with Vice-President Humphrey, the administration's liaison with the cities, and filled his ears with their complaints. On his recommendation, the president appointed a team to investigate the OEO and placed at its head a skilled efficiency expert, Bertram Harding, deputy director of the Internal Revenue Service. Harding helped to force out Haddad, Boone, and other militants and in June 1966 was rewarded by being appointed Shriver's top assistant.

During 1966 Congress cut OEO appropriations and tried to pare down the community action programs. That was also the year when the OEO got into trouble with the liberals and the left for bowing to Senator John Stennis's attack on its Head Start program in Mississippi, perceived by the senator as radical and a threat to his power.

Still, the OEO continued to harbor community action militants at the lower echelons and continued to foment and focus community discontents.

The prize case of community action–sponsored confrontation is San Francisco, a city famous for flamboyant gestures and extraordinary social tolerance. There Wilfred Ussary of CORE, the militant black civil rights organization, headed the local CAP and used it to build a Black Power machine in direct opposition to Mayor John F. Shelley. Ussary's community organizers menaced whites and spent OEO money to launch civil rights protests. Ussary himself, at a staff meeting in September 1966, proclaimed, "Old Whitey's got to go. We're going to raise hell tonight." He also threatened physical violence against one of his colleagues, a black clergyman who had objected to Ussary's rhetoric and tactics and had sent letters of protest to Shriver and the FBI.[35]

Ussary's extremism was soon overshadowed by Charles Sizemore's. A tall and menacing black militant associated with the radical Black Student Union at San Francisco State College, Sizemore's appointment as director of the summer program to reduce juvenile delinquency at the Hunter's Point black ghetto was apparently inspired by the theory "set a thief to catch a thief." When, shortly after his appointment in June 1967, Sizemore heard that he would have to cut back the number of jobs for black youths on his payroll, he dispatched thirty toughs under an aide to confront Mayor Shelley at city hall. If the mayor did not come up with the cash to restore the jobs by five that evening, they told him, "This goddam town's gonna blow."[36]

The mayor somehow managed to scrape up $45,000 before time ran out and saved the cut jobs, and perhaps the city. But that was not the end of Sizemore's colorful activities that summer. He hired black militants like Bobby Seale of the Black Panthers to give lectures to ghetto young people. Seale told his youthful auditors to "remember, when you . . . steal from the white man . . . you are dealing with real politics."[37] When Sizemore took a bunch of black teenagers to a downtown theater, they celebrated the occasion by beating a bartender and looting several Geary Street stores.

These incidents led the OEO to clamp down on local agency officials. Yet scandals continued to erupt, the worst in 1968 when Chicago officials discovered an OEO program virtually run by the Chicago youth gangs, the Blackstone Rangers and the East Side Disciples.

The Rangers were organized in 1960 by Southside Woodlawn ghetto youths to defend their turf on Blackstone Avenue against their rivals. With several thousand members, by 1968 the Rangers were a power in Woodlawn and extorted money from ghetto merchants, engaged in petty crime, and waged open war against their rivals, a coalition called the Disciples, with an arsenal of guns, knives, and bicycle chains.

In June 1967 the OEO funded a "high risk" job-training program for the Rangers and the Disciples in the hope of deflecting their members' energies into more useful channels. The OEO set up four training centers and gave trainees $45 a week to attend classes. It paid Rangers "president" Eugene ("Bull") Hairston and "vice-president" Jeff ("Black Prince") Fort $500 a month to serve as project "teachers" and leaders. The money ran out in May 1968, but the OEO quickly submitted a request for $1 million to continue the project.

By this time the enterprise had set off alarms among the more conservative citizens of Chicago, including the police. On June 20 Senator John McClellan's Permanent Investigations Subcommittee opened hearings on the project that attracted attention in most of the nation's press. Some of the testimony was sensational. On the first day the superintendent of the Cook County jail testified that the Rangers were a "black Mafia" being trained by the OEO in the skills of organized crime. A Chicago police official told the subcommittee that crime in Woodlawn had become worse since the OEO had entered the picture. The police had managed to break up the gangs, but now, under the OEO's funding, they had united again. George "Mad Dog" Rose described how one of the project training centers, the First Presbyterian Church, had been used as a storehouse for gang weapons and marijuana and had served as a community hall for wild parties. The pastor of the church, John K. Fry, knew what was taking place, he said, but was unconcerned. Worse, he was a virtual Fagin who had counseled the Rangers on how to extort thousands of dollars from Woodlawn merchants.

During the weeks of hearings the OEO had its share of defenders. Fry denied Rose's charges. The weapons at the church had been brought there under an agreement with the police to disarm the Rangers. Bertrand Harding, the OEO's acting director since Shriver's resignation in the summer, identified Rose as an ex-convict and insisted that his testimony could not be taken seriously. Senator Charles Percy of Illinois, Dirksen's more-liberal colleague, expressed his confidence in the black director of the Woodlawn organization that had coordinated the project and said he hoped that others would not be discouraged from supporting similar projects. Yet it is clear that the Chicago gangs project drove another nail into the OEO's coffin.

Cleveland had its own version of knavery disguised as community participation. There, during the summer of 1968, $31,000 of OEO money was funneled through the Reverend DeForest Brown to militants in Hough, the city's black ghetto. The chief beneficiary of this largesse was a Black Muslim named Fred Ahmed Evans, a tough with a dishonorable discharge from the army, who wore a handmade African dashiki and a skullcap. Evans and his disciples called their group New Libya and trained for the "final day" of showdown with the white man. In mid-July, after they had gunned down a uniformed traffic guard, they got into a shoot-out with the police in which three men died and twelve were wounded. Evans and his followers were finally captured, but not subdued. When he was asked what he thought he was accomplishing, he replied: "It's only the beginning. . . ."[38]

But no scheme connected with the OEO could have been more fiendishly devised to arouse middle-class fears and resentments than the welfare rights movement.

An important feature of most CAPs was the neighborhood service center, usually a noisy ghetto storefront office crowded with rickety desks and battered typewriters where young poverty officials talked to clients and planned their next assault on inequality. The centers were supposedly "neighborhood city halls" that dispensed aid and advice to poor people threatened with displacement by urban renewal or entangled in the legal system. Their chief function, however, was to guide the poor through the complexities of the welfare rules and guarantee that they got the share of city and federal welfare services that they were legally entitled to. The net effect was to enlarge enormously the welfare rolls in each of the communities where they operated.

The staffs of the service centers quickly developed an adversary relationship with welfare and city officials determined to keep costs within limits. So did their clients. One effective device for assaulting the supposedly insensitive establishment was through welfare mothers' organizations. Traditional "welfare" administered by the city was an intrusive, time-consuming, often degrading process, and the service center workers had no trouble finding and exploiting a deep pool of resentment among slum women. Before long, in scores of cities, groups of women with children, but no husbands, were ready to picket, sit-in, and, at times, even physically assault, welfare agencies and welfare officials.

At first these protest efforts were scattershot affairs. They soon became part of an organized movement.

As early as 1964–65 small groups of welfare mothers in the Minneapolis–St. Paul area and elsewhere had come together to defend their legal rights and to work for common concerns. In 1966 Dr. George A. Wiley, a black civil rights activist who had surrendered a promising academic career to work for CORE and the poor, established the Poverty Rights Action Center in Washington, D.C. The process culminated in the formation, primarily on the East Coast, of the National Welfare Rights Organization in 1967 and of Direct Action Recipients of Welfare the following year in Minneapolis.

These bodies were not merely welfare client defense agencies. They had a radical philosophy inspired by Richard Cloward and his collaborator Frances Fox Piven as spelled out in their 1966 article, "A Strategy to End Poverty." If enough families could be placed on the welfare rolls, these activists announced, the burden on the taxpayers would become intolerable and the system would break down. There would then ensue a political crisis that would lead to "a guaranteed annual income" (GAI), the Piven–Cloward solution to the welfare muddle. The GAI was not merely another welfare device, however. Unlike welfare, it was redistributive, shifting income from the middle class to the poor. As the two activists expressed it, "a federal program of income redistribution" had "become necessary to elevate the poor en masse from poverty."[39]

The two professors of social work were not merely militant in their ends; they were militant in their means. They envisaged a strategy based on disruption. Militant confrontations with the authorities "would exacerbate strains among Negro and white working-class and middle-class elements in the urban Democratic coalition." This "strategy of crises" would be the instrument of reforming "the traditional means of distributing income in the country."[40]

The welfare rights militants were most effective in New York, where Cloward and Piven were headquartered and where the nation's most liberal mayor, John V. Lindsay, ran an administration exceptionally responsive to the demands of the black and Hispanic communities. Lindsay's human resources administrator, Mitchell Ginsberg, and Dr. Jack Goldberg, his commissioner of social services and welfare, a former consultant to the OEO, accepted their chief's view that the militants spoke for the entire community.

Though Cloward and Piven had formulated the "overload" theory back in 1966, it was only in 1967 and 1968 that it began to be widely applied. The two activists had hit on an ingenious approach. New York had on the books a rule that besides their regular semimonthly welfare checks for food and rent, eligible welfare clients were legally entitled to an additional "special grant" to provide a minimum standard of furniture, household equipment, and clothing. The city had seldom authorized this allowance, however, and few welfare clients bothered to apply for it. But now the Cloward–Piven-inspired citywide Coordinating Committee of Welfare Groups, headed by Hulbert James, determined to force the city to comply with its own disused rules.

In March 1968 James and his group began to mimeograph lists of items that welfare clients were entitled to and to distribute them by the thousands throughout the ghetto. In April mobs of organized welfare clients descended on New York welfare centers to demand special grants for necessary items. Demonstrators jammed the centers, sometimes camping out overnight. Their applications, completed by activist legal services lawyers and OEO service center militants, produced mountains of paper and blew the circuits of the welfare bureaucracy. They also raised the city's welfare outlays on the special grants from $20 million in 1965 to $90 million in 1967–68.

At this point even the most liberal New York politicians bridled. Late in the year city officials proposed to put an automatic flat ceiling of a hundred dollars a year per client on the special grants. This would hold down costs, while at the same time, they hoped, it would end the disorders at the welfare centers.

The militants were equal to the challenge. They were not primarily interested in getting more money for welfare clients. They wanted to destroy the "bankrupt," "antiquated," "lawless," and "self-defeating" welfare system as a whole as a first step to redistributing income in American society. If city bureaucrats believed they had put a damper on disorder, they were mistaken. Welfare activists, Cloward and Piven reported in the fall, would counter the city's moves by urging clients to "spend the rent," that is, use their rent money for other purposes. With no money to pay the landlords, they would be evicted, of course. "But evictions will provoke street confrontations with the police and marshals and may constitute an even greater threat to placidity in the ghettos."[41] The authorities would face another dangerous challenge.

The poverty program organizers were indeed provocateurs. But the militancy of the ghettos was as much indigenous as borrowed. During 1966–67 the Black Power movement took root in the inner city, and the white organizers often found themselves outstripped by their clients in their confrontational enthusiasm. By 1968 ghetto entrepreneurs had learned major lessons on how to manipulate the system for their advantage. They knew that "The Man" felt both guilty and afraid and that to squeeze him for money and favors you only had to play on both feelings simultaneously. To get your way you collected the brothers and descended on the local OEO office in force, looking fierce, indignant, dangerous, and determined. Then you shouted, banged on floors and tables, and talked tough and profanely. In the black community, according to the journalist Tom Wolfe, this was called "mau-mauing," after the black Kikuyu rebels whose terrorist tactics had driven the white colonial regime from Kenya back in the 1950s.

Mau-mauing started with blacks, but in places like San Francisco it quickly became a general Third World technique effective for restoring welfare cuts and getting the bureaucrats to cough up extra money or jobs. As Wolfe noted, it also brought a psychological dividend: "You made the white man quake. You brought *fear* into his face."[42]

There is a side of militancy that critics either missed or deplored. The War on Poverty *did* create community competence of a kind. By 1966 or 1967 a black antipoverty cadre had emerged with new-honed political skills. In a number of cities with large black ghettos—Newark, Cleveland, Detroit—these men and women would use the antipoverty programs to organize power bases that prepared the way for the black mayors who would appear at the decade's end.

But whatever the long-term gains, corruption, venality, waste, and militancy undermined public support for the War on Poverty. Growing skepticism about OEO claims further weakened public backing. The OEO puffed its programs immoderately. It spent thousands on slick brochures touting its activities and glamorizing its field workers. The OEO public affairs department churned out an ocean of upbeat press releases. These pronouncements were long on rhetoric and short on facts. In 1965 the OEO's annual report acknowledged that "the most significant results" of its first year were "*not* measureable in terms of expenditures, or people helped. . . ." Rather, the agency had created "a new and growing concern for a minority who might otherwise be doomed to a life of poverty." A year later its chief contribution, its own releases admitted, was that it had alerted "the conscience of the country to the problem of poverty. . . ."[43]

OEO officials not only fudged when called to account; they sometimes deliberately misled the public. At one point Shriver claimed that 80 percent of Upward Bound's graduates went to college. He neglected to add that half of these were flunking out. A 1967 OEO statement noted that 53 percent of Job Corps trainees were being placed in jobs. But as Congressman Charles Goodell of New York observed, pre-OEO job training programs had placed an even higher percentage. Two years after it began the War on Poverty had run into the same credibility gap as the war in Vietnam.

The conservative and liberal press recounted the horror stories—the first with glee, the second with regret. In 1968–69 two books, Daniel Moynihan's *Maximum Feasible Misunderstanding* and Edward Banfield's *The Unheavenly City,* savaged the War on Poverty as devisive and counterproductive. Well before this, Sargent Shriver, convinced that the poverty program would be his political graveyard, tried to desert. The president, fearing his departure would damage the administration's image, refused to let him go. Then, in March 1968, he bailed him out by appointing him ambassador to France. By this time the president himself had few illusions left and had begun to call the CAP leaders "kooks and sociologists."

Yet it is easy to see that, even without the excesses, the War on Poverty was doomed. In 1966 the Democrats lost their swollen congressional majorities. The Ninetieth Congress that convened in January 1967 was not the Johnson rubber stamp of its predecessor, and it threatened to kill off the poverty program entirely. Fortunately for the program's defenders, now mostly OEO bureaucrats, benefit recipients, and a portion of the academic—social science community, it was rescued at the last minute. But the price was high. Hereafter, local officials would run the CAPs; they would no longer act as independent power centers and dispensers of jobs and money. In this new form, in late 1967, Congress extended the Economic Opportunity Act for an additional two years.

But if the flesh survived, the spirit had departed. After 1968 the War on Poverty and the Great Society lost their forward thrust.

The loss of momentum was not solely the effect of waste, corruption, and resentment. In 1968 the economy lost its steam and with it the sense of well-being, the margin of material comfort that had made the whole thing possible. That year the specter of inflation abruptly appeared to haunt the American consumer. In 1968 too the United States dollar ceased to be the linchpin of the world economy. Neither of these dangers was mortal. Yet their psychological effects were profound. Suddenly the American mood of confidence and optimism deflated. As the business historian Robert Sobel has said, "The 'American Century' ended sometime in the 1960s and this became apparent to many in 1968."[44]

Americans did not abruptly become poor. Nineteen sixty-eight would be prosperous to the end with GNP rising from $794 billion to $864 billion. But it would also be full of economic shocks and alarms that would highlight the fragility of America's economic performance.

The weakness would first become apparent in the international economy. The United States had enjoyed a favorable balance of trade ever since the end of the nineteenth century, when its wheat, cotton, coal, steel, farm machinery, and a cornucopia of other products had been the cheapest and best in the world. During these years America had become the world model of productivity, its factories in Pittsburgh, Detroit, Chicago, and Buffalo the envy of Europe. During and following World War I, America had also become the world's largest creditor, with capital to spare for other nations' needs and large annual returns of interest to add to its earnings on the international accounts books.

World War II had confirmed the country's economic and industrial lead. Alone among the major belligerents, the United States had escaped physical destruction and had emerged as an international economic colossus, with 60 percent of world manufacturing output and a quarter of the world's total international trade during the late 1940s.

Clearly, it could not maintain this extraordinary position for very long. Europe recovered, in part because of American Marshall Plan aid, and was soon able to supply its impoverished population with homebuilt, homegrown goods. The Japanese too regained their feet and, freed of past dreams of glory, applied their fierce ingenuity to the task of getting rich. Before long both Western Europe and Japan were meeting most of their own people's needs.

Yet for most of the 1950s and 1960s the United States managed to sell more abroad than it bought. In 1964 the trade surplus was $6.7 billion, the highest level since 1947. American success depended in part on low and stable prices. It also depended on superior American technology, organization, and marketing and managerial skills. American wages were far higher than those of every other country in the world, but the foreign producers' wage advantage was offset by American efficiency and know-how. The period was, in the words of a *Fortune* magazine writer, "a cushioned era."[45] Then, rather abruptly, America lost its industrial preeminence, its ability to surpass its world competitors in price and quality.

The decline was quickly reflected in foreign trade. By the mid-sixties Europeans and Asians were not merely supplying their own needs and beginning to compete with the United States in foreign markets; they had begun to penetrate the vast American domestic market as well. German-made Volkswagens began to crowd American streets and highways. By mid-decade two new cars, the Toyota and the Datsun, appeared on the roads of both coasts and were attracting the eyes of the curious. In 1967 the United States imported 767,000 cars. By 1968 sales of Volkswagens, Toyotas, Opels, and others were running at a still higher clip, and by the end of the year total car imports were expected to cost the country over $1 billion.

But the car invasion was not all. Italian and Spanish shoes and leather goods, German cameras, Taiwanese and South Korean radios, tape recorders, and TVs, Japanese and British bicycles and motorcycles—all had begun to push American-made goods out of the domestic market. The country was no longer even self-sufficient in steel, the key measure in the past of any nation's industrial standing. At the end of the 1950s the United States was a large net exporter of steel. In 1967 it imported almost a billion dollars' worth more than it sold.

The slide of America's international competitiveness would become catastrophic in the next two decades. But by the opening months of 1968 it had already begun to frighten knowledgeable observers. In June *Fortune* magazine noted that heavy imports of raw materials like oil and copper were one thing, but America was losing the international competition in industrial goods, "the very area of economic life where we thought we had special competitive strength."[46]

The trade imbalance aggravated the deficit in the balance of payments, the net of all international transactions between this country and the rest of the world—trade, interest payments, overseas investments, tourist spending, foreign aid, and other international transactions. The payments deficit was not new. Ever since the fifties the total United States international balance sheet had been in the red. The fault at this point was not American weakness. On the contrary: the nation's enormous international power and its resulting political commitments were responsible. Free World leadership did not come cheap. The United States had to bolster its friends and allies, actual and potential, all over the world to the tune of billions in gifts each year lest they falter in their resolve to defend themselves against their Communist enemies—and ours. American strength was also displayed in the billions left in Europe by rich American tourists or transferred abroad by American corporations eager to buy up foreign companies. From 1950 on, in only one year did the United States fail to send more dollars abroad than it received back. By 1968 the cumulative postwar American balance-of-payments deficit had reached the gigantic total of close to $40 billion.

For most of the postwar period the American payments deficit caused little trouble. Foreigners' willingness to hold American dollars seemed limitless. And why not? They were the paper gold that kept the international monetary system afloat. And they were surely as sound as the American colossus itself. Certain that the dollar was as secure as anything in an uncertain world, Europeans, Asians, Latin Americans, and Africans stuffed the notes that poured from the U.S. Treasury presses into strong boxes and mattresses as enthusiastically as their fathers had squirreled away gold sovereigns in the past.

All was well until 1965 or 1966 despite the oceans of green that had flowed out of the country. Then came the surge in imports of late 1967 and early 1968. Now we were also sending dollars abroad to pay for the excess of imports over exports.

By itself this wave of money would have weakened confidence in the ability to exchange dollars for gold on demand. Even more serious, however, was the swelling American budget deficit. Beginning in late 1965 the Treasury's tax take fell behind its expenditures. In the 1966–67 fiscal year the government spent almost $9 billion more than it took in. In the period July 1, 1967–June 30, 1968, fiscal 1968, its excess of outlays over income soared to over $25 billion. By early 1968 the cumulative deficit of the previous three years had reached almost $38 billion, an enormous sum for the day.

The deficit was caused by the Vietnam War, the most expensive effort since Korea to bolster the Free World. Between 1965 and 1966 the annual Defense Department budget leaped over $8 billion. Between '66 and '67 it went up another $13 billion, and the following year another $10 billion. Domestic costs, especially Great Society welfare and poverty programs, also rose, but at a slower pace.

The president hid the cost figures for Vietnam in the general defense budget and refused to admit how much the country was paying for the war. His lack of candor was in part inbred. Johnson was by nature a devious man who seemed incapable of telling the truth when a fiction was more interesting or convenient. He lied about his parents, his childhood, his college years, his trip to California as a teenager. He now lied about the war's costs. He also feared that the American people would not accept the sacrifice, would demand either that he deescalate or, equally unacceptable, cut back drastically on domestic programs. Faced with the prospect of abridging the war or the Great Society, the president preferred to deceive.

For a time it worked. In 1966 Johnson was able to induce his Council of Economic Advisers to play down the ill effects of the budget deficit. "Defense procurement by itself," the CEA's 1966 report stated, "will not be placing extreme demands on particular industries."[47] In his own Economic Report of early 1966 the president anticipated critical questions about the war's economic impact: could the country avoid major industry or personnel bottlenecks? Could it avoid a destructive wage-price spiral? Could the United States move ahead with Great Society programs and still meet its defense needs? "My confident answer to each of these questions," he replied, "is YES."[48] When a *Fortune* magazine researcher contacted the Pentagon for figures on the amount being funneled directly into Vietnam, he was stonewalled. "We have no intention of cost-accounting the war," an official told him.[49]

Yet the war's costs could not be hidden for long. Johnson had escalated the war with the American economy "already in a roaring boom."[50] War outlays soon poured billions more into the nation's income stream. Deficit spending is fine when there are jobless workers and idle factories; it will put people and machines back to work. But when the economy is hurtling along at top speed, deficits can only mean more dollars to buy more things than can be produced. This is the classic formula for inflation: more dollars chasing fewer goods.

From 1961 through 1964 consumer prices had not risen faster than 2 percent annually. By the mid-sixties Americans had come to take price stability for granted. Then in 1965 came the administration's commitment to winning a ground war in Vietnam and the surge in military spending. By December 1967 the consumer price index was rising 0.4 percent in a single month, almost 5 percent a year, revealing an economy beginning to overheat.

Americans were unnerved by inflation. Since the beginning of the decade they had come to assume that price stability was the normal state of affairs. Price increases of even 4 or 5 percent a year evoked frightening images. Americans remembered the 50 percent leap in living costs in 1946–47 when Truman and Congress had ended the wartime Office of Price Administration and allowed prices to find their own level. If they were older, they recalled the 1920s German hyperinflation when it took wheelbarrows full of paper money to buy the daily newspaper and thick rolls of thousand-mark notes to purchase a postage stamp.

The experts too were unprepared for inflation. Robert Sobel has said that the American economy in the late sixties was like French military preparedness in 1940. We had erected an economic Maginot Line of safeguards against the *last* war, the Great Depression, a time when prices for everything went down, down, down. But we were not ready for the new onslaught, inflation. Nineteen sixty-eight would be the start of the great inflation surge that would not be checked until the 1980s and then only at appalling human cost.

Inflation further eroded America's foreign trade position. The country's trade deficit was worsened by the price shifts. With American prices rising, foreign cars, machinery, luxury goods became more attractive to consumers. Simultaneously, expensive American products became even less appealing to foreign buyers.

Most portentous of all, American budget deficits and the zooming trade imbalance undermined international confidence in the American dollar. Foreigners had been happy to hold any amount of Uncle Sam's obligations; by the opening months of 1968 they held over $31 billion. They now began to ask nervously: "Will the United States be able to fulfill its gold-redemption commitments?"

The American dollar was already under attack as the Western world's measure of value for political reasons. Charles de Gaulle, the savior of France from the Nazis, had returned to power in 1958 determined to break the economic and political dominance of the "Anglo-Saxon" powers and to restore France to its rightful "grandeur." As leader of the Free French government-in-exile during the war, de Gaulle had been snubbed and humiliated by Churchill and Roosevelt, and the proud general was prepared for revenge against the "Anglo-Saxons." In 1963 he vetoed Britain's application for admission to the European Common Market, the economic union that had partially merged the economies of most Western European countries and made them a formidable rival to the United States. This was Britain's punishment for maintaining a "special relationship" with the United States. Then, two years later, he began to cash in France's dollars for gold, pulling millions out of Fort Knox and sucking them into the subterranean vaults of the New York Federal Reserve Bank, where foreign nations kept their gold stocks. The general argued that his motives were economic: the unadorned gold standard—as opposed to the Bretton Woods system—was the only international exchange that really worked. He also claimed that the Bretton Woods arrangement benefited the United States disproportionately. But clearly his attack on the postwar monetary system was another case of anti–"Anglo-Saxonism."

The French war against Bretton Woods and against the preeminence of the dollar helped destabilize an already shaky gold exchange standard. As early as the opening months of 1965, foreign holders of American dollars, frightened by the Vietnam escalation, rushed to convert them into gold. Suddenly the gold reserves dropped hundreds of millions of dollars until they approached dangerously close to the point where they were not enough to meet the minimum legal "gold cover" for American currency required by U.S. law. Johnson intervened by removing the gold-cover requirement on several billion dollars of federal reserve notes. The crisis eased and everyone relaxed.

It soon resumed. In 1967 de Gaulle struck against the British pound, his financial allies doing what they could to undermine confidence in its convertibility into gold. In mid-November 1967 the pound was officially devalued from $2.80 to $2.40. Less gold would now be needed to make it exchangeable. In the process of trying to stabilize the international exchanges the United States lost $1 billion in scarce Treasury gold.

The next few weeks were a time of further uncertainty. In the wake of the pound devaluation, American Treasury officials flew to Basel to confer with the Gold Pool countries, a group of seven nations organized in 1961 to shore up the gold exchange standard by providing extra gold in emergencies. Unfortunately, the unscheduled and unexplained move only suggested that the administration was running scared. Soon after, Secretary of the Treasury Henry Fowler remarked to reporters that the dollar "was on the front line."[51] It was a foolish statement that only added to the bankers' and speculators' jitters.

By the end of 1967 the whole Bretton Woods monetary structure was swaying dangerously, threatening to bring the Free World economy down with a crash. Americans' view of the decade's agenda would be profoundly narrowed.

During the month of December 1967 the United States gold loss was $900 million, the largest for any month on record. It was this massive drain that had prompted Lyndon Johnson to issue his New Year's Day guidelines for curtailed tourist spending, private foreign investment, and United States government expenditures abroad.

For the moment this was the easiest way out. The United States could also have devalued—raised the price of gold to, say, forty dollars an ounce. But this might have thrown the world economy into chaos. The new guidelines promised to avoid such a drastic consequence. But they were also not enough.

On March 1 the greatest wave of speculation since the Great Depression hit the international gold market. In the next ten days $1 billion in gold—nine hundred tons—changed hands in London, where most of the world's buying and selling of the yellow metal was conducted. This was twenty to thirty times the normal amount. Speculators, anticipating devaluation and the increased price of the precious metal, sent gold mining stocks soaring in New York, London, and Johannesburg. By now it was clear that the panic was feeding on itself and that if it continued much longer would bring the entire postwar international monetary order down with a roar. The public, however, ignorant of finance, caught the jittery mood and held its breath.

On March 10 the seven Gold Pool countries convened again in Basel and pledged support for the dollar. But these were just words and had little effect. On Wednesday evening the thirteenth, after the London Gold Exchange had closed for the day, Johnson called Prime Minister Harold Wilson on the hotline connecting the White House to No. 10 Downing Street. Shortly before midnight, Wilson, accompanied by the chancellor of the exchequer and the economic affairs secretary, went to Buckingham Palace. In matters of such grave importance practice dictated that the sovereign be consulted. A little after 1:00 A.M. Queen Elizabeth issued a proclamation closing the Gold Exchange as well as the United Kingdom's foreign exchange markets, stock exhanges, and the foreign departments of all British banks.

The crisis was far from over. On March 14 gold sales topped $400 million, an all-time record for a single day. That weekend American tourists in Europe found that no one would take their travelers' checks or exchange dollars for the local currency. During the next few days the politicians and the central bankers scurried around frantically looking for a more permanent solution. On March 16–17 the Gold Pool central bankers came to Washington and agreed to abandon the practice of selling government gold to private buyers. Speculators could continue to buy and sell to one another, but they could not draw gold out of treasuries and central banks thus playing hob with the backing of the world's major currencies.

The action of the Gold Pool was confirmed in Stockholm at the end of the month. There, at a meeting of the Group of Ten, a consortium of ten major industrial nations organized in 1960 as a monetary stabilizing force, the "two-tier" system adopted by the Gold Pool was made permanent. Central banks could continue to exchange their currencies for gold at thirty-five dollars an ounce, but everyone else would have to pay the market price, whatever it might be. This policy would preserve the gold backing for the dollar at the old rate and retain its role as a stable reserve for the world's currencies, but would protect the gold at Fort Knox. The Group of Ten also agreed to establish a new system of Special Drawing Rights (SDRs) that would allow the United States and other countries to substitute a new kind of "paper dollar" for actual gold in meeting trade deficits. The changes announced at Stockholm took much of the pressure off the dollar, and peace proponents viewed it as encouragement of the United States in its Vietnam madness. During the meeting Stockholm students demonstrated outside the conference hall carrying signs that read: SDR EQUALS SUPPORT FOR MASS MURDER.[52]

The day following the adoption of the two-tier system the price of gold on the international exchanges fell by several points. The crisis was over. But something else had happened, too. The United States had surrendered financial leadership of the Free World.

Few Americans understood or seemed to care about the gold crisis. A reporter for *The New York Times* found that the man-in-the-street was indifferent to financial events in London, Stockholm, and Washington. "I have other problems now," one woman hurrying down Fifth Avenue told him. "I figure our leaders know what they're doing. I hope," said a man unloading a truck on West Forty-third Street.[53]

Yet the crisis did affect ordinary Americans. Vietnam might be the major cause of the budget deficits, but domestic programs were also expensive. During the worst days of the panic the papers were full of reports that in order to save the world monetary system American spending—for whatever purposes—would have to be brought under control.

The gold crisis placed an enormous strain on the president. March 14, Lady Bird Johnson noted in her diary, was "one of those terrific, pummeling White House days that can stretch and grind and use you. . . ." She, though only on the edges of the maelstrom, was deeply affected. "What must it be like for Lyndon!"[54]

Indeed, the president was concerned with more than international finance. However much he hid it from the general public, he understood the connections between gold, inflation, Vietnam, and the Great Society. The only way to continue the war, preserve international monetary stability, and achieve his domestic goals, all at the same time, was to raise taxes. In effect, Americans would have to pay for the war and the Great Society by taking more money out of their pockets; they could no longer be financed by printing money. Perhaps the people would be willing to pay for the war, since that involved the Communist menace abroad and the national safety. But after three and a half years of confrontation, waste, and disorder, would they also be willing to pay for the Great Society?

Johnson resisted the idea of a tax increase for months after his advisers told him that it was necessary. He understood the need, but he could not bite the bullet. In January 1967 he finally asked Congress to impose a 6 percent surcharge in all income tax returns to take effect after June 30, that is, in fiscal 1968. But he remained sensitive to any discussion of Vietnam costs. In May Paul Lazarus, Jr., president of Federated Department Stores, told the Business Council that Vietnam would create a 1967–68 revenue shortfall of $15 billion to $18 billion. Supreme Court Justice Abe Fortas, LBJ's adviser and close friend, was on the phone in hours complaining to Lazarus that the claim was exaggerated and would seriously hurt the country.

Congress itself was reluctant to act. Nineteen sixty-eight was an election year. You do not impose new burdens on the voters when they are about to decide your political fate. Congressional opponents of Vietnam who saw new taxes as further fuel for the detested war were also skeptical. Republicans had still another motive: if prices rose, they could blame the Democrats for fiscal mismanagement in the upcoming campaign. The most serious hurdle of all was Wilbur Mills, chairman of the all-powerful House Ways and Means Committee.

Congressman Mills of Searcy, Arkansas, was a short, moon-faced man with thick eyeglasses, a broad nose, and smooth, slicked-back hair. He looked like a nondescript small-town accountant or dentist, and Lyndon Johnson called him "that prissy, prim, and proper man."[55]

Appearances were deceiving. A shrewd lawyer with a Harvard degree, Mills had a secret life, it seems, that included a yearning for the presidency, a drinking problem, and a yen for pretty women. But at this point the public knew him only as a hardworking conservative southern Democratic who considered himself the watchdog of the Treasury against the liberal spenders.

Like many southern conservatives, Mills detested the Great Society. His views on the government's role and responsibilities might have supplied the text for the Reagan revolution fifteen years later. He questioned the very premise of the Great Society: that a rich nation owed its benefits to all its citizens. America's economic surplus should not be poured out in charity programs. "My philosophy," he stated, "is that government is not entitled to all of the increment that comes from a tax system when the economy is booming." He did not agree with people who believed that Treasury surpluses belonged "to the government for new programs. . . ." Rather, "There should be periodic tax reductions . . . , and they should go back to the private sector."[56]

From the first, Mills had cast a dubious eye at the figures and forecasts of the Council of Economic Advisers, especially the data on Vietnam War costs. At the hearings on the president's proposed 6 percent tax surcharge, held in the large, ornate House Ways and Means Committee room at the Capitol in August 1967, Mills listened patiently to Secretary Fowler and other Treasury officials when they testified for the surcharge, but chided them for overestimating revenues and underestimating costs. The chariman made it clear that there would be a stiff price for any tax increase: the administration would have to retrench, cut the budget. "If I'm going to be for an increase," he stated, "I want some degree of assurance that the action is going to be temporary, and I know it's not going to be temporary unless federal spending is cut back."[57]

Despite the pleas of Fowler and Federal Reserve Board Chairman William McChesney Martin, Mills vetoed a surcharge in October. Vague promises to reduce spending were not enough, he announced. There must be a firm commitment to specific reductions and a bipartisan Program Evaluation Commission to study and evaluate all federal spending programs. But "as of now the tax bill is dead."[58]

For several months the tax surcharge remained frozen. Then, as Mills prepared to return to Searcy for Thanksgiving, Fowler gave him an administration proposal promising to cut or postpone expenditures drastically. The Treasury would reduce its outgo by an amount equal to every additional dollar earned by the tax increase. Mills took this document home with him, and when he returned to Washington held further hearings. By this time the British devaluation had churned up the international monetary system, and when Fowler once again appeared he could marshal new arguments for the surcharge. The international monetary system was tottering, and the United States, he told the committee, had never before confronted a monetary problem "more decisive for our country and the free world."[59] The secretary also brought further concessions: the administration would cut the budget for fiscal 1969 by $4.1 billion. It would also accept Mills's proposal for a bipartisan task force to evaluate federal spending programs and establish legislative priorities. The new plan represented progress, Mills said.

While Mills and the Treasury haggled over terms, Johnson continued the impossible fight for stable prices, the war in Vietnam, and the Great Society all at the same time. In his January budget message the president asked for a 10 percent tax surcharge, an increase over the 6 percent of the previous year. This would reduce the deficit for 1969 to only $7.9 billion, he delcared. He admitted that "we cannot do everything we would wish to do,"[60] but at the same time he recommended increases for his Model Cities program, for manpower training, and for child health care.

In his Economic Report to Congress three days later Johnson acknowledged that the economy was in trouble. Growth was "too fast for safety," he admitted, and with wholesale price rises in the second half of 1967 exceeded "in only four other half-year periods in the past sixteen years," the country faced the prospect of severe inflation. The "first and foremost" task of 1968 was "to put our fiscal affairs in order." Yet the president was still not prepared to abandon the Great Society. "The war on poverty must go forward," he announced. "The exceptional economic benefits" that Americans had enjoyed in the previous seven years imposed "obligations" on them "to the more than ten million households still in poverty."[61]

During the months that followed, Johnson waffled over the costs of the Great Society. In late February the National Advisory Commission on Civil Disorders, headed by Governor Otto Kerner of Illinois, made its report on the causes, course, and cures of ghetto riots. Johnson disliked the commission's pessimistic conclusions that America was "moving toward two societies, one black, one white—separate and unequal" and its charge that the riots were at heart caused by an intractable "white racism." (See chapter 3.) But he also objected to its proposals for sharp increases in poverty outlays that would, as the Budget Bureau told him, double the $30 billion already appropriated for the poor. What he needed, he said, was more votes, not more bright ideas on how to spend money. Johnson greeted the report with the less than resounding endorsement that it was "worthy of study."

During the months ahead, the president continued to twist and turn. In a mid-March speech to the National Alliance of Businessmen he noted that "some desirable programs of lesser priority are going to have to be deferred. . . . Hard choices are going to have to be made in the next few days."[62] A day later the newspapers reported that the president would accept budget reductions of $8 to $9 billion. Yet just a few days earlier, in his annual health message to Congress, he had asked for $58 to $237 million additional in the 1969 fiscal year for postnatal care for "needy" mothers and a Health Manpower Act to "train more health workers and train them better and faster."[63]

At the end of January the president sent his top team of economic advisers to the Hill to beg once more for action on the tax surcharge. They failed. Chairman Mills was not impressed with their prediction of an overheated economy and runaway inflation—not when there was no accompanying plan to cut back. The spending increase for the 1969 fiscal year was simply "too damned much," he told the president's emissaries. At this latest rebuff, Secretary of the Treasury Henry Fowler "for just an instant . . . buried his face in his hands."[64]

For weeks the struggle was a standoff. Then came the March gold crisis. On the thirteenth a blue-ribbon panel of advisers led by former Treasury Secretary Douglas Dillon warned of "the grave consequences" to the country's "international trade and financial position" of inaction on taxes.[65] A month later Martin of the Federal Reserve Board joined the battle. The nation was "in the midst of the worst financial crisis since 1931," he warned. "We are faced with an intolerable budget and also an intolerable deficit in our international payments," and both would "have to be corrected over the next few years or the United States is going to face either an uncontrollable recession or an uncontrollable inflation."[66] In the face of the worsening economic and financial news, on April 2 the Senate broke the logjam by appending a 10 percent tax surcharge and a mandatory $6 billion reduction in total federal spending for 1969 to a minor tax bill sent over from the House. But the House continued to resist.

By this point the president had already ordered his poverty agencies to cut back on spending. Toward the end of March the commissioner of the New York City Community Development Agency announced that the OEO was slashing funds to city remedial and adult education programs and to some neighborhood projects. The cuts, he said, would be "devastating."[67]

But Mills was still not satisfied and refused to be moved. He pooh-poohed the gold crisis. The United States had the strongest economy the world had ever seen, he told a business group later in the month, and the country would be better off focusing on its overall productive power than worrying about day-to-day gold fluctuations.[68]

In early May—after further Johnson concessions on domestic spending—Mills changed his tune. On the sixth he and a bare majority of the Ways and Means Committee endorsed the $10 billion tax increase coupled with a federal spending cut of $6 billion. The measure now went to a joint House-Senate conference to reconcile differences.

Johnson still refused to give up. The House budget cuts were too severe. They would kill off all that he had tried to do. In the spring he told his cabinet that if he were "a dictator and . . . could write my own ticket" he "would add to the budget instead of taking from it and . . . wouldn't have a ten percent surcharge either."[69] At this May cabinet meeting the president apparently actually asked his official advisers for their opinions of the surcharge. The financial people and the hawks, more concerned with the war than the poor, told him that failure to enact a tax bill would be disastrous. Defense Secretary Clark Clifford declared: "Whatever has to be done has to be done to get this tax bill. We'll do it." But the liberals—Attorney General Ramsey Clark, Robert Weaver of the Department of Housing and Urban Development, Stewart Udall of the Interior Department, and Labor Secretary Willard Wirtz—urged Johnson to resist the drastic cuts. Wirtz was adamant: "I wouldn't pay one single penny, not one single penny. . . . Don't go below your budget, Mr. President. Don't surrender."[70]

The split in the cabinet mirrored the divisions in the country at large. The business community placed price and monetary stability ahead of the Great Society. The liberals, organized labor, and the civil rights organizations reversed the order. In Congress the differences offered some hope of rescuing his programs, and Johnson decided to test the waters with a motion asking the House members of the House-Senate conference committee to reduce the budget cut from $6 to $4 billion. No luck. On May 29 the administration's scheme went down to defeat 259 to 137.

The president now threw his full support behind the bill in the House-Senate conference committee. On May 30 LBJ told a press conference that if Congress "will vote for the conference report containing the tax increase and the $6 billion expenditure cut, I shall approve it."[71] The liberals would not say die, however. In the House the big-city delegates vowed to restore any cuts in welfare programs that Mills had forced from the president. Sixteen Senate defenders of the Great Society attacked the measure when it returned for approval from the joint conference committee. Philip Hart of Michigan sounded a note of apocalypse. Invoking the name of the young militant Black Power leader who had been blamed for stirring up the ghettos, Hart declared that no one should "put the finger on Stokely Carmichael if there are riots this summer after we pass this bill." The blame, he said, would rest with Congress for cutting money for education, welfare, and antipoverty programs.[72]

The protest came to nothing. On June 28 Johnson signed the bill—this time without ceremony.

This was not the death knell of the Great Society. The reform impulse spluttered on a bit more. In August Johnson signed into law the Housing and Urban Redevelopment Act, touted as the most comprehensive housing bill to be passed since 1949. It authorized $5.3 billion spread over three years to build or rehabilitate more than 1.7 million housing units and to provide rent subsidies for low-income families. Johnson characterized it, in his self-contratulatory way, as "the most-comprehensive, the most-massive housing program in all American history."[73]

The momentum continued even into the fall. In October the president signed a bill extending through June 1971 work-study programs and insured loans to college students and funding for Upward Bound, the Teacher Corps, and other educational programs.

One striking phenomenon of the months following the surcharge is the extent to which existing programs inflated as more and more poor people cracked the code of the system and learned how to scoop up benefits. In the fall election campaign Richard Nixon and Spiro Agnew, his running mate, would attack "the spending of public dollars to buy off young militants" and promise to cut out the "welfare cheats,"[74] but outlays for the poor and dependent continued to climb long after 1968.

In fact, under Nixon they rose to levels well above Lyndon Johnson's. In LBJ's last fiscal year, federal expenditures on "human resources" for the poor were about $10.6 billion. By 1971 they had risen to almost $23 billion. This represented not only a large increase in dollar amount but also a surge in the proportion of the federal budget.

Yet this was not the Great Society; it was at most inertia. Nixon was indifferent and inattentive to domestic issues and despite all his conservative rhetoric did little to stop the continued growth of welfare costs. And so they soared. Yet in June 1968 the Great Society, already badly wounded at the hands of its friends and enemies alike, lost its forward movement and its inner spirit. After fiscal 1969, as a commitment, an idea, the Great Society was dead.

So was the unbounding economic optimism of the 1960s. All through 1968 the stock market had taken a roller-coaster ride, roaring higher at news of technological breakthroughs or new mergers and plunging with each alarm on the international monetary front. On December 3, despite all the market to-ing and fro-ing, the Dow Jones reached 991, the highest point since the great postwar bull market began in 1949. Thereafter, for a decade stocks would slide, the Dow declining fully a half in constant dollars. As Robert Sobel says: "There can be little doubt that the longest and in many respects most powerful upward surge in the history of Wall Street ended sometime during the post-election season and before New Year's Day" of 1968.[75]

For America the seventies would be a decade of obstinate inflation, slumping productivity, and declining international competitiveness. Economic growth rates would drop from a yearly average of almost 4 percent in the period 1947–67 to under 3 percent in the next dozen years. At the end of the eighth decade of the century, millions of American families would be worse off than they were in 1968. In later years, as Americans looked back to that year, most would remember the war, the domestic turmoil, the violence. But a few would also recall that they, and the country as a whole, had never felt so flush and that for a time the feeling had engendered an extraordinary outpouring of social sympathy and generosity.

2

No Wider War

IN 1968 Americans could not escape Vietnam even on New Year's Day. Three years of steady media drumbeat had not driven the war from the front page.

On January 1 the big *New York Times* Vietnam story was the skirmish at My Tho in the Mekong River Delta near Saigon. Just ten minutes past midnight, while the city's bells were pealing the new calendar year, a Vietcong unit had ambushed the South Vietnamese Second Marine Battalion. Nineteen marines had been killed and forty-seven wounded. Thirty of the enemy were reported dead in the firefight.

There was also a dispatch by Raymond Apple, a Columbia-educated journalist who had come to Vietnam in 1965 to establish the *Times*'s Saigon bureau. Apple was about to return home and this would be his final story from Saigon. The *Times* man was straining to be fair, but his exasperation broke through. American officials in Vietnam, he wrote, were under growing pressure from their bosses in Washington to produce evidence of progress, especially by the South Vietnamese government and the Army of Vietnam (ARVN), the South Vietnamese armed forces. At the U.S. Embassy officials were saying that the "American people will no longer tolerate the Vietnamese caring less about winning than we do." They denied that field representatives had been told to falsify figures or pull their punches, but, Apple wrote, there was strong pressure to fudge the weaknesses of our Asian ally. After all, 1968 was an American election year, and as one bureaucrat had remarked at a recent briefing session, the "people we work for are in the business of reelecting President Johnson in November."[1]

The Vietnam news on the first day of the new year was not good. But neither was it bad. It was just another twenty-four hours in what was becoming America's longest, most discouraging war. In early 1965, shortly after his landslide victory over Barry Goldwater, Lyndon Johnson had committed the United States to military defeat of the Vietcong–North Vietnamese forces and had steadily increased the nation's investment of men and money. On January 1, 1968, there were five hundred thousand American troops in Vietnam and almost sixteen thousand Americans had died in action. In the next three months the tide of war would crest in a furious storm. Powerful men in high places would rethink Vietnam, escalation would cease, and the war would finally begin to recede.

The war had begun in 1945 as a revolt against the French colonial regime by the Vietminh, the Vietnamese Communists, led by Ho Chi Minh, with their base in the northern portion of the country and their capital at Hanoi. Ho had proclaimed Vietnam's independence in September 1945, but the Vietminh had been forced to fight for eight bitter years to achieve even a portion of it. In 1953, after the French defeat at Dienbienphu, the Geneva Conference of the interested parties officially confirmed North Vietnamese independence and recognized a distinct South Vietnam with its capital at Saigon, the two separated by a "demilitarized zone" at the seventeenth parallel. Within two years, the powers at Geneva had declared, there would be "general elections which will bring about the unification of Viet Nam. . . ."[2]

For a time Ho and his colleagues, intent on consolidating their control in the north and certain that the promised plebiscite would favor the reunification of all Vietnam under their control, bided their time. Then, when it became clear that there would be no election, they lost patience. Vietminh partisans, who had either been withdrawn from the south or told to lay low, were now reactivated. As Vietcong—to use their enemy's term—they were soon carrying out guerrilla warfare against the Saigon regime under Ngo Dinh Diem. In December 1960 the Vietcong, or "Cong," as the Americans called them, formed the National Liberation Front (NLF) and announced a program that combined "agrarian reform," a "democratic culture and education," and a "foreign policy of peace and neutrality" with "peaceful reunification of the country."[3]

The NLF professed to be a "united front" that included bourgeois liberal elements as well as Marxists, and claimed to represent all indigenous "progressive" elements of the south. In reality, it was Communist-run, its strings pulled in Hanoi by Ho, a founder in the 1920s of the French Communist party and a devoted disciple of Lenin. This pedigree did not mean that thousands of peasants did not support it. Whether repelled by the corruption, elitism, and tyranny of the Diem regime or attracted by Vietcong promises of land and bread, many southerners embraced the VC. The guerrillas moved "among the people like fish in water,"[4] the Communists would say, providing them with food, shelter, and information. Each year many young peasants joined the VC, impressed by the dedication and bravery of its cadre and believing its promises of beneficent social change.

It was difficult for the United States to avoid responding to the crisis in Vietnam. The great cold-war superpower rivalry that erupted within two years of Hitler's defeat in 1945 quickly took control of American foreign policy. Every event, everywhere in the world, soon became part of the fierce Soviet-American competition. The struggle in part was over power, dominion, and national security. It was also between rival political-economic systems, Western liberal capitalism pitted against Eastern Leninist socialism.

In Europe the rivalry produced a series of crises over Germany, Berlin, and Czechoslovakia that led to the North Atlantic Treaty Organization (NATO), a defensive alliance with the European democracies, and to the "containment policy" to seal off the Soviet Union and its satellites from expanding westward toward the continent's heart. In Asia and Africa, the collapse of the old European colonial empires created vast power vacuums that sucked in the superpowers, especially after the Soviet Union proclaimed its support for "wars of national liberation."

By 1947 the American government had begun to see the Vietnam struggle in a new light. Then in 1949, after the Chinese Communists under Mao Tse-tung drove Chiang Kai-shek and his pro-American Nationalists out of mainland China and proclaimed a Communist People's Republic, American foreign policymakers discovered the "domino effect": if Vietnam fell to the Communists, other Asian nations would inevitably follow until the entire Far East had been lost to the Free World.

These concepts were still only half-formed when in June 1950 waves of Communist North Korean soldiers, intent on forcibly unifying the divided Korean people, swept across the thirty-eighth parallel separating the Korean Peninsula into two political halves. American forces from Japan and the continental United States under the command of Douglas MacArthur were soon locked in bloody combat with the North Koreans all across the mountainous peninsula. In November, with MacArthur's troops approaching the North Korean–Chinese border, thousands of Red Chinese troops poured into Korea and threw the Americans and South Koreans back beyond the original north-south dividing line. The Americans and their United Nations allies rallied and pushed the Communists back to the thirty-eighth parallel. There the two sides settled down to a frustrating and costly war of attrition that tried the patience and distorted the judgment of the American people.

The outbreak of the Korean War confirmed official American doubts of Ho's intentions. He was clearly a Sino-Soviet surrogate in a Communist struggle to dominate the whole of East Asia. The American analysis was fundamentally wrong. Ho was certainly a confirmed Marxist who had the support of the Soviet and Chinese Communist regimes. But the Communist world was not a simple monolith. Red China would soon break with the Soviet Union to pursue an independent course, and Ho would be in neither's pocket. He and his government could not be counted on to follow the Sino-Soviet agenda when it did not suit their purposes. Yet perception is everything in foreign policy. To an increasing number of high-placed Americans it seemed as clear as day that Ho was a Soviet-Chinese proxy whose victory in Vietnam would advance the cause of world communism.

Even in democratic nations foreign policy is usually determined by elites closely connected by birth, schooling, or occupation, or by all three. This may be a heritage of the time when diplomacy was a sport of cultivated and cosmopolitan gentlemen with supple social skills and vast command of languages. Such men make the conduct of foreign relations and their country's connection with the world their special concern. They are drawn to government by a sense of service, but not generally to the gritty, slippery realm of party politics or domestic law making. Their natural habitats are not the parliaments or the city halls, but the embassies and the foreign chancelleries.

In other Western countries this foreign policy elite has usually been recruited from the old aristocracy. America's equivalent has been the wealthy old Protestant families whose sons attend private boarding schools, graduate from Harvard, Yale, or Princeton, and enter law, banking, the universities, and private foundations. However informally, these clans constitute a patriciate that shares with other nations' elites a sense of responsibility—of noblesse oblige—toward the rest of their society.

In this century the progenitor of the foreign policy elite was Elihu Root, a Wall Street lawyer, Theodore Roosevelt's adviser and secretary of state, and then Republican senator from New York. The bearded, austere but witty Root believed foreign policy was the bailiwick of informed gentlemen. Like his successors, Root was an eastern internationalist who refused to accept the isolationist, America-should-go-it-alone views of his midwestern fellow Republicans.

Root passed his attitudes on to Henry Stimson, graduate of Andover, Yale, and Harvard Law School, who became a partner in Root's law firm in 1897. True to the foreign policy elite ethic, Stimson took frequent sabbaticals from his lucrative professional life when called by his president. During the 1920s he served as governor general of the Philippines under Calvin Coolidge and became Herbert Hoover's secretary of state. Many of the foreign policy elite circle have been nominal Republicans, like Root and Stimson, but that has seldom affected their decision to serve. In 1940, when Franklin Roosevelt, seeing war approaching in Europe, asked Stimson to join the cabinet as secretary of war, he did not hesitate.

Stimson in turn attracted to government service a circle of young men with backgrounds and credentials like his own—John McCloy (Peddie School, Amherst, Harvard Law), Robert A. Lovett (the Hill School, Yale, Harvard Law), W. Averell Harriman (Groton, Yale), Dean Acheson (Groton, Yale, Harvard Law), Charles E. ("Chip") Bohlen (St. Paul's, Harvard), George Kennan (St. John's Military Academy, Princeton). These men rose to high positions in the diplomatic service or the State Department, though many were sojourners in government rather than permanent residents. All were internationalists who early saw the danger of Hitler and helped guide the country into war in 1941 and afterward helped guarantee that it did not return to isolationism.

They were also authors of the post–World War II containment policy that marked the early stages of the cold war. None of them was a fanatical anti-Communist, though they had little use for Russian Bolshevism. The danger from the Soviet Union was its expansionism, they said. Like Hitler's Germany, the USSR was an expansionist totalitarian state that must be checked to preserve the Free World, the leadership of which had irrefutably devolved on the United States.

Most of the foreign policy elite were "Atlanticists," who felt that Europe and the Soviet threat must be first on America's agenda. They scorned the Far East priority of the right-wing "China Lobby" that had supported Chiang Kai-shek before 1949, and resisted its scheme to "unleash" Chiang so he could invade the Communist-controlled mainland from his Taiwan refuge. Yet it was Secretary of State Acheson who had midwived U.S. intervention in Korea to stop the North Korean Communists, and his fellow foreign policy elitists had seconded his decision.

However uneasy about fighting a land war in Asia, Acheson, Harriman, and their colleagues favored aiding the French in Vietnam if only to help out an important and hard-pressed

European ally. By 1954 the Americans had spent a billion dollars on Vietnam, providing almost 80 percent of French war costs.

After the Geneva accords American anti-Communist aid went to Diem, the head of the Saigon government, an aloof mandarin who came to power as premier in 1954. But American officials had few illusions about his leadership. In 1961, following an official visit to Saigon, Vice-President Lyndon Johnson would call Diem "the Winston Churchill of Asia." When asked by reporter Stanley Karnow if he had really meant it, Johnson replied: "Shit, Diem's the only boy we got out there."[5]

John F. Kennedy continued the Vietnam policies of his predecessor. The new president was as wary of international communism as Eisenhower had been and if anything more disposed to assert American power around the world. Americans, he declared in his inaugural address, would "pay any price, bear any burden, meet any hardship, support any friend, oppose any foe to secure the survival and success of liberty."[6] Vietnam was not exempt from the tough-minded formula.

Kennedy's position was endorsed by the foreign policy elite. By 1960 most of these men, except the hardy septuagenarian Averell Harriman, had left public life, but their influence continued through younger figures like the Bundy brothers, MacGeorge (Groton, Yale) and older brother William (Groton, Yale, and Harvard Law), and Paul Nitze (Harvard), and through the prestigious Council on Foreign Relations and its influential journal *Foreign Affairs*. By the opening years of the 1960s they were key components of the "Eastern Establishment," a nebulous but powerful political entity made up of opinion leaders and "influentials" associated with the better universities, the more-serious media, and the leading circles of corporate law. Kennedy made Mac Bundy his national security adviser and brother William, Dean Acheson's son-in-law, his deputy assistant secretary of defense for international security affairs. Harriman, meanwhile, after a single term as governor of New York, was called back to Washington as "roving ambassador" and stayed on as assistant secretary for far eastern affairs. Paul Nitze, William Bundy's predecessor at Defense, later became secretary of the navy.

Kennedy was at first as committed to the Diem government as Eisenhower. As a member of Congress he had called the Diem regime "the cornerstone of the Free World in Southeast Asia. . . ."[7] In early 1961 he authorized an increase in the number of American military advisers and approved augmented American economic support to enable Diem to increase his army by another twenty thousand men.

In October 1961 Kennedy dispatched General Maxwell Taylor, a handsome military intellectual and future chairman of the Joint Chiefs of Staff, and Walt Rostow, his deputy national security adviser, to South Vietnam to survey the ground and report back what was needed to stop the Communist advance. The Taylor–Rostow report repeated the domino formula of the Eisenhower administration and recommended an increase in the number of U.S. military advisers and the dispatch of American-manned military helicopters to help the South Vietnamese. In a section directed to the president's eyes only, it also suggested sending eight thousand American combat troops. These would be disguised as logistical support forces sent to aid sufferers from a major flood in the Mekong River Delta.

Back in Washington, Secretary of Defense Robert McNamara and the Joint Chiefs of Staff rejected the Taylor–Rostow report as inadequate. Budding "hawks," they favored a much more aggressive line. Eight thousand men would not "tip the scales decisively. . . ." The United States would only find itself "mired down in an inconclusive struggle." Showing that "we mean business" would require at least six divisions, two hundred thousand men.[8]

Kennedy spurned this startling proposal, but authorized more advisers and other forms of aid. By 1963 several hundred American pilots were flying noncombat missions in South Vietnam and more than ten thousand uniformed American troops, including Green Beret counterinsurgency forces, were working as instructors with the South Vietnamese army and government.

This war on the cheap did not work. The Diem regime seemed incapable of winning "the hearts and minds" of the South Vietnamese people. Diem was both corrupt and intolerant. He let

his family and associates use their connections and offices to line
their pockets. A Catholic, he favored his own religious community
and treated the South Vietnamese Buddhist majority harshly. In
mid-1963 he tripped off a virtual war with the Buddhists that
damaged his regime's reputation irrevocably in the United States
and around the world. One of the indelible images of a war full of
atrocities is the grisly photograph of a protesting Buddhist monk
in saffron-colored robes enveloped in flames on the streets of
Saigon.

Thich Quang Duc's immolation was so effective as anti-Diem
propaganda that six other suicides by fire soon followed. Washington was appalled. When the American ambassador in Saigon
defended the regime, Kennedy replaced him with Henry Cabot
Lodge, the blue-blooded former Republican senator from Massachusetts.

The anti-Buddhist campaign toppled Diem and his regime.
For months a group of South Vietnam army officers and public
officials had been plotting Diem's overthrow, but they wanted
American support. Kennedy at first waffled. Finally, at the end of
August 1963 he authorized Lodge to stop all American aid to
Diem, the signal the insurgent generals wanted. On November 1,
they attacked the presidential palace. Diem and his brother, the
notorious anti-Buddhist Ngo Dinh Nhu, had escaped but were
captured in Saigon's Chinese quarter, where they had taken
refuge, and were assassinated with a spray of bullets from
automatic weapons and repeated knife stabs.

John F. Kennedy died three weeks later from a rifle volley as he
rode through the streets of Dallas. At the time few people saw it as
divine retribution, though the thought would later surface in the
peace movement. The coup, however, would be a blow to the
South Vietnamese cause and to the American policy of containment in Southeast Asia.

Lyndon Johnson knew a lot about domestic affairs, but little
about foreign policy. When it came to taxes and patronage, pork
barrels and roll calls, he was a master. No one could size up a
congressman or a state governor more quickly and get him to do

his bidding. But his virtuosity stopped at the water's edge. Foreign policy required different skills and different insights. International relations was not some ethereal realm where only angels played, but Johnson's homespun versions of bluff, cajolery, manipulation, and browbeating did not suit the subtleties of an unimaginably complex world. Townsend Hoopes (Phillips Academy, Yale), who would serve LBJ as deputy assistant secretary of defense for internal security affairs, says bluntly that "he was out of his depth in dealing with foreign policy. . . ."[9]

The new president's understanding of foreign affairs was fixated at the 1930s and 1940s, when the German, Italian, and Japanese aggressors had threatened the Western democratic powers. He had learned too well the lessons of Munich, where the French and British had abandoned democratic Czechoslovakia to appease Adolf Hitler. That notorious compact had only whetted the aggressor's appetite and had not bought peace. After Munich, *appeasement* became an odious word that implied a foolish weakness in the face of a bully that only postponed the day of reckoning.

To Johnson, Communist policy in the Far East was indistinguishable from Hitler's in 1930s' Europe. Like the Nazi dictator's, it posed a serious danger to order and stability in the region and the world. "So I knew," he told his biographer Doris Kearns after retirement, "that if the aggression succeeded in South Vietnam, then the aggressors would simply keep on going until all of Southeast Asia fell into their hands, slowly or quickly. . . ."[10]

But the president was also driven by other demons. The victory during the late 1940s of the Communists in China over America's friend Chiang Kai-shek had traumatized the nation. Conservatives, and members of the pro-Chiang China Lobby, had accused the Democrats of "losing" China—as if that vast land was American property to be disposed of at our whim—and the claim had fueled the McCarthyite witch hunt against liberal New Dealers. Whatever the cost, LBJ resolved, some latter-day Joseph McCarthy must never be allowed to destroy him with the charge that he had "lost" Vietnam.

Behind Johnson stood a team of more sophisticated and diplomatically adept men. But many were afflicted by their own false perceptions. To Secretary of Defense Robert McNamara, a former Ford motorcar executive "whiz-kid," the figures proved beyond a shadow of a doubt that the war was winnable. A man with "a very thin background in foreign affairs,"[11] McNamara believed what the generals told him. Secretary of State Dean Rusk was obssessed by China and cast Mao in the role of the Asian Hitler. If he was not stopped, Armageddon would shortly ensue. The most hawkish of all was Walt Whitman Rostow, a former Rhodes scholar and MIT professor of economic history. Rostow was an intellectual whose insights into economic growth and development were often brilliant but unsound. The conflict in Vietnam, he believed, was a test of America's ability to prevent "wars of national liberation" from defeating the Free World in its struggle with communism.

None of the three men was a member of the foreign policy elite inner circle, but Johnson retained the Bundys, Harriman, Nitze, and others from the previous administration and constantly called on Acheson, McCloy, and other Establishment sages for free advice. The president was of two minds about these men. He made fun of Acheson, whose Anglophilism and British guardsman's mustache made him an obvious target for any coarsegrained, self-made Texan, and lamented that he would never get credit for anything he accomplished in foreign affairs because, unlike the "cookie pushers," he "didn't go to Harvard." Yet he bragged about his Rhodes scholars and assorted house intellectuals: "Goddamn, I made it without their advantages and now they're working for me."[12]

Johnson's close link to the foreign policy elite began during the 1964 presidential campaign when he asked McGeorge Bundy to organize a peace panel of prominent foreign policy leaders to support his campaign against Goldwater. Bundy was able to recruit McCloy, Lovett, Acheson and a dozen others to the Johnson cause. After election in his own right, LBJ continued to call on these men for advice. Before long Mac Bundy, with tongue partly in cheek, had labeled them "the Wise Men." The group never had a precise membership, but it included Acheson, Harriman, the Bundys, McCloy, Lovett, Kennan, plus anyone else the president felt could give him disinterested advice based on long experience in political and international affairs. Almost all could trace their attitudes and perspectives to the Root–Stimson tradition of patrician leadership.

As a whole the Wise Men did not find the emerging Vietnam policy congenial. Most of them believed that Europe should come first and associated the focus on Asia and the Pacific with the right-wing China Lobby. Yet they would confirm Johnson's decision to escalate the war.

But that was still in the future. From the outset Johnson was committed to the domino theory. Only days after coming to office he told a small meeting at the White House that he did not intend to "lose Vietnam." Soon after he signed an "action memorandum" pledging to help the South Vietnamese "win their contest against the externally directed and supported Communist conspiracy."[13]

Unfortunately, in Saigon the conditions for survival were worse than ever. The generals who took over after Diem were even more incompetent and far more lethargic than their predecessor. Disturbed by their ineptitude, Johnson sent McNamara to Saigon to look things over. The secretary of defense made optimistic noises publicly but reported back serious doubts to his chief. The regime was losing control in the countryside, he told the president. The South Vietnamese army was losing more weapons to the Vietcong than it was capturing. The United States should watch developments closely and prepare for "more forceful moves if the situation does not show early signs of improvement."[14]

McNamara was only hinting at the "escalation" that other advisers were openly demanding. According to the statement prepared by the Joint Chiefs in early 1964, South Vietnam was "pivotal" to America's "worldwide confrontation" with Communist power. Defeat would damage American credibility and trustworthiness in Asia as well as other parts of the world. But defeat in South Vietnam could not be avoided unless we changed our tactics. At present, we were "fighting . . . on the enemy's terms" under "self-imposed restrictions." That must cease. The United States should undertake joint actions with the ARVN, including commando raids and air strikes against North Vietnam, and overview flights in Cambodia and Laos to gather intelligence information. American troops in substantial numbers might also be needed. Most important, an American commander must take over "the actual direction of the war."[15] Curtis LeMay, the tough-talking air force commander, was putting it more bluntly and coarsely. The United States must bomb North Vietnam to hit the source of the enemy's support: "We are swatting flies when we should be going after the manure pile"[16]

The Joint Chiefs were talking about the "Americanization" of the war. It would take an agonizing decade to extricate the United States from the course of action they recommended.

Johnson was slow to accept the hawkish advice of his chief idea men. Nineteen sixty-four was a presidential election year, and he intended to swamp his Republican opponent and show that he was no mere "accidental president." He could not hand the American people a major land war in Asia and expect the overwhelming mandate he so passionately desired.

The president was not a fool who took the generals at their word. But there is little evidence that at this point he had serious nonpolitical qualms about escalation. Johnson merely wanted to keep the war out of the election campaign. Such a position was not at odds with a desire for standby authority to escalate if and when needed.

During the spring and summer of 1964, William Bundy and Rostow, now chairman of the State Department policy planning council, prepared a document for Congress giving Johnson authority to order American military forces to the defense of any Southeast Asian country threatened by aggression or subversion. Johnson hesitated to submit the resolution to Congress during the election year. In mid-July the Republicans had nominated the trigger-happy air force reserve major general and United States senator from Arizona, Barry Goldwater, as their presidential candidate. The Democrats' strategy called for tagging Goldwater as an extremist and warmonger, and at times they were shamelessly demagogic. It would not do to destroy the effect by requesting a new grant of presidential war powers.

But then a propitious moment arose. On August 2, as the *Maddox*, a U.S. destroyer equipped with electronic gear to detect Communist installations along the Vietnam coast, approached the

Red River Delta, three North Vietnamese patrol boats emerged from shore. The North Vietnamese let loose with torpedoes and guns but did no damage. The *Maddox* returned the fire, hitting all three boats and badly damaging one. In the next few days the *Maddox,* now joined by the USS *Turner Joy,* was sent out again to cruise the North Vietnam coast to "assert the right of freedom of the seas."

What followed is a comedy of errors. It is still not clear that the attempt to provoke the North Vietnamese to action worked. The two destroyers, their radars sweeping the horizon, their sonars beeping away, encountered severe rain squalls that made detection of the enemy difficult. The ships' officers would later report that in the melee the American destroyers had successfully evaded twenty-two torpedoes and sunk two or three Communist vessels. It is entirely possible they had fired at phantoms.

It made no difference. The president ordered jets from two American aircraft carriers to bomb North Vietnamese patrol-boat bases and an oil-storage depot. The evening of August 5 Johnson went on the air to tell the American people that the country was responding "to repeated acts of violence against the armed forces of the United States. . . ."[17] The next day he sent Congress a revised version of the resolution prepared by his aides weeks before that authorized him to "take all necessary measures to repel armed attack against the forces of the United States and to prevent further aggression," and to "use armed force" to assist our allies in Southeast Asia.[18]

The Tonkin Gulf Resolution would later become the focus of a furious storm. The administration would treat it as the moral and legal equivalent of a declaration of war; its antiwar opponents would denounce it as a colossal fraud and deception. Yet few people opposed it in August 1964. The House of Representatives passed it unanimously. In the Senate the curmudgeony Republican senator from Oregon, Wayne Morse, and Democratic Senator Ernest Gruening of Alaska cast the only dissenting votes. Gruening presciently denounced the resolution as a "predated declaration of war."[19] There were other doubters, but they were reassured by William Fulbright of Arkansas, the courtly former Rhodes scholar who chaired the powerful Foreign Relations

Committee. There is every reason to believe that the American people—those who bothered to notice the resolution at all—supported it with equal enthusiasm.

Johnson was reticent about Vietnam during the election campaign. "Not a single speech of President Johnson's was devoted to . . . [the Vietnam] conflict," Richard Goodwin, one of his chief speech writers, would later note.[20] When the president did mention the war, it was to reassure the public that he did not "intend for American boys to do the fighting for Asian boys" or for the United States to "get tied down in a land war in Asia."[21] As far back as June, Johnson had used the phrase "we seek no wider war" to calm public fears.[22] Over and over, during the campaign and beyond, he would repeat "no wider war" or "no larger war" on appropriate occasions.

But the president would not, or could not, keep the conflict confined or the commitment limited. Within days of the Tonkin Gulf Resolution, General Taylor, Lodge's replacement as ambassador in Saigon, and General William Westmoreland, the new American field commander in South Vietnam, were warning the White House that Communist infiltration from the north was accelerating and that firmer measures must be adopted or the south would collapse.

The Cassandras were not wrong. During 1964 the Vietcong forces had expanded to 170,000 men, mostly recruited in the south, but some inserted from the north. Thirty thousand of these guerrillas belonged to elite battalions newly equipped with automatic weapons provided by the Chinese and the Soviets. The weapons were transported south over the network of paths through the mountains and jungles that came to be called the Ho Chi Minh Trail. Against these revolutionaries were pitted the ARVN troops commanded by Saigon, but this force was timidly led by a privileged officer class riddled with corruption. Worse still, Diem's successors were soon battling for control and in December Nguyen Khanh was overthrown. Eventually, a measure of stability would be restored by General Nguyen Van Thieu and Air Vice-Marshal Nguyen Cao Ky, who appointed themselves head of state and premier, respectively, and between them would rule South Vietnam for the next decade.* As 1964 drew to an end, existing indirect American support seemed inadequate to shore up an independent and stable South Vietnam and prevent a Communist takeover.

The solutions proposed by Taylor, seconded by William Bundy, were sustained bombing of North Vietnamese bridges, railroads, and oil depots to hamper the infiltration of men and weapons from north to south, and the mining of Haiphong harbor to impede the flow of Soviet and Chinese supplies. Johnson had little faith in bombing as a way to stop the infiltration or to force a North Vietnamese retreat, but early in 1965 he agreed to send national security adviser McGeorge Bundy to Saigon to size up the situation on the ground.

Bundy arrived on February 4, just two days before Soviet premier Alexei Kosygin reached Hanoi to discuss Soviet help to Ho and his government. As Bundy was preparing to leave for Washington on February 7, the Vietcong suddenly struck at the American base near Pleiku, unleashing a shower of mortar shells over the unsuspecting Green Berets and other advisers. Eight Americans died, more than a hundred were wounded, and ten U.S. planes were destroyed or badly damaged. All but one or two of the attackers escaped.

By the standards of a later day the toll was minor, but Bundy was shocked. Joining Taylor and Westmoreland in the latter's Saigon headquarters, the three put their heads together to consider what course to recommend. A strong-willed and some-times brusque man, Bundy seemed the most bellicose of the three: Westmoreland would later say that having "smelled a little gun-powder he developed a field marshal psychosis."[23] But they all agreed that the Pleiku assault could not be allowed to go unpun-ished. That afternoon Bundy phoned the White House and proposed that the United States commence bombing targets in the north. This time the president approved, and that same day forty-five navy planes hit an enemy military barracks just over the

---

* In September 1967 their power was confirmed by a general election, but their narrow victory failed to provide the mandate needed to make the administration strong.

line in North Vietnam. Premier Kosygin immediately promised to supply North Vietnam with "all necessary assistance if aggressors dare encroach upon [its] independence and sovereignty."[24]

The air strike on Februrary 7 was the forerunner of a massive and systematic bombing campaign launched several days later. Designated rather poetically "Operation Rolling Thunder," the attack was designed to cripple North Vietnam's economy and to diminish sharply its military capability. It did neither. Americans should have learned from World War II that even an advanced nation like Germany could not be destroyed by conventional high-explosive and incendiary bombing. How much less vulnerable was an economy as rudimentary as North Vietnam's? By April, after two months of steady pounding with TNT and napalm, it was clear that little if anything had been accomplished.

Dubious or not, most Americans approved of LBJ's response. Polls showed that 70 percent of the public favored a bombing campaign as the only way to "save" Vietnam. But within one influential public sector, the liberal academic community, the air strikes created consternation.

Many academics, appalled by Goldwater's right-wing ideology and saber-rattling, had supported the president enthusiastically in November, as had the politicized portion of the student body. Even Students for a Democratic Society (SDS), the voice of the emerging student "New Left," had proclaimed it would go "part of the way with LBJ."[25] Now, feeling utterly betrayed, both students and faculty launched a campaign to force the reversal of American Vietnam policy. Operation Rolling Thunder marks the true beginning of the anti-Vietnam movement. (See chapter 5.)

By now lies, half-truths, and betrayal had become the norm of administration policy. In announcing Rolling Thunder, Johnson carefully concealed the dangers of the new policy to avoid giving alarm. The operation, he told the public, was to be "a program of measured and limited air action"[26] against targets close to the seventeenth parallel. Initially, it was indeed limited, but when it failed to bring the enemy to heel, it was followed by another wave of attacks and then a succession of others, each one described as restricted or measured and touted as decisive—and each one as fruitless as its predecessors. By the time the mass bombing ceased for good in late 1972, American B-52s and other aircraft had dropped over one million tons of bombs on North Vietnam and many millions more on the Vietcong south of the seventeenth parallel. All told, American aircraft dumped more than three times the bomb tonnage in Vietnam as in all of World War II, the greatest war in history.

Rolling Thunder was the classic fatal first step. The air campaign raised worries about the security of American planes and air crews scattered throughout the south. The airbase at Danang, along the northern coast, seemed especially exposed, and in February 1965 Westmoreland requested two battalions of marines to protect it from attack. His purpose had only been, "Westy" later wrote, "to secure a vital airfield and the air units using it."[27] But the thirty-five hundred men in full battle gear who waded ashore onto the Danang beach on March 8 breached a vital barrier. There were now combat troops under independent American command in Vietnam, not merely advisers.

The administration soon crossed another Rubicon. On April 1 Johnson decided to send Westmoreland two more marine battalions and almost twenty thousand support troops. The new contingent would be assigned a new mission as well: they would not be restricted to protecting air bases and other installations, but would be allowed to foray into the countryside to attack the Vietcong enemy. Once again the president misled the media and public. No "far-reaching strategy" was "being suggested or promulgated,"[28] he told reporters. He also ordered the secretaries of state and defense and the director of the CIA to cover up. The operations, he informed them, should be carried out as "rapidly as practicable, but in ways that should minimize any appearance of sudden changes in policy. . . ."[29]

Thereafter "escalation" became a remorseless process, like some appalling addiction that demands ever-growing dosages to achieve its effect. In June 1965 Westmoreland submitted a request for 100,000 men, including thirty-five battalions of combat troops. These would be sent on "search and destroy" missions against the Vietcong in the countryside, while ARVN troops would be employed in "pacification"—occupying Vietcong-free areas and protecting civilians. Johnson approved 50,000 and then a further 100,000 soon after. By the end of 1965 there were over 184,000 American troops in Vietnam.

Those who remember Johnson as a crude, insensitive tyrant, indifferent to the human and political costs of Vietnam, misread the man. During the spring of 1965 he began to have nightmares about what he called "that bitch of a war."[30] Was he doing the right thing? His doubts pushed him once more to the Wise Men, perhaps only to have his acts confirmed, and in July he summoned the group, including McCloy, Lovett, and Acheson, to Washington for a day of consultation and cross examination. Johnson himself was not present at the meeting at the State Department, but Bill Bundy, Rusk, and McNamara stood in, asking the crucial questions about Vietnam.

If Johnson wanted a claque he got it. As Bundy reported, most of the sages favored "making whatever combat force increases were required." Several, in fact, "thought our actions had perhaps been too restrained, and had been misconstrued by Hanoi that we were less than wholly determined."[31] The group explicitly endorsed the domino theory. If Vietnam fell, they agreed, Thailand would soon follow and Japan and India would be in danger. Europe too would be affected by our failure to stop the Vietnam Communists. Our NATO allies would lose their faith in our will to fend off Soviet aggression and would be tempted to make their separate arrangements with the USSR.

Thus reinforced, through 1966 and 1967 Johnson authorized virtually every troop and arms request Westmoreland made, hoping that one more massive draught of military power would finally end the awful pain. By mid-1968 the number of American combat troops in Vietnam would total 542,000. The president was not opposed to negotiations. He launched periodic "peace offensives," offering to negotiate a settlement. Each of these collapsed over such irreconcilable issues as the reinforcement of Vietcong cadres during a truce, the recognition of the Vietcong as legitimate parties to any negotiations, the timing of bombing halts, and like matters that one side or the other considered crucial. The ultimate snag, however, was that Hanoi wanted a unified Communist Vietnam, while Washington wanted an independent non-Communist South Vietnam. Neither would yield the main point.

The fighting pitted American firepower against Communist flesh and blood. The Vietcong suffered horrendous human losses, but were able to raise a steady supply of new recruits from among the displaced villagers, many of them disgusted by corrupt and venal South Vietnamese officials and the insensitive Americans. What they lacked in numbers, the Vietcong made up in dedication or—as their opponents preferred to say—in fanaticism. Vietcong troops could live on a handful of rice or some wild roots or fruit, eked out with an occasional sequestered chicken. They could survive in dirt bunkers and tunnels while enemy bombs and shells pounded them mercilessly. Patriotism and idealism, instilled by dedicated Communist cadres, stiffened their resolve, but so did the summary execution of traitors and informers.

With each passing month, the direct North Vietnamese involvement grew. At first Hanoi relied primarily on its surrogates, the Vietcong, to carry on the fight. Then, from 1967 on, in response to American escalation, it dispatched over a hundred thousand regulars across the Demilitarized Zone (DMZ). Over a half million North Vietnamese soldiers would die before the war had ended.

By late 1967 the United States was floundering in what everyone had feared: a major land war on the Asian continent. It had become a nightmare from which there seemed no escape. By now even McNamara was in such anguish that his friends feared for his mental balance. To clear his mind about how the country had arrived at its impasse, in June 1967 he ordered the collection of classified government dispatches, memos, and position papers that, when stolen by Daniel Ellsberg and published by *The New York Times,* would be called the "Pentagon Papers."

In November 1967 Johnson summoned the Wise Men once again to Washington to advise him what to do. Eleven came, including Harriman; Acheson; Maxwell Taylor; Mac Bundy, now head of the Ford Foundation; George Ball, the dovish former undersecretary of state, now also back in private life; Robert Murphy, a former State Department official under Dulles; Supreme Court Justice Abe Fortas, LBJ's longtime crony; the former ambassador to Saigon, Henry Cabot Lodge; Clark

Clifford, a prominent Washington lawyer and all-purpose presidential troubleshooter; and several others.

The pundits assembled once more in the State Department diplomatic reception room to listen to briefings by Earle Wheeler, head of the Joint Chiefs of Staff, and Secretary Rusk. Both made the same points: the United States was winning the war in the field; the American people were being misled by the media. The Wise Men bought this view almost without demurrer. "I detect in this group no sentiment for our pulling out of Vietnam," Walt Rostow informed the president in his memo of the meeting.[32]

The next day Johnson met with the Wise Men personally in the White House Cabinet Room. A doting grandfather, he held four-month-old Patrick Lyndon Nugent on his lap like some sort of live security blanket. Acheson and Mac Bundy said they doubted that bombing would bring Hanoi to the negotiating table, but they and the others strongly endorsed staying in Vietnam till victory. "Getting out of Vietnam is as impossible as it is undesirable," Bundy declared. The trouble was weak public support. The administration must emphasize "the light at the end of the tunnel," a phrase that would ring ironically down the years ahead.[33] Clifford, the urbane, silver-haired smoothie, reminded the group that the Korean War had had its critics, too. Like that one, this war was right and necessary. The one discordant note was sounded by George Ball, who had held off to the end. As the Wise Men left the room, he burst out: "I've been watching you across the table. You're like a flock of buzzards sitting on a fence, sending the young men off to be killed. You ought to be ashamed of yourselves."[34] His charge shocked his listeners, but did not change any minds. To the foreign policy elite, the war was still "Go."

January in Vietnam is a special month, full of celebrations. To Westerners and the westernized it included the Gregorian calendar's New Year's Day, of course. For the Vietnamese, westernized and traditional alike, it is notable for Tet, celebrated in 1968 on January 30.

Tet is the Vietnamese name for an ancient holiday, the new year as calculated from the lunar calendar of 13 twenty-eight-day months. It has been described as a "combination of All Soul's Day, a family celebration, a spring festival, a national holiday, and an overall manifestation of a way of life."[35] It is the biggest holiday of the Vietnamese year, and in 1968 it would usher in the Year of the Monkey.

The celebration lasts for a week, but preparations for its observance begin months before with the purchase of new clothing. People bring flowers from the countryside to decorate homes, offices, and public buildings, and line up at the stores to buy noodles, rice wine, tea, and the traditional cakes of sticky rice.

Ever since 1963 the Communists had proclaimed cease-fires for Christmas, the Western New Year, Buddha's birthday, and Tet. Since 1965 the South Vietnamese and Americans had followed suit. In 1968 the My Tho ambush on January 1 and sixteen other incidents had violated a seventy-two-hour truce proclaimed by the Vietcong guerrillas to mark the Western New Year's holiday.

My Tho was followed three weeks later by a North Vietnamese artillary attack at dawn on the marine garrison at the Khe Sanh, near the Laos–South Vietnam border. Yet taken as a whole, during January a palpable calm rested over the rice fields, the jungles, and the villages of Vietnam. For ten days preceding the thirtieth, even the American bombers had stopped their runs across the border, though mostly to avoid harming a Romanian diplomat visiting Hanoi. On January 17 Westmoreland reported that the Communists "seem to have temporarily run out of steam."[36]

The calm hid preparations for the most concentrated and ferocious campaign since the end of World War II to drive the foreign enemy from Vietnam. The attack, said a secret Communist report, would "decide the fate of the country" and "end the war."[37] The North Vietnamese called the operation the "General Offensive and Uprising." The rest of the world would know it as the Tet Offensive.

Hanoi had ordered the attack in July to break the military stalemate that had lasted since the American troop buildup of mid-1965. The Communists did not expect to defeat the Americans in the field; they lacked the firepower to do so. Their goal was primarily psychological. They would engage the ARVN and inflict such punishment that the enemy's will to fight would crumble. In every major city people would rise up against the South Vietnamese government, creating chaos and destroying the regime's ability to function. The discouraged Americans would then cut their losses and depart, and Ho Chi Minh and his colleagues would finally achieve what they had sought for twenty years—the reunification of north and south under a Communist administration. And there was another reason for the attack as well, the Communist cadres told the brave men who were to risk their lives: Uncle Ho was very old and it was essential to liberate the south before he died.

The plan was a high-risk gamble. While units of the North Vietnamese army kept the Americans occupied at their bases, the soldiers of the National Liberation Front would launch surprise attacks in every province of the south. This time they would ignore the villages and concentrate on the cities, simultaneously hitting them from within and from without.

Tet was a distinct operation, but it was only the capstone of an offensive that had begun the previous fall against American outposts in the highlands and along the Cambodian and Laotian borders. Pleased to see the enemy come out of his hole and face him, Westmoreland had used American brute firepower to great advantage in search-and-destroy missions. At the same time American bombers and heavy artillery had blasted the North Vietnamese regulars at Conthien, Dakto, and other spots. At Dakto 300 B-52 missions and 170,000 artillery shells had reduced the jungle to splinters and killed thousands of the enemy.

The Americans knew that more was in store. There were ten thousand U.S. intelligence experts in Vietnam, and they had done their job. Captured documents, loose-lipped prisoners, the unexpected assaults in the highlands and along the frontiers—all revealed that a major push was imminent. On January 5 a U.S. press release from Saigon quoted a North Vietnamese document that described the General Offensive and Uprising, including the plan to "take over towns and cities."[38]

But it was one thing to suspect that the enemy had something up his sleeve; it was another to know when he intended to pull it out. It was like Pearl Harbor almost a generation before: American officials were certain that something was up but could not time the strike or tell precisely where it would fall. Above all, no one guessed that a surprise attack would come at the Tet holiday. Several years later Westmoreland told an interviewer: "I frankly did not think they would assume the psychological disadvantage of hitting at Tet itself, so I thought it would be long before or after Tet."[39] It was not the first time, nor would it be the last, that the Americans miscalculated the enemy's intentions and capacities.

The Tet holiday began after midnight on Tuesday, January 30, Vietnamese local time. A half hour into the Lunar New Year two small vehicles pulled up to a pagoda adjacent to the South Vietnamese government radio station at Nha Trang, a medium-size city halfway up the coast. Several men in ARVN uniforms leaped out. Corporal Le Van Thang thought they might be Vietcong in disguise and radioed news of their arrival to his headquarters. When his superiors confirmed his suspicions, he spread the alarm and fired a warning shot. The ersatz ARVN fired back. Five minutes later mortar shells fell near the Nha Trang government Navy Training Center, and at 2:00 A.M. Regiment 18-B of the North Vietnam People's Army tried to force its way into the city.

The poorly coordinated assault failed dismally. Regiment 18-B collided with a superior ARVN force and never entered Nha Trang. ARVN troops also broke up a "spontaneous" pro-Communist demonstration that erupted at a nearby suburban hamlet, while in the city itself infiltrators managed to capture only two strategic posts and then were quickly dislodged. Fourteen hours after the attack began the city was declared free of enemy forces.

Six other towns along the coast and in the mountains, including the country's second largest city, Da Nang, felt the brunt of Communist blows that same night. In each the attacks failed and the Communists took heavy casualties, over 5,400 killed and 704 captured, according to American reports. Hundreds of South Vietnamese civilians also died in the gunfire and flames.

At 9:45 that morning the Americans and South Vietnamese officially canceled the Tet truce and ordered all men back to their units. Yet even now they were not fully aroused to the danger. President Thieu, celebrating the holidays in My Tho, his wife's hometown, refused to return to Saigon. The Americans were no more alert. There had recently been a deluge of "maximum alert" orders. This seemed another cry-wolf occasion, and they moved sluggishly to meet the emergency.

In Saigon the only excitement until early Wednesday morning, the thirty-first, was provided by fireworks explosions, echoes from the noisy Tet celebration. With its cafés, music halls, racetrack, and luxurious bordellos, the city had been considered the Paris of the Orient during the French colonial regime. Now crammed with two million inhabitants, it was still a community of brilliant contrasts. Along the tree-lined boulevards were the gaudy villas of the rich. In the back alleys lived thousands of poor folk, many refugees from the war in the countryside. Chinese immigrants occupied the shacks of the Cholon slum, where they ran the gambling and vice rings. A melange of rich and poor, East and West, the city smelt at once of incense and excrement. It had been spared the turmoil that had afflicted the countryside the past three years, and its people were complacent.

At 3:00 A.M. a massive blast rocked the U.S. Army's Tactical Operations Center near Long Binh, fifteen miles from the capital. The adjacent ammunition dump had come under heavy enemy rocket and ground attack and erupted like Stromboli. Nearby was Bien Hoa air base, where more planes landed and took off than at any airport in the world including Chicago's O'Hare. Bien Hoa was the assigned target of the Vietcong Fifth Division, and soon it too was shuddering under rocket and small-arms fire. Other Communist troops meanwhile pressed in on Tan Son Nhut. There, besides the big airbase with its hundreds of planes and helicopters, the American Vietnam command and the Vietnamese Joint General Staff maintained their headquarters. At one point the VC breached the base's defensive perimeter and seemed on the verge of disrupting the very nerve center of American–South Vietnamese operations.

By this time chaos reigned in Saigon itself. The Vietcong detachments that infiltrated Saigon had entered the city by public transportation undetected and had assembled at "safe houses" to receive their weapons and instructions. Like most VC, the guerrillas were largely ignorant young peasants. Saturated in Marxism-Leninism, they had little idea what they would do once they had accomplished their immediate missions. The truth was they were suicide squads, being sacrificed to shake the enemy's morale and confidence.

The Saigon phase of Tet was a series of five separate operations. The attack on the heavily defended presidential palace was carried out by fourteen Vietcong—thirteen men and one woman—who approached in three trucks, one jammed with TNT. Guards stopped them at a side gate, and they fled to a nearby house where they held out against government troops for fifteen hours until most had been killed.

Another small Vietcong contingent failed to take the headquarters of the South Vietnamese navy. They penetrated the wall surrounding the building, but then all but two were killed by gunfire.

Minutes before, a group of Vietcong had blasted their way into the government radio station armed with diagrams of offices and studios and a set of keys that would open all the locked doors. Seizure of the station was a vital piece in the overall Tet offensive plan. As ready students of modern social science, the Communists knew that whoever controlled information controlled power. A North Vietnamese radio technician accompanied the commandos, and they carried propaganda tapes announcing the General Offensive and Uprising and the liberation of Saigon.

The invaders met their match in Vu Duc Vinh, the station's director. The day before, Vinh had arranged to shut down the station's transmission in the event of attack, and now on signal the technicians at the transmitter, fourteen miles from the studio, cut the lines. The Vietcong commandos held the station for six hours before being driven out but were never able to broadcast their tapes. It was a strategic victory for the South Vietnamese government, but it had its comic side. At the transmitter Colonel Vinh found himself without political material, and while the city rocked with explosions, Saigon radio filled the air with a mishmash of Vietnamese martial music, Viennese waltzes, and Beatles and Rolling Stones rock.

The Vietcong attempt to take the main Saigon prison and liberate its political prisoner inmates was even less successful. The Vietcong unit assigned to the mission, Regiment 165-A, encountered government troops before it reached its objective and was wiped out in a firefight at a nearby cemetery.

Each of these forays by itself would have been front-page news. Not since before the American arrival in force three years before had the people of Saigon itself heard gunfire and seen blood on the streets. But none would have the impact of the assault on the U.S. Embassy compound on Thong Nhut Boulevard.

The embassy was an unusual six-story structure set in a compound enclosed by a high wall. Completed in 1967, the building was protected by a stone rocket shield and capped by a helicopter pad. Seven years later this cement slab would be crowded with frantic Americans and Vietnamese clamoring to be taken out of the capital before the Communists arrived. Within the compound wall, besides the main chancery building, was a two-story villa built by the French years before and retained as a guest house when the new embassy was erected. In January the villa was occupied by George Jacobson, a former Army colonel now a civilian embassy staff member, and Robert Josephson, a retired army noncom, also on the embassy staff.

The embassy was an inspired target. Though "Pentagon East" was at Westmoreland's headquarters in Tan Son Nhut, the embassy was a vivid symbol of the American presence in Vietnam, and its capture, the Communists were certain, would resound throughout the world as proof of American impotence and inability to win the war. General Giap would commit almost seventy thousand of his troops to the Tet offensive, but it was the nineteen invaders of the embassy compound who would capture the world's attention.

The Vietcong commandos had gathered at 59 Phan Thanh Gian Street at a house adjacent to a small auto repair shop owned by a Vietcong sympathizer. The hideaway was stocked with TNT and ammunition shipped there three months earlier from Battalion Four headquarters near the Michelin Rubber plantations thirty miles north of the capital. The Vietcong soldiers themselves had recently infiltrated the city dressed as civilians on their way to celebrate the Lunar New Year.

Just after midnight on Wednesday the guerrillas broke out the weapons and explosives that had been cached in the garage. By 2:45 A.M., hidden in a light truck and a taxi, they were on their way to their target.

The small convoy approached the compound minutes later, and even before stopping, the VC started firing at two American MPs at the side entrance. The MPs fired back and then slipped back through the side gate. Inside the compound, they quickly flashed a "Signal 300," the MP code for an enemy attack.

Before help could arrive, the VC commandos had blasted a hole through the front wall and entered the compound. The two American military policemen killed the first two Vietcong who came through the three-foot wide gap, but died themselves, shot in the head and chest. At this point a jeep with two more MPs, responding to the alert, arrived at the embassy. Both men fell in a fusillade from the Communist soldiers.

The surviving VC commandos were now inside the compound, but they were outside the chancery building itself. Fortunately, Sergeant Ronald Harper, one of the marine guards inside, had beaten the invaders to the teakwood doors and slammed them shut in their faces. The VC fired rifles and antitank rockets at the locked doors and lobbed grenades through the holes. Harper and another marine were both wounded. A third marine guard on the chancery roof pumped .38 rounds at the invaders until his revolver was empty. The bullets missed their targets, but the VC remained outside.

By now Captain Robert O'Brien, head of the marine security guard detachment, had arrived at the compound with his men; they found themselves locked out and the enemy within. The captain sent an MP for grenades to blast through the gates. He

returned empty-handed with the incredible story that the grenades were out of stock; none were available. Unable to break in,
O'Brien's detachment took position outside the embassy wall. The
besiegers were now themselves besieged.

Several Americans and South Vietnamese remained inside the
chancery building itself. Ambassador Ellsworth Bunker had been
spirited away to a secret refuge elsewhere in the city soon after the
firing broke out. But Harper and two other marines were still in
the building, while a night staff of six other Americans and two
Vietnamese employees were trapped on the upper floors. Meanwhile, in the villa behind the chancery, Jacobson and Josephson
had been rudely shaken from their sleep by the racket. Neither
man had a proper weapon, but once awake, Jacobson had gotten
hold of a hand grenade. Either less lucky or less ingenious,
Josephson had to settle for a bent coat hanger.

Though the MPs had been on the scene for many minutes, it
took an excruciatingly long time for other forces to react. An hour
after the break-in Ambassador Bunker requested help for the
embassy from the Vietnamese police. They refused on the
grounds that it was too dangerous: in the dark no one would be
able to distinguish friend from foe. Westmoreland was more
cooperative. Soon after 4:00 A.M. the general dispatched a military
police battalion to clear out the embassy compound.

The Vietcong soldiers held off the enemy for the next five
hours, hiding behind the large flower tubs in the garden and
returning the growing barrage of fire from surrounding
buildings. In the chancery building itself the Americans were in a
strange position. They were trapped and in imminent danger of
death, but their telephone lines were open and the civilian
employees in the CIA room on the top floor could talk directly to
officials at the State Department Operations Center in Washington and at the White House Situation Room, halfway around the
world. Philip Habib, a high State Department official, would later
recall how he could distinctly hear the sounds of explosions over
the long-distance lines as he talked to the frantic embassy personel
twelve thousand miles away.

At dawn the rescue forces finally discovered the hole the VC
commandos had blasted through the compound wall the night

before. Robert Furey, an embassy security officer, slipped cautiously through the opening only to encounter a wounded Vietcong lying on the lawn directly in front of him. The man had a grenade in his hand. Furey raised his rifle but before he could fire he was knocked back by a blinding flash. The Vietcong soldier had pulled the pin, but had been too weak to throw the grenade and had blown himself up.

Soon after, the military police finally battered their way through the compound gates and debouched onto the lawn. Simultaneously, a 101st Airborne Division helicopter landed on the embassy roof. Five paratroopers, weighed down with rifles, grenades, and combat knives, leaped off; the major in charge was the surprisingly named Hillel Schwartz. They quickly determined that there were no VCs in the building. By this time most of the nineteen invaders were dead or dying.

There was a final episode at the villa where one wounded VC had sought refuge. The man's bloody footprints on the floor below revealed his presence to Jacobson, hiding on the second-floor stairwell. The colonel called for help on his still working telephone and braced to meet the enemy with his lone grenade. Fortunately, he was spared the encounter. What followed was the stuff of a Sylvester Stallone epic. MPs and marines quickly surrounded the building and opened fire on the Vietcong inside. The rescuers tossed a gas mask and a .45 revolver up to Jacobson and then lobbed a tear gas grenade into the villa. The acrid fumes filled the ground floor rooms, forcing the Vietcong soldier upstairs. As he climbed the stairs, the man fired his AK-47 automatic rifle ahead of him, chipping pieces of plywood off the walls and ceiling over Jacobson's head. When he reached the stairwell turn, Jacobson leaped up and pulled the trigger of his revolver at point-blank range. The man dropped. Jacobson seized his automatic weapon prepared to meet any other enemy, but the battle was over. No one was left.

At 9:15 A.M. the embassy was declared officially secure. Five minutes later General Westmoreland came to inspect the damage. He shook hands with Sergeant Harper and then put in a call to Habib in Washington to tell him all was well. Waiting outside was an excited crowd of reporters who had just crossed the scarred and bloody lawn and seen the Vietcong and American bodies. "The enemy's well-laid plans" had gone "afoul," the general said.[40] No one believed him—not standing amid the rubble and gore of the embassy compound.

The battles in and around the capital were only a portion of the offensive fury that broke out on the thirty-first. That same day Vietcong forces attacked Ben Tre, My Tho, Vinh Long, Can Tho, and other towns in the Mekong Delta. In fact they hit most of the provincial capitals and many of the Delta's district capitals.

The Communists displayed amazing élan and courage. But the price was high. The guerrillas seized public buildings and private residences, hiding behind South Vietnamese civilians, and had to be blasted out. At Ben Tre, a Delta city of thirty-five thousand, American planes dropped napalm and hundreds of five-hundred-pound bombs on the enemy; American guns smothered the town with 155 mm. shells. Five hundred, perhaps a thousand, civilians died. It was at Ben Tre that an anonymous American major told Peter Arnett of the Associated Press: "It became necessary to destroy the town to save it."[41] To the peace movement the phrase became an ironic icon of the brutal, senseless Vietnam War.

Some of the bloodiest fighting of the Tet offensive occurred at Hue. This beautiful northern city, with its charming boulevards and park-lined River of Perfumes, had been the old capital city of the Emperor Gia Long. Its temples, palaces, towers, and moats had been modeled on the Chinese Imperial City of Beijing. Until Tet, it had been an island of peace in the war-torn land. It was about to join the rest of the country as a scene of slaughter and beastliness.

Shortly after 3:00 A.M. on the thirty-first, Communist forces struck Hue with an artillery barrage. Soon after, two North Vietnamese battalions charged across the bridges spanning the moats and penetrated the Citadel that formed the two-square-mile heart of the Imperial City. The Vietcong's purpose was to terrorize, to destroy morale, and to disrupt and divide the enemy, not to occupy the city permanently.

The Communists' first targets were the billets, residences, and offices of American advisers and of South Vietnamese administrators and military personnel. These people were to be treated harshly. "Cruel tyrants and reactionary elements" were to be shot.[42] The others were to be taken prisoner, but killed if they could not be removed to safekeeping. According to the orders given the "provisional battalion," foreign civilians—except for the French, who, for political reasons, were to be handled gently— were to be arrested. These orders were death sentences for hundreds of Hue's residents—civil servants, military men, students, and Catholic priests and laymen—who were shot, bludgeoned, incinerated, or buried alive. Almost three thousand people were slaughtered. Most were South Vietnamese, but the victims also included three German doctors, two French priests, and the Americans Stephen Miller, a member of the U.S. Information Service, and Courtney Miles of NBC International.

The task of recapturing Hue took more than three weeks and turned much of the beautiful city into rubble. The fighting resembled the bloody house-to-house encounters of World War II, with the attackers forced to root the occupiers out with small arms, bayonets, and grenades. It was bloody, gut-wrenching, high-adrenalin work. Reinforced by three marine battalions, the counterattacking ARVN forces, composed of many outraged city natives, fought well, proving that the South Vietnamese were not hopeless soldiers when properly motivated.

The fighting within the Citadel was agonizing. Ground taken during the day was lost at night. American marines died from sniper fire and from grenades. A marine officer called it "face-to-face, eyeball-to-eyeball confrontation" and remembered the "horrible smell" of the bodies buried under the debris. "You tasted it as you ate your rations, as if you were eating death."[43]

On February 24 the last Communists were cleared out and the red-and-yellow banner of the South Vietnamese Republic run up the flag tower at the Citadel's south wall. The next day a South Vietnamese Ranger task force retook the captured Cambodian pagoda in the Gia Hoi district, the last VC stronghold. After twenty-five days Hue was finally free, but the charming city was left a "shattered, stinking hulk, its streets choked with rubble and rotting bodies."[44]

Hue was the longest-running battle of the Tet offensive, and its conclusion marked the end of Tet proper. But to the Americans the military crisis continued for some weeks longer.

The most serious fear was the possibility of a second round of attacks against the cities. When this did not materialize, the anxieties of Westmoreland and the administration shifted to the Communist assault on the marine base at Khe Sanh that had been gathering momentum ever since late January.

In Saigon and Washington, Khe Sanh, an isolated outpost in the far northwest corner of South Vietnam, seemed a possible reprise of Dienbienphu, the decisive 1954 Communist victory that had led to the French withdrawal from Vietnam. The comparison was misleading. American ground firepower in 1968 far exceeded that of the French in 1954. The Americans also had inexhaustible air power. Moreover, Communist aims at Khe Sanh were different. At Dienbienphu their goal had been to break French morale and force them to negotiate. The Khe Sanh attack was probably intended only to draw American forces away from the cities to maximize the impact of Tet.

Yet almost everyone drew the Dienbienphu parallel. Westmoreland ordered his staff to analyze the 1954 battle for lessons on how to lift the new siege. The media, in their quest for drama and easy comprehensibility, found the analogy irresistible. The "historical ghost" of the French debacle, declared Marvin Kalb, a CBS State Department correspondent, was "casting a long shadow across Washington."[45] The president himself made the analogy and became obsessed with the battle. He didn't "want any damn Dinbinphoo," he told General Earle Wheeler of the Joint Chiefs.[46] Johnson had Pentagon experts construct a sand table model of the Khe Sanh plateau in the White House Situation Room and late at night would pore over it in his bathrobe while consulting the latest dispatches and aerial photographs from Saigon.

In the end Khe Sanh was successfully relieved. All through February American planes and artillery pounded the Communist forces in the mountains surrounding the base. American B-52s dropped one hundred thousand tons of explosives over a five-square-mile patch, producing crushing Communist casualties: ten thousand dead to five hundred for the Americans. During the two-month siege, scores of cargo planes and helicopters flew in supplies and carried out the wounded.

Gradually, the punishment became too great for even the most-dedicated revolutionaries to bear, and by mid-March Communist units began to withdraw. On April 1 a combined U.S.–South Vietnam force launched a drive from the east toward the besieged base and on the fifth linked up with the marines. The ordeal was over.

One incident late in Tet would not come to the attention of the American public until the following year: the massacre of more than three hundred Vietnamese civilians at the hamlet of My Lai, near Quang Ngai, by soldiers of Charlie Company of the Americal division led by Captain Ernest Medina and Lieutenants William L. Calley, Jr., and Steven Brooks.

My Lai was by no means the only incident of brutality toward civilians during the Vietnam War. Like all civil wars—and all wars at all times—Vietnam was studded with atrocities. Guerrilla warfare, relying on stealth and ambush and destroying the enemy's morale, is certain to be especially vicious. Even regular troops, like the American "grunts," quickly forget the Geneva Convention rules and revert to savagery. Understandably, the apologists of Charlie Company pointed to the brutal behavior of the Vietcong–North Vietnamese at Hue at almost the same time. Yet My Lai—and the almost successful effort to cover it up— remains one of the most shameful pages in the annals of the United States Army.

The atrocity can be explained, if not excused. The American soldiers were young, uneducated, inexperienced, and jumpy. Many saw VC killers lurking behind every hedgerow and under every peasant hat. The troops were angry. Guerrilla warfare brings death in covert, nasty ways: from hidden mines underfoot; from booby-trapped souvenirs; from civilians—even women and old men—in disguise. After months in the hostile alien land most grunts despised the people—"gooks," "dinks," "slopes." An ugly joke circulated around the GI bars in 1968 that the solution of the Vietnam mess was to "load all the Friendlies onto ships and take them out to the South China Sea. Then you bomb the country flat. Then you sink the ship."[47] Charlie Company itself had recently lost several men from mines and enemy fire, and the survivors thirsted for revenge.

Vietnam was fought by the nation's blue-collar youth and underclass. In World War II the nation's elite—the sons of Joseph Kennedy, Edsel Ford, and Franklin Roosevelt—had gone forth to do battle for their country against its enemies. In Vietnam, virtually every middle-class draft-age man who could wangle it got an educational deferment or a psychological 4-F, or decamped for Canada. By 1968 middle-class draft evasion and draft avoidance was fast pushing the nation's entire Selective Service System to the point of collapse.

Like most American combat troops in Vietnam, the soldiers of Charlie Company were ill-educated young men of working-class background; almost half were black. The favorite reading matter in the unit was comic books, scarcely the fount of an enlightened moral code. In only a few cases did traditional religious training make up for deficient education.

The junior officers who commanded the platoons that did the dirty work were themselves young, inexperienced, and poorly educated. Captain Ernest Medina was a Mexican American raised in Colorado who rose from the ranks and won his commission through Officer Candidate School. Lieutenant Calley was a callow Miamian, a junior-college dropout who had worked as a bellhop, restaurant dishwasher, and railroad switchman before enlisting in the army. An undeveloped moral sense is not confined to the poor and the ignorant, of course. One of the least endearing figures of the Vietnam War was Colonel George Patton III, commander of the Eleventh Armored Cavalry Regiment, stationed just south of Quang Ngai. Son of the dashing tank commander of World War II, Patton was born to wealth and privilege. His advantages did not curb his truculence. Patton would tell his men before going to battle: "I do like to see the arms and legs fly." That Christmas the Pattons had sent cards to their friends and relatives reading: "From Colonel and Mrs. George S. Patton III—Peace on Earth." Attached were color snapshots of dismembered Vietcong soldiers.[48] Yet it is easy to understand how twenty-year-old youths raised on comic books and TV, without traditional religious training, sometimes behave badly when frightened and excited.

The My Lai mission was to destroy a supposed Vietcong base and wipe out the crack Vietcong Forty-eighth Battalion of 250 men. The grunts were apprehensive. Before they left Landing Zone Dotti, their bivouac area, Captain Medina had told them that it "looked like a tough fight." They would be outnumbered two to one.[49] According to some of the men, Medina had also given them a blank check to kill. "Well, boys, this is your chance to get revenge on these people," one soldier reported him as saying. "When we go into My Lai, it's open season. When we leave nothing will be living. Everything's going to go."[50]

At 7:30 A.M. the First Platoon, under Lieutenant Calley, arrived by helicopter at a rice field adjacent to the hamlet. The men had been told "this is what you have been waiting for—search and destroy."[51] Soon after landing they saw an old man standing in a rice field waving his arms. Someone thought he was a VC and cut him down with automatic rifle fire. When they examined the body, they found he was unarmed. Minutes later Lieutenant Steven Brooks's Second Platoon landed, followed by the Third with Captain Medina and his company command post.

At 8:00 A.M., as the troops approached My Lai hamlet, some Vietnamese fled across the adjacent fields. They too were gunned down. The villagers who remained in their thatch-covered houses, hoping for the best, were no more fortunate. The soldiers swept into the village firing into the houses indiscriminately, although no one had attacked them. They set fires to many of the dwellings and then bayoneted the inhabitants as they fled the flames. Some of the soldiers ordered civilians into the bunkers that many war-wise Vietnamese families had constructed inside their thatch houses as shelters against bombs, and then tossed grenades through the entrances. One young soldier picked up a fifty-year-old man, threw him down a well, and then lobbed a live grenade after him.

The worst of the carnage took place at a drainage ditch just to the east of the village where the soldiers had collected as many as 150 civilians, mostly women and children. Lieutenant Calley arrived at about 8:45 A.M., and when some of the villagers tried to crawl out of the ditch he opened fire. He ordered his men to join him and all but a few did, pumping bullet after bullet into the writhing mass of human beings. At one point a crying two-year-old tot escaped from the ditch. Calley pushed him back and then shot him. Soon after, he told his men to take a break from the hot work.

Meanwhile, the Second Platoon under Lieutenant Brooks was engaged in its own dirty work at the nearby sub-hamlet of Binh Tay. Brooks's men at one point rounded up a group of ten to twenty women and children, brought them to the southern edge of the village, and made them squat in a circle. The troops fired several rounds from a grenade launcher into the group and then finished off the survivors with rifle fire. Earlier, Brooks's men had raped and sodomized a number of young Vietnamese women.

The worst of the horror was over at 9:30 or 10:00 that morning. By the time Captain Medina ordered a lunch break shortly after eleven o'clock, 347 villagers were dead. According to the official Peers Commission investigation, "There were quite possibly several unarmed VC (men and women) among the group and many more who were active and passive supporters of and sympathizers with the VC forces."[52] But only three or four "confirmed VC" were found among the dead. In addition only three enemy weapons were discovered. My Lai was clearly a low-yield operation.

Tet was not a military defeat. American and South Vietnamese losses were far smaller than those of the Vietcong and North Vietnamese. By one American estimate the Communists had lost thirty-three thousand men through mid-February, compared to a tenth that number for the U.S.–ARVN forces.

Vietcong losses were especially brutal. Tet had brought hidden VC cadres to the surface and thousands were killed, leaving a vacuum that remained hard to fill for many months. In the campaign's wake, Communist influence in the hamlets and villages fell off sharply. Hanoi had also failed to achieve its domestic political objective. The South Vietnamese people did not repudiate the "puppets" in Saigon and embrace the National Liberation Front. In fact for a time Tet improved the performance of the

ARVN and the South Vietnamese government. The brutality of the Communists at Hue and elsewhere outraged many South Vietnamese until now indifferent to Communist success. Government support grew. Saigon officials began to exhibit greater energy and during the post-Tet period established an effective People's Defense Force to arm the rural population against the guerrillas.

Yet Tet marked the high point of the American political and military commitment in Vietnam. Thereafter it would steadily decline.

In a sense this curious result is a classic instance of mass optical illusion. Almost everywhere in the United States, even in the White House and the Pentagon, Tet was perceived as an astounding defeat for the American cause. The first reports over the wire services and the early TV stories from Saigon emphasized the attack on the embassy. These gave the impression that the Vietcong had actually penetrated the chancery itself; the supposedly "terrorist-proof" building, the very heart of American power in Vietnam, had been captured. Then, when the building was cleared, the failed attack became a "symbolic" triumph for the Communists.

Like so much else about Vietnam, Tet was as much a media artifact as a real event, a tight knot of reality and appearance. During the days and weeks that followed, the media touted Communist success. In a February 1 NBC TV "special" on Tet, Robert Goralski, the network's Pentagon correspondent, declared that "even the American military . . . admired what the Vietcong were able to do and what they had seized." Joseph C. Harsch of ABC chided American officials for lack of frankness. What Washington needed, he said, was another Winston Churchill who would "admit frankly the fact that after two years of massive American military intervention in Vietnam, the enemy has been able to mount and to launch by far the biggest and boldest and most sophisticated offensive of the whole war."[53]

As the days passed the media perspective became even more negative. The reporters and commentators were in part victims of their profession's inherent limitations. They strained for the vivid vignette that would stand out from the gray fact and rivet the reader's attention. They talked inevitably of blood, fear, rage, and destruction. TV, even more than print, reached for the striking image, and the cameramen scrambled to supply the networks with footage of shattered and burning buildings, bandaged American grunts, and heaped-up civilian bodies. After three years of chronic, low-grade fever, the 105 degrees of Tet was a news bonanza.

Given this barrage, no amount of explanation could blunt the impression of Vietcong prowess and power, and even administration officials found it hard to swallow the official line out of Saigon that the Communists were losing. Harry McPherson, a White House aide and Johnson speech writer, later recounted how, during Tet, he would watch the TV reports in the evening and the next morning go to see Walt Rostow, now McGeorge Bundy's successor as national security adviser, to ask what had really happened. Rostow would show him the cables from Saigon describing brutal Communist losses. Yet, McPherson recalled, "I mistrusted what he said. . . . Like millions of other people who had been looking at television the night before, I had the feeling that the country had just about had it, that they would simply not take any more. . . ."[54]

Vietnam was a "living room" war. The first had been World War II, when radio had brought the voice of Edward R. Murrow and the sounds of Nazi bombs on London into American homes. Now sight was added to sound. For the first time Americans could see their own young men killing and dying on a foreign battlefield within hours of the events themselves. The picture, amplified many times by TV's immediacy, was appalling.

During and after Tet, where the media did not project the image of defeat, they focused on allied brutality. The statement by the American major about destroying Ben Tre to save it was the verbal complement to images of giant, vulturine B-52s pulverizing the green Vietnam mountains and plains. The equivalent World War II image—Flying Fortresses over Germany—had sent a thrill through American hearts twenty-five years before. But then we had been fighting the powerful and fearsome "Nazi war machine." Now the bombing seemed an obscene display of American brute strength directed against a weaker antagonist, little brown people clad in black pajamas. Here was another reason to deplore the American presence in Vietnam.

No film footage did as much damage as AP photographer Eddie Adams's 35-mm shot taken on a Saigon street on February 1. As Adams and an NBC television crew drove across embattled Saigon, they spotted some South Vietnam marines force-marching a small, tousle-haired man along the street. Though dressed in a civilian plaid shirt, black shorts, and sandals, he was a captured Vietcong officer. Adams and the NBC crew were following the party down the street when suddenly General Nguyen Ngoc Loan, head of the South Vietnam national police, appeared. A brutal man, chosen in 1963 to suppress the dissident Buddhists, Loan had done his job ruthlessly. The general stopped the party and waved away onlookers. Then, with his right hand inches away from the captive's head, he pointed a revolver and fired just as Adams tripped the shutter of his Leica. One of the NBC crew had also been filming and got a motion picture of the same scene.

The still of the captured Vietcong caught at the moment of death made the first page of *The New York Times* and appeared in scores of other American papers the next day. That evening twenty million Americans saw the filmstrip on NBC's "Huntley–Brinkley Report." The network had edited out the spurt of gore as the bullet passed through the victim's head, but what remained was a sickening image of the brutality of our esteemed ally. Here was another horrifying image of the Vietnam War to add to the others.

The administration was furious at the media coverage of Tet. It was biased and hostile, White House and Pentagon spokesmen charged. Several times during the crisis administration officials lost their tempers at the correspondents. At a "backgrounder" press conference for reporters on February 9, Secretary Rusk listened to the newsmen's skeptical comments about American intelligence effectiveness in Vietnam. The usually unflappable Georgian finally blew up. "There gets to be a point when the question is whose side are you on," he lashed out. "I don't know why . . . people have to be probing for the things that one can bitch about."[55]

Washington's short fuse derived partly from worry over what seemed to be a deteriorating American world position. January 1968 had not been a good month for the United States. Tet seemed part of a new global Communist drive to put the Free World on the defensive. On the twenty-first, thirty-one North Korean commandos had been intercepted in Seoul, the South Korean capital, while on a mission to assassinate president Park Chung Hee, an American ally. Two days later North Korean patrol boats on the Sea of Japan seized the U.S. Navy intelligence ship *Pueblo* in what the Communists claimed was their territorial waters. The ship and its eighty-three crew members had been taken to Wonson in the north, and the Americans were being threatened with trial as common criminals.

This was America's first serious hostage crisis, and it provoked the same outrage as the others to come. On January 25 Johnson called back fifteen thousand air force and navy reservists to active duty to meet the emergency. That same day the United States asked the U.N. Security Council to consider the incident. The acute phase of the *Pueblo* crisis would be over in a few weeks and then settle down into months of dreary negotiations. In December the men were finally released, but the ship was retained. Through February and March, however, it did not seem paranoid to believe that a concerted Red Chinese campaign was under way to drive the United States out of the Far East.

The administration was obviously defensive and hypersensitive, but the media did report Tet as more of a disaster than the facts warranted. This overreaction requires some explanation.

The newsmen in part were responding to the administration's blatant overselling of American progress. The reporters and correspondents already shared the broad public perception of a yawning "credibility gap" between what the president and his colleagues claimed and what was actually taking place in Vietnam. Tet made the disenchantment far worse.

The journey of Walter Cronkite from faith to doubt was both a paradigm of media disillusion and a powerful additional push to public disenchantment. By 1968 Cronkite was already the "dean" of American TV reporting. His "CBS Evening News" reached twenty million viewers five days a week, the largest news audience in the country. Avuncular, slow-talking, deep-voiced, sincere, Cronkite inspired confidence; people knew he would not lie.

Until Tet, Cronkite had strongly supported American intervention in Vietnam. After a 1965 visit to the Far East, he had announced that "Communism's advance must be stopped in Asia and . . . guerrilla war as a means to a political end must be finally discouraged."⁵⁶ He accepted the administration's claim that the United States was not just resisting communism, but helping to build an new, independent Vietnamese nation. This "nation building" goal, he believed, justified the costs. During the next two years, while his fellow journalists grew cynical about American purposes and skeptical of American victory, the administration waged a successful struggle for Cronkite's heart and mind.

The first bulletins on Tet stunned Cronkite, and he flew to Saigon to see for himself, arriving in the capital on February 11, while fighting was still going on in the city's outskirts. He reported his first impressions back to his viewers soon after. "First and simplest, the Vietcong suffered a military defeat," he declared. But the Tet offensive had also "widened a credibility gap" in Vietnam between what "the people are told and what they see about them."⁵⁷

In succeeding days Cronkite toured the other Tet battlefields including Hue, where the marines and the ARVN were still painfully digging out the Communists. The scene reminded him of ravaged World War II Europe, where he had been a young reporter for United Press. Amid the destruction and carnage he could see little of the nation building the administration had been talking about these past three years.

Back home Cronkite prepared a "Report on Vietnam" based on his visit. Nine million Americans viewed the half-hour special on Tuesday, February 27, and its effects were devastating. The audience saw film clips of a concerned-looking Cronkite with pipe and steel helmet holding forth amid the ruins and rubble. At the end of the on-site visuals he delivered his final estimate of recent events live from his desk in New York. Hiding behind "the referees of history," he called Tet a draw. Khe Sanh, then still under siege, might yet be a catastrophe, but the battle there too was a probable "standoff." He doubted that the South Vietnamese government could pull the country together, especially now that the cities had become major Vietcong targets. Cronkite's conclusion was grimly pessimistic. Taken together, it seemed "now more certain than ever that the bloody experience of Vietnam is to end in a stalemate." It was increasingly clear that the Americans would shortly be forced "to negotiate, not as victors," but at most, "as an honorable people who lived up to their pledge to defend democracy, and did the best they could."[58]

Cronkite's response was a classic rebound effect: from total belief to total doubt. The Fourth Estate refused to accept the administration's viewpoint for other reasons as well. The press did not like Lyndon Johnson. He was an inconsiderate man who would call press conferences and announce presidential trips at the last minute, forcing reporters to abruptly change personal plans. Several veteran White House newsmen admitted frankly that they didn't "care for him as a person."[59]

The post-Tet media response was more than personal animus, however. Reporters and journalists were no longer Hildy Johnsons, Hecht–McArthur *Front Page* characters, cynical, tough-talking men and women trained primarily in the rough school of hard knocks. Most were now college-educated, often with advanced degrees from good journalism schools. They were part of the "new class" of urban liberals that was beginning to emerge, especially in the cities of the Northeast. The old reporters could have identified with the self-made president; they might even have admired his fancy footwork. The new breed considered him a rube and found his cornball folksiness insincere and unappealing. They also shared the anti-Vietnam skepticism of their counterparts in other professional networks. By 1968 it was fashionable among academics, writers, and other intellectuals to disbelieve almost everything that emanated from the White House. Whatever an individual correspondent's own views, he or she found the anti-Vietnam peer consensus a powerful intimidating force. William S. White, one of LBJ's few friends among the newsmen, noted that "every journalist I know who consistently supported Viet Nam was truly punished" by members of the press, especially in the East. On the other hand "nobody was punished in the press because he was a dove."[60]

The president and his advisors struggled to neutralize the media's bleak picture. Westmoreland must make a brief comment to the press every day "to reassure the public here that you have the situation under control," Johnson ordered.[61] On February 2 he told a news conference that "the stated purposes of the general uprising have failed." Under questioning Johnson admitted that the enemy was also trying for a "psychological" victory, but said he was confident that when the American people knew the facts, they would not be discouraged at what had happened.

Of course he was wrong. We know today that Communists suffered a severe military defeat at Tet. But they also won the psychological victory that Johnson discounted. Despite "scientific" polls, it is always difficult to judge changes in the climate of opinion, but it is now clear that Tet was a psychological watershed for the American public. After January 1968 millions of Americans sensed that the war could not be won.

The earthquake in mainstream public opinion after Tet was a critical ingredient in the retreat from Vietnam. But major foreign policy decisions are not referendums, even in democracies. The important thing was that Tet was also the turning point for the foreign policy elite that had led the nation into the Vietnam embroilment. Over the next two months they would make the decisions that halted the forward momentum of the War and begin the process of winding down.

Despite the brave public face, the administration itself was shaken by the massive Communist offensive. For weeks after the initial Tet attacks had been contained, the president and his close advisers continued to worry about Khe Sanh and the rumored second round of assaults on the cities. To prevent any further setbacks the White House offered Westmoreland additional men and equipment. "If you need more troops," General Wheeler cabled Westmoreland, "ask for them." "The United States Government is not prepared to accept a defeat in South Vietnam."[62]

Defying five thousand years of precedent, Westmoreland was less anxious for reinforcements than his civilian superiors. He already had a half million troops, and unless the situation worsened at Khe Sanh he saw no need for more. But the "nervous Nellie" in the White House insisted that everything be done to avoid a catastrophe in Vietnam, and Wheeler fed Westmoreland the lines to use for extracting more men.

The Joint Chiefs had their own reasons for prompting Westy. America had military and political commitments around the world, not just in Vietnam. Every man in Vietnam, they feared, weakened America's defenses in Europe, Korea, and other crucial areas. The nation's Strategic Reserve, the pool of military manpower needed to fulfill America's worldwide obligations, was now dangerously depleted. The only way to deal with the drain was to call back to service men in civilian occupations. The Joint Chiefs understood that a reserve call-up was political dynamite. Young men would have to leave their jobs, their schools, their wives and families, and put on their tight old uniforms. Americans were not willing to fight an unlimited war in Vietnam, and the effects of a recall in an election year would be politically explosive. On the other hand, perhaps it could be justified both to the president and the American people if it was made clear that the alternative was actual combat defeat.

Westmoreland finally got Wheeler's oblique message and on February 8 cabled the Joint Chiefs that he might require another division of American troops by the end of the year. A White House meeting on February 12 considered the Vietnam reinforcement problem. Wheeler favored a call-up; McNamara opposed it. Johnson told the conferees to study the problem further. But he did authorize sending Westmoreland a brigade of the Eighty-second Airborne Division and a marine regimental landing team.

Though the number was small, the Joint Chiefs considered this a further erosion of the American strategic military reserve. The next day they proposed mobilizing 46,000 reservists at once, with another 140,000 to be readied for quick call-up. They also recommended that Congress authorize extending enlistment times for all military personnel and grant the military authority to selectively call reservists to active duty.

That same day, at another White House meeting, the president balked again. He recalled how Kennedy had been criticized when he had activated the reserves following the rancorous 1961 summit meeting with Nikita Krushchev at Vienna. And what about the reservists called to active duty following the *Pueblo* incident? That move had been a waste of time; the men had not been used for any serious purpose. No, he would not take the drastic step until he was satisfied that it was needed and could be done with minimal political and economic effects.

By this time the Eight-second Airborne had been ordered to Vietnam, and Johnson decided to go to Fort Bragg to personally see the unit off. It was a solemn occasion for the president. His own sons-in-law, Charles Robb and Pat Nugent, were servicemen and soon to leave for Vietnam duty. He truly had no heart for sending young men to be shot at and killed in Southeast Asia. Many of the paratroopers had just returned from a tour in "Nam" and were not overjoyed to be going back again. As the president went down the helmeted ranks shaking hands and talking with many of the men, he was heavyhearted.

Particularly distressing was an exchange with one soldier. Had he been in Vietnam before? the president asked. "Yes, sir, three times." Was he married? Yes, he was. Did he have any children? Yes, a boy. How old was he? "He was born yesterday morning sir." The president asked no more questions. As he wrote in his memoirs: "It tore my heart out to send back to combat a man whose first son had just been born."[63]

Like so much else about the Vietnam War, the story contains a falsehood. Many of the men actually on orders to leave for Southeast Asia were drowning their sorrows at an off-base beer party and were not on the inspection line. The paratroopers Johnson met were largely substitutes filling in to make the ceremony look good. Yet this time the president was probably not a party to the deception, and there is no reason to doubt that his anguish was genuine. It is possible that the policy turnabout soon to take place had its origins in this painful send-off ritual at Fort Bragg.

On February 23 General Wheeler arrived in Saigon to help evaluate the situation on the ground and to provide Johnson with the information he needed to make a decision on reinforcements. "Bus" Wheeler, a distinguished-looking, articulate staff officer, was tired and pessimistic, Westmoreland later reported, as much a victim of press negativism as any common citizen. His attitude was not improved by a rocket attack on his billet that evening that forced him and his party to hastily move their quarters to a better-protected spot.

After two days of consultation, the two senior officers and their staffs concluded that 206,000 more American ground troops must be sent to Vietnam. These would be doled out in three increments as needed through the end of the year. A portion of each would be deployed to stop the enemy attack in Vietnam, to restore security in the towns, cities, and heavily populated sections of the countryside, and to regain the military initiative. The rest would be used to bring America's depleted Strategic Reserve up to strength and would be ready, if needed, to be deployed to Vietnam as well. The total would raise the U.S. manpower commitment in Vietnam to almost three-quarters of a million troops. Stripped of its qualifiers, the Wheeler–Westmoreland scheme was a call for continuing and expanding the bankrupt search-and-destroy tactics and for further Americanization of the war. If implemented, it would be still another installment in the escalation process that had deposited the United States in the Vietnam quagmire.

Wheeler and his aides wrote their report winging back from Saigon. It was finished when they arrived in Honolulu and by the president's request cabled ahead to Washington. There it would set in motion the process of taking the United States out of Vietnam.

The Wheeler report reached the eyes of high Defense Department officials at a February 26 Pentagon luncheon presided over by McNamara. The president had seen McNamara's loss of faith during the previous months as faintheartedness and had eased him out of the Pentagon with a nomination as president of the World Bank. The secretary of defense was about to leave the cabinet and had only three days left in office. Good soldier to the end, McNamara had nevertheless convened the February Pentagon meeting in the president's absence in Texas.

The Wheeler report shocked the diners. McNamara himself declared its implementation would cost $10 billion. The civilian service chiefs expressed doubts that more troops were needed in Vietnam. McNamara told them to have their experts analyze the report from the perspective of their own branches. They should consider alternative responses, but concentrate on the immediate issue of the manpower increase.

Back in Washington, the president listened to his advisers discuss the report during the next few days in a series of White House meetings. Wheeler himself was present at a breakfast session on February 28 to present his case and the new secretary of defense–designate, Clark Clifford, sat in. Everyone was impressed with the tone of urgency that Wheeler injected. Despite the soothing official line on Tet, the general conveyed a sense of alarm. "He came back with a story that was frightening," Clifford later recalled. "We didn't know if we would get hit again, many South Vietnamese units had disappeared, the place might fall apart politically."[64] Johnson himself listened carefully and decided to appoint a study group under Clifford to consider the Wheeler document and report back to him as soon as possible.

The president trusted Clifford as he did few other men in Washington life. Tall, sleekly handsome, articulate, soft-spoken, the incoming defense secretary had served presidents since Harry Truman just after World War II. But he preferred private life and the rewards of Washington corporate law. He was reputed to be the highest paid professional in America, earning a half million dollars a year from his legal practice. His success by itself commended him to LBJ, a man who respected wealth and corporate power, his hill country populism notwithstanding.

Clifford had resisted a dozen efforts to recruit him for long-term office, and only LBJ's awesome persuasive powers could get him to accept the Defense portfolio. His coyness had hurt him. Dedicated federal bureaucrats considered him a dilettante, a man more interested in good living than public service. At the Pentagon, moreover, many of the high civilian functionaries were McNamara men who inevitably resented their chief's successor.

But now, after Tet, there were more important considerations as well. Tet had crystallized the growing doubts of American policies among high civilian Pentagon officials. It had revealed, Townsend Hoopes later wrote, "the doubters and dissenters to each other, as in a lightning flash."[65] The Pentagon people feared that Clifford was a hawk of hawks who would turn back official thinking to 1965, when everyone at the White House and the Pentagon believed that brute force alone could win victory in Southeast Asia. On February 13, two weeks before Clifford took office, Hoopes, hoping to change his incoming boss's mind, wrote him a long letter calling "the idea of a U.S. military victory in Vietnam . . . a dangerous illusion," and criticizing Westmoreland's costly and ineffective search-and-destroy policy.[66]

The skeptics' dovish disquiet was not misplaced. Clifford had endorsed the bombing campaign and had condemned any unilateral halt as beginning the slide to certain defeat in Vietnam. During the Wise Men meeting the previous November, he had been as hawkish as the others. But now the doves were wrong about him. In 1967 he had gone to the Far East at Johnson's behest to push America's Asian allies to commit more troops to the Vietnam effort. He discovered that the putative "dominoes" were reluctant to comply. As he later wrote, the visit had left him "puzzled, troubled, concerned," and inclined to think that perhaps "our assessment of the danger to the stability of Southeast Asia and the Western Pacific was exaggerated."[67]

By the time of his nomination Clifford's faith in bombing and a hard line generally had begun to recede. During his confirmation hearings the secretary-designate had endorsed a version of Johnson' so-called San Antonio formula calling for a bombing halt when and if the North Vietnamese promised to negotiate. During the talks, the formula provided, the Communists could continue their normal military activities, but not expand them. This was not yet the unconditional bombing cessation that the North Vietnamese insisted on, but it went a considerable distance toward meeting their demands. Meanwhile, several of McNamara's dovish civilian subordinates—Paul Warnke and Paul Nitze, as well as Hoopes—had launched a campaign to educate their new chief to the necessity of deescalation.

The Clifford Task Force held its first meeting the afternoon of February 28 with McNamara, defense secretary for two more days; Rusk; Treasury Secretary Henry Fowler; Taylor; Rostow; CIA Director Richard Helms; along with William Bundy, Habib, Nitze, Warnke, Wheeler, and others from State and the Pentagon, present. As Clifford understood their mission, they were to consider only *how,* not *whether,* to meet the Wheeler–Westmoreland request for more men. But it did not take long before the Task Force's members' sense of their responsibility expanded under the influence of a searching and honest discussion.

Fowler provided an eye-opener at the first meeting. If Wheeler got what he asked for, the treasury secretary said, there would have to be substantial increase in the federal defense budget. Congress was already up in arms over inflation-inducing federal deficits and would insist on raising taxes to finance any manpower increase in Vietnam. The legislators would also demand dollar-for-dollar cuts in domestic Great Society programs. (See chapter 1.) The political and financial pain of any further troop buildup would be, in a word, excruciating.

At the next meeting, on February 29, Clifford raised the "whether" issue for the first time. Should the United States continue its present policy in Vietnam? Was there any chance of success even if we sent many more than 206,000 troops? To help decide the issue, he commissioned experts at Defense, State, the Joint Chiefs, and the CIA to prepare studies of the military, diplomatic, and financial implications of granting the troop request and to consider alternatives to further escalation.

This was a critical step. As we have seen, many Pentagon civilians had lost their faith in American policies in Vietnam. These men were now being asked to write the studies that would decide the fate of those policies.

One of the most prominent was Alain Enthoven, a former Rhodes scholar with a Ph.D. in economics from MIT. Like almost everyone else in a high government position, Enthoven was a committed cold warrior. He did not doubt that the Soviet Union and Red China were threats to the West. But he no longer believed that further investment in Vietnam served our purposes. Enthoven composed a devastating critique of American policy which concluded that after a half million troops, 1.2 million tons of bombs, and 400,000 attack sorties in a year, "we have achieved stalemate at a high commitment. A new strategy must be sought."[68]

Enthoven rejected the troop increase out of hand as being no more likely than previous reinforcements to defeat the enemy. He did not recommend withdrawal. The "price of quitting now would include the undermining of our other commitments world-wide, bitter dissension at home, and a probable resurgence of active Chinese-USSR territorial aggrandizements."[69] The Communists could be stopped without paying a further price by reequipping the South Vietnamese so that they could carry on by themselves. In effect, what Enthoven and his staff were proposing instead of further escalation was *Vietnamization* of the war, though the term had not yet been coined.

Many of the other papers prepared for Clifford and the task force conveyed a similar message. One of the most thoughtful was put together by Paul Warnke's staff at the Pentagon's International Security Affairs office. The authors of this document included some of the brightest young men in government service—Leslie Gelb, Morton Halperin, Herbert Schandler, Richard Holbrooke, and others. Several had served in Vietnam; others came from the universities. They had long deplored the military focus in Vietnam and now saw the opportunity to drive home the point that only a political solution was possible. As Halperin later said, Clifford had thrown them the ball and their aim was to "turn him around."[70]

The central thrust of the Warnke group's paper was that further escalation would simply provoke counterescalation with no net gain. At home the higher financial outlays, increased U.S. casualties, and apparent confirmation of American warmonger-ing would trip off further draft evasion and further peace demonstrations and unrest in the cities. Like Enthoven, the

Warnke group stopped well short of recommending withdrawal, however. We should continue our military commitment at existing levels, but only to buy time for the South Vietnamese to "develop effective capability." Once again the answer was Vietnamization.

The papers commissioned on the twenty-ninth were considered in Clifford's new Pentagon office on Friday morning March 1. This was the first of many daily staff meetings that overlapped the less frequent task force conferences. Reading about these sessions today makes us impatient. The discussions seem circuitous, evasive, Aesopian. The doves did not propose getting out, but rather adopting a strategy of "population security along a demographic frontier." In ordinary English this meant giving up the search-and-destroy missions in the difficult mountain-and-jungle terrain of Vietnam's interior and concentrating on protecting the cities. The net effect would be to limit the American military commitment and American casualties. But no one yet talked of getting out and leaving Vietnam to the Vietnamese.

Clifford's report to the president on March 4 was even more oblique. It recommended increasing our forces in Vietnam by 22,000 men, an early call-up of 245,000 men to strengthen the Strategic Reserve, additional pressure on the South Vietnamese government to improve its military and political performance, no new peace initiative, and reserving decision on the full Westmoreland troop request pending further study of possible new approaches to Vietnam. There were eight appendices clipped to the document explaining the reasoning behind each recommendation. Taken as a whole it was more a proposal for slowing escalation than reversing it, though it did hold out the possibility of a more thorough reassessment following another major study.

The president saw the Clifford report in the Cabinet Room the afternoon of March 4. He had just flown in that noon from Ramey Air Force Base in Puerto Rico, where he had spent the weekend with Pat Nugent, his Vietnam-bound son-in-law. His mood was confident; Westy had sent him an optimistic review of the post-Tet fighting and a positive appraisal of the future.

Johnson was in a conciliatory mood. The Clifford proposal had advised against further peace moves, but now Secretary Rusk unexpectedly suggested that perhaps a limited halt in bombing—outside of battlefield areas—would be useful to start peace negotiations. Since the rainy season, making flying dangerous, was about to begin anyway, it would entail little added military risk. In the past Johnson had been skeptical of a bombing halt. In late 1965 and early 1966 the United States had stopped the bombing of North Vietnamese and Vietcong targets for over a month to bring the Communists to the bargaining table. The move had not only failed; the enemy had used the pause as an opportunity to rush new men and supplies into the south. And there had been other bombing halts to establish goodwill. None had worked. Hanoi had insisted that these gestures were tricks or too little by themselves to warrant concessions.

The president himself believed that this time the circumstances might be riper. If Westmoreland was right, Tet had been enormously expensive to the enemy. Perhaps Hanoi would now be more conciliatory. He picked up the suggestion and told Rusk to prepare a bombing-pause statement.

The next day at lunch the discussions continued with Rusk making his partial-bombing-halt proposal again and Rostow, the hawk, advising Johnson to ask the American people to gird their loins for an all-out, knockdown drive in Vietnam. Johnson unexpectedly sided with the doves. Clifford should take whatever steps were needed to beef up the ARVN—more helicopters, more U.S. automatic rifles. The United States, he said, was about to "make a basic change in strategy."[71]

On Sunday, March 10, page one of *The New York Times* carried an account of the Wheeler–Westmoreland troop request and the debate it had set off in the administration. Hoopes apparently had leaked the basic story, and it had then been fleshed out by reporters Neil Sheehan and Hedrick Smith with bits and pieces gleaned on Capitol Hill, at the State Department, and elsewhere in the vast whispering gallery of Washington.

The piece was a reasonably accurate report that laid out in detail the various positions of administration officials. It also placed the debate in context. Tet, the *Times* reporters noted, had profoundly changed official attitudes and created the "sense that a watershed has been reached. . . ."[72]

The *Times* is a powerful journalistic force, especially in foreign affairs. Its front page is routinely photographed by the Associated Press and sent out to its hundreds of press subscribers around the country who then, especially on overseas news, follow the "Newspaper of Record's" estimate of what is important. It is a morning newspaper, but its early editions appear late the evening before.

That Saturday night the mighty and the inquisitive had gathered at the Gridiron Club dinner at the Statler-Hilton hotel in Washington. This is an annual white-tie occasion when government officials, industrialists, and news media bigwigs get together for an evening of dining and jollity. It features a series of skits poking fun at politicians and other prominent public figures. During the course of 1968's festivities, someone handed Ben Bradlee, executive editor of *The Washington Post,* a copy of the Associated Press handout. Bradlee was startled and began to buttonhole administration officials among his fellow guests. He quickly concluded from their evasive answers that the report was correct.

The dinner almost ended there. In minutes the other newsmen and publishers present had caught on, and there was a rush to the nearest phones to tell editors and subordinates to stop the presses. The food got cold.

On Sunday and Monday newspapers all over the country blared out news of the troop request and the administration debate. Few of the papers had anything good to say about the Westmoreland–Wheeler proposal. Rostow would later insist that the leak had "churned up the whole eastern establishment and created a false issue. . . . It overrode the hopeful news and had quite substantial effects on public opinion."[73]

On March 12 Dean Rusk appeared before the Senate Foreign Relations Committee to testify on Vietnam. The proceedings promised to be rough. Committee chairman Fulbright was now

Johnson's chief congressional adversary on Vietnam and had become the president's sworn enemy. Johnson gave the senator little credit for an honest difference of opinion. The man's motives were egotistical. "Fulbright's problem," LBJ claimed, "is that he's never found any President that would appoint him Secretary of State. . . . He wants the nation to stand up and take notice of Bill Fulbright, and he knows the best way to get that attention is to put himself in the role of critic."[74] Fulbright had one of the more impressive intellects in the Senate; by 1968 the disenchanted Johnson was calling him "Senator Halfbright."

Now, in March 1968, Fulbright once more placed the administration's policies in Vietnam under a harsh spotlight. For almost eleven hours, spread over two days, the senators grilled Rusk before the television cameras. They bore in particularly hard on the troop-request report. Had Westmoreland asked for the additional men as reported? Rusk's answer was misleading. When he saw the news story, he had talked to the president about it, he said. Johnson had responded that he had not come to any conclusions about any future course. Rusk himself would not speculate about numbers of men or other future plans. The administration intended to examine every option from every angle, "but we have not come to conclusions" and the president did "not have specific . . . action recommendations in front of him at the present moment."[75]

Rusk was not the only high administration official who spent time on the Hill during March. Accompanied by General Wheeler, Defense Secretary Clifford made the rounds of House and Senate committees concerned with military affairs and learned that there were now more doves than hawks in Congress. No one was happy with a reserve call-up, and some influential conservatives like Senator Richard Russell of Georgia, head of the Senate Armed Services Committee, even thought the whole Vietnam involvement a monumental mistake. Senator Henry Jackson of Washington, one of the capital's most consistent cold warriors, later recalled how strongly affected Clifford had been by the skepticism he found in Congress.

Fulbright had called Clifford to follow Rusk before the Senate Foreign Affairs Committee. The secretary asked to be excused since he was new to the office and preoccupied with the war. Besides, he told the senator confidentially, he and his staff were engaged in a fundamental review of Vietnam. The two men agreed that it would be better to postpone Clifford's appearance until after the administration's discussions had been completed so as not to jeopardize the possibility of change.

The request nonetheless had a strong effect on the secretary. Nitze was later to note that "When Clark Clifford had to face up to the possibility that he might have to defend the administration's policy before the Fulbright committee, his views changed."[76] It was at this point, says the historian Herbert Schandler, that Clifford crossed the line into the deescalation, negotiated peace camp.

Meanwhile, the president's own attitudes were shifting in subtle ways. Johnson never ceased to believe that South Vietnam was a country in its own right, not just part of a larger Vietnam, and that Communist aggression against it must be stopped if aggressors everywhere were to be discouraged. But after Tet he could no longer deny that there were limits to America's capacity to achieve what it wanted. By March 22 he had categorically decided that he would limit new Vietnam troop deployments to a token number; the 206,000 figure was not acceptable. Fortunately, this resolution coincided with an unusual burst of energy in Saigon. Soon after Tet, President Thieu ordered an increase of sixty thousand men in the Vietnamese armed forces and invoked a dormant law authorizing the drafting of eighteen-year-olds. On March 21 he made a speech attacking corruption and declaring that the South Vietnamese people "must make greater efforts and accept more sacrifices because this is our country . . . and this is mainly a Vietnamese responsibility."[77] These signs of renewed vigor eased the president's mind. Perhaps the South Vietnamese were in fact capable of defending themselves against the aggressors. Yet Johnson would continue to waver to the very end.

Clifford was not the only top adviser who was shifting ground. By March Harriman was certain that the war was a mistake, and he soon convinced Acheson, already deeply disturbed by the reports of the Vietcong's kamikaze determination, to take a stand against further involvement. On March 14 Acheson went to the

White House to tell the president the war was unwinnable. Johnson kept him waiting until 2:00 P.M. and then delivered one of his pep talks: Tet was a victory, Westy had assured him he could win with just a few more thousand troops, the Joint Chiefs were optimistic. Acheson interrupted: "Mr. President, you are being led down the garden path." He did not believe the generals. The key issue was whether the South Vietnamese could be stiffened enough to take over their own defense. If not, the president would have to find a "method of disengagement."[78]

The next day another adviser, U.N. Ambassador Arthur Goldberg, sent Rusk a memo proposing that the United States stop *all* naval and air bombardment of North Vietnam for a time to determine if the Communists would negotiate. We should not ask them to promise negotiations first, he said. The president was willing to consider a partial halt but not the complete cessation that Goldberg proposed. The scheme seemed a surrender to the enemy, and at a meeting the following day Johnson used some colorful, down-home language to describe it. Nevertheless, he sent both Rusk's partial bombing halt proposal and Goldberg's total one to Ambassador Bunker in Saigon for his view of their effects on South Vietnam. Bunker's response was not surprising: a total bombing halt would be very disturbing to the Saigon government, while a partial halt, particularly if accompanied by more military aid, would be easier to sell.

During these last days of March, Johnson was irritable and restless. Even a weekend stay at the LBJ Ranch did not help. On Sunday the seventeenth the president and Lady Bird watched a TV special on Vietnam where Vice-President Humphrey nobly defended the administration's policies. But he and Rusk, Lady Bird wrote in her diary, were virtually the only remaining public supporters of the president. "I have a growing feeling of Prometheus Bound, just as though we were lying there on the rock, exposed to the vultures, and restrained from fighting back."[79]

Part of Johnson's irritability focused on Clifford. LBJ felt betrayed. He had thought Clifford more steadfast than McNamara. He was not. And besides, his position seemed purely negative. He opposed existing policy, but it was not clear what alternative he favored. At times during these weeks the president expressed his displeasure with Clifford by excluding him from meetings. Fortunately, he retained his respect for the man and continued to listen.

Johnson had been preparing a major address on Vietnam for some time and had called in his fellow Texan and chief speech writer, Harry McPherson, to help out. The speech became the subject of a late afternoon White House meeting on March 20. There, in the Cabinet Room, Rusk, Clifford, Goldberg, McGeorge Bundy, Supreme Court Justice Abe Fortas, and others argued over a formula for convincing Hanoi that the United States was sincere in its desire for talks and providing some inducement to the Communists to come to the bargaining table. Though the meeting ended without a clear resolution, the consensus seemed to be that a bombing pause would achieve nothing. The president now decided to delete any mention of a peace initiative from his address.

Clifford himself had no firm idea of how the administration should proceed toward the shining goal of disengagement in Vietnam. Yet he knew that the processes of the previous three years must be reversed. His solution was another meeting of the Wise Men.

The pundits—the same men who met in November plus Cyrus Vance, former deputy secretary of defense, and General Matthew Ridgeway, MacArthur's successor in Korea—assembled in the State Department on Monday afternoon, March 25. They found waiting for them a heap of briefing documents that they were asked to read. That evening, at dinner with several cabinet officers, they discussed the war, and it quickly became clear that much had changed since the previous fall. Walter Isaacson and Evan Thomas, in their study of the Wise Men, believe this gathering to have been the "highwater mark of U.S. [postwar] hegemony." They were about to reverse "the momentum that they had done so much to generate. . . . Though few were conscious of it, they were at one of history's turning points."[80]

After dinner the briefings began in the State Department Operations Center on the floor below. The Wise Men listened to still hawkish staff people at State, Defense, and the CIA, who emphasized the devastating costs of Tet to the attackers and the quick recovery of the South Vietnamese forces. Clifford, Goldberg, former Treasury Secretary Douglas Dillon, and the others grilled them closely about the South Vietnamese government and the war. They were not convinced by what they heard.

The Wise Men met alone the next morning and resumed their discussion. Overnight, for many, convictions had jelled into near certainty. Mac Bundy's brief notes summarized the group's majority position: "There is a very significant shift in our position [since last November]. . . . We hoped then there would be slow but steady progress. Last night and today the picture is not so hopeful. . . ." Acheson said bluntly: "We can no longer do the job we set out to do in the time we have left and we must begin to take steps to disengage."[81] Maxwell Taylor, who remained a hawk, recalled that he could find no better way to perceive it than as a victory of *The New York Times* over his "Council of Foreign Relations friends."[82]

At eleven o'clock Johnson met the pundits at the White House. The president arrived with Wheeler, Westmoreland, and Creighton Abrams, Westy's deputy commander and soon-to-be successor, in tow. At breakfast with the president earlier, the generals had spoken optimistically of the strategic situation in Vietnam. Johnson felt that the administration briefers had been too pessimistic the previous evening and decided to bring military men along to talk to the savants. Don't give them "an inspirational or a gloom talk," he told them. "Just give them the factual, cold, honest picture as you see it."[83]

The military men performed as expected. Wheeler, recently back from another trip to Vietnam, reported much better conditions on the battlefronts since Tet and much better spirits in Saigon. The big problem was morale in the United States. "Most of the setback was here," he noted, "which was one of their [the enemy's] objectives." Abrams declared that the ARVN units had fought well during Tet. If they had not, he pointed out, "we would have had a catastrophe. . . ."[84] One of the Wise Men asked Abrams if the Communists were capable of mounting another Tet. The answer was a categorical No. Another savant asked the general if the South Vietnamese could assume a larger share of the fighting once the current military buildup was completed. The answer was Yes.

The generals' views made little difference. At lunch with his Wise Men, without the officers or the administration functionaries, Johnson listened to McGeorge Bundy, acting as a general spokesman for the group. Since the meeting in November, Bundy told him, there had been a "significant shift" in viewpoint. Bundy quoted the statement that morning of Acheson, the group's elder statesman. The president jotted down the words "Can no longer do job we set out to do" and underlined them boldly.[85]

Johnson resisted the advice he was hearing. He thought the pundits had been misbriefed and asked to see the staffers they had talked to. But he himself was shaken, and he moved one more step toward acknowledging that he lacked the political resources to continue on the existing course. Clifford later declared: "The meeting with the Wise Men served the purpose that I hoped it would."[86]

Now the process began that led to the hardest decision that Lyndon Johnson made as president.

He had served only one full term and was eligible for reelection. Only within a very small circle of his family and closest associates had he hinted that he might not run in 1968, and even the political inside dopesters failed to guess that he might renounce the White House. The man was too power-mad, too egomaniacal to step down when the Constitution allowed him four more years.

All through 1967, the press and the politicos assumed that LBJ would be the Democratic candidate in '68. Among the antiwar people, Johnson had become the symbol of the war, and his defeat for the Democratic nomination the focus of liberal doves' hopes for an early withdrawal from Vietnam. In the summer of 1967 a goggle-eyed dynamo of a New York lawyer, Allard Lowenstein, had begun a dump Johnson movement. That November Senator Eugene McCarthy of Minnesota, under Lowenstein's urging, announced his intention of challenging the party chief. In early March, the following year, McCarthy came to within an eyelash of defeating Johnson in the New Hampshire Democratic primary. Soon after, the dreaded enemy, Robert Kennedy, junior senator from New York, also announced his candidacy. (See chapter 5.)

LBJ was a man who needed public applause and love like other men need light and air. He now found himself faced with the terrifying possibility of repudiation. "I felt that I was being chased on all sides by a giant stampede coming at me from all directions," Johnson later told Doris Kearns.[87] A brooding LBJ in the guise of King Lear was *Time* magazine's Man of the Year in January. The depiction reflected the president's own deepest anguish.

The story of the McCarthy and Kennedy insurgencies and the forces behind them will be told in detail later. (See chapter 5.) They shaped Johnson's decision to remove himself from politics and return to the ranch. So did his health.

Johnson did not come from a long-lived family. His father had died of a heart attack at sixty; his uncle George at the same age. In 1955, he himself, while Senate majority leader, had suffered a massive myocardial infarction and spent six weeks in the hospital followed by three months of bed rest at home. Ever since his childhood, when he had been forced to sit next to his paralyzed grandmother, he had suffered from a recurrent nightmare of his own physical paralysis by stroke. Later in life the dread was compounded by the experience of Woodrow Wilson, whose stroke while president had left him for a time unable to speak, move, or write, though his mind remained unimpaired.

The president's health was a major concern of Lady Bird, too. In September 1967 at the ranch, she told close family friends and political advisers, John Connally and Jake Pickle, that she would be horrified if Lyndon was incapacitated. It would be better if he withdrew while still physically strong. He had mellowed enough to find outlets for his boundless energies in the hill country, and he could afford to "come down off the mountain."[88]

By the fall of 1967, according to Lady Bird, the only decision left to make was not whether, but when—and how—to withdraw. But in public the president never seemed to waver. In late February he amused White House guests from the National

Governors' Conference with the opening words of his welcome speech: "Distinguished Governors, charming ladies, friends—and favorite sons—I am delighted to welcome you to the White House—temporarily."[89] He brought back his former press secretary George Reedy to help organize his reelection campaign and conferred with the columnist Robert Spivack about how to shape the impending contest. James Rowe, one of the president's oldest friends, took charge without a White House demurrer of a new Citizens for Johnson–Humphrey Committee.

His reelection run seemed a foregone conclusion. In mid-February, Carl Rowan, writing in the *Chicago Daily News,* asserted what almost everyone believed: the chances of LBJ not running for reelection, "can't be better than a million to one."[90]

Health concerns, fear of repudiation by the voters, the possible ignominy of defeat by "pipsqueak" Bobby, all influenced Johnson's decision to renounce a second full term. But Johnson's presidency was ultimately a casualty of the war. What changed Johnson's mind was the conclusion that it would require a dramatic gesture to bring the North Vietnamese to the bargaining table.

Johnson's big speech on Vietnam was scheduled for March 31. He would, he concluded, announce a bombing halt based on Rusk's suggestions. He would also use the speech as the occasion to withdraw from the 1968 race. Coupling the two would convince the Communists that his proposal was "a serious and sincere effort to find a road to peace."[91]

Yet to the very end he hesitated, as if some stroke of good fortune might restore the splendid days of 1964 and 1965 and permit him to enjoy four more years of accolades and triumphs. The speech drafting had been assigned to Harry McPherson before the tortuous Vietnam reappraisal process was more than a hint, and by March 10 McPherson had collected ideas and composed paragraphs that emphasized the need for further sacrifice to win the war. Then, as the president's thinking changed, so did the speech. By March 27 he and his aides were on the sixth or seventh draft.

That day, McPherson, Clifford, Rusk, Rostow, and William Bundy met at the State Department and composed a statement pledging the United States to cease bombing unconditionally north of the twentieth parallel. By the evening, however, Johnson was waffling again. It was not until the following day that, crablike, the bombing-halt clause crawled into the speech. Later, on the twenty-eighth, the president authorized Rusk to inform the South Vietnamese government of the plan and solicit its approval.

On Saturday, the thirtieth, with Clifford, Wheeler, Rostow, William Bundy, and McPherson present, the president, in shirt-sleeves and loosened tie, went over each word in the final draft. Clifford was careful to see that not only was the bombing-halt clause retained but that the address as a whole was couched in a conciliatory tone. Johnson had already told key members of Congress that he intended to reduce the air war and had received Ambassador Bunker's report that he had informed the South Vietnamese and gotten their approval. The president raised no further objections.

The address had originally ended with a peroration invoking a favorite Johnson image of defiance: Colonel William B. Travis and his outnumbered Texans at the Alamo. Obviously, that now had to go, and normally McPherson would have arranged the alternative. But Johnson told him that he would write his own conclusion. At the end of the meeting the uneasy McPherson came up to Clifford and asked, "Clark—what's up, is he going to say *sayonara?*"[92] Clifford told him not even to think about such a thing.

Sunday, March 31, began hectically for the president and Lady Bird. At 7:00 A.M., their older daughter, Lynda, flew in from California on the "red-eye special" after seeing her husband off for Vietnam. The First Lady urged Lyndon to get his sleep, but he insisted on being at the White House door when Lynda arrived in the official car. The president helped Lady Bird put the exhausted young woman to bed.

Later that morning Johnson went to church, stopping off on the way back to say goodbye to the vice-president and Mrs. Humphrey, who were leaving for an official visit to Mexico. But the rest of the day was spent working with his aide Horace Busby in the Treaty Room, giving a final polish to the speech scheduled for nine that evening on national television.

In December, during his whirlwind around-the-world trip, Johnson had asked Busby to prepare some lines renouncing a second full term. He considered reading this statement at the conclusion of the January State of the Union Message, but of course had not. In late March he asked Busby to try again, and on March 30 showed the result to his press secretary, George Christian.

In his memoirs, *The Vantage Point,* Johnson gives the impression that by this time his decision was firm. It was not. The events of that final Sunday polishing session show that the president remained hesitant almost to the last minute. The one interruption that day occurred when Johnson joined a group of senior Democratic leaders to discuss the forthcoming presidential campaign. The politicos told him that he would probably lose badly to Eugene McCarthy in the Tuesday Wisconsin primary. Despite Wisconsin, they thought he could get the nomination and win in November. He would have to limit his appearances, however, to avoid antiwar heckling and violence. The president said nothing to deflate their optimism and returned to the Treaty Room to continue polishing his evening address. Later that day former North Carolina Governor Terry Sanford, just selected to head the Johnson–Humphrey reelection committee, left for Milwaukee, still believing that he was in charge of LBJ's reelection campaign.

The broadcast at nine that evening originated from the Oval Office. Several days before, when political reporter and historian Theodore White interviewed "Mr. Big" for his book on the 1968 presidential election, he had been shocked by Johnson's exhausted slouch and defensiveness. "The eyes, behind the gold-rimmed eyeglasses, were not only nested in lines and wrinkles, but pouched in sockets blue with a permanent weariness," White wrote.[93] But LBJ now seemed calm and at ease—philosophical, one would say of a more cerebral man.

On camera, seated as his desk, the president opened with a statement that he wanted to speak "of peace in Vietnam and Southeast Asia." He mentioned the San Antonio formula and how

North Vietnam had rejected it. Despite that rebuff, he was "taking the first step to deescalate the conflict," he declared. "We are reducing—substantially reducing—the present level of hostilities." "And," he added, "we are doing so unilaterally, and at once." Bombing of North Vietnam would henceforth be limited to the region just north of the DMZ, and even this limited bombing might come to an early end if "our restraint is matched by restraint in Hanoi."

Hoping to make the peace gesture more concrete, Johnson announced that he was designating Harriman and the American ambassador to Moscow, Llewellyn Thompson, as negotiators with the Vietnam Communists. "I call upon President Ho Chi Minh to respond positively, and favorably, to this new step toward peace."[94]

The speech reviewed American goals in Vietnam and asserted that substantial progress had been made in building a durable South Vietnamese government. Johnson summarized the costs of the Vietnam War and pleaded with Congress to raise taxes to pay for it. As he approached the end, he prayed that his offer would not be rejected and that it would lead to an early peace.

At 9:35 the president raised his right arm as he glanced at his wife sitting out of camera range. It was a prearranged signal that he would read an addendum to the thirty-page speech he had just completed. His voice now took on a more personal tone as he told his viewers: "For thirty-seven years in the service of our Nation . . . I have put the unity of the people first, . . . ahead of any divisive partisanship." But now the nation was seriously divided. In the four years since the duties of the presidency had devolved on him, much had been accomplished. These gains were now threatened by "suspicion, distrust, selfishness, and politics. . . ."[95] Believing this, he had concluded that he should not permit the presidency to become involved in the noisy contentions of the coming election year.

Alert viewers across the country could see what was coming, though the thought had barely time to form before he resumed. "Accordingly, I shall not seek and I will not accept the nomination of my party for another term as your President."[96]

No one interrupts the president of the United States when he is speaking on prime-time television to seventy million people. But the audience of friends, family, advisers, and reporters in the Oval Office shot to their feet as if their chairs had been electrified, drowning out the president's last few words. In millions of living rooms around the country the range of reactions was similar: surprise, joy, dismay.

The speech was the most memorable Lyndon Johnson had ever made. In the next two days the White House received forty-nine thousand telegrams. There were also thirty thousand letters. Many of the messages were cordial. His friends expressed dismay at his departure; some of his opponents, now that he was going, forgave him.

Not everyone took the peace offer seriously. Senator Fulbright, for one, attacked the proposal as "a very limited change in existing policy . . . not calculated to bring a response from North Vietnam."[97]

This time the senator showed that he really was, occasionally, only "half bright." On April 3 as the president was chatting with Senator Scoop Jackson of Washington and his family in the Oval Office, Tom Johnson, one of the White House staff, rushed in from the Press Room clutching a piece of ticker copy. He gave it to George Christian, who handed it to the president. It was a bulletin reporting a broadcast from Hanoi Radio: the North Vietnamese were willing to talk!

Soon after, the Situation Room forwarded the full North Vietnamese statement. Hanoi had attacked American policy generally and insisted that "the U.S. government had not correctly and fully responded to the just demand of the DRV [Democratic Republic of Vietnam] government, of U.S. progressive opinion, and of world opinion." But it was prepared to overlook the limitations of the American action. "On its part, the DRV government declares its readiness to send its representatives to make contact with U.S. representatives to decide . . . the unconditional cessation of bombing and all other war acts against the DRV so that talks could begin."[98]

The president showed the bulletins to Jackson. He then left

the Oval Office and walked into the Cabinet Room where Robert Kennedy and Ted Sorenson, the New York senator's campaign aide, were waiting. After his withdrawal Johnson had promised to confer with each of the major candidates on the latest domestic and foreign developments, and Kennedy had come for his briefing. Lyndon Johnson surely felt a surge of triumph as he handed his adversary the dispatches.

The Vietnam War still had almost five more years to run before the last Americans fired their last shots. Actually, more Americans would die in Southeast Asia after April 1968 than before.

Yet the spring of 1968 was the turning point of America's longest—and least successful—war. Peace talks began in Paris on May 10 in a mood of great optimism. The American negotiators were so certain that an agreement was imminent that rather than finding long-term accommodations, they rented hotel rooms for the delegation.

The talks bogged down in a few weeks over U.S. demand for a complete withdrawal of DRV troops from the south and North Vietnamese insistence on a complete bombing halt before even considering negotiations. Then, when the Americans agreed to stop the bombing, more trouble would develop over seating the National Liberation Front delegation. Not until January 1973 would the two sides sign a treaty that ended America's involvement.

But 1968 was the war's high tide. Many Americans would be sent to Vietnam over the following years as replacements for men who had served their year's tour of duty. But the total number of troops would never exceed the mid-1968 peak of 540,000. By the end of 1970, Vietnamization had reduced to 334,000 the number of Americans fighting and dying in the jungles and the rice fields.

In later years the peace movement would claim chief credit for American disengagement in Vietnam. As we will see, there was some reason for their belief. Hawks would blame the media for American withdrawal. The press and TV, they said, had distorted the Communist success at Tet and turned the mainstream public against the war. There was some truth to this view, too. But in the end it was the foreign policy elite's loss of faith after Tet that turned the tide. The Wise Men would forgather once more in 1971—to defend NATO, their creation, against a congressional challenge—but they would never again affect the course of American foreign policy. When they abandoned containment, they put a period to their own existence.

3

We Shall Overcome—Someday

RICHARD G. HATCHER was inaugurated mayor of Gary, Indiana, on the first day of 1968. The occasion would not usually have rated national press attention. A smoky steel town just across the state line from Chicago, Gary had only 178,000 people, making it 500 or more steps down from the nation's largest city. But the media were present in force, and newspapers across the country carried the details of the inaugural ceremony at the city's Memorial Auditorium. Three thousand guests, including a score of celebrities, attended. James Farmer, recent head of CORE, the Congress of Racial Equality, was there. So was Dick Gregory, the activist comedian. Richard Hatcher was different: he was black.

Hatcher was not the first black mayor of a northern city. Carl Stokes of Cleveland, though elected at the same time, had been sworn in a few months earlier. But Hatcher had challenged an entrenched white political oligarchy, and the campaign had been particularly bitter.

The media treated the victory as the culmination of the decade-long civil rights movement that had changed the social face of America. In fact, as 1968 began the civil rights movement was in crisis. By the end of the year it would be virtually dead.

For over a decade, ever since the landmark 1954 Supreme Court *Brown* v. *Board of Education of Topeka, Kansas* decision outlawing school segregation, the "second Reconstruction" had moved from victory to victory, leveling the monstrous edifice of Jim Crow that had shadowed southern race relations since the 1890s. But now that little remained of publicly enforced discrimination, equality of white and black in America remained far off. The movement was at an impasse.

The crusade against segregation had enlisted many thousands, whites and blacks. At the van had been the "Big Five" civil rights organizations.

The oldest and largest of these was the National Association for the Advancement of Colored People (NAACP). Formed in 1909 by white liberals and northern-born black rebels, the NAACP had assaulted segregation with a barrage of articles, speeches, lobbying activities, and legal actions. NAACP attorneys had been the first to challenge Jim Crow in the state and federal courts, and the head of its Legal Defense Fund, Thurgood Marshall, had argued the *Brown* case. In 1968 the NAACP's executive director was Roy Wilkins, a Missouri-born, northern-educated journalist.

The Urban League, founded in 1910 by white philanthropists and black and white academics, was another joint black-white effort. Its mission was to smooth the transition of Negroes moving from the rural South to the North's industrial cities. It too employed words as its major weapon. The league advised new arrivals from the South and tried to find them jobs. It trained a whole generation of black social workers in the problems of the emerging black urban ghettos and provided a respectable outlet for white liberal energies and money. Its head in 1968 was Whitney Young, Jr., a six-foot-tall two-hundred pounder with a disarming smile.

Both the NAACP and the Urban League relied heavily on white philanthropy. Moorfield Storey and William Walling, both upper-class white reformers, were the first officers of the NAACP. Arthur Spingarn, another white man, was an early head of its legal committee, and the league's first chairman was Edward Seligman, a white professor of economics at Columbia. In the early years many members of the league's staff were white.

Both senior civil rights organizations held optimistic views of

America's racial ills and their cure. Of all the groups in American life, they said, Negroes had been the most harshly victimized by prejudice. But the injustices they suffered had been through denial of America's most fundamental principles of equality, not some ineradicable white racism. Education, agitation, legislation, adjudication would ultimately overwhelm bigotry and usher in a epoch of racial justice.

Change denied is change radicalized. The glacial pace of racial advance during the first generation of the twentieth century provoked a more militant response. In 1942 a group of pacifists and socialists, black and white, including James Farmer, a Texas-born black minister's son, Homer Jack, a prematurely gray white biologist turned Unitarian minister, and Bernice Fisher, a divinity student at the University of Chicago, founded the Congress for Racial Equality in Chicago. CORE was interracial, like its predecessors, but its founders were impatient with mere words. CORE preached nonviolent civil disobedience as a way to attack discrimination, whether legal Jim Crow in the South or the informal exclusion practiced by northern businesses, clubs, professional bodies, and landlords. "All of us," Fisher later recalled, "were afire with the ideas of Gandhian nonviolence."[1]

CORE tested Gandhiism in 1942 with a sit-in campaign to force the Jack Spratt coffee house in Chicago to serve black patrons. The owners at first resisted aggressively. At one point the mangager smashed the dishes the waitresses had used to serve the mixed-race test group. At another, George Houser, an early black CORE leader, remembered, he served them "meat with egg shells scattered on it, or a plate of food salted so heavily that it could not be eaten. . . ."[2]

Eventually the restaurant owners surrendered, but a 1946 attempt to test a recent Supreme Court decision outlawing Jim Crow seating on interstate buses failed. CORE riders through Virginia, North Carolina, and Kentucky who refused to take the segregated seats at the back of the bus were arrested, and several served twenty-day terms at hard labor on the road gang. The "Journey" received some publicity, but segregation remained.

American racial attitudes were changing. World War II, a victory over the most malevolent bigotry of modern times, gave racism a bad name. The new postwar prosperity blunted the edges of economic competition and permitted greater social tolerance. Meanwhile, the black community was growing in self-confidence and wealth. By now there were thousands of college-educated black professionals and businessmen, and black voters in the northern cities had become a powerful political force. The black churches too, long the nurseries of charismatic black leadership, were now stronger and richer. Yet in 1946 enormous areas of American life were still segregated, either legally or by venerable practice, and black Americans, measured by every index of social and economic standing, belonged to an inferior caste. CORE's direct action was premature. The bus riders had collided head-on with a set of social values still deeply entrenched. But they were part of the racial past and were ripe for rapid change.

The *Brown* decision created the modern civil rights movement. Now, for the first time, the federal government promised to intervene effectively in favor of a colorblind society.

The struggle to implement *Brown* gave birth in 1957 to the Southern Christian Leadership Conference (SCLC). Its womb was Montgomery, Alabama, "Cradle of the Confederacy," where, almost a century before, a convention of angry proslavery secessionists had proclaimed the Confederate States of America.

The SCLC was brought forth in pain and sorrow. The occasion was a bus boycott called by Montgomery's black leaders in December 1955 to protest the arrest of Mrs. Rosa Parks for refusing to take her Jim Crow seat at the back of a Montgomery city bus following a hard day's work at a downtown department store. The event was not entirely spontaneous. Mrs. Parks had not intended to defy the law, she later said. "I simply decided that I would not get up, I was tired. . . ."[3] But she was not a political innocent. Mrs. Parks was a dedicated antisegregationist who had worked for the Montgomery chapter of the NAACP and had taken courses in race relations at the Highlander Folk School, an early community-action training institution located in the Tennessee mountains. Nor was the boycott a spur-of-the moment event. For many months black Montgomery leaders had been looking for an occasion to challenge the city's segregated transit system and had rejected several other cases as vulnerable to attack. Mrs. Parks, a sweet-faced lady of impeccable reputation, seemed above reproach. Here was the perfect opportunity to defy the insensitive and brutal bus company and strike a blow for black dignity.

Mrs. Parks was booked on Thursday. On Friday a coalition of black ministers and civic leaders announced a boycott of city buses for the following Monday, the day of Mrs. Parks's trial. The Montgomery leaders asked the young and eloquent new preacher at the Dexter Avenue Baptist Church, Dr. Martin Luther King, Jr., to lead the boycott movement. Though he had arrived with his new wife in Montgomery only a year before, King had been jolted by the ugly racism of the city and accepted the leadership role. His life and that of the nation would never be the same.

King was an extraordinary man. But he was not a plaster saint. He belonged to the black bourgeoisie that would later suffer so much abuse from militants, and he shared their middle-class virtues and failings.

He had led a sheltered life. His father, "Daddy" King—the Reverend Martin Luther King, Sr.—presided at Atlanta's Ebenezer Baptist Church, one of the richer black congregations in a southern city where racism seldom showed itself brazenly. The King family was protective and sheltering. His childhood years had been spent, King said, in "a very congenial home situation," one "where love was central and where lovely relationships were ever present."[4] The young Martin enjoyed boisterous sports and exhibited more than his share of adolescent agony and self-pity. In college, he also had a streak of the dandy. His friends teased him for it, calling him "Tweed" to mark his natty sports jackets.

King could not elude segregation, of course. In 1943, while returning by bus from an oratorical contest in south Georgia with his high school teacher, the fourteen-year-old boy was forced by the driver to surrender his seat to a white rider. "It was," he later wrote, "the angriest I have ever been in my life."[5] Through elementary and high school he attended segregated schools; there were no others in the South. He took his B.A. at the all-black Morehouse College, a branch of all-black Atlanta University. Then, in 1948, he escaped Jim Crow for a time by going north to study theology and philosophy. In 1953, while taking his Ph.D. at Boston University, he met Coretta Scott, a young Alabama voice student at the New England Conservatory of Music, and married her that June. The following year he accepted the call to become pastor at Montgomery's Dexter Avenue Church at $4,200 a year, the highest salary paid any Montgomery black minister. He was now back in Jim Crow land.

King's philosophical studies had exposed him to the egalitarian social views of Walter Rauschenbusch, a founder of the liberal Prostestant Social Gospel movement of the early twentieth century. He had also encountered the pacifism of the Reverend A. J. Muste, the prominent Christian Socialist, and the nonviolent protest philosophy of Mohandas Gandhi, the Indian political leader whose civil disobedience tactics in 1948 had ousted the British Raj from his homeland. King was intrigued by nonviolence as a protest tactic, but he was not yet a full believer in the value of Gandhi's *satyagraha* against the oppressor.

The fiery, yearlong Montgomery bus strike in 1955–56 tempered and matured King. Black Montgomeryans organized car pools or walked to work to avoid patronizing the Jim Crow bus line. The boycott cut deeply into the bus company's revenues. A few local whites admired the dedication of the city's blacks, but most were fearful and indignant. The Ku Klux Klan bombed King's house and those of other boycott leaders and burned black churches. King and other Montgomery blacks were arrested. Hotheads in the black community were ready to riot, but King restrained them. "We are not advocating violence," he told his followers. "We must love our white brothers no matter what they do to us."[6] This was still the innocent spring of the civil rights movement, and his Christian message earned the admiration and goodwill of moderate Americans everywhere.

Victory in Montgomery came through a Supreme Court decision on December 20, 1956, declaring Alabama's Jim Crow transportation laws unconstitutional. Shortly before 6:00 A.M. the following morning, King and his associates boarded a Montgomery city bus, paid their fares, and sat down in front seats. "For the first time in this 'cradle of the Confederacy' all the Negroes entered buses through the front door," noted *The New York Times*.

"They did not get up to give a white passenger a seat. And whites sat with Negroes."[7]

King's Montgomery success led to the formation early in 1957 of the Southern Christian Leadership Conference. Dedicated at first to ending Jim Crow on public transportation, it soon added all segregation as well as restored black suffrage to its agenda. Around him at the SCLC King collected a roster of unusually able aides and allies—Bayard Rustin, a courtly black Quaker with beautiful diction, long active in CORE and pacifist causes; Ralph Abernathy, the plain-spoken, twenty-nine-year-old black pastor of Montgomery's First Baptist Church; Reverend Fred Shuttlesworth, a slender, intense man who headed Birmingham's Bethel Baptist Church; Wyatt Tee Walker, a tall, Baptist preacher from Petersburg, Virginia, with the air of an aristocrat; Andrew Young, a youthful, well-spoken, Congregational minister; and Ella Baker, a prim but passionate former field secretary for the NAACP. Some of these people were relatively new to struggle, others—like Rustin and Baker—were battered veterans of the civil rights wars.

During the next decade, with the SCLC in the lead, the civil rights movement rushed from victory to victory, demolishing segregation and restoring long-denied voting rights by political pressure, legal challenge, and the tactics of nonviolence and civil disobedience.

The SCLC, like its predecessors, retained its faith in biracialism. Whites were a major source of funds and organizational skills. Among King's closest advisers was Stanley Levison, a New York lawyer with a radical past; the Reverend Glenn Smiley, a white pacifist minister, tutored King on Gandhian nonviolent protest when he was still unclear about its precise shape. Whites also marched, demonstrated, and risked their lives with SCLC.

In 1960 the civil rights movement spread from adults to young people, in the process creating the Student Nonviolent Coordinating Committee, the last of the Big Five.

SNCC derived from a youthful escapade in Greensboro, North Carolina, the site of the all-black North Carolina Agricultural and Technical College. There, on February 1, 1960, four black students from the college, fired up by a semester of late-night discussions of justice, injustice, courage, and hypocrisy, sat down at the segregated Woolworth's lunch counter and ordered coffee and doughnuts. The young men had already bought some school supplies and had the receipts to prove it. When the waitress said "I'm sorry, we don't serve you here," they answered politely, "in fact we've already been served."[8] That day they sat dumbly at the counter, ignored by the waitresses. And the day after, and the day after that. It took a year before the students had desegregated Greensboro's lunch counters. Long before this, the sit-in tactic had spread to other schools in the Greensboro area and then to black schools throughout the South.

The sit-ins took courage and awesome self-control. White hoodlums pushed lighted cigarettes against the backs of black girls at the counters; they blew cigar smoke in the protesters' faces, spat at them, and dumped french fries in their laps. Discipline held and the protesters' self-restraint and Christian forbearance was inspiring. "We wanted to make . . . clear to everybody," recalled Franklin McCain, one of the four original Greensboro students, "that it was a movement . . . seeking justice more than anything else and not a movement to start a war. . . ."[9] White students at Michigan, Swarthmore, Berkeley, Harvard, and other liberal campuses, already disenchanted with fifties' conformity, were soon picketing local Kresge and Woolworth stores to express their support. In 1961 a group of white student leaders organized the Northern Student Movement to raise money for their black colleagues and to coordinate white student support.

In April 1960 a group of sit-in leaders meeting in Raleigh at the call of the SCLC's Ella Baker formed the Temporary Student Nonviolent Coordinating Committee. They soon dropped the "temporary," creating the acronym SNCC, pronounced "snick." From the outset the new organization committed itself to nonviolence. It was "the foundation of our purpose, the presupposition of our faith, and the manner of our action," its founding manifesto stated.[10] But its tactics would be direct action, not the slow course of suits and legislation. It would be unbureaucratic and undogmatic, and ready to improvise. And it would be interracial—whites and blacks together.

*   *   *

During the next five years the civil rights movement cut like a cyclone through the tangle of segregation. The year after the sit-ins belongs to CORE under James Farmer, who, in the decade and a half since the 1946 bus-rider challenge to interstate transportation segregation, had worked as field secretary for SLID, the youth affiliate of the old-line social democratic League for Industrial Democracy; as an organizer for the New York City municipal workers' union; and as assistant to Roy Wilkins at the NAACP. In 1961 Farmer was offered the post of national director of CORE, the organization he had helped found twenty years earlier, and accepted enthusiastically. CORE promised to be feisty and aggressive, qualities that suited him. When he told Wilkins his plans, the head of the NAACP wistfully remarked: "You're going to be riding a mustang pony—while I'm riding a dinosaur."[11]

Farmer opposed piecemeal and localized civil rights agitation, local demonstrations by local people. Let the critics of "outside agitators" be damned. The civil rights drive must become national, must "establish the position that we were entitled to act any place in the country, no matter where we hung our hat and called home, because it was our country."[12] His first project at CORE was the "freedom rides" through the South, in imitation of the 1946 Journey, to test again the courts' ruling on interstate bus seating.

The first freedom riders—seven blacks and six whites—set out on two intercity buses from Washington, D.C., in early May 1961. They intended to ignore Jim Crow seating on the buses and at the depot lunch counter and restroom facilities. Pledged to absolute nonviolence, they expected to run into a hornets' nest.

They did. At Rock Hill, South Carolina, a mob of angry whites blocked the entrance to the white waiting room and beat John Lewis, then a member of the Nashville SCLC, and Albert Bigelow, a white pacifist, when they tried to enter. As they moved south, the mobs of white racists, alerted by the media, grew larger and more savage. In Alabama the Klan intercepted the first bus just over the Georgia state line. At the Anniston depot an angry crowd of whites wielding chains, bats, and iron rods smashed windows and slashed at the tires. The police held the crowd back so that the Greyhound with its passengers could escape, but the Klansmen pursued and forced everyone out on the highway with an incendiary bomb that filled the cab with choking smoke. The Trailways bus encountered even greater ferocity when it arrived at Anniston. Klansmen climbed aboard and beat the occupants brutally. A blow to the head left Walter Bergman, a retired white schoolteacher, permanently brain-damaged.

More mayhem followed. When the second bus arrived in Birmingham, another gang of white toughs pounded the passengers with iron pipes, key rings, and fists, while the Birmingham police, in cahoots with the Klan, stood by and watched. By this time even the bravest civil rights defenders had reason to hesitate. When they discovered that no bus would agree to carry them to their next stop, Montgomery, they accepted a Justice Department offer to fly them to New Orleans and safety. The price was simply too great for even the bravest to pay.

The freedom rides were only one front of the biracial war against segregation and disfranchisement of the early 1960s. In many southern towns and cities, impatient black leaders challenged local resistance to desegregation and voter registration. They often turned to King to show them how the weak could humble the mighty.

King's function was to inspire. The SCLC was not an efficiently run organization. Its chief asset was King's eloquence and passion. His most powerful weapons were his resonant baritone and his command of the Old Testament prophetic mode. His words poured out like organ chords, and their Biblical sonorities touched deep layers of recognition in Americans, black and white alike.

The King preaching style had once been common among Protestant ministers generally, but now was little heard from white urban pulpits. It survived among black clergymen, like some ancient insect caught in amber. And black preachers and congregations contributed other qualities of their own. Sermons in black churches were dialogues. Congregations echoed the words of the preacher, urged him on to further efforts amidst shouted "amens." Students of rhetoric called it antiphony.

King's eloquence and forensic skills were not always enough. At Albany, Georgia, where King and the SCLC came in December 1961 to lead a local desegregation and voter registration movement, he met defeat. King and the SCLC led sit-ins and walk-ins to desegregate the city's parks, theaters, lunch counters, and libraries. Police Chief Laurie Pritchett promptly hauled the demonstrators off to jail.

But Pritchett was a shrewd man who had studied up on Gandhian techniques so he could foil them. "I did research," he later said, and "found his [King's] method was . . . to fill the jails. And once they filled the jails, we'd have no capacity to arrest and then we'd have to give in to his demands."[13] He soon changed his tack, arranging for sheriffs and jailers in towns as far away as a hundred miles to take in arrestees. He was also careful to avoid rough treatment and by refusing to create martyrs avoided the wave of liberal sympathy the Albany movement needed for success. When city officials offered the Albany movment's leaders a deal—desegregation of bus and train depots in return for ending demonstrations—they accepted. The local officials then reneged on their promises. "We killed them with kindness," a city official later explained.[14] King was not a party to the agreement, but SNCC, already resentful of his celebrity, accused him of betraying Albany's blacks.

Despite Albany, the weapon of nonviolence as wielded by King and the SCLC would bring down the whole baroque structure of southern segregation in a few years.

From Albany, the following year King and the SCLC moved on to Birmingham, Alabama's chief industrial city, a community "trapped for decades in a Rip Van Winkle slumber."[15] King and his colleagues brought an agenda: desegregation of lunch counters, department store fitting rooms, drinking fountains, and rest rooms; a biracial committee to work out a desegregation timetable for other spheres of city life; improved job opportunities for Birmingham blacks; amnesty for any demonstrators arrested.

Birmingham was one of the most intransigent cities in the Deep South. Jim Crow was everywhere and often took bizarre forms. City officials had pulled a book featuring friendly white and black rabbits off the kiddie library shelves. They had surrendered the city's minor league baseball club so that Birmingham could avoid the ignominy of having to play integrated International League teams. Birmingham whites had objected to playing "Negro music" on "white" radio stations. The city was so totally segregated, King once declared, that he felt he was "within a cab ride of being in Johannesburg, South Africa."[16]

The city was also an armed camp. Andrew Young called it "the most violent city in America."[17] The Klan was a power in Birmingham and had been implicated in a score of bombings of civil rights leaders' homes. Wags nicknamed the city "Bombingham." Worse still, the police were enthusiasts of the wrong side. Led by the beefy, bespectacled Eugene "Bull" Connor, they were tough, brutal men who despised blacks and often treated them like vermin. Connor had promised Birmingham citizens that he would not tolerate sit-ins in their city. And behind the city police chief were the Alabama state police under the orders of recently elected Governor George Corley Wallace, an avid segregationist. Blacks in turn were armed to the teeth to protect themselves against what they considered racist hoodlums in uniform. Until King and the SCLC put their foot down, some carried guns to demonstrations so they could "kill me a cracker."[18]

King and the SCLC came to Birmingham at the invitation of Fred Shuttlesworth, founder of the local SCLC affiliate, the Alabama Christian Movement for Human Rights. King's motives were mixed. He could not refuse Shuttlesworth's request. The man had been bombed, beaten, and jailed; his wife had been stabbed. He deserved every ounce of support he could get to desegregate the hate-filled city. But King had other reasons to chose Birmingham as well. If this city could be cracked by the nonviolent approach, few places could stand against it. "It was our faith," King later declared, "that 'as Birmingham goes, so goes the South.'"[19]

The campaign was a triumph for nonviolence. The first stage of "Project C" (for "confrontation"), started slowly with sit-ins at downtown lunch counters. The police made arrests and the media took notice. On April 6 fifty blacks led by Shuttlesworth marched to city hall. Connor arrested the whole crew. The following day, Palm Sunday, the police rounded up and booked a second group led by King's brother, Alfred Daniel. By this time the SCLC had announced a black boycott of downtown stores that threatened to cut sharply into busy Easter shopping.

On April 10 city officials secured a court injunction forbidding racial demonstrations. King defied the order. On Good Friday, King and Abernathy led a march of fifty men and women on city hall. As the small group paraded down the street, a thousand blacks cheered them on. Bull Connor let them go only eight blocks before intercepting them. As King and Abernathy knelt to pray, detectives and motorcycle cops seized the marchers by the seats of their pants and threw them all into paddy wagons to be booked and jailed. The media once more paid attention.

King spent his time in jail composing a nineteen-page letter defending "nonviolent direct action" as a civil rights strategy. His "Letter from Birmingham Jail," written on toilet paper scraps and sheets of personal stationery supplied by a black trustee, defended the SCLC against charges of "unwise and untimely" action by a group of white Birmingham clergymen. Blacks had waited "more than 340 years" for their "constitutional and God-given rights." Perhaps it was easy for those "who had never felt the stinging darts of segregation to say, 'Wait,'" but when, like black people, "you have seen vicious mobs lynch your mothers at will and drown your sisters and brothers at whim; when you have seen hate-filled policemen curse, kick, and even kill your brothers and sisters; when you see the vast majority of your twenty million Negro brothers smothering in airtight cages of poverty in the midst of an affluent society . . . —then you will understand why we find it difficult to wait."[19] The letter was smuggled out page by page by King's lawyers and typed up at Project C headquarters. Eventually reprinted in a hundred periodicals and anthologies, it was the most eloquent defense of nonviolent civil rights published by an American.

King was tempted to remain in jail to challenge his arrest head-on. But he feared that his absence from the day-to-day operations of Project C would weaken it, and he decided to accept bail. Once free, he confronted the decline of media interest. "The press is leaving," he told Reverend John Thomas Porter, a former assistant at his Montgomery church, "we've got to get going."[20] Soon after, he authorized the "Childrens' Crusade," a calculated attempt to provoke the police and so capture the attention of the media and incite a great wave of northern sympathy.

On May 2, six thousand black children, some as young as six, marched from the Sixteenth Street Baptist Church to downtown Birmingham. The police arrested almost a thousand and carted them off to jail, stuffing the cells to capacity. The following day, Connor's men intercepted a march of twenty-five hundred black youngsters carrying banners reading FREEDOM. Connor stood by, cigar clamped in his mouth, and ordered his men to "let them have it." Fierce jets of water from high pressure hoses shot out at the demonstrators, knocking down children and adults alike. People were swept off curbs and slammed against walls. Some had their clothes ripped off. When outraged black bystanders hurled bottles and bricks at the firemen and police, Connor unleashed attack dogs who charged the crowd, slashing at running protesters with their fangs.

The media covered the violence minute-by-minute, and the American public was stunned by the brutal encounter. President Kennedy told an Americans for Democratic Action audience that it made him "sick." He disputed the timing of the demonstrations, but he understood, he said, why the black people of Birmingham were "tired of being asked to be patient."[21]

On May 4 Burke Marshall of the Justice Department Civil Rights Division and Assistant Deputy Attorney General Joseph Dolan flew to Birmingham to try to negotiate a settlement. Their boss, the attorney general, dispatched a barrage of phone calls to southern officials and prominent northern businessmen with subsidiaries in the South or connections with the Birmingham business community. Already hurt by the boycott that had reduced retail sales by one-third in the previous month, the city's merchants, manufacturers, and bankers were petrified by the chaos they saw ahead. Now that all the jails were filled, Connor would have to stop the demonstrators by direct physical interdiction, and massive destruction of property did not seem inconceivable. Though reluctant to submit to coercion, the city leaders concluded that it was better than a total collapse of order. "The idea of negotiation," one white businessman noted, "was offensive to all present," but further violence was "an . . . even more disastrous alternative."[22] On May 10 they agreed to accept all the protesters' major demands.

Birmingham was a turning point for the civil rights movement. In its wake, a wave of boycotts, sit-ins, marches, and strikes rolled across Dixie. The bigots used every legal weapon to stop the movement. In June Governor Wallace stood at the door of the University of Alabama's administration building trying, despite a federal court order, to prevent two black students from enrolling in the state university. President Kennedy federalized the Alabama National Guard, and the next day Wallace yielded. When peaceful resistance failed, the segregationists turned to violence. On June 11 a sniper shot and killed Medgar Evers, the NAACP Mississippi field secretary, in Jackson, Mississippi. On September 15, a Sunday, fifteen sticks of dynamite went off outside Birmingham's Sixteenth Street Baptist Church where the protesters of May had forgathered. Four black girls, changing to their choir robes, were crushed to death under falling debris, and twenty-one other Sunday School students were injured.

Birmingham also brought gains. During the spring and summer of 1963, scores of southern towns desegregated their bus terminals, parks, and playgrounds, and hired black policemen. The campaign also confirmed mass white support. Millions of white Americans, particularly the educated northern middle class, had watched the firehoses, the snarling dogs, and the flailing nightsticks, and were revolted by the racial system that produced them. The deep pockets of white liberals yielded up their resources. Millions poured into the major civil rights organizations.

Birmingham and the Wallace challenge convinced President Kennedy that the federal government needed new weapons against disfranchisement and segregation, and on June 11 he announced that he would introduce a bill to make a national "commitment . . . to the proposition that race has no place in American life or law."[23] A week later the Civil Rights Act, barring discrimination in public accommodations and in employment, creating an Equal Employment Opportunity Commission and a Community Relations Service, and declaring illegal various schemes to prevent registration of black voters, began its yearlong progress through Congress.

The high point of the summer was a mass demonstration on the Washington Monument Mall in Washington, D.C., in support of the pending bill. The largest demonstration of the civil rights era, it would be a love feast where white liberals and black civil rights moderates celebrated the unity of all decent Americans in the cause of racial equality.

Over 250,000 people, a third of them white, gathered at the Mall on August 28. Many of the black marchers were working people or rural southern folk who had never been to their nation's capital. They had come to celebrate the wonderful advances of the past few years and to express their yearning for dignity. The whites were mostly prosperous northerners—housewives, clergymen, lawyers, academics, students—people for whom the experience of discrimination was vicarious. Products of a liberal subculture that had evolved since World War II's end, many had long dreamed of a society that would fulfill the ancient but long-delayed promise of American equality. They had been drawn to Washington by a powerful surge of sympathy for black aspirations. It was their orderly and middle-class way to express brotherhood.

The actual "march" consisted of a slow human current circling the Lincoln Memorial. When this ended, the vast crowd settled down on the grass in front of the Monument and around the edges of the Reflecting Pool to listen to the speakers. They took off their shoes and unwrapped picnic lunches.

Much of what they heard was routine and predictable. The fiery John Lewis, now SNCC chairman, disgusted with the federal government's failure to protect civil rights workers in the South, had intended to indict the government and to urge blacks to take matters into their own hands by marching "through the heart of Dixie the way Sherman did."[24] But he had been stopped by the moderates, and the revised speech was less incendiary. The rest was standard civil rights rhetoric. Not until after the footsore, the sunbaked, the replete, and the bored had begun to drift off did King speak. It was the event that made the 1963 March on Washington a historic event.

King was now the uninaugurated "President of the Negroes." As he stood on the podium facing out to the vast crowd, he was at the height of his powers. He was not a handsome man like Wilkins or Young. He was short, and though only thirty-five, he was already portly. His forehead sloped; his jaw jutted. But he had the ability to make his words soar and carry others with him. Even with a racially mixed audience he could invoke the responsive mode and make a speech into an anthem.

King's "I have a dream" speech had its prosaic and commonplace stretches. But at the end, when he stopped reading his prepared text, it took off. Its peroration invoked the image of humanity as one "beloved community." He had a dream, he said. It was a vision of the future—of little black boys and girls holding hands with little white boys and girls, of the sons of former slaves and former slaveowners sitting down together at the table of brotherhood, of one day the nation's "jangling discords" transformed into "a beautiful sympathy of brotherhood." He ended with the crescendo that has echoed down the years: When we let freedom ring "from every state and from every village and from every hamlet, we will be able to speed up the day when all of God's children, black men and white men, Jews and Gentiles, Protestants and Catholics, will be able to join hands and sing in the words of the old Negro spiritual, 'Free at last, free at last; thank God Almighty, we are free at last!' "[25]

For King, the SCLC, and the biracial, nonviolent civil rights movement, 1964 was the best year. On January 3 *Time* named King Man of the Year and cited him for stirring "in his people a Christian forbearance that nurtures hope and smothers injustice."[26] In July, Lyndon Johnson, surrounded by his cabinet and all the major civil rights leaders, signed the Civil Rights Act of 1964. That October King received the Nobel peace prize in Oslo.

Early in 1965 King and the SCLC shifted emphasis from desegregation to full voting rights for all blacks in the South. King's first target was the small Alabama black-belt city of Selma, and his strategy was to provoke the local authorities to a violent reaction that would revolt the nation and assure passage of a tough federal voting rights bill.

It worked beautifully. Sheriff Jim Clark was as much of a coarse bigot as Bull Connor. He was determined to preserve the South's "way of life," he told his wife, and would "not let the niggers take over the whole state of Alabama."[27] He played his part as villain to the hilt. On March 7 his men beat, whipped, and gassed six hundred SCLC marchers as they tried to cross the Edmund Pettus Bridge on a fifty-mile walk to Montgomery to protest the killing of a black civil rights worker, Jimmie Lee Jackson, by a trigger-happy state trooper. The media spread the horrifying pictures around the country and the world. ABC broke into its movie *Judgment at Nuremberg,* a dramatization of the 1946 Nazi war crimes trial, with footage of the Alabama atrocities. The lesson could not have been sharper. Within a matter of hours, hundreds of white clergymen were streaming into Selma at King's call to join a "minister's march to Montgomery."

One of the ministers, James Reeb, a Boston Unitarian, would provide an invaluable white martyr. On the evening of March 9, he and two fellow Unitarian ministers had dinner at a black-operated restaurant. On the way back to SCLC headquarters, they were attacked by four white men brandishing two-by-fours and screaming "You want to know what it's like to be a real nigger?"[28] All three clergymen were badly hurt. Reeb's skull was crushed and he died two days later without regaining consciousness.

Several days later Johnson called Governor George Wallace of Alabama to the White House where he dressed him down for his obstructionist tactics on voting rights and his resistance to admitting blacks to the segregated state university. On March 15 the president went before Congress and delivered a speech in support of a federal voting rights bill that might have been written by King himself. The president ended on a ringing peroration. The cause of black Americans "must be our cause too," the president declared. "Not just Negroes, but . . . all of us . . . must overcome the crippling legacy of bigotry and injustice. And . . . We . . . Shall . . . Overcome."[29]

Congress applauded almost every sentence and at the end, deeply moved by the echo of the civil rights anthem, gave LBJ a standing ovation. Even SNCC's militant John Lewis called the speech "historic, eloquent, and more than inspiring."[30] Soon after, a federal judge lifted an injunction earlier imposed on the march from Selma to Montgomery, and three hundred civil rights workers crossed the Pettus Bridge unimpeded and headed down the highway to the state capital. Four days later, before twenty-five thousand cheering people at the capitol steps, King and his colleagues conducted a victory rally. King was at his most eloquent, building to a ringing climax with repeated "how long would it take" to achieve a just society, followed by "not long, not long." On August 6 the president signed the Voting Rights Act, which swept away virtually every legal impediment to a free and democratic ballot.

After Selma the biracial civil rights movement retreated. By 1966 it was suffering severe inner strain. By 1967 it had lost most of its white liberal support and was floundering.

The internal tensions came primarily from the left of the movement, from the militants of SNCC and CORE. These were young men and women, and they brought to everything they did the natural zeal, impetuosity, and impatience of the young. To them compromise seemed surrender; deliberation, cowardice.

But there was more to their position than the hot blood of youth. Both organizations had been at the frontier where the civil rights movement nakedly faced the savages. In such ventures as the freedom rides they had exposed themselves directly to the unmediated fury of the white South's racism and had suffered brutally. After the bus-depot beatings it was hard to believe that the "beloved community" was just over the horizon.

The disenchantment was reinforced by the Mississippi Freedom Summer of 1964. For SNCC, Mississippi was the great challenge. The poorest—and the blackest—state in the Union, it was a "closed society," a community determined to use every means, legal or violent, to preserve the racial status quo. It was into this cauldron of white fears and racist rage that Bob Moses, a New York–born schoolteacher with a Harvard M.A., plunged SNCC during the summer of 1964.

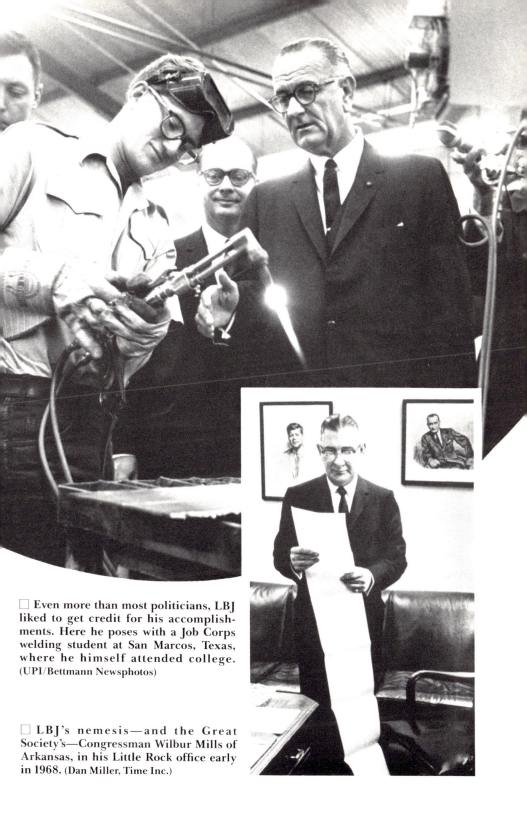

☐ Even more than most politicians, LBJ liked to get credit for his accomplishments. Here he poses with a Job Corps welding student at San Marcos, Texas, where he himself attended college. (UPI/Bettmann Newsphotos)

☐ LBJ's nemesis—and the Great Society's—Congressman Wilbur Mills of Arkansas, in his Little Rock office early in 1968. (Dan Miller, Time Inc.)

☐ A black bureaucrat telling reporters about the Great Society's plans to rehabilitate the Bedford-Styvesant ghetto in Brooklyn. "Bed-Stuy" is still a squalid slum today. (Bob Gomel, *Life*)

☐ A concise, graphic expression of one reason why the Great Society closed up shop. (Benst, *Newsweek*)

SPOTLIGHT ON BUSINESS

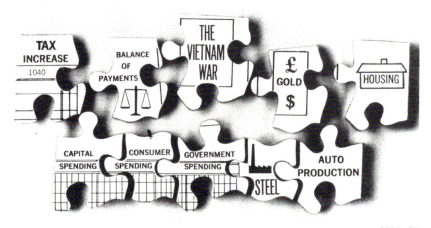

Economy '68: In the eighth straight year of prosperity, can the pieces still fit together?

☐ This picture of a South Vietnamese official executing a Vietcong suspect during the Tet offensive possibly did more to damage the Saigon government than Tet itself. (AP/Wide World Photos)

☐ Ambassador Ellsworth Bunker (*middle, white hair, white shirt*) and reporters inspect the U.S. Embassy grounds soon after the last Vietcong intruder had been killed. (Dick Swanson, *Life*)

☐ American marines during the battle to recover Hue, here hiding behind a wall to escape deadly sniper fire. (UPI/Bettmann Newsphotos)

□ Ambassador Bunker and General William Westmoreland pay their respects to twenty-seven U.S. MPs killed in Saigon during the Tet offensive. (UPI/Bettmann Newsphotos)

□ LBJ, Westmoreland, Secretary of Defense Clark Clifford, and Secretary of State Dean Rusk, April 1968, following meetings on how to implement policies in Vietnam in the wake of Tet. (AP/Wide World Photos)

□ LBJ's surprise announcement: "I shall not seek and will not accept . . . another term as your President." (AP/Wide World Photos)

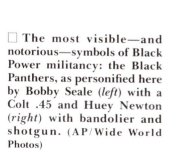

Martin Luther King, Jr., August 1963, at the Lincoln Memorial delivering his soaring "I have a dream" speech. (Magnum)

The most visible—and notorious—symbols of Black Power militancy: the Black Panthers, as personified here by Bobby Seale (*left*) with a Colt .45 and Huey Newton (*right*) with bandolier and shotgun. (AP/Wide World Photos)

☐ A dramatic picture of the balcony of the Lorraine Motel just moments after King's assassination. Distraught associates, including current mayor of Atlanta Andrew Young, point toward where the shots rang out. (Joseph Louw, *Life*)

☐ A Washington, D.C., clothing store on Seventh Street after being ransacked by a rioting mob following King's assassination. (*The Washington Post*)

☐ Rain and mud—almost as much as indifference and backlash—helped defeat the Poor People's Campaign at Resurrection City. (AP/Wide World Photos)

☐ Mario Savio, standing on the steps of Sproul Hall, tells Berkeley students about the Free Speech Movement's intention to call a general strike against the University of California administration. (UPI/Bettmann Newsphotos)

☐ Bernardine Dohrn, fierce revolutionary, shortly to become a Weatherman leader, soon after to retreat underground. (Tom Copi)

☐ The sign perched on *Alma Mater*'s lap in front of Columbia's Low Library says it all— as seen by students and faculty alike. (Claus Meyer, Black Star)

☐ An unusual shot of the rostrum during the June 1968 SDS national convention, East Lansing, Michigan. This was the last such convocation before the organization split and collapsed. (Tom Copi)

☐ Here's the intrepid San Francisco State president S. I. Hayakawa, tam-o'-shanter and all, atop the infamous, offending sound truck, yanking out wires. (AP/Wide World Photos)

Moses proposed a bold but risky scheme. Acting under an umbrella organization called the Council of Federated Organizations (COFO), SNCC would bring to Mississippi hundreds of volunteers to establish "freedom schools," set up a shadow Mississippi Freedom Democratic party (MFDP), and induce thousands of black farmers who had never exercised the franchise in their lives to register and vote. Most of the volunteers would inevitably be white, for only a major white presence would attract the indispensable media attention. A critical, though only whispered, part of this formula was that only white casualties would lead to federal intervention.

The issue of white volunteers was divisive. SNCC still accepted the principle of a biracial movement, white and black together. But black separatism was quickly gaining ground.

The mood shift had several causes. The young white men and women attracted to SNCC were useful for their skills and their connections with the "white power structure." But they were also aggressive and assertive. By the end of 1963, 20 percent of SNCC's entire staff was white, and many black workers feared a takeover of the organization.

SNCC was also responding to the new black nationalism that was abroad in the nation. One part of this new position derived from the Nation of Islam, the Black Muslims.

Founded in the 1930s by a mysterious black prophet, W. D. Fard, and invigorated by Elijah Muhammad, a former Detroit automobile worker, the Black Muslims celebrated racial pride. Blacks must not be ashamed of their history and their racial characteristics. In their original home they had been noble and creative people; indeed, they had been the "original men" from whom all the other races had derived. It was slavery, not inherent black qualities, that had produced the "shiftless" and dissipated "Negro." Muhammad forbade his followers to gamble, drink, smoke, fornicate, or consume conspicuously. Muslims had to hold jobs and contribute to the movement a substantial portion of their income.

Self-respect does not mandate xenophobia, but in fact the Muslims' teachings were profoundly antiwhite. White people, Muhammad declared, had been created by an evil black scientist,

Yakub, whose aim was to wreak destruction on his own kind. He attacked Christianity as a slave religion imposed by white men to foster love for the oppressor. He told his followers to surrender their "slave names" and adopt Muslim ones. He and his followers called white people "blue-eyed devils" and the "human beast." They were "liars and murderers" and the "enemies of truth and righteousness."[31] The Muslim doctrine was nationalist and separatist. Blacks must reject integration, even if offered, and separate themselves in every way from the white community. *Muhammad Speaks,* the official statement of the Muslim program, declared that all Americans "whose parents or grandparents" were descended from slaves "be allowed to establish a separate state or territory of their own—either on this continent or elsewhere."[32]

By the early sixties the Black Muslims' most articulate spokesman was Malcolm X, a former convict converted to the Nation of Islam while in prison. Malcolm was eloquent and shrewd, adept at getting media attention. He denied he was a racist. "I've never been a racist," he asserted on one occasion. "I believe in indicting the system and the person that is responsible for our condition."[33] But at times he was deliberately inflammatory and offensive. At one point he talked about how black jet pilots would one day bomb white city neighborhoods. When 120 white Atlantans, the pride of the city's cultural elite, died in a plane crash in France, he publicly thanked Allah for the disaster. In November 1963, with the nation in shock over the assassination of John Kennedy, Malcolm calmly observed that the "chickens had come home to roost."[34] By February 1965, when he was himself assassinated by a rival Black Muslim group, he had modified much of his antiwhite position, but his separatist black nationalism had already left a deep impression on many youthful civil rights workers.

These young people had also been influenced by the collapse of world colonialism and the rise of an independent black Africa. In 1965–66 the achievements of new black countries like Ghana and Malawi were still limited; the promise of the future seemed immense, however, and black Americans, most for the first time, were caught up emotionally in the affairs of the "dark continent." Pan-Africanism in turn stimulated a new black pride—in part borrowed from the Muslims—that was defined by its contrast to white aesthetics, culture, dress, and values. John Lewis noted the effects of the new perspective on SNCC staffers in the spring of 1964. Even in SNCC, he noted, though "we talk about integration, about the beloved community," separatist changes could be observed. "The way they dress, the music they listen to, their natural hairdos—all of them want to go to Africa. . . ."[35]

The young militants were also affected by Marxism. Some of the white volunteers in Mississippi had come from leftist families and left behind a residue of Marxist ideology when they returned home. Mainstream Marxism was suspicious of nationalism; class, not nation or race, was what counted. But in several Third World varieties it fused the three. In 1963, *The Wretched of the Earth*, by Frantz Fanon, a black doctor from Martinique who had fought with the Algerians against the French, gave the nationalistic yearning of Third World peoples a strong Marxist twist. Fanon's book became a virtual bible for the black militants.

Most of all, however, the new attitude was created by growing despair and disenchantment with the glacial progress toward full equality. Despite misgivings, SNCC authorized a hundred white volunteers for the Freedom Summer project. But they could not curb the enthusiasm of the students themselves or the boundless energies of Allard Lowenstein, the rumpled, passionate young New York lawyer and political activist who was determined to make Freedom Summer a spectacular success. Lowenstein traveled the northern campus circuit during the winter and spring of 1964 delivering the message that if Mississippi, the South's "festering sore," could be cured of racism, the rest of Dixie would follow.[36]

Eventually, almost a thousand white college students spent all or part of their 1964 summer in Mississippi working for COFO and either CORE or SNCC, its two main constituent organizations. Even before most of them arrived, however, they learned that three COFO field workers, Michael Schwerner and Andrew Goodman, both white, and James Chaney, black, had disappeared after leaving Meridian near the Alabama line to investigate reports of a church burning in Neshoba County. Investigators soon found their torched car. Six weeks later the FBI discovered their bullet-ridden bodies buried in an earth dam near the inappropriately named town of Philadelphia.

In June, after news of the COFO workers' disappearance, President Johnson had ordered the FBI to protect the Freedom Summer volunteers. But the federal presence was at best fitful and half-hearted. White racists succeeded in imposing a reign of terror on Mississippi, bombing houses of civil rights supporters, burning thirty-five black churches, and beating scores of COFO and SNCC workers. Local authorities were worse than useless. They helped the racists, arresting hundreds of civil rights volunteers on flimsy pretexts.

The summer brought good things. At the freedom schools, black children heard plays, poems, and stories by black writers for the first time. At the local community centers black Mississippians learned to speak up and speak out. Freedom Summer was valuable propaganda for the civil rights movement, adding several vivid additional chapters to the movement's martyrology.

Yet the experience also had its debit side. Shared danger is supposed to create bonds among people. Sometimes it fails. For the black SNCC and COFO workers, the white volunteers seemed like sunshine soldiers who could return to their campuses and comfortable northern homes, while they, the regulars, would remain to face the brutes and murderers alone.

Cultures clashed. White volunteers from Swarthmore or Oberlin or Berkeley were not—or not yet—used to the mores of black youths. To relieve pressures the black COFO workers drank a lot and smoked pot. Sex was another safety valve for young men and women under terrible strain. One serious difficulty was interracial sex. There's no blinking at the fact that some male SNCC workers induced white female volunteers to climb into their beds to prove their lack of race prejudice. Black women deeply resented this exploitation.

The experience was more disillusioning for blacks than for whites. Despite the tensions, most white students came to admire the bravery and understand the feelings of the SNCC people. The experience drove them to the left. Mere goodwill clearly could not destroy racism. Moreover, the American government could not be relied on to fight injustice. Back on their home ground many would perceive their role as insurgents. The emerging student movement would soon absorb their new radical perspective.

For SNCC the most disturbing event of the summer actually took place in distant Atlantic City, New Jersey. One of COFO's more successful summer projects was the scheme to enroll all those excluded by the lily-white regular state Democratic organization in the Mississippi Freedom Democratic party. The MFDP signed up sixty thousand adults, mostly illegally disfranchised black people, and, in a Freedom Primary, selected forty-four delegates, mostly black, to go to the Democratic National Convention to challenge the regulars as the state's delegation.

Their arrival in Atlantic City in August precipitated a crisis. LBJ looked forward to a celebration of the party's achievements and his nomination by acclamation. None of the party leaders wanted a bruising convention floor fight, especially one with racial overtones. The administration forces suggested a compromise that allowed two MFDP representatives to be seated as delegates-at-large and promised better ways of choosing state delegates next time, for 1968. King, Rustin, and James Farmer of CORE urged acceptance of this half-a-loaf. Johnson was a friend of the black man; his opponent, Barry Goldwater, the Republican nominee, was a racial conservative endorsed by the segregationist enemy. But SNCC's Forman, Lewis, and Moses, fresh from the terrors of the Klan and redneck sheriffs, denounced the scheme as immoral and its supporters as sellouts.

Despite their opposition, the convention formally adopted the compromise proposals, and SNCC members returned to Mississippi embittered by what they considered a liberal betrayal. "The masters of political power," announced Charles Sherrod, a member of the SNCC leadership circle, were still not ready to trust blacks with "real power." "We are not only demanding meat and bread and a job, but we are also demanding power, a share in the power." The only question was whether blacks would share power "in reconciliation" or "in rioting and blood."[37]

*　　*　　*

Though SNCC and CORE's ideologies and tactics diverged from the civil rights mainstream, their targets remained the denial of voting rights and equal access to public facilities. But as the decade approached its midpoint, it became impossible to ignore the seething urban ghettos of the North, where jobs and housing came first on the want list.

Until 1920 blacks had been only a tiny fraction of the North's urbanites. During the next four decades, immense waves of migrants from the corn, tobacco, and cotton fields of the old Confederacy began to roll north to the factories, slaughter houses, kitchens, laundries, docks, and construction sites of the North and West. By 1960 Los Angeles's population was 13 percent black, New York's 14 percent, Chicago's 23 percent, Philadelphia's 26 percent, Newark's 34 percent, Baltimore's 35 percent, Detroit's 41 percent, and Washington's 54 percent.

As poor blacks moved in, middle-class whites moved out. The whites left behind were the working poor, who shared with the black newcomers the emigres' leavings in housing, city services, schools, and hospitals. These had never been opulent for the poor, but now, with fewer families used to urban living and fewer to pay sales and property taxes, they deteriorated. Once-handsome neighborhoods of row or frame houses turned into wretched slums, where yards were trash dumps, windows were filthy and broken, and abandoned automobiles defaced the streets. Once-decent schools became blackboard jungles for the teachers and prisons to keep undisciplined young men off the streets during daylight hours. Once-adequate hospitals turned into bedlams with jammed emergency rooms and corridors overspilling with patients' beds. Worst of all, whole communities deteriorated into besieged encampments where decent folk huddled behind triple-locked doors after dark.

The departure of the lawyers and executives, teachers and accountants, also removed a buffer that had separated blacks from the white working class. In the schools, in the shops, on the streets, they now confronted one another in a raw, direct way, without middle-class reasonableness and politesse to mediate. Meanwhile, the upsurge of black self-awareness had produced antibodies among the whites whom black city dwellers rubbed against. These were the social types that sociologist now called "white ethnics"—Poles, Italians, Greeks, Irish, Hungarians—people at times as obsessed with race and tribe as blacks and often with as long a list of grievances.

A minority of the black newcomers and a somewhat larger proportion of their children found a distinctly better life in the northern cities. Most did not. They often lacked skills and education, and when they did not, they frequently encountered a wall of bigotry among employers and unions that denied them their just place in the job market. It is hard to recall today how cruelly and blatantly unfair was the economic discrimination black Americans experienced as recently as 1950.

The effects of poverty were compounded by residential segregation. White Americans were fiercely protective of their urban turf. They might accept a black fellow employee in the workplace or a black diner in the adjacent restaurant booth, but their blood ran cold at the sight of a black family moving into the neighborhood. Obviously, black families found places to live in the northern cities, but they were in the decaying areas that whites were fleeing. There, prejudice decreed, they must be confined. Before long the black neighborhoods were ringed with invisible barriers that held in the undesirable aliens as effectively as the physical walls of medieval Jewish ghettos.

It is natural to extrapolate the black ghetto explosions of the mid-1960s directly from the poverty and social pathology that discrimination created. It is also simplistic. Discrimination was receding by the late 1950s, and with each passing year blacks were closing the gap with whites. This was true in education, where more and more black youths remained in school and an ever-larger proportion were attending colleges and professional schools. Black health had improved so that by the early 1960s the life-expectancy difference between the races had narrowed. Only the relative standing of median white-black family incomes seemed to be stuck. But in absolute terms black family incomes were rising, and even the ratio was about to improve. In 1960 black families earned 48 percent the income of white families; in 1970 it would be 61 percent.

But tell that to an eighteen-year-old black youth with learning difficulties doomed to be a career delivery boy at the local A&P when he dropped out of school. Tell that to an eighteen-year-old unmarried mother deserted by her children's father and living on welfare. Tell that to an intelligent but unskilled twenty-five-year-old "blood," full of the prides, the juices, and the yearnings of his age and his status but without the means to legitimately satisfy them. People like this did not consult the Census Bureau and Department of Labor statistics. All they could see was that if you were black, you were poor, and you were powerless to change it.

No doubt, then, the ghettos were crammed with men and women who were wronged by white society. But as countless social psychologists have told us, anger is also a response to dashed expectations. It can almost be plotted as a ratio between desire and reality. The desire in this case is not some absolute wish; we would all choose paradise now. It is, rather, the sense that we deserve something and that what we deserve is attainable.

Ever since the end of World War II, black Americans had experienced a revolution of rising expectations. The war to destroy Nazi racism had stigmatized all racism and delegitimized the South's Jim Crow. After 1945 fewer young black men and women in the South saw any reason to acquiesce in a regime of legalized racial oppression. The civil rights assault on segregation and disfranchisement can be viewed as an effort to bring reality into line with desires given legitimacy by new, more democratic attitudes.

But what about economic equality? Why weren't there proportionately as many black as white doctors, lawyers, mayors, judges, college professors, airline pilots, scientists, skilled craftsmen, executives, and millionaires? America talked about equality; it made equality the right of all. But blacks were not equal. They were the last and the least in American occupational life. They were the people who got the crumbs off the groaning national table.

Black Americans had been in this position long before the 1960s, of course. But it no longer seemed necessary or tolerable. Never before was the nation so rich, so able to afford abundance for all its members. Some part of postwar prosperity had been shared by the black community. During the sixties, as we saw, the share would actually increase. During these same years the number of blacks classified as "craftsmen and foremen" grew by 57 percent at a time when the total number of these skilled workers increased by only 12 percent. The advance was enough to awaken appetite but not to satisfy it.

Unfortunately, the economic inequalities of industrial America did not yield to quick remedies. No one in a pluralistic society with many power centers and decision centers could push a button and give everyone a personally rewarding, well-paying job. Obviously no society can provide such a regime—else we *would* have paradise now. Militant blacks wanted compressed into ten years what it had taken the Irish three generations and the Jews two generations to achieve. This did not mean that it was not possible to attack job discrimination, whether institutionalized or personal, through the legislative process. It clearly was. It did not mean that government could not provide a floor under those unable to help themselves. It clearly could. It did not mean that public agencies could not support training programs to improve the skills of the poor. They clearly had to. Under the label of the Great Society, America in the 1960s tried all these approaches to match results with expectations. But as the decade reached its midpoint, the effects of all these programs seemed at best marginal—and the ghettos could not wait.

One other grievance marked the ghetto mood. Ghetto residents believed that the police were a brutal, racist, repressive force. Overwhelmingly white, they despised and feared ghetto blacks and treated them like dirt. At the same time they ignored the real crime of the ghettos and were often on the take. And the police were only a small piece of the whole. The entire criminal justice system, it was said, was rigged against blacks, who seldom got a fair day in court.

The charges were true. But they were not the whole truth. White cops were recruited from the working class. They were the whites closest to blacks in status and most threatened by black aspirations. They came to ghetto assignments predisposed to consider blacks inferior. Ill-equipped by their training to understand the sources of the ghettos' social ills, after a month or two on the beat in poverty-stricken, chaotic Watts, Bedford-Stuyvesant,

Hough, Woodlawn, Clinton, and East Oakland, many could not help concluding that ghetto people were responsible for their own plight.

And they were also responding to the hostility they encountered. In the ghettos, hate begat hate. Call a cop a "white honky" and likely as not he will prove you right. Before long the police and the residents were caught in a classic vicious cycle that had no apparent beginning and no apparent end.

A final ingredient in the poisonous brew was militancy itself. Anger, at least anger turned outward, is often enlarged by a process of sharing. Exchanges of atrocity stories, positive reinforcement through approval, channeling of ill-focused feelings—all can increase the intensity of resentment and rage. Later in this decade, women would call a similar process consciousness-raising. The militancy of the mid- and late-sixties served as a consciousness-raiser for much of the black community.

Malcolm X had preceded everyone else in this campaign to heighten anger, and his influence went deep in the ghettos. His militancy was reinforced by the black intelligentsia, the men and women most sensitive to the slights and humiliations of bigotry and closest to the astonishing changes in Africa. By mid-decade these intellectuals were talking about apocalypse. "There is *no* reason that black men should be expected to be more patient, more forebearing, more farseeing than whites; indeed, quite the contrary," wrote James Baldwin in his prophetic 1963 book, *The Fire Next Time*. If whites failed to accept the "total liberation" of blacks, there would be murder and riot in the cities. Unless white America yielded it could expect, in the words of the Negro spiritual, "the fire next time."[38]

The growing militancy at the top seeped down to the ghettos. By the late sixties little knots of militants plotted and planned and talked of revolution in most of the black slums. But most ghetto rioters were not revolutionaries. They were unemployed black youths who seldom read Malcolm X or James Baldwin, if they read anything. Yet somehow the angry, retributive thoughts and words were absorbed and would soon be heard above the clamor of the sirens and gunshot blasts.

The seething ghetto angers and resentments boiled over in the mid-1960s as furious, destructive riots. Riots are complex social events with many causes. The urban explosions of 1964–68 were race riots—of a sort. Unlike those of the past, they were not *between* the races, at least not in the usual sense. Blacks, though instigators, did not, ordinarily, attack whites. But they did attack white property, especially white stores and buildings, though in some cases it is difficult to distinguish between the destructive and the acquisitive urges. The sixties' riots were riots of rising expectations. The people who took to the streets were men and women frustrated by the failure of America to deliver *now* on its promises of abundance and equality.

The first of the new crop came in 1964 with upheavals in New York's Harlem and in the ghettos of Rochester and Philadelphia. Somehow, these did not sear themselves into the nation's collective consciousness. Watts, the following summer, did.

The rioting in this palm-lined Los Angeles ghetto began on August 11 and lasted for six days. By the time the National Guard had smothered the flames, there were thirty-four dead, nine hundred injured, and nearly four thousand in the hands of the police. Property damage, mostly burned and looted stores, totaled $200 million by some estimates.

Nineteen sixty-six was worse. There were explosions in Chicago and in Milwaukee, Dayton, San Francisco, and other cities. The riots in Cleveland's Hough were particularly ferocious and destructive. In at least five cities the rioters overwhelmed the local police and the authorities were forced to call in the National Guard.

Nineteen sixty-seven was the culminating year. There were 150 racial uprisings, including fearsome rebellions in Newark and Detroit. In the decaying New Jersey city the police and the Guard killed 25 blacks while trying to stop the looting and the arson. Detroit, then a booming center of the still unchallenged American auto industry, exploded a few days later over police brutality. The untrained, trigger-happy Michigan National Guard fired off thousands of rounds at looters and suspected snipers. Forty-three people died and a thousand were wounded. The property destroyed was vast, almost all of it in black neighborhoods, though frequently white-owned.

The ghettos seethed through the whole year, but summers were by far the most dangerous times. Young men were out of school and many were unemployed. They hung out on the street corners, bored with the slow weeks of doing nothing. The ghettos broiled. Few people had air-conditioning and the discomfort level soared. It did not take very much to create a spark, and the initial surge of adrenalin quickly activated the pent-up wrath and frustration of the whole community, including adults and respectable working people. By 1966 the expression "long, hot summer" had become shorthand for what seemed chronic ghetto insurrection.

The civil rights movement was profoundly affected by the ghetto uprisings. King flew to Los Angeles at news of Watts and with Rustin and Andrew Young toured the still-smoldering ghetto trying to cool the fierce resentments. At least one of his biographers sees this visit as a turning point in his career. King, David Lewis writes, learned from Watts "the superficiality of civil rights gains. His national role as champion of massive federal assistance to the urban poor was henceforth a moral necessity."[39] What remained, he says, was merely the choice of a northern city to test the capacity of the civil rights movement and the SCLC to change the lives of the ghetto poor.

Watts and the other riots further radicalized the civil rights militants. Watts had proven, one CORE field secretary declared, that black people would "refuse to walk peacefully to the gas chambers." CORE's Floyd McKissick was moved to remark that "many good things have occurred for blacks as a result of violence."[40] CORE and SNCC moved further from integrationist, nonviolent principles.

The heightened militancy led to a shift in leadership. In January 1966 McKissick succeeded James Farmer as CORE national director; in May Stokely Carmichael succeeded John Lewis as SNCC chairman. McKissick was a Durham, North Carolina, lawyer who believed that nonviolence was "a dying philosophy" that had "outlived its usefulness."[41] Carmichael was a tall, gifted, West Indies–born New Yorker, a graduate of elite

Bronx High School of Science, equally at home in bib-overalls speaking to southern black farmers and in a European-cut suit telling college kids about Thoreau, Camus, and Sartre. Carmichael had been at Selma and had joined the march along Route 80 to Montgomery, but he no longer had much faith in biracialism. While "black and white together" trekked triumphantly to the state capital, he had boldly recruited among the Lowndes County black farmers who lined the road. These became the basic human material for an all-black Panther party sworn to challenge the local white Democrats and the Lowndes County power structure.

By early 1966 both SNCC and CORE had begun to talk about excluding whites from membership, but the flight from the integrationist past accelerated during the march to support James Meredith's one-man voting rights demonstration in Mississippi.

The man who had integrated Old Miss in 1962, Meredith had set out on June 5 on a "walk against fear"—a 225-mile march from Memphis to Jackson to encourage timid blacks to register to vote. The second day, just inside the Mississippi state line, a white man fired a load of birdshot into Meredith's back, legs, and neck, wounding him severely.

The attack brought the major civil rights leaders to a hurried conference in Memphis. All agreed that the incident could not be allowed to go unanswered; the march, however mistaken to begin with, must be resumed. "We had an understanding . . . ," recalled SCLC's Andrew Young, "that if you let people stop you from doing something through death then it only encouraged them to kill you whenever they wanted you to stop. . . ."[42] But Roy Wilkins of the NAACP and Whitney Young of the Urban League wanted an interracial, nonviolent march to build support for a pending 1966 civil rights bill, while McKissick and Carmichael demanded a demonstration that would encourage all-black community organizing. They also wanted the marchers to call for protection on the Deacons for Defense, a black paramilitary, Louisiana-based group.

King found himself caught in the middle. His entire career had been built on nonviolence and the goal of a colorblind, biracial society. How could he accept the guns and the anger of the young militants? He argued with McKissick and Carmichael, pointing out how many whites had been beaten or even killed in the civil rights cause. To reject white participation would be "a shameful repudiation" of the entire movement since the 1950s.

The CORE and SNCC leaders remained unconvinced, and their attacks finally drove Young and Wilkins to leave the conference and the march. When King too threatened to withdraw, Carmichael and McKissick reluctantly accepted the nonviolent, interracial plan.

The march turned into a victory for the militants. King had commitments in Chicago to help with a new poor people's campaign, and he could only participate sporadically. Carmichael and McKissick were present through the whole demonstration and had as unintentional allies rural white bigots who heckled, harassed, and attacked the marchers. From the beginning the participants took their cues from Carmichael, chanting such slogans as: White blood will flow; Seize power; and Hey! Hey! Whattya know? White folks must go—must go![43] The journalists who accompanied the marchers reported the angry rhetoric with relish to their readers.

At Greenwood, Carmichael was arrested for putting up a tent on the grounds of a local black high school. CORE and SNCC held a rally to protest, and it was here that white Americans heard a new term: *Black Power.*

After McKissick and King had spoken, Carmichael, just released from jail, jumped up on the flatbed truck being used as a platform and delivered an angry attack on his tormentors in the dialect of his rural black audience.

It was the twenty-seventh time he had been arrested, he shouted, "and I ain't goin' to jail no more." Blacks must stop pulling their punches. "The only way we gonna stop them white men from whippin' us is to take over." Blacks had been saying "freedom" for six years. It hadn't worked. "What we gonna start saying now is Black Power!" The crowd bellowed in unison: "Black Power!" Now another SNCC worker vaulted onto the platform beside Carmichael and yelled: "What do you want? Say it again." The crowd went crazy. "Black Power! Black Power! Black Power!"[44]

King knew the dangers of the Black Power slogan and for the remaining days of the march sought to blunt its edge. The SCLC contingent tried to drown out the militants' chant with their own "Freedom Now! Freedom Now!" King told reporters that "we must never forget that there are some white people in the United States just as determined to see us free as we are ourselves."[45] But the new, angry blast became louder and louder. By the time the marchers reached Jackson on June 26, the white public had become aware of a frightening new turn in the civil rights movement.

The year that saw the advent of Black Power also marked the birth of the Black Panthers in Oakland, California. The Panthers borrowed their name from Carmichael's Lowndes County political party, but they were a distinctly urban phenomenon. The founders were Huey Newton and Bobby Seale, two older black students at Merritt College, a two-year school that catered largely to East Oakland's black ghetto youth. Newton, the charismatic youngest son of a Louisiana railroad brakeman, met Seale, a former GI who had spent time in the stockade for protesting a racial incident, in 1965. Both were already convinced that separatism was essential for an effective black protest movement.

In September 1966 Seale and Newton composed a platform for "the Black Panther Party for Self Defense" and the following month ran off a thousand copies at night on an antipoverty-program mimeograph machine. This document demanded freedom for blacks to determine their own "destiny" in their own "community." It contained proposals for making the ghettos virtually independent of the larger society. The key plank was a statement justifying the carrying of arms by ghetto residents to defend the black community against "racist police oppression and brutality."[46]

The Panthers and the police were at war from the outset. To discourage police brutality, Panthers carrying rifles, cameras, and tape recorders began to shadow police patrols. It was not a crime in California at this time to carry loaded weapons, if visible, but it gave the police the jitters and led to a number of near shoot-outs. The Panther "police alert patrols" probably had little effect on the cops' behavior, but the Panthers' macho and defiant image was a powerful magnet for adventurous black youths, who were soon flocking to Panther headquarters to sign up.

One early Panther recruit was Eldridge Cleaver, an athletically built, Arkansas-born ex-convict with a gift for words and a powerful attraction to and for white women. In 1967 Cleaver had just been released from prison where he had served nine years for rape, an "insurrectionary act," he declared, against white society.[47] In prison he had written a number of essays that had impressed Edward Keating, editor of a California left magazine, *Ramparts*. Keating hired Cleaver to write for his journal and had the prison essays polished for publication. They appeared to wide acclaim as *Soul on Ice* early in 1968. By this time Cleaver had become the Panthers' "minister of information" and editor of their bimonthly publication.

The Panthers broke into the headlines in May 1967 when thirty of them armed with rifles, shotguns, and pistols suddenly appeared at the state capital in Sacramento to protest a bill making the carrying of loaded weapons a criminal offense. Looking back, the incident seems comical. The young men, in their leather jackets, black berets, and shiny combat boots, made a frightening sight as they strode down the unfamiliar marble halls of the huge capitol building. Actually, they had no idea where they were going and were merely following the crowd of excited capitol reporters and photographers who were backing up as fast as they could ahead of them snapping pictures and shouting questions. The Panthers probably intended to go to the visitors' gallery, but the reporters' backpedaling course drew them directly into the Assembly Chamber, where the legislators were startled out of their wits by the sight of thirty husky black men armed to the teeth.

The Panthers quickly retreated from the chamber. Just outside they paused briefly to read their statement protesting the pending gun-restriction legislation and then departed for Oakland. That might have ended the matter, but on the way back a Panther car broke down and was forced to stop at a service station. Here the police caught up, arrested the lot, and charged them with a flock of crimes and misdemeanors.

The Sacramento demonstration brought the Panthers a flood

of notoriety. *The New York Times* sent a reporter to interview Newton. Seale was invited to give a talk to the Berkeley student body. Both men made the most of the occasions to shock "Whitey." They would personally "kill" any police officer caught "brutalizing" a black person, they said. Newton noted that a Panther member when cornered, like the animal itself, would pounce on his assailant and destroy him, "thoroughly, wholly, absolutely, and completely."[48] Statements that outraged white middle-class Americans, thrilled ghetto youths. More recruits signed up; new Panther chapters were organized.

Through 1967 the chief targets of Panther rhetoric continued to be the police. In May *The Black Panther,* the organization's official publication, carried the first of many cartoons depicting a pig wearing a police uniform. The ironic caption read: "Support Your Local Police." The cops' response was predictably hostile. After Sacramento they stepped up their harassment of Panthers, especially those who violated the new state law prohibiting the carrying of loaded firearms on the streets or in automobiles.

In October the mutual hostility and suspicion erupted in a shoot-out between a car full of Panthers and the Oakland police. In the fusillade one policeman was killed, another wounded. Huey Newton ended up in the hospital with bullet wounds, charged with murder. For the next year the Black Panthers would be preoccupied with defending their leader and getting him released. The slogan Free Huey would soon dominate every Panther meeting and statement.

The Panther preoccupation brought them into alliance with Bay Area white radicals. In late 1967 the radicals—antiwar militants, present and former Berkeley student leftists, and a sprinking of older leftists—had organized a statewide Peace and Freedom party and were trying desperately to get the 105,000 signatures needed to get on the California ballot in 1968. The radicals owned a sound truck and had access to liberal money; the Panthers had numbers and influence in the ghettos. In exchange for Peace and Freedom's support for the Free Huey campaign, Seale and Cleaver promised to canvass in the ghettos and get militant blacks to register for the new party.

The alliance opened a split between the Panthers and other

black separatists who saw the pact as a betrayal. Newton, Seale, and Cleaver did not care. Except at the very beginning, the Panthers were never unquestioning nationalists. At times they continued to express contempt for whites, but they also made fun of the Pan-African pose of wearing dashikis and changing English "slave names" to Swahili ones. Influenced by their white allies, they adopted a version of Marxism that identified the ghettos with Third World revolutionary anticolonialism. More and more they spoke of the Panther party as the "vanguard" of a revolution that would overturn capitalism and racism in American simultaneously. Before very long they would foist this view on their white allies.

By 1965 Martin Luther King had heard the cry of the ghetto and had concluded that biracial nonviolence must be converted into an instrument for ending the centuries-old economic inferiority of black Americans. If he failed, the civil rights movement faced only two possibilities: futility or destruction. If black and white together in peaceful protest could not resolve the economic plight of black people in Chicago, Detroit, Newark, or Cleveland, then despair or race war were the only alternatives. Bayard Rustin had reached a similar conclusion. "The civil rights movement," he declared in early 1965, "is evolving from a protest movement into a full-fledged *social movement*. . . . It is now concerned not merely with removing the barriers to full *opportunity* but with achieving the fact of equality."[49]

King's decision to shift his efforts north came soon after the victory at Selma. For some time Al Raby and Meyer Weinberg, two Chicago civil rights activists who had been fighting local de facto school segregation, had been urging King to bring his skills to bear on the Windy City. For a time King held back, then, in the summer of 1965, he made a tour of four northern cities—Chicago, Cleveland, New York, and Philadelphia—to scout the terrain for the new urban campaign. The reconnaissance decided the issue. In late August the SCLC announced that its target would be Chicago, a community with almost a million blacks and some of the most squalid and oppressive black slums in the country.

In fact, Chicago was not an ideal choice. It was run like a Central American republic with Mayor Richard Daley as the *Caudillo*. Daley did not use guns or strong-arm tactics to get his way; he used patronage and cash, but he managed to run the city the way he wanted. Chicago would fit his own lower-middle-class idea of a respectable, orderly community. Black Chicagoans were not outside the pale. In fact, most of the city's traditional black leaders were deeply in the mayor's debt. But he had little use for the new breed of militants who wanted quick change. They were dangerous troublemakers who must be stopped.

The city was also a capital of white backlash. It was a collection of tightknit ethnic neighborhoods—Polish, Baltic, Irish, Jewish, Italian, German. Many of these people were homeowners whose small frame houses and handkerchief-size lawns and backyards were all they had to show for decades of hard work. Black neighbors alarmed these men and women because their presence threatened to undermine the value of the family home and the order and stability of the community. Add to these fears the ethnics' deep-rooted race prejudice and their tribal suspicion of all outsiders, and you have an inflammable mixture that would have daunted any civil rights leader.

But not King and the SCLC. With little advance preparation King arrived in Chicago in late January 1966 and established headquarters for his "Chicago Freedom Movement" in a tenement apartment in the North Lawndale ghetto. Soon after, he told the Chicago press that he would lead a ghetto rent strike if the landlords did not quickly improve their properties. Meanwhile, he said, he would do a study of the city's job and housing conditions. Later that day he met with the Chicago police chief and told him that he might have to use nonviolent civil disobedience to achieve the ends of the new Chicago campaign.

King's drive and determination were not enough; the Chicago movement quickly faltered. The SCLC was unable to devise a coherent strategy to end housing segregation and to improve the job opportunities of Chicago blacks. But the most serious problem was Richard Daley. The mayor was suspicious of King and the SCLC. He would brook no illegality, no disorder. He feared the outsiders would trip off the kind of trouble that had ravaged Watts, and he also worried that King would unhinge the complex set of relationships he had constructed with the city's old-time black leaders. He quickly mounted an effective campaign to convince the city and the black community that his administration had already alleviated the worst housing and school conditions in the city's working-class districts. With Great Society poverty funds becoming available, the economic plight of the poor would also soon be relieved. Besides, the problem of poverty was not created in Chicago. "It was created," he told audiences of civic leaders, "a thousand miles away in Mississippi, Georgia, and Alabama." In any case, civil disobedience was not the answer. Clergymen should "deliver sermons on the moral responsibilities of landlords and tenants and how members of their congregations could get job training and improve themselves."[50]

During June King spent much of his time on the Meredith march and came to understand, as never before, the strength of the angry black nationalist mood. He returned to Chicago convinced, Andrew Young said, that the SCLC had to "deliver results—nonviolent results in a Northern city—to protect the nonviolent movement."[51]

Back at the North Lawndale headquarters, King announced that on July 10 the SCLC would hold a march on city hall to make Chicago "a just and open city."[52] This would be the real beginning of the Chicago campaign. Soon after, the Chicago Freedom Movement announced its three goals: "power for the powerless," equal "opportunity and results," and an "open metropolis."[53]

"Freedom Sunday" proved to be a scorcher with the temperature close to 100 degrees. Everyone who could manage was at the beach, and only thirty thousand people turned up at Soldiers Field to hear King kick off the campaign. King made some specific proposals. Minority people should withdraw their deposits from any bank that discriminated against them and boycott any company that refused to employ them. If Daley refused to help, they should vote for his opponent in the approaching mayoralty election. King completed the demonstration by affixing to a city hall door his equivalent of Martin Luther's 1517 ninety-five theses demanding an end to police brutality, housing discrimination, and denial of jobs on racial grounds.

The small turnout on Sunday had encouraged the mayor, and when, on Monday, King and ten other black leaders came to city hall to confer, he fended them off. The city had already done so much for racial justice, he said. "What would you do that we haven't done?" he asked.[54] King now raised the stakes. On July 30 he announced that the SCLC and its supporters would march through a number of all-white neighborhoods at the edges of the ghetto to protest the exclusion of black people. King knew that this would be inflammatory, but he denied any intention to precipitate a confrontation. In any case the SCLC could not be deterred by threats.

The marches were as dangerous as predicted. On July 30, hecklers, carrying signs reading WHITE POWER and NIGGER GO HOME, screamed obscenities and hurled rocks and bottles at five hundred protesters as they marched through a Lithuanian-Irish neighborhood on their way to Halvorsen Realtors. Both Al Raby and divinity student Jesse Jackson were hit by missiles. The next day the protesters returned, and once again angry whites shouted abuse and threw stones. On neither occasion did the police show much zeal in protecting the demonstrators. On August 5, King himself, accompanied by Raby and gospel singer Mahalia Jackson, led six hundred demonstrators through a neighborhood of Poles, Lithuanians, Germans, and Italians. In Marquette Park they were surrounded by a thousand hostile people waving Confederate flags and Nazi swastikas and shouting, "We want Martin Luther Coon!" "We hate niggers!" "Nigger go home!" "Get the witch doctor!"[55] Suddenly the mob unleashed a barrage of bottles, bricks, and rocks. King was hit in the right temple and knocked to one knee. Stunned and shaken, he bent his head and continued to kneel under the rain of missiles. He soon recovered and continued the march.

Once out of the park the procession, though police-protected, was dogged by an angry crowd screaming insults and pelting the marchers with salvos of missiles. On the way back they ran a similar gauntlet. When they reached the park, they found another twenty-five hundred hecklers who chased their buses and cars as they pulled away. One man screamed at the demonstrators: "I worked all my life for a house out here, and no nigger is going to get it!"[56] King admitted that he had "never seen anything so hostile and so hateful as I've seen here today," but declared he would continue the marches and "bring this hate into the open."[57]

The demonstrations continued for another week accompanied by the same violence. On August 19 Daley secured a court order enjoining large marches in the city. King countered with the announcement that he would lead a large interracial demonstration through Cicero, a suburb where the court order did not apply.

Alarms instantly went off. Cicero was a mostly Slavic community where for many years the "Mob" had been a power. Its people were notorious for their racism, and in the past attempts by blacks to buy property had provoked riots and cross burnings. Not long before a young black man looking for work in the neighborhood had been murdered by white hoodlums. The community exemplified the very worst of white blue-collar bigotry, and city officials were in terror of a racial bloodbath.

Virtually every responsible leader begged King to back off. The only enthusiasts were the extremists of both sides. White bigots licked their chops at the prospect of catching King and his supporters on the streets of Cicero. SNCC and CORE militants, for their part, looked forward to a showdown with the honkies.

The march never took place. Faced with the prospect of mass mayhem, Daley cracked and agreed to consider the SCLC's demands. On August 26 King, Daley, Archbishop John Cody, various union officials, and influential Chicago businessmen met for two hours at the Palmer House hotel and hammered out a "Summit Agreement."

The agreement contained ten points pledging the city's real estate agents, banks, municipal agencies, unions, and other groups to work for open housing and to provide aid to enable black families to buy homes anywhere in the city. In reality it was little more than a pious statement of intent, without effective enforcement machinery. King accepted it because it avoided what might have been a massacre. And who knew? Perhaps it might make a difference! King hailed the Summit Agreement as the "most significant program ever conceived to make open housing a reality. . . ."[58] He agreed to postpone the Cicero march indefinitely, but warned that "if this agreement does not work, marches would be a reality."[59]

After the first flush of enthusiasm, civil rights leaders felt an enormous letdown. The militants pronounced the Summit Agreement a "sellout," and SNCC and CORE defiantly conducted a small-scale Cicero march of their own that narrowly escaped becoming a slaughter. But even King's colleagues were disheartened. The Chicago campaign was Selma, not Birmingham. The downcast Al Raby noted that people considered King a messiah, and he really wasn't.

A January 1967 Gallup poll showed that Martin Luther King was no longer one of the ten most admired Americans. His downfall had not been Chicago; it was Vietnam.

King had doubts about the Vietnam War from the beginning of American escalation in early 1965. War offended his pacifist, nonviolent principles, and this war, an assault on dark-skinned people, seemed from the outset to be particularly heinous.

As the war intensified, King found additional reasons for opposing it. Growing manpower demands hit the ghettos particularly hard. Before long a disproportionate number of black youths were fighting and dying in Southeast Asia. The war also threatened to drain all energy and money out of the War on Poverty. Here again black Americans would be the heavy losers.

King's antiwar stand was easily misunderstood. He had never accepted liberal cold-war precepts. Indeed, he was probably not a liberal, but a socialist of sorts. Certainly, at the end, he talked about such things as the "restructuring of the whole American society."[60]

On the other hand, he was not "soft on Communism." The red-obsessed FBI director, J. Edgar Hoover, thought he was a tool of the Communist conspiracy and as early as 1952 had begun to investigate King's associates. At least one, Stanley Levison, had once been a Communist party member. But it is clear that King's disgust with the Vietnam War derived from his pacifism and the perceived costs to the black community rather than any sympathy for international communism.

Though warned that speaking out would imperil the civil rights alliance with the Johnson administration, King could not remain silent. As a "moral leader" he felt called on, he said, to declare himself on a "question that deals with the survival of mankind."[61] In August 1965 King denounced American intervention as likely to endanger "the whole of mankind."[62] Johnson tried to silence him. In September he asked U.N. Ambassador Arthur Goldberg to explain the Vietnam situation to King. The two conferred, but King did not change his mind. In fact, in the press conference that followed the meeting he added to the furor by endorsing the admission of Red China to the United Nations and its inclusion in any Vietnam negotiations.

King avoided further statements on the war through most of 1966. But as the human and economic costs mounted, he found himself drawn into the organized anti-Vietnam movement. In late February 1967, at Los Angeles, he devoted an entire speech to the war's iniquities, calling it a struggle to "perpetuate white colonialism."[63]

In early April he addressed a meeting at New York's Riverside Church sponsored by Clergy and Laymen Concerned About Vietnam where he labeled the American government "the greatest purveyor of violence in the world today. . . ."[64] Later that month he was the leading speaker at the massive antiwar rally and march mounted by the Spring Mobilization Committee in New York (see chapter 5). Simultaneously, in San Francisco, Coretta King spoke at the Mobilization's West Coast demonstration.

King's anti-Vietnam stand cost him dearly. The liberal media, still hawkish on Vietnam, told him to stick to his civil rights business. Conservatives warned he would alienate white Americans from the civil rights movement. Most serious was the wrath of Lyndon B. Johnson.

The FBI had begun to tap King's phone conversations as far back as early 1963. At the time the Bureau's chief concern had been the supposed Communist affiliations of Levison. Later, when King criticized the FBI publicly for its failure to protect civil rights workers in Albany and elsewhere, Director J. Edgar

Hoover found an added reason to keep secret tabs on King's activities. Wherever King went, FBI agents loaded with sophisticated electronic gear followed to pry into every SCLC strategy meeting and into every private moment of King and his associates.

And they uncovered some personal scandal. King was not a perfect human being. He was a lusty man with strong appetites who enjoyed female company; women, in turn, no doubt ignited partly by his world celebrity, found him fascinating. By the mid-sixties, moreover, he and Coretta, alienated by money differences and his insistence that she stay home and care for the children, had grown apart. Though full of guilt, he did not always resist the sexual temptations that fame and his personal charm created. The FBI had graphic sound recordings of parties and bedroom interludes that involved interracial sex.

LBJ had listened with relish to the FBI tapes of some of King's peccadilloes. Now, in the wake of King's powerful attack on his Vietnam policy, the president authorized the FBI to show its salacious report on King to leading liberals in Washington and around the country in hopes of discrediting the man. When one White House aide protested, Johnson exclaimed: "God damn it, if only you could hear what that hypocritical preacher does sexually."[65]

His Vietnam position also hurt him within the civil rights movement itself. Whitney Young and Roy Wilkins opposed his stand as a sacrifice of racial goals. At one point Young and King crossed swords in public following a fund-raiser on Long Island. As they were leaving the reception, Young told King that his anti-Vietnam position would lose the movement large amounts of money. King angrily shot back: "Whitney, what you're saying may get you a foundation grant, but it won't get you into the kingdom of heaven." Young, now angry himself, accused King of indifference to the fate of the ghettos and pointed to King's well-tailored suit and elegant shoes. "*You're* eating well!" he exclaimed. King retorted that he opposed the war because it hurt the ghettos. At this point one of the fund-raiser's sponsors pulled the two men apart.[66]

There were some gains. King's anti-Vietnam stand almost

reconciled the civil rights left to him. By now King had become an object of fun to the young radicals. They referred to him as "De Lawd," after the sanctimonious main character—God as a southern black preacher—in Marc Connelly's popular play of the 1930s, *Green Pastures*. But they heartily endorsed his anti-Vietnam stand for they themselves believed the American role in Southeast Asia totally depraved.

Unfortunately, the civil rights movement did not need further support from the left. It needed to retain some portion of the white liberals, the "community of conscience," that had provided so much of its money and political firepower ever since the 1950s.

But white liberals were finding it increasingly difficult to participate in the civil rights movement. In December 1966 SNCC voted to exclude all whites from membership. CORE did not officially eject whites from its ranks until the summer of 1968, but well before this most white members and workers had been pushed out of local chapters and the national office. Whites might have been willing to accept a sideline role, but except for the most militant members of Students for a Democratic Society (SDS) and a small sliver of what the columnist Tom Wolfe would later call the "radical chic," even this limited participation became difficult as Black Power rhetoric escalated.

Here SNCC set the pace. In May 1967 it elected H. Rap Brown, chairman. Brown made Carmichael seem like a cream puff; Brown's tongue was a deadly blunt instrument. Soon after his election he told reporters that "the white man won't get off our backs, so we're going to knock him off." He called President Johnson a "wild mad dog" and a "honky cracker" and threatened to shoot Lady Bird if someone gave him a gun.[67] On July 25, at Cambridge, Maryland, during a major Eastern Shore desegregation campaign, he announced that "if America don't come around, we're going to burn it down. . . ."[68] An hour or two later a riot broke out in the Cambridge business district, and black protesters burned and looted stores. The authorities accused Brown of inciting the violence, and he was arrested and indicted.

One of SNCC's most wounding acts was its attack on Zionism. Soon after Brown's arrest, SNCC's newsletter featured an article accusing Israel of taking over Palestinian Arab land "through terror, force, and massacres."[69] The article was not a fluke. For many months SNCC and much of the black left had been cultivating ties with Third World groups. It was a natural ideological progression for a movement increasingly alienated from mainstream America, but it also reflected a growing anti-Semitic current within the black community that stemmed in part from hostility to white Jewish landlords and merchants in the ghettos. It may also have been reinforced by useful ties, financial and otherwise, with Al Fatah and other Arab nationalist organizations.

SNCC's anti-Israel position proved a financial disaster. Jews had been the staunchest white supporters of the civil rights movement. Now many were outraged. The American Jewish Congress called the newsletter article "shocking and vicious anti-Semitism."[70] Jews, like other white Americans, had been offended by the Black Power movement, and Jewish contributions to civil rights organizations had been dropping off for some time. Now they plummeted. Cleveland Sellers, a SNCC leader, would later note that donations "from sources just stopped coming in. . . ."[71]

In June 1967 the Supreme Court upheld the conviction of King and seven of his associates for demonstrating without a permit in Birmingham four years before. In October King, Abernathy, Shuttlesworth, Wyatt Tee Walker, and four others went to jail for four days. Ever since late summer King had been mulling over the next big step for the SCLC, and in those few days of enforced inactivity he consulted with Abernathy and Walker. Together they sketched in the outlines of King's last great campaign.

The plan was not another march like those in the Chicago suburbs. King had no reason now to believe that these were productive. In the end the Chicago campaign had accomplished very little. King may also have flinched at the prospect of again subjecting his supporters to the fury of a white backlash mob. These people seemed to be more dangerous than the dogs and fire hoses of the police and state troopers of the South. He also believed that marches in northern cities merged with the general turbulence of city streets and that their message was lost in the background noise.

Yet the civil rights movement was in crisis and something had to be done or it would die. If the SCLC failed to seize the initiative, there were only two possibilities: the moderates would allow it to settle back on its laurels with much of its work still undone; or the Black Power extremists would gain control and propel the country into race war.

The blueprint drawn up in Birmingham municipal jail was elaborated in a series of SCLC staff meetings in November. King now talked less about race and more about class. "Something is wrong with capitalism as it now stands in the United States," he told his colleagues. "We are not interested in being integrated into *this* value structure. . . . A radical redistribution of power must take place."[72]

As presented to an early December SCLC meeting, the proposal called for a prolonged, massive campaign to force Congress to enact bold new laws to improve the lot of the poor. The Poor People's Campaign would be interracial. Blacks would be its core, but there would also be Native Americans—the new name for Indians—Hispanics, and whites.

It would also be coercive. King no longer saw the federal government as a benevolent force that he could count on. Its actions in Vietnam had made that clear. The campaign would entail massive civil disobedience in the nation's capital to "cripple the operations of an oppressive society." In the spring, thousands of the nation's dispossessed would descend on Washington and camp out on the Mall. They would disrupt the operations of the government. They would create "major massive dislocations" until Congress met their demands. The plan drew inspiration from the veteran's Bonus Army of 1932 that had demanded early payment of a promised World War I soldiers' bonus. But it was also a logical projection of what had gone before in the civil rights and peace movements. As King explained to his supporters, the Poor People's Campaign would be his "last, greatest dream."[73]

The Poor People's Campaign was unveiled at a press conference on December 4 at the Ebenezer Baptist Church in Atlanta. As King spoke, he was in a somber mood. The campaign, he told reporters, was "a last desperate demand" by blacks. It was an attempt to avoid "the worst chaos, hatred, and violence any nation has ever encountered." Given the angry mood of the ghetto, it would be "risky," but failure to act would be "moral irresponsibility."[74]

In the weeks following the official announcement, King came under sharp attack for putting the government and the nation in jeopardy. Wilkins accused him of bowing to the militants. The NAACP's Dr. John Morsell charged that the scheme "would be met with as insurrection and put down as such and that would lead to violence."[75] Lyndon Johnson, as usual, personalized the move. It was an attack on him, a man who had done more for Negroes than anyone who had ever occupied the White House. Johnson appealed to King to reconsider the operation and when he refused, warned against fomenting any deliberate disorder. He would clamp down hard on lawlessness "in whatever form and in whatever guise."[76]

It was following the announcement of the Poor People's Campaign that King became a target for the FBI's COINTELPRO operation. Launched in the early 1960s to infiltrate and harass several Marxist groups, in 1967 COINTELPRO added "black nationalist hate groups" to its list of public enemies deserving of investigation and subversion, and in March 1968 it named King specifically, along with Carmichael, Rap Brown, and Elijah Muhammad of the Black Muslims, as a full target. Simultaneously, the Bureau prepared an enlarged edition of the King corruption-and-peccadilloes book, sending copies of the twenty-one-page report to the president, the State Department, military leaders, and the CIA to "remind top-level officials . . . of the wholly disreputable character of King."[77]

In January King met with the SCLC staff in Miami to get final approval for the Washington project. He gained his point, but only after a struggle. By now a number of SCLC members feared it was chimerical to expect poor people with widely differing ethnic backgrounds to cooperate. Rumors were also circulating that Carmichael and Brown were determined to infiltrate the project with their supporters and turn it to violence. In fact, in 1967, Carmichael, no longer active in SNCC, had set up headquarters in Washington and early in the new year had established a "Black United Front" to push for black control of the District's local police and schools. With his Washington base, would he try to incite a violent confrontation for the sake of showing "the naked face of power"? Political extremists were beginning to talk the revolutionary language of "the worse is the better," and Carmichael and his allies might well seize the chance to destroy any possibility of a middle course between acquiescence and revolution.

King denied the likelihood of serious violence. In February he told a reporter that if the demonstrations in Washington became violent, "we shall call them off."[78] But he was not as confident as he claimed to be. He knew he could not guarantee that there would not be a major confrontation with the authorities.

Despite the doubts and the warnings, King pushed ahead. Soon after Miami, he dispatched forty SCLC staff workers to six southern states and nine of the major riot-torn cities to recruit the three thousand poor people who would form the nucleus of the campaign. King would not reveal full details of the SCLC's plans. He wanted, he said, to maintain "the element of surprise" so as to keep the authorities off balance. But he did describe how the "core group," trained in nonviolence, would "set the tone" of the demonstrations. As they proceeded, thousands of others would join in, but with the nonviolent foundation laid, they would abide by the same set of principles.

During these early months of 1968, the mood of the SCLC leaders was far more somber and apprehensive than at any time in the past. No one at Atlanta headquarters had a clear idea where the campaign was heading. In February the writer Jose Yglesias heard Andrew Young, SCLC's executive director, tell a caller that he had no idea how long the campaign might last. As near as he could figure, "by the end of June we will have gotten some response or all of us will be in jail."[79]

Some of the uncertainty came from breaking new ground. King admitted to Yglesias that with the adoption of the Poor People's Campaign the organization was "engaged in the class struggle." The gains that the civil rights movement had fought for thus far had not cost anyone a penny. But the SCLC, he acknowledged, was now calling "for a redistribution of economic power."[80] King insisted that the SCLC's demands did not go beyond what the American people were willing to support, but obviously he felt uneasy and unsure.

King's mood fed his personal insecurities. He had long believed that he was a marked man. Now, with the movement about to challenge the economic status quo, he expected that the hatemongers and the bigots would soon be zeroing in. He could not allow his personal fears to deter him, but he sensed impending danger.

On February 4 King delivered the Sunday sermon to his congregation in Atlanta. It was a foreboding and a personal testament. "Every now and then I think about my own death," he told his flock. He did not wish to dwell on it in a morbid way. But practically speaking, what would he want said on the occasion? King now quietly delivered his own eulogy. He did not want anyone to mention his prizes and his honors. He wanted them to talk of how he had "served." He wanted them to say that he had been a "drum major," a drum major for justice, for peace, for righteousness. The "shallow things" did not matter. He only wanted to leave a "committed life behind."[81]

Toward the end of February, King squeezed concessions out of Carmichael and Brown. The two militant leaders would agree not to "fight" the Poor People's Campaign. In fact, they would join it, and on King's terms: nonviolence. Though King had neutralized the Black Power activists, he remained as opposed as ever to their views. "We have not given up on integration," he told reporters after the meetings with Brown and Carmichael. "We still believe in black and white together. . . . We need . . . to bring the coalition of conscience together."[82]

Soon after, King and his colleagues completed the detailed plans of the Washington campaign. Though he hoped to preserve racial amity, he was willing to risk class antagonisms. The campaign would have three phases. It would start in late April with a trek of the core group to Washington, perhaps in part by mule train, the standard transport of impoverished southern rural black folk. In the capital they would settle in a shantytown on the Mall and serve as the magnet for a giant demonstration much like the 1963 march.

Nothing in this was either very new or very threatening. In

phase two, however, the demonstrators—the core group joined by thousands of black Washingtonians and white college students—would disrupt government agencies and court mass arrests. The demonstrators would pack the jails until Congress passed an "economic bill of rights" that would assure full employment for those able to work and provide a guaranteed annual income for those who could not.

The most radical part of the plan, phase three, would only be invoked if Congress failed to act. The SCLC and its followers and allies would launch boycotts of a number of major industries and of selected big-city shopping centers. SCLC supporters might also attempt sit-ins at factories to shut them down. The campaign would be accompanied by supportive marches around the country and by further disruptive demonstrations in Washington. The pressure point of phase three would be the business community, which would, if all went well, force Congress to meet the SCLC's demands.

At the end of February, King's new militancy received unexpected support from the seven-month-old National Commission on Civil Disorders, chaired by Governor Otto Kerner of Illinois. The commission report was the high-water mark of 1960s' white racial liberalism. Its widely quoted conclusion was that the nation was "moving toward two societies, one black, one white—separate and unequal." The report, much of its telling summary written by New York City's reform mayor John Lindsay, was a classic expression of white liberal guilt. It placed the blame for black poverty, rage, and disorder solely on "white racism." Race prejudice, it stated, had "shaped our history decisively," and it now threatened to blight our future. The report ignored any black responsibility for civil disorder.

The commission made 160 recommendations. Several suggested improving ghetto-white relations through a shibboleth of the era: improved communications. A number called for open-housing laws, like those King had demanded in Chicago. Most, however, focused on a massive transfer of income from taxpayers to ghetto dwellers through a system of uniform federal welfare payments, federal income supplements based on need, and the construction of six million units of new housing for people unable to pay market rents or prices.

Black leaders from every part of the civil rights movement hailed the Kerner report. Young was pleased with its attack on white bigotry; King called it "a physician's warning of approaching death with a prescription to life."[83] Even McKissick praised it for its honest admission of white racism.

But the general public's response boded ill for the Poor People's Campaign. Though the curious white public bought almost three-quarters of a million paperback copies of the report, many must have disliked what they read. Certainly most politicians found it distasteful. Richard Nixon, campaigning for the Republican presidential nomination in New Hampshire, attacked it for its "tendency to lay the blame for the riots on everyone except the rioters."[84] Nixon was a conservative, but Vice-President Humphrey, a man with a proud record of civil rights advocacy, did not like the indictment of whites and commented that the report's conclusions were "open to some challenge."[85] Many key politicians, including the president himself, saw the recommendations as utopian. Johnson was offended by the report's failure to give him credit for what his administration had already accomplished, and he was appalled by the $30 billion price tag of the Kerner program. He did not need further suggestions on how to spend money, he commented; what he needed was more votes in Congress.

On March 14 King convened a meeting of fifty-three nonblack minority groups in Atlanta to plan their role in the approaching Washington campaign. He told reporters that most of the three thousand demonstrators scheduled to arrive in Washington on April 22 had already been recruited and trained. He also described his plans for a nineteen-day tour across the country to talk to community groups, businessmen, and black nationalists to muster support and raise money.

Soon after, King was on the road. SCLC planners contemplated a "tent city" on the Mall to shelter the core group of demonstrators. This would cost an estimated four hundred thousand dollars. With the SCLC now so closely associated with the antiwar movement, the money springs had dried up, and it looked as if financing would be a major problem. Only King's own dynamic presence could reassure the skeptics and overcome growing resistance. The fund-raising trip was exhausting. Toward the end, in New York's Harlem, King admitted that he was "very tired."[86] He had been getting only two hours of sleep a night for the ten previous days. His friends thought he was emotionally exhausted as well. Coretta King heard him remark during this period that he yearned "to take a year off from everything and reflect on all the problems and just see where we're going, what I do from here."[87]

King had clearly taken on too much. In addition to the Poor People's Campaign, he had been drawn into a strike of Memphis garbage workers, mostly black, against the city. He knew that he already had his hands full but could not resist the pleas of the city's black leaders that he speak out in support of the strikers. In some ways the Memphis situation resembled the planned Washington campaign itself. The sanitation workers were poor men who were being exploited. "If we don't stop for them," he told his colleagues, "then we don't need to go to Washington."[88]

On March 18 King interrupted his transcontinental tour and flew into Memphis, checking into the Lorraine Motel near the riverfront. That evening he conferred with James Lawson, one of the Memphis black leaders, and then hurried to Mason Temple where he gave a rousing speech to seventeen thousand cheering black strike supporters. King depicted the Memphis strikers as the prototypes of all impoverished people and proposed a march downtown on March 22 to support their cause. After the meeting he told Lawson and his colleagues that he would personally lead the demonstration.

King arrived back on Memphis on March 21, ready to fullfil his commitment. That evening a blizzard descended on the city and the march was postponed until the twenty-eighth.

Meanwhile, King tried to staunch a wound that was threatening to drain the blood from the civil rights movement: black anti-Semitism. On March 25 he flew to a Catskill Mountain resort north of New York City to ask a convention of Jewish religious leaders to support the Poor People's Campaign. The meeting went well. The rabbis opened with a rendition of "We Shall Overcome" in Hebrew, a gesture that touched King deeply. Most of the session was devoted to questions; King was simply too tired to give another speech.

He told the rabbis that blacks would have to gain a measure of autonomy and power; token acceptance of a few within the existing power structure was not enough. How could ghetto life be improved? By massive investments within the ghettos themselves and by simultaneous efforts to permit blacks to find good housing outside. Then came the crucial question: would the Reverend King comment on the "vicious anti-Semitism" of Carmichael and Rap Brown?

King had no difficulty giving his listeners the response they sought. He despised the militants' views, he said. He condemned anti-Semitism wherever he saw it. One evil in society could not be overcome by embracing another. "For the black man to be struggling for justice and then turn around and be anti-Semitic," he declared, "is not only . . . irrational . . . but . . . very immoral." A question about the militants' support for the Arabs against Israel followed. King said most of the right words: Israel was "one of the great outposts of democracy"; its security must be assured. He marvelled over how the Jews had transformed the desert "into an oasis of brotherhood and democracy."[89] But he also noted the Arab need for economic security. This could be satisfied by a Middle Eastern Marshall Plan. The formula was conventional and shallow, but it seemed to satisfy the Jewish religious leaders, who pledged that they would support his Washington campaign.

On March 28, as promised, King was back in Memphis to lead the downtown march and rally. At 11 A.M. six thousand marchers left the Clayborn Temple AME Church for city hall with King and Ralph Abernathy in the lead. Most were men and women committed to a peaceful demonstration, but tagging along was a contingent of "Invaders," college-age ghetto disciples of Rap Brown who believed the country ripe for revolution. Three blocks into the march those in front heard the sound of shattering glass.

The Invaders were smashing store windows and looting. As police in full riot gear moved in, King decided to call off the protest. He would never lead a violent march, he said. King and Abernathy were whisked away by car and watched the rest of the demonstration on their motel TV set.

The march quickly turned into a riot. The police shot off mace and tear gas at looters; they pounded rampaging Invaders into submission with their clubs. Black youths replied with bricks and bottles. When the mayhem stopped, sixty people had been hurt and a black youth of sixteen fatally shot. The mayor quickly imposed a curfew and the governor dispatched national guardsmen who quelled the disorder by evening.

The Memphis riot almost undid the Washington campaign. If a supposedly peaceful demonstration had degenerated into violence, how could King expect to contain his followers in the capital when his avowed purpose there was to create disorder? Senator Robert Byrd of West Virginia called Memphis "a preview of what may be in store" for Washington and urged a federal court order to block the campaign.[90] *The New York Times,* on the thirtieth, advised King to call off the Washington campaign. "None of the precautions [King] . . . and his aides are taking to keep the capital demonstration peaceful" could guard against a repetition of Memphis, it warned.[91]

King himself was discouraged. The Washington campaign might indeed be doomed. But he also feared that if he canceled it, he would lose his credibility as a leader; people would say he was "at the end of his rope." He must continue. At a press conference before he left Memphis, he insisted that he had no idea of the Invaders' presence or that any Memphis blacks were planning violence, and promised to return to the city "as quickly as possible" to resume the sanitation workers' campaign. He would also not abandon the Poor People's Campaign. Memphis had demonstrated beyond doubt that racial and economic issues were connected. SCLC staff workers, he emphasized, were "eminently qualified" to keep the Washington demonstrations peaceful. True, riots were "part of the ugly atmosphere of our society," and he could not guarantee that they would not occur during the coming summer. But the SCLC's "demonstrations will not be violent."[92]

But King faced a barrage within the SCLC as soon as he returned to Atlanta headquarters. At a meeting at Ebenezer Baptist Church, many of his closest associates deplored the decision to return to Memphis. James Bevel, the SCLC's chief antiwar activist, even attacked the Poor People's Campaign. Bevel, an ordained minister from Mississippi who wore overalls and an orthodox Jewish skullcap on his shaved head, spoke of how difficult he found it to communicate to people the meaning of the campaign. He did not "know how to preach people into the Poor People's campaign."[93] After listening to the attacks and protests for several hours, King simply left the room.

King's gesture worked. When he returned to the church that afternoon, he found a chastened collection of SCLCers. He was right after all, they told him. They might have to postpone the Washington demonstrations for a few weeks, but it was necessary to return to Memphis to properly finish the job they had undertaken. Their support did little to cheer King, and he left the church depressed and touchy, snapping at his young aide, Jesse Jackson, when he tried to get his attention.

King's mood changed a few days later. In Washington on the thirty-first he watched the president's TV speech on Vietnam. King was as astounded as most Americans when Johnson announced that he was withdrawing from the presidential race. He was also immensely encouraged. Maybe this meant peace in Vietnam and also a president who would be more sympathetic to black aspirations. He returned to Atlanta in better spirits, ready to finish up in Memphis and then take on the biggest project in his life.

King and his associates were not the only ones who expected to be in Memphis during the opening days of April. James Earl Ray, an escaped white convict, was also anxious to get to the city. Ray was planning to kill King.

Driving east from California in a white Ford Mustang, Ray had begun to stalk King about mid-March. During the next few weeks he followed him from Selma to Atlanta and then to

Memphis. On March 28 he bought a small-caliber rifle in Birmingham and the next day exchanged it for a more powerful Remington Gamemaster equipped with a telescopic sight.

Ray, who had been in and out of jail most of his adult life, was probably a paid assassin whose only motive was money. The evidence that he was himself a bigot is weak. Yet he was doing the work of bigots. His two brothers, John and Gerald, both criminals like James Earl, were associated with J. B. Stoner, the racist head of the National States Rights party, and with members of George Wallace's prosegregation American Independent party.

There is evidence that James's brothers helped him escape from the Missouri State Penitentiary in late April 1967. There is also evidence that they had connections with John Sutherland and John Kauffmann of St. Louis, both arch racists who hated King and had offered money to eliminate him. A House of Representatives Select Committee on Assassinations concluded in 1979 that through intermediaries including his two brothers, Sutherland and Kauffmann probably paid James Ray to get the "big nigger."[94]

King, of course, knew nothing of the conspiracy to destroy him when he and his party arrived in Memphis the morning of April 3. His presence in Memphis was an important local event, and a crowd of reporters was waiting at the airport when his plane landed. His friends and associates in the Memphis strike whisked him past the reporters and brought him to the Lorraine Motel, where he and Abernathy checked into room 306 on the second floor overlooking a courtyard parking lot. The Memphis media noted King's arrival, and one radio station even broadcast the name of the motel and his room number.

That evening King addressed an audience of two thousand at Mason Temple. The weather had been stormy, and King expected a small turnout. He was tired and reluctant to go and had appeared at the church only when Abernathy called with the news that the crowd was large and enthusiastic.

His talk was extemporaneous and full of forebodings that events would soon turn into prophecy. King dwelt on life and death. He was glad that God had allowed him to live in the mid-twentieth century. With all its griefs and pains it had been a time of great challenges and great progress. He talked about the time back in 1958 when he had been stabbed in New York by a demented woman and had narrowly escaped death. He was glad that he had survived, for in the ten years since then so much progress had been achieved by black people. It did not matter what happened to him now, he told his listeners, "because I've been to the mountain top." "Longevity has its place," he intoned. Like everybody else he wanted to live a long life. But that did not matter anymore. He had looked over Jordan and seen the Promised Land. He might not get there with his listeners, but he knew the Negro people would get there. In this, his last speech, he ended on a triumphant note. "And so I'm happy tonight. I'm not worried about anything. I'm not fearing any man. Mine eyes have seen the glory of the coming of the Lord."[95]

James Earl Ray arrived in Memphis on April 3 and put up at the New Rebel Motel on the city's outskirts. The next day he moved to Bessie Brewer's rooming house adjacent to the Lorraine Motel. The first room Mrs. Brewer showed him faced the front of the building. He could not see the Lorraine from it and asked for another. Room 5B was more satisfactory. It was in the rear of the building, and from its window you could see the back of the Lorraine across the courtyard. Ray took it. That same day he bought a pair of binoculars at the York Arms Company on South Main Street.

On Thursday, the fourth, King slept late. His brother Alfred Daniel had arrived from Louisville at midnight, and the two had stayed up talking and reminiscing almost until dawn. Once awake, King occupied his day with plans for the march aborted so abruptly a few weeks before. During what remained of the morning he conferred with the Invaders and other militant youth groups. He could not get them to agree with his nonviolent tactics and dismissed them angrily.

The afternoon was more relaxed. Martin spent more time with his brother and made plans with Abernathy for dinner that evening at the home of one of his prominent supporters, the Reverend Samuel Kyles.

By 5:30 King was bathed, shaved, and dressed. Kyles arrived to escort the party to his home for dinner, and he and King joked about the food that Mrs. Kyles planned to serve. When Abernathy asked for a minute to put on some aftershave lotion, King went out on the balcony overlooking the courtyard with Kyles to get some air. Below in the parking lot Jesse Jackson, James Bevel, Andrew Young, and several other King aides were waiting for the chauffeur to leave with the dinner group. King bantered with them.

At six o'clock, as King stood alone on the balcony, a shot rang out. A soft-nosed .30 caliber bullet smashed into his face on the right side, severing vital arteries and severely damaging his spinal column. King crumpled and quickly lost consciousness. Andrew Young rushed up from the lot and felt his pulse. Kyles, who had just stepped back into the room, turned and knelt down. Then he turned away and sobbed.

As King's life ebbed, James Earl Ray was seen running down the corridor from the bathroom in the rooming house. Minutes later he rushed from Mrs. Brewer's carrying a small suitcase that he dropped in front of Canipe's Amusement Company. He then jumped into a white Mustang and roared away. The police quickly recovered the bundle. It contained two cans of beer, a local newspaper, a portable radio, a bottle of aftershave lotion, a pair of binoculars, and a .30-06 rifle with telescopic sights. Many of the items had Ray's fingerprints on them; the radio had a half-scratched-out serial number that proved to be Ray's inmate number at the Missouri State Penitentiary.

An ambulance arrived five minutes after the shot, and King was rushed to St. Joseph's Hospital. Surgeons worked furiously to save him. At 7:05 they pronounced him dead.

Within hours racial violence erupted in 110 American cities. The apostle of peaceful change was honored by a holocaust that exceeded in fury and cost any of the previous "long, hot summers." Ironically, King had warned of this possibility in his last fund-raising letter accusing the government of "playing Russian roulette with riots" and "speculating in blood" by doing too little about the ghettos' problems.[96]

The worst explosion took place in Washington, D.C., within a mile of the White House. Though the capital was more than 65 percent black, it was not a slough of despair. It had a black mayor and a predominantly black city council who, though appointed, exercised substantial power. It also had a large black middle class composed of federal workers with decent jobs and steady incomes. These characteristics made for stability and a stake in the city's well-being. Yet the district had its share of unemployed youths, crumbling slums, and racial resentments. It was also the focus of the impending Poor People's Campaign, making the murder a special provocation. Finally, it was where Stokely Carmichael had located his militant Black United Front.

News of King's death was on the airwaves by 8:15 Thursday evening. Many of Washington's youths who hung out at the corner of Fourteenth and U streets carried transitor radios, and in minutes everyone knew of the assassination. When a black *Washington Post* reporter arrived at the intersection, she found the atmosphere tense. A reporter for NBC News, discovering she was the only white woman in the crowd, made hasty preparations to leave. As she searched for a taxi, an elderly black woman told her she hoped no cab would stop for her.

People were very angry. In the People's Drug Store, a busy anchor point of the Fourteenth Street ghetto shopping district, a small crowd huddled around a radio listening to the president. Johnson had just canceled a visit to Hawaii to speak to the American people. Whatever his private thoughts, his words were appropriate. "America is shocked and saddened by the brutal slaying tonight of Dr. Martin Luther King. . . . I know every American of good will joins me in mourning the death of this outstanding leader and in praying for peace and understanding throughout this land." But his remarks only provoked his drug-store listeners. "Honkie," one exclaimed. "He's a murderer himself. . . . This will mean one thousand Detroits."[97]

While Johnson was still speaking, a small crowd of thirty young men burst into the store. One of them was Carmichael, clad in army fatigues. "Martin Luther King is dead," they shouted. "Close the store." The white manager did not argue. As the lights began to go off, the group left to repeat their actions at other stores along Fourteenth Street.

The violence did not start until about 9:30 when someone kicked in the People's Drug Store windows. Soon after, a youth smashed the glass door of the Republic Theater on U Street, and another slipped inside and came out with a huge bag of popcorn. Carmichael, according to reports, tried to stop the store trashing and calm the crowd. "You really ready to go out and kill?" he shouted at one enraged youth. "How you gonna win?" But Carmichael had not become a sudden convert to nonviolence. His point was only that no one was prepared as yet for violence. "We're not ready," he yelled. "Let's wait till tomorrow." When someone else smashed through the window of the Belmont TV and Appliance Store, Carmichael ran up with a large revolver and grabbing one youth by the shoulder told him, "If you mean business, you should have a gun. You're not ready for the 'thing.' Go home. Go home."[98]

The crowd was in no mood to listen even to Carmichael's qualified restraint. Store windows and doors were soon shattering all along Fourteenth Street, and looters were running through the streets loaded down with liquor, clothing, and appliances.

At 12:30 A.M. arsonists set the riot's first fires. When the firemen arrived, the crowd attacked them with bottles, stones, and cans. The police quickly appeared and lobbed 100 tear-gas canisters at the mob. They scattered, some to go home, but many to reassemble a short distance away and resume the stone throwing. By the time the first night's rioting had subsided, 150 stores had been looted, 7 fires had been set, and more than 150 adults and 50 juveniles had been arrested. There were also 30 injured, including 5 policemen and a fireman. It is possible, though not certain, that a white man, caught in the ghetto, had been beaten to death.

Thursday night was only the beginning of Washington's ordeal. Meanwhile, riots almost as wounding erupted in a dozen other cities.

In Chicago, rioting broke out on Friday in the city's West Side ghetto, and West Madison Street soon became a red streak of fire across the city. The turmoil had begun about 1:30 in the afternoon when bands of young men surged down the street laughing and shouting. A barrage of bottles turned store windows to shards and opened holes through which eager hands pulled TV sets, sports jackets, and whiskey bottles. For a while nothing seemed beyond reach of the ingenious. One band of youths smashed an automobile showroom window and tried to drive off with a sleek new car. Its undercarriage became stuck on the lower edge of the window frame, and all the thieves could do was to pummel the car to vent their frustration.

That first day Illinois national guardsmen arrived to impose order. They failed, and the violence continued into Saturday. Mayor Daley now imposed a 7:00 P.M. to 6:00 A.M. curfew on everyone under twenty-one. Daley was the toughest of the city officials. He believed that his police superintendent had been too lenient with the rioters, and after the worst of the turmoil was past he announced that in the future the police would shoot to kill any arsonist and shoot to wound any looter. Four months later, when the city hosted the Democratic National Convention, the mayor's shoot-to-kill order would be remembered.

By Saturday disorders had burst out in Philadelphia, Detroit, San Francisco, Pittsburgh, Boston, New York, and dozens of other large and small cities. Baltimore ignited on Saturday afternoon and after a relatively quiet night rioting resumed the next morning. By dusk on Sunday two major fires and many smaller ones were raging in the East Baltimore ghetto. On Sunday Governor Spiro Agnew imposed a curfew and forbade all sales of liquor, firearms, and gasoline in small containers.

In three of the cities—Baltimore, Chicago, and Washington— federal troops had to be brought in when state and local forces proved inadequate. Washington, where the federal government exerted direct authority, was the earliest to turn to the military. The first soldiers arrived in the capital on Saturday, and by that evening nine thousand were patrolling its ravaged streets. In Chicago, when the rioting resumed on Saturday and spread to the

South Side, Illinois Lieutenant Governor Samuel Shapiro requested federal troops, and on Sunday five thousand men of the First Armored Division from Fort Hood, Texas, and the Fifth Mechanized Division from Fort Carson, Colorado, arrived by plane. The army came to Baltimore on Sunday evening after Agnew discovered he could not control the violence with city police and national guardsmen alone.

Though virtually no city with a black population escaped turmoil, for its magnitude and its symbolic meaning the explosion in Washington made the most powerful impression on the public mind both in the United States and abroad.

Many of the city's rioters on the second day were students from the District's predominantly black high schools. The school authorities had tried to keep them in class, but they had walked out. All through the day they swelled the crowds of looters who were stripping bare the shelves and storerooms of ghetto merchants.

The looting was not confined to the poor or to teenagers. Washington reporters wrote of well-dressed adults lugging bags of shoes and purses and garbage cans filled with liquor bottles out of wrecked stores. On Friday a middle-class couple with their two teenage children were seen leaving Grayson's Dress Shop carrying dozens of plastic-draped dresses and ladies' coats still on hangers. Two women in their twenties staggered down the street under the weight of a box piled high with bolts of expensive yard goods. A woman government worker with a master's degree, arrested for looting a liquor store, later wrote a pseudonymous article for *The Washington Post* describing how for "ten seconds" she "felt that the system had finally given me something for nothing."[99]

A few of the rioters were more intent on destruction than booty. Most of the arsonists were either vandals or people who wanted to cover up their looting. A few were revolutionaries, however, for whom firebombing was a political statement.

Several days after order was restored, a *Washington Post* reporter made contact with a small cell of dedicated revolutionaries who talked about their role during the disorders. They had come together as a group in February, they said, for the purpose of armed rebellion. King's assassination had caught them by surprise, but they had seized the opportunity to serve as catalysts for violence in places where little if anything was happening.

The revolutionaries claimed credit for much of the arson. They had used their supply of Molotov cocktails and explosives to destroy stores and other property, and others had followed their lead. Their purpose had been to maximize the disorder and to prepare the ground for revolution. But they also had immediate ghetto interests in mind. When the *Post* reporter asked how they had picked their targets, they told him: "First of all, like they were the biggest Jews and the biggest exploiters in the community and we wanted to make sure they never did get back."[100]

The *Post*'s discovery of a revolutionary cell confirmed people's suspicions that part of the Washington violence was the work of outside agitators. During the disorders themselves, the Washington authorities worried about Stokely Carmichael. Would the Black Power advocate throw fuel on the fire? They would have been delighted to nail him for inciting to violence, and they shadowed him closely.

Carmichael actually played a canny game. On Friday morning he held a press conference. "When white America killed Dr. King," he announced, "she declared war on us." He talked about retaliation and about how black people would have "to get guns."[101] This was as bloodthirsty as any extremist—or white bigot—could want. But Carmichael was not simple-minded. Immediately after the news conference he went to a student-sponsored rally at his alma mater, Howard University. The outdoor meeting rang with militant antiwhite denunciations, and Carmichael, when he spoke, again condemned "Whitey." But though he talked of imminent disaster, most of his pronouncements sounded more like apocalyptic predictions than calls to action. Clearly, the example of Rap Brown was in his mind; he did not want to land in jail. In the end, there would be no legal grounds to charge him with inciting to riot.

Whatever the causes, the arrival of troops on Saturday quickly ended the Washington disorders. The soldiers stayed until April 16, and when they left the nation's capital was calm. The destructive impulse had exhausted itself elsewhere, as well. In all, around the country, there had been thirty-nine deaths, twenty thousand arrests, and $45 million worth of property damage.

On Monday, April 8, Coretta King and Ralph Abernathy, King's designated successor as head of the SCLC, came to memphis to lead the postponed March for the sanitation workers. Fifteen thousand people walked in silence as a memorial to King. At the Memphis City Hall Coretta told the crowd, "We must carry on because this is the way he would have wanted it." She proved as fine a master of biblical prose as her husband. We must, she intoned, "go forward from this experience, which to me represents the Crucifixion, on toward the resurrection and redemption of his spirit."[102] On April 16 the city of Memphis recognized the sanitation workers' collective bargaining rights and raised their wages.

Martin Luther King's funeral was held on Tuesday, April 9. Though King had requested a simple ceremony when his time came, it was an elaborate rite of national mourning.

Eight hundred people crowded into the modest church where King had been pastor. Seated on the narrow wooden pews were many of the nation's famous, including Vice-President Humphrey, Senators Robert Kennedy and Eugene McCarthy, former Vice-President Richard Nixon, Jacqueline Kennedy, and Attorney General Ramsey Clark. The nation's black leaders and celebrities were also there: the entertainers Harry Belafonte, Sammy Davis, Jr., Mahalia Jackson, Diana Ross, and Lena Horne; Thurgood Marshall, the first black Supreme Court Justice; the civil rights leaders Whitney Young and Roy Wilkins: and, of course, a full roster of King's SCLC lieutenants. The Black Power militants, however skeptical of King, buried their disagreements with him in death and came to pay their respects. Carmichael arrived with six bodyguards and insisted that all of them be given seats in the jammed church.

Abernathy officiated at the obsequies—sermons, hymns, tributes, and a tape of King's "drum major for justice" sermon of February. The temperature in Atlanta was in the eighties, and the participants sweltered while the speakers droned on. Well past noon the discomfort of the indoors was exchanged for the torture of a three-and-a-half mile procession in the blazing Georgia sun to the Morehouse College campus where King had taken his degree twenty years before. The coffin was carried on a mule-drawn farm cart to symbolize King's Poor People's Campaign, while behind trudged fifty thousand dripping people, including all the celebrities.

The cortege arrived at 2:30 in the afternoon, and another long round of eulogies, hymns, and sermons ensued. At 4:30 Bishop William Wilkes of the AME Church delivered the benediction, and soon after King's body was brought to Southview Cemetery and laid to rest. The whole overblown ritual had lacked the dignity the man deserved, but it was all atoned for by his epitaph. On his marble monument they inscribed: FREE AT LAST, FREE AT LAST, THANK GOD ALMIGHTY, I'M FREE AT LAST.

King's death did not abort the Poor People's Campaign, but it probably guaranteed its failure. For all his enthusiasm and good intentions, Abernathy was not the man of destiny King had been, and he was unable to fulfill his predecessor's hope that the nonviolent, biracial civil rights movement could survive. His failure would mark its demise.

For almost fifteen years Abernathy had labored in King's shadow. He had been second in command but lacked the broad education, worldliness, and personal magnetism of his chief. Born in a small Alabama town, he was closer than King to the black people of the rural South. His lack of sophistication, however, placed him farther from the white liberals whose support, though weakened, was still essential. Many within the civil rights movement doubted his ability to carry on effectively. One former SCLC staff member told a reporter, "He lacks Doc's all-round abilities, and he's going to have to rely heavily on the staff to see him through. He can't dominate the situation as Doc did, and he must adjust to that fact."[103]

On April 26 Abernathy and his aides arrived in Washington to lobby for the coming campaign. They conferred with labor leaders and liberal business groups and extracted pledges of support. On the twenty-eighth Abernathy returned with an advance guard of one hundred black, brown, yellow, and white "poor people" to present the campaign's economic demands to Congress and the administration. The delegations were not awed by their audience. They tongue-lashed officials over the inadequacy of federal programs and the white racism they claimed was implicit in the government's behavior, and demanded major changes in the way the poor were treated.

Soon after, caravans of poor people began to leave Memphis, Chicago, Albuquerque, Jackson, the Bay Area, and elsewhere headed for the capital. The best-publicized was the Memphis group of fifteen hundred that set out from the Lorraine Motel in a mule train with Abernathy in the lead wearing the campaign uniform of blue jeans. In each case, supporters along the way provided buses, food, and shelter. In many cities the campaigners marched and held rallies to recruit and raise funds for the main event.

Abernathy and the SCLC had momentum going for them. If mainstream Americans had been appalled by the postassassination violence, they had also felt a surge of guilt. In the wake of the murder Congress passed another civil rights bill, the last of the 1960s series, prohibiting discrimination in housing nationwide. This measure seemed likely at the time to end one of the major grievances of black Americans. But to express white America's ambivalence about recent events, the new law also made it a crime to cross state lines with the intent to create a riot or to make or transport firearms or instruct anyone in their use for a riot. It would soon become a two-edged sword wielded primarily against the left.

The same ambivalence appeared in negotiations between the SCLC and the federal and city authorities for the planned "tent city's" site. After the disorders earlier in the month, the politicians were understandably uneasy about the campaign. Conservative Senator Russell Long of Louisiana expressed the feelings of many of his colleagues when he insisted that the government must not "bend the knee" to the demonstrators.[104] But administration and District officials proved willing to negotiate, especially after the SCLC threatened to squat on government property if it could not get a permit, and on May 11 the Interior Department and the

SCLC struck a deal. The city would set aside fifteen acres of West Potomac Park, just off the Mall near the Lincoln Memorial, for an encampment. The eight-page permit forbade firearms, liquor, and open fires, and required that the residents provide sanitation facilities, remove garbage, and abide by local safety regulations. One provision that officials would later regret excluded the U.S. Park Police from the site unless invited. The permit would run for a month, until June 16. To reassure the timid, the federal government announced that it was prepared to call on eight thousand troops and the D.C. National Guard in an emergency.

The first residents of the shantytown, soon called Resurrection City—mostly children and young people from the Deep South—arrived in Washington on the weekend of May 11–12. They were housed in a Catholic church in Arlington, across the river. On Sunday the first Resurrection City structures of plywood, plastic and canvas began to rise in West Potomac Park. That same day three thousand demonstrators staged a march through the neighborhood burnt out by the previous month's riots. Among the bus loads of demonstrators who reached the capital over the weekend were a contingent of Invaders from Memphis, members of the teenage group who had rioted during King's first march in support of the sanitation workers. It was an ominous note.

The first two hundred residents of Resurrection City moved in on May 15 while the A-frame structures were still going up. Reporters came to watch, but were kept outside the snow-fence barrier that rimmed the camp. They were not ignored, however. Reverend Bernard Lafayette, the campaign's national coordinator, told them that as far as the SCLC was concerned the June 16 deadline was pro forma. "The permit may run out," he noted, "but we will not be run out. We got our permission to stay here from the American Indians."[105]

There were problems from the start. Money was tighter than anticipated, and construction material ran out after 150 of the scheduled 600 shanties has been erected. These provided shelter for only 500 demonstrators, though thousands more were expected to pour into the city to take part in the scheduled mass demonstrations. On May 16 Mayor Walter Washington met with federal and District officials in an emergency session that lasted for two days to consider the inadequate planning and the housing crisis. They concluded that the building program must be speeded up and that meanwhile the new arrivals would be deflected from the already overcrowded churches where they were being housed and sent elsewhere.

Among the new people just in by bus from the Midwest was a contingent of Blackstone Rangers from Chicago and Commandos from Milwaukee, the latter led by Father James Groppi, a radical white priest. Like the Memphis Invaders, they had been recruited as marshals to keep order in the encampment on the principle, apparently, of set a thief to catch a thief. These ghetto youths were part of the group brought to Sts. Paul and Augustine's Church for processing. It took five hours for the campaign officials to collect names and addresses and to assign people to billets. By the time they got to the Rangers and Commandos, most of them had disappeared and could not be found.

The initial problems were never really solved. The marshals enjoyed their authority too much and flaunted it, ordering press photographers and reporters around and preventing them from interviewing Resurrection City residents or campaign officials. Even liberal reporter Mary McGrory of the *Washington Star* found their manner insufferable. The young black men, she wrote, were "pushing people around in a style to which they have become accustomed. Their orders were numerous and arbitrary. They shouted 'make way,' joined hands, shoved organizers, sympathizers, and curious indiscriminately, intervened swiftly in any dialogue between poor and press."[106]

Worse was to come. As the days passed, boredom set in and the marshals began to revert to blatantly delinquent behavior. They were soon spending their evenings roistering in the Fourteenth Street strip and other sleazy Washington hangout neighborhoods, returning drunk to the encampment to stage wild parties with whiskey brought in illegally. They assaulted newsmen, including several black reporters, stole from encampment residents, and beat several people, mostly whites, who crossed them. On May 22 the SCLC staff finally lost patience with the marshals and loaded two hundred on buses for the trip back to

Memphis and Chicago. Some returned, however, for the free food and the easy prey. Ghetto teenagers from the District soon joined them, and the troubles continued.

To control the rowdies Reverend James Orange organized the Tent City Rangers, reliable young men in their twenties. They were unable to police the encampment. Till the very end Resurrection City remained unsafe for its more orderly inhabitants.

Ethnic divisiveness was another source of trouble. As promised, the campaign was an interracial affair. A clear majority of the Resurrection City population was black, but there were whites—mostly radical students—some Asians and Puerto Ricans, a contingent of American Indians, and a sizable group of Mexican Americans from the Southwest. The Mexican American leader was the abrasive Reies Lopez Tijerina, founder of the Alianza movement in New Mexico.

Alianza was dedicated to recovering lands supposedly taken away from Spanish-speaking New Mexicans by the Anglos after they acquired the Southwest in 1848. In 1967 Tijerina and some of his followers had shot it out with lawmen after their suit to regain the claimed lands failed in the courts. Now, at Resurrection City, Tijerina proved touchy and assertive of his group's prerogatives. He claimed that the blacks made all the decisions and ignored the others. Abernathy and Andrew Young replied that Tijerina was only interested in publicizing Alianza's demands.

Rains of heroic proportions made everything immeasurably worse. The deluge began on May 23 and continued for a month with only brief breaks. The rain penetrated the shanties, soaking everything. Puddles of water, ankle-deep and even hip-deep, quickly filled the streets between the structures. Mud was everywhere, sometimes sucking the boots off people's feet as they tried to get around. Garbage, old clothing, packing cartons, and liquor bottles sank into the muck, making footing even more difficult and the atmosphere noisome. Despite the physical discomfort— and making it worse—over twenty-five hundred people had been jammed into the fifteen acre site before the campaign ended.

With each passing day Resurrection City became less and less useful as a dramatization of the plight of the nation's poor. The public—even the liberal public—saw the squabbling, the menace, the chaos, and many concluded that the cause was hopeless.

Meanwhile, the political strategy of the campaign became a scattershot of uncoordinated actions. The campaign leaders had planned a mass demonstration on Memorial Day, but because of unforeseen delays they were unable to carry it off. Fortunately, the federal authorities granted the campaign leaders an extension of their permit from June 16 to the twenty-third.

Hoping to retain liberal support as long as possible, the campaign leaders avoided premature confrontations with the government. Most of the forays in the early weeks, accordingly, consisted of treks to government agencies to present a set of demands, some speechmaking, and then a return to camp. One exception was a demonstration on June 3, when seventy-five Indians in warbonnets led a Resurrection City delegation to the Supreme Court to protest a recent decision denying fishing rights to some Washington State tribes. Refused admission to the court's stately white marble building, the Indians pounded on the great bronze doors. A small group was finally allowed in. Meanwhile, on the plaza outside the building, the waiting crowd had become restless and began to throw stones at windows and scuffle with police. Americans take the dignity of the Supreme Court seriously. The incident got a bad press.

The high point of the campaign was supposed to be "Solidarity Day," a convocation of poor people's delegations from all over the country. SCLC leaders hoped that the turnout would exceed the throngs of the 1963 March on Washington, where King had given his "I have a dream" speech. To assure an impressive showing they turned over the details of the demonstration to Bayard Rustin, who had managed the 1963 operation so skillfully.

Rustin was not a good choice for a campaign that sought to push beyond the mainstream. A moderate, close to the country's trade union leadership, he still cherished the black-liberal alliance of the recent past. On June 2, without consulting Abernathy or Lafayette, he issued a statement with a redefined set of campaign legislative goals. It was a less militant platform than the SCLC leaders wanted, leaving out the demands of the ethnics and conspicuously lacking any attack on America's Vietnam involvement. Hosea Williams, the campaign direct action coordinator, dismissed it as "a lot of jazz and foolishness." Abernathy repudiated the document, calling it a "misunderstanding of goals,"[107] and Rustin promptly resigned. During the next few days the newspapers headlined the event as CONFUSED GOALS, LEADERSHIP CRISIS PERILS POOR MARCH, and DISSENT JEOPARDIZES THE POOR PEOPLE'S CAMPAIGN.[108]

On June 12 and 13 almost two inches of rain fell on Resurrection City in twenty-four hours. To the good Christians in the SCLC it looked like the biblical flood, and some talked of abandoning the encampment. But the campaign struggled on, its leaders hoping that Solidarity Day would redeem the early failures.

Success continued to elude Abernathy, Young, Bevel, and the rest. The problem was in part the leaders themselves. They lacked the capacity to inspire and move that King had possessed; they could not command the respect he had enjoyed in the nation at large. King's stature had compensated for the general inefficiency of the SCLC in the past. Without it, the SCLC's organizational incompetence became painfully apparent.

But that was not all. Unlike Selma and Birmingham, the Poor People's Campaign had no villain, no Jim Clark, no Bull Connor. The president might have stood in, but he had renounced reelection and no longer seemed a worthy opponent. There was also the confusion of voices in Resurrection City. No one who read the papers could doubt that the campaign was beset with disunity and inner conflict. Not that the SCLC's previous campaigns had been entirely free of dissension, but never before had the fissures been so widely publicized. It was difficult to wholeheartedly endorse a project so riven internally.

But most important, times had changed. Gone was the vision of a colorblind society where race would be irrelevant. Instead, race had become virtually the most significant thing about anyone. Race obsession was not merely an affliction of black militants or white backlash extremists. It had been foisted on people generally by the ghetto disorders and the hateful rhetoric of the *enragés* of both races. King might have soared above the anger and resentment; his successors could not.

Solidarity Day was scheduled for June 19—"Juneteenth," the anniversary of Texas's slave emancipation in 1865. It started well. For a change the skies were clear, and it would remain rainless, but hot, for the rest of the day. At daybreak, cars and buses began to arrive in the District with loads of out-of-town participants. By noon a large crowd had gathered at the Washington Monument and was waiting for the ceremonies to begin. Campaign leaders would later claim that the turnout was as great as in 1963. But the best estimates are that it was less than a hundred thousand, probably only a third of the "I have a dream" total.

The social profile of the participants was about the same as in 1963: white, liberal suburbanites; college students; church groups; members of established civil rights organizations. But there was an enormous difference in the spirit, the "feel" of the demonstration. Nineteen sixty-three had pulsed with optimism and enthusiasm; 1968 was heavy with portent. Speaker after speaker warned of the consequences of failure to respond to the poor's needs. Even Whitney Young expressed deep fears. "This may be," he declared, "the last march which is nonviolent and which brings blacks and whites together. . . . The nation and the Congress must listen to us now before it is too late—before the prophets of violence replace the prophets of peace and justice."[109] It was an election year, and a flock of congressmen and political candidates, including Vice-President Humphrey and Senator Eugene McCarthy, made their appearance. But this did stop Abernathy from bitterly attacking the administration for burning the Great Society "to ashes by the napalm in Vietnam" and insisting that it was impossible to trust the elected officials of the nation."[110]

The crowd, fired up at first, faltered during the long day. Speeches went on interminably, and the ceremonies were not over until 7:00 P.M., more than two hours late. And they were numbingly dull. Only Coretta King received an attentive hearing. People soon began to drift away, so that by the end only a few thousand stalwarts were left to hear Abernathy finish his hour-long address. This was mostly a rehash of old slogans made notable only by his threat to remain in Washington past the deadline if the campaign's demands were not met.

With few exceptions the media reports on Solidarity Day were negative. None of the reporters could avoid an invidious comparison between what they had just seen and the glorious August day in 1963. THE MARCH 5 YEARS LATER; FRUSTRATION REPLACES HOPE, read *The Washington Post* headline.[111] In part, surely, the newsmen were expressing the country's general disenchantment with the civil rights movement as a whole.

Late that evening, back at Resurrection City, the young militants helped confirm the press's skepticism by a fit of violence following a late evening dinner at the Statler-Hilton hotel. Arriving back at the encampment shortly after 1:00 A.M., the diners encountered a group of park police and began to taunt them. A scuffle erupted when the militants began showering the cops with bottles and cans. Police reinforcements armed with shotguns soon arrived, and it appeared that blood would flow. Fortunately, several SCLC leaders came up just in time and managed to separate the two sides before anything serious could occur.

Later that day a group of militants marched on the Department of Agriculture and demanded to see Secretary Orville Freeman. When told they must wait and that the secretary would see only a twelve-person delegation, they marched around the building and blocked entrances. These tactics had been promised since the Poor People's Campaign was first proposed by King in December, but had never been used. Now the authorities quickly gathered up fifty of the demonstrators and hustled them off to jail.

Soon after, another contingent of militants appeared and blocked rush-hour traffic leaving the city along two main streets adjacent to the Agriculture building. The police now threw off their restraint and waded into the crowd cracking heads with their clubs. The melee continued for half an hour, and then another 150 Resurrection City people led by Hosea Williams and Jesse Jackson appeared. Jackson stopped the attacks and calmed his people down with appeals for nonviolence. He then marched them back to the encampment.

They did not stay. Enraged by several panicky motorists who had barreled through demonstrators injuring several, a crowd streamed out of Resurrection City toward Seventeenth Street. They were intercepted by the police and began to throw bricks, rocks, and bottles. For a time the police merely dodged, but then lost patience and used tear gas to drive the crowd back to the encampment. For the remainder of the night, hundreds of armed District policemen ringed the camp, while inside a fierce debate took place on how to deal with the new crisis.

The militants demanded revenge and direct action against the police in the name of the black revolution. Bevel, who claimed to be as radical as anyone, denounced senseless violence. He particularly attacked the toughs who, he said, got their kicks from assaulting people and were indifferent to the consequences.

In the end Bevel's caution prevailed. By now, however, the public as well as Congress and the authorities had lost all patience with the Poor People's Campaign. That same day the disgust reached a peak when Alvin Jackson, the deputy chief marshall at Resurrection City, quit and in a statement to the *Washington Daily News* described a virtual reign of terror at the encampment. The reason why people were leaving, he said, was not mud, poor food, and leaky shelters, but because when campaigners came home from a day of picketing they found "their belongings stolen or their wife raped. . . ." There were "rapes, robberies and cuttings every day" in Resurrection City, and when the culprits were caught, nothing could be done to punish them.[112]

During the next few days what remained of the campaign fell apart. On June 21 Tijerina and the other Mexican American leaders virtually wrote the campaign off. Many Chicanos had already departed for home, and after Solidarity Day the Mexican Americans' role became nearly invisible. The same day District and federal authorities meeting in closed session refused to renew the Resurrection City permit beyond its June 23 expiration date. By now District and U.S. Park Service officials, even Walter Fauntroy, an SCLC leader himself, agreed that the situation had gotten out of hand. The campaigners would have to take the shanties down and start vacating on Sunday at 8:00 P.M. Officials discussed what they would do if the Resurrection City inhabitants defied their orders. Some believed that the National Guard or federal troops might be needed.

In reality, many SCLC leaders had come to see Resurrection City as a noose around their necks. But it was also a symbol of defiance, and its abandonment would be a defeat. On Saturday Abernathy told reporters that "we're not making plans to leave." In fact, a "new phase" of the Poor People's Campaign would begin on Monday after the permit expired. The two intervening days would be spent on a "spiritual rededication" to nonviolence.[113] The new phase would specifically exclude the violence-prone troublemakers.

The end came on Monday. SCLC officials had decided not to fight it out. They would not leave voluntarily, but they would allow themselves to be arrested as a protest.

Their scenario was essentially carried out. Before daybreak a thousand District policemen gathered at the Reflecting Pool. At dawn amplifiers began to repeat the message: "The permit for use of this property has expired. You must leave the camp by 10:40 this morning to avoid arrest and prosecution."[114] At 11:10 Chief John Layton ordered a man to climb a powerline pole and cut off the camp's electricity. The freedom songs blaring over the camp public address system stopped dead.

The police had always kept to their side of the snow-fence barrier. Now, with sixty reporters and photographers slogging through the mud behind them, they pushed it aside and searched the huts. Only a few were still occupied, and their inhabitants were arrested. Several of the shanties were booby-trapped and burst into flame when their doors were opened.

About a hundred remaining campaigners were gathered at the culture tent near the center of the encampment, singing songs and clapping their hands rhythmically. They allowed themselves to be arrested, and most marched off without protest to waiting buses to be taken for booking. Later that day Abernathy and two hundred other SCLC leaders and supports were arrested, as agreed, while demonstrating on Capitol Hill.

That evening rioting broke out near SCLC headquarters at

Fourteenth and U streets. Police quickly cleared the streets with tear gas and Mayor Washington imposed a curfew. The disorders soon ended and did not resume the following day.

SCLC leaders and supporters met on Thursday night at the New Bethel Baptist Church to consider future options. Many in the audience came from Resurrection City. Jesse Jackson, the chief speaker, proposed organizing forty local Poor People's Campaigns in cities around the country. The focus of the New Phase would be citywide boycotts that would "share the pain" of poverty in America with other people. Until now, he said, "only the poor have been suffering and it is now time to set up a redistribution of the pain."[115] Bevel suggested that the campaign branch out to involve all of Washington. "The white folks took our town [Resurrection City], and now we are going to take their town."[116]

During the next few weeks Abernathy and Bevel tried to transfuse some new life into the Poor People's Campaign. Bevel stumped the black neighborhoods of Washington seeking support for a mass protest against the destruction of Resurrection City. From jail, Abernathy, hoping for another Selma response, called for a mass convergence of the nation's clergymen on Washington. They would defy the authorities and court arrest. As at Selma the nation's conscience would be aroused.

Nobody came. Nor did anything come of the New Phase boycotts. On June 30 Jackson told *The New York Times* that "it really looks as though we'll have difficulty pulling through with anything."[117] A week later he admitted in private that the boycott proposal had made so little impression on public opinion that there was scant chance that the scheme would get off the ground. On July 7 Jackson told a group of refugees from Resurrection City to return home. Round one was over, and there was no point in hanging around for a delayed round two.

By mid-July Jackson and Bevel had vanished from view, and whatever was left of the Poor People's Campaign devolved on second- and third-echelon leaders. They conducted a few meetings and rallies in the Washington area, but attendance was poor.

Abernathy was released from jail on July 13. Two hundred people showed up to express their support. He visited the campsite, which had now been cleared of all its structures and reseeded. Its emptiness seemed to depress him, and he left quickly without a word.

The New Phase never amounted to anything. The defeat in Washington had eroded support for the SCLC both among liberals and in the black community. When, in September, the SCLC finally got around to drawing up its fall plans, they amounted to little more than a voter turnout drive in the ghettos to defeat Nixon in November.

In the real world, few things end cleanly. This applies to the civil rights movement as much as to any other historical event.

The SCLC did not disappear. It struggled on through the 1970s with reduced funds and diminished expectations. Some of the money it received Coretta King apparently diverted to the Martin Luther King, Jr., Center for Social Change, a move resented by SCLC veterans. In 1977 Abernathy was deposed in a SCLC power struggle, and by the spring of 1979 there was serious talk of disbanding the now feeble creature that King had given life.

SNCC's decline was more precipitous and more complete. By the end of 1968 it was little more than a handful of ineffectual activists without a following. In June it replaced Rap Brown, mired down in defending himself against federal indictment, with quiet-spoken Phil Hutchings. Under his leadership SNCC cultivated a more moderate image. In July it expelled Stokely Carmichael for his newly formed alliance with the Black Panthers.

The move to the right did not help. With each month more and more supporters, especially the veterans, drifted away. And those who did not were often forced out. At the December staff meeting in Atlanta, Cleveland Sellers and Willie Ricks were attacked for their association with the Panthers, whose willingness to ally themselves with white radicals was considered anathema by the Black Power nationalists. Sellers and Ricks counterattacked by charging SNCC with associating with paramilitary groups. They too were expelled.

SNCC clung to life for a few more years but as a shadow

organization. By 1970 there were only two active chapters—New York and Atlanta. Soon after, it quietly expired.

CORE did not disappear, but it ceased to matter. In 1968 Roy Innis, a passionate black nationalist though not a political revolutionary, became its head. He called the new CORE "a Black Nationalist Organization" with "separation" as its goal. His program emphasized community self-help and black capitalism and proposed a constitutional amendment that would recognize blacks as a "nation within a nation."[118] Even as a black separatist organization, CORE sank into obscurity. By 1969 it was left with a tiny staff, limited funds, and a handful of chapters. It had been eclipsed in the public consciousness by the even more militant Black Panthers.

The Panthers became notorious in 1968. On April 6 an Oakland police squad car pulled up to a parked car containing Eldridge Cleaver, Bobby Hutton, and several other Panthers. The police, according to Cleaver, suddenly fired a shotgun at him. This set off a wild shoot-out in which Hutton was killed and nine other Panthers including Cleaver were arrested and sent to the state prison at Vacaville.

Despite his previous criminal record, Cleaver was released on bail in time to spend the summer and fall campaigning as presidential candidate of the Peace and Freedom party. His campaign was a farce. Nobody expected Cleaver to get a million votes, but his supporters did hope he would advance the antiwar, left agenda. Instead, he rejected his radical allies and took up with the Berkeley counterculture. He soon took on their most antisocial characteristics. As an associate later said, during the campaign he "was stoned out of his mind half the time. . . ."[119] After the election, afraid he would be returned to prison, Cleaver jumped bail and fled to Algeria where he became a spokesman for anti-American agitation.

Meanwhile, Panther chapters were being decimated by police raids and attacks in the Bay Area and around the country. The Panthers were clearly the targets of brutal official racism, but they often brought trouble on themselves by their paramilitary poses and their angry antiwhite rhetoric.

Despite the mayhem, Panther attitudes splashed over onto the XIX Summer Olympic Games held in Mexico City in October when several black American athletes, disciples of Professor Harry Edwards of San Jose State College, turned their awards ceremony into a Black Power political statement. A twenty-five-year-old bearded black sociologist, Edwards was a former college athlete himself. He had personally felt the sting of racism, but his black nationalist attitudes derived from the Black Muslims, Malcolm X, and the Panthers in Oakland, fifty miles to the north, as much as from his own trauma. In November 1967 Edwards had convened a meeting of black athletes and issued a call for blacks to boycott the Mexico City games to protest the presence of a South African team and to dramatize the dependence of America's international athletic standings on black prowess. Sixty black athletes had signed the boycott announcement.

But Edwards was bucking a powerful current. Sports had been the escape hatch from poverty and obscurity for generations of young black men, and he was asking them to place principle and racial solidarity before the precious chance to make it in America. In the end, the boycott effort had to be abandoned, but Edwards convinced several San Jose State track and field stars, Tommie Smith, John Carlos, and Lee Evans, to make the games a showcase for a black nationalist protest.

As expected, America's black athletes dominated the running events at the Summer Olympics. Tommie Smith won the gold medal and John Carlos the bronze for the 200-meter dash. James Hines won a first for the 100 meters, Lee Evans for the 400. Hines, though he had never supported the boycott plan, had already asserted his position by refusing to accept his award from the hands of Avery Brundage, the crusty old racist who headed the International Olympic Committee. When Smith and Carlos came to the platform to accept their medals and bask in the crowd's applause, they were prepared for something more dramatic. Just before the ceremony the two men had grabbed several props for their intended performance. Smith had tied his wife's black scarf around his neck; Carlos had donned a black shirt borrowed from a Jamaican athlete. Both were wearing black leather gloves. As they walked toward the awards platform, sprinter coach Stan Wright, himself black, rushed to tell the U.S. track coach Payton Jordan of what was about to happen. "They'll regret this for the rest of their lives," Wright remarked.[120]

The ceremony provided still another memorable image of 1968. As the band played "The Star-spangled Banner," Smith and Carlos, wearing black stockings without shoes, stood on the platform, their heads lowered, their arms raised in the Black Power salute. The white Australian silver medal winner appears bemused between them. The U.S. Olympic Committee, threatened by Brundage and the International Committee with retaliation, suspended both men and ejected them from Olympic Village, where the American team was housed. It was an empty gesture. Smith and Carlos had already won their medals; both had been staying in Mexico City hotels with their wives. It is hard to believe that either man regrets today what he did two decades ago; it was probably the most notable event in their lives.

For a time in 1968 SNCC and the Panthers sought a merger. It did not succeed. SNCC objected to the Panther ten-point program as reformist rather than revolutionary. The Panthers in turn called SNCC a bunch of black hippies. A July meeting of SNCC and Panther leaders failed to settle the differences. The trigger-happy Panther representatives threatened to shoot the SNCC people. Violence was averted, but all chance for cooperation evaporated. As one SNCC member said, "I can't work with anybody I don't feel right turning my back on."[121]

The Panthers would limp on for another few years, but they never became an effective force for racial change. A few white radicals continued to champion their cause out of revulsion at the way they were treated by the police and the authorities. But raids, indictments, and what can only be described as official murder wore away even their limited support, and the Panthers were gone by 1973 or '74.

The only civil rights organizations to survive relatively intact were the NAACP and the Urban League, the most conservative. In fact, if we look at their financial resources, they actually gained in the years immediately following the Poor People's Campaign. Forced to share civil rights contributions from whites and blacks with CORE, SNCC, and the SCLC during the mid-1960s, their income soared when their competitors to the left collapsed at the end of the decade.

Money did not bring happiness. The NAACP proper was soon engaged in a bitter fight with its own offspring, the Legal Defense Fund. The fight dissipated its energies and resources. After 1968 the NAACP was primarily a watchdog of past legal achievements and a guardian of 1960s' gains. During the following decade the NAACP sought to improve the economic well-being of blacks through the device of affirmative action. Some progress was made in getting blacks admitted to professional schools, union apprenticeship programs, and a wide range of private and public jobs. But the process proved glacially slow, and "equality of results" is still a distant goal.

No one can tell whether King would have been more successful than his successors in moving from de jure to de facto equality for blacks in America. American society has always cherished a rough equality, but it has never been friendly to redistributive schemes. Its principle—though not always its practice—has been: everyone starts at the same time, but the outcome at the finish line is not assured. If King had lived, could he have forced white middle-class America to change this principle? His successors have not sought direct income redistribution. Rather, they have turned to affirmative action, preferential treatment in jobs, and other benefits for minorities. These policies have not produced the millennium, and meanwhile the social pathologies of the ghettos have worsened. There is no way of telling whether King's survival would have made a difference. But what is clear is that his murder in April 1968 ended the second American Reconstruction, the sweeping crusade that finally, after a century, fulfilled the promise of the first Reconstruction.

4

The Left Could Not Hold

ON NEW YEAR'S DAY, 1968, Bernardine Dohrn ate a late breakfast in her Greenwich Village apartment and in the afternoon took a walk through New York's Lower East Side. That evening she packed for a long-planned trip to Europe. On January 2 she was in London, and her brief diary jottings, found in an abandoned appointment book by investigators for the Illinois Crime Commission, describe a lecture at the London School of Economics and a pilgrimage to the offices of *New Left Review*, the journal that had contributed its name to the 1960s movement she would soon join.

An attractive woman of twenty-six, Dohrn had grown up, a rather ordinary middle-American child, in Whitefish Bay, near Milwaukee. After college she tried graduate study in history but found it dull and took a law degree at the University of Chicago.

In 1966–67, while working with Martin Luther King's Chicago Project, Dohrn met some of the white activists in Jobs or Income Now (JOIN), a community action venture of Students for a Democratic Society (SDS). SDS was the nation's largest and most-influential radical organization, but Dohrn herself was still only at the fringes of the radical movement.

Dohrn's first job with the National Lawyers Guild moved her further left. The Guild was a left-wing professional association placed on the attorney general's list of "subversive" organizations during the McCarthy era. Formed in the mid-1930s as an alternative to the conservative National Bar Association, it had supported many left-liberal causes over the years including arms to Loyalist Spain, federal antilynching statutes, civil liberties protection for radicals, and union exemption from antitrust laws. In the sixties it had become active in the civil rights movement, defending the Student Nonviolent Coordinating Committee (SNCC) against the attacks and legal maneuvers of the Mississippi authorities during the summer of 1964 and that fall pleading the Mississippi Freedom Democratic party's case before the Atlantic City presidential nominating convention.

During the year that Dohrn remained in the guild, she became close to members of the SDS New York regional office. A few weeks after her trip to Europe, she led an SDS-sponsored conference on women's issues. On June 14, at the big 1968 annual SDS convention held at Michigan State University, she was nominated for SDS interorganizational secretary. Before the vote the delegates questioned her about her beliefs and qualifications. Someone asked: "Do you consider yourself a socialist?" Dohrn did not hesitate: "I consider myself a revolutionary communist."[1] She won without opposition. Many in the audience now considered themselves "revolutionary communists," too. The New Left had repudiated its own origins and embraced Leninism.

In 1968 SDS was the keystone of the New Left. It was the largest of the New Left organizations with anywhere from 50,000 to 100,000 members and perhaps 350 chapters scattered across the nation's 2,500 campuses. These figures only hinted at its influence, however. SDS had many thousands of hangers-on. Rebellious college students naturally gravitated toward the most notorious antiestablishment organization at hand. Many never paid dues or carried membership cards, but they attended SDS meetings and turned out for SDS-sponsored rallies, especially during moments of high crisis and excitement. Thousands of young men and women would later claim they were SDS members though they had never formally joined.

Organized by the socialist League for Industrial Democracy

(LID) as its student auxiliary (SLID) during the 1930s, SDS had gone through several bewildering incarnations. In 1935 it had merged with the Communist-front National Student League to form the American Student Union. When the American Communist party (CPUSA) abandoned its "united front" policy following the Hitler–Stalin pact of September 1939, both student groups had passed unnoticed off the scene.

After the war LID revived the student league, but it proved a feeble body. The parent organization itself was scarcely robust. During the fifties LID lost much of its radical fire, preserving a touch of its socialist past as a badge of honor but devoting much of its limited energies to fighting the Communists at home and supporting anti-Soviet American policy abroad.

Though still proclaiming its socialism, SLID fell victim to the sweeping anti-Communist hysteria of the 1950s that we call McCarthyism. During these years it excluded from membership all who advocated "dictatorship and totalitarianism and . . . any political system that fails to provide for freedom of speech, of press, of religion, of assembly, and of political, economic and cultural organization. . . ."[2] Despite its identification with cold-war attitudes, however, it attracted such young men as James Farmer, Aryeh Neier, Michael Harrington, and Gabriel Kolko, who, in different ways, would become leaders of 1960s' dissent from the cold-war consensus.

As the nation's hysteria abated, as Americans tired of cold-war confrontation, as the Soviet Union under its post-Stalin leaders began to grow more cautious and less paranoid, the SLID transmuted into SDS.

The agent for change was a prematurely balding, scholarly graduate student of twenty-four at the University of Michigan, Robert Alan Haber. In the spring of 1960 a ten-thousand-dollar gift from the liberal United Automobile Workers of America enabled LID to appoint a field secretary to help the organizing efforts of its newly renamed youth auxiliary, Students for a Democratic Society. Haber was a logical choice. His father, a University of Michigan labor sociologist, had belonged to LID, and the younger Haber had himself been active in the tiny remnant that passed for a left campus political movement in the mid-fifties. In 1960 Haber was looking for a way to transform his passionate social sympathies into a vocation. His success in organizing a "Human Rights in the North" conference at Ann Arbor in the spring of 1960 impressed the LID elders and brought him the job of SDS field secretary.

Haber was a harbinger. He felt changes of air pressure, shifts in mood, alterations in the tone of voices before almost anyone else. And clearly, something was in the air as the new decade opened. McCarthyism had almost run its course. The senator himself had been repudiated by his colleagues and in 1957 had died, unlamented, of cirrhosis. As the decade wound down, the liberal and left opinion makers and intellectuals were beginning to shake off their terror of public disgrace and professional ruin.

Many were also reverting to their normal adversary relationship to American society. During the fifties, America's victory over Hitler, its astounding postwar prosperity, its clear moral superiority to the Soviet Union under its paranoid dictator and totalitarian party, had reconciled many of the country's artists, writers, and academics to their own liberal capitalist nation. For a number of years intellectuals joined the American celebration, commemorating and venerating the country's past, its institutions, its values, its success. When one-time socialist Daniel Bell published *The End of Ideology* in 1960, he was expressing the new-found faith of his kind in pragmatic liberalism after a long addiction to heady utopianism. The era would be a lost generation for the left.

But Bell's book was also the era's swan song. Even as it was making its way to press, the shoots of early radical renewal were beginning to poke through the frozen soil. On a few major cosmopolitan campuses around the country, young men and women, many the children of "Old Left" parents, began to stir.

In 1959 at the University of Wisconsin, a group of pioneers founded *Studies on the Left*, a scholarly journal dedicated to "the radicalism of disclosure." Two years earlier, left students at Berkeley had organized the campus political party, SLATE, to restore some ideological bite to student politics. SLATE sought to replace the mindless student pep-rally, "sand box" politics of the day with campaigns for greater student freedom, lower campus bookstore prices, an end to nuclear testing and capital punishment, and a reduction in cold-war Soviet-American tensions. The University of Michigan had acquired its equivalent of SLATE when Tom Hayden, the live-wire editor of the *Michigan Daily*, the campus paper, visited Berkeley in the summer of 1960. A skinny senior with a bulbous nose and deep acne scars, Hayden was impressed with the SLATE people, and when he returned to Ann Arbor in the fall he recruited Haber to help him launch VOICE, a new activist student party.

Other campuses were nurseries for student radical journals, clubs, and political parties during the last years of the fifties or the first of the sixties—Harvard, Swarthmore, Oberlin, Reed, and Antioch among them. Several also sheltered the meager remnants of Old Left student groups like the Young People's Socialist League and the Trotskyist Young Socialist Alliance.

The location of the small, pioneer New Left tribes was not random. They had surfaced at either elite liberal arts schools or large, cosmopolitan state universities, and flourished among a student clientele that came disproportionately from the professional middle class, often left and frequently Jewish. Many of their members were "red diaper babies," the children of 1930s' radicals fulfilling their parents' aborted social yearnings.

But the young activists were not merely carbon copies of their elders. Their radicalism was "new"—in several important ways. First, it was not pro-Soviet, as so much 1930s and early 1940s leftism had been. New Leftists seldom had much use for the USSR. Their hero countries were Red China and Fidel Castro's Cuba, places that seemed to have escaped the coercive bureaucratic rigidities of the Soviet Union under Stalin and his heirs. But they were not dedicated anti-Communists. Too young for the fierce left internecine battles of the thirties, they belittled the dangers to an independent left of the disciplined Communist *apparatchiks* who still abounded and deplored the nation's seeming obsession with the Communist menace.

At first the New Left was not even Marxist. Theirs was a "post-scarcity" leftism nourished on affluence and infused with the belief that whatever else its failing, modern capitalism had proved its ability to create material abundance. In standard Marxism, capitalism was doomed to escalating crises that would ultimately tear it apart. But postwar American did not look much like capitalism in its final days. The nation had never before been so prosperous, and the benefits of soaring production and national income seemed to seep down even to the working class. In 1958 John Kenneth Galbraith, a witty liberal, published the best-selling *The Affluent Society*, confirming the essential conquest of private poverty while deploring the survival of "public squalor." Even when the left rediscovered poverty soon after, it never could entirely shake off its belief that America had put scarcity behind it.

Yet the new radicals did not join the postwar celebration of America. American life continued to provide enormous scope for dissenters and naysayers. Affluence creates its own special discontents. Influenced by Paul Goodman's *Growing Up Absurd* and the works of Jean-Paul Sartre and Herbert Marcuse, the emerging New Left grappled with existential questions like alienation, aesthetic and moral squalor, and meaninglessness. Their primary concern was not for the "quantity" but for the "quality" of life in recent America, for despite affluence, the young radicals believed, Americans had not succeeded in creating a humane, open, interesting society or in giving meaning to the lives of ordinary people. What was wrong with the country, wrote Berkeley graduate student Robert Scheer in 1963, was not poverty, but "the reality of life in Los Angeles, Syracuse, and Sacramento, with their bowling alleys and shopping centers, and those vast stretches of America which are a blight upon the idea that man is sensitive, searching, poetic, and capable of love."[3] In later years, when the international left rediscovered the early, "humanistic" Marx of the *Economic and Philosophical Manuscripts*, it would consider views such as these within the Marxist canon. But in 1960 they appeared a new departure for the left.

The emerging New Leftists also rejected the Marxists' faith in the proletariat as the prime agent of revolutionary change. In the Orthodox Marxist credo, capitalism's decline must cause ever-increasing "immiserization" of the working class until it rose up in wrath and overthrew the system. But clearly American workers were not a seething, discontented, class-conscious proletariat, ripe for revolution. They were fat and contented, and their leaders, the trade union heads, were prime defenders of the existing social order and of American cold-war foreign policy. It was difficult to see how such people could ever be counted on to disturb the status quo.

If not the proletariat, then who? Here the young radicals seized on the insight of sociologist C. Wright Mills, a maverick motorcycle-riding Columbia professor who refused to join the fifties' celebratory consensus. Mills had trained at Wisconsin during the tail end of its left-liberal era and remained a naysayer all his life. In two best-selling books he attacked the new labor leadership as coopted and described the new white-collar middle class as unable to protect itself against the true "power elite" who ruled in capitalist America. In 1960, Mills wrote an open letter to the editors of the British *New Left Review* that became a key New Left manifesto.

Where, he asked, in an era of fat complacency, could new political ideas and new actions to advance social change come from? Mills disparaged the old Marxist "labor metaphysic." The working class had been coopted and had turned soft. There was only one "agent" for change in the new postwar world: "the young intelligentsia." Only they were "thinking and acting in radical ways"; and only they could supply the brains and the bodies for revolt.[4]

Mills, with his authentic Texas earthiness and his passionate commitment to social justice, made a deep impression on the young activists now beginning to assemble on liberal campuses. They read his work and were flattered by his faith in their political potential. His views were also convenient for the young intellectuals. It was astounding good fortune that the campuses, where the activists were, were just the places where the revolution would begin. They quickly seized on his ideas. As early as March 1961 Haber was writing an LID elder that "if any really radical liberal force is going to develop in America, it is going to come from the colleges and the young. Even baby steps toward our vision of a 'social transformation' are going to have to be [taken] on campuses."[5] They also adopted his term *New Left* to distinguish themselves from their predecessors.

This picture of a middle-class, student-centered left was incorporated into SDS's eloquent Port Huron Statement adopted in June 1962. Written largely by Hayden, Port Huron was the New Left's Declaration of Independence. It identified the signers as "people of this generation, bred in at least modest comfort, housed now in universities, looking uncomfortably to the world we inherit." It named the ills of the nation as racial bigotry, the cold war, apathy, alienation, and "meaningless work." It talked about transforming formal, sclerotic representative government through "participatory democracy" that would give people a sense that they could control their lives. It concluded that the university could be the source of change, for it was "the central institution for organizing, evaluating, and transmitting knowledge," and was open to new intellectual and ideological currents.[6]

Despite their emphasis on their own role, for the next two years SDSers tried to fight someone else's revolution. SDS members were active in SNCC and in Martin Luther King's Birmingham campaign during 1962 and early 1963. Some went to Mississippi during Freedom Summer in 1964. They also picketed northern dime-store chains and collected money to support the southern black students' lunch-counter desegregation campaign.

In 1963–64 SDS's major effort, however, was the ill-conceived Economic Research and Action Project (ERAP), a community action, back-to-the-people movement based on a set of debatable premises: that full employment was about to end and bread lines were imminent, and that the white working class could be induced to join with blacks to build an "interracial movement of the poor." Theory was reinforced by a restlessness among the SDS first generation that had written the Port Huron Statement. Now in their mid-twenties, they were finished with college and uncertain about how to merge their skills and social sympathies. ERAP would be only the first of many attempts to solve the SDS "alumni" problem.

Community action and organizing, as we have seen, were very much in the air during the early 1960s, and Haber and Hayden had little trouble getting funding. With the proceeds of a small United Automobile Workers' grant, during the spring of 1964 SDS established ten projects in major cities including Newark, Chicago, Cleveland, Boston, and Baltimore. With the arrival of summer vacation, college students joined the small initial cadres. In all perhaps 150 young men and women participated in the ERAP that first summer.

The activists rented apartments or old slum houses and lived on forty-two-cents-a-day diets of beans and rice. They distributed leaflets explaining that they wanted to help the jobless solve their unemployment insurance and welfare problems. They held evening meetings to talk about community issues and how to force the bureaucrats and politicians to meet neighborhood needs. ERAP projects often overlapped the federal government's Community Action Programs and ran into many of the same difficulties with city hall. Local political leaders resented the outsiders' "meddling" and "troublemaking," and the police often harassed them.

But there were more serious problems than official hostility. The anticipated economic slump never materialized. In fact, during the four years following 1964 the economy would thrive beyond anything within recent memory. As Lee Webb, a Boston SDSer with the Chicago JOIN project, later said, "Just as we got to Chicago lines at the unemployment compensation center started to get shorter."[7] The experience only confirmed the SDSers' view that the failings of capitalism lay in the existential and cultural realms, not the economic.

And there were other problems at ERAP, as well. The ERAPers quickly discovered that they did not understand the poor and vice versa. In fact, it was not the proletariat who came to the evening meetings; it was the underclass, the *lumpenproleteriat*, of semidelinquents, drifters, welfare mothers without husbands, winos, and drug takers. Disorganized, demoralized, antisocial, passive, they expected little of society and were often as happy to rip off the ERAPers as the "system." Many came to the meetings for handouts or diversion. Slum youths were drawn by the prospects of making out with the ERAP women.

The ERAP projects were also impeded by the activists' self-doubts. Participatory democracy meant that people must achieve control over the decisions that affected their lives. But how could the ERAPers avoid imposing their own wishes and desires on the apathetic people they wanted to help? The students had a different agenda from their clients. As one Newark ERAP worker noted, "We are trying to make people think and change their values. . . . When we find a woman at home every day watching soap opera . . . we don't try to force her attention from the TV to the rats and the roaches, but we try to make her think what it is about her life that makes her watch that soap opera every day."[8] Wasn't this manipulative? No matter how they examined the issue, the radical students could not solve the dilemma of how to square the theory of participatory democracy with the realities of apathy and manipulation. It undermined their will and exhausted their energies.

As a major SDS program, ERAP lasted through the summer of 1965. Thereafter, though the Chicago JOIN project, the Cleveland project, and one or two others continued for several more years, the program wound down. Yet the idea of community organizing would never vanish. It was amazingly durable and survives today as the "New Citizen Movement" with some of the same people still active as leaders.

As ERAP passed through its brief rise and decay, events in distant California were refocusing attention on the campus scene in a sensational way.

The University of California at Berkeley in 1964 was a giant, in enrollment, affluence, and intellectual standing. The flagship of a distinguished seven-campus system, it had twenty-seven thousand students and more Nobel Prize winners than any other university except Harvard.

Berkeley was a liberal institution in a liberal community. The Bay Area had a reputation for left politics that went back at least to the beginning of the century. During the 1930s the Communist party had enjoyed a substantial following in northern California and had published a West Coast newspaper, *The People's World.* The 1940s brought World War II pacifists and refugees from McCarthyism to San Francisco and the East Bay Area. In the 1950s, while the rest of the country apparently slumbered, San Francisco had cohosted with New York an antibourgeois cultural revolt, the Beat Generation.

The university was colored by the Bay Area's left politics. Most Berkeley undergraduates were fresh-faced young Californians innocent alike of ideology and complexity. But there was a leaven of red-diaper babies who had created SLATE and had defied the House Un-American Activities Committee when it came to northern California in 1960 on one of its periodic Communist-hunting expeditons. By the fall of 1964, moreover, several hundred civil rights veterans, tempered in Freedom Summer or in local Bay Area civil rights sit-ins and protests, were active on campus. The civil rights activists had offended local conservatives and clashed with the powerful *Oakland Tribune,* run by Republican Senator William Knowland.

The Berkeley graduate students, many of them politically sophisticated young men and women from the major eastern and midwestern cities, formed another pool of potential militants. And student militants could count on the Berkeley faculty to a point. The most prestigious universities, we know, had the most liberal faculties, especially in the humanities and social sciences. At Berkeley, faculty liberalism was reinforced by sensitivity to civil liberties violations created by years of feuding with the University's Board of Regents over a special faculty loyalty oath imposed in 1948 at the onset of the McCarthy era.

In the fall of 1964 the president of the university system was Clark Kerr, a labor economist supposedly wise in the ways of negotiation. Kerr was a Quaker, a liberal, and a former member of LID. At the end of the 1940s he had served as chairman of the Berkeley Committee on Privilege and Tenure that had fought the regents' mandatory loyalty oath. When he became president of the entire University of California system, he dropped the oath. But nothing in his past had prepared him for the experience he would undergo after classes resumed in the fall of 1964.

Like most adults in that year, Kerr was not attuned to the emerging antiauthoritarian temper among the advanced young. The university still considered itself *in loco parentis*, the protector of students' health and safety and the guardian of their manners and morals. Berkeley had the usual set of parietal rules governing student dormitory hours, dress, and behavior. It also had rules regarding political activity on campus. These were designed to assuage the legislators' fears that the state-supported institution might become politically partisan and were surprisingly strict for a liberal campus. Practice mitigated theory, however. The university allowed students to use the Bancroft Strip, an area just outside Sather Gate, to recruit for political causes and to hold rallies.

The confrontation known as the Free Speech Movement (FSM) began on September 15 when the dean of students, Katherine Towle, informed the heads of all student organizations that beginning the following week, all soliciting for candidates or political parties and all efforts to raise money for off-campus causes would no longer be permitted on the Bancroft Strip. For years student organizations had set up manned bridge tables on the strip as stations for political and social advocacy. There the interested or curious could find literature on the civil rights movement, vegetarianism, sexual freedom, peace, the Young Republicans, and almost anything else, and talk to an eager young advocate about his cause. This boisterous, vibrant, ever-lively scrap of land was an integral part of the Berkeley "scene," and helped make the university a magnet for every young maverick and gadfly in the country. It would not be abandoned without a fight.

On the seventeenth, representatives of eighteen student groups, including the Young Republicans, met with the dean to protest the new regulations. She agreed to allow distribution of "informative" literature but not advocacy of "a specific vote, [or] call for direct social or political action."[9] The university would also not permit fund-raising or recruiting for off-campus causes.

In past years the dean's proposal would have seemed a reasonable compromise. But the storm fast gathering did not occur in a vacuum. The political climate had changed drastically over the past year or so. Recently, Berkeley students had picketed the *Oakland Tribune* for its racist hiring practices. Earlier in the summer the strip had served as a recruiting ground for anti-Goldwater pickets at the San Francisco Republican convention. In the fall of 1964 several of the tables at Bancroft and Telegraph avenues were manned by tempered veterans of Freedom Summer, young men and women who had faced a lot tougher adversaries than Dean Towle, Clark Kerr, or the regents.

The sides had already been drawn. Conservative regents and administrators feared the university was becoming a staging area and resource for advocates of radical social and political change and wanted to stop it forthwith. Student activists saw their expanding political activities jeopardized, especially their fund-raising and protest actions for SNCC and the Congress of Racial Equality (CORE). Neither side was altogether frank about its goals. The regents and administrators ignored ideology and talked about orderly procedures and discipline. The students focused on free speech, both out of principle and because its appeal went beyond the radical agenda that many Berkeley students would support.

But the clampdown on student freedoms was only one element in the rebellious brew. Campus activists by now had come to see the university itself as a valid target. The administration and the regents were guardians of a corrupt and privileged order and the university an integral part of the modern American Leviathan. Just recently, in his Godkin Lectures at Harvard, Clark Kerr had talked proudly of how the universities were at the forefront of the "knowledge industries" and how they had "become a prime instrument of national purpose."[10] If Kerr was right, why should they be exempt from criticism and attack?

There were other grievances. Not only was the university a slavish "servant of power"; it was a pedagogic failure. Professors were self-serving careerists who ignored their students; administrators were petty bureaucrats, enslaved to the "power structure," and ignorant of real education. The universities were too large, too impersonal, too indifferent. As a comment on the university's dehumanization, student militants in the weeks ahead would carry signs echoing the directions on the IBM punch-card system that Berkeley and other swamped colleges used to keep track of their business: I AM A STUDENT. DO NOT FOLD, SPINDLE, OR MUTILATE ME. As more and more campuses followed the Berkeley road to violent disruption, the student left and its defenders would blame much of the chaos on the colleges' educational bankruptcy.

The indictment was valid only in a roundabout way. Future pollsters would learn that most students—and especially the activists—enjoyed their courses and admired their instructors. Yet the colleges' size and impersonality inevitably affected the course of campus events. Students did not become rebels or revolutionaries because they didn't like Sociology 23 or History 101, or because their instructors had long lines outside their offices at advising time. But many dissenters were clearly moved by a desire for connections, by a yearning for community, that the overcrowded universities of the sixties could not easily provide.

In the past these needs could be satisfied by campus fraternities, debating societies, or clubs. After years of attack as exclusive and privileged, however, these organizations had lost their legitimacy, certainly for the incipient activists. The "Movement" took their place. Not only did it provide adventure and scope for youthful energies; it also evoked a fervent sense of belonging. In 1966 a veteran of the Free Speech Movement about to unfold would describe his experience:

You were for once free of the whole sticky cobweb that kept you apart from each other and from the roots of your existence, and you knew that you were alive and what your life was all about. . . . The F.S.M., with its open mass meetings, its guitars and songs, its beards and long-haired chicks, made the aloofness and reserve of the administration . . . the formality of the coat and tie world, seem lifeless and dull by comparison.[11]

Whatever its sources, confrontation in Berkeley proceeded with tragic inevitability. The students refused to accept Dean Towle's new rules and on September 30 set up unauthorized tables on the Bancroft Strip. When the administration cited five of the rules breakers for disciplinary action, their supporters marched, five-hundred strong, into Sproul Hall, the administration building, and demanded that all be subject to discipline alike since all had broken the rules. Dean Arleigh Williams refused to see them en masse and told them to leave. They refused and began a sit-in. Seven hundred Berkeley students bedded down on the floors of Sproul Hall, prepared to spend the night.

The next day the crisis reached a new stage. Whatever their original intentions, the protesters abandoned the Sproul sit-in at 2:00 A.M. so that they could be fresh for actions the following day. At nine that morning, the "United Front"—representatives of the major student campus groups affected by Dean Towles's order—defiantly set up advocacy tables in front of the administration building. At about 10:30 A.M. Dean George Murphy approached the CORE table and warned Jack Weinberg, the student manning it, that if he did not leave he would be arrested by campus police. Weinberg, a CORE member and former mathematics graduate student, refused to yield and when the campus police dragged him to a police car went limp in classic civil rights fashion. Observing this struggle was a large crowd that had gathered earlier to see what would happen after the previous day's events. Largely United Front partisans, the onlookers were outraged, and a few began to sit down around the car to block its departure. Hundreds more quickly followed their lead. The crowd was soon singing an old radical song: "We're fighting for freedom, we shall not be moved."[12]

For the next thirty hours three thousand excited people surrounded the car with Weinberg and several campus guards trapped inside, while United Front members delivered speeches from its top attacking the administration. One of the most eloquent was Mario Savio, a tall, frizzy-haired philosophy undergraduate who, at Weinberg's urging, had spent the previous summer in McComb, Mississippi, working for the Council of Federated Organizations (COFO) and SNCC. A New Yorker of working-class Italian background, Savio had confessed to a friend a few months earlier that he was tired of reading history—"I want to make it."[13]

Now, standing barefoot on the roof of the car, he made clear that he had mastered the special rhetoric of the civil rights movement. The Berkeley administrators, he charged, were Nazis.

The campus guards were copying the SS officer Adolf Eichmann who had only "done his duty" while herding Jews to the gas ovens.

During the next hours, with Weinberg and his captors still uncomfortably stranded in the squad car, the students and the administration tried to end the impasse. At 7:30 the following evening Savio once more clambered on top of the stranded squad car, its roof now comfortably flattened by all the students who had used it as a speaking platform. The FSM and the administration had concluded an agreement, he told the crowd. The university would not press charges against Weinberg, it would appoint a joint student-faculty-administration committee to examine the issue of campus political activity, and it would submit the cases of the suspended students to a faculty discipline committee. In return the students would suspend their protest. The crowd shouted their approval. Many drifted off for home; others stayed on campus that evening to hear folksinger Joan Baez, a resident of nearby Carmel, perform at a victory concert.

The student uprising at Berkeley was far from over. On October 4 the activists formally organized the Free Speech Movement, with an executive committee to make policy decisions and a smaller steering committee to handle day-to-day strategy. FSM leaders pledged not to disband until the campus was declared a free speech haven.

During the next few weeks, calm prevailed on the eucalyptus-lined campus. The FSM had little to do. In November the administration issued revised rules on campus political advocacy that seemed to grant the FSM almost all it wanted. Then, during Thanksgiving vacation, it undid all the good work by insisting that four students, including Savio, answer charges for the squad-car incident.

The day after classes resumed the FSM issued an ultimatum: if the disciplinary proceedings against the four students were not dropped within twenty-four hours and "freedom of political activity" not assured, they would occupy Sproul Hall once more and then, if necessary, proclaim a student strike boycotting all university classes.[14] Soon after, the Graduate Coordinating Committee of the FSM, representing the activist graduate students and teaching assistants, announced it would support any strike that might be called.

The events of the next two weeks are central to the New Left legend. Never before, in living memory, had students tried to shut down a major American university. In future years the sit-in and strike would take on a heroic aura and become the stuff of myth.

The occupation began with a mass rally at noon on December 2 at Sproul Plaza, just outside Sather Gate. No student demonstration of the sixties could proceed without musical accompaniment, and Joan Baez was present to warm up the six thousand students, observers, and Berkeley street people with the strains of Bob Dylan's "Blowin' in the Wind." Savio followed with a moving speech that rang the changes on dehumanization and alienation and the necessity for the individual to resist injustice. The university was a "machine" that ground up students as raw material, he said. It was necessary to stop that machine, "to put your bodies upon the gears, and upon the wheels, upon the levers, upon all the apparatus, and you've got to make it stop."[15] When he finished, to the background of Baez's "We Shall Overcome," over a thousand people followed him and the other FSM leaders into Sproul Hall to occupy the building and close down the administration.

The students occupied the first four floors of the building, distributing themselves along the corridors one- or two-deep to avoid disrupting operations. They sang songs and conducted "freedom school" classes, but they kept the noise level down. When evening approached FSM monitors brought in food from outside.

Kerr wanted to wait the occupiers out. They would become bored and tired soon enough, he believed, and leave. And a few did. Baez for one, certain that nothing was going to happen that night, left. But the governor, Pat Brown, was under enormous pressure to take action. He had been accused of a feeble response at the time of the squad-car siege and was sensitive to further accusations of weakness. He decided to evict the protesters.

At 7:00 P.M. campus police locked the doors, letting people depart if they wished, but allowing no one else to enter. Nothing further happened for eight hours. By 1:00 A.M. the lights had been turned out at Sproul, and most students had bedded down for the night. Then, a little after three o'clock, the Berkeley campus chancellor, Edward Strong, entered the building and, moving from floor to floor, announced that "failure to disperse will result in disciplinary action."[16] Soon after, six hundred police invaded Sproul and, starting at the top, moved down floor by floor arresting students and loading them into waiting buses and police vans. Most students exited on their own legs, but some went limp and had to be dragged out, not always gently. Eight hundred were arrested and processed at the Santa Rita Rehabilitation Center. All were released on bail by December 4.

While students were still being cleared from Sproul, the FSM announced a "massive, university-wide strike" to commence immediately.[17] By morning picket lines protesting the police "bust" blocked the entrances to classroom and office buildings. Soon after, the students established a "strike central" to drum up campuswide support and to coordinate strike activities. Nothing was left to chance. FSM workers tore pages from the student directory and, assigning a page per volunteer, telephoned every student they could reach asking them either to join the strike or to respect the picket lines. The campaign was effective. Most classes in the arts and sciences, the university's core, ceased to meet. In all, about half the Berkeley student body followed the FSM's lead.

Outraged at what they perceived as a brutal police violation of university sanctuary, the Berkeley faculty quickly joined the fray. At an excited ad hoc meeting, they denounced the decision to call the police and adopted resolutions demanding that all disciplinary actions pending against students be dropped, that no student be prosecuted by the university for advocating off-campus actions, and that an academic senate committee, composed of faculty, take over the job of discipline for rules infractions arising from political activities. The faculty, in effect, were proposing to override the administration's mandated disciplinary responsibilities.

On Monday, December 7, Kerr appeared before sixteen thousand students, faculty, and staff at a mass open-air meeting at the Greek Theatre on campus. He proposed light punishment for the illegal tables, the squad-car incident, and even for the Sproul occupation. He refused, however, to consider leniency for any of the strikers. Not only was this plan too begrudging; it was also doomed by the rough handling of Savio by two guards as he tried to gain the microphone. Kerr quickly called the guards off and Savio had his say, but the incident further poisoned administration-FSM relations. That afternoon, at Sproul Plaza, an FSM rally shouted down the administration's proposal.

The following day the university's Academic Senate, the official voice of the full-time Berkeley faculty, met at Wheeler Hall to consider what to do. Excitement was high; almost one thousand faculty turned out, three to four times the usual number. A group led by sociologist Lewis Feuer supported student political advocacy only if it was "directed to no immediate act of force or violence. . . ."[18] Feuer was a former radical, but he feared student militancy. In 1930s' Weimar Germany, he warned, Nazi student organizations, claiming university sanctuary, had browbeaten and terrorized Jews, liberals, socialists, and other groups opposed to their program. Such practices must not be allowed to happen again. The Feuerites were a minority. The senate endorsed unregulated student political activity and recommended that the university drop all charges againat anyone accused of rules violations before the strike began. Three thousand students had been waiting quietly outside Wheeler Hall, straining to hear the debate on the public address system. When the faculty filed out, they cheered. An FSM handbill appearing soon after proclaimed: "Happiness Is an Academic Senate Meeting!"[19]

The fight was almost over. Though composed of conservative lawyers and businessmen, the regents in essence accepted the faculty proposal on December 18 and the campus quieted. On January 2, as students were streaming back from Christmas vacation, the regents fired Berkeley Chancellor Edward Strong, Dean Towles's superior, and replaced him with the more permissive Martin Meyerson, dean of the College of Environmental

Design. Meyerson immediately issued a new set of advocacy and speech rules that gave the FSM virtually everything it wanted. On January 4, the FSM held its first legal rally on the steps of Sproul.

In a strict sense the Free Speech Movement was over. The FSM Steering Committee lingered on for some months longer, but its essential political work was done. Radicals had won their campaign to turn the Berkeley campus into a recruiting ground and staging area for political activities in the society outside. In the years to come, this privilege would be used to the hilt by an amazing spectrum of Bay Area advocates, activitists, militants, rebels, utopians, mavericks, crazies, and cranks.

Its effects became apparent almost immediately in the curious "Filthy Speech" episode. By now, besides its political dissenters, Berkeley also harbored a community of cultural rebels, young men and women who were stretching the limits of the older bohemia by experiments with lysergic acid diethylamide, LSD. In the next two years Berkeley's Telegraph Avenue environs and the Haight-Ashbury district in neighboring San Francisco would attract thousands of young people from mid-America to the new "hippie" scene. It was not a local rebel, however, but New Yorker John Thomson, who created the new incident when, on March 3, he stationed himself on the steps of the student union with a sign bearing a single vivid word: Fuck. When a student wag asked him what part of speech he meant, he added an exclamation mark. Soon after, Thomson was arrested for outraging public decency.

Today the incident seems trivial. Yet the Thomson episode seriously tarnished the image of the FSM. The "counterculture" was still a fresh phenomenon, and most FSM leaders understood Marx better than Freud. Could obscenity really be a free speech issue? Their ambivalence marked a seam that, though papered over at times, would always exist between the political left and the counterculture.

Though dubious, the FSM sent a delegation the following day to ask Meyerson to have the charges dropped. The chancellor refused to act, and the FSM leaders held an "obscenity" rally on the student union steps where the incident was treated as something of a joke. A student read portions of D. H. Lawrence's banned erotic classic, *Lady Chatterley's Lover;* the chairman of the campus Conservative Club revealed he had ordered for distribution a thousand FUCK COMMUNISM signs. Several students were arrested for using obscene language. The FSM's pro-Thomson effort, however feeble, placed it on the defensive. People began to call the latest protest the Filthy Speech Movement, a label that seemed to trivialize the events of the previous months. Many of the FSM's faculty supporters defected. Mark Schorer, of the Berkeley English department, denounced the defenders of Thomson as childish. The latest FSM cause, he said, was in "the panty raid, booze, and sex division of protests."[20]

In late April Meyerson dismissed one FSMer from the university for obscenity and suspended three others. At a noon rally that day Savio declared that the "honeymoon with Marty" was over. Yet the campus did not rise at his urging. A few days later the faculty endorsed Meyerson's actions, and when student elections were held the following week, SLATE and other pro-FSM tickets did poorly. In a matter of days Savio himself resigned from the FSM, and on April 29 FSM announced that it would become the Free Student Union (FSU), committed to defending student causes in general. By April 30, two thousand students, the *Daily California* reported, had joined FSU. But nothing happened; the new organization sank without a trace.

By June 1, with the campus settling into its summer torpor, FSM was gone.

Despite the final diminuendo, the Free Speech Movement at Berkeley accelerated SDS's retreat from the slums and return to the campus. Surely no one could now doubt that students were a powerful force for change. Writing in *Studies on the Left*, Larry Spence noted that Berkeley had disproved "the vulgar Marxist belief . . . that men must be hungry or unemployed or discriminated against to participate in radical political action. . . . Men must be *conscious*, not hungry to attempt the reconstruction of society." The Berkeley revolt had demonstrated, he wrote, "that such a radical consciousness can be created by means of successful acts of social dislocation. . . ."[21]

Though SDS's small Berkeley chapter had not taken a prominent part in the rousing events of the fall and winter, the FSM
captured the attention of SDSers around the country and confirmed their vision of students creating a "revolution for themselves." As one anonymous SDSer noted in December 1964, "The
revolution may come from the universities after all if Berkeley is
any indication."[22]

But now another distraction from the goal of transforming
American society intruded: the Vietnam War.

During the 1964 presidential election SDS had expressed its
ambivalent support of Johnson over the trigger-happy Barry
Goldwater with slogans like Part of the Way with LBJ and
Johnson with Open Eyes.[23] Within months this attitude changed.
Once president in his own right, Johnson became as bellicose as
his opponent. In February 1965 he ordered the massive bombing
of North Vietnam and soon after dispatched the first American
combat troops to Southeast Asia. By early 1965 he had become
the left's prime villain.

SDS opposed the Vietnam War from the outset. Some of SDS's
founding members had belonged to TOCSIN, an antiwar organization at Harvard. Others came from the Student Peace Union
(SPU), an undergraduate organization that endorsed nuclear
disarmament and an early end to nuclear testing. Among SDS's
early programs was the Peace Research and Education Project,
headed by Richard Flacks, a graduate student in sociology at the
University of Michigan, heir to a family left tradition. In October
1963, TOCSIN's former head, the tall and owlish Todd Gitlin,
like Stokely Carmichael a Bronx High School of Science graduate,
organized a joint SDS-SPU peace and disarmament demonstration in Washington. The postwar peace movement was in the
doldrums in 1963, and the media noticed the event only because President Kennedy took pity on the shivering picketers
outside the White House and ordered hot coffee sent out to
them.

SDS continued for a while to be ahead of the pack. In
December 1964, still months before the American bombing
attacks, SDS decided to protest the growing U.S. presence in

Vietnam by another Washington march. Planning for the April demonstration lagged at first. Flacks, Gitlin, and other peace people notwithstanding, many SDSers were not interested in foreign policy. The "bomb" was real enough, but the rest was too abstract, too remote from American life. Vietnam itself seemed too narrow an issue, one that could easily evaporate if in the end the United States proved flexible. It would be a mistake, many felt, for SDS to become a "single issue organization," to put all its chips on the Vietnam number.

The February bombings abruptly changed the picture. SDS's proposal was carried along in the flood of campus outrage that produced the sweeping campus teach-ins and the new crop of antiwar ad hoc committees, and on April 17 there were twenty thousand protesters on hand in the capital, twice the number expected.

The Washington march put SDS on the map. *The New York Times* gave the story three columns and an eighty-point head on the front page. The *Times* quoted Paul Booth, a young Swarthmorean, on SDS's idealistic goals and purposes. "We are working on domestic problems. . . . We feel passionately and angrily about things in America, and we feel that a war in Asia will destroy what we're trying to do here."[24] Students everywhere took notice, and in the fall when classes resumed hundreds approached the local SDS representative and signed up. By the end of the 1965 school year SDS counted eighty chapters and a total dues-paying enrollment of about two thousand. Many more "unsigned members" were soon turning to SDS as a rallying point for campus antiwar action.

SDS's newfound celebrity did not improve relations with the parent LID. Ever since the Port Huron Statement the more-conservative League elders had been suspicious of their offspring. Port Huron had been insufficiently anti-Communist, they felt, and they had summoned Hayden and Haber to headquarters to scold them about their "United Frontism." The two student leaders had been properly contrite, and this early breach was quickly closed. But SDS's anti-Vietnam position now upset the LID members who prized their ties with the Johnson administration and the nation's cold-warrior trade union leaders.

Relations between juniors and seniors reached a crisis point after SDS dropped its Communist exclusion policy at its June 1965 convention held at Kewadin, a small resort town in northern Michigan. A number of Kewadin delegates, aware of the aggressive new Marxist-Leninist youth groups, had objected to dropping the constitutional clause excluding Communists. "If I'd wanted to [work with Stalinists], I'd have joined the Du Bois Clubs," one exclaimed.[25] But the resolution won the support of the younger members who, even more than the veterans, saw anti-communism at a musty survival of the bad old McCarthy days, and it passed handily.

Both the LID and SDS had a point. The league and other democratic left groups certainly exaggerated the Communist party menace at home. But, at the same time, SDS's anti-anti-communism was naive. The Marxist-Leninist left had noted the upsurge of insurgency among the young and was preparing to take advantage of it by its traditional infiltration and takeover tactics. Within the student movement, Old Left would soon confront New Left, and in the struggle that followed SDS would be destroyed.

The Marxists' new youth drive produced two separate student groups, both organized by the offspring of Old Leftists. The Du Bois Clubs, named after the prominent black Communist, W. E. B. Du Bois, was the offshoot of the CPUSA, Moscow's American satellite and a member of the Kremlin-oriented world Communist movement. One of its founders was Bettina Aptheker, an FSM activist and the daughter of the Marxist historian, Herbert Aptheker. The Progressive Labor (PL) party was a Maoist group that supported the policies of the People's Republic of China. Its intellectual positions were even more dogmatic and its attitudes more anti-American than those of the CPUSA. Fred Jerome, one of its organizers, was the son of Communist party intellectual V. J. Jerome.

Both groups, but especially PL, were more conservative than the mainstream SDS in matters of dress, taste, and personal style. SDSers wore jeans and sandals; the SDS women wore their hair long; many of the men sported beards. Mainstream SDS mores were not sharply different from those of the emerging counterculture: relaxed sex, humor, communalism, a little pot, rock music. PL outlawed beards and marijuana and ordered couples living together to get married. PLers wore jackets and ties and often looked—and acted—like junior executives. The "revolution," they insisted, must be taken seriously. PL was the more aggressive of the two Marxist organizations and the graver threat to SDS's integrity.

The critical difference between Old Left and New Left, however, was not style, but ideology. At its best, and in its prime, mainstream SDS was undogmatic. It did have a central vision—of students, intellectuals, and the professional middle class leading a new kind of revolution against conformity, rigidity, powerlessness, and repression. But this was not sharply defined, and SDS was not intolerant of conflicting ideas or their disseminators.

To both the Du Bois Clubs and Progressive Labor, the material relations of life were pivotal to human history, and class struggle was the chief mechanism of mankind's progress to ever higher stages. Acting through a "vanguard party," students might help raise the proletariat's collective consciousness. But students, the enlightened bourgeoisie, and the professional classes could play only an adjunct role to the class-conscious workers.

PLers and Du Bois Club members had infiltrated SDS even before it rescinded its exclusion clause. After Kewadin they joined SDS en masse and PL, especially, soon became a key SDS faction.

By the fall of 1965, the tensions between the LID and SDS over the exclusion issue had become intolerable. Paul Feldman of the LID Board of Directors accused SDS of "agnosticism" on communism and failing "to judge the Communist side in the war by the same standards applied to the American role." He wondered if SDS had any rightful place in the LID, an organization "in principled opposition to Communism and all other forms of totalitarianism."[26]

In the past the LID's contribution of $3,600 to SDS's annual expenses had been indispensable. By the fall of 1965, SDS had become sufficiently famous, or notorious, to have its own source of funds, and in October the two groups decided to go their own ways. Soon after, SDS abandoned its New York office and moved its headquarters to West Madison Street in Chicago.

*   *   *

The next two years represent the second generation in SDS's short, incandescent life. The transition was marked by both a change of personnel and a shift in tactics and goals.

By the time of the June 1965 Kewadin convention, the original SDS leadership had begun to drift away from day-to-day management of office affairs. Finished with college courses and degrees, the veterans found it difficult to justify staying active in campus politics. Some like Hayden, Gitlin, and Oberlin graduate Paul Potter, joined ERAP community action projects; others like Haber, Booth, and Richard Magidoff, an Ann Arbor VOICE founder, drifted into the Radical Education Project (REP) or went off to the new radical think tank, the Institute for Policy Studies, where they could speculate about the future of America. A "new breed," attracted to SDS by the antiwar movement and the growing disenchantment with the liberal consensus, soon took command.

The new leaders came from a different division of America. They attended less prestigious schools, were more Protestant than their predecessors, less learned in left lore and left history, and more often from conservative families. They came from the all-American heartland, not from the alien, outward-looking coasts. Their journey to the left had been much harder than for the Old Guard. In Texas, Jeff Shero later recalled, "To join SDS meant breaking with your family, it meant being cut off. . . . If you were from Texas, in SDS, you were a bad motherfucker, you couldn't go home for Christmas. Your mother didn't say, 'Oh, isn't that nice, you're involved. We supported the republicans in the Spanish Civil War, and now you're in SDS and I'm glad to see you're socially concerned.' In most of those places it meant, '*You Goddamn Communist.*' "[27] Geography would provide their name; they would be called—imprecisely—the Prairie Power faction.

The new breed, with the enthusiasm of fresh converts, were more anarchistic than their predecessors. But they were not a mob of shoot-'em-up cowboys. Prairie Power leaders Greg Calvert and Carl Davidson were intellectuals who sensed the need for a theory of social change to fit the circumstances of modern

American life. Both young men were from working-class backgrounds and grew up in small towns, Davidson in Pennsylvania, Calvert in the Pacific Northwest. But they had better-than-average educations. A large man with a Pancho Villa mustache, Davidson had been a philosophy major at Pennsylvania State University; Calvert, middle-sized and rotund, had finished most of a Ph.D. in French history at Cornell University and at the time he joined SDS was a history instructor at Iowa State College.

Both valued the original insight of SDS that a modern, affluent society could not count on the working class for revolutionary change; only the ethical, aesthetic, and psychological discontents of the professional and middle classes could fuel a movement for fundamental social change. If anything, they carried this idea theoretically further than their predecessors.

Davidson's formulation of the middle-class revolution concept, "student power," was the more instinctive, less abstract, of the two. At SDS's Clear Lake, Iowa, national convention in August 1966 he pointed out how completely capitalist America relied on the universities. They produced society's business elite, its legal defenders, its propagandists, its apologists, its protectors. What if students organized and refused to cooperate with the system, refused to play these roles? "We might then have a fighting chance to change that system."[28] Davidson's formula for converting passive young men and women into committed rebels was for student militants to organize and demand control over grading, parietal rules, curriculums, and the like. These matters need not be taken seriously in themselves. The ultimate purpose of the campus agitation was to raise consciousness, not to reform university practices. Davidson's "Toward a Student Syndicalist Movement" was presented as a position paper to the SDS annual convention at Clear Lake, where its clarity and directness made a powerful impression.

In early 1967 SDS discovered the French neo-Marxists, a circle of left intellectuals who sought to adapt Marxist theory to two obviously disquieting facts of late-capitalist society: the eclipse of the proletariat by the technical-professional classes, and the increase and spread of material abundance. To "save the appearances" of the traditional Marxist formulas of working-class leadership and increasing misery under capitalism, they posited a "New Working Class" of academics, engineers, social planners, scientists, and salaried professionals. Though not impoverished, the "new workers" were powerless to make decisions and their impotence created deep frustration. Capitalist society paid them off with the modern bread-and-circuses of mass consumption, but they were alienated and hence a potential revolutionary force. Davidson quickly added this argument to his previous student-power idea. The university uprising was nothing less than "the revolt of the trainees of the new working class against the alienated and oppressive conditions of production and consumption within corporate capitalism."[29]

During the next few months, the New Working Class theory was further refined by a group of SDSers from New York's New School. In early 1967 these young men—Bob Gottlieb, David Gilbert, and Jerry Tenney—presented a paper to a REP-sponsored Princeton conference that identified students as "the structurally relevant and necessary components of the productive processes of modern capitalism." If they could be kept from being coopted, their sense of frustration would give them "an immediate stake in radical change."[30] Greg Calvert heard the Gottlieb–Gilbert–Tenney "Port Authority Statement"—a jocular play on Port Huron and the New York City bus terminal—and it struck him with the force of revelation. Staying up most of the night, he revised his own talk to include the Gottlieb–Gilbert–Tenney insights.

The following day he presented what would be the most complete formulation of the New Working Class idea. Calvert posed the question of why people became revolutionaries and concluded that it was out of inner, personal need, not sympathy for anyone else. Liberal reformers were moved by guilt to fight someone else's battles. True revolutionaries fought their own. This principle clearly justified the black militants' expulsion of whites from the civil rights movement. But did middle-class whites themselves have any valid motives for revolution?

Calvert took issue with orthodox Marxists who insisted that revolutionary mass movements were "built out of a drive for the acquisition of more material goods." No, revolutions were

"freedom struggles" created by the perception of a chasm between human potential and human reality. At times, and in
certain places, they might well be struggles for material abundance. But when material abundance had been achieved, as in the
modern industrial West, "the drive for freedom will rest on
different perceptions and will set different goals."

Calvert was trying to address a central dilemma for the
mainstream New Left: that a large proportion of the middle class
were gratified with material abundance and pleased with their
lives. Without question people who had reached the years of
discretion during the calamitous 1930s and early 1940s, reveled in
the postwar suburban house, the color TV, the family car; these
were unexpected bonanzas and they yearned for no meaning
beyond them. But this was a "false consciousness." Middle-class
Americans were not really masters of their fate. The members of
the New Working Class merely occupied slots within "the same
exploitive system" as the old working class. Calvert went on to
second the views of Davidson and Gottlieb that the universities
were the crucibles of the New Working Class and concluded with
the observation that "white Americans as well as black Americans
are beginning to recognize their common oppression and are
raising their demands for freedom which can be the basis of a
movement which could revolutionize America."[31]

Berkeley had demonstrated that students were powerful when
they united to defy authority. But the Free Speech Movement had
limited civil liberties goals. Student power and the New Working
Class gave campus confrontation more ambitious objectives. The
universities were factories where radicals—or at least white radicals—were manufactured. Campus issues were inherently trivial,
but they could be made into effective insurrectionary tools. By
presenting university officials with demands they could not meet,
the authorities could be forced into repressive missteps. In this
way, people could be made to see the "naked face of power"
behind the mask of benevolence. Once enlightened, they could be
enlisted in the case of revolution. In the course of their university
experience, young men and women would begin what the radical

German student leader Rudi Dutschke called "the long march through the institutions" that would lead eventually to capitalism's overthrow.

This position seemed cynical and dishonest to the unsympathetic. At the end of the turning-point year, John Searle of Berkeley's philosophy department, in a satiric piece for *The New York Times Magazine*, noted that "any old issue would do" for student militants so long as it raised a "Sacred Topic," one that touched some fundamental principle that the university administration could not yield. The Sacred Topic would then be the occasion for forcing a confrontation that would radicalize the campus.[32] To the militants, however, universities were pivotal institutions of the capitalist state, serving that state's exploitative purposes and recruiting and training the servants of power. Targeting them for disruption seemed a legitimate exercise of revolutionary tactics.

The growing disenchantment with the universities followed the rising trajectory of antiwar feeling. In 1964–65 students knew little of the universities' involvement in military research, and what they knew did not seem especially deplorable. Then, as Vietnam moved center stage, their membership in weapons development and counterinsurgency consortiums; their permission for napalm manufacturer Dow Chemical, the CIA, and the military services to use campus facilities for recruiting; and their willingness to provide the Selective Service System with class ranking and examination results to determine draft deferments— all came to seem sinister.

Campus rage at the Vietnam War dragged SDS into the antiwar movement willy-nilly. Students were indifferent to the Chicago leaders' fears of single-issue advocacy and joined SDS to express their antiwar feelings. But SDS was not the only student antiwar group. By 1967 campus anti-Vietnam activists could join the Resistance and the Student Mobilization Committee, groups that opposed the war without all the Hamlet-like dithering of SDS. On many campuses SDS found it either had to take a more active antiwar role or lose out to the competition.

SDS soon found itself cooperating with the other antiwar organizations. SDSers made up the "Armies of the Night" shock troops, who broke through the flailing clubs and tear gas of the paratroopers at the October 1967 Pentagon demonstration and poured onto the lawn in front of the "Warfare State" national headquarters. That same month SDS provided bodies for the Dow Chemical Company protest at the University of Wisconsin and for the massive demonstration to stop military inductions at the Oakland army center. At the very end of the year, the SDS National Council finally announced an official change of policy. In the spring SDS would sponsor ten days of antiwar activity that would zero in on "financial and corporate industrial targets."[33] The campaign would nail the Vietnam War as an integral part of American capitalist imperialism, not the unfortunate aberration the liberals said it was.

The National Council resolution was a clue to forces that were straining the very existence of SDS. The New Working Class theory was Marxist, or neo-Marxist, but not rigidly or uncompromisingly. It avoided the elitism that assigned the discontents of an alienated bourgeoisie to the proletariat. It retained the sense that oppression was not merely economic deprivation, but cultural and psychological as well. It was not weighted down with a century of struggle over dogma and definitions and entangled in battles over obscure theoretical fine points. But equating the Vietnam War with imperialism was to accept an orthodox Leninist view of capitalism as in its last desperate years. Despite twenty years of sustained Western economic growth and prosperity, SDSers were now supposed to believe that capitalism was in its death throes, its "final stage." It was as if the experience of the whole postwar era had been erased from memory.

In any movement of the young, creeds, like "generations," follow in rapid-fire succession. The New Working Class analysis lasted scarcely two years as a quasi-official SDS position. As early as the fall of 1967, Davidson, one of its fathers, had begun to backtrack. In a September issue of *New Left Notes* he called the idea that students were oppressed "bullshit," and claimed that they were "being trained to be the oppressors and the underlings of oppressors."[34] Calvert and Gottlieb kept the faith, but their voices came to seem more and more isolated.

The New Working Class theory in part fell victim to the very middle-class guilt it was supposed to avoid. SDSers were especially sensitive to the claims of blacks and other Third World people that they, and they alone, felt the full force of oppression and that only they could make the revolution. Davidson noted the "arrogance of it all" when white students manned the draft resistance tables in the student union building. "We organize students against the draft when the army is made up of young men who are poor, black, Spanish American, hillbillies, or working class. Everyone except students."[35]

It was also a casualty of the bloated apocalyptic rhetoric that marked the decade's end. How could alienated social workers, engineers, and computer programmers compete for media and movement attention with dudes wearing Afros or Pancho Villa mustaches and screaming "burn it down," "get the honkie," and "revolution now"? By the beginning of 1968, as we have seen, a note of nihilism, despair, and rage—some sincere, some self-dramatization—had diffused through the civil rights movement. These were heady attitudes that thrust their professors to the head of the revolutionary line. SDS soon found that it must either join the race or be left behind.

SDS's encounter with Progressive Labor was another part of the retreat from the middle class. By the summer of 1966, PL's presence began to gall, with many mainstream members beginning to resent the "Old Lefty phrase mongering" that had settled over all discussion. At the Clear Lake national convention, John Maher, a Boston SDSer from a rich Houston family, proposed that PLers and Du Bois Clubbers be compelled publicly to identify themselves so that other members could evaluate their positions. His opponents accused Maher of red-baiting and defeated his resolution.

PL's challenge to SDS intensified in late 1967 when the Red Chinese party line, following a shift in Beijing's foreign policy position, decreed that Ho Chi Minh and the North Vietnamese were Soviet puppets. The attack on Ho, hitherto the wise, avuncular sage and tribune of the people, caused large defections from PL's ranks, especially among adults. To offset their losses PL leaders redoubled their efforts to infiltrate SDS chapters. In late May they began to advertise a summer "work-in" scheme in various SDS forums. Students would get jobs in factories during their summer vacations. "To be with, to move, and move with American workers we've got to work with them," a PL article in *New Left Notes* announced.[36] The "worker-student alliance" expressed PL's position that factory workers would make the revolution. But the work-in scheme contained a hidden clause: the experience would make new recruits for PL's views within SDS.

The summer work-in proved a dud. Not only had it been advertised too late, but few students found the idea of propagandizing among factory workers congenial. Yet PL never abandoned the idea of a worker-student alliance and in various forms would use it to batter at the students-first emphasis of the second-generation SDS leadership.

PL was never a very large group. At the end of 1967 its total membership was probably under a thousand. Yet what it lacked in numbers, it made up in energy and dogmatic persistence. Jeff Shero, one of the Prairie Power leaders, described the effect of the PL presence on SDS deliberations and discussions at this time:

They'd raise questions that'd take up everybody's time, their theoretical Marxist questions . . . and you had to deal with it, and it skewered all debate—even if like eighty percent of the people thought that it was nuts. . . .

PL had a comprehensive ideological structure with which they could interpret the world, and at any time on any subject they could give a classic Marxist analysis of what the problem was and rally their solid support behind that. And then you'd have the other people who were trying to debate and discover what America was all about, the American system and how it worked, but were uncertain and needed to talk out things, and had a lot of ambiguity. But there was no way to organize ambiguity and searching against a classic Marxist analysis. They had an ideological tradition—and it was almost impossible to solidify a counteranalysis to that.[37]

Shero's attitude was shared by many mainstream SDSers: PL was aggressive and disruptive. But these very qualities attracted others, and where PL did not beguile, it insinuated. Once attracted to its tough posture, recruits were seduced by its dogmas. Before long SDS leaders found themselves competing with PL and the other, smaller groups, to fall in with Marx and Lenin.

As 1968 approached, the problem of what to do about SDS alumni became more urgent. More and more of the original SDS membership were finishing their B.A.'s or leaving school and yet wanted to continue to work as radicals. How could such people retain a radical vocation? Where could they find young men and women of like mind?

One option for SDS alumni was reform electoral politics. The idea for a left-liberal coalition to end the Vietnam War and to strengthen the social reform agenda originated with the California Democratic Council, a left wing of the state Democtratic party increasingly alienated from LBJ by the war. In early 1966 the council and a group of like-minded easterners established the National Conference on the New Politics. Though SDS officially refused to endorse the New Politics conference, Paul Booth, Lee Webb, and Arthur Waskow were prominent early members and organizers. All three had been early SDS leaders, Booth at Swarthmore, Webb at Boston University, and Waskow, slightly older and a former legislative assistant to Wisconsin Democratic Congressman Robert Kastenmeier, an "at-larger."

In 1966 the New Politics conference supported longtime Berkeley activist Robert Scheer in his primary campaign against the incumbent Democrat, Congressman Jeffrey Cohelan, a liberal hawk, in the East Bay district of northern California. Scheer lost, but the New Politics inpulse grew stronger as the 1968 presidential campaign approached.

The effort to create a left electoral alternative to Johnson and the Democrats came apart in the late summer of 1967 at the New Politics convention in Chicago, a convocation of liberals, radicals, mavericks, naysayers, Johnson-haters, peace advocates, civil rights activists, Black Power nationalists, and everyone else who believed American society had not lived up to its promise of peace and equality.

Two days into the speeches and workshops, the black militants dropped a bombshell. The convention must allot blacks 50 percent of all committee representation, endorse the political self-determination of all black people, extend "total and unquestionable support" to all wars of national liberation including that of the Vietcong, support black control of social, economic, and political institutions in black communities, and provide financial reparations "for the historic physical, sexual, mental, and economic exploitation of black people. . . ." Two further demands were even more humiliating than these: the convention must endorse on trust the resolutions of the recent Newark Black Power conference even though no one had read them, and it must condemn the "imperialist Zionist war." If this manifesto was not accepted by 1:00 P.M., CORE national director Floyd McKissick warned, the black delegates would pull out.[38]

Consternation! But also some twisted pleasure. The ultimatum provides an illuminating glimpse of the left-liberal mind-set during these last years of the decade. The convention could not approve such a platform without destroying all hope of a left-liberal coalition. Yet it did. Harvard professor Martin Peretz, one of SDS's largest benefactors, and other Jewish delegates stormed out. Several other white delegates denounced the crude manipulation. But for every one who resented the Black Power assault, another enjoyed the abasement. As Bertram Garskoff of the Ann Arbor Citizens for Peace chortled, blacks *were* the movement. "We are just a little tail on the very end of a very powerful black panther. And I want to be on that tail if they'll have me."[39]

In the end the convention failed to endorse a new party or recommend candidates for 1968 and settled for a vague promise to work in the neighborhoods for peace and social justice. In mid-1968 the New Politics conference simply disbanded. Though the left would field a presidential ticket in 1968 under the label Peace and Freedom party, it would be a feeble effort more symbolic than serious.

The alumni problem also inspired more direct solutions. In 1966 at its Clear Lake convention, SDS considered the issue of an "adult" New Left organization without taking action. Meanwhile, here and there small clusters of radical professionals began to coalesce spontaneously, creating what they were soon calling Movement for a Democratic Society.

In July 1967 the alumni issue drew 250 delegates to a conference at Ann Arbor sponsored by SDS's Radical Education Project. Many who came were plagued by ambivalence and revealed it in the speeches and seminars that marked the occasion. Some saw no way that radicals could practice as professionals in America. Social work was irretrievably committed to social control, declared a Columbia-trained professional. "If you can afford to be a full time revolutionary, then fight for socialism elsewhere." The American legal system was "the rationalization of force, coercion, and murder and the means by which obedience is extracted" from the masses, said Ken Cloke of the National Lawyers Guild. It was only a fig leaf for the power structure.[40]

Even those delegates who condoned traditional careers for radicals warned against the wrong priorities. Radicals could practice a profession, declared Barbara and Al Haber, but they must never put "the code of ethics and responsibility of their professions" before the cause. They "should have no 'ethical' scruples about providing 'cover' to movement people, using politics as a criterion in giving recommendations, references, jobs." They must "not respect the confidentiality of documents, meetings, privileged information, etc., if their contents would be valuable to the movement." This course, they agreed, presented "moral problems," but conscience could be assuaged if radical professionals were candid about their "politics and values."[41]

The Radicals in the Professions Conference produced little more than a newsletter of radical alumni activities. But other efforts bore riper fruit. In 1968 "Port Authority" author Bob Gottlieb and some friends helped organize Movement for a Democratic Society chapters among teachers, social workers, programmers, writers, and several other professional groups in New York. That March, in Chicago, radical young college teachers and graduate students established the New University Conference, (NUC), the most substantial result of the alumni impulse.

The debate at NUC's founding convention highlighted the radical intellectuals' ambivalence toward universities and academic careers. Universities had enormous power to coopt radicals, the historian Staughton Lynd warned. "Whatever our social origins," he noted, "the university is a marvelously effective instrument for making us middle-class men." Richard Flacks, now a University of Chicago sociology instructor, countered with a version of the New Working Class idea. "Despite itself," he announced, "the university and the educated middle class have been a major source for whatever alternatives to capitalist values have persisted in this society." Radicals must not abandon the universities but turn them "into a major arena of struggle against imperialism, against militarism, against capitalist culture and ideology, and for the creation of an alternative culture and ideology, and a new class to carry that alternative into the rest of society."[42]

The disagreements did not keep the Chicago convention from creating a permanent body combining the functions of a trade union, radical intellectual center and support group, and left gadfly within higher education. The NUC story belongs properly to the years from 1969 on, but in 1968 it made its presence dramatically known at the Modern Language Association (MLA) meeting in New York during the December holidays.

The annual academic association meetings in America are held in large downtown hotels of major cities, preferably ones with good restaurants, luxury shopping, and some night life. People come for the urban flesh pots, for the publishers' cocktail parties, for the chance to see old friends, to interview or be interviewed for jobs, to preen over their new books, and— occasionally—for intellectual exchange. This year the MLA would be forced to debate a political agenda, as well. The NUC planned to announce the radical presence in the MLA and had mailed out hundreds of handbills and placed a notice in *The New York Review of Books* promising "to stir things up. . . ."[43]

The radicals were a distinct minority within the association, but circumstances would play into their hands. The convention was meeting in a national atmosphere charged with political alarm. The previous August, at the Chicago Democratic convention, student radicals and peace advocates had been savagely beaten by Mayor Daley's police. Just two months before, Richard

Nixon, the voice of reaction, had been elected president. To many academics, especially the younger ones, *Götterdämmerung* seemed near.

The radicals established their advantage on the opening day of the meeting when Americana Hotel security guards asked three MLA activists led by Louis Kampf of MIT to remove five hand-lettered posters they had affixed to the white stone pillars at the hotel's entrance. The placards, they said, defaced hotel property. The signs summarized the radicals' agenda: literature must be "liberated" from its current bourgeois spirit, the MLA must be made revelant, and the association must cancel its arrangement to meet next year in Mayor Daley's repressive Chicago. Kampf was particularly solicitous of one that read: THE TIGERS OF WRATH ARE WISER THAN THE HORSES OF DESTRUCTION, an opaque quotation from William Blake that seemed to convey the activists' contempt for the MLA's establishment types. The professors refused to comply with the demands, and in the scuffle that followed they bested the security guards. The hotel management promptly called in the city police, who arrested the brawny trio.

News of the incident electrified the conventioneers. Even the moderates, reacting tribally, were outraged at the arrest of their fellow academics. That evening the insurgents called a protest meeting that drew eight hundred people, many of them angry middle-of-the-roaders. There members attacked the MLA as a reactionary body dominated by a privileged clique of senior professors and demanded that the charges against Kampf and his colleagues be dropped.

On Saturday the radical caucus held sessions on curriculum changes, racism, high school teaching, and the special professional concerns of graduate students and women, the MLA proletariat. At an NUC-sponsored session, Noam Chomsky, the radical linguistics theorist, denounced American policy in Vietnam. When the Chomsky meeting adjourned, the fiery Maoist, Bruce Franklin of Stanford University, led a sit-in in the Americana lobby to protest the Kampf arrest.

The radicals got their revenge on Sunday at the annual MLA business meeting. As usual, the association's slate of future officers had already been selected by a nominating committee. The NUCers would have none of this establishment–old-boy stuff and decided to challenge the official slate by offering Kampf's name for second vice president, the officer in charge of the next MLA convention program and the person who automatically received the presidental nomination the year after. No one expected the radical motion to carry, but MLA members were still angry and Kampf was swept to victory by a wave of sympathy. Following this success, the insurgents went on to pass resolutions condemning the Vietnam War, attacking the draft, supporting black nationalist writers Eldridge Cleaver and LeRoi Jones, and canceling the 1969 MLA meeting in Chicago. The whole thing was a radical blowout. As Florence Howe, one of the discipline's most dedicated militants, remarked after the convention, "From any point of view, NUC at the MLA was an incredible success."[44]

Nineteen sixty-eight witnessed two of the most spectacular campus revolts of the decade.

Despite all the media attention, the Free Speech Movement at Berkeley had not released a flood of imitative campus rebellions. The calm was brief. Nineteen sixty-seven would see an acceleration of university disruption. Then, during the 1967–68 academic year, political upheavals would rock almost three-quarters of all American campuses.

Many of the uprisings were spontaneous events, spawned by the interplay of late sixties' *Zeitgeist* and unpredictable local happenstance. But some were informed by the Calvert–Davidson student-power strategy to raise the revolutionary consciousness of undergraduates and to accelerate the revolutionary impulse through deliberate confrontation.

The student-power formula was probably never applied in pure form anywhere. Yet in 1968 it was possible to see its outlines in the major disruptions on both coasts, at Columbia University in New York and at San Francisco State College.

As 1968 began Columbia seemed an ideal target for radical revolt. The university was vulnerable by sixties' criteria. Though its best days were behind it, it was still rich and powerful and that alone made it worthy of attack. It was also locally unpopular. Like most universities during the decade, it was growing fast. Perched on a confined tract on Morningside Heights, with black Harlem immediately to the east, it had bought up neighborhood residential buildings and moved their tenants out to solve its own space problems and "improve the neighborhood." The evictees had protested, but fruitlessly. As 1968 began, Columbia seemed to many local people a harsh, self-serving landlord.

The university also had a black problem. By 1968 Columbia and other major universities had recruited small contingents of black and Third World students. Many of these young men and women felt overwhelmed and insecure and sought one another out for emotional and intellectual support. Self-segregation encouraged nationalist militancy and reinforced the view that the university was only another "honkie" institution, essentially alien and antagonistic. In 1964–65 the black students at Columbia had organized a Student Afro-American Society (SAS) that had 150 members during the opening of the 1968 spring semester. At first SAS had functioned as a cultural solidarity group. By early spring it had shifted with the times to political activism and had found an important issue in the university's relations with the Harlem community to the east, on the flats below Morningside Heights.

One of Columbia's highest priorities was a new building to replace its decrepit gymnasium. During the early 1960s, the city had granted it space to build the gym in Morningside Park, a steep strip of trees, boulders, and underbrush, entered only by the foolhardy or suicidal, that marked its physical separation from Harlem. In return for the right to build at the top edge of the park, the university agreed to devote part of the new facility to community use.

Had the gym been built when first proposed, this concession might have sufficed. By the late sixties, however, the Harlem community's new assertiveness demanded more. The university responded by agreeing to build a separate swimming pool in the new building for the "community," but still the militants balked. By early 1968 black activists were calling the gym an imperialist white intrusion into Harlem. As the spring semester began, SAS proclaimed that the gym symbolized Columbia's racism and indifference to the concerns of black Americans.

The university was vulnerable in other areas as well. Columbia was a member of the Institute for Defense Analysis (IDA), a consortium originally of five schools founded in 1956 to evaluate weapons and do other research for the Defense Department. Columbia had joined in 1959, and President Grayson Kirk became an IDA trustee. Radicals, predictably, would see the university's IDA membership as confirmation of its complicity with the American "war machine," a relationship also displayed in its willingness to allow on-campus recruiters for the armed services and for firms engaged in war work.

But the ingredients for trouble went beyond Columbia's misdeeds. The campus chapter of SDS was one of the most militant in the country. Organized in early 1968, it had first been rather moderate in its tactics, concentrating on matters directly associated with the Vietnam War—the draft, off-campus corporate and military service recruitment policies, and secret university military research. Through the early months of 1968 its "praxis-axis" leaders were Ted Kaptchuk, a thoughtful senior majoring in Eastern religions, Ted Gold, the bespectacled son of a New York doctor and a Teachers College professor of education, and Dave Gilbert of "Port Authority" fame. All three were cerebral types who accepted the New Working Class analysis and favored slow "base-building" for Columbia SDS through propaganda, dorm discussions, and other educational processes.

Pitted against the praxis-axis was the "action faction," or "the Kamikazes," as they sometimes called themselves. These were young men of a different breed. John Jacobs ("JJ") was a Columbia dropout who affected a "biker" personal style—duck-tail haircut, leather jacket, and gold chain; Tony Papert was a PL-affiliated premed transfer from Princeton; Mark Rudd was a swaggering junior from Maplewood, New Jersey, the son of a real estate agent who, though an army reserve officer, claimed to be delighted that "Mark has time to spend on . . . politics."[45] They and their followers scorned their opponents' timidity. Only through militant confrontation, Rudd believed, was the individual compelled to "commit himself to the struggle to change society as well as share the radical view of what is wrong with society."[46] Rudd was clearly committed to the student-power approach to larger ends. As he later admitted, "The essence of the matter is that we are out for social and political revolution, nothing else."[47]

Rudd was not a captivating young man. Arrogant, shambling, heavy-jawed, he went out of his way to be crude. He threw around "fuck" and its variations like an army drill sergeant. It was he who popularized the ghetto expression "Up Against the Wall, Mother-fucker" as an epithet against the authorities and the police. At one point, during a conference with some senior faculty, Rudd put his dirty feet on the table under their noses and told them that what they were saying was "bullshit."

Rudd later explained his nasty behavior as a tactic to undercut deference to faculty and administrators. But even his SDS associates considered him arrogant and self-serving. The April–May campus rebellion made Rudd a "movement heavy," and he was soon surrounded by an entourage of female groupies attracted by his sudden fame. He used his celebrity to his sexual advantage, and even his colleagues were soon calling him "Mark Studd" behind his back.[48]

Rudd came to Columbia in the fall of 1965 and joined SDS soon after the chapter was organized. He quickly became known as a hard-liner. During the 1967–68 winter break he visited Castro's Cuba, and when he returned to Columbia he was elected head of the SDS chapter, replacing Kaptchuk.

A week or two later an official of the New York Selective Service office came to campus to talk about the draft. The praxis-axis circle planned to attack him verbally. Rudd had other ideas. As the Selective Service representative rose to speak, Rudd shoved a lemon meringue pie in his face and ran from the room unrecognized in the confusion.

Rudd's next sally against the war makers and racists was an anti-IDA demonstration in March that led to the suspension of five SDS leaders. In April Rudd's credentials as a tough hombre were validated when he shouted during the solemn campus memorial ceremonies for Martin Luther King that the service was an "obscenity" and the "racist" Columbia administration was "committing a moral outrage against Dr. King's memory."[49]

The spark that finally detonated the campus started as a noon rally on Tuesday, April 23, at the Sundial, a bronze plaque embedded in College Walk between Low, the administration building, and Butler Library, which housed the main university book collection. SDS intended to protest the IDA affiliation, university racism, and the disciplinary action against the IDA demonstrators. It seemed indifferent to the gym issue. The protesters were to assemble at the Sundial and then, in defiance of the rules, enter Low, where they would announce their demands to the administration. If challenged, they would leave quietly.

Things turned out differently. By noon a hundred SDSers and four hundred supporters had gathered at the Sundial. Nearby were a thousand onlookers, students and some faculty, waiting to see what would happen when SDS invaded Low. There were also several hundred counterdemonstrators—many athletes, or jocks—carrying signs: SEND RUDD BACK TO CUBA, ORDER IS PEACE.

The rally began with Ted Gold's attack on the Kirk administration's disciplinary policy followed by a speech by Cicero Wilson, an intense black sophomore who was the newly elected president of the Student Afro-American Society. Until now, SAS had ignored SDS. In fact, it had engaged in little campus political activity of any sort. But it was beginning to stir, and the burly, heavy-featured Wilson now denounced the university's gym project and attacked Columbia's white liberals and radicals for failing to take racism seriously. Waving his fists in the air, he warned that if they did not act, they would "be responsible for a second civil war."[50] Wilson concluded by asking his listeners to support SDS's demand for an open hearing on the student suspensions.

At this point a message arrived from Vice-President David Truman offering to meet with the accused students. A pleasant-looking midwesterner with thinning gray hair, Truman had been a popular dean who made it a point to remember students' names, personalities, and problems. Although a busy man, his door, as they said, was always open. He and his colleagues knew about the plan to invade Low and also feared a clash between SDS and the conservative jocks and fraternity "Greeks." The note was intended to defuse the confrontation and make negotiation possible, but it confused Rudd and the other SDSers who now wavered, not knowing what to do. Suddenly, SDSer Tom Hurwitz, a red bandanna around his head, shouted: "Did we come here to talk or did we come here to go to Low?"[51] At that, a small crowd of SDSers advanced on the administration building. On the steps they collided with a platoon of counterdemonstrators and a scuffle broke out. The radicals then tried to enter the building by a side door, but the guards inside got to it first and after a shoving match with the students locked it securely.

A flustered SDS contingent, surrounded by the curious and skeptical, reassembled outside Low to consider what to do next. At this point pure chance set off a portentous chain of events. Suddenly someone screamed: "Gym site! Gym site!" At this signal a detachment of demonstrators chanting "Gym Crow must go"[52] took off for Morningside Park determined to have something to show—no one knew what—for the day's effort.

These events of April 23—in fact much of what took place during the whole week following—have the quality of improvisation. Certainly most of SDS's moves in late April and early May were ad-libbed in the heat of battle. But if the day-to-day tactics were extemporized, the action faction never lost sight of its larger goal: to create maximum disruption as a means to revolutionary ends.

At several points SDS made its aims overt. In a position paper composed early in the spring semester, Rudd had announced two targets for SDS: student "radicalization" and striking a blow at the U.S. government's war effort. The campaign would start with praxis-axis–type position papers, dorm canvassing, and petitions against the ROTC, but end with a "mass action" sit-in at Low in April followed by a general student strike.[53] Another early 1968 SDS document, "Proposal for a Spring Offensive Against Columbia—Racism," is a scenario for campus disruption that faithfully anticipated coming events. There would be a takeover of Low and Kirk's office in the building. Then "open struggle perhaps with city cops will develop. WE FIGHT! Community support, black students, lib[eral]s begin to come in."[54] Both schemes contain elements of whimsy and fantasy. Still, taken in conjunction with the student-power position and the action faction's proclivities, they suggest more contrivance in what followed than the militants and their partisans would admit.

Once arrived at Morningside Park, the SDS and Afro society members tore down sections of the wire fence that enclosed the gym site. The police rushed in to protect it, and in the fracas several people were hurt and a white student, Fred Wilson, was arrested and charged with felonious assault.

As more and more police arrived, the crowd retreated to the Sundial where they once again milled around indecisively until someone suggested that since Low was defended they should invade nearby Hamilton Hall, the main classroom and faculty office building for undergraduates at Columbia College. At Hamilton the demonstrators encountered Dean Henry Coleman and two other college administrators returning to their offices following lunch and told them their demands: drop the IDA, drop the gym, and drop the charges against the five SDS leaders and against Fred Wilson. He had no power to change the president's disciplinary procedures, and he certainly would not consider any proposals under duress, Coleman replied. Rudd was blunt: "I guess we're going to keep you here."[55] Coleman and his colleagues walked to the dean's office and locked the door. The battle for Morningside Heights had begun.

The ad-lib invasion of Hamilton Hall soon turned into an occupation. The students established a steering committee and drew up a set of six demands: (1) the university must cancel all pending disciplinary action against the SDS leaders and grant a general amnesty to all participants in the current demonstration; (2) it must rescind the ban on indoor demonstrations; (3) it must suspend gym construction at once; (4) it must resolve all future disciplinary actions in open hearings before students and faculty under standard courtroom due process rules; (5) it must get out of the IDA; and (6) it must use its good offices to get the charges against Fred Wilson dropped.

This was a sophisticated and hedonistic student generation. The protesters quickly phoned the newspapers, local radio stations, and the TV networks, and contacted their local allies in the city, bringing a swarm of white radicals, black militants, and reporters rushing to Hamilton. They brought in food, blankets, and guitars, and hung portrait posters on the pillars in the Hamilton lobby: Lenin and Che Guevara for the whites; Stokely Carmichael and Malcolm X for the blacks. Professor F. W. Dupee, of Columbia's English department, with the litterateur's yardstick of virtue, was impressed. "Compared to the radicals of the Thirties, so stodgy and uninventive, these youths seemed to unite the politics of a guerrilla chieftain with the aesthetic flair of a costumer and an interior decorator."[56]

Four buildings besides Hamilton—Low, Mathematics Hall, Fayerweather, and Architecture—would be occupied by radical students before the police were finally called in and the protesters forcibly removed. During these seven days, a half dozen groups maneuvered to sway the course of events and to shape the uprising to their own ends.

The white SDS radicals were frank about their goals: they hoped to precipitate a revolution in "Amerika."* Mark Rudd later noted that the only " 'good' function" the university served was "the creation and expansion of a revolutionary movement." Anything else, he insisted, was a "passive capitulation to reformism. . . ."[57] The mechanism of the revolutionary process was to be the student-power approach of Davidson and his colleagues. As Carolyn ("Rusti") Eisenberg, a radical history graduate student, wrote, "Clearly one of the main objectives of the Columbia action was the *radicalization of new students.*"[58]

Except for the frank revolutionary rhetoric, this was not new. Student-power, after all, was the logical extension of the middle-class student focus that had given birth to SDS. But the Columbia

---

* This Germanic spelling, increasingly common in radical polemics from 1968 on, was intended to convey the similarity between contemporary America and Nazi Germany.

uprising saw one of SDS's other early principles, participatory democracy, virtually abandoned. SDS functioned through the Columbia rebellion as a "vanguard." As Eisenberg noted, it tried throughout to "stay ahead of the movement. . . . Its task was to seize [the] initiative even during the crisis, thus setting the terms of conflict, to which others—allies as well as opponents—would have to respond."[59] Herself a member of the campuswide Strike Coordinating Committee formed after all five buildings were occupied, she attacked SDS for its domineering role. The coordinating committee was supposed to be a representative body but was really under the thumb of SDS, functioning as a "cadre."

The priorities of the black students in Hamilton were much more specific and immediate. Columbia must provide a more-comfortable environment for them. They also wanted to see the gym project abandoned. Well disciplined and tightly controlled by their leaders, they were suspicious of the anarchistic white radicals and resented, as blacks had in the early days of SNCC, their tendency to take charge. Early on Wednesday morning they told the SDS leaders: "We want to take a stand here. It would be better if you left and took your own building."[60]

Rudd and his colleagues on the steering committee were in no position to argue with SAS. By this time in sixties' insurgency, black militants had achieved a powerful moral hold over white radicals. Blacks clearly were the chief victims of America's injustice and oppression, and it was hard for middle-class white radicals to deny them anything. And there was another consideration. During the first hours at Hamilton, black delegations from nearby Harlem, including Muslims, Mau Maus, and other *enragés,* had turned up to show their "brothers" support. Rumors were soon circulating that they had brought guns. Though they talked tough, at this point at least, the white radicals had no actual experience with violence. As they caucused, they were afraid that a race war might soon break out at Hamilton with themselves caught in the cross fire. "It was fascinating," said a white student who attended the meeting, "here they were presenting this grandiose vision of revolution and a new world, while the blacks were downstairs scaring the shit out of everyone."[61] Choosing discretion over valor, at 5:00 A.M. a sleepy band of white Barnard and Columbia undergraduates stumbled out of Hamilton into the April dawn.

What to do now? It would be humiliating to give up. Some of the Hamilton occupiers had slipped away to catch up on badly needed sleep, but about two hundred remained. Their natural target was Low, the administration building, where the previous day they had been repulsed. This time, using a loose board as a battering ram, they smashed the glass doors and broke into the building. They were soon amusing themselves pecking away at President Kirk's office typewriters, drinking his sherry, and smoking his White Owl "President" cigars. The students ransacked Kirk's files and later photographed some papers concerned with the IDA that they distributed to the underground press. But they did little real physical damage. On Thursday city police came to remove a $450,000 Rembrandt and other works of art on the president's wall. The students did not object.

Wednesday was strategy day for the white radicals. The Low contingent analyzed, theorized, argued, and debated. SDS "heavies" held meetings in the offices of the college humor magazine, where the action faction and the praxis-axis wrangled bitterly until Rudd temporarily resigned in a huff as chapter president. Hour after hour: meet, meet, talk, talk, scheme, scheme. Intellectuals, even impetuous young ones, often make unconvincing revolutionaries.

That evening Avery Hall, home of the School of Architecture, was "liberated" by the socially conscious architecture students. On Thursday afternoon some SDSers forced their way into Fayerweather, the classroom and office building for the graduate school history and social science departments. Observing the takeover from a unique vantage was Mark Naison, taking his doctor's orals from a committee headed by Richard Hofstadter, Columbia's star intellectual historian. Through the din of angry voices, breaking furniture, and falling plaster, the committee continued to ply Naison with questions. They seemed "tickled pink," he reported, "at the prospect of keeping the institutional ritual alive amidst the surrounding chaos. . . . They regarded themselves," he concluded, "as the carriers of the light of civilization among the depredations of the strange new barbarians."[62]

A final occupation took place on Friday, the twenty-sixth, when raiding parties from Low and Fayerweather seized Mathematics Hall.

During the occupation, Hamilton remained a distinct sovereignty under black rule, but the four other buildings were governed jointly by the Strike Coordinating Committee, composed of elected representatives from each group. They also shared a bureaucracy of typists, telephone answerers, and mimeograph machine operators located at "Strike Central" in the "unliberated" dorm, Ferris Booth Hall. The addition of Fayerweather, Avery, and Mathematics Hall brought older students from the graduate and professional schools into the action. Though Columbia SDS was all-male like Columbia College itself, by the second or third day many women from Barnard and the graduate schools had joined the demonstration, creating a major problem with Booth's bathroom facilities. Times were indeed changing, and the radical women refused to tolerate any chauvinism from their male colleagues. When, on Thursday evening, the Fayerweather leaders issued a call for women to cook for the occupiers, a female Fayerweatherite made her outrage known in emphatic terms. "Liberated women do not cook," she shouted. "They are not cooks."[63]

During the occupation students moved freely back and forth between three of the buildings—Avery, Fayerweather, and Mathematics—and between these and the rest of the campus. An army of outsiders soon reinforced the original occupiers. The Columbia uprising was a news event of extraordinary resonance. Here was no disturbance at some isolated college town in the provinces. This was a revolt in the nation's media nerve center, and it brought the intellectual celebrities—Dwight Macdonald, Susan Sontag, Norman Mailer, Stephen Spender, and others—rushing to the campus from Greenwich Village and the Upper West Side to get the feel of revolution by mingling with the insurgents in their liberated buildings. It was not quite October 1917 at Moscow's Smolny Institute, perhaps, but it was the closest thing available.

The occupation also lured "Movement" celebrities. Tom Hayden suddenly materialized from Newark and took virtual command at Mathematics Hall. There he was joined by an East Village collection of "hippies, winos, drop-outs, [and] neighborhood people with a program of revolutionary politics and life style," who went by the euphonious name of "Motherfuckers."[64] At Hamilton, Rap Brown and Stokely Carmichael came to cheer and encourage the brothers. The campus swarmed with reporters and television crews delighted with such colorful, outrageous events in their own backyard.

Free building access was denied only at Low. Security guards left the students already there, but refused to allow anyone else to enter the building.

Life in the occupied buildings was a mixture of exhilaration and boredom. There were too many speeches, too many repetitive rap sessions. At Low, Tony Papert delivered lectures and conducted discussions of Marxism-Leninism. Many of the undogmatic found them dull. There were more amusing doings, too. In Fayerweather the students held a movement wedding, with the Reverend William Starr, a Protestant minister, officiating. The bride, dark-haired Andrea Burrow, carried a bouquet of roses and wore a tan mantilla, a heavy sweater, jeans, and white sneakers; the groom, Richard Egan, wore maroon jeans, a white, high-collared Nehru jacket, beads, and black boots. During the ceremony, Starr noted that the bride and groom wanted "to become one because of the experiences of the past few days." He concluded by pronouncing them "children of the new age." Andrea and Richard asked to be called "Mr. and Mrs. Fayerweather."[65]

Fayerweather students, by far the most relaxed and with it, also put on a show of flashing strobe lamps. There and at Mathematics Hall, a student Pied Piper with a tin whistle led exuberant snake dances through the buildings' rooms and corridors.

The Columbia insurgents, like the Berkeley free speechers four years before, found a new sense of community in their shared struggle that contrasted powerfully with the usual anomic mood of university life. "I was overwhelmed by the suddenness [with which] . . . I could function in a group," one student later told the social psychologist Robert Liebert. "It was the beginning

of a new vocabulary—'brother,' 'friend'—a vocabulary of camara-
derie, where people didn't talk before."[66] Another rebel told the
Cox Commission, which later investigated the Columbia uprising,
"here [in Fayerweather] was a single commune in which adult
hypocrisies did not apply any longer, where people shared and
shared alike. . . ."[67]

The new bonds could not cover up differences of ideology and
style, however. There was the rift between the Rudd–Jacobs
leaders, who aped the youth culture, talking dirty, swaggering,
and dressing like bikers or slum whites, and the Progressive Labor
apparatchiks like Papert, who wore jackets and ties, cut their hair,
and kept their language clean to avoid offending the adult
blue-collar proletariat. There was also a tension between liberals and radicals. Of the four "communes," as the buildings
were called, Mathematics and Low were the most radical.
Fayerweather, with a large proportion of older graduate students,
sheltered most of the liberals. It was also the most contentious
place, where fist fights erupted several times over ideology and
tactics. Fayerweatherites were the strongest critics of SDS's vanguard role.

Ranged against all the protesters was the self-designated
"Majority Coalition." In reality, like SDS and its active allies, it
represented only a sliver of Columbia opinion. Numbering about
two thousand, Majority Coalition members were more likely than
their opponents to be jocks, Greeks, and business and engineering
majors. They took authority seriously and issued a stream of
handbills and manifestos attacking the rebels' "tasteless, inconsiderate, and illegal manner" of conducting their protests.[68]

From Tuesday, April 24, through the following Monday,
university officials, New York City politicians and community
leaders, faculty coalitions, and student constituencies negotiated
to end the building occupations. Many feared campus violence.
The Majority Coalition, outraged at the interruption of classes
and what they considered SDS's truculence and arrogance,
threatened to storm the buildings and evict the occupiers by brute
force themselves. When radical sympathizers tried to throw food
and supplies to the occupiers of the quarantined Low, Majority
Coalition students batted the cans and packages down with sticks.

They also scuffled with black militants from Harlem who tried to enter Columbia buildings. Through the whole occupation liberal faculty and the administration had some reason to fear that Columbia would break out into a bloody student civil war if the strike continued.

During the week's occupation, the black students maintained an autonomous status and a separate policy, scarcely noticing the doings of the white left. The blacks held some special cards. Their backing from the black community made the white radicals' support seem feeble; almost every black New York Democratic politician showed up at Hamilton to express sympathy. Even more useful, a steady stream of menacing-looking Black Power nationalists visited the strikers. Their appearance on campus evoked visions of apocalypse. After the riots of the past three years, the possibility of the ghetto below the cliff swarming up to destroy Columbia was never far from anyone's mind. As Diana Trilling, wife of Columbia's famous literary critic, noted: "With Harlem on its borders, a measurable catastrophe might have become an unmeasurable disaster—the university might be over-run or burned down."[69]

Though they were happy to play on white fears, the Hamilton students themselves were not Black Power nihilists. Unlike the white radicals, only a small percentage were humanities majors; the rest were in the "practical fields" that promised a direct job at graduation. Columbia must drop the gym and recognize their special needs, they insisted. But they saw little reason to scuttle their chance to make it into the middle-class world by destroying the university. The poet Stephen Spender, one of the campus pilgrims during the week's occupation, concluded that the members of SAS acted "not as if they were black power fanatics who worked to destroy the university and then the society . . . , but as though they were a foreign power which had a cold but realistic relationship with another power—the university—in which each party, though they were enemies, understood that much might be gained by respecting the other's integrity."[70]

Dean Coleman was the first beneficiary of this measured response. When informed that the forcible detention of the dean could be considered kidnapping, the SAS leaders let him go.

Coleman and the other captive administrators in Hamilton walked free on Wednesday afternoon after twenty-six hours of incarceration.

Talks with the white radicals followed a more-convoluted course. Much of it was conducted through the faculty serving as an intermediary authority.

The Columbia faculty was liberal even for an Ivy League school. The campus had a handful of conservatives who detested the student leftists and supported the administration. Orest Ranum, a historian of seventeenth-century France, publicly denounced the uprising. The only Columbia faculty member to teach classes in academic robes à la Oxford, he became the symbol of the tory opposition. But the hard-line conservatives were neither numerous nor, except for Ranum, outspoken.

Each campus revolt of the sixties thrust the local left faculty into positions of prominence, and so it was at Columbia. A circle of younger professors, including Richard Greeman of the French department, Robert Zevin of Economics, Immanuel Wallerstein of Sociology; and Jeffrey Kaplow and Robert Fogelson of History, sympathized with the student occupiers and pleaded their case with Kirk and his colleagues. Though mostly junior, for a time they became the big names and power brokers on campus.

A majority of the Columbia faculty were neither radicals nor tories, but as good liberals they were essentially prostudent. Led by Alan Westin of the government department, a bespectacled New Yorker with a Ph.D. in political science and a law degree from Harvard, they spoke through the Ad Hoc Faculty Group (AHFG), organized on Wednesday at an extemporized meeting near *Alma Mater,* the allegoric statue in front of Low. The AHFG quickly adopted five resolutions: the Columbia board of trustees should immediately cease construction of the gym; the administration should delegate all disciplinary power to a tripartite committee of students, faculty, and deans; the students should evacuate all buildings, and if they did so the faculty would use their influence for a solution that included the preceding points even if it required boycotting classes until they were accepted; the faculty would physically interpose themselves between building occupiers and the police or other intruders; the faculty would resist attempts to expel any student for acts committed thus far. The liberals rejected only one of the students' six demands: the general amnesty in advance.

The next four days were a blur of faculty-student-administration meetings and discussions. Wallerstein, whose special field was modern Africa, served as the intermediary between AHFG and the black students in Hamilton, frequently climbing over barricades to get into the cordoned-off building. Westin and his colleagues met with Rudd and the other leaders of Strike Central and with Kirk, Truman, and other administrators. The AHFG also intervened between groups of angry students determined to teach the other side a lesson. It was an exhausting schedule for many. David Goodman, a young research assistant in the Latin American Institute, told a *Times* reporter, "I've had about 12 hours sleep in the past few days."[71]

The sticking point was the general amnesty. The student radicals refused to accept any penalty at all for their actions. Whether this was only militancy or a tactic to scuttle negotiations is not clear, but it prevented agreement. Administrators and moderate faculty found it hard to swallow. At times even the most sympathetic professors wavered in the face of SDS intransigence. On Friday evening Rudd, apparently determined to offend the faculty, told a meeting of the ad hoc group that its approach was "bullshit." "There is only one solution," he told the professors. "Recognize that these are political acts and the reasons behind them are political. . . . Amnesty is the only solution. I ask that this group grant us amnesty with the understanding that what we did was right."[72]

The radicals were not the only intransigents. The trustees refused to accept the right of any group except the administration to deal with student discipline. They also reiterated their faith in the value of the gym project.

The ad hoc group kept trying. On Sunday morning it came up with a "bitter pill" proposal. If the students accepted the AHFG's original terms and the administration did not, the faculty would interpose between the students and the police. If the students did *not* accept the proposals but Kirk *did*, the faculty would *not* place their bodies on the line. In effect, the faculty promised to throw their weight on the side of whichever group accepted its terms.

Kirk and Truman accepted key provisions of this proposal, though with a flock of qualifiers. The student radicals rejected it outright. Surrendering the amnesty demand would not only expose the demonstrators to punishment, the protest leaders believed, it would also end the revolt before the campus had become thoroughly politicized. Reinforcing the students' intransigence were the AHFG's handful of radical members, who advised the militants privately that the longer they held out the more faculty support they would win.

By Monday afternoon it seemed that only police action could break the impasse. Hoping to avoid an uncontrollable racial explosion, moderate black leaders, representatives from Mayor John Lindsay's office, university officials, and the police negotiated round the clock with the SAS students in Hamilton. The black students finally concluded that they had nothing to gain from a bloody confrontation and agreed to leave the building quietly when the police came and to accept arraignment on trespassing charges.

The white radicals prepared to resist. For a time the Low occupiers considered Tom Hayden's ingenious scheme to put Columbia's valuable collection of Chinese porcelain on the building's window ledge and threaten to drop it piece by piece to the cement below if the police broke in. In Avery the architecture students collected liquid soap from the janitor's room and spread it on the stairways to make the cops slip when they invaded the building. At Mathematics Hall the students adopted another of Hayden's plans: half the students would sit on the steps of the lower floors to impede the police while others barricaded themselves in upstairs classrooms.

SDS intended to extract maximum moral advantage from the impending police action. Off-campus, action-faction leaders briefed novices on how to provoke the police into violence to create as much outrage as possible. Students should insult the cops' female relatives, one SDS leader suggested. The police were mostly prudish Irish Catholics who would blow up if a student, especially a girl, told them "their mother sucks black cocks" and similar things.[73] Roger Kahn, an honest reporter, though generally sympathetic to the students, noted that some occupiers actually used such verbal kamikaze tactics when the police arrived.

The administration hoped to keep violence to a minimum. It failed. Members of New York's Tactical Patrol Force and plainclothesmen started emptying the buildings early Tuesday morning after issuing a formal warning at each and allowing a short interval for anyone to leave who wished.

The cops were not gentle. They beat students with their nightsticks and dragged them down the stairways with their heads bumping on each step. Outside the buildings, they roughed up anyone, student or faculty member, who tried to block their entrance, and chased and clubbed unfriendly spectators who came to watch the action. The ambulance from nearby Knickerbocker Hospital made more than a dozen trips carrying the injured to the emergency room. St. Luke's got another eighty-seven casualties. Most of the victims were students, but there were also some faculty. James Shenton, a popular American history professor, wound up at St. Luke's with an injured shoulder. Robert Zevin of the Economics department suffered face and scalp cuts, while A. Bruce Goldman, the campus rabbi, was knocked semiconscious by the police. In all, over a hundred students, faculty, and others were injured, though none critically. Over seven hundred students and their friends and allies were arrested and carted off in vans to the Tombs for booking.

The Columbia occupation and bust had immense repercussions. Locally, the impact was just what the revolutionaries wanted: it radicalized the campus. Surveys taken before the police action show a majority of the student body favoring the radicals' main goals, but only 20 percent endorsing their tactics. Police brutality absolved the occupiers of any blame for their inflexibility and truculence. How could you blame these brave young men and women when they had been so horribly brutalized by the "pigs"? Even some conservatives were so repelled by the unfettered police violence that they reconsidered their positions. A member of the student Majority Coalition told a psychiatrist: "I had always respected the police. . . . In this case the police action revolted me. I became a striker."[74] "My attitude changed as soon as the cops charged," declared Corwin Moore, a freshman from Old Lyme, Connecticut. "Whatever enmity I had against the demonstrators, I now have against the administration."[75]

On Tuesday evening, with broken glass, splintered wood, and torn clothing still strewn over the campus, angry students, faculty, university employees, and Morningside Heights "community people," rushed to join the Strike Coordinating Committee, and prepared for a showdown with the administration. The nonacademics were a token added to satisfy a recent split-off from the Progressive Labor wing of SDS calling itself the Labor Committee and headed by a strange, older Trotskyist, named variously Lynn Marcus or Lyndon LaRouche. In the 1980s LaRouche would become notorious as the leader of an organization as extremist as the Labor Committee, but at the opposite end of the political range.

On Wednesday the coordinating committee announced its official demands: no reprisals against anyone involved in the building occupations and inclusion of strike leaders in a "restructuring" of the university. Until these demands were met, students would boycott all classes.

The faculty ad hoc group also met in emergency session just hours after the police invasion of campus. Shocked and angry, its members came within an eyelash of condemning the administration and supporting the student strike. In the end Westin, fearing, he said, to split "the faculty along . . . lines that would be irretrievable in the next few years," refused to endorse the resolution and walked out of the meeting.[76] Westin's unexpected defection stunned the members. The AHFG took no action and never met again, a strange conclusion for the majority faculty organization.

The student strike lasted for the rest of the spring semester. The administration tried to deprive it of steam by suspending classes for a week and allowing students to skip final exams without penalty. Yet four to six thousand supported the strike and even after classes officially resumed on May 6 many stayed away. To fill the class void, the coordinating committee set up its own "free university" with the standard repertory of the other alternative schools that had sprung up around the country— classes in Marxism, guerrilla warfare, Zen, and sexual liberation. Launched with enthusiasm, it quickly petered out.

The first few days following the bust seemed to usher in a revolutionary dawn on Morningside Heights. Exhilarated strikers met in "communes" and debated weighty issues: the nature of education in a free society, how the university could be made more democratic, and what the world would be like after the revolution. On May 5 Herbert Marcuse, the celebrated radical philosopher, came to Columbia and engaged in a dialogue with fifteen top SDS leaders. He and the Columbia SDSers agreed that the intelligentsia were a potentially revolutionary force and that the new advanced capitalist societies produced their own unique set of "contradictions." Marcuse disappointed the student radicals, however, by asserting that, despite all their failings, universities were still centers of critical thought worthy of preservation even in their existing form.

The euphoric mood did not last. As the days passed more and more students returned to classes or drifted home for an early summer vacation. The Strike Coordinating Committee tried to revive enthusiasm with demonstrations against tight security on campus and the IDA. But they were ineffectual.

Meanwhile, a serious rift developed within the coordinating committee itself between the hard-core SDS and a more moderate faction—Students for a Restructured University—drawn into the Strike Coordinating Committee primarily by outrage at the police bust. On May 16, the moderates withdrew from the coordinating committee. Though they praised SDS for opening their eyes to "the political realities of our common situation," they deplored its simple "moral blacks and whites" and its conclusion that a "free university" was "impossible in an unfree society." They themselves were uneasy with the "prospect of an indefinite future of polarization and unrest" and would be content to work for making Columbia a better place now without waiting for the revolution.[77]

Cooling fervor and liberal defection did not deter the militants, and for the remainder of the semester they kept the campus in an uproar. On May 17, SDS sponsored a campus rally that drew 700 people from around the city. While Rudd was orating, a student informed the crowd of a spontaneous takeover by angry tenants of a nearby Columbia-owned apartment house. The crowd rushed to the building to join the disaffected renters. The police arrived soon after and, this time, gently removed the protesters, arresting 117.

Violence would erupt on campus one more time. On May 16 the administration had sent disciplinary letters to SDS leaders Rudd, Morris Grossner, Nick Freudenberg, and Ed Hyman. They were to come to the dean's office on May 21 to discuss their actions during the April building occupation. The summons set off a new round of demonstrations and a reoccupation of Hamilton Hall on the twenty-first. This time the administration called the police immediately. The Tactical Patrol Force arrived at Hamilton just after midnight and rounded up the protesters. Before the operation was over, however, someone set several fires in the building, in the process destroying the notes and papers of Professor Orest Ranum. One of the Hamilton Hall occupiers was Bernardine Dohrn, who had been drawn to the Columbia scene like so many other radicals by the sense that great events were transpiring.

With the end of the academic year an uneasy peace settled over the campus. Most students returned home and slipped easily into their summer routines of jobs, dates, weekends at the shore. But Columbia was not forgotten like so many other campus revolts. Much of its impact came from the sheer attention it received. No campus uprising of the decade, before or after, would get such voluminous press and TV coverage. But it was more than media hype. Columbia detonated while major student revolts flared in Germany and France. The spring uprising at Nanterre, a satellite of the Sorbonne in Paris, almost destroyed the Fourth French Republic. For weeks, as the radical students rioted in Paris, the world waited to see if 1968 would join 1789, 1830, and 1848 as a critical date in the development of Western revolutionary consciousness. That winter and spring the German universities were also racked by student uprisings led by the *Sozialistischer Deutscher Studentenbund*, the German SDS.

The sense of the student revolt as an international phenomenon amplified the events at Hamilton, Fayerweather, and Low. Given Nanterre, the Sorbonne, and the recent disorders at the Free University of Berlin, the unrest on American campuses no longer seemed adolescent high jinks. Here was something not visible before. As *Fortune* magazine declared of Columbia's SDS, "These youngsters . . . are acting out a revolution—not a protest, and not a rebellion, but an honest-to-God revolution."[78]

Fortune was right. The events on the Columbia campus mark a watershed in the New Left student movement. SDS had bandied about the term *revolution* before the events of April and May. The ultimate goal of the student-power movement, after all, was to create a revolutionary climate among students and New Working Class professionals. It did not presuppose an actual blood-will-flow-on-the-streets revolution, however, but a process of slow infiltration and takeover of establishment institutions. Rudi Dutschke's "long march through the institutions," rather than barricades and bombs, was to be the model for fundamental change, with violence employed only tactically.

The events at Columbia changed these perceptions, at least for a small group of radical leaders. Could the universities, after all, be the ultimate source of revolutionary change? Or did radicals have to leave their sheltered halls to be effective? The example of the French and German students who fought the police from behind barricades in Paris and Berlin, the guerrilla war in the ghettos, and the paramilitary actions of the Black Panthers made antirecruiter protests and attacks on university war complicity seem pallid. However sound in theory, it was difficult to wait for the slow social processes of advanced industrial societies to tilt the balance to change. In France the students had almost brought down the government. Why were American student radicals wasting their time with the IDA and gymnasiums? Juan Gonzales, a member of the steering committee, raised the issue soon after the second Hamilton occupation. "If our goals went beyond the university," he explained, then "we should have been willing to leave it. . . . Were we students who were politically active, or activists who happened to be students?"[79]

The media did not follow the ongoing debates among SDS

intellectuals very closely, but by the end of the 1967–68 academic year no one who paid attention could doubt that SDS and the campus militants had much more in mind than reforming the universities. In June Tom Hayden, always a bellwether, wrote "Two, Three, Many Columbias," proclaiming the revolutionary potential of the Columbia experience. Hayden envisioned students destroying buildings next time, not just occupying them, and the government forced to send federal troops "to occupy American campuses."[80] The article's title was inspired by "Two, Three, Many Vietnams," a slogan of Che Guevara, the Latin-American expert in guerrilla warfare.

At Columbia itself, SDS probably made as many enemies as friends. But at other campuses the Battle of Morningside Heights confirmed SDS as the most radical, most exciting, most effective instrument for fundamental social change. Rudd became a hero among campus dissenters for the very swagger, verbal violence, and boorishness that repelled the general public.

During the summer months, he and other Columbia SDSers fanned out north, south, and west to tell of the recent events on Morningside Heights and to whip up student revolutionary fervor. An FBI report to the director from the Denver office in late June tells of a speaking tour of Colorado colleges by an unidentified member of the Columbia Strike Coordinating Committee. He had come, the young man told his student audience, to clear up certain "myths" about the Columbia uprising. But he was also there to spread the revolution. "Take over this university," he urged. "This is your institution, baby. Let's bring down the University the way we did Columbia."[81]

Columbia sent SDS's campus stock soaring. Carl Davidson estimated that national membership had leaped to seven thousand, local chapter membership to six times that number, in the wake of the Columbia upheaval. During the 1967–68 academic year, according to the Educational Testing Service, about 2 percent of all American college students—well over 140,000 young men and women—considered themselves affiliated with SDS. SDS had also broadened its base. Once confined to the elite and the large cosmopolitan colleges, SDS chapters could now be found on smaller campuses, at Catholic schools, and even in the high schools, where teenybopper radicals now imitated their college big brothers and sisters. And SDS was only the cutting edge of the student insurgency. The number of students calling themselves either radicals or revolutionaries was even larger, almost 13 percent of all college undergraduates, according to one survey.

SDS held its 1968 convention at the Michigan State Student Union in East Lansing from June 9 to 15 in a hall decorated with red-and-black banners and posters of Lenin and Trotsky. The delegates matched the decor. Many sported red arm bands and carried Mao Tse-tung's "little red book" of revolutionary aphorisms and mottoes.

The National Office delegation was the largest present. They were themselves in transition. Most still believed that middle-class people were potentially revolutionary, but their faith was weakening. Rudd and his Columbia colleagues were a new element in the mix. They scorned the more sedate and contemplative approach of Calvert, Davidson, and other middle-period leaders and favored the "action" approach they had applied at Columbia.

The Columbia circle found allies in a group from Ann Arbor that included Diana Oughton and Bill Ayers. Both Oughton and Ayers were paradigms of late New Left social types. A pretty, light-haired young woman from a wealthy Illinois family, Oughton as a little girl belonged to the 4-H club and the Congregational church and rode horses. After Bryn Mawr she joined an American Friends Service Committee program that took her to Guatemala where she lived in a small rural community and worked with the impoverished Indians. Here the contrast between affluent America and dirt-poor Guatemala radicalized her. Ayers too came from a rich midwestern family. He attended the University of Michigan and joined Beta Theta Phi, a fraternity famed for its jock membership and wild parties. Ayers was drawn to political activity after Johnson's escalation of the Vietnam War in 1965 and was arrested at a sit-in at the Ann Arbor draft board.

In a different era, the two might have met at a debutante ball.

In fact, they met in Ann Arbor in 1966 as teachers in the Children's Community School, a permissive private elementary school that scorned the traditional three Rs and aimed at producing liberated children for the new age. They soon became lovers and reinforced each other's rebellion against their upper-bourgeois parents. Both young activists came to East Lansing bitterly disappointed at the recent failure of their "alternative" school and were looking for a way to express their rage at American society.

East Lansing also swarmed with young members of the Old Left—Du Bois Clubbers, Trotskyists, Anarchists. The largest Marxist-Leninist contingent, however, was Progressive Labor, represented by fifty or so disciplined, well-scrubbed, well-groomed young men and women who spoke as one on all issues and now, for the first time, directly challenged the SDS New Left leaders for control.

The initial clash came over a position paper by Bernardine Dohrn and two other National Office leaders that noted the revolutionary promise of students, professionals, and welfare mothers, but said nothing about the mainstream proletariat. PL responded with ridicule of the New Working Class drift and a loud defense of traditional Marxist doctrine. The National Office group struck back with a scheme to tighten up SDS's weak structure for the unspoken, but understood, purpose of foiling PL's drive to take over. Its members also made explicit their suspicion of PL. It was an unprincipled "external cadre," charged one NO leader, that was trying to use SDS as a recruiting ground and packed meetings "in order to manipulate acceptance of a line. . . ." Tom Bell, a founder of the Cornell SDS chapter who refused to allow his true-red "communism" be impugned by anyone, rose shaking with anger to denounce PL for its obstructionism. It wasn't possible to have a debate without running into the PL line, he announced, and as a result nothing ever got done. Unless SDS took action against PL, it was in imminent danger of collapsing. A PLer promptly shouted "red-baiting," setting off a five-minute demonstration of foot stamping and shouts of "PL out! PL out!"[82] Any LID elder present at Ann Arbor could have been excused a quiet "I told you so!"

In the end, the convention failed to adopt any coherent program for the year ahead. It did elect new officers, however, with NO leaders Dohrn and Mike Klonsky chosen interorganizational secretary and national secretary, respectively, and Fred Gordon, an outsider and relative unknown, elected education secretary. It was on this occasion that Dohrn bluntly labeled herself a "revolutionary communist." In addition, the NO managed to elect most of the eight-member National Interim Committee, the body that provided continuity between major SDS meetings and conventions.

During the summer SDS seemed rudderless and hesitant. PL turned once again to summer work-ins as a way to stimulate revolution and this time induced 350 young radicals to take jobs in factories and construction sites where they could rub shoulders with the proletariat. Most student energies were deflected into the antiwar movement, however, though SDS continued to avoid taking the lead.

Not so SDS veterans. It was two first-generation SDSers, Tom Hayden and Rennie Davis, who conceived the National Mobilization Committee's anti-Vietnam demonstration at the Democratic National Convention in Chicago that exploded in headlines in late August. But Hayden and Davis represented the "old-fashioned" New Left politics of the past, not the radical "communism" of the present. To the new leaders they seemed hopelessly out of date. Two weeks before the convention, Klonsky, the new national secretary, told the readers of *New Left Notes* that the politic position of Davis and Hayden "doesn't even matter."[83]

But SDS could not entirely ignore the growing excitement as the date of the Democratic convention approached. In July the National Office urged members to turn out in force to proclaim their opposition to the war. They also decided to send a cadre to Chicago to recruit among the young supporters of Eugene McCarthy, the Minnesota antiwar senator who was still challenging the front-runner, Vice-President Hubert Humphrey, Johnson's heir, for the presidential nomination. Certain to be disillusioned when Humphrey won the nomination, the NO reasoned, these naive liberals would be ripe for plucking by SDS.

Events in Chicago enhanced SDS's fascination with violence.

The SDSers who came to the convention were far more impressed by the black militant Blackstone Rangers and the white street kids who threw rocks, broke windows, and fought the cops than with the "Clean for Gene" McCarthyites. Many were drawn to force and repelled by it simultaneously. Hitting and fighting had been taboo to middle-class kids. Yet nursery admonitions could not eradicate the normal furies and rages of existence, and they could be set loose when properly triggered. Despite the plan to propagandize only, some SDSers merged with the mobs that took on Mayor Daley's cops in the Chicago parks and the streets around the convention hotels and experienced the exhilaration of anger explosively released. It was powerful stuff.

The turn to violence reinforced the retreat from the New Working Class concept. By now many student radicals had carried their revolt to the point of class self-contempt. Suffering from what the French call the *nostalgie de la boue,* the yearning for mud, they had begun to worship the underclass. However frightening, the resolute acting out of white working-class youths or ghetto blacks now seemed more authentic and valid than the feeble verbalizing of middle-class activists.

Chicago also confirmed the growing sense that the country was on the verge of cataclysm. How else to interpret the behavior of Mayor Daley's police except as a measure of the power structure's desperation? And if the authorities resorted to naked power, why should the left balk? On Labor Day weekend following the convention, a small group of SDSers who had been in the thick of the street actions at Lincoln and Grant parks met at a secluded farm near Downers Grove, Illinois, for rest and rehabilitation. Many were charged up with adrenalin. Chicago, Klonsky pronounced, had revealed the establishment's willingness to use any means to keep power. Carl Oglesby, reflecting the old SDS, objected. Chicago showed that the "ruling circles" were divided over the war. Klonsky denounced him "as the most dangerous man on the left."[84]

Chicago had made a deep impression on a small circle of radicals who lived together in a commune on Felch Street in Ann Arbor's black ghetto. Oughton and Ayers were members of this group, and they, and several other commune members, had been at the Democratic convention. The Felch Streeters had joined a "hit-and-run squad" that fought Mayor Daley's cops on the streets and returned to Ann Arbor high on violence. They called themselves the "Jesse James Gang" to proclaim their toughness and resolved to remake the Ann Arbor SDS. Until now, they said, SDS had been "a polite, inoffensive part in the drawing room of the university."[85] No more.

At the first fall meeting of VOICE, the University of Michigan's SDS chapter, the Jesse James Gang challenged the regulars, who now seemed too sedate and indecisive. The *enragés* demanded "aggressive confrontation politics" and turned the chapter meetings into shouting matches. After a month of struggle that included threats of personal violence, the rebels drove the regulars out. VOICE, the source of the Port Huron Statement, was now another force for "action" rather than protest within SDS. As Ayers announced soon after victory: "We are tired of tiptoeing up to society and asking for reform. We're ready to kick it in the balls."[86]

Autumn 1968 was a tumultuous period for the student left. "Columbia and Chicago," reported Ayers and Terry Robbins, his associate as SDS midwestern organizer, ". . . have contributed to a new atmosphere of . . . aggressiveness and the possibility for continued, prolonged action."[87] The new semester was scarcely under way when violence swept the nation's campuses. At the university of Michigan 200 students were arrested at a sit-in in support of Ann Arbor welfare mothers. On the first day of registration, 240 black students locked themselves into the student union and had to be dragged out by the police. Arson and bombing attacks, a new tactic, struck ROTC facilities at the universities of Berkeley and Delaware and Oregon. Radical students at the University of Washington in Seattle that fall danced by the light of a burning ROTC building to the chant:

> This is number one,
> And the fun has just begun,
> Burn it down, burn it down, burn it down.[88]

The rhetoric was even more heated than the actions. This fall counterculture papers, like SDS-affiliated *RAT* in New York, began to publish directions for making bombs and Molotov cocktails. In mid-October, at the SDS National Council meeting in Boulder, Colorado, the most popular literature was *Sabotage*, an anonymous pamphlet with the straight poop on revolutionary arson and bombing. The delegates walked off with every copy. Pacifism and pacifists, once respected if not followed, had by now become anathema. Just before Christmas *New Left Notes* published a statement of the SDS chapter at San Francisco State College condemning pacifism as a smoke screen for oppression. It was used "to keep people in their place and we must use any means necessary including people's violence to defeat them."[89]

The statement was not surprising. By Christmas 1968 the decade's most ferocious and sustained campus disruption was under way at San Francisco State.

By now most cosmopolitan campuses had a substantial roster of black students. As at Columbia, many only wanted a chance to learn useful skills and make it in the larger world. But an aggressive minority sought to transform the university itself. The colleges must create new black studies programs, recruit more minority students, hire more black faculty, and provide more scholarship aid to black, brown, and working-class students. Each of these demands, except the last, violated some important university principle or threatened some aspect of the meritocratic system that had been built up over the years by American higher education. Conservatives predicted they would lead ultimately to politicized universities on the Latin American model.

At San Francisco State in the fall of 1968, the spokesman for these ultimatums was George Murray, an English instructor and the Bay Area Black Panther minister of education. A man who had announced that white people did not belong to humanity, Murray had been a firebrand on campus all through the semester. In October, at Fresno State, he had exhorted students "to kill all the slave masters," including President Johnson, Chief Justice Earl Warren, and Governor Reagan. Shortly after, he advised black students at his own college to carry guns on campus to defend themselves against "racist administrators."[90] Under great pressure from the conservative and moderate forces in the state establishment, on November 2, SFS president Robert Smith suspended him.

Murray's suspension set off a four-month strike of unprecedented fury. The result might have been expected. No school in the country had a more combustible human mix. Besides the black nationalists, organized as the Black Student Union (BSU), State had militant Asian, Chicano, and other Third World groups. In the spring of 1968, these activists established the Third World Liberation Front (TWLF). The school also attracted radicals from the Berkeley free speech and anti-Vietnam battles. State had active SDS, Du Bois Club, and student Trotskyist chapters as well. To top it off, just a few miles to the east was the hippie capital of the nation, Haight-Ashbury, and many State students moved easily between the chaotic world of the counterculture and the structured one of higher education.

There was also the college faculty. The California State College system was a distinct notch below the university in funding and prestige, but State's location in the nation's most liberal metropolis had attracted an able and unusually independent faculty. Only a minority would have called themselves radicals, but many of the humanists and social scientists—even more than at other cosmopolitan schools—were antiwar and civil rights activists and antiestablishment in their general attitudes. A fair proportion of the left-liberal and radical faculty belonged to local 1352 of the American Federation of Teachers (AFT), a militant group that had long fought the State College administration and trustees over salaries and faculty autonomy. This strong left-liberal leaning would affect the course of events.

Just a week before Murray's dismissal, the BSU had issued a set of demands for a black studies program with power to set curriculum and hire and fire whom it pleased, open admissions to San Francisco State for all black and Third World applicants, and a black financial aid officer to replace the white one currently in charge of distributing scholarship and work-study money. Now they added reinstatement of Murray to the list. Soon after, the Third World Liberation Front joined the strike and added its own demand for an autonomous School of Ethnic Studies.

On November 5, with the strike set for the following day, Stokely Carmichael appeared on campus to inspire the troops. His message was incendiary. The strike must have goals beyond any academic program. It must "heighten the contradictions," for by so doing people were made politically "aware." His final note was ominous. "It is easy to die for one's people. It is more difficult to work and kill for one's people."[91] Carmichael certainly did not speak for most of the black students, but from the outset the San Francisco State strike would be conducted with a wild intemperance that surpassed anything hitherto seen on an American campus.

The strike began the next day with a rally in Main Auditorium. Here Ben Stewart of the BSU announced that the strikers would use disruption as their basic tactic. Through a "war of the flea," he said, students could harass the enemy to death. After his pep talk, commando groups fanned out across campus and burst into classrooms forcing instructors and students to disperse. A larger force invaded the Business and Social Sciences Building and scattered books, papers, and equipment. The next morning, during an SDS campus rally, the BSUers stuffed toilets and lit wastepaper-basket fires in several campus buildings. On Thursday, the eighth, the BSU escalated its attacks. At noon, five masked students burst into the chemistry department office, overturned desks and filing cabinets, and fled in a waiting car. Another party of black students invaded the anthropology department office and broke several windows before escaping. The invaders left behind a casualty, a black girl who had given herself a bad shock when she cut the cord of an electric typewriter.

On November 13, after a clash between strikers and the San Francisco police Tactical Squad, President Smith closed the campus and canceled all classes. It would remain closed "until we can rationally open it," Smith told a news conference.[92] This was exactly what the strikers wanted, and conservatives and moderates roared that Smith had knuckled under. On November 18, State College Chancellor Glenn Dumke, an ally of Governor Ronald Reagan, ordered the campus reopened. Smith resisted and on the twenty-sixth he was fired. His successor, the trustees announced, would be Samuel Hayakawa, a professor of English. When Reagan heard of the choice, he remarked: "I think we have found our man."[93]

And they had. The stocky sixty-two-year-old Japanese-American with the embroidered tam-o'-shanter was an ardent conservative who had no patience with radical and disruptive students. Despite his own Asian origins, he despised the Third World radicalism of the strikers. He also loathed the "cult of alienation among intellectuals" and cherished traditional university values.[94] Hayakawa immediately ordered classes to resume and then announced a series of tough regulations to restore the campus to normal. Due-process disciplinary procedures would be suspended for the emergency, and the faculty would meet classes or face punishment. "I want to make it clear to everyone," he announced, "that I will break up this reign of terror."[95]

Hayakawa became a conservative folk hero when he took a little direct action of his own against the strikers soon after the Thanksgiving recess.

The incident began when radical students brought a sound truck to a campus rally in violation of the president's rules and parked it a hundred yards from his office. Disturbed by the noise, Hayakawa stormed out and demanded that the students remove the truck. They refused, and the outraged little man scrambled atop the truck's cab intending to shout his orders to disperse. With TV cameras whirring away, he tried to speak, only to be drowned out by the sound equipment. Furious, the 153-pound Hayakawa grabbed the wires connecting the amplifiers and speakers, and with a mighty heave tore them out. Then, with radicals crying "On strike. Shut it down," he was helped down off the cab and escorted back to his office by a bodyguard of conservative and moderate students.[96]

Over the next few days the scrappy little man became a national celebrity. The National Council of Churches selected him as Man of the Year. In a Gallup poll the public chose him as the country's top educator. Invited to the annual Washington Grid-iron Dinner, he received a standing ovation from the assembled press lords and Washington politicians.

But the incident did not make his life on campus any easier.

During the weeks preceding the Christmas recess, the BSU, SDS, the TWLF, and their supporters continued their guerrilla war to shut the college down. The strikers held daily noon rallies that routinely turned into raids on classrooms and administrative offices. The Tactical Squad and the California highway patrolmen would then arrive, and the two sides would tangle in bloody clubbing and rock-throwing melees. These confrontations did not happen on rainy days. This was California and revolution was possible only when the sun shone.

In January the American Federation of Teachers, representing the left-of-center faculty, joined the strike on the students' side. The AFT endorsed the militants' demands: the retention of George Murray, autonomous ethnic and black studies programs, and amnesty for the strikers. But they also demanded better grievance procedures for themselves, a reduced teaching load, a greater faculty voice in running the college, and an improved sabbatical policy. In return for their support, the BSU and the Third World Liberation Front promised to desist from their hit-and-run tactics.

San Francisco was a union town, and the AFT received some backing from militant city trade unionists. But only a handful of their colleagues in the State College system came to their defense. Besides the absence of moral support, there was the dearth of money. Few professors could forgo their monthly paychecks, and by early March they and their families were facing empty larders and stacks of unpaid bills. As Herbert Wilner would later recall, "There was . . . rhetoric, and . . . dialectic, and that stuff could go on till doomsday." And "there was that other little detail: money."[97] Realism quickly took hold. On March 5, after Hayakawa and the trustees had promised a grievance procedure that would protect them from retaliation, the union settled.

The AFT surrender made it impossible for the students to continue. But they refused to end with a whimper. On the evening of March 5 a bomb exploded prematurely outside the Creative Arts Building, severely injuring a BSU member. The police discovered two more unexploded bombs in one of the rooms, one with enough dynamite to destroy the entire building.

On March 18 the students, too, finally quit after Murray gave his approval.

The San Francisco State strike was a disaster by any normal measure. Murray was not rehired and the student strikers did not get the general amesty they had demanded. They did get a black studies program, but this soon became just another academic department, firmly under the control of the president and the trustees. More important for the student left, the strikers' excesses and Hayakawa's success in dealing with them reinforced the hard-liners among legislators and college administrators around the country. It was now clear to conservatives that a tough policy was the best policy after all. The lesson would be widely applied during the months and years that followed.

Yet radicals pronounced San Francisco State a victory. It had been an important learning experience, they said. Achieving stated campus goals was less important than the new forms of disruption employed. The "tactics of the flea," announced Todd Gitlin, now living in the Bay Area, represented "a quantum leap in the history of the student movement."[98] The strike was an "astonishing success" for the "freshness and originality of its tactics . . . ," wrote two young radicals in April.[99]

But San Francisco State was not only a telling lesson in militant deployment; it also demonstrated, the tough-minded said, that the Third World "colonies" in the United States were the most reliable sources of rebellion. It was one thing for student radicals to observe ghetto militancy from a distance through the media, but at State white and Third World activists had actually collaborated. Here were tough and determined allies willing to put their lives on the line for their principles. The insight would be portentous.

In the interval between the National Council meetings at Boulder, Colorado, in mid-October and at Ann Arbor in late December 1968, SDS took a fatal step toward dissolution. During these weeks the National Office searched for a formula to assimilate the new tactical militancy and the new Third Worldism and at the same time adapt to PL's aggressive proletarianism. In the process SDS virtually abandoned its view that advanced capitalism oppressed through alienation, rather than material deprivation, and that change in America was only possible on middle-class terms.

Boulder had been another battle between the anti-Maoist National Office faction and Progressive Labor for control. PL tried to get SDS to adopt its Student Labor Action Project, a version of its worker-student alliance, but the National Office was able to vote it down two to one after a bitter battle. After the vote, one NO leader was seen jumping up and down and shouting "We won. We smashed the PL bastards!"[100]

Yet the Progressive Labor challenge profoundly altered the position that SDS had taken since its founding. In a stream of position papers that poured out of Chicago that fall, the National Office leaders began to backtrack on the critical issue of the "true" revolutionary agent. In early October one entitled "The False Privilege" called on students to shed their middle-class affiliations and identify with "the exploited class, the working class."[101] Soon after, Jim Mellen, a stocky older member of Ann Arbor's Jesse James Gang, circulated a proposal announcing that "Students for a Democratic Society recognizes that a revolutionary transformation of the United States Society depends upon the organization of a massive popular movement of the poor and working people."[102] Both of these papers were preliminary; the key document of SDS's turnaround was "Toward a Revolutionary Youth Movement," nicknamed RYM I.

RYM I's chief author was National Secretary Mike Klonsky, a skinny blond Californian with a pugnacious jaw whose father had been a Communist party official on both coasts. Klonsky was a rough-hewn character, very different from his predecessors as SDS's head, and a good specimen of the leaders that the overheated times were beginning to raise up. Richard Flacks, one of the Old Guard, later called him a "hood" and was certain that he joined SDS deliberately to sabotage it.[103]

Whatever Klonsky's hidden motives, RYM I marked a giant step toward ending SDS's commitment to the "New" Left and a virtual surrender to the old Marxism of the 1930s and 1940s. "Students alone" could not "bring about the downfall of capitalism," it stated. They would find it hard to accept this fact since they had been instilled with racist and anti-working-class views. But radical students now must reach out to "new constituencies" both on and off campus and transform "SDS into a youth movement that is revolutionary."

Only the Talmudists of the left could tell how this statement distinguished the NO from its sworn enemy, Progressive Labor. But there was a difference—still. The National Office leaders separated themselves from PL by retaining a cultural component in their thinking. The oppressed, RYM I stated, were not just defined by their relations to "the means of production" as in the traditional Marxist canon; that is, they were not just assembly-line workers, miners, hod carriers, and the like. They were also the alientated young, members of the "youth culture," whether rich or poor, bourgeois or proletarian. Klonsky and his colleagues were certain that there existed a whole new class of young men and women oppressed by the schools, the courts, the police, and their parents, who were raw material for revolution. "The struggle of youth," RMY I stated, "is as much a part of the class struggle as a union strike."

The RYM I statement also refused to consider America's racial minorities just another part of the proletariat. PLers, like most orthodox Marxists, saw the plight of nonwhite racial minorities as a version of capitalism's exploitation of the working class. They deplored nationalism as "bourgeois" and were uncomfortable with the separatist impulses that had eclipsed the civil rights movement. RYM I accepted the distinctiveness of minority oppression. Blacks and other minorities were "internal colonies" of the United States, and hence their struggle was really an anti-imperialist struggle. In fact, it placed them at the cutting edge of revolution.[104]

PL came to Ann Arbor armed with its own resolution and supporting position paper: "Fight Racism; Build a Worker-Student Alliance; Smash Imperalism." Introduced by four students at San Francisco State, it was as predictable, as musty, as antique, as the Old Left phraseology of its title.

"Fight Racism" reinterated the position that all exploited groups—blacks, browns, women, as well as workers—were mem-

bers of the proletariat. Liberation movements were frauds. Black
nationalism, for example, was "an ideology the ruling class relies
on to split the movement." "Cultural oppression" was also pho-
ney. Students were not "niggers too," as some New Left rhetoric
would have it. Though they were exploited and misled, their
oppresion was mild by comparison with that of Third World
peoples. Under the head "specific proposals," the PL paper
emphasized the need to relate student struggles "to working-class
struggles." Students must support the demands of campus cafete-
ria workers and janitors and cleaning people, for example. They
must support local blue-collar strikes and keep in close touch with
the local labor movement. "Only when the student movement is
united with the masses of the working people in this country," it
concluded, "will we be on the way to crushing the imperialist
system."[105]

Anyone today who follows the circuities of the argument must
be puzzled by the fiery debate they provoked. Could such abstract
positions really have meant so much? Only when we remind
ourselves of the ancient history of left sectariansim and fissip-
arousness does the life-and-death struggle make much sense.

The debate at Ann Arbor between the National Office spokesmen and PL was passionate. Few of the twelve hundred delegates
and observers probably understood the buzz words and all the
twists and turns of the arguments. Yet most perceived the power
struggle between the NO and PL, and when the vote was called
lined up for or against the two major factions. The result was a
National Office victory. But it was close. The RYM I resolution,
the chair announced, had been carried by just twelve votes.

RYM I preserved some part of SDS's heritage. But it was a
small fragment. The December 30 vote destroyed the SDS that
had been launched at Port Huron in June 1962. With it went
much of the New Left, for SDS was its core organization.

It had become the custom in SDS's short life to conclude major
meetings with a fund-raising session. Held just before people
returned to campus, it was a time when disagreements were
forgotten and everyone sang political songs while emptying their
pockets into the communal collection bucket. This time the two
sides, still unreconciled, flung slogans at one another and tried to

shout down their opponents. When the NO people struck up the old Wobbly tune, "The Workers' Flag is Deepest Red," the PLers hurled back "Don't use the red flag againt the red flag." NO's "Solidarity forever," was muffled by the chant: "Defeat false unity."[106] It boded ill for the future.

The future came six months later at SDS's annual convention held in Chicago. There, on June 18, the National Office "collective" appeared with a new document in hand, "You Don't Need a Weatherman to Know Which Way the Wind Blows."

The cryptic "Weatherman" title came from a protest song by Bob Dylan, a youth culture hero, and represented a continued clutching at cultural straws. But the contents proclaimed a final surrender to Third Worldism. During the months after Ann Arbor, in part to fend off the feared PL takeover, the National Office leaders had joined forces with the Black Panthers. The Panthers, as usual, set their price for friendship high: virtual surrender to their claim that "Revolution would come from a Black Thing." The group at Chicago headquarters was also affected by the heady contact with Cuban revolutionaries and North Vietnamese during a winter trip to Havana.

The "Weatherman" document came down unequivocally on the side of Third Worldism. It opened with a quotation from one of Mao Tse-tung's lieutenants that the "principle contradiction" in the contemporary world was the struggle against American imperialism. It went on to announce that white adults in America—both middle-class and working-class—were hopeless as agents for revolution since they benefited from "white skin privilege." The cutting edge of world revolution was the Third World peoples, whether at home or abroad. The role of American youth, including college students, was to show solidarity with these struggles. The youth movement had no legitimacy of its own.

These views were more extreme versions of RYM I's. But the "Weatherman" document also announced two new positions. Young Americans must accept the need for "armed struggle." Rallies and demonstrations were things of the past; it was now war for liberation. The second flowed from the first. SDS must change from a broad membership body and become a small "cadre" group centrally controlled that could achieve "effective secrecy."[107] Here the influence came not only from the Panthers but also from SDS's recent experiences at Columbia, Michigan, and San Francisco State. It is no accident that "Weatherman" authors included members of the Ann Arbor Jesse James Gang and that its chief draftsman was John Jacobs, the notorious "JJ" of the Columiba action faction.

The ninth annual convention of SDS at Chicago was its last. The opening session in the decrepit old Coliseum on South Wabash Avenue began hours late on Wednesday, June 18, in part because of tight security to avoid "pig" infiltration. The debate was acrimonious and unremitting with manifestos from various anarchists, the Trotskyists, a "Marxist-Humanist" group, and a number of other splinters, as well as the NO and Progressive Labor. Most of the delegates tried to read "Weatherman," but it was hard to penetrate its abstractions and codes. Like many others, Susan Stern, a pretty SDS camp follower from Seattle, supported it only because it was vouched for by people she respected.

The battle between PL and the National Office began early and never let up. At times the exchanges deteriorated into shouting matches with Klonsky and Jared Israel of the Harvard PL contingent and other leather-lunged delegates screaming charges and epithets at one another. A series of votes on minor issues soon made it clear that the NO could not dominate the sessions. PL had at least a third of the delegate voters, as many as the NO, with another third a swing group between the two.

To break the impasse, the NO tried to use the Third World as a club against its opponents. On the second evening contingents from the Chicago Panthers, the Puerto Rican Lords, and the Mexican-American Brown Berets turned up at the Coliseum and addressed the delegates on the NO's behalf. The tactic backfired. Rufus Walls, the Illinois state Panther minister of information, attacked PL as a bunch of "armchair Marxists" and placed the Panthers on the side of the NO. But then he undid all the good by speaking his sexist mind on women's liberation. The Panthers believed in the freedom of love, he said; they believed in "pussy power." Pandemonium! PLers and the large radical feminist contingent were on their feet screaming "Fight male chauvisnism!" Walls was unperturbed. "Superman was a punk because he never even tried to fuck Lois Lane," he shot back.[108] The disastrous evening concluded with a fistfight between NO and Pl partisans.

On Friday evening SDS fell apart. The split began with Panther leader Jewel Cook's menacing statement that if PL did not change its position on the issue of "the self-determination of all oppressed people," the Panthers would consider its members "counter-revolutionary traitors" to be "dealt with as such." SDSers would be "judged by the company they keep and the efficiency and effectiveness with which they deal with bourgeois factions in their organization."[109] Once again the Coliseum's naked rafters reverberated with shouts and denunciations. With this as their parting shot, the Panthers stalked off the stage.

Whether this scene was planned or spontaneous, it set in motion the quick process of disintegration. As the Panthers left the hall, Rudd was heard through the hubbub: "Right! We should do it. Let's split the organization right now. All those who want to expel PL move to the next room."[110] Jeff Gordon of PL rushed to the microphone and tried to calm the crowd, but Bernardine Dohrn settled the issue by announcing that anyone ready to consider reading PL out of SDS should accompany her. While PLers chanted "Sit down" and "Stay and fight," clusters of NO supporters followed Dohrn to an adjacent caucus room. There the talk was inconclusive, and not until Saturday morning was the decision made. Then, after listening to Dohrn deliver an eloquent rehearsal of SDS's origins, the group expelled PL from SDS by a vote of 500 to 100.

That evening, armed with a written rationale, the NO people returned to the main hall to declare themselves to the whole convention. Dohrn took the microphone and denounced PL as racist and reactionary. The rest of SDS could not live with such people, and PL was hereby expelled. The hall rang with roars of outrage: "Shame! Shame! Shame!" Dorhn managed to get through her speech, and then, after one last shout into the mike—"Long live the victory of the people's war"—she marched out of the hall followed by the whole of the NO contingent.[111]

The next day PL returned to the Coliseum and, declaring itself the real SDS, proceeded to elect national officers. It also voted to move national headquarters to Boston, where much of its strength was concentrated. A few miles away, the supporters of the "Weatherman" document convened in a Congregational church and elected Columbia's Rudd, Bill Ayers of the Jesse James Gang, and Jeff Jones, an Antioch dropout active in the New York office, as national officers. They then adjourned after vowing to meet with the Panthers the following month to form a "United Front Against Fascism" and to mount a "mass action" in the fall against Vietnam.

SDS-PL was to last for several years as a front for the Progressive Labor party. It never enjoyed a following and died a quiet death in 1972–73, after the United States and the People's Republic of China established diplomatic contact.

The "real" SDS turned to terrorism. In October, to repay old scores, "Weather people," men and women, dressed in combat gear, brawled with Mayor Daley's police on the streets of Chicago. The Days of Rage and a series of "raids" on working-class neighborhood high schools were supposed to convince "youth" in the abstract that Weathermen were tough hombres who could be counted on in a pinch. Heads were bloodied, windows smashed, desks overturned. But the forays only convinced most street kids that the radical students were crazy. The response, in turn, forced SDS to rethink its youth position. Maybe, the conclusion emerged, *all* white people, not just adults and not just workers and bourgeoisie, were hopelessly lost.

SDS, in its final Weatherman guise, convened publicly for the last time at the end of 1969. The three-day meeting, held in a squalid ballroom in Flint, Michigan, was billed as a "national war council" that would broaden public support. It was really a display of how far SDS had removed itself from the realities of American life.

Through the noise, the smoke, and the confusion emerged a grotesque culmination of the Weatherman line that white people in America did not count, that only Third World peoples could make a revolution. Every speaker denounced the "honkies" and heaped praise on Panthers and Third World revolutionaries. A bearded Mark Rudd declared that white people were under the spell of "Moby Dick"—"white skin privilege"—as much as any Captain Ahab, and like the demented sea captain must destroy the white whale or fail the revolution. Self-hate and nihilism infused every statement and remark. "We're against everything that's 'good and decent' in honky America," declared John Jacobs. "We will burn and loot and destroy. We are the incubation of your mother's nightmare." At one point the leaders considered whether killing white babies was a revolutionary act! The answer: "All white babies are pigs."[112]

The most notorious of the verbal extravagances was Bernardine Dohrn's eulogy of Charles Manson and the Manson "family," who had just been arrested for the beastly murder of the pregnant actress Sharon Tate and four others at a Los Angeles mansion. The satanic Manson, who preyed on women and despised blacks, was a Weatherman hero because he personified evil to white, conventional America. Dohrn crowed over the murders. "Dig it, first they killed these pigs and then they ate dinner in the same room with them, then they even stuck a fork into the victim's stomach! Wild!"[113]

Following the war council, a quarter of those at Flint—about a hundred militants—signed up with small "affinity groups" and went underground to become terrorists. Before slipping out of sight, most tried to get their hands on money to stay afloat in the "belly of the beast." Diana Oughton asked a friend to buy some travelers' checks, give them to her, and then report them stolen. Oughton would cash them and the friend would not lose anything. Other Weather people tried to borrow money from parents, relatives, and friends, and there were rumors that during these weeks of early 1970, some were dealing in hard drugs to get cash. One quick three hundred dollars came from the sale of SDS's archives to the Wisconsin Historical Society just before the Chicago police swooped down on the West Madison Street headquarters to sequester all materials for use in prosecutions for the Days of Rage. The American public took little notice of these events, but it was about to be abruptly jolted to awareness of enemies within.

On or about the first of March, Diana Oughton, Cathy Wilkerson, Kathy Boudin, Terry Robbins, Ted Gold, and other young Weatherman revolutionaries, moved into an elegant townhouse in Greenwich Village owned by Wilkerson's father, a radio station owner vacationing in the Caribbean. On March 2, one male member of the Greenwich Village group bought two fifty-pound boxes of dynamite from the New England Explosives Corporation of Keene, New Hampshire, for fifty dollars. Four days later a white station wagon delivered some cartons to the Wilkerson townhouse. They apparently contained dynamite, blasting caps, sections of metal pipe, and several cheap alarm clocks.

A few hours later, just before noon, someone attached a wire to the wrong terminal. A tremendous explosion reverberated through the house and the neighborhood, collapsing walls, virtually obliterating Robbins, and mangling Oughton almost beyond recognition. Gold, on the first floor, was killed by falling beams. Five other people in the house escaped without serious injury, three, never conclusively identified, by scrambling out the back and disappearing. Wilkerson and Boudin, the latter totally naked, stumbled into the street and were taken in by a neighbor lady who offered them a shower and clothing. The two women threw on the garments and, while their benefactress returned to the blast site, fled, neither one to surface for over a decade.

Yet the New Left did not end with a T. S. Eliot bang. The collapse of SDS wrecked its center and demoralized the survivors. But the radical political impulse of the sixties did not suddenly dissipate. It took the economic slump of the early 1970s to destroy the illusion that abundance was guaranteed and that dropout students could drop in again any time they wanted. The final withdrawal of American troops from Vietnam in 1973 removed another reason for dissent. Yet echoes from the Weather Underground and other terrorist groups would reverberate until the early 1980s. And a trained ear can still detect the faint voices of the sixties' New Left in the environmental movement, the anti-nuclear campaign, the radical faculty circles flourishing on cosmopolitan campuses.

Still, it was in 1968, the turning-point year, that the New Left lost its way. When SDS, its heart, adopted the Revolutionary Youth Movement resolution at its Ann Arbor National Council meeting at Christmastime 1968, it abandoned the insight that had set it apart from sterile traditional Marxism. From then on young radicals could respond to the claims of advanced capitalist society only with bombs and impotent rhetoric.

5

Good Night, Sweet Prince

SENATOR EUGENE MCCARTHY of Minnesota remained in Washington over the 1967 Christmas recess to prepare for the political trial ahead. On January 1 he held a press conference to explain his decision to seek the Democratic nomination against an incumbent president of his own party.

He was concerned for the young, the senator said. They were "on the edge of almost complete alienation from politics," and he hoped to restore their faith in the system. He wished for "a reasonable—not perfect—settlement of the war" and would seek solutions for "the internal problems of poverty and unrest in our cities. . . ." His candidacy had not taken off, he admitted. But "I'm not gloomy. I knew it was going to be slow and hard going and that there was not going to be any great sweeping popular response immediately."[1] The press conference was a perfect measure of the man: diffident, tentative, principled—and touched with a trace of tragic failure.

In the weeks since his November announcement to run, things in fact had not gone well. McCarthy had launched his campaign in Chicago on December 2 at a rally of Concerned Democrats arranged by the indefatigable Allard Lowenstein, the sparkplug of the "dump Johnson" movement. The senator was late, and Lowenstein had warmed up the audience of four thousand antiwar partisans with a Johnson-bashing pep talk that had brought roars of approval. When McCarthy finally wrested the microphone from the flamboyant Lowenstein, his brief remarks seemed juiceless. Tall, lean, ascetic, donnish in his bearing and words, the senator quoted the socialist thinker Charles Péguy and the historian Arnold Toynbee, and alluded to Hannibal and Tiberius Gracchus. He referred to the mistakes of the "administration," but he refused to attach the president personally. Even his criticism of the United States' Vietnam policy seemed tepid. The nation must seek "an honorable, rational, and political solution," but he was "not advocating peace at any price."[2]

The audience had been disappointed, and for the remaining weeks of the year the effort to deny a sitting president his party's renomination had appeared little more than a quixotic gesture. As a friend of the liberal activist attorney Joseph Rauh said during these slow weeks, "Gene's entry into the race is the greatest thing that could happen to Johnson; he's so weak he makes even Johnson look good."[3]

The war had made McCarthy a candidate. By 1968 millions of Americans despaired of victory in the Vietnam conflict and yearned to extricate the United States from the sickening trap we had created for ourselves in Southeast Asia.

Vietnam had evoked an insurgent response as early as the mid-1950s, when France sought American help to save its crumbling Indochinese empire. During the Eisenhower years, fear of another interminable land war on the Asian continent had prevailed over the cold-war reflex of the day. When America finally took the plunge in the sixties, many critics would continue to emphasize the practical realities: Vietnam was unwinnable, the wrong war in the wrong place.

But resistance to Vietnam was not only expedient; it was also ethical and ideological. From its beginnings America had had its share of religious pacifists—Quakers, Mennonites, and others—who believed that war violated the higher moral law. Since before the Civil War there had also been a secular peace movement that condemned war as wasteful and inhumane. During World War I, peace advocates had founded the Women's International League for Peace and Freedom and the pacifist Fellowship of Reconciliation. In the 1920s other pacifists had added the War Resisters League to the list.

World War II, a "good war" against the unspeakable Nazis, had weakened the peace movement. But by the mid-fifties, with the political intolerance of Joseph McCarthy receding and public anxiety over the "bomb" on the rise, the peace movement returned with a rush. In 1956 David Dellinger, Bayard Rustin, and A. J. Muste founded *Liberation,* a "Third Camp" journal—neither pro-American nor pro-Soviet—dedicated to peace and social justice simultaneously. In 1957 liberals organized the National Committee for a Sane Nuclear Policy (SANE) to press for an end to nuclear testing and to promote the "concept of a higher loyalty—loyalty by man to the human community."[4] The following year Gandhian civil disobedience pacifists founded the Committee for Nonviolent Action. Soon after, moved by the same rebound forces that energized the reemerging campus left, a group of midwestern student pactifists and socialists launched the Student Peace Union (SPU). By 1960 the SPU and affiliated single-campus peace groups such as Harvard's TOCSIN had five-thousand members.

The signing of the Soviet-American limited nuclear test ban in 1963 deflated public fears of nuclear fallout and slowed the organized peace movement's drive. The earliest murmurs of America's Vietnam involvement alarmed the peace forces and tripped off several organized protests, but these made little public impression. Then, in February 1965, came Johnson's "Operation Rolling Thunder" order to engage in saturation bombing of North Vietnam. Overnight, peace became an electrifying issue in the press and on the nation's campuses.

It was never easy to separate the anti-Vietnam and the broader pacifist components of the sixties' antiwar movement. All pacifists denounced America's Vietnam role, but not all anti-Vietnam activists opposed war in general. The nonpacifists belonged to a broad phylum of social and political types. Men like Norman Cousins of the *Saturday Review* and Eric Fromm, the famous psychiatrist, founding fathers of SANE, were liberals who had long been working to smooth the sharp edges of American life without altering its basic outlines. To their left were various Third Camp radicals including the *Liberation* circle and the group around *Dissent*—Irving Howe, Michael Harrington, Norman Mailer, Paul Goodman, Dennis Wrong, and Sidney Lens—and the fellow-traveling journalists of *The Monthly Review* and the *National Guardian*. The Old Left Stalinists of the Communist party, the Trotskyists of the Socialist Workers party, and the Maoists of Progressive Labor, along with their student affiliates, were other active elements in the anti-Vietnam camp.

SANE and Turn Toward Peace harbored most of the liberals. Women Strike for Peace, founded in 1961, attracted liberal women and incipient feminists. The Marxists avoided a peace vehicle of their own, following instead the venerable "United Front" policy of alliance with liberals and, in this case, pacifists, which enabled them to exert influence far beyond their own small and suspect limits. The front groups also served as a recruiting ground for new members for revolution. The Trotskyists, especially, were able to use the peace movement for ulterior purposes. Barred from membership in SANE and Turn Toward Peace, they thrust their way to the very center of the various umbrella anti-Vietnam organizations, winning for themselves a powerful position, disproportionate to their numbers, in the community of sixties' dissent.

Various passions, attitudes, and agendas inspired the nonpacifist peace movement. Radicals, like the Trotskyists and the New Left, were implicitly anti-American. The United States was the capitalist motherland, and all its activities abroad were inevitably in the service of the ruling class and inevitably depraved. The National Liberation Front and the North Vietnamese, by contrast, were in the van of the world struggle of oppressed peoples against capitalist neocolonialism. Trotskyists avoided anti-American displays, but the young New Leftists would defiantly parade through city streets waving Vietcong and North Vietnamese flags to thrust their views into the faces of their opponents.

As the war expanded and intruded into every cranny of national perception, it also created a powerful tide of moral revulsion among millions in the political center. Americans fight best when charged by righteous wrath or a sense of mission. In Vietnam, the American capacity for indignation favored the enemy. Americans in Southeast Asia seemed brutal ravishers of a weaker people. The disproportion in American and enemy power and in technological prowess by itself was too great to sustain the image of a just war and awakened the root-for-the-underdog reflex among millions of ordinary citizens. B-52s and napalm against rifles and sharpened sticks made laughable America's claim that it was fighting a dangerous enemy in freedom's name. Equally repulsive was the ruthlessness of an antiguerrilla war. In September 1965 the distinguished University of Chicago political scientist, Hans Morganthau, described how counterinsurgency imposed brutal tactics on the United States. Americans in Vietnam had "tortured and killed prisoners; . . . embarked on a scorched-earth policy by destroying villages and forests; . . . killed combatants and noncombatants without discrimination because discrimination is not possible."[5]

Indignation was also fed by distaste for our South Vietnamese allies. Here was no virtuous little Finland or Poland, weak nations victimized by powerful neighbors. The regime in Saigon was itself an undemocratic and corrupt government that did not deserve our help. Anger was also encouraged by a distaste for Washington's deceptions and cover-ups and for a draft system that virtually exempted the white middle class and ensnared only the poor, the black, and the brown.

The sixties' peace movement was not always peaceful. Liberals often spurned the Trotskyists and the Communists either on principle or out of fear of being stigmatized. Radicals, in turn, called their liberal opponents red-baiters. The left disagreed with the center over the nature of the war and how to end it. Most liberals considered the war a blunder, an avoidable mistake without larger significance. The United States should arrange a withdrawal that would preserve autonomy for South Vietnam. *Negotiation* was the key liberal term. Radicals considered the war "imperialistic," a symptom of America's inherently depraved capitalist system, and insisted that the United States withdraw without conditions. The radical slogan was: Out now!

At times these differences broke into open warfare. In 1965 Robert Pickus of SANE's West Coast office disowned the organizers of the Students for a Democratic Society (SDS) April peace rally in Washington as more "hostile to America than to war" for their willingness to accept marchers of every political persuasion.[6] Bayard Rustin, another anti-Marxist, tried to "torpedo the march because . . . communists had taken over in some places."[7]

Until his death in February 1967, the sun that held the peace movement's separate spheres on course was Abraham Johannes Muste, an ordained Protestant minister whose life had been one long crusade for peace and social justice. By the time of the anti-Vietnam movement, "AJ" had spent half a century as a preacher, trade union activist, and one-time Trotskyist ideologue who fought for civil rights and civil liberties, an end to war, and economic equality from the bases of the Fellowship of Reconciliation, the Committee for Nonviolent Action, and an assortment of other radical and nonconformist organizations.

By the mid-1960s he was the grand old man of the peace movement. Tall, gaunt, ascetic, he looked like an El Greco monk in rumpled modern dress. An imperious father and often inconsiderate husband, he was not without personal faults. But the universal respect his selfless devotion to peace and social justice conferred made him almost the only person who could keep the diverse peace groups pulling in one direction. As David Dellinger, another radical pacifist, wrote after Muste died, "He managed to work creatively with those who shared only a part of his philosophy or strategy, without sacrificing the integrity of his own deepest beliefs. . . ."[8]

Muste's skills would be sorely needed in 1966 and 1967, the last two years of his life. But for a time after Operation Rolling Thunder, pacifist headquarters on Beekman Street in lower Manhattan would take second place to the nation's campuses as the antiwar center.

Johnson's decision to bomb North Vietnam sent a shock wave through American colleges and universities. Many of the nation's liberal professors disliked LBJ despite his New Dealish positions and policies. The attitude was partly snobbery. The president's folksiness seemed phony, his Texas persona alien. Yet in the fall of 1964, their fear of his bellicose opponent, Barry Goldwater, had led them to suspend their disbelief and toil for his election. Their outrage over the bombing, when it came, was reinforced by the feeling that they had been duped. At Ann Arbor in early March, professorial mortification created a new form of protest, the teach-in, and restored a new incandescence to the smoldering antiwar movement.

The teach-ins were an unplanned byproduct of academic anger. No one knew that something original was to be added to the protest arsenal when on Thursday, March 11, a group of twenty-five University of Michigan professors, mostly of junior rank, met in a suburban Ann Arbor living room to consider how to respond to the new Vietnam provocation. Everyone's first thought was another "We view with alarm" public statement to be published in the local paper. This would achieve little, but everyone would feel a bit better. Then, William Gamson of the Department of Sociology proposed something new: why not call off classes for one day and fill the time with a round of special lectures and seminars describing the issues in Vietnam and the dangers of America's involvement? The plan had the appeal of novelty, and before they adjourned that evening the group had composed a call for a work moratorium for circulation among their colleagues the following day.

What seemed fresh over coffee the night before seemed unworkable in the full glare of day. The student response was enthusiastic. Ann Arbor was already at the cutting edge of the student left revival, and Vietnam, with its specter of personal danger and death, was a special abomination to the young. But many faculty were repelled; in early 1965 a work stoppage seemed a drastic tactic. Administrators were shocked. Professors were not "workers" like truck drivers or janitors; they were professionals, and could not strike. The university president, backed by the governor and the legislature, threatened disciplinary action against any faculty member who refused to meet his classes. After several days of canvassing, few senior professors, though protected by tenture, were willing to lend their names to the project.

On the evening of March 17 faculty and students met and during an eight-hour session worked out a formula that broke the impasse. The seminars, lectures, and rallies would be scheduled after classes to meet the objections of the administration and state officials. Then, if the Ann Arbor demonstration succeeded, the teach-in plan would be broadened into a national protest to be held in Washington. With the work stoppage dropped, the university administration agreed to provide auditoriums and classrooms and suspend dormitory curfews for women students.

Student response was spirited. The militants, of course, needed no urging. VOICE members and other leftists were soon manning the phones, the typewriters, and the mimeo machines alongside the faculty. Conservative and moderate undergraduates, impressed by the visits of activist professors to the dorms and the fraternity and sorority houses to discuss the teach-in, also signed on. One sophomore realist put his finger on a success factor easily overlooked by people over thirty. The administration's waiver of curfew rules for the women undergraduates, said Jared Stamel, "undoubtedly gave a big stimulus to the event."[9]

The marathon of speeches, discussions, and lectures began at 8:00 P.M. on March 24 with three thousand students and several hundred faculty present; six hundred survived until the cold Michigan morning twelve hours later.

The teach-in was acclaimed an immense success. Yet the praise emphasized its effects on the already converted. Like so many other protests of the decade, it was a deeply moving event to participants. "We are not now wholly the same people we were before the teach-in," wrote one upbeat faculty organizer soon after.[10] "This teach-in shows me what a university has to be," exclaimed one self-described "lowly freshman."[11] Peace was clearly as effective as free speech or civil rights in momentarily forging a close community out of the buzzing confusion of campus life.

Perhaps this sense of community is the ultimate motive for events like the Michigan teach-in. Clearly it was not a triumph for free inquiry. The model at Michigan was "protest, not discussion; monologue, not debate," admitted Marc Pilisuk, one of the organizers.[12] The students did not get an objective view of

Vietnam, though as promised, the other side was allowed to conduct a virtually unnoticed counter-teach-in the following evening. On March 24 speakers and discussion leaders like Carl Oglesby of SDS, Arthur Waskow of the left-liberal Institute of Policy Studies, and Professors Frithjof Bergmann, Kenneth Boulding, and William Gamson were neither neutral nor expert on Southeast Asia. Their message was simple: the United States must get out of Vietnam unconditionally; we had no business there. Not everyone present admired the partisanship. As one undergraduate, overheard by a *Michigan Daily* reporter, exclaimed: "This thing isn't fair at all. They aren't presenting the other side."[13]

Whatever its failings, the teach-in idea proved eminently exportable. During the planning stage, the Ann Arbor faculty pushed the scheme vigorously among their colleagues on other campuses. After the big event at Michigan, the Inter-University Committee for Debate on Foreign Policy, headed by the radical Cornell economics professor Douglas Dowd, took up the work. Columbia students and faculty held their own teach-in on March 26. Other campuses—Western Reserve, Michigan State, Chicago, New York University, Pennsylvania, Wisconsin, UCLA, Oregon, and scores more—soon followed. The Michigan pioneers often supplied experience and speakers. Sometimes the teach-ins included defenders of America's Vietnam policy; usually the sessions were one-sided, in part because the State Department and other Vietnam supporters refused to participate in events they believed irretrievably biased.

The promised national teach-in took place in Washington's Park Sheraton Hotel on May 15 with a live debate as the centerpiece and a roster of satellite panels. The audience numbered some five thousand, mostly antiwar students, some from as far away as California. The debate was widely reported. Special telephone hookups brought it to thousands of students on campuses around the country; radio and TV stations picked it up; the wire services carried extensive reports. It was the first time something approaching a national debate over foreign policy had ever taken place.

Unlike the campus events, the national teach-in was reasonably balanced. National security adviser McGeorge Bundy, dispatched by Johnson to check out the crisis in the Dominican Republic, missed the proceedings, but Berkeley political scientist Robert Scalapino, Johnson policy planner Walt Whitman Rostow, and others defended the administration. The attackers endorsed a range of positions. George M. Kahin of Cornell and Hans Morgenthau of Chicago accused the United States of confusing an internal civil war with an act of aggression by the north against the south. Isaac Deutscher, the Trotskyist historian and biographer, denounced America as the leading imperialist nation and the major force in perpetuating the cold war. Somewhere in the middle, expressing the growing doubts of Senator Robert Kennedy, was the historian and former White House aide, Arthur Schlesinger, Jr. Schlesinger called Johnson's bombing policy ineffective and admitted that the country's commitment in Vietnam might have been a mistake. Unconditional withdrawal, however, would undermine confidence abroad in our foreign policy and play into the hands of the Red Chinese.

Balance did not extend to the audience. Participants were impatient with any speaker who failed to denounce the war. They greeted Schlesinger and his qualified defense of the president with a chorus of boos.

For a time the teach-ins dominated the antiwar movement. They ceased during the summer, but resumed in the fall and flourished on campuses for another year or two. Eventually, they even spread abroad—to Toronto, Tokyo, London, and Paris— wherever opponents of American foreign policy flourished. They effectively mobilized antiwar sentiment, reaching thousands of students and faculty and, until their novelty wore off, attracting widespread public attention. They also served as a training ground for antiwar activism. The interuniversity committee provided speakers, reading lists, and literature to antiwar organizers. During the 1966 congressional primary campaign, it supported several "peace" Democrats' challenges to proadministration incumbents.

*　　*　　*

In a roundabout way, the teach-ins also spawned the International Days of Protest, the first of the big-time street demonstrations for peace. The event connecting the two was the giant Berkeley anti-Vietnam teach-in of May 21–22, staged by the Vietnam Day Committee (VDC), a creation of Free Speech Movement veterans looking for a new cause after the fall victory over Katherine Towle and the University of California's Board of Regents.

The VDC was the brainchild of Stephen Smale, a brilliant young Berkeley mathematics professor from a far-left family, and Jerry Rubin, an irreverent graduate student dropout from Cincinnati. Smale was thirty-five, eight years older than Rubin, and a scholar of international reputation, but boyish in manner and appearance. Rubin, a former sportswriter for a Cincinnati daily, was a five-foot-four-inch imp who turned left politics into a hilarious clown act that often infuriated his more sober allies. Both men were natural-born gadflies who delighted in confounding the pompous and the established.

Their handiwork, Vietnam Day, was a nonstop, thirty-six-hour marathon of speeches, rock music, and street theater that set the style for many later antiwar demonstrations. Thirty thousand people attended some part of the rally on the Berkeley campus, with up to a third that number present at any given time. The organizers invited Robert Scalapino and others to present the administration's side, but neither he nor any other pro-administration speaker showed up. "Veal Scalapino," one wit noted, had turned into "chicken Scalapino."[14]

Vietnam Day's success led its impresarios to convert the VDC into a permanent organization. Incorporating all shades of political opinion from Trotskyist to liberal, it soon became the major hub of dissent in the Bay Area, a focus for every naysayer and maverick, social and political, around. Soon after, Smale and Rubin, impressed with the international opposition to Vietnam, called for an International Days of Protest to be celebrated by rallies in cities all over the world where people opposed America's Vietnam policy.

One of the Vietnam Day speakers had been Staughton Lynd, a

young history professor from Yale whose blond, all-American good looks disguised a passionate commitment to social justice. The son of the sociologists Robert and Helen Lynd of *Middletown* fame, Lynd was by 1965 a radical, a civil rights activist, and a fierce opponent of the Vietnam War who had moved well beyond his parents' mild socialism. At the Berkeley teach-in he proposed a new "Continental Congress" where inarticulate and powerless Americans could speak out against war, racism, and inequality. This idea struck a receptive chord and soon evolved into an "Assembly of Unrepresented People" to meet in Washington to forge a coalition of the forces of civil rights, social change, and peace.

The assembly, held from August 6 to 9, 1965, to commemorate the twentieth anniversary of the atomic bombing of Hiroshima and Nagasaki, drew a wide spectrum of insurgent organizations including the Student Nonviolent Coordinating Committee (SNCC), the Committee for Nonviolent Action, the War Resisters League, the VDC, SDS, Women Strike for Peace, and the Student Peace Union. The conference-cum-demonstration was a four-day affair of al fresco workshops at the Washington Monument on peace, poverty, civil rights, civil liberties, and "free universities"; a roster of insurgent speeches; and an antiwar march to the Capitol. The march was modest in size, but there were enough hecklers and arrests to draw wide media attention. The *Life* magazine cover of August 16, 1965, showed David Dellinger, Bob Parris (Bob Moses) of SNCC, and Staughton Lynd covered with red paint thrown by an American Nazi. The judge fined the Nazi ten dollars; he sentenced Dellinger to forty-five days in jail.

Out of the assembly came the first anit-Vietnam umbrella coalition, the National Coordinating Committee to End the War in Vietnam (NCC), with headquarters in Madison, Wisconsin. The brainchild of a hundred young activists at the Washington rally, the NCC proved to be a feeble body. Though it had assumed responsibility for the October International Days of Protest, the actual work of organizing the demonstrations de-volved mostly on local groups around the country only loosely tied to the committee. In the end the VDC in the Bay Area and the Fifth Avenue Peace Parade Committee in New York did most of the work, a bicoastal pattern that would last as long as the peace movement.

As became the norm, the New York demonstration was the larger of the two. The Fifth Avenue Peace Parade Committee was a coalition of New York–based radical pacifists, SANE-type liberals, Old Left Trotskyists, Communists, and Progressive Laborites and assorted New Leftists from SDS and other organizations. Keeping this babel from collapsing into total confusion was "AJ," whose charm and persuasive powers could get the radical lions to lie down with the pacifist lambs—and also keep the lions from tearing one another to pieces. As it was, he barely headed off a major donnybrook over whether the official slogans should emphasize a negotiated Vietnam withdrawal as demanded by the liberals or the Out Now! approach favored by everyone else. After days of bickering the committee discovered a rallying cry all would accept: Stop the war in Vietnam!

In the end, thirty thousand protesters marched down Manhattan's Fifth Avenue from Ninety-first to Sixty-eighth streets under the parade committee's auspices. Despite some heckling and tomato throwing, most of the people lining the street were friendly or at least tolerant. Adult marchers carried banners and placards, some with blowups of a Vietnamese mother and child, others with an enlarged detail of Picasso's celebrated antiwar painting, *Guernica*. Children carried brightly colored, slogan-inscribed helium balloons. Actors from the Bread and Puppet Theater, the then New York–based counterculture theatrical troupe, wore enormous papier-mâché masks and costumes depicting a villainous LBJ and his pitiful Vietnamese victims. Another group wearing skeleton masks satirically played the "Marine Hymn" on children's musical instruments.

In the Bay Area the Vietnam Day Committee's plans miscarried. Theoretically hospitable to all antiwar factions, the VDC was actually controlled by a new breed of wild and woolly leftists and counterculture street people who itched for some dramatic blow against the establishment. In a series of raucous meetings in Berkeley they had shouted down their sobersides Trotskyist opponents and committed the VDC to shutting down the Oakland Army Terminal, the shipping point for munitions and supplies going to Vietnam. This scheme failed. On October 15, fifteen thousand chanting VDC protesters and allies came up against four hundred armed and helmeted Oakland police at the Oakland-Berkeley city line and were turned back. The next day, five thousand of the marchers returned to the scene of their defeat and again tried to approach the army terminal. Once again the police blocked the way. This time they also encountered a crew of black-jacketed, booted Hell's Angels motorcyclists who charged shouting "America for the Americans!" Marchers, police, and bikers were soon in a wild free-for-all that produced one broken leg, one deep scalp wound, and a scattering of bruises and contusions. Not until November 20—after securing a favorable court order—did the demonstrators manage to cross into Oakland, and by then hardly anyone noticed.

For the next two years the peace movement ballooned to match the escalating war. During the October 1965 antiwar demonstration, a disciple of Dorothy Day's Catholic Worker movement, David Miller, became the first person to publicly burn his draft card in defiance of a federal law defining such an act as a felony. Nineteen sixty-six was the year the antiwar protest achieved real momentum. In the spring a Minnesotan, Barry Bondhus, poured two buckets of human feces over the files of his local draft board. Wags would call it "the movement that began the Movement."[15] GI antiwar resistance began that July when three Fort Hood, Texas, soldiers refused to obey assignment to Vietnam. The peace activists improvised a Fort Hood Three Defense Committee and beat all the relevant protest and propaganda drums to prevent the military authorities from sending the rebellious soldiers to the stockade. The three men spent two years in jail, but the campaign would keep the antiwar volume on high for many months.

Nineteen sixty-six also marked the first demonstrations against Dow Chemical Company, the producer of napalm, the nightmarish inflammable jelly that fastened onto its victims flesh and killed or produced horrible disfiguring burns. It was also the year Harvard SDSers cornered Secretary of Defense Robert McNamara, trying to escape in his limousine while on a visit to the university, and made him listen to a barrage of charges that he and his colleagues were lying about Vietnam. McNamara, his face contorted and grim, was heckled unmercifully. He would never allow himself to be publicly grilled again on Vietnam.

This was also the year of the Fulbright hearings, when administration spokesmen stubbornly defended the American Vietnam involvement in three week-long televised Senate meetings conducted by the head of the Senate Foreign Relations Committee. For the first time a national audience witnessed respectable, level-headed men attacking the war and denying its necessity.

In 1966, too, with Vietnam troop deployments edging up to four hundred thousand, the peace forces established the November 5–8 Mobilization Committee, the first of several "Mobilizations," to coordinate and direct anti-Vietnam activities for the fall.

"The Mobe's" nebulous autumn project was a program of marches, teach-ins, rallies, and leafletings designed to influence the 1966 Congressional and local elections. The most visible demonstration was another parade committee march and rally in New York where the speakers included Edward Keating of the leftist Catholic magazine *Ramparts* and Allen Ginsburg, the Beat Generation poet laureate.

Soon after, the November 5–8 Mobe evolved into the Spring Mobilization to End the War in Vietnam. The Spring Mobe was charged with more than an ad hoc mission. As its founding document declared, it intended to "broaden . . . the influence of the peace movement as much as possible" and to "widen the movement into such localities and professional milieux including . . . labor, literary, military, civil rights, traditional peace groups, religious, electoral, as are not presently organized or which need organizational assistance."[16] In December a group of Trotskyist and Dubois Club students established the Student Mobilization Committee to cooperate with the adult organization.

The Spring Mobe's April 1967 actions were the most impressive demonstrations for peace yet. By now the anti-Vietnam movement had spread beyond its original base of chronic dissenters and longtime antiwar advocates. In New York several of the less conservative unions joined the proceedings.

Another recruit was the Catholic left, the small group around Dorothy Day's *Catholic Worker* and the Berrigan brothers—the Jesuit Daniel and the Josephite Philip. These Catholic mavericks had been fierce opponents of Vietnam since the beginning, but the Catholic clergy had taken little part in formal antiwar demonstrations. Now Monsignor Charles O. Rice agreed to join the New York march and to provide a visible Catholic presence to the demonstration. The biggest addition, however, was Martin Luther King and the Southern Christian Leadership Conference.

The civil rights left had already proclaimed its abhorrence of the Vietnam War. Malcolm X had called the war an imperialist attack on "little rice farmers, peasants, with a rifle. . . ."[17] In January 1966 SNCC announced that it supported draft evaders who refused "to . . . contribute their lives to U.S. aggression in the name of the 'freedom' we find so false in this country."[18]

The attacks of the civil rights left were predictable—and inconsequential. The views of its center and right were neither. King's Southern Christian Leadership Conference along with the National Association for the Advancement of Colored People and the Urban League were members in good standing of the Johnson coalition. Grateful for the greatest outpouring of civil rights legislation since Reconstruction, they had given the president their political power of attorney. Could they now afford to offend the touchy leader when there was still so much more to accomplish?

The NAACP and the Urban League would never take a forthright stand against the war. But King, a pacifist, a man of the left, a defender of the Third World, could not avoid confronting the Vietnam issue. In 1965, and again the following year, he had spoken out in favor of a negotiated settlement "even with the Vietcong."[19] But he had curbed his criticism to return the administration's goodwill.

In late 1966, with plans for the spring demonstrations gathering momentum, the Mobe leaders tried to get King to join. King felt he could no longer refuse, but he set conditions: the Communists must be excluded, and Stokely Carmichael must be taken off the program. The Mobe leaders would not yield, and it looked as if they would have to do without King. Then David Dellinger made a case to King's lieutenants that they could not resist. The Mobe, he told them, was "going to have the biggest antiwar march that ever took place . . . with or without Martin Luther King," and King "was going to be left behind in history if he didn't come."[20] King agreed to participate and then berated the NAACP for refusing to take a "forthright stand" on Vietnam.[21]

Among the peace forces, the one holdout against the Spring Mobe was SANE. Back in 1960 SANE had purged itself of Communists following a searing red-baiting attack by Senator Thomas Dodd of Connecticut. The attack had made the organization sensitive to any charge of disloyalty, and it resisted association with radicals. Recently, SANE officials had heard that some of the groups planning to march were determined to carry Vietcong flags. Worse still, some of the April marchers would be avowed Communists. SANE leaders balked. The famous pediatrician, Dr. Benjamin Spock, SANE's cochairman, tried to change his colleague's minds, but failed. In the end SANE refused to endorse the demonstration. Feeling rebuffed, Spock resigned from the national organization later in the year and moved to the peace movement's left.

In January the Spring Mobe appointed the Reverend James Bevel its national director. Bevel was a prominent member of the SCLC, and the move was obviously intended to cement King's participation. But he also proved to be an effective organizer. He could rouse people to action and was full of bright ideas. At one point he burst into the Mobe's New York office exclaiming: "What this demonstration needs is some Indians."[22] As he explained it, there were fifteen thousand Indians serving in Vietnam, a far-higher proportion than their numbers in the general population, and they deserved to be represented. And they were: Chiefs Lame Deer and Henry Crow of the Rosebud Sioux and Mad Bear Anderson of the Tuscarora, carrying signs comparing General Westmoreland to George Custer of Little Big Horn disaster fame and proclaiming GREAT WHITE FATHER SPEAKS WITH FORKED TONGUE! led the first platoon of New York marchers on April 25.[23]

In New York, demonstration day, cloudy and threatening, began with a draft-card-burning ceremony at the Sheep Meadow in Central Park conducted by seventy young men, mostly from a Cornell University group called "We Won't Go." As the cards were tossed into a flaming coffee can, onlookers intoned, "Resist, resist." The Mobe moderates had opposed the ritual, fearing angry public reaction. But the card burners and their supporters had refused to listen. Part of a new antidraft movement among college activists, the militants were determined to stop "the war machine" by clogging its wheels, and the card burning was intended to advertise their plans. But it was also an existential act, an "act of witness," and a gesture of group solidarity. Martin Jezer, an editor of *WIN*, a War Resisters League publication, was one of those who joined the Cornell contingent. He would later write: "The burning of my draft card was, symbolically, my graduation or entrance into this world."[24]

The march itself, the largest since the Vietnam War began, set forth from the park at noon with King, Spock, and Monsignor Rice in the fore as it moved south and east to United Nations Plaza. One hundred thousand people had collected at U.N. headquarters by 2:00 P.M., and more would arrive during the proceedings. As people waited for the official ceremonies to begin, folksingers entertained with protest songs including the old radical standby, "This Land is Your Land."

The crowd was typical of the broad-gauged sixties' demonstrations. Representatives of each of the 1960s' ameliorist social typology were there—clergymen, nuns, writers, professors, students, doctors, lawyers, suburban housewives, professional reformers, and an assortment of young people carrying flowers and signs, some bedaubed with paint. There was one enormous gap: the blue-collar working class. This omission would not be limited to the 1967 Spring Mobe march. Blue-collar Americans during these years would associate the antiwar movement with disrespect for flag, for family, for country. Many labor leaders shared the view of their rank and file and in addition were trapped in the same Johnson coalition as the civil rights movement. How could they repudiate a man who had brought the country full employment and conferred such real benefits on organized labor? Peace activists would agonize over labor's demurrer from the antiwar movement but never find a remedy.

King's keynote speech at the plaza demanded an end to the bombing operation. Spock emphasized the ecumenicism of the antiwar movement. "People of all ages, people of all shades of political opinion" were welcome into the movement, he announced. Despite King's objections, Carmichael spoke, calling the United States "brutal and racist," and, as feared, his appearance provoked Black Power outbursts. With people still dribbling in from the park, a torrential rain suddenly descended, sending everyone scrambling for cover and abruptly ending the rally. Despite the sudden conclusion, the event clearly had been an outstanding success. As he stood on the speakers' platform, King turned to Dellinger and remarked in wonder: "It's more [people] than the August '63 civil rights march."[25]

The San Francisco march and rally were less successful. The weather was cold and wet in the Bay area, and only fifty thousand people came to Kezar Stadium for the ceremonies. The audience flagged quickly. Some of the promoters tried to repeat the recent groovy Be-In at Golden Gate Park (see chapter 6) and hired acid-rock bands like Country Joe and the Fish, Moby Grape, and a truckload of musicians from Haight-Ashbury, the lively new hippie capital, to belt out antiwar songs. The dedicated antiwar people were too uptight for this "flower child" outburst. The march organizers sent the Jug Band packing and nervously warned everybody to be careful about the stadium grass. By the time Coretta King rose to speak, the audience had thinned out to a handful.

The significant event at Kezar Stadium, though barely noticed at the time, was a brief talk by a jacketless, bearded young man named David Harris, the former student body president at Stanford University. Harris and his friends had been living in a commune in a strange atmosphere of SNCC stoic pride, biker bravado, and Quaker pacifism. Most of the young men at Cooley Street, including Harris, were college dropouts or recent graduates and could feel the hot breath of the Selective Service on their necks. It focused their minds wonderfully on the draft issue. In March 1967 Harris and his close friend Dennis Sweeney hit on the idea that if enough young men refused induction, it would be impossible to prosecute them all and the draft would collapse.

Without new cannon fodder, the war itself would soon follow the draft to extinction. They called their scheme "resistance," and Harris told the Kezar Stadium audience that he and his colleagues intended to call a national draft-card turn-in for mid-October to put their plan into effect. Harris's minute or two at the podium would mark a major turn in the antiwar movement.

By the spring of 1967, the opposition to Vietnam had begun to change the direction of national politics. Two years after Rolling Thunder, a large part of the president's own party had deserted him on Vietnam and were looking for an alternative candidate for 1968.

The estrangement was most intense on the party's left, among the reform clubs, councils, and associations that had emerged during the 1950s as part of the decade's Adlai Stevenson liberalism. The reform Democrats' agenda for the nation was the New Deal welfare state rounded out by national health insurance and laws to foster racial equality and a juster distribution of wealth. In local politics, they opposed the old-fashioned Democratic bosses and party pols and sought to replace them with men and women like themselves—college-educated, principled, humane. In their social contours, they resembled the good-government mugwumps of the late nineteenth century and the Progressives of the years just before World War I—white, upper-middle-class, well-educated—though they were more often of immigrant stock than their predecessors. Many deplored the excesses of the McCarthyite witch hunters, but refused to accept "totalitarians" into their organizations. While they endorsed the anti-Soviet containment policies of Truman and his successors, they generally rejected the two-sided cold-war model of "them" and "us."

The new Democrats clustered in local Democratic reform clubs in big cities like New York, Chicago, San Francisco, and Los Angeles. In California they belonged to the California Democratic Council, founded in 1953 to preserve the liberal momentum of the first Adlai Stevenson presidential campaign. In Chicago they formed the Independent Voters of Illinois and the Democratic Federation of Illinois. In New York they ran the Village Independent Democrats, the West Side Democrats, and other reform clubs. Their national forum was Americans for Democratic Action (ADA), formed in 1947 with Eleanor Roosevelt, Arthur Schlesinger, Jr., Mayor Hubert H. Humphrey of Minneapolis, Protestant theologian Reinhold Niebuhr, Walter Reuther of the United Automobile Workers, and liberal Supreme Court Justice William O. Douglas among its charter members.

ADA endorsed John Kennedy for president in 1960 but refused to support Johnson on the same ticket. The months following Kennedy's assassination changed ADA's collective mind, and no organization fought so hard to get LBJ returned to the White House in 1964. Thereafter, the Great Society programs of 1965–66 tightly locked ADA, and the reform Democrats generally, into the Johnson "consensus," along with the moderate civil rights leadership, the trade unions, and the academic community.

Allard Lowenstein was the quintessential reform Democrat. A dark, intense New York lawyer addicted to college-style wrestling, he was already a seasoned veteran of liberal causes while an undergraduate at the University of North Carolina at Chapel Hill in the 1940s. Lowenstein was an early leader of the National Student Association, America's response to the Soviet-dominated World Federation of Democratic Youth, and in later years a receiver of, and conduit for, CIA money going to the American student movement. It is moot whether Lowenstein lent himself to the CIA's cold-war purposes. If so, he behaved strangely. In the late fifties, as foreign policy adviser to Hubert Humphrey, then United States senator from Minnesota, he was a major supporter of African decolonization, an effective antiapartheid propagandist, and a determined enemy of the Spanish dictator Francisco Franco. In the early sixties Lowenstein, by this time a professor at North Carolina State in Raleigh, became an effective catalyst in the civil rights movement. It was Lowenstein's idea of a "freedom vote" by Mississippi's disfranchised black voters that produced the Mississippi Freedom Democratic party and its disruptive challenge to the lily-white regulars at the 1964 Atlantic City Democratic convention. It was his whirlwind campus-circuit recruiting campaign for the 1964 Freedom Summer project that attracted to

Mississippi the hundreds of white students needed to make it a media success in the North.

Lowenstein's recent biographer, Richard Cummings, sees the CIA's anti-Communist hand in all these activities. His thesis is grossly overstated. But Lowenstein always remained hostile to Soviet policy and determined to keep alive a viable liberal alternative to the far left. He was especially concerned about the ideological seduction of the young. Lowenstein kept close to the undergraduate culture even after he had reached his late thirties, and David Harris has charged that he was a covert homosexual whose interest in young men was not entirely political. However mixed his motives, his fear that Vietnam was destroying the faith of the young in liberalism and wrecking the Great Society drove him into leadership of the antiwar movement.

In the summer of 1966, though preoccupied with courting Jenny Lyman, whose Boston Brahmin father disapproved of her hyperthyroid Jewish suitor, Lowenstein brooded over the war. He concluded that Johnson would have to be replaced by an antiwar figure even at the risk of destroying the liberal coaltion. At this point—and for long after—his ideal candidate was Robert Kennedy, the martyred president's younger brother, now senator from New York. In December Lowenstein and Curtis Gans, a one-time member of SDS now an ADA staffer, drafted a paper for ADA that demanded deescalation and a negotiated peace in Vietnam, with the Vietcong treated as a legitimate party to any settlement. That fall and winter a half dozen paid public letters making the same points appeared in *The New York Times*. Signed "student council presidents," "peace corps returnees," "college editors," all were actually composed by Lowenstein.

In early April 1967, just before the spring Mobe, Lowenstein, James Wechsler of the *New York Post*, and the liberal activist attorney Joseph Rauh, Washington counsel for the United Automobile Workers, introduced a resolution at the annual ADA convention opposing LBJ's bid for a second term unless he abandoned his hard line on Vietnam. The motion threatened to tear ADA apart. The moderates shouted that it would destroy the Johnson–Great Society coalition and ultimately ADA as well. Lowenstein defended the resolution from the floor in a spontaneous burst of eloquence that brought a roar of applause. When the Wechsler motion carried by a majority of three to one, Gus Tyler, an old-line anti-Communist trade union leader, remarked: "This is the end of ADA."[26]

The epitaph was premature, but over the next few months the divisive debate continued within ADA over whether it was worth breaking liberal ranks over the Vietnam War. Rauh, who had presented the brief for the Mississippi Freedom Democrats at the 1964 convention, soon backed off, probably swayed by the prowar position of Reuther and the United Auto Workers, his employers. The dump-Johnson people did not have an alternate candidate, he noted, and without a candidate, there was no movement. Rather than trying to replace Johnson, why not insist on inserting a peace plank in the Democratic platform at Chicago? Through the summer the debate continued in the pages of the ADA magazine with articles by Rauh, Curtis Gans, Gus Tyler, and others defending or attacking the dump-Johnson strategy.

Though Lowenstein retained his connection with ADA, he and Gans decided to find another base for their effort to deprive LBJ of the renomination. In early August Lowenstein flew out to a California Democratic fund-raising dinner on the same plane as Robert Kennedy and managed to spend several hours with the senator talking about a possible candidacy. "If you want to run, we'll let you," Lowenstein joked.[27] In a more serious vein, he told Kennedy he was determined to forestall Johnson. "With you we could do it more easily—but we're going to go it with you or without you." Like almost everyone else, Bobby still considered any attempt to replace Johnson harebrained. Stopping Johnson was as likely as "a priest in Bogotá deposing the Pope," he said, and he declined the honor.[28]

But the trip was not wasted. In California Lowenstein conferred with Gerald Hill, the California Democratic Council's chairman, and the two decided to proceed with the dump-Johnson movement. Late that night, by phone, they roused Gans in Washington and asked him to head the national office of a new organization, the Conference of Concerned Democrats, to find an alternative to LBJ and develop a constituency to get their candidate elected. Gans told them he was about to begin his two-week reserve training stint with the marines but would be ready to move on September 1.

The quest for candidate and voters was arduous. Back from Parris Island, the obliging Gans resigned from ADA and set up the headquarters of the Concerned Democrats in his Washington living room. Gans was the inside man. He and his wife, Genie, extracted likely names from anti-Vietnam petitions and any other source they could find. They arranged these by order of prominence and by precinct and handed them to Lowenstein, the outside man, who promptly set off to make contact and stir up interest.

The standard Lowenstein foray was a whirlwind of meetings—with students, political leaders, and the general public. Gans would often precede him to prepare the way, but Lowenstein would do all the talking, whether in small private confabs or at great mass meetings before university audiences. The two traveled to thirty-four states, devoting particular attention to the early-primary states of Minnesota, New Hampshire, and Wisconsin and to the two behemoths, New York and California. The response was encouraging. Students cheered themselves hoarse at the rallies, and in Wisconsin and New Hampshire a number of influential politicians signed aboard the dump-Johnson campaign.

On September 23 the ADA national board met in Washington to consider once more the issue of an alternative to LBJ. The night before, Senator Kennedy had invited some political friends to his home in McLean, in suburban Washington. Lowenstein arrived with Jack Newfield, a liberal *Village Voice* reporter; Arthur Schlesinger and James Loeb, a New York newspaper publisher, were already there. The small group debated whether Bobby should become a candidate for the Democratic nomination, with the senator hanging on the discussion. Lowenstein, his stockinged feet tucked under him, argued from his armchair that the war must be stopped at all costs. In any case, if Johnson lost a few of the primaries he might step down. Newfield seconded Lowenstein. Schlesinger, who favored the Rauh proposal for getting a negotiated peace plank into the 1968 Democratic national platform, responded that it would be impossible to defeat

Johnson. In any case, '68 would be a Republican year, and it was better if Bobby waited until '72. At this point the senator himself intruded: "I think Al may be right. I think Johnson might quit the night before the convention opens. I think he is a coward."[29]

Yet Kennedy remained unconvinced by the two anti-Johnson partisans. Like all the Kennedys, Bobby despised LBJ: Here was the coarse and boorish satyr to the martyred president's Hyperion. The clan had never forgiven LBJ his good luck to have survived; he had never forgiven them their resentment of his survival—or their sense of superiority. For a year following his brother's death, Bobby had unhappily continued as attorney general and, when passed over for vice-president in 1964, had run for the U.S. Senate from New York and won.

He would "have a problem" if he ran against Johnson, he now remarked. "People would say that I was splitting the party out of ambition and envy. No one would believe that I was doing it because of how I felt about Vietnam and poor people."[30] The meeting soon adjourned; Bobby would not run.

The next day the Concerned Democrats suffered a serious setback when ADA refused to endorse the dump-Johnson movement. "Al wanted a resolution . . . without a candidate and I said no," Rauh later recalled.[31] ADA was still unwilling to break up the Great Society coalition for something as quixotic as trying to deprive an incumbent president of his party's renomination.

During the next weeks, the quest for a challenger continued. Lowenstein and Gans approached George McGovern, the liberal South Dakota senator. The answer was No. The boyish Frank Church of Idaho was next. Another no. General James Gavin, a high military officer opposed to Vietnam, said he was interested, but only in the *Republican* nomination, and that ended that. The insurgents even considered the Harvard economist, John Kenneth Galbraith, a genial, witty, and articulate man, who, as luck would have it, was Canadian-born and hence ineligible for the office.

One of the few possibilities remaining was the senator from Minnesota, Eugene McCarthy. Unfortunately, he seemed to lack interest in any higher office. At McGovern's suggestion Lowenstein and Gerald Hill talked to McCarthy at breakfast in his hotel suite while they were both in Los Angeles in late October. The senator surprised them. He plied Lowenstein and Hill with questions: Would labor support him? What about money? Would there be enough volunteers? The two advocates were full of quick optimism, and after listening to their remarks, the senator broke into a broad grin. "I guess you can cut it down to one."[32] "I was ecstatic, it was like music, like an organ welling up in my ears," Lowenstein later told the historian Theodore White.[33] Lowenstein phoned Gans and sped back to Washington. They would not reveal McCarthy's decision until the big Chicago meeting of the Concerned Democrats in December. But they finally had their candidate!

The peace movement did not hold still for mainstream constitutional processes to divert the United States from its evil course. In May 1967 representatives of the Spring Mobilization met in Washington and decided to schedule a major civil disobedience action for late October in the nation's capital. The delegates also dropped *Spring* from the organization's title and renamed it the National Mobilization Committee to End the War in Vietnam, usually shortened to "the Mobe."

During the summer doldrums, the peace forces kept busy with a broad schedule of activities. They sponsored a series of non-binding war-peace referendums in liberal communities to demonstrate public disapproval of Vietnam. In late June members of the Los Angeles Peace Action Council and the student Mobe demonstrated outside the Century Plaza Hotel, where the president had come to address a Democratic fund-raiser. The police used clubs to break up the crowd. Hundreds were injured, sixty sent to hospitals, and fifty arrested. The Los Angeles demonstration was the first time that anti-Vietnam protesters had clashed violently with police.

The big fall antiwar demonstration was actually a collaborative effort of the more radical peace forces. The main event was the Mobe's October civil disobedience demonstration in Wasington. But in addition there were the Resistance-sponsored antidraft action, a California-based Stop the Draft Week, and a "peace torch" marathon with runners carrying coast to coast a lighted torch from Hiroshima, site of the first atomic bomb explosion, to advertise the horrors of war.

The fall project took an absurdist turn when, during the late spring, the Mobe's David Dellinger asked Jerry Rubin of the Vietnam Day Committee to come east and direct the Washington action. Rubin jumped at the chance and arrived in New York from California accompanied by two Bay Area buddies. The Californians were bursting with strange ideas. In the two years since the big Berkeley VDC teach-in, Rubin and his friends had been swept up in the Haight-Ashbury hippie street scene. Rubin now saw the world through a hallucinogenic fog of pot and LSD and wore beads and sported a crown of wild, curly hair. The demonstration, he insisted, must target the Pentagon. Peyote-using Indians considered five-sided figures symbols of evil, and an "exorcism" of the Pentagon, the most famous five-sided building in the world, would inspire the public.

One of the Californian's first moves after reaching New York was to survey the emerging East Village counterculture. In a matter of hours Rubin had discovered his doppelgänger, Abbie Hoffman, another frizzy-headed absurdist, and soon after found himself with his friend in the visitors' gallery at the New York Stock Exchange showering dollar bills on the delighted floor traders below to advertise the hippies' contempt for material culture.

While the Mobe's seedy headquarters on New York's Beekman Street acquired West Coast Day-Glo colors, the other antiwar groups made their own fall plans. The Resistance movement got a big boost with the release of "A Call to Resist Illegitimate Authority," composed by Marcus Raskin and Arthur Waskow of the leftwing Institute for Policy Studies. Proclaiming support for draft refusal and pledging the signers to contribute bail money and help families of draft resisters, the document had been circulating in the antiwar community for some months to mixed responses. Norman O. Brown, the counterculture guru, would not sign. His reason was unfathomable, like much of his prose. Neither would Hans Morgenthau, the anti-Vietnam University of Chicago political scientist. Morgenthau posed the sensible objection that those not of draft age should not encourage young men to do illegal things. Allen Ginsburg signed with a characteristic demurrer. He did not like the "humorless prose." "You'd be better off telling people to goof off or fuck off from the draft," he wrote the editors, "than all this gobbledygook which takes too long to read."[34] Yet in the end there were 158 signatures of prominent writers, academics, clergymen, and journalists affixed to the statement when it appeared as a paid advertisement in *The New York Review of Books* and *The New Republic* in late September.

The October actions in the flesh were the most massive and militant antiwar protests to date. In California, Stop the Draft Week metamorphosed from a peaceful draft-card turn-in into clashes with the police that sharply raised the violence level of the antiwar movement. On the culminating day, Friday, October 20, ten thousand protesters from Berkeley, Stanford, San Jose State, and several Bay Area high schools, equipped with helmets and shields, fought the police in a five-hour hit-and-run battle at the Oakland induction center that resembled a choreographed ballet. The protesters blocked induction-center entrances and stopped buses bringing inductees to be signed up. When the police charged, they broke and ran and then reassembled for another foray. Though the induction procedures were delayed only for a few hours, radical leaders gushed over the new "mobile tactics" and promised to use them widely elsewhere.

The demonstrations in Washington were more massive, if more pacific. For a time, it looked as if Rubin, Hoffman, and their colleagues would turn the Pentagon march into a freak show. At a Mobe press conference on August 28 to announce the October plans, Hoffman told reporters that they intended "to raise the Pentagon three hundred feet in the air." Rubin was less imaginative, but more frightening. "We're now in the business of whole-sale disruption and widespread resistance and dislocation of . . . American society," he announced.[35] Matters got even more hairy a few days later when an article by Keith Lampe, one of Hoffman's counterculture friends, appeared in the *Mobilizer*, the Mobe's official publication. Lampe, in Hoffman's later words, was "a zany peace creep who liked to dress up as a keystone Kop,"[36] and "On Making a Perfect Mess" promised zonked-out-of-the-head chaos for Washington. Lampe anticipated a colorful series of events on October 21–22:

A thousand children will stage Loot-Ins at department stores to strike at the property fetish that underlies genocidal wars. . . .
Hey, who defoliated the White House lawns? . . .
Hey, who kidnapped the guard at the Tomb of the Unknown Soldier? . . .
During a block party in front of the White House a lad of nine will climb the fence and piss, piss, piss. . . .[37]

Lampe's article was the last straw. The moderate Mobe leaders squelched the offending *Mobilizer* issue and took over publication of the paper. But serious damage had been done. Many SANE members boycotted the demonstration as did the SCLC, Negotiations Now, and the Quaker American Friends Service Committee.

Despite the defections, the Pentagon march in October would provide something for almost everyone. The Resistance people held their draft-card turn-in at the Justice Department, where they, and their big box of cards, were politely received. The Trotskyists, the moderates of Women Strike for Peace, and the liberal trade unionists got their rally at Lincoln Memorial with speeches, songs, and uplift followed by a slow procession to an officially designated Pentagon parking lot across the Potomac River. The action types and student radicals had their chance to shout obscenities, hurl eggs and bottles, carry the Vietcong flag, and violate the agreement with the General Services Administration. Norman Mailer and several other celebrities won their brief martyrdom in jail for cutting the wire fence at the Pentagon entrance and charging up the stairs. Mailer also got a best-seller and Pulitzer Prize–winner, *The Armies of the Night*, out of his few hours outside the Pentagon.

The demonstration officially ended at dusk, but several thousand protesters, mostly students, remained, huddled in blankets in front of the huge building, after the crowds departed. Some tried to get the troops who faced them in battle gear to defect. "Join us! Our fight is not with you!"[38] Some put flowers in the gun barrels of the impassive young men in uniform. A photo of this gesture remains one of the many indelible images of the sixties antiwar movement.

The air became cold as the evening wore on, and someone shouted "Burn a draft card! Keep warm!"[39] Hundreds of small flames were soon twinkling across the Pentagon plaza. After midnight the reporters and TV crews left, and the federal marshalls, now unobserved, began to rough people up until sociologist Sidney Peck, a Mobe official, shouted that the protesters' demonstration permit was still valid and the Mobe would file charges. At dawn most people had drifted away, and student leaders, preferring to seem in control, advised the crowd to disperse. In a few minutes the plaza was empty.

Peace leaders proclaimed the Pentagon march a colossal success. "I felt," Peck later observed, "that now there was a resistance movement. . . ." He could foresee "that . . . people on a mass basis . . . would [now] refuse to be complicit, . . . would refuse to pay taxes, to do research, to accept the draft, . . . refuse to fight, to produce and transport the weaponry. . . ."[40]

None of this ever occurred. There were never many resisters in Peck's sense. To the very end, in fact, a majority of Americans would remain on the sidelines. The war seemed to many people like some chronic family problem: deplorable, but also so tangled as to be insoluble. Yet Peck was not entirely wrong. The peace movement did not end the war, but it deserves some of the credit for forcing reconsideration of Vietnam. Each new antiwar demonstration helped "bring the war home," convincing an ever-widening circle of influential and articulate Americans that if only for the sake of civil peace Vietnam must be ended. By raising the price of fighting the war, the peace movement accelerated American disenchantment among the people who made the decisions.

No one was as convinced of the march's success as the president and his aides, though their response was naturally the reverse of Peck's. The peace movement was encouraging the enemy to hold out despite punishing military costs, they charged, and there was a serious danger that the United States would be beaten, not by the Vietcong and North Vietnamese, but by our own inner disagreements. The president warned that the protesters were postponing peace. The war would end sooner, he said, if Americans were united rather than divided.

Johnson's private view of the peace activists was not publishable. They were traitors, collaborators with the enemy who must not be allowed to defeat the United States. Besides the demonstrations, Johnson was enraged by the meetings from 1965 on between antiwar leaders and the North Vietnamese in Indonesia, Cuba, Europe, and North Vietnam itself. Just the previous September, an American delegation of peaceniks, radicals, and mavericks had spent eight days in Bratislava, Czechoslovakia, where they had met with Vietcong and North Vietnamese representatives. A secret intelligence report on this meeting had convinced at least three Republican congressmen, including Gerald Ford, that the Pentagon march had been carefully plotted with the enemy to help subvert American morale.

The charges of aiding the enemy were overwrought, but they should not be dismissed entirely. The Vietnamese Communists did not expect to defeat the Americans on the battlefield. Victory, they knew, would come only by undermining the American will to fight, and they welcomed such events as the Pentagon march as signs of declining American resolve. Four days after the demonstration, dispatches from Hong Kong reported that a North Vietnamese newspaper had praised "the American people's growing movement against the U.S. ruling circle's aggression in Vietnam" as "a valuable support for the Vietnamese people."[41]

The meetings with American dissenters in Bratislava, Jakarta, Havana, and eventually in Hanoi itself were an effective part of the Vietcong–North Vietnamese psychological war against the United States. They did not make converts. The visitors were already hostile to American policy; but the pilgrimages inevitably hardened and invigorated their anti-American views. Ever since the eighteenth century, the Russians had been adept practitioners of the Potemkin Village trick of prettied-up false fronts to impress influential visitors. The North Vietnamese had learned the technique well from their mentors, and their receptions invariably left the American visitors breathless over the warmth, compassion, bravery, determination, and yearning for peace of the Vietnamese people. The pilgrims' fulsome accounts of these meetings in books, articles, and interviews—given what we know of North Vietnamese rigidity and truculence—attest to the amazing effectiveness of Hanoi's psychological warfare.

But nothing can excuse the administration's response. Johnson did not stop with polite admonitions against the peace movement. Instead, as with Martin Luther King, he authorized a campaign of surveillance and disruptive tactics against the offender that foreshadowed the even more deplorable activities of the Nixon era.

In 1965 the FBI launched a "dirty tricks" operation of false mailings against the Berkeley Vietnam Day Committee to mislead peace protesters about the time and place of demonstrations. Early in 1967 the CIA began to investigate the foreign connections of the antiwar publication *Ramparts*. That fall, after the Pentagon march, Johnson ordered the CIA to look carefully into the issue of North Vietnamese–peace movement collaboration. The agency did its duty but found nothing incriminating and told the president so. Johnson refused to believe the report and remained certain to the end that the Communists were actively financing the peace movement and providing its marching orders.

COINTELPRO, launched by the FBI in the spring of 1968, shortly after the Columbia student uprising, was primarily an anti–New Left operation. But J. Edgar Hoover and his colleagues had difficulty defining what the New Left was, and COINTELPRO spent more time harassing the peace movement and its leaders than the student radicals. Before the Democratic convention in August, for example, the Mobe's Sidney Peck found himself facing a massive IRS tax audit designed to keep him too busy verifying his returns to carry out the Mobe's program for the convention. The agency also tried to destroy peace leaders' personal reputations. FBI agents, for instance, mailed anonymous letters to newspapers accusing David McReynolds of the War Resisters League of homosexual activities. Johnson himself had not approved the COINTELPRO operations, but his suspicions obviously encouraged the director's activities.

The government also took more direct steps to squelch the

antiwar movement. The Vietnam War was both futile and foolish, but no one who directly defied the Selective Service laws could have expected to avoid prosecution at some point. The laws derived from the state's legitimate right to protect its citizens against foreign enemies. You could call them props of an evil war, but in a democratic nation where the courts and legislatures functioned, redress was ultimately available through constitutional processes, however slow. Any other response invited the sort of chaos that no society could easily condone. The civil rights activists broke the law too, but the laws they violated were usually local ordinances that offended the nation's collective conscience and challenged superior federal enactments and legal decisions. It is a measure of the late sixties' "resistance" mood that so many people despised constitutional processes and dismissed the consequences of disobeying federal statutes.

The administration's crackdown on draft resisters began in 1965 when it indicted David Miller and several other militants for draft-card burning. Shortly after the Pentagon march, General Lewis Hershey, head of the Selective Service System, directed local draft boards to classify as I-A—eligible for immediate induction—all "misguided registrants" who participated in "illegal demonstrations" or interfered with the operation of the Selective Service Act.[42] The government also came down hard on men like the Fort Hood Three, military personnel who refused combat assignment out of conscience.

Until the end of 1967, however, the government's targets had been limited to draft-age young men or members of the armed forces. Antiwar leaders, even those close to the draft-resistance movement, had been left alone. Then in early January 1968, a federal grand jury in Boston indicted Dr. Spock, Yale Protestant chaplain William Sloane Coffin, Marcus Raskin of the Institute for Policy Studies, Michael Ferber of the Resistance, and Mitchell Goodman, an antiwar writer, for conspiring "to counsel, aid, and abet young men to violate the draft laws."[43] The case went to trial at the end of May, and three weeks later all but Raskin were convicted. Sentence was delayed for appeal, and in the end no one was punished. But the Resistance trial and other federal

prosecutions depleted the peace movement's energies and financial resources and slowed its momentum.

The shouts, the chants, the placards, the crowds in the streets
could be heard and seen in the caucus rooms and convention halls
where the politicians gathered, and they affected their actions.
From the outset Gene McCarthy proved an unpredictable candidate. His refusal to wait until the Concerned Democrats' early
December meeting in Chicago to announce his decision to run in
the primaries against LBJ had made the kickoff rally a dud.
During the weeks that followed, he had done little to inject life
into his campaign, scorning emotional fireworks and traditional
hoopla—marching bands, straw hats, screaming fans. He admitted that he found it hard to emote "for effect." His low-key
style impressed one supporter as a "real asset" that contrasted
"nicely with President Johnson's . . . flamboyance,"[44] but it
miffed Lowenstein, whose modus operandi was frenetic action.
For his part McCarthy found Lowenstein trying: he had too many
irons in the fire, the senator felt, and he clearly continued to
prefer Bobby as the candidate.

Meanwhile, a rift over money opened between Lowenstein
and Gans. The dump-Johnson organization had accumulated
large debts, and Gans, who had personally received only a
pittance for months, blamed his poverty on Lowenstein, the man
who managed the finances. When McCarthy set up his own
campaign organization independent of the Concerned Democrats, Gans signed on as director of operations under overall
campaign manager Blair Clark, a former vice-president of CBS
News. Lowenstein remained a McCarthy supporter, but his
relations with the senator would never be very cordial again.

The state that held the earliest primary, New Hampshire, was
the obvious place to to kick off the McCarthy campaign. The
victory that McCarthy would win there would deflect the course of
American political history.

The ball was almost fumbled. The senator preferred to start
with Massachusetts. With its large delegation, it was the better test

in the Northeast; New Hampshire would prove nothing, he believed. Fortunately, Gerry Studds and David Hoeh, two New Hampshire academics prominent in the state Democratic party, refused to take no for an answer. As teachers—Studds at the elite preparatory school, St. Paul's, and Hoeh at Dartmouth College—they regretted the profound disillusionment of the young with the war and the electoral process that seemed unable to end it. McCarthy, with his dry wit and almost Yankee demeanor, could restore the cynics' faith and carry the state against the pro-Johnson Democratic regulars. The two men bombarded the candidate and his aides with memos, phone calls, and letters, asking them to reconsider. They also submitted a detailed campaign plan that estimated total costs at a puny fifty-five thousand dollars. The strategy worked. On January 2, while Hoeh was having dinner with Clark at Manchester's Wayfarer Hotel, McCarthy called and told them that he had changed his mind. A week later Hoeh rented a storefront office in Concord, the state capital, for student volunteers. It would be the first of hundreds.

The campaign began with New Hampshire still locked in winter's freezing grip. "The state was covered in snow," McCarthy later wrote, "all the trees, excepting the evergreens, were lifeless and black. Most houses had storm windows and storm doors; long underwear flapped frozen on the wash lines."[45]

The local citizens, whatever the optimists had predicted, were not noticeably warmer. New Hampshire was at heart a conservative state. Its leading newspaper, the Manchester *Union-Leader,* was published by William Loeb, a choleric supporter of the far right-wing John Birch Society. It was a Republican state, with 50 percent more registered GOPers than Democrats. Many of its Democrats, moreover, were French and Irish Catholic blue-collar workers employed in defense industries and easily aroused by patriotic calls to support "our boys" in Vietnam. Yet at its southern end, where it touched Massachusetts, it had a stretch of true McCarthy country. Here, in what was virtually a suburb of Boston, were the lawyers, engineers, high-tech businessmen, academics, and middle-class housewives who formed McCarthy's natural constituency.

Two things turned unpromising New Hampshire into a triumph for the insurgent spirit of the day. The first was the Tet offensive. The North Vietnamese–Vietcong attack during the Lunar New Year converted thousands of believers into doubters. Even Americans who did not suddenly become doves lost faith in the ability of the United States to achieve victory in Southeast Asia. Polls would show that many who voted against Johnson in March were angry at him not for waging war, but for not waging it vigorously or effectively enough to ensure victory.

The second was the Children's Crusade. One of the senator's new staff, taken on with Clark, was Sam Brown, a pale-cheeked young divinity student from Council Bluffs, Iowa. Brown had been your ordinary clean-cut mid-American WASP undergraduate when he encountered McCarthyism—the red-baiting kind—at Redlands University in southern California. He was repelled. Soon after, he met Lowenstein at a National Student Association meeting. The two events together produced a potent synergism, and by the time Brown came to the Harvard Divinity School he was a confirmed social activist and peace advocate.

Brown was the "student coordinator," who, with a gaggle of Ivy League graduate-student lieutenants, arranged the volunteers' housing, meals, schedules, and tasks. The students themselves were self-selected. The earliest had come in January from the cluster of private and public colleges in Amherst, Massachusetts. They had been reinforced when news of the exciting battle shaping up to the north spread by word of mouth to Cambridge and New Haven. Then, on the Washington Birthday weekend, three student-packed buses, the forerunner of scores more, had arrived from the Washington–Baltimore area. In all, the two or three thousand "kids" who turned the New Hampshire campaign into a triumph came from a hundred different schools scattered from Michigan to the west to Virginia to the south. One of the most effective was the candidate's own bright-eyed daughter, Mary, who took a leave from Radcliffe College to join her dad's campaign.

Most of the student volunteers were nubile young people, and a major New Hampshire attraction—besides peace and freedom—was girls—or boys. But there were also some young married couples like the Stavises, two graduate students from New York, drawn by less gonadal concerns. Just finished with their semester's course work at Columbia and NYU, Ben and Rosann took the bus for Concord on St. Valentine's Day, arriving with their suitcases at state headquarters in mid-morning. Before they could wash or change their clothes, they were put to work cleaning, wire stringing, and stacking flyers and pamphlets. The next day as Ben shivered in the fifteen-degree cold trying to identify voters' party affiliation from an outdoor roster, he suddenly realized that the campaign really needed him. The Stavises had expected to stay only a week or so. That day they agreed to remain until after the primary, still a month away. They would hang on until the end of the line in late August.

Few of the student volunteers were deep-dyed radicals; most believed in "the system," though for some the attitude was wait-and-see. But there was a serious style problem. Accoutered in the grungy clothes and exuberant hair styles of the elite colleges, many looked like hippies and bomb throwers by Granite State standards. Sam Brown "kept his hair at a perfect length,"[46] according to the Stavises, and it was his responsibility to reduce the culture shock to a minumum. "Straights"—girls willing to wear modest hemlines and demure blouses, and boys beardless and shorn—were assigned to ringing door bells and handing out campaign literature on the streets. "Nonstraights" were kept indoors, out of sight, stuffing envelopes, making phone calls, and writing press releases. Eventually many nonstraights, craving the personal contact and the fresh, if frigid, air, exchanged jeans and T-shirts for skirts and sports jackets, removed excess hair, and were reclassified. The process gave birth to the famous slogan Clean for Gene.

By the end of February, it was becoming clear that a real challenge to the president was shaping up in New Hampshire, that this was not the pushover campaign it had first seemed. The student volunteers were really making a dent. Even the most stony-faced Granite Staters found the students hard to resist. As one New Hampshire Democratic leader remarked, "These college kids are fabulous. . . . [They] knock at the door and come in politely, and actually want to talk to grown-ups, and people are delighted."[47]

And the kids were not alone. With New Hampshire the antiwar movement had a real candidate making a real fight, and it loosened the pockets of the affluent liberals of New York, Boston, Washington, and Chicago. The campaign soon became a magnet for adult celebrities like the actor Paul Newman and folksingers Peter, Paul, and Mary, who came to canvass in person. It also brought into the McCarthy camp maverick political pros, like speech writer Richard Goodwin, a Kennedy man willing to take second-best to end the war if Bobby would not do it. Dark, scowling, deep-voiced, Goodwin had worked for the Kennedys and then for LBJ, but had deserted the administration over Vietnam. In New Hampshire he proved a skillful strategist who, for example, instantly saw the gaffe of the regulars' coercive scheme to test the loyalty of Democrats by issuing Johnson pledge cards and made it into a major McCarthy plus.

The voters made their decision on March 12, a clear, crisp New England day. The regulars had proclaimed that McCarthy would get less than a quarter of the vote, up from a puny 12 percent predicted by a Gallup poll in January, but still no catastrophe for the president. The media, however, smelled an upset, and the major TV networks were ready with crews to interview the candidates and flash the results.

The media of course were right. Early news had the small towns going for Gene. But would the cities support him? During the evening wait, a press aide rushed in with the news that a poll watcher had discovered that three dead men had voted in Manchester. The McCarthy wit leaped out. "Don't release it. They were ours; it was the Resurrection. They came back to vote for us."[48] The cities, too, soon got in line. By midnight the senator was running 40 percent plus to the president's 50 percent, a stunning upset. On the Republican line Richard Nixon, had done even better: 79 percent to Nelson Rockefeller's 11 percent.

McCarthy appeared at the Manchester Sheraton ballroom close to midnight for the victory celebration and was greeted by "Chi-ca-go, Chi-ca-go," from the volunteers. He modestly declined credit for the results and praised the revelers as "the most intelligent campaign staff in the history of American politics."[49] Soon after, he returned to his suite and received a congratulatory call from Kennedy. He was in bed by 1:00 A.M.

When all the absentee ballots, write-ins, and crossovers were counted, McCarthy, the challenger from nowhere, came within 230 votes of the incumbent president. Everywhere the victory was interpreted as a referendum for peace. It was not. The Tet offensive *had* shifted public opinion sharply in favor of the dove position. Between February and March, Gallup polls reported a drop in hawks from 60 percent to 41 percent of Americans and a corresponding leap in doves from 24 percent to 42 percent. But McCarthy had not been perceived by everyone as a peace candidate. As the scientific polls showed, three out of five McCarthy supporters in overwhelmingly hawkish New Hampshire deserted the president because he was not hawkish *enough*. The truth is that for many reasons Lyndon Johnson had ceased to be a popular president and was no longer liked even by loyal voters of his own party.

But political outcomes in America are not decided by scientific polls. The startling results in New Hampshire registered as a peace vote and set in motion powerful political forces. To Bobby Kennedy in New York they were an electric shock jolting him to action.

The senator from New York was a strange amalgam of pride and humility, of action and thought. The third son, the runt of the litter, he grew up in the shadow of two older, bigger, smarter, handsomer brothers. He had to compensate by extra effort, extra work, extra determination. From the first the Kennedys were groomed for public power, power made possible by the patriarch Joseph's enormous wealth, but if Joe Junior and John were to be the monarchs, Robert, at best, was destined to carry their trains. He had accepted the role gracefully and had served as John's attorney general with no thought except to make the administration look good. As the country's chief law officer, his civil rights role had been subordinated to the administration's need to hold the white southern Democrats without losing the black northern ghettos; his anticrime campaign had been designed to make JFK's presidency seem tough on criminals. So long as his brother lived, there was little to distinguish Robert, except the money and the Harvard education, from any other Irish-American pol—tribal, loyal, competitive, pragmatic, and sometimes—as his enemies insisted—"ruthless."

John's assassination transformed Robert's life. It is tempting to say that the tragedy deepened his personality. It no doubt did, but not to the extent the sentimentalists believe. Unlike Joe Junior and John, Bobby probably never needed a demonstration that life was full of ironies and defeats, though the assassination certainly confirmed these truths and amplified the kinder side of his nature. More important, the events that awful day in Dallas changed his image. The sharp and sometimes ugly lines of the scrappy, ruthless, shallow loyalist were now softened. He too had suffered, and the pain made him seem more human. Image makes a difference in American electoral politics.

It is often said that Bobby had great inner capacity for growth. This is also unnecessarily sentimental. More to the point, his brother's death changed his circumstances. As attorney general after November 1963, he was no longer right-hand man to the shining young monarch, his older brother, but to a stranger, someone coarse, alien, and resentful of the Kennedys. He was, besides, the successor, out from the shadow, his own man for the first time, beholden to no one yet responsible for the family's reputation. It is hard not to believe that his growing differences with LBJ over Vietnam were fed by the need to assert an independent course for himself. Then, with the run for U.S. senator from New York, he acquired a new constituency, more liberal, less Irish than his brother's when he was in Congress. He also acquired a new layer of advisers to add to those he had gathered as attorney general and as the successor to King Arthur in Camelot. Adam Walinsky, Peter Edelman, Jeff Greenfield, Tom Johnston, and Frank Mankiewicz all came from a more issue-oriented, liberal milieu than Bobby himself, and all except Mankiewicz were under thirty. These young men alerted the senator to what was happening in America and put him in touch with the left intellectuals, the student leaders, the ghetto militants.

Surely the new Bobby of the eighty-five-day run for the Democratic presidential nomination—the gentle, self-mocking, compassionate, empathetic people's tribune—was as much a product of the new facts of late sixties' America and the new men and women around him as of the existential growth potential of the man himself.

The results in New Hampshire were a very large new fact to Bobby and his advisers: Johnson was beatable. The senator would have to declare or someone else would run off with the nomination. Nothing would ever persuade the McCarthy people that Kennedy had not used Gene as a stalking horse to test the dangers of the nomination quest and then to be replaced by the real hunter. That the New York senator now jumped into the ring was a measure, they said, of the Kennedy arrogance, of the Kennedys' assumption that the presidency was theirs by divine right. The renewed charges of "ruthlessness" and "opportunism" would haunt Bobby throughout the short remainder of his life.

The truth was more complicated than this. Before leaping into the contest, Kennedy tried to strike a deal with Johnson. Two days after New Hampshire, he, Ted Kennedy, and Ted Sorensen met with Defense Secretary Clark Clifford and proposed that if the president issued a statement that the war must be "reevaluated" and agreed to appoint a commission with a roster of "independent" members to consider America's future course in Vietnam, he would stay out of the race. Clifford apparently took the proposal to Johnson, who rejected it out of hand. LBJ's published response at the time was that it would help Hanoi, that it was a political deal and no way to run a war, and that it was an abdication of presidential power. One of his aides was quoted as saying the proposal was "the damnedest piece of political blackmail" he had ever encountered.[50] We can be certain that LBJ's own words were even more pungent.

But besides, McCarthy himself was partly responsible for his rival's behavior. He seemed interested primarily in changing American policy in Vietnam, not actually in winning the nomination—or the office. If New Hampshire suddenly whetted Bobby's taste for the presidency, it had the same effect on Gene. It could also be argued that McCarthy never had a chance to win in

November. Bobby did. But whatever the merits of the case, the thousands of young men and women who had worked for Gene in New Hampshire would never forgive Kennedy for trying to steal what they had won with pain, sweat, and sacrifice.

Yet Kennedy tried to avoid a grudge fight with his rival. On the day following the primary, the two men met at Ted Kennedy's Washington office and Bobby told Gene of his decision. He tried to explain it on grounds that McCarthy could accept. He had been prompted by the administration's growing intransigence on Vietnam; by Nixon's victory in the New Hampshire Republican column; by the increasing administration indifference to the crises of the cities; and by the obvious fact that the Democrats were already so deeply divided that his candidacy could scarcely make things worse. The effort at peace did not work. Outwardly calm, McCarthy inwardly seethed. He had no objections to Kennedy's running, he replied, though since he did not intend to withdraw, the field would be getting crowded. Kennedy should delay his announcement, however, or if he could not, confine his primary campaigns to a few states where the McCarthy forces did not intend to compete. Despite the bland words, he later remarked that "Kennedy was fattening me up for the kill."[51]

For a few weeks McCarthy and Kennedy loyalists tried to strike a deal. On March 15, Ted Kennedy, accompanied by an entourage of both candidate's supporters, flew to Green Bay, Wisconsin, to see if the two sides could avoid a damaging donnybrook. The party arrived late and was greeted in the McCarthy hotel suite by the senator, the senator's independent-minded wife Abigail, Mary, his daughter, and some of the McCarthy staff. McCarthy was not interested in a joint effort; nor was he willing to withdraw. He still felt resentment. As he later explained, Bobby had let him do the preliminary work himself. "It was," he remarked wryly, "a little lonely up there in New Hampshire."[52] Ted left the Northland Hotel at three that morning with no pact in hand.

Back in Virginia, a party at Hickory Hill, the Kennedy estate, was winding down. Scheduled weeks before as a birthday celebration for Bobby's wife, Ethel, now, after the momentous events of the past week, it became an important business meeting as well.

While the rich, the stylish, the literate, and the famous clustered around the piano to sing songs, in another room Schlesinger, Walinsky, and Greenfield worked on the paragraphs that would publicly announce the senator's decision to run.

The birthday festivities tapered off at about eleven o'clock. The political meeting continued, but the conferees adjourned without a completed draft of the statement since no one knew what Ted and McCarthy had arranged. At 2:00 A.M. Bobby went to bed asking someone to wait up for Ted's call from Green Bay. Ted himself arrived at five-thirty and awakened Schlesinger. "Abigail said no," he reported. "They won't cooperate."[53]

Bobby and his weary advisers assembled again in the Hickory Hill breakfast room at seven the next morning and finished composing the announcement that the senator was in the race. At ten o'clock, Kennedy appeared with his family and entourage to face the media in the old Senate Caucus Room, where John had declared his candidacy eight years earlier.

Bobby had not slept much, but he was dapper in a blue suit and red-and-blue-figured tie that Ethel had picked out for him. He also wore the prized Kennedy-loyalist badge: a gold PT-109 tie clasp commemorating his brother's World War II naval exploits. Alert and serious, he told the assembled reporters and colleagues that he was not running "merely to oppose any man . . . ," but because the country was in peril—in Vietnam, in the ghettos, in its international economic relations.[54] Kennedy tried to head off the surge of criticism from the McCarthyites that he knew would come and praised McCarthy's "remarkable New Hampshire campaign. . . ." It had revealed how deep the divisions were in the party and the nation, and until that had been made clear his own participation would have been seen as a clash of personalities rather than a disagreement over issues. The reporters' response to his defense boded ill. Barely muffled guffaws from the press section greeted the words that his candidacy "would not be in opposition" to the Minnesota senator's, "but in harmony."[55]

Kennedy and his party escaped from the Capitol after a bruising round of reporters' questions and raced to National Airport to make the New York St. Patrick's Day Parade on time.

They had hurried for nothing. For redressing all those years of WASP scorn and rejection, the Kennedys had earned a special spot in the hearts of most Irish Americans. And Bobby, in some ways, was more Irish than his cooler, more intellectual older brother. But he was also a dove, and no group of New Yorkers was more hawkish than the Driscolls, O'Briens, and Scallys of Astoria, Inwood, and Hell's Kitchen. As the candidate marched down Fifth Avenue, he could hear catcalls and cries, "You'll never make it, ya bum!"[56] At one point a young fellow marcher carrying a St. Francis College banner turned on him angrily and was about to punch him in the nose when the cops grabbed him.

Bobby went to Boston the next day for another St. Patrick's Day Parade, this time with his brother, the junior senator from Massachusetts. Perhaps it was Teddy's presence, or the fact that the Boston Irish accepted him as their own, that made the crowds far warmer. They cheered as the brothers strode along side by side. On the flight back to New York, Bobby's aides discussed the differences between the two receptions and concluded that there were three things a campaigning politician should always avoid: racetracks, sporting events, and the New York St. Patrick's Day Parade.

Kennedy's talk of healing party divisions may have been opportunism, but the problem was real. As 1968 opened, the Democratic party seemed to be decomposing into its constituent elements. Writing on the first day of the year, the pundit Walter Lippmann declared that even if Johnson were reelected "the decline and disintegration of the Democratic Party" would "not be stopped."[57]

The Democrats did not suddenly discover disunity in 1968. Back in the twenties, Will Rogers, the cowboy humorist, had proudly proclaimed: "I'm not a member of any organized political party. I'm a Democrat."[58] But the disunity had seldom before been so thorough or so visible.

On the party's left, the war and the McCarthy candidacy had produced turmoil. ADA had split into "pragmatists," who felt the organization must preserve itself as a "responsible vehicle for the liberal-labor-minority coalition within the Democratic Party," and "moralists," who agreed with John Galbraith that they would "have a great deal of difficulty with their consciences if they didn't support McCarthy."[59] In February, ADA's national board voted to endorse McCarthy, the first time in twenty years it had failed to support an incumbent Democratic president. John D. Roche, a former Brandeis professor and one of ADA's mainstays, resigned on the spot. Two days later the presidents of three major AFL-CIO unions—I. W. Abel of the United Steel Workers, Louis Stulberg of the International Ladies' Garment Workers Union, and Joseph Beirne of the Communications Workers of America— submitted their resignations from the ADA board. The protest soon spread to the membership, with several prominent liberals resigning during the next few days. By the time of the ADA national convention in mid-May, most of the dissenters were gone, and the convention confirmed its national board's action with only a handful of nay votes. But the organization was seriously shaken and entered the fall campaign less able to provide support for the Democrats than in past years.

More serious was the disaffection of the right. From Reconstruction on, the Democrats, the party of sectional reconciliation and white supremacy, had counted on the South as the most loyal part of the nation. For the next fifty years it was virtually impossible for the party to exercise power without southern support.

During the 1930s, New Deal agricultural relief, flood control, and welfare programs had confirmed southern fidelity. They had also created in the North a vast new Democratic constituency among the urban children and grandchildren of European immigrants and among the millions of blacks, newly arrived and newly enfranchised, in the big-city ghettos. These changes had shifted the party's center of gravity away from Dixie to the urbanized North and East.

After World War II, as racial justice encroached on economic justice in the party's agenda, southern Democrats grew restless. In 1948 southern conservatives stalked out of the national convention to protest the adoption of the strong civil rights plank introduced by the young mayor of Minneapolis, Hubert

Humphrey, and ran a separate presidential slate under the States Rights Democratic party (Dixiecrat) label. By the early 1950s the southerners were back in the party, but the seams remained; and as the civil rights movement forged ahead, it left behind growing numbers of fearful men and women—in the North as well as in the South—who believed that blacks were making gains at their expense. The mood was given the name *backlash,* and it meant trouble for the Democrats.

Backlash voters were spread across the social and—to some extent—the ideological spectrum. In the South they included the crude and brutal bigots of the Ku Klux Klan and whites, primarily of rural birth, whose sense of worth depended on the continued existence of a black undercaste and who condoned lynching and bombing to protect the racial status quo. The southern blacklash also included men and women comfortable with the urban and industrial present who acknowledged past racial injustices, but were unsettled by the speed of racial change and claimed the civil rights movement had gone too far too fast.

Backlash in the North was a more complex phenomenon. The North had its quota of coarse racists who despised blacks and condoned violence to keep them in their place. More common were the offended moderates who had accepted desegregation and enfranchisement, issues that concerned the South, but panicked when the civil rights movement became militant and aggressive and turned its attention north to tackle housing segregation and economic discrimination.

In the North, too, crude racism was largely a lower-class phenomenon, expressed most directly by blue-collar workers and members of the bottom layers of the middle class. "Ethnics" mostly—the children and grandchildren of Eastern and Southern European immigrants—they denied that their ancestors had either enslaved blacks or received the government largesse that blacks were now demanding and getting. Why, then, should they pay? Like rural southern whites, they were socially insecure and resented being jostled by blacks demanding their place in the sun.

In the North, especially, racial backlash often took disguised or displaced forms. By the closing years of the sixties, urban Americans began to feel besieged as crime and disorder seemed to take over their neighborhoods. The perception was not a mirage. Crime was in fact becoming a scourge in American cities as the decade waned. During the 1950s the rate of violent crime was both low and level; homocide rates actually declined in the fifties. Then, beginning in 1964, the incidence of violent crime mysteriously began to soar and continued to climb into the 1970s.

It was not necessary to be personally mugged or burglarized to feel the effects of the crime surge. By 1968 the air was charged with stories about the worsening plague. In August J. Edgar Hoover reported that the number of felons had risen 89 percent between 1960 and 1967, nine times the population rate increase. In December the FBI announced that violent crime for the first nine months of the year was 19 percent higher than for the same period the year before, with homocide up 21 percent. In March *The New York Times*'s Sunday Week in Review section contained a full-page advertisement of a family planning group headed: HAVE YOU EVER BEEN MUGGED? WELL, YOU MAY BE!"[60] The text made the blunt point that if there were fewer slum babies there would be fewer crimes.

Crime was clearly a racial issue. Much of the deluge was a byproduct of demography—the postwar baby boom had raised the proportion of crime-prone young males in the population— and blacks were also the most frequent victims. But many of the criminals were black slum dwellers, and the advent of the crime plague seemed to correspond with the influx of blacks into the city ghettos. In the minds of many urban whites, moreover, the muggings, armed robberies, and rapes were bracketed with the ghetto riots that had swept the cities from 1965 onward as examples of social chaos. By 1968 the phrase *law and order* had become a verbal code for demands that blacks be kept from disturbing the social peace.

But backlash was not only antiblack. Backlash voters deplored the disrespect and insubordination that had infected the entire society. They deplored the antics of the rebellious white students. Many had not gone to college, but they prized the "advantages" of a college education and were outraged at the contempt that privileged students showed for them. They feared the growth of drug use and illegitimacy and were disturbed by the increase in school truancy. They were shocked by the sexual revolution that had legalized pornography and made publicly acceptable forms of sexual expression and practice that had once only flourished underground. They were patriots and were enraged by the Vietcong flags and the attacks on the United States that they saw and heard at antiwar rallies.

Backlash voters looked for villians. Some blamed the influence of Dr. Spock and the permissive approach to child rearing he and his social scientist allies had preached over the previous decades. These, they said, had delegitimized the family and undermined authority. Start with Spock's child-care approach and you ended up with Mark Rudd and Tom Hayden. Others blamed the courts. The Miranda decision, requiring that accused lawbreakers be informed of their legal rights and other rulings of "activist" federal judges, had made it easier for criminals and drug dealers to escape punishment and allowed obscenity, pornography, and sexual perversion to be openly displayed and practiced. A Gallup poll of March 1968 showed that 63 percent of Americans considered the courts "too soft" on criminals; another 1968 poll showed that 78 percent believed that "life today" was getting worse "in terms of morals." In 1968 various "decency" groups, angry at Justice Abe Fortas, Johnson's longtime friend, for his rulings in favor of sexually explicit writing, helped defeat his nomination as Chief Justice of the Supreme Court.

Backlash Americans also blamed liberals and, what to many seemed the same thing, intellectuals, for the country's descent into chaos. The radical college professors who praised the student militants, and the administrators who failed to punish them as they deserved, were encouraging campus anarchy. The writers, playwrights, journalists, and artists who signed antiwar petitions and marched with King, Spock, Muste, and the rest were encouraging draft evasion and hatred of America. They also resented the rich liberals, mostly WASP, who defended the black militants, the minorities, and the troublemakers on spurious humanitarian or ideological grounds. Such "limousine liberals" did not themselves bear the brunt of school desegregation—they could afford private schools for their children. They did not pay the price of crime—they were protected by doormen and guards; they traveled by car and taxi. They could ignore open housing ordinances—many lived in expensive suburbs that no black family could afford. They could support job quotas for minorities—their jobs were not threatened by black competitors. Among New Yorkers the prototype of the breed was Mayor John Vliet Lindsay—St. Paul's, Yale, and Yale Law School—who, his critics said, seemed to think the white working class a lost cause and had placed all his political chips on the liberal professional class and the black ghettoites.

Blacklash Americans had many ways of expressing their anger at the disintegration of order and deference. They demanded stricter laws and tougher punishments for criminals. Even Johnson could not withstand the pressure and in June 1968 would sign the Omnibus Crime Act making permission to wiretap easier to obtain and permitting criminal prosecutors to use evidence in court obtained in ways not previously acceptable. He later told his biographer Doris Kearns that he had wanted to veto the bill but feared the political consequences. "Nixon . . . forced me into it by all the election bullshit blaming the Democrats for crime in the streets."[61]

Backlash activists at times resorted to vigilantism. The Klan was one of the chief beneficiaries of outrage at the ghetto rebellions. "A week after the riot in Newark, we chartered six new units in New Jersey alone," the Klan's Imperial Wizard told an *Atlanta Constitution* reporter in January 1968.[62] In March, when the Chicago school authorities tried to bus black students to all-white schools on the northwest side to meet desegregation guidelines, vigilantes hurled a firebomb through the window of the school principal two hours before classes were to begin. Even in liberal Brooklyn the vigilante spirit flared up in 1968. That spring Rabbi Meir Kahane founded the Jewish Defense League (JDL) after a series of muggings of elderly Jews by black ghetto youths. The JDL was not homicidal like the Klan, but its members were moved by the same distaste for the changing racial status quo and were not averse to physical violence.

*   *   *

The most distinctive expression of the backlash spirit in 1968, however, was George Corley Wallace, the former Democratic governor of Alabama. Wallace was the Platonic ideal of the southern demogogue. His background was the poverty of the rural South, but not its Tobacco Road caricature. His brother Jack remembered, "We had patched overalls on, but they were clean. We grew most of our own food and in the summertime we spent a good bit of our time helping mother shell peas and snap beans."[63] For extra money young George picked cotton and pecans and sold magazines.

All three of the Wallace boys had to work their way through college. George, the oldest, shoveled coal and waited on tables for twenty-five cents an hour in the Tuscaloosa boarding houses where the middle-class University of Alabama students lived. He managed to get through law school just after Pearl Harbor and during World War II was a flight engineer on B-29 bombing missions over Japan. Wallace was mustered out in 1945 with a 10 percent disability from the effects of meningitis. By this time he was a married man. His wife was Lurleen Burns, a pretty young woman who clerked in a Tuscaloosa Kresge five-and-dime store and one day had sold him brilliantine at the notions counter.

Wallace was always a politician. In college he was constantly electioneering and got himself voted class president by taking on the fraternity machine. During the war he bombarded Barbour County citizens, many total strangers, with letters and cards from every place he was stationed, keeping in touch with the folks who would be politically useful when the fighting was over. In 1946 he cashed in, running successfully for the state legislature from Barbour County, getting more votes than his two opponents combined.

Wallace came to Montgomery as a protégé of Governor James Folsom, one of the Deep South's better types of politician. "Big Jim" was a Populist, a man whose career was built on concern for the "little man" and suspicion of the "foreign" corporations from the North that exploited him. Folsom was not a racist, though racism often went with Populist territory. And neither was Wallace. George had returned from the war convinced that whites would have to treat blacks better in the future and did not change drastically until after *Brown* v. *Board of Education* challenged the whole Jim Crow structure in 1954. The decision restored race, in slow decline as a political issue, to a central place in southern politics. In 1958, after a six-year stint as a state circuit judge, Wallace ran for governor and lost to John Patterson, who had positioned himself as the more zealous defender of white supremacy. The defeat held a lesson for Wallace. "John Patterson outniggered me," he told his friends, "and boys, I ain't going to be outniggered again!"[64] He ran again in 1962 and this time he opened the racial appeal full throttle. He won, and in January he concluded his inaugural address on the state capitol steps with the cry: "Segregation now! Segregation tomorrow! Segregation forever!"[65]

Wallace was a middling good governor. He built fourteen new junior colleges, fifteen new trade schools, and initiated a $100 million school construction program. He also launched the largest road-building project in the state's history. One of Jim Folsom's old allies asserted that Wallace's "economic programs surpassed the fondest dreams of every liberal in the state."[66] Unfortunately, the money came largely from sales taxes, which placed a disproportionate burden on the state's poorer citizens. At the same time he used state agencies such as the Highway Patrol and a special state tribunal to bolster his personal power and to intimidate opponents of his racial policies. He achieved national notoriety and local fame when, in the first year of his governorship, he "stood at the schoolhouse door" defying a federal court order to desegregate the University of Alabama and yielding only to federal bayonets. The formula of defiance, compliance, and martyrdom in sequence made him a hero to racial conservatives and a potent political force.

Wallace understood the furies and resentments of white working-class Americans and saw their political potential. In 1964 he decided to run in the Democratic presidential primaries in Wisconsin, Maryland, and Indiana. In a year when Johnson would rack up the greatest popular presidential vote majority in history, Wallace won over 30 percent of the primary vote in each state—crossovers from the Republicans, white working-class

Democrats threatened with neighborhood racial change, or non-voters alienated from the regular electoral process. A shocked LBJ coined the phrase *white backlash* to describe the phenomenon. Overnight, Wallace became the prime spokeman for the backlash constituency and a frightening threat to the liberal consensus.

Wallace's try for the Democratic nomination in 1968 faced one large hurdle. Under Alabama law he was not eligible for reelection in 1966 and so would have no political base two years later when he would need it. He was equal to the challenge. In 1966 Lurleen, already sick with the cancer that would soon kill her, ran in George's place with the promise that her husband would be always at her side to advise her. She won the Democratic nomination and in November swamped her Republican opponent. Wallace was now assured of the limelight for his larger national purposes. On February 7, 1968, he announced in Washington that he would run for president on a third-party ticket.

Wallace was not a telegenic candidate. Physically, he might have been cast as a Snopes in a dramatic adaptation of a Faulkner novel. He was stumpy and had a paunch, a bulbous turned-up nose, and smooth, black, combed-back hair so thin that the pink scalp showed through. He always looked rumpled, with baggy suits and plastic-tipped White Owl cigars poking out of his jacket breast pocket.

He was a limited man, shrewd but uncultivated. He spoke with a "grits-and-gravy voice"; his grammar was often shaky. As a private person, his biographer Marshall Frady has said, he was scarcely aware of his surroundings. He didn't care for money, food, family, or home. He had no hobbies. He was totally political. But Wallace knew one thing: millions of white Americans were disgusted with the state of the nation and wanted an alternative. He knew who the new folk villains were. He would denounce "the rich folks" who could "send their chillun to a private school . . ." while Birmingham steelworkers were getting "run over and trampled."[67] He attacked the "pointy-headed" intellectuals: "Hell, . . . when they've gotten into power" they "made some of the bloodiest tyrants man has ever seen."[68] He ripped the liberals: if he had his way he would "bring all those briefcase-toting bureaucrats [of the Department of Health, Education, and Welfare] to Washington and throw their briefcases in the Potomac River. . . ."[69] He execrated the radicals: the "activists, anarchists, revolutionaries, and Communists" should all be jailed.[70]

Wallace ran under the label of the American Independent party, a skeleton organization of Alabamians with little experience in national politics. Even before the candidate's formal announcement, these rank amateurs had been trying to get their candidate on the ballot in all fifty states. They called their drive "Mission Impossible," but by the fall they had succeeded. The candidate himself was their chief attraction, traveling the circuit on a slow propeller plane with his entourage, working up enthusiasm for the ballot petition campaigns. A timid flyer, Wallace would sit quietly close to the pilot's cabin, his feet up against the bulkhead, rising only to make a prudent visit to the men's room before arriving at the next stop.

Wallace's reception in the South was always enthusiastic. Everyone assumed he would be savaged in the North and the West, and at times he was. In Minneapolis on the July Fourth weekend, hecklers drowned out his words and wrecked the auditorium where he was to appear. The rally was canceled. But his reception was often favorable. Away from Dixie the candidate pulled his punches, a trifle. He criticized the civil rights movement and defended separation of the races, but avoided overt racism. His message was that the nation was simultaneously overgoverned, underdisciplined, and chaotic, views that appealed to many northern audiences. He announced that he would "slash foreign aid, . . . cut out millions of dollars from the Health, Education and Welfare Department, . . . chase the federal government out of the schools and the hospitals, . . . stop the breakdown of law and order, . . . put law violaters in jail, . . . and jail those Americans who openly advocate the victory of the Communists. . . ."[71] There were hecklers at times, but he often left his rallies with hundreds of signatures on the local American Independent party nominating petition.

All of this was expensive; the ballot drive would ultimately cost $2.5 million, about a dollar a name. Some of the money came from the sale of Wallace "kits": buttons, ties, bumper stickers, hats, and other campaign paraphernalia. Some was collected at the rallies by pretty, hat-passing southern girls in white blouses and fifties' beehive hairdos. Conservative fat cats rained checks on their favorite candidate. H. L. Hunt, the Texas oil tycoon, sent $500,000. Leander Perez, the racist boss of Louisiana's Plaquemines Parish; Colonel Sanders, the Kentucky Fried Chicken king; and Edward Ball, a Florida millionaire, were other big contributors. For a time one of Wallace's most-enthusiastic supporters was John Wayne, the Hollywood actor. Wayne sent three $10,000 checks, the last one inscribed "Sock it to 'em, George!"[72]

There would be, all told, fourteen Democratic primaries from March to July, but many were nonbinding, small-state, or so strongly skewed to one candidate that they were not worth contesting. Only four or five after New Hampshire meant any-thing, and in each of these Eugene McCarthy and Robert Kennedy collided head-on.

McCarthy's next stop after New Hampshire was Wisconsin, a state bordering his own home base and a liberal, good-government bastion. Here was friendly territory where there would be a plentiful supply of university students and faculty, liberal lawyers and professionals, and even some dovish trade union leaders.

His first appearance in the Badger State came at St. Norbert's College three hours after Kennedy's announcement. The senator was heartened by the standing ovation he got from the 750 students who packed the small school's auditorium and was pleased when they cheered the priest who referred to McCarthy's rival as "Bobby-come-lately." His optimism was reinforced by his feeling that his "national staff" had been tempered in the fires of New Hampshire and could be expected to be even more effective the second time around.

It was still winter in the Midwest when the staffers began to arrive in mid-March, just after New Hampshire. Most had adopted a personal compaigning specialty, something he or she did well. Some mustered crowds for rallies; others managed the car rentals; some were good at contacting labor union or farm leaders. There were money raisers and telephone canvassers and ticket arrangers and speech writers. Most of the staff were graduate students. They got five dollars a day and a room in a private house or a hotel and ate and slept irregularly. Besides the veterans there were the locals. Most of them were older liberals, Stevensonians long active in the state Democratic party's reform wing. At times, inevitably, the two groups clashed. The locals resented the national staffers as whippersnappers and know-it-all intruders; the veterans deplored the locals' inability to understand the nature of the new kind of campaign they had pioneered. They soon coined the acronym *NTTL*, Never Trust the Locals, to express their contempt.[73]

Besides the locals-veterans division there was a Senate staff–campaign staff split. The people who had surrounded the senator in Washington, his family, Jerome Eller, his Senate administrative assistant, and others, displayed a proprietary attitude toward the candidate and disliked the neophytes under Gans and Blair Clark. McCarthy's personal secretary-cum-valet went out of his way to be nasty to the campaign staff, sneering out their names when they received telephone calls in the candidate's suite. The senator himself was a source of discord. He was lackadaisical about details and seemed to spend as much time writing poetry as discussing strategy or planning future moves. Jeremy Larner, one of his young speech writers, also believed he was too susceptible to flattery and too inclined to place "pets" in strategic positions where they insulated him from important facts and events.

However serious, the campaign's defects would not affect the outcome in Wisconsin. The splash McCarthy made in New Hampshire gave him national stature. "Where he once went unnoticed, a reporter for the *Washington Star* wrote, "people now stop him on the street. When he visited a local television station last week . . . the secretaries . . . lined a stairwell to shake his hand as he left the building."[74] His newfound celebrity would help immensely in Wisconsin.

Bobby was not on the ballot, but the president was, and as primary day approached it became clear that Wisconsin would be a worse rout for LBJ than New Hampshire. On March 26 Larry O'Brien, the veteran Democratic campaigner, arrived in

Milwaukee to assess the damage and reported back to his chief that it did not look good. On March 30, after O'Brien had returned to Washington, a McCarthy poll showed that over 60 percent of the Democratic voters would choose the senator. The predictions for Wisconsin would affect Johnson's decision on March 31 to renounce a second full term.

The president's withdrawal came as a complete surprise to the McCarthy Wisconsin team and produced something of a let-down. That evening Larner was unceremoniously awakened at McCarthy's Milwaukee headquarters by journalist-historian Theodore White pointing at the TV screen and gasping: "Johnson snapped. His nerve snapped."[75] Later, downstairs at the hotel bar, Larner noticed some disconsolate academics from Madison hunched over their drinks. What was bothering them? Johnson could come back; and besides it was American institutions, not a single man, who had caused the war. Larner concluded that they really missed not having Lyndon to hate.

In the end, the senator won over 56 percent of the vote to the president's 35 percent, a stunning victory. Yet it is not clear that the results were any more a mandate for peace than they had been in New Hampshire. McCarthy carried all forty-one Madison precincts, for example, but a simultaneous citywide plebiscite calling for an immediate cease-fire and troop withdrawal in Vietnam went down to defeat by 27,000 to 20,000. As in New Hampshire, the primary in Wisconsin was a vote against the president for more than one reason.

The first one-on-one confrontation between Gene and Bobby came in Indiana in April and early May. It was a confused and inconclusive race that served as a shakedown cruise for Kennedy but proved very little.

Indiana contains pockets of liberalism in the university center of Bloomington, the suburbs of the few large cities, and in industrial Lake County, where the smoky steel mills of Gary dominate the landscape. The rest of the state is aggressively provincial, small-town America epitomized, a place where the favorite poet is still James Whitcomb Riley and the favorite song-writer Paul Dresser ("On the Banks of the Wabash"). There are rural and small-town Indiana Democrats along the state's

southern tier of counties, but they are as southern in origins and
orientation as the Kentuckians across the Ohio River. Even the
state's metropolis, Indianapolis, is a big conservative hick town,
boastful of its downtown war memorial and proud to be national
headquarters of the American Legion.

The problems for the two maverick Democrats were compounded by the favorite-son candidacy of Roger Branigin, the
Democratic governor. Branigin had been chosen by the state
leaders, who despised and feared Gene and Bobby, to stand in for
Johnson before he had removed himself from the race. After the
renunciation, despite an appeal by Ted Kennedy, he remained in
the running as surrogate for Vice-President Humphrey, the man
the mainstream party leaders now hoped and expected to take
LBJ's place. "Governor Branigan has the organization," said a
McCarthy supporter, assessing the strengths and strategies of the
candidates, "and is appealing to the pride of the voters. Kennedy
has the money and is appealing to the emotions of the people.
McCarthy just has the appeal of his logic."[76]

Bobby had not been idle since his announcement in mid-
March. After the St. Patrick's Day parades he had given two
speeches in Kansas, two more in the South, and then had made a
nine-day campaign swing to the West Coast and back with stops in
the Southwest, the Mountain States, and the Midwest. He had
won the young and militant and lost many of the middle-aged and
moderate. Everywhere he was mobbed by adoring young people
screaming "Sock it to 'em, Bobby."[77] They surrounded his car
trying to touch him. They elbowed one another and shoved
notebooks, programs, and bits of paper at him for his signature.
"Oh, he's real!" cried a teenage admirer. "He's real!" Signs and
posters proclaimed his popularity. BOBBY LUV IS SUPER GROOVEY,
read a placard in a Fort Wayne auditorium.[78]

Blacks, too, responded passionately to Kennedy, a candidate
who made racial justice and civil rights as much a part of his
campaign as Vietnam. When Kennedy toured the riot-torn area
of Washington, D.C., after Martin Luther King's assassination, he
was hailed by black mourners. "I knew you would be the first to
come here, darling," said one woman as she grabbed his hand.[79]

Kennedy had given the public the kind of fire they wanted and had not gotten from Gene. American policy in Vietnam was bankrupt. We were supporting a corrupt regime in South Vietnam; the Saigon government refused to draft eighteen-year-olds, while the United States did; we were making a desert in Southeast Asia and calling it peace. The country was paying dearly at home for its folly abroad. The war was costing the United States $85 million every day. That was the price "of a moderate program to bring jobs to young people in the ghetto for an entire summer. . . ."[80] Disunity and strife were tearing the country apart. "We have seen tanks patrolling American streets, machine guns fired at American children."[81] And who was responsible for such things? Some people blamed the anarchists, but the guilty were those who had rejected the American tradition of generosity. Such people were "calling upon the darker impulses of the American spirit."[82] He was running to end such things.

The words themselves seemed inflammatory to middle-of-the-road Americans. But even more disturbing was the glandular response of the crowds. They shrieked and waved and chanted and clapped and sang. They pawed the candidate when they could and tore off his tie and his cuff links. In Kalamazoo, a housewife chased Kennedy to his car and grabbed his right foot. I "couldn't get a hanky or anything," she explained, "so I just took his shoe."[83] Much of what happened was the mass frenzy of celebrity chasers, the people who had gone gaga over Frank Sinatra in the forties and the Beatles in the early sixties. But it seemed to mean more. One of the reporters who accompanied Bobby to Kansas and the South said that the reaction on the campuses had been downright "scary."[84] Before the tour was over, the columnists were beginning to use the word "demagoguery" to describe the Kennedy campaign.

His advisers urged Bobby to take a calmer approach in Indiana. "You have made your point about nomination and razzle-dazzle," said Arthur Schlesinger, "now . . . it is time to slow down."[85] The candidate listened. His new tactics mixed liberal rhetoric with pragmatic substance, an approach that would serve him for the rest of the campaign.

Indiana could not be treated like California or a large university campus, and the candidate's message in the Hoosier State was that private enterprise, not government handouts, would be the ultimate salvation of the poor. He had already initiated a program in Brooklyn's black Bedford-Stuyvesant ghetto to attract job-creating capital to the inner city, and he touted this model for helping minorities, catering thereby to black separatists and white businessmen simultaneously. He also touched on the law and order issue, reminding the voters that he had been U.S. attorney general, the man responsible for enforcing the federal laws, and promising to make the streets safer.

Though the McCarthy and Kennedy forces went one-on-one for the first time in Indiana, the encounter was not at first bruising. Both sides shared a common grievance against the state's largest paper, the *Indianapolis Star,* whose publisher, James Pulliam, though a Republican, supported Governor Branigin. The *Star* was indecent in its favoritism and mentioned the other two candidates only to make them look bad. It was particularly critical of Kennedy, frequently running derisive cartoons and harsh editorials. One cartoon, on April 21, depicted Ethel and Bobby as Bonnie and Clyde desperadoes hurtling along the state's highways in a fancy convertible scattering money in handfuls over the landscape.

Though many of the younger McCarthy workers remained resentful of Kennedy's opportunism, the pragmatists assumed that if their candidate failed they could always go over to Bobby, who at least was on the right general track. Why create an impossible breach? Even the Kennedyites' attempt to buy off McCarthy workers, and their dirty tricks, like trying to rent away the McCarthy people's headquarters hotel, the seedy, half–burnt-out Claypool ("Cesspool"), failed to arouse great passion.

Then, late in the campaign, the Kennedy people attacked McCarthy's congressional record. As representative and senator, they charged, he had been a chronic absentee, had favored the oil lobby, and had missed an important vote to invoke cloture thereby jeopardizing the 1968 Civil Rights Act. To the McCarthy loyalists this was hitting below the belt, and thereafter neither side gave the other quarter.

The results on May 7 gave Kennedy 328,000 of the 776,000 votes cast, 42.3 percent. Branigin got almost 31 percent, and McCarthy 27 percent. It was a victory for Bobby, of course, but not an overwhelming one. He had not swamped his rival and had not even picked up many reliable delegate votes. The sixty-three Indianans plus alternates who would be going to Chicago in August would be pledged to him for only one ballot; thereafter they would be free to vote their personal preferences. Since they would actually be picked by the party regulars at the state Democratic convention in June, it was certain that their votes would go to Humphrey if the Chicago convention went into a second round of candidate voting. The Indiana vote, though muddied by the Branigin presence, reflected the real candidates' constituencies. McCarthy had won the professional and executive suburbs; Bobby had carried the blacks and the white blue-collar Democrats.

A week later Bobby took Nebraska's handful of first-round votes away from McCarthy, son of the Midwest, senator from farm-state Minnesota. Kennedy, Boston-born, representing urban New York, obviously had little credibility in the farm belt. He tried humor instead. In Crete, a town of thirty-five hundred southwest of Lincoln, he announced that he was doing better than anyone else in helping the farmer: his ten children were consuming twenty-six quarts of milk a day! At another Nebraska rally, a small scrap of paper blew out of his hand. He quipped: "That's my entire farm program; give it back quickly."[86] Humor—plus money and superior organization—did the trick. The final vote gave Bobby his first absolute majority—almost 52 percent to Gene's 31 percent.

Oregon was Bobby's first defeat, the first electoral defeat for any Kennedy. The state, as Bobby remarked, was one "giant suburb," its people presperous, well educated, middle class.[87] Many Oregonians refused to think of the problems besetting other parts of America. "I'm not saying we don't have our troubles like everyone else," declared one Portland resident, "but in ten minutes' time I can be off fishing and forget about them."[88] Without a significant black and ethnic population, the state baffled Bobby and his aides. "How do you get a handle on a state

like this?" inquired an uneasy Kennedy campaign worker at one
point.[89] Bobby could not even seize the antiwar issue. The state
was strongly anti-Vietnam, and its Democrats had organized early
for McCarthy, the first antiwar candidate to declare. The
Kennedy forces tried to ignore Gene and concentrate on
Humphrey, who, released by LBJ's renunciation, had announced
as a candidate in late April. It didn't work. The McCarthy people
bought TV time for a joint Gene–Bobby debate and then when
Kennedy turned them down called him a coward. If he was
unwilling to debate someone from his own party, the Minnesota
senator declared in Portland's Memorial Coliseum the evening of
May 25, how well would he handle Nixon after the convention
and, still more to the point, how could he hold his own against
foreign leaders if elected? The cowardice charge mushroomed
the next day when McCarthy and Kennedy almost bumped into
one another while campaigning at the Portland zoo. Still unwilling
to give his opponent free media exposure, Bobby bolted for his
convertible before the photographers could snap pictures of the
two candidates together to cries from the McCarthy forces of
"Coward!" "Chicken!"[90]

One event of the Oregon campaign would have portentous
consequences. Both candidates strongly favored Israel in its
struggle for survival, whether out of personal conviction or to
attract Jewish American support. But Bobby, with his New York
base, was the more outspoken. "The United States must defend
Israel against aggression from whatever source," he declared in a
speech at Portland's Temple Neveh Shalom toward the end of the
Oregon campaign. "Our obligations to Israel, unlike our obligations toward other countries, are clear and imperative." The next
day his talk was reported in a Pasadena, California, paper that ran
an accompanying photograph of Kennedy wearing a yarmulke,
the head covering of orthodox Jewish males. The piece was seen
by a Palestinian Arab refugee, Sirhan Sirhan, now living with his
family in the Los Angeles area. Sirhan wrote in his notebook:
"Robert F. Kennedy must be assassinated before June 5, 1968."[91]
It was the day after the California primary.

The Oregon results restored McCarthy's campaign credibility.
The Minnesotan got almost 45 percent of the vote, with Kennedy

taking about 39 percent, and most of the rest going to the president, who was still on the ballot. As Kennedy would later say, he always did best where people needed things. In Oregon everyone seemed to have pretty much what he wanted. On the way to California, Bobby and Richard Tuck, one of his staff, playfully discussed airlifting a ghetto into Oregon. "But will they *like* it there?" Bobby asked. "I mean, it's *Oregon*—all those roses."[92]

California, with its 174 delegates—over 13 percent of those needed to win in Chicago—was the final and biggest prize. The state was a microcosm of America—with the past lopped off. It had its industrial wage earners, but they worked in aerospace factories or made computers. It had its farmers, but they were agribusiness specialists and workers. It had its moguls, but most of them were first-generation, self-made men. It had its students, but they were generally screwier and more rebellious than anywhere else. It had its ethnics, but they were disproportionately Mexican—Chicanos, they were now being called—rather than Southern and Eastern Europeans. The Golden State was split unevenly by a cultural fault line at the Tehachapis, with a more liberal, maverick community to the north and a more conservative, conformist one to the south. Neither part had more than traces of an America preceding 1900, though even more than the north, the south seemed to have been born yesterday.

California marked the return of Vietnam to the political agenda. For a time after the early April announcement of U.S.–North Vietnam peace talks, the Vietnam issue had gone into eclipse. By May, with the talks stalled by procedural disputes, it returned. On a foray into northern California from Oregon on May 22, McCarthy blamed American intervention in Vietnam on the misconception that the United States had "a great moral mission to control the world." The Minnesota senator was not afraid to criticize the Vietnam policies of the martyred brother. The delusion, he said, went back to the 1950s and was shared by the John F. Kennedy administration as well as by Republicans. And it still flourished. He was not "convinced" that either of his two Democratic opponents "has entirely renounced those misconceptions. . . ."[93]

After his announcement, Bobby never emphasized the Vietnam issue as much. He had, after all, shared in his brother's decisions to launch the Bay of Pigs invasion, send advisers to Vietnam, and confront the Soviets during the Cuban missile crisis. It was not hard to depict him as a cold warrior. Besides, he never could bring himself to criticize the United States as freely as McCarthy. On a pre-Indiana trip to California, he had encountered young supporters of the new radical Peace and Freedom party at a San Francisco rally. They had called him a "Fascist pig" and screamed "Victory for the Vietcong."[94] Kennedy put away his prepared text and defended himself. He wanted to keep America from getting mired down in other Vietnams, he said, but he could not support victory for the Vietcong.

Radical hecklers notwithstanding, California was better Kennedy country than Oregon, and Bobby's campaign was soon back on the track. Here he had a solid base in the black and Mexican ghettos of the Bay Area, the Central Valley, and Los Angeles. The Kennedy personality had a natural appeal for both communities. Bobby's passion, impetuousness, and generosity— even his "ruthlessness"—were magnetic to people whose cultures valued "heart" over "head" and prized "male" action over "feminine" thought. The McCarthy people would try to steal slices of the minority pie, but their man was too cerebral, too cool, too unwilling to bend in style or content to black and brown needs to make much headway.

Besides his style and personality, Kennedy had his alliances. He had befriended Cesar Chavez, the head of California's mostly Mexican farm workers' union, in his fight to organize the state's agribusiness workers. "He came without asking anything of us," Chavez explained, "he came without expectations of any benefit to him."[95] Chavez' *campesinos* would gratefully repay his generosity by getting out their fellow Mexican Americans en masse on primary day.

He also had the support of black groups like the Sons of Watts in Los Angeles and Assemblyman Willie Brown of San Francisco's Bay Area Black Caucus. The New York senator's visits to Watts, downtown Los Angeles, and the Central Valley farm towns were delirious love feasts of cheering, crying, shouting people reaching out to the candidate as he rode along in his open car, trying to touch him as if to absorb his mana, his magic. After the disaster of Oregon, their love drained away his fatigue and revived his spirits.

The day after the Oregon primary, a chastened Kennedy, no longer so certain of success, had agreed to debate his opponent on ABC TV's "Issues and Answers." The debate took place on Saturday evening, June 1, at ABC's San Francisco studios and was broadcast over 171 TV outlets nationally, live or on film. The format resembled that of the Nixon–John Kennedy debates eight years earlier: a panel of three reporters asking the candidates prepared questions. Both sides prepped carefully for the meeting. The McCarthy people put together a briefing book of expected questions and suggested replies. The New York senator spent the day before in tough trial-run sessions with advisers. McCarthy arrived at the studio looking cool and nonchalant; Bobby appeared six minutes later, looking nervous.

The first question from the panel was on Vietnam, and it opened a small crack between the candidates. McCarthy favored accepting the Vietcong as part of any future South Vietnamese government. Kennedy opposed any American attempt to force the South Vietnamese to accept the National Liberation Front. The next query concerned the McCarthy camp charge that Bobby, as a cabinet member, was implicated in the cold-war policies of his brother and Lyndon Johnson, including the Dominican invasion, and hence unsuited to be a candidate. McCarthy denied that he or his supporters had read Kennedy out of the race because he had shared in earlier White House foreign policy decisions. Kennedy responded that he wasn't even in the government during the Dominican affair.

Neither senator came off as the ideal candidate. McCarthy, as expected, was cool, but also distracted and at times seemingly baffled. Kennedy, as anticipated, was aggressive, but also precise and factual. The one big difference between them came over how to deal with the housing and economic problems of minorities, and here a curious transposition of viewpoints occurred. Nothing so frightened white suburbanites as the prospect of ghetto blacks suddenly appearing in their midst. A desire to escape this contamination was what had propelled many of them to the suburbs in the first place. Now McCarthy, the favorite of the suburban liberals, repeated a position he had taken some days earlier in a speech at Davis: unemployed ghetto dwellers had to be relocated in new federally constructed housing in the suburbs where the jobs were. Kennedy, the tribune of the nation's minorities, also had his prepared position on the ghettos: they must be made livable by infusions of private capital to provide jobs and housing for their residents. Ghetto folk, in effect, could stay at home; no need for them to relocate. It could be argued that McCarthy's position represented the now-outdated integrationist viewpoint and Kennedy's the new separatist mood of the militant black leadership. But Kennedy added a remark during the debate that throws this explanation out of kilter. Backtracking a little, he declared that he was not opposed to "moving people out of the ghettos." Then he paraphrased the McCarthy position in words that played to every suburbanite nightmare. His opponent was "going to to take ten thousand black people and move them into [southern California's] Orange County."[96] The McCarthy staff in the studio expected their candidate to jump on this demagogic statement, but he let the chance pass and the debate soon after wound down.

That evening the Kennedys briefly attended a star-studded gala at a San Francisco hotel but left early. On Sunday Bobby and Ethel went to mass at a small Catholic church near the Fairmont, their Nob Hill hotel. That day, McCarthy finally took Bobby to task for his Orange County remark. It was "scare tactics" that "could increase suspicion and mistrust among the races," he declared, and a "crude distortion of his position."[97]

June 3 was the last day of the campaign, and it must have passed like a blur for the candidates. Both shuttled back and forth between the Bay Area and the Los Angeles basin. On Tuesday, election day, Kennedy relaxed at the Malibu home of film director John Frankenheimer, where six of his ten children were enjoying a California vacation. He would not have a chance, he knew, to spend time with his kids for the next few weeks. The New York primary was on June 18, and he had a full schedule of meetings and rallies starting on Friday. He made the best of the hours while the California voters were expressing their preferences and surfed with the children for a while. But the day was foggy and cool, and they soon gave it up for a romp in the Frankenheimer pool.

McCarthy too was in Los Angeles on election day, staying at the Beverly Hilton with Abigail, Mary, and his close staff. The mood at the hotel was downbeat. The McCarthy people had expected their candidate to trounce Kennedy at the debate, and at best they had drawn a tie. Crowd turnouts, on the days immediately following, had been down from earlier in the campaign. The "steam had suddenly left the campaign."[98]

California was crucial. Kennedy had been saying that if he lost he would withdraw in favor of McCarthy. McCarthy had made no such promise, but most of the staffers believed that their candidate had to win to remain viable. "Enjoying the Don Quixote role," Gene, if badly beaten, might remain in the race "to the bitter end," staffer Ben Stavis believed, but then the campaign would be no more than a "holding action."[99] In that case, staffers would desert to Bobby en masse. Many had already contacted the Kennedy people to line up jobs in case of a decisive California defeat.

Kennedy won, but it was not a landslide. RFK took 46 percent of the vote to McCarthy's 42 percent, with 12 percent for California Attorney General Thomas Lynch, Humphrey's stand-in. In the winner-take-all contest, however, he would have gotten the state's whole convention delegation. His vote, as expected, was concentrated among blacks, Chicanos, and blue-collar union workers. He had also pulled even with Gene among the Jews. McCarthy carried the educated suburbanites and Democrats in conservative communities such as San Diego. To the end the pattern had held, and the seers who watched the returns come in predicted that it could assure victory for Bobby in November if he won at Chicago.

The prediction would never be tested. Kennedy arrived at campaign headquarters at the Ambassador Hotel at seven o'clock and went to the Royal Suite on the fifth floor. A hundred

Democratic leaders, top campaign staffers, and favored reporters were already crammed into the living room watching TV and drinking. In the bedroom area were gathered the inner Camelot circle—Ted, Pat Lawford, Ted Sorensen, Stephen and Jean Smith—along with a few privileged outsiders. Downstairs in the hotel's Embassy Room, listening to a live rock band, were the junior staffers, boys wearing Kennedy straw hats, girls dressed in blue skirts, white blouses, and red sashes. Even before the polls closed at 8:00 P.M., CBS had predicted a comfortable Kennedy victory, and everyone was in a raucous good mood.

Minutes after the first projections, the networks were dunning the candidates for statements. McCarthy, at the Beverly Hilton, obliged. He and his people, he said, had given their best shot in Oregon, where there no minorities to distort the results. They had proved there—and now, it seemed, in California—that they had the independent voters, those any Democrat needed to win in November. The statement sounded like the alibi it was.

Kennedy cautiously resisted the reporters' prodding and spent the early and mid-evening making calls back east to find out the results in the South Dakota primary, also held that day, and to discuss strategy for New York. One call, shortly before 11 o'clock, went to Allard Lowenstein. "Al" was still supporting McCarthy, and Kennedy wanted to know if, with victory now in sight, he would switch allegiance. Lowenstein was not at home, and Bobby, now certain of the optimistic reports, left the suite to speak to the network news team interviewers. He returned and asked Richard Goodwin to call Al again. Goodwin got through and put Lowenstein on hold as the senator went down to the Embassy Room to make his victory speech.

Kennedy arrived in the bright, noisy, crowded room a little before midnight. Ethel, wearing an orange-and-white miniskirt and white stockings, stepped up on the small platform with him to face the battery of microphones and share the glow. The crowd cheered when it saw its hero, and Ethel waved at them.

Bobby was at his relaxed best. He noted Don Drysdale's record-breaking sixth shutout just pitched for the Dodgers that evening and said he hoped "we have as good fortune in our campaign."[100] He praised his supporters and campaign workers, mentioning by name as many as he could get in including Roosevelt Grier, the massive Los Angeles Rams tackle who had served as a bodyguard and expediter during the campaign. He also thanked his cocker spaniel Freckles, and—though he noted he was not putting things in the "order of importance"—his wife. The serious part of the statement suggested the themes he intended to emphasize during the weeks to come: reconciliation with the McCarthy people, reconciliation between the races, peace in Vietnam. He ended with "thanks to all of you, and on to Chicago, and let's win!"[101]

It was past midnight when Kennedy and his party left the room for a press conference with the print correspondents. To avoid the excited well-wishers clamoring to touch the senator, they escaped through a corridor that passed close to the hotel kitchen. The passageway was lined with equipment and admiring kitchen workers, and no one paid much attention to a slight, dark-haired young man who had asked if the senator would pass that way and then stationed himself near a steel tray-stacker to wait. As Kennedy was answering a radio reporter's question, Sirhan Sirhan raised his right arm over the Kennedy aides and fired a volley of shots point-blank into the senator's head. Kennedy threw his hands up toward his face and collapsed onto the cement floor. As he lay on his back with his eyes open, blood flowed from behind his right ear.

It took several seconds for spectators to realize that the volley was not the sound of firecrackers. Others had been hit in the barrage and were down, but people only a few feet away were still unaware of what had happened. Those who saw Sirhan tried to knock the .22 from his hand, but he resisted furiously and Grier and others had to wrestle him to the ground. It took minutes before anyone could pry his fingers off the gun. By now the crowd had become aware of what had happened, and "the kitchen erupted into madness."[102] Crazed with grief and anger, people rushed to pummel the still-struggling gunman and would have killed him if Rosie Grier had not fended them off. Meanwhile, the newsmen in the adjacent press room had rushed in to find out what had happened, and they pushed and shoved to get pictures or a view they could later report. "Give him air," begged Ethel

Kennedy. "Please give him air." "This is history," shouted a photographer, not missing a beat as his flashgun popped.[103] The senator was now lying, still conscious, in a small clearing protected by his aides, a jacket under his head, his shoes off, his tie loosened. A kitchen boy, Juan Romero, had put a rosary in the senator's limp hand and was on his knees by his side praying. Ethel, who was pregnant with their eleventh child, knelt down to take her husband's hand. She whispered to him and stroked his brow.

The medics arrived at 12:23 A.M. As they whisked him to the waiting ambulance, Kennedy lost consciousness. At Central Receiving Hospital his heart stopped, but they revived him and while administering oxygen, plasma, and dextrose, rushed him off to another hospital for surgery. One bullet, the critical one, had entered behind Kennedy's right ear and lodged in the center of his brain. It took three expert neurosurgeons almost four hours to remove most of it. But the effort was fruitless. At 1:44 A.M. on June 6, twenty-six hours after the shots rang out, Kennedy died. At his bedside were Ethel, his sisters Jean Smith and Pat Lawford, his brother Ted, his brother-in-law Stephen Smith, and Jacqueline Kennedy.

During the next days the American people went through another dark agony of the soul, wondering, as they had in November 1963 and again the previous April, if the whole society was not deathly sick and on the verge of collapse. To black Americans Martin Luther King's murder had been the cruelest blow, but even whites who deeply admired the civil rights leader felt somewhat excluded from the grief. Now all could share the pain. There were, of course, those impervious to Bobby's charms, but his appeal had not been circumscribed by race, religion, or ethnicity. The anguish spilled over the barriers between Americans. Jean Smith later recounted how, as she left the Receiving Hospital, two black women had run over and said: "God bless you, sweetheart. We'll pray for you . . ." and then had sat on the grass moaning and crying.[104]

Thousands of Americans, tuned in to get the final primary results, had seen the tragedy on their TV sets. A continent away, Lowenstein, ironically, was on telephone hold with the senator's suite at the very moment the shots ran out, but only learned about the shooting when his wife rushed in to tell him what she had seen on her set. He dropped everything, and an hour later was in the air headed for Los Angeles to see if he could help.

The body lay in state at New York's St. Patrick's Cathedral, and it seemed as if everyone whose life Bobby had touched came to pay their respects. The roster of mourners reads like the cast of the era's dramas: statesmen—Averell Harriman, Robert McNamara, Douglas Dillon, and Lord David Cecil; intellectuals and literati—Robert Lowell, Truman Capote, William Styron, Milton Friedman, Isaiah Berlin; entertainers—Kirk Douglas, Jason Robards, Shirley MacLaine; journalists—Stewart Alsop, David Brinkley, Jimmy Breslin, Joseph Kraft; civil rights militants—Floyd McKissick and Julian Bond. Even radicals. At 1:00 A.M. on Friday morning Tom Hayden accompanied Jack Newfield to the cathedral to stand vigil at the coffin. Hayden hunched down in an empty pew and quietly wept. Thousands of anonymous New Yorkers, too, wound through the cathedral nave to get a last glimpse of Bobby. "Our friend is gone," sobbed a black woman outside the cathedral. "Oh, Jesus, he is gone. Jesus. Jesus."[105] It was a tribute to the man's humanity and ability to express the deep inner yearnings of Americans.

The ride by train to Washington's Arlington National Cemetery was an instance of real life's revenge against man's staged solemnities. The train developed brake trouble, and the four-and-a-half-hour trip took over eight hours. The day was a scorcher and few of the cars were air-conditioned. The mourners—family and close friends—sweated and suffered, many taking solace from the abundant supply of free drinkables in the club car. By the time the train reached Union Station, half the guests were quietly sodden.

The worst part was the accident, however. Subdued crowds lined the right of way for much of the 225 miles from New York to Washington. At Elizabeth, New Jersey, the crowd spilled over onto the northbound track, not knowing that the trains to New York were still running. At 1:24 P.M. the Admiral, bound from Chicago to New York via Philadelphia, roared by. As the funeral party watched from their windows in horror, it hit a clump of trackside mourners, killing two and injuring six others.

In Washington the casket was placed in a hearse, and a small cortege of cars with the president, vice-president, and immediate family members followed it to the cemetery. As the motorcade crossed the city, thousands of Washingtonians, many black, lined the streets. It was well after sunset, and as the cars passed, spectators held up lighted candles or struck matches. A brief stop at the Lincoln Memorial to express sympathy for the Resurrection City campers included a choral performance of "The Battle Hymn of the Republic." Then across Memorial Bridge and into the cemetery.

The gravesite had been chosen by Robert McNamara, Bobby's colleague in the JFK and Johnson cabinets. It was just twenty feet from John's plot. The graveside ceremony was simple and dignified, with Patrick Cardinal O'Boyle of Washington reciting the prayers. The most touching moment came when Jacqueline Kennedy led her two children to their own father's grave for them to place sprigs from their uncle's wreath. A hundred mourners accompanied Ethel and the children to Hickory Hill for a drink and a snack. They all left by four, Sunday morning, and it was over.

The death of Robert Kennedy made a difference. It was not pure campaign rhetoric that he could have unified the nation. He had his enemies, fierce ones—bigots of both races, confirmed Kennedy-haters, extremists of farthest right and left. Even level-headed, decent Americans often disliked the Kennedy mystique. These people would never have voted for him as the Democratic presidential candidate. The remote fringes would have gone in any case for Wallace and the American Independent party or for Eldridge Cleaver and Peace and Freedom.

During his last political journey he had not won the independent voters of the suburbs and the front offices or the campus intellectuals. But many of these people would surely have come over when faced with the alternative of Richard Nixon in November. If Tom Hayden could cry at the funeral, could the McCarthy students and all but the most ferocious campus radicals have remained aloof? And even many backlash voters would have defected. Polls consistently showed that many of the Irish, Italian, Polish, and German voters who formed the Wallace community of resentment liked Bobby and were willing to give him their votes. He had the Hispanic and black vote sealed up tight, of course, and these minority folk, often alienated from the civic process, would have come out to vote for him in record numbers. Add the left liberals to the independents, to the ethnics, to the blacks and Chicanos, to the trade unionists, to the regular dyed-in-the-wool party voters, and you had a combination hard to beat. McCarthy could not have done it; Humphrey did not do it. Kennedy might well have.

Would it have changed anything? To try prophesy, it probably would have brought America's Vietnam War to an end long before 1973. It might also have restored the forward momentum of liberal reform, revitalizing the Great Society, though undoubtedly under a different name. One can easily imagine a second President Kennedy extracting from a weary society one further burst of effort to reduce national inequalities of wealth and power.

But Robert Kennedy was gone, and the nation continued on its headlong retreat from the Johnson consensus years.

6

The Personal Is Political

NEW YEAR'S DAY MORNING, 1968. Five people—Abbie Hoffman; his wife, Anita; Jerry Rubin; his girlfriend, Nancy Kurshan; and Paul Krassner, editor of *The Realist*—lie sprawled on pillows in Hoffman's Lower East Side pad coming down from an LSD trip. Krassner rises unsteadily to his feet and elevating his arm observes: "Look, when you make the peace sign of the *V* the extension of your arm makes it a *Y*." The first letter. Anita chimes in: "I love you very much." The second letter: *I*. Rubin supplies the two *P*s, Hoffman the other *I*, and Nancy the final *E*. "YIPPIE."[1] Thus, according to Hoffman, on the first day of 1968 was born Yippie and the scheme for thousands of "dope-taking, freedom-loving, politically committed activists"[2] to take over the Chicago Democratic convention and transform it from the ex-pected "Festival of Death" to a Festival of Life.

The story, of course, is whimsical—like almost everything that Hoffman said and wrote. The Yippie movement was not con-ceived in one spontaneous, drug-driven swoop on January 1, 1968. It had a history. The weirdo Berkeley street people as far back at least as the Free Speech Movement had dabbled in politics. The drug culture on both coasts that had surfaced during the last years of the 1950s was never completely apolitical. Most recently, the Pentagon "exorcism" ritual of the October National Mobilization to End the War in Vietnam demonstration had blended cultural dissent with political insurgency. Yet the Hoffman account contains symbolic truth. It was in 1968 that the "personal became political." That year groups of vocal Americans would organize to demand that "square" and "straight" society let them love and live as they wished. The process would gather into a loose political coalition sexual libertarians, druggies, gays, and feminists, and would profoundly alter how Americans perceived and behaved.

The cultural insurgency politicized in 1968 was a long time in ferment. Bohemia was invented by the artists, models, entertainers, students, and marginal intellectuals of Paris during the middle of the nineteenth century as an antidote to the smug and repressed ethic of the newly enfranchised bourgeoisie. Bohemians defined themselves by reference to their opposites. If the new class of businessmen and public functionaries was prudent, rational, discreet, and moderate, bohemians were rash, passionate, spontaneous, and extravagant. Bohemians' lives defied bourgeois patterns. They rejected steady jobs and lived along the margins of the economy. They repudiated monogamy and families and assumed informal and often promiscuous sexual relationships. They replaced the somber colors and tailored cut of bourgeois dress with flamboyant hues and flowing lines. They ignored the bourgeoisie's strict sex role divisions; bohemian women wore short hair and pants; bohemian men, long hair and ruffles.

Classic nineteenth-century bohemia also developed an ideology. It was aggressively aesthetic. Music, painting, poetry, and sculpture were more than adornments; they were central to existence itself. But the arts of bohemia were not the polite and conventional arts of the official academies. They reached for the new, the outrageous, the impudent, and the loosely structured. Bohemia invented the avant-garde that revolutionized literature, the visual arts, and music toward the end of the nineteenth century.

For a portion of bohemia, politics was irrelevant. But many of the artists, writers, and intellectuals who congregated in the garrets and lofts of the cities' bohemian quarters were also radicals. The mood here too was antibourgeois, antagonistic to the political hegemony of the middle class closely tied to the conservative or liberal parties of the nineteenth-century capitalist state. In the large cosmopolitan cities of the Western nations, the socialists and anarchists invariably lived in cozy proximity with the avant-garde artists and writers. No manifesto of protest or revolution could be circulated without a long list of famous "advanced" painters, novelists, intellectuals, and assorted literati affixing their signatures.

America was behind Europe in its cultural development, but by the opening years of the twentieth century, small pockets of men and women with advanced social and aesthetic views had begun to collect in New York's Greenwich Village, San Francisco's Barbary Coast, New Orleans's French Quarter, and a few other urban enclaves. There they developed bohemias with the same mixture of long-haired men and short-haired women obsessed with freedom as in the major European capitals.

America's bohemian communities continued to flourish through the 1920s and 1930s and then, in the years immediately following World War II, went into eclipse. The darkness was brief. The timid conformity of American life during the fifties generated the inevitable reaction in the form of the Beat Generation.

The Beats were the direct ancestors of the counterculture. Young men and women living mostly in New York, San Francisco, and Los Angeles, their sensibility was molded by association with black jazz musicians. Music has been a part of the self-defining journey of successive American generations, and the incipient young rebels of 1946 were inspired by the complex, cerebral improvisations that came from the horns of Charlie Parker, Miles Davis, Dizzy Gillespie, and Thelonious Monk. And along with the sounds came the language, the dress, the pot, and the personal style affected by the black jazz musicians. Like the new bop artists, they were "cool"—detached and relaxed, remote from the driving enthusiasms of their cultural predecessors in the hot, aggressive thirties and forties. The pose resembled feline detachment, and it was no accident that "cool cat" became the ultimate term of praise. They also borrowed marijuana, a drug that produced a kind of exaltation, one that could be shared but also allowed a private kind of "high."

The new bohemians were rebels of a sort. But they were not political. They despised the square suburban America of the day with its repressions, its empty strivings, its plastic goals, its prudent rationalism. The proper response was not agitation, however; it was withdrawal. Beats eschewed Marx and Debs and read D. T. Suzuki, the Zen Buddhist popularizer, or Alan Watts, his Western interpreter and disciple. They replaced the outward struggle for utopia by the inward struggle for personal nirvana or satori. There was another Beat mood, equally personal but less contemplative. Beats were exponents of the ecstatic, the Dionysian. They denounced the sexual repression of square America and exalted the orgy as the ideal peak experience. As one critic has written, the Beats "spoke primarily for the beleaguered self, for the holiness and spontaneity of the natural man."[3]

The image was valid for the lowest levels of Beatdom where the teenage dropouts and runaways, the "weekend" beatniks, forgathered. But it does not do justice to the cultural pioneers of North Beach and the East Village.

The Beat mood was created by a group of young men and women who went to Columbia in New York just after the war and hung out in the bars and coffee shops in the university's cultural shadow on Morningside Heights. With the inevitable rebelliousness of bright adolescents, they refused to accept the self-congratulatory mood of postwar America.

At the center of the Columbia group was Jack Kerouac, a handsome French Canadian originally from Lowell, Massachusetts, who had come to the university in 1939 on a football scholarship and then dropped out. During the war Kerouac spent some time in the navy but then returned to the Columbia neighborhood, living with Edie Parker, an art student from Michigan, and patronizing the West End Bar on Broadway.

Edie's apartment was a gathering place for the local aesthetes and nonconformists, and there Kerouac met Lucian Carr, a startlingly handsome Columbia freshman from St. Louis, and Allen Ginsberg, a curly-haired young Columbia undergraduate from Paterson, New Jersey, already struggling with his homosexuality and yearning to be a great writer. Through Carr, Kerouac and Ginsberg met William Burroughs, at thirty older than the others. A Harvard graduate who had knocked about and worked as a bartender, an ad man, a detective, and a pest exterminator, Burroughs was distantly related to the adding-machine family and used the small monthly sum they sent him to support his drug habit. In 1950 he would publish *Junkie*, an account of his drug life that would evoke the jagged rhythms of life on heroin.

Another important character who breezed through New York was Neal Cassady, a semidelinquent from Denver who had come to Columbia just after the war to learn how to write. Cassady was a Western primitive who left the deep mark of his wild, spontaneous personality on the crowd at Edie Parker's. In October 1946 he and Kerouac made a picaresque journey to California and back in a silver Hudson Hornet that became the basis for *On the Road,* Kerouac's 1958 stream-of-consciousness novel that suddenly alerted the general public to the Beat phenomenon.

The new cultural stirrings were bicoastal. In these same early postwar years, in San Francisco's North Beach, Kenneth Rexroth, Lawrence Ferlinghetti, and various refugees from the experimental Black Mountain College in North Carolina came together in a literary movement that paralleled the New York mood in its worship of the spontaneous, the primitive, the outlaw. In Ferlinghetti's City Lights bookstore the new poets and hangers-on found a setting and a patron. Ferlinghetti not only sold books, he also published them, and soon made City Lights Books into a major disseminator of Beat poetry. The city also pioneered the public poetry reading, where visiting and local bards recited their works to adoring audiences.

Allen Ginsberg arrived in 1953 to survey the San Francisco scene and stayed to write "Howl," a turbulent, drug-induced wave of words that announced America's guilt for destroying "the best minds" of his generation and described the country as Moloch, the monster of repression and greed.

Moloch! Solitude! Filth! Ugliness! Ashcans and
    unobtainable dollars! Children screaming under
    the stairways! Boys sobbing in armies! Old men
    weeping in the parks!
Moloch! Moloch! Nightmare of Moloch! Moloch the
    loveless! Mental Moloch! Moloch the heavy
    judger of men!
Moloch the incomprehensible prison! Moloch the
    crossbone soulless jailhouse and Congress of
    sorrows! Moloch whose buildings are judgment!
    Moloch the vast stone of war! Moloch the
    stunned governments![4]

In October 1955 Ginsberg organized a poetry reading at the
Six Gallery, an old garage with a dirt floor, one bathroom, and a
stage, with Rexroth as master of ceremonies and himself and four
local poets as performers. His whimsical postcards advertised the
occasion as a "charming event" with "wine, music, dancing girls,
serious poetry, free satori,"[5] and the turnout was over a hundred.
But charm was not its strong point. In town on a visit, Kerouac set
the audience mood by drunkenly pounding a gallon jug of wine to
show his enthusiasm. The highlight of the evening came when
Ginsberg, himself half-drunk and swaying to the poem's ca-
dences, read "Howl." No one had ever heard it, and the audience,
intoxicated on words and Burgundy, roared and stamped its
approval. The response, said Philip Lamantia, a poet friend of
Cassady's, was "like bringing two ends of an electric wire together."[6] Many who attended that night would remember the event as
the dawn of a new aesthetic age.

Howl and Other Poems appeared as one of City Lights' Pocket
Poets Series in 1956 to wide critical notice, if not always acclaim.
In 1957 *Evergreen Review,* an influential forum for the cultural
avant-garde, published an entire issue devoted to the San Francisco renaissance. Soon after, Viking Press issued *On the Road.* As
luck would have it, Gilbert Millstein, a *New York Times* editor
friendly to the new aesthetic mood, reviewed it for the *Times Book
Review* and called it "an authentic work of art" and "the most
beautifully executed, the clearest and most important utterance

yet made by the generation Kerouac himself named years ago as 'beat'. . . ."⁷ The book became an instant best-seller and thrust the Beat writers and their special world to cultural center stage.

The term *Beat* may have been coined by Kerouac in 1948 when he described his friends as weary with "all the forms, all the conventions," members of a "beat" version of the 1920s' "Lost Generation" of writers and artists.⁸ Kerouac meant the novelists and poets who were helping to produce a cultural metamorphosis. But Beatdom also threw off a ring of camp followers, the beatniks, for whom it was primarily a mode of personal response to the humdrum world of fifties' America. By the time the Beat writers burst into the public's consciousness, a Beat lifestyle had coalesced among the young, signaling a new bohemia.

Like every generation of bohemia, the beatnicks flourished in cities. Young men and women seized by the beatnik urge left the suburbs and small towns and settled in the decaying low-rent neighborhoods of the metropolises. In San Francisco's North Beach, Venice West in Los Angeles, or New York's Lower East Side (the East Village), whole neighborhoods of beatnik pads appeared. The beatniks professed contempt for American materialism, and they furnished their apartments with bare mattresses, cheap prints, and dime-store cushions. Yet even at the lowest beatnik levels, the arts—especially music—had a special place, and the new bohemians could seldom forgo fancy phonographs or expensive guitars.

The public, with some justice, saw the beatnik phenomenon primarily as a life-style. To readers of *Life* or *Look* or the Sunday supplements a beatnik was a scruffy young man, bearded and wearing sandals, or a short-skirted female waif with long black stockings, mascara-ringed eyes, and pale skin. These beings used a strange vocabulary of terms such as *dig it, cool man, far out,* and the word *like* as a ubiquitous connective between thoughts, and seemed to function in a perpetual drug-induced haze. Their lives apparently consisted of languor interrupted by ecstasy. But however dubious, in the mid-fifties the Beat scene was the only revolution around, and to the farseeing it appeared a foretaste of more to come.

☐ A famous picture: antiwar "flower power" confronts "the war machine" during the march on the Pentagon of October 1967. (Paul Conklin, Monkmeyer)

☐ A protest against the draft in downtown San Francisco, late April 1968. Everything looks better in the City by the Bay. (UPI/Bettmann Newsphotos)

□ Eugene McCarthy and his "Clean for Gene" supporters in Manchester during the momentous New Hampshire presidential primary. (Charles Harbutt, Archive Pictures)

□ Robert Kennedy speaks to a Jewish congregation in Portland during the Oregon primary. This photo, reproduced in a Southern California newspaper, supposedly enraged Kennedy's pro-Palestinian assassin, Sirhan Sirhan. (AP/Wide World Photos)

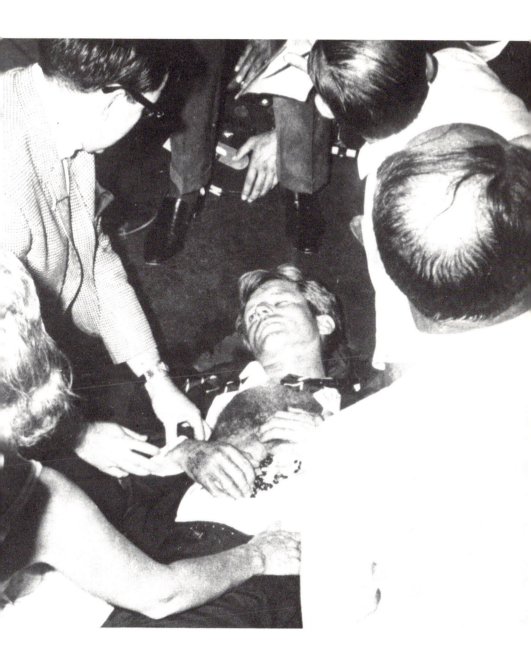

☐ Still alive, Robert Kennedy lies
on the floor of Los Angeles's Ambassador Hotel with rosary beads
slipping from his hand, awaiting
the arrival of medical help.
(UPI/Bettmann Newsphotos)

☐ Timothy Leary about to marry Rosemary Woodruff in a Neo-American Church ceremony at Millbrook, New York. The boy to his right is his son, Jackie. (AP/Wide World Photos)

☐ Allen Ginsberg and Beat poet Gary Snyder at the January 1967 Be-In in San Francisco's Golden Gate Park— living ties between the bohemia of the 1950s and the 1960s. (Gene Anthony)

☐ The Charlatans, a "non-famous" acid-rock band, giving a free concert at Golden Gate Park during the Summer of Love. (Gene Anthony)

☐ A Digger handing out free bread—literally, this time —to hippies in the Haight-Ashbury. (Gene Anthony)

☐ The Beck–Malina Living Theater returns from exile in Europe in 1968 only to find that Americans have caught up to and passed them by in cultural radicalism. Here they perform at Yale. (Ben Martin/*Time*)

☐ Women's liberation protesters on the Boardwalk in Atlantic City during the 1968 Miss America Pageant. The picture held by the young woman on the right is a vivid example of sexism prevalent at that time and it was much cited by feminists. (AP/Wide World Photos)

☐ George Wallace at the podium of the American Independent party rally at New York's Madison Square Garden, October 25, 1968. Fifteen thousand people came to cheer—and boo. (Hy Simon/Pictorial Parade)

☐ Richard Nixon greets well-wishers at Willingboro, New Jersey, late September 1968. (UPI/Bettmann Newsphotos)

☐ Yippies and other protesters atop Civil War General "Black Jack" Logan's statue in Grant Park during the Democratic National Convention in Chicago. (Art Shay, Time Inc.)

☐ Antiwar demonstrators coming up against a line of Mayor Daley's police at the Chicago convention. (Robert Cottrol, *Time*)

In March 1969 the federal government indicted seven antiwar—New Left activists (as well as Bobby Seale) for conspiracy to instigate a riot at the Democratic convention. Seated before the mike in this photograph are Jerry Rubin and Nancy Kurshan, his wife. Looking on (*from left to right*): John Froines, a guard (not identified), Abbie Hoffman, Lee Weiner, David Dellinger, Tom Hayden, and Rennie Davis. (AP/Wide World Photos)

Vice-President Hubert Humphrey and his wife, Muriel, outside the polling station in their home community, election day 1968. (Pictorial Parade)

This is the view that America and the world saw from the Apollo 8 space capsule as it orbited the moon at Christmastime 1968. (National Aeronautics and Space Administration)

*   *   *

The novelist Alan Harrington called hippies "no more than Beats plus drugs."[9] Change *drugs* to LSD and it would be hard to find a better one-sentence description.

Beats and beatniks were not unfamiliar with drugs. They had borrowed marijuana from black musicians. They used heroin and cocaine occasionally. And Ginsberg and some of the others had experimented with peyote, a mind-altering substance extracted from a Mexican cactus plant. But the shift that vastly accelerated the whole pace of cultural change came with psilocybin and lysergic acid diethylamide, LSD.

LSD was discovered in 1938 by Albert Hofmann, a Swiss chemist experimenting with ergot derivatives for Sandoz Laboratories, a Basel pharmaceutical firm. Hofmann ignored the new substance for five years but had not forgotten it. Then, in 1943, as he prepared a new batch, some of the crystals stuck to his fingers. The chemical was absorbed through his skin and in a few minutes he found himself overcome by "a remarkable . . . state of intoxication . . . characterized by an intense stimulation of the imagination and an altered state of awareness of the world." As he lay in a daze, "there surged up from me a succession of fantastic, rapidly changing imagery of a striking reality and depth, alternating with a vivid, kaleidoscopic play of colors."[10] The bespectacled Swiss scientist had just taken the first LSD trip.

In 1947 published reports on LSD appeared in the scientific journals. Soon after, the CIA, ever alert for new ways to defend freedom and democracy, began to experiment with the chemical that it feared—and hoped—could "destroy integrity and make indiscreet the most dependable individual."[11] The Agency was soon testing the effects of acid on its own personnel and on unsuspecting patients in federal prisons and drug treatment centers. Some of these experiments produced "bad trips" when subjects writhed in terror or sank into near coma. In one case, an army civilian scientist committed suicide by jumping out of his hotel room after taking LDS. The Agency was not deterred. For a number of years a CIA employee, George Hunter White, ran "safe houses" in New York and San Francisco where uninformed subjects, prostitutes and their "johns," were slipped LSD in their drinks or food and then observed through one-way mirrors to see the weird results of mixing LSD and sex.

Besides its own experiments, the CIA awarded contracts to selected university scientists and private researchers. The ironic effect was to expand the circle of LSD initiates far beyond the cold-war–defense community. By the early fifties clusters of scientists, academics, sensation-seekers, and creative artists had taken notice of the hallucinogenic phenomenon and were anxious to learn more. Some were doctors or psychologists who believed that an LSD trip imitated schizophrenia and would help them understand the causes of insanity or allow them to modify irrational or antisocial behavior. Others were seeking personal enlightenment or escape from life's dreary round.

Mystical states had always intrigued Western intellectuals and artists if only because they challenged the rationalism of the surrounding bourgeois world. Scholars had explored the mystery cults of the late classical world, the shamanistic religions of premodern peoples, the exalted emotional states of Western saints and martyrs, the secrets of Eastern holy men and prophets. Some had noticed the use by non-Western wizards and sorcerers of natural substances to produce heightened mystical experiences and sought out opportunities to test their effects personally.

One of the first psychedelic pilgrims was the English novelist Aldous Huxley, whose *Brave New World* had described a future dystopia chemically reinforced by "soma," a drug that induced a sense of well-being and so bolstered a coercive and exploitative social system. Drugs did the Devil's work in the novel, but Huxley's fascination with altered states of mind led him to mescaline, an extract from the peyote cactus used by the Indians of the Southwest and Mexico to induce a religious trance. In 1953 he took some at his Hollywood Hills home. "It was without question," he later wrote, "the most extraordinary and significant experience this side of the Beatific Vision." When he looked at a small vase of flowers, he saw what "Adam had seen on the morning of creation—the miracle, moment by moment, of naked existence . . . flowers shining in their own inner light and all but

THE PERSONAL IS POLITICAL

quivering under the pressure of the significance with which they were charged."[12] In 1954 Huxley's *The Doors of Perception* described the experience and introduced the subject of chemically altered mental states to a still wider audience of literate Americans.

Time-Life publisher Henry Luce and his wife, Clare Boothe, had already begun to use LSD recreationally in the company of Huxley and Christopher Isherwood, another English novelist. In 1957 Luce published a seventeen-page *Life* article, "Seeking the Magic Mushroom," by banker R. Gordon Wasson, recounting his visit with his wife to a remote part of Mexico where they partook of "God's flesh," a fungus containing a powerful hallucinogenic drug, and had experienced brilliant visions. If thousands read the Huxley book, millions read the Wasson article. Back in Basel, soon after, Dr. Hofmann extracted the essence of the mushroom and named it *psilocybin*.

Three young men exposed to these early glimpses of heaven-in-a-pill would create a movement and a world view out of the psychedelic experience. One was Allen Ginsberg.

By 1958 or 1959 the beatnik phenomenon had begun to tail off. The Beat poets had deserted North Beach and scattered through the Bay region. In New York the Columbia area had ceased to attract rebels and dissenters. The party, it seemed was over.

But some of the Beats, notably Ginsberg, bridged the gap to the counterculture era by way of psychedelics. Ginsberg first took peyote in the mid-fifties; "Howl" mentions "peyote solidities of halls . . ." In 1959 he tried LSD at the Mental Research Institute in Palo Alto, one of the private research groups that supplied the drug to volunteers and recorded their responses. At his own suggestion, the experimenters turned on a stroboscope lamp while he was under the influence and the flickering light produced a bad trip. Ginsberg felt his "soul being sucked out through the light into the wall socket and going out."[13] Despite the terrifying encounter, Ginsberg was impressed with the power of LSD to change perception.

Another father of the psychedelic revolution was Timothy Leary, a chiseled-featured Irish American who had come to

Harvard to teach clinical psychology after a successful career with the Kaiser Foundation Hospital in Oakland. A Berkeley Ph.D., Leary at thirty-nine was in the throes of a mid-life crisis following two failed marriages. In the summer of 1959 while vacationing in Cuernavaca, Mexico, he swallowed seven black teonanácatl mushrooms washed down with a beer chaser. The results were profound. "It was above all and without question the deepest religious experience of my life," he later wrote.[14]

Leary returned to Harvard and, in collaboration with Richard Alpert, a younger Harvard colleague, launched a research project to test the effects of psilocybin, the essential ingredient of "magic mushrooms." The two professors first gave the drug to inmates of the state maximum security prison at Concord to see if it would affect the recidivism rate. The results were promising: only a quarter of those who took the drug returned to prison as compared with the usual four-fifths. But the two experimenters quickly went beyond conventional behavior-control research. They themselves became confirmed trippers and salesmen for mind-altering drugs and were soon scattering psilocybin wholesale around the Cambridge community. Before long they had established a headquarters in Newton where they proselytized for instant spiritual enlightenment through drug ingestion.

The place attracted a constant stream of graduate students and local celebrities. Ginsberg came from New York in December 1960 with his lover Peter Orlovsky. This time, in the more congenial setting of the Leary–Alpert mansion, he had a good trip and became convinced that psilocybin was the key to transforming the world's consciousness. Before he left, he had provided Leary with the addresses and phone numbers of some of the most important musicians, artists, publishers, poets, and writers in New York, people who could spread the psychedelic gospel and help to alter the very basis for human perceptions. Leary quickly followed up on the suggestion, and soon half the creative people in New York were experimenting with the magic-mushroom essence. Neal Cassady also flew up to Boston to try the new drug, and so did the poet Charles Olson, a former rector of Black Mountain College and a Beat founding father.

In the spring of 1962, a tall, balding Englishman with a mysterious past, Michael Hollingshead, showed up in Newton with a mayonnaise jar full of something new—LSD-laced syrup. Leary took some and the Harvard professor was stunned by its explosive effects. It was, he wrote, the "most shattering experience of my life."[15] Alpert and Ralph Metzner, another of his psilocybin-project associates, soon tried the stuff and became instant converts. Though Leary refused to accept undergraduates as subjects, he did not exclude Harvard graduate students. Before long, Leary noted, "every weekend the Harvard resident houses were transformed into spaceships floating miles above the Yard."[16]

The doings of the Leary–Alpert group soon became a scandal, and the Harvard administration clamped down. In March 1962 the two were called before a faculty committee and accused of conducting their research in an irresponsible way. The story of the stormy meeting was picked up by the *Harvard Crimson,* and it brought the incident to the attention of the U.S. Food and Drug Administration. Though psychedelic drugs were not illegal, a month later the FDA told Leary that he could not continue his experiments without an M.D. present.

That summer Leary and Alpert moved the scene of their operations to a more congenial locale. The two LSD gurus had concluded that the quality of a trip depended on "set and setting," that is the attitude of the tripper and the trip's physical and psychological surroundings. In July they established a psychedelic summer camp at Zijuatenejo on Mexico's West Coast where thirty guests—Harvard graduate students, some Cambridge proto-hippies, a few academics, and Peggy and Tommy Hitchcock, two rich enlightenment seekers—tripped to their hearts' content. While the guests beachcombed, meditated, and bodysurfed, Leary rearranged an English translation of the *Tibetan Book of the Dead* to make it suitable for LSD acolytes to use as a spiritual guide during their experiences.

In the fall the two high priests reestablished themselves in another Newton house where twelve people, including two of Leary's children, lived as an extended family. By this time Alpert and Leary were embarked on a mission they believed would simultaneously change world consciousness and the face of national culture. During their final months in Newton, they set up the International Foundation for Internal Freedom (IFIF) and announced that they would establish a chain of centers across the country staffed by medical, social, and legal advisers where artists, writers, and "searchers for meaning" could "explore their internal geography."[17] At its national headquarters the IFIF would publish a journal, the *Psychedelic Review,* edited by Ralph Metzner. The IFIF's announcement brought hundreds of membership applications, each enclosing the required ten-dollar initiation fee.

In May Leary flew down to Mexico to start the first of the IFIF's summer sessions, while Alpert stayed behind in Boston to take care of the organization's booming business affairs. It was in Zijuatenejo that Leary heard that Harvard had fired both its mind-bending professors, himself for nonperformance of duties and Alpert for continuing to dispense psilocybin.

The summer was like Club Med plus LSD. The IFIF had taken over the entire Hotel Catalina and filled it with members who tripped once a week and spent the rest of their time playing chess, strumming guitars, listening to talks on mysticism, and discussing their acid experiences. Dining was by candlelight on the outdoor patio. Unfortunately, the little ersatz nirvana attracted unwashed, unkempt, and unemployed beatniks who wanted to join the festivities. At first Leary allowed them to stay for twenty-four hours, but he was soon forced to turn them away. Back in Mexico City the disgruntled rejectees told the American colony of lurid doings at the Hotel Catalina.

In June, six weeks after it began, the authorities ended the idyll by ordering the hotel closed and expelling Leary and his colleagues from Mexico. Leary and Alpert visited Dominica in the Caribbean for an alternative location, but the scheme became entangled in local Dominican politics and quickly collapsed.

For a time it looked as if the plan to turn America on was dead. Then partial salvation came as a gift from William Hitchcock, brother of Tom and Peggy, a rich stockbroker with the Lehman firm of Wall Street bankers. The brothers had just bought a sixty-four-room mansion on four thousand acres at

Millbrook, New York, two hours by car from New York City. Bill Hitchcock, a Leary disciple, offered the use of the main house for the Leary–Alpert operation, and in mid-September the IFIF, renamed the Castalia Foundation and drastically scaled back, relocated in Dutchess County. Millbrook would be a community of seekers and searchers where, through experiment and study, the secrets of the inner world would be revealed, and then, through the foundation's publications, this new knowledge would be transmitted to all mankind. On the model of utopian communities of the past, Millbrook would become a light unto the nations, a redemptive community.

The actuality was somewhat different. Thirty men and women, many from the Harvard core group, came to live at the mansion, tripping together on a regular basis and carefully transcribing their feelings and responses. Visitors, especially the paying and unfamous, were treated to seminars on Buddhism, yoga, and the psychedelic experience, generally without exposure to LSD. The setting was stunning. Millbrook was furnished with gorgeous Persian carpets, dazzling crystal chandeliers, and magnificent fireplaces; its walls were covered with paintings designed to reproduce and reinforce the psychedelic vision. Yet the environment was also orgiastic and chaotic. The permanent residents, including children and pets, remained stoned for days on end. People pranced through the rooms, grounds, and corridors—often clothesless—and made love at whim. Millbrook was not only an avatar of the psychedelic era; it also helped pioneer the sexual revolution.

The center's influence radiated in a wide circle from Dutchess County. Besides the paying weekend seminar people, influential visitors descended on Millbrook to satisfy their curiosity or gain enlightenment. Musicians like Maynard Ferguson and Charlie Mingus, already hip to marijuana, came to learn about acid. Alan Watts, the Zen philosopher, was another visitor, as was the radical psychologist R. D. Laing. Through Viva Superstar, a beautiful blond actress, the Millbrook community established a connection with the avant-garde New York artist Andy Warhol. Paul Krassner of *The Realist* also made a pilgrimage to the psychedelic mansion. Krassner later claimed that he had not enjoyed the experience. He had discovered that he really did prefer reality to fantasy.

Millbrook professed to be more than a hedonic commune. It was, its founders insisted, a shrine for the new revelation. As a clinical psychologist trained in the 1950s, Leary saw modern civilization as the product of the id's repression by the ego and the superego. He wanted, he said, to change Western consciousness— to replace guilt, achievement, and the work ethic by spontaneity, the pleasure principle, and joy in idleness. He would later embody his philosophy in the simple slogan "Turn on, tune in, drop out." Leary never shucked off entirely the academic's bondage to rationality and control and would be criticized for it by the fringe to his left. But in his own eyes he was the apostle of the Dionysian, the antithesis of bourgeois America and all its rigid values and empty strivings. Millbrook would be the mother church of a new faith that would challenge the decaying old square world.

Leary's lofty if disquieting goals were not inconsistent with blatant hucksterism; at times turn-on became put-on. He often seemed a con man who cut his message to fit his clientele's cloth. In an 1966 interview for *Playboy*, the mouthpiece for Hugh Hefner's sexual-freedom message, he asserted that LSD was "the most powerful aphrodisiac ever discovered by man. . . . In a carefully prepared, loving LSD session, a woman will inevitably have several hundred orgasms." Speaking for himself, his "participation in every form of sensory expression" had "multiplied a *thousandfold*." In his opinion, "the sexual impact" was "the open but private secret about LSD."[18]

Leary was also an impressive showman. When psychedelics became the sophisticates' rage during 1965 and 1966, he put on "celebrations" for his newly formed League for Spiritual Discovery, light and sound shows where paid audiences, through slide projections, strobe lights, and booming rock music, experienced a simulated LSD trip. Paul Morrissey, a filmmaker friend of Andy Warhol, after seeing one of these performances in the East Village, exclaimed: "God, Doctor Leary is wonderful! What a medicine show!"[19]

Yet the comparison with religion was not mere metaphor. Several Indian tribes of Mexico and the Southwest treated peyote as a sacrament, and one flourishing Indian religious group, the Native American Church, had incorporated the divine cactus into its rituals. Millbrook too begat a formal religion—after a fashion.

One of the Millbrook circle was Arthur Kleps, an upstate New York social worker who had experimented with mescaline in 1960 and then, four years later, abruptly appeared at Millbrook's door after reading about Leary and Alpert in *The New York Times.* Kelps did not fit comfortably into the Millbrook community. He was too irreverant and incorporated an even larger dose of the charlatan and the self-promoter in his personality than the other Millbrook people. In 1966 he seceded from Millbrook and founded the Neo-American Church.

The new faith was a mixture of the serious and the clownish, like almost everything touched by LSD. Acid and other psychedelics would be "sacraments" that would expedite "enlightenment," Kleps declared.[20] All well and good, but then Kleps made himself high priest of the new religion with the title of Chief Boo Hoo and adopted as his church's symbol a three-eyed toad over the motto Victory Over Horseshit.[21] Kleps frankly admitted that his purpose was "money and power" and devoted the last twenty pages of his *Catechism and Handbook,* the Neo-American Church's bible, to a catalog of items that members could buy, including a self-destruct box that went up in smoke when opened and a certificate testifying that the Chief Boo Hoo had never heard of the bearer and was totally indifferent to his existence.

On the West Coast, the Prometheus of the psychedelic culture was Ken Kesey, a burley Oregonian with prematurely thinning hair and an antic style. In 1960 Kesey was a graduate student in English at Stanford University, living with his wife in Perry Lane, a small beatnik community transplanted from North Beach to Palo Alto. Needing money, he volunteered as a subject in drug experiments at the local Veterans' Administration hospital, where the doctors placed him in a room, gave him pills, and recorded his responses. One out of every three pills was LSD, and the effects were fantastic. Sounds had color, small objects appeared huge, figures glowed and pulsated. With his perceptions transformed by acid, Kesey wrote his novel about the inanities of psychiatric treatment at a state mental hospital and finished it in June 1961. *One Flew Over the Cuckoo's Nest* appeared the following February to glowing reviews and made him a celebrity.

Perry Lane soon became a mecca for all the cultural dissenters around. The Texas novelist Larry McMurtry came to visit. Richard Alpert showed up as did a wild-haired young musician, Jerry Garcia. Neal Cassady of *On the Road* fame not only made an appearance but stayed on to become a leading man in the Kesey comedy that soon followed. By now the Perry Lane community was completely turned on, consuming vast helpings of Kesey's LSD-laced venison chili and peyote buttons supplied by a mail-order house in Laredo, Texas.

In July 1963 the owner of the Perry Lane tract sold the property to a developer, and Kesey and his entourage moved to a house in the redwoods at La Honda, south of Palo Alto. There they improved on Perry Lane, creating their own version of set and setting. This was not Buddhism and incense à la Millbrook. Instead, there were rock and bop blasting out of speakers strung from tree to tree and fantastic mobiles and pulsating nonobjective paintings dangling from bushes and limbs.

In the spring of 1964, Kesey and his friend Ken Babbs had a brainstorm. Kesey and four or five friends would buy a station wagon and drive to New York for the World's Fair, arriving in time for the publication date of Kesey's new novel in July. Then someone saw an advertisement for a 1939 International Harvester bus fitted out with benches, bunks, a sink, a refrigerator, cabinets, and shelves—all for fifteen hundred dollars. This was it! The deal was concluded, and the La Honda crew, now calling themselves the Merry Pranksters, swarmed over the vehicle, wiring it for sound, painting it with swirling Day-Glo mandelas, and cutting a hole through the roof so a passenger could sit on a raised platform with his head and upper body poking through the top.

In early July Kesey as Swashbuckler, Babbs as Intrepid Traveler, Mike Hagen as Mal Function, Steve Lambrecht as Zonker, and others nicknamed Mountain Girl, Gretchen Fetchin the Slime Queen, Doris Delay, Hardly Visible, and the like, set off for New York. The driver was none other than the holy primitive Neal Cassady, a little the worse for wear after two years in San Quentin for possession of one stick of marijuana. On the rear of the bus was a sign reading CAUTION: WEIRD LOAD; one in front said FURTHUR, with two whimsical *u*'s. In the refrigerator were pitchers of orange juice spiked with grade A acid.

The trip east is the nearest thing we have to a counterculture epic. Kesey decided to film the whole thing, perhaps as a commercial venture, and a partial record exists of the pranks, trips, encounters, and mishaps. Days were not comfortable. The bus rattled and strained and bounced hard over every bump. Bathroom stops at rural filling stations were chancy. The station operators complained about the strain on their septic tanks of a dozen people all relieving themselves at once, and Kesey had to point out how much gas the bus took so they would let the Pranksters use the facilities. Nights were even worse. It was hard to sleep going seventy miles an hour over rutted roads in a vehicle without springs. Meanwhile, day or night, everyone was strung out on acid, pot, and then, for variety, Benzedrine—speed.

But there were compensations. The dope was good, and weird, wonderful things happened when acid mixed with velocity, a screaming hi-fi, a whizzing landscape, and freaks confronting squares. And there was good sex, or at least lots of it. There was a sleeping bag on the shelf of the "love bunk." That's where you crawled when you wanted to make it. It was always occupied, and Tom Wolfe, the historian of the Pranksters, asserts that it got such hard use that mere proximity was enough to impregnate any virgin.

There were visits along the way. In Houston they stopped at Larry McMurtry's house on Quenby Road and there were forced to abandon Stark Naked, a junior Prankster, who flipped out and thought McMurtry's son was her own long-lost Frankie. On out across the Deep South with a stop in New Orleans and then to Pensacola to visit a friend of Babbs.

They reached New York in mid-July and looked up Kerouac and Ginsberg, who were in town. Cassady did the introductions. It was an awkward encounter: Beat meets counterculture—only the second word did not yet exist. The two groups eyed each other across the chasm of acid. There was a generational thing, too. As Wolfe says, "Kerouac was the old star. Kesey was the wild new comet from the West heading christ knew where."[22] In short, it didn't jell.

The next stop was Millbrook. The Learyites were the only other acid community yet born, and the Pranksters were eager to meet their East Coast blood brothers. They arrived, speakers blaring and a Prankster hurling green smoke bombs off the top of the bus. "We're here! We're here!"

Silence. After a minute or so Alpert, Peggy Hitchcock, Maynard Ferguson, and a few others appeared and gave the cavorting Pranksters a cool, appraising eye. Then Peggy Hitchcock invited them to tour the mansion. Leary himself did not materialize. According to Tom Wolfe's version, he sent a message that he was on a serious three-day trip and could not be disturbed. Leary claims that he had the flu and was in bed with a fever. But in any case, he later wrote, he did meet with Kesey and Babbs before they left, and both parties promised to stay in touch. Whatever happened, the Pranksters departed convinced that their free-wheeling American brand of psychedelia, not Leary's set and setting amidst Far Eastern gewgaws, was how the future would go.

The trip back was charged by speed, not acid. The LSD had run low, and Alpert had refused to replenish their supply. When the Pranksters reached La Honda, at least one, Sandy Lehmann-Haupt, was deep in speed paranoia. Soon after set-down Kesey took the bus and the Prankster crew down to Big Sur to conduct a seminar for Fritz Perls, the Gestalt psychologist who had established Eselen, a group therapy center for up-tight achievers, on grounds a thousand feet above the crashing Pacific waves. There Perls and his assistants showed the paying guests how to forget past and future and live Now. Kesey was to be a "resource person" who would demonstrate how to live for the present. For Sandy Lehmann-Haupt, it was almost curtains. While on a candlelight procession from the grounds down to the shore, he flipped out, and ran screaming down the highway toward Monterey. The police picked him up and held him in the town jail until his brother, Christopher, flew in from New York and took him back for medical attention.

Kesey and his friends spent most of the time from the fall of 1964 through the following spring making a movie out of the forty-five hours of color film they had shot on the trip. They also became more and more immersed in the acid dream. In the summer Kesey met the Hell's Angels through reporter Hunter Thompson and in August invited the bikers to visit La Honda. The association was improbable at first thought and fitting at second. Acid heads and bikers were both outlaws in the square-straight world. Both built their lives around moving down the highway.

The meeting was a wild success. A lot of people besides the regular Pranksters, including Alpert, Ginsberg, and many of the old Perry Lane bunch, turned up at La Honda for the fun. Kesey had stretched a fifteen-foot-long banner across the place reading THE MERRY PRANKSTERS WELCOME THE HELL'S ANGELS, and everyone awaited the roar of the Harley-Davidsons with hearts pounding. At a little after 3:00 P.M. the formation rumbled over the bridge and stopped in a whirl of dust in front of the house. Forty shaggy, sweaty bikers in sleeveless denim jackets with skull-and-cross-bones insignia dismounted and looked around curiously. What the fuck was this all about! The Pranksters and their guests were already floating on acid and pot. Ginsberg, beard down to his sternum, was hopping around clashing finger cymbals and chanting Hare Krishna, Krishna Hare, and so forth. Everyone was weaving to Bob Dylan's nasal "Mr. Tambourine Man" and other good music and was too zonked to be afraid of the baaad nasties. The Pranksters' cool—plus big ice chests of beer and batches of acid—kept the peace. The cops hovered just off the property waiting to move in at the slightest sign of violence or overt law breaking. The occasion never came, and when the Angels roared off two days later, a kind of alliance between the two outlaw cultures had been forged.

*   *   *

In early 1965 path crossed path, event piled on event, A met B, and the counterculture came to full flower.

LSD was crucial, of course, and here Leary and Kesey were Johnny Appleseeds planting their magic packets on fertile ground at a hundred places across the continent. The turn-on community, hitherto a small band of initiates, soon swelled into a psychedelic nation.

Of the two, Leary was the more peripatetic. By the fall of 1965, his roadshow of lectures, sound, strobe lights, and yogic exercises traveled an East Coast circuit with periodic forays to the Midwest and California. Leary did not distribute acid, but many of the more sophisticated, seventy-five dollars a crack "clients" bought their own and floated through the sessions. Kesey confined himself to the Bay Area, but here his influence would be profound.

Kesey and Leary provided the psychedelic movement's software, as it were. The key hardware developer was a shrimpy, dark-haired character with a nasal voice and a patrician pedigree named Augustus Owsley Stanley III, called by his middle name. Owsley had drifted to the West Coast and by early 1965 had taken up with Melissa Cargill, a young University of California chemistry major. For a time they manufactured methedrine at his Berkeley apartment, and then, after California narcotics officers closed them down, they began to turn out acid. The Owsley enterprise shifted to high gear with the advent of Tim Scully, a Berkeley science whiz who helped create the purest, strongest acid anyone had ever seen. The Owsley tablets, color-coded for each new batch, established the standard and brought the promoters a flood of money. Cynics were happy to make note of the profits, but Owsley and company saw themselves as benefactors and social engineers as much as entrepreneurs. As Scully later said, "We believed that we were the architects of social change, that our mission was to change the world substantially. . . ."[23]

Together Owsley and Kesey created the amalgam of acid and rock music that made up the Bay Area psychedelic culture.

From the mid-fifties on, rock and roll was the music of adolescent rebellion in the cities and the suburbs of the land. With its pounding rhythmic beat, it expressed the exploding sexual energies of the newly pubescent. In Elvis Presley—of the swiveling hips and bedroom eyes—the young soon had a hero, admired all the more for the embarrassment and dismay he caused his elders. The Beatles too from the beginning were a rallying point for youth rebellion. Their music at first avoided political and social comment, but their funny "mod" haircuts offended parents on two continents and so had special meaning for the young. Then, with *Rubber Soul* in late 1965, intimations of something more than "Yeah, yeah, yeah" began to creep into the Beatles' lyrics, things hinting at freedom, protest, and getting high.

But in mid-decade rock still competed with folk as the music of dissent. Ever since it had been discovered by thirties bohemians and radicals and proclaimed "the people's" music, folk music had conveyed an insurgent message. It was no accident that Joan Baez had been the troubadour of the Berkeley Free Speech Movement. In 1965 the freshest voice on the folk scene was Bob Dylan, a skinny Jewish kid improbably from Hibbing, Minnesota. Back in 1965, when he first arrived in New York, Dylan was only distinguishable from all the others who strummed the acoustic guitar and warbled "Barbara-Allen" and "Shoo-tail Fly" by his hoarse and adenoidal tone. He soon moved on, however. In 1965, at the Newport Folk Festival, decked out in dark glasses and an outrageous polka-dot Carnaby Street shirt, Dylan went "electric." He was soon composing songs about anomic lives and relationships that were implicitly critical of society—"It's Alright, Ma," "Like a Rolling Stone," "Gates of Eden," and others—that celebrated the pleasure of acid or denounced the Vietnam War.

Dylan's merger of rock with LSD was anticipated in the Bay Area. During the mid-sixties, a number of local rock groups with such colorful names as Country Joe and the Fish, the Jefferson Airplane, the Lovin' Spoonful, the Family Dog, and Big Brother and the Holding Company performed in halls in San Francisco, Marin County, or the East Bay area. One of these, the Grateful Dead, formerly the Warlocks, was led by Jerry Garcia, Kesey's friend from Perry Lane. Many were still pretty amateurish, but they had their followers and their promoters.

The Bay Area fusion of acid and rock was the work of Kesey and Owsley together, though the collaboration would be a case of parallel effort rather than direct cooperation. Owsley would supply the LSD and some of the money, and Kesey would supply the energy and the organizing—or, often, dis-organizing— genius.

The new mixture started as the Acid Test, a total experience combining music, dance, lights, and images all swept along on a blast of LSD that participants would take before or during the test. To this day it is not clear what was being tested, except the subjects' mental fortitude.

The first test was a small affair in late November at Ken Babbs's house outside Santa Cruz, down the Peninsula, with the music supplied by the Pranksters themselves and the Pranksters' intercoastal film epic as the major feature. The next took place at a private house in San Jose, but this time Garcia and his Grateful Dead played to three or four hundred kids recruited from the recently adjourned Rolling Stones concert at a nearby audi-torium. The third Acid Test, at Muir Beach, added the strobe lights. Despite the name, relatively little acid had circulated at the first two tests. But by now everyone had gotten the idea that you were expected to be stoned, and the third test was a shrieking, blasting, overload, short-circuit experience. It was even too much for Owsley, who was hurled into a bad trip by the sheer volume of stimuli and reacted by threatening to cut off everyone's acid supply.

Owsley soon had second thoughts and became a major spon-sor of the Trips Festival of January 1966. He not only supplied the acid but also became the Grateful Dead's angel, pouring money into their electronic equipment so that no other group in the world had so many giant speakers, mixers, microphones, control panels. Out of these began to come a new sound, acid rock, the special music of the counterculture.

The Trips Festival of January 21–23 at Longshoremen's Hall put the acid rock scene on the map. Bill Graham, former manager of the San Francisco Mime Troupe, who had become a major rock promoter through sponsoring benefit concerts for the troupe at the Fillmore auditorium, handled the business details. Free publicity was provided by Lou Gottlieb, formerly of the folk group the Limelighters, now working as a music columnist for the

Chronicle. On Tuesday Gottlieb called the Trips Festival an event of "major significance in the history of religion." The Almighty was "vouchsafing visions" to certain people that far exceeded those of St. Theresa. Everyone should go, he said.²⁴ But the biggest boost of all, probably, was Kesey's bust early Tuesday morning on a rooftop in North Beach for possession of pot. This was Kesey's second arrest for possession, and it looked as if the famous novelist might be put away for as much as five years without chance of parole. The publicity was priceless.

The festival was a bang-up success, grossing $12,500 with little overhead. Two weeks later Graham was running weekly trips at the Fillmore and was on his way to becoming the Florenz Ziegfeld of the rock business. For the customers it was the beginning of the psychedelic era. Tom Wolfe describes the event as "the first national convention of an underground movement that had existed on a hush-hush cell-by-cell basis."²⁵ When Wolfe wrote his book on Kesey and the Merry Pranksters, the word had not yet been coined, but what he meant was that the counterculture had just been born.

The emergence of the counterculture can be followed through its sounds. It can also be tracked through its sights and, as it were, its feels.

Spectacle, movement, light, and color were sensory elements of the new consciousness. The posters that advertised the trips and the tests represented a new pictorial art that combined Eastern—predominantly Indian—motifs with the bursting stars, flaming mandalas, and undulating lines of acid visions, the turn-of-the-century elegance of art nouveau, and Viennese artist Alfred Roller's fat, space-filling letters. Wesley Wilson, a former San Francisco State College student who ran a low-priced print shop, though not a trained artist, gradually elevated the acid rock posters to a fine art by a process of trial and error. The style was further refined in 1966 by a Vietnam deserter named only "Dangerfield," who did designs for *The Oracle,* a new under-ground newspaper that began to publish that fall.

The acid-influenced poster art merged with pop art to produce a whole new visual sensibility. Pop was an attempt to destroy the distinction between the everyday and high art. Its predecessor as the reigning style was abstract expressionism, a genre that replaced the visual representationism of traditional art by pure lines, curves, spots, loops, and splotches of color. It was a painter's kind of painting that seemed far removed from everyday experience. The pop art of Warhol, Claes Oldenburg, James Rosenquist, and Roy Lichtenstein chose as its subject matter the most utterly banal—Campbell's Soup cans, ice cream cones, giant hamburgers, automobile-engine parts, silk-screened Marilyn Monroes—and presented it in the most naive, direct way. It was a revolt of the commonplace against the cerebral and in a significant sense reflected, and at the same time mocked, the plastic, commercial sensibility of the time. Pop was incorporated into the "comix" genre of the underground press that would soon appear in the campus neighborhoods and the hippie enclaves.

Hippies were actors in the drama of the streets; in some ways theater was the art form closest to the counterculture. It was also a vehicle for spreading the counterculture sensibility.

Theater has been a vehicle for social and political dissent since ancient times. Before World War I "serious" theater exploring radical ideas and avant-garde techniques, as opposed to Broadway diversions, found a home in the "little theater" movement. In the 1930s there was the left-wing agitprop theater of Clifford Odets and various Communist party sympathizers. During the 1950s the experimental impulse spawned "off-Broadway," and when that became too establishmentarian and popular, gave rise to "off-off-Broadway."

The first of the postwar experimental groups was the Living Theater of Julian Beck and Judith Malina, two pacifist-anarchist-bohemian New Yorkers who began to present avant-garde plays in their Manhattan living room soon after VJ Day. The Becks served up strong fare for the late forties and fifties—Gertrude Stein, Bertolt Brecht, Paul Goodman, and Frederico Garcia Lorca—playwrights whose radical politics or radical techniques shocked conventional audiences.

By the mid-1950s the Becks had moved their productions to a loft over a vegetable market on Manhattan's Upper West Side.

Toward the end of the decade, following a further move to the Village, they fell under the spell of the French critic-actor-playwright Antonin Artaud, whose "theater of cruelty" rejected the formal quality of the contemporary commercial stage and demanded that the theater return to its "original function" of revelation, challenge, spectacle, and ecstasy. Artaud emphasized the physical over the verbal and believed it essential to dissolve the barriers between the active performer and the passive spectator.

By this time the Becks had become active in the civil rights and pacifist movements. They also began to produce protest plays such as Jack Gelber's *The Connection*, a frank and sympathetic drama about drug addicts, and Kenneth Brown's *The Brig*, a surreal depiction of dehumanizing marine corps cruelty toward military prisoners. As pacifists, the Becks refused to pay federal taxes on their Living Theater earnings, and in 1964 the federal government ordered them shut down. They defied the authorities and staged a benefit festival behind locked doors. Arrested and tried, they turned the trial into a three-ring circus and were sentenced to several months in jail. After a brief incarceration at Danbury Federal Prison, they left the United States for a long stay in Europe. They would return in 1968 only to find that in the intervening years of fulminating social change, their vanguard absurdist-anarchist approach had become dated.

When the Becks fled to Europe, they left behind Joseph Chaikin, their Brooklyn-born principal actor, who had established a theater laboratory within the Living Theater company to try out "different ideas . . . about ensemble playing and different improvisational things."[26] The laboratory soon evolved into an association of actors, directors, playwrights, and critics called the Open Theater.

Chaikin's company, like its predecessor, was both experimental and radical. It avoided the standard repertory and explored the unstructured realms of dream, myth, and poetry, where words were only one component of performance and where the boundaries between audience and performer tended to disappear. Improvisation on broad themes figured prominently in its performances. The Open Theater was also a theatrical school where members spent much of their time in exercises to perfect their technique and to see how far they could push the limits of the stage. Chaikin was a political activist like his mentors. He believed that every member of the company, in addition to being gifted, must be "politically oriented." The stage should function as "a weapon." The Open Theater company members shared "a political attitude, unlike Lincoln Center, unlike the commercial theater."[27] During the sixties the Open Theater presented two successful commercial plays, both political, Megan Terry's antiwar *Viet Rock,* and *America Hurrah,* Jean-Claude van Itallie's absurdist attack on American society.

In all, five major companies would make up what R. G. Davis calls the Radical Independent Theater. (There was also one Spanish-language group, Luis Valdez's El Teatro Campesino.) In New York, besides the Beck and Chaikin companies, there was the Performance Group of Richard Schechner, a professor of theater at New York University and the editor of the influential *Drama Review.* In 1968 Schechner and his associates performed *Dionysus in '69,* a parable of liberation set among the Greek gods that included improvisation and direct involvement of the audience in on-stage nude gropings.

Another New York–based radical theater group was Peter Schumann's Bread and Puppet Theater, founded in 1960. Modeled after European Punch-and-Judy street theater, it employed larger than life-size puppets, masks, signs, and music to convey its didactic radical messages. Bread and Puppet performed primarily on the streets and became an essential part of almost every New York anti-Vietnam demonstration.

None of these, however, created such large cultural waves as Ron Davis's San Francisco Mime Troupe.

Davis had started as a dancer and was converted to mime after seeing a brilliant performance by Marcel Marceau, the French pantomimist. In 1957 Davis went to Paris to study the art with Etienne Decroux, returning to America after six months and settling in San Francisco. The most interesting theater in the city during those yeasty days was the Actor's Workshop, run by two San Francisco State College professors, Herbert Blau and Jules Irving. Davis auditioned for the workshop and was hired as an assistant director.

Davis was too independent-minded to remain within the workshop mold for long, however, and like Chaikin soon established a little subgroup of his own within the company that gave mute mime performances with improvised props. In 1963 he broke with the workshop over the issue of accepting foundation support, a policy, he felt, that made art a servant of establishment culture. He soon moved his Mime Troupe to an abandoned church in the Mission District. When the audiences were slow in coming, he went to them, putting on performances in local San Francisco parks.

The Mime Troupe quickly assimilated the growing cultural and political activism of the Bay Area. In 1965 Davis and Saul Landau concocted a "minstrel show," performed by white actors in blackface, that flayed racism with ridicule. The troupe presented the minstrel show in the Bay Area along with pieces by Bertolt Brecht, the German Marxist dramatist, and revivals of sixteenth- and seventeenth-century Italian commedia del l'arte pieces updated to emphasize anticapitalist or antiwar themes.

That year the Mime Troupe found itself at the intersection of the New Left and counterculture. Early in 1965 Davis hired Bill Graham to serve as the troupe's business manager. A little later Peter Berg, a short, blond young man nicknamed "the Hun," joined as playwright and adapter. In August the company tried to perform in Lafayette Park in defiance of a San Francisco Park Commission order revoking their performance permit for obscenity. The cops intervened, and Davis, the activist reporter Marvin Garson, and a Mime Troupe actor were arrested. To pay the legal fees for this bust, Graham threw the Appeals Benefits, featuring the Fugs, the Jefferson Airplane, the Family Dog, and other icons of the emerging acid-rock scene, and launched himself on his rock music–promoter career.

That May, Davis presented a manifesto to his colleagues aligning the Mime Troupe with SNCC, CORE, and SDS. Berg called the approach "guerrilla theater," and the term was soon adopted by a rash of small and ephemeral street-theater groups that appeared in college towns and metropolitan centers around the country performing skits attacking racism, the Vietnam War, and the establishment. But Davis committed the Mime Troupe to more than leftist agitprop. Its members would also, he stated, "exemplify the message that we asked others to accept" by living without the sexual, material, and psychological hang-ups of the bourgeoisie.[28] Out of this rich compost of left politics–cum-pot, LSD, and free love would shortly spring the Diggers, a ragtag of street activists and cultural anarchists who would set the tone for the counterculture capital, Haight-Ashbury.

Deep social ferment is usually accompanied by an assault on the sexual customs of the day. The attack may come from the crusaders for "purity," as in the Methodist revival of early nineteenth-century England and America. In our own day, it has more often come from the opposite direction, from the zealots of instinctual "liberation."

The sexual revolution of the 1960s appeared at the crossroads of several long-term trends. Its intellectual roots go back to Freud's discovery of the psychic costs of repression and the vulgarization of his ideas during the 1920s and after into a creed of hedonism. By the early sixties the intellectual rationale for instinctual liberation had been established by the neo-Freudians Wilhelm Reich, Herbert Marcuse, Norman O. Brown, and Paul Goodman.

An Austrian-born psychiatrist who practiced his therapy and developed his theories in 1920s' Vienna, Reich tried to fuse Freud and Marx. Repression, he insisted, was the hallmark of authoritarian regimes. "Suppression of . . . natural sexuality . . . makes the child . . . obedient, . . . good, and adjusted in the authoritarian sense," he told Viennese workers. "It paralyzes the rebellious forces, because any rebellion is laden with anxiety. . . ."[29] By contrast, sexual freedom would hasten the triumph of socialist equality. Doing his part for the revolution, Reich fought for free abortion and disseminated birth control information and devices to unmarried adolescents at his clinics in Viennese working-class neighborhoods.

In 1930 Reich moved to Berlin where he joined the Communist party and continued to proclaim the linkage between repression and Fascism, a theme made urgent by the growing menace of Hitler. By 1933 Reich's sexual radicalism had offended the repressed German Communist leaders, and they expelled him from the party. Hitler came to power soon after, and Reich fled Germany, first to Vienna, then Copenhagen, then Oslo.

He arrived in the United States in August 1939, just days before Nazi troops swept into Poland, and reestablished himself in New York as a teacher, a writer, and a therapist. In the 1940s he "discovered" "orgone" energy—a sort of biological electromagnetic field. The orgone force, he concluded, was everywhere and had immense therapeutic value. A patient could sit in an orgone energy accumulator, a large metal-lined box, and the energy he absorbed could cure cancer, reduce the incidence of colds, and promote the healing of burns and wounds. In later years his disciples would also recommend the accumulator as a way to increase sex drive and potency. Before long, Reich was manufacturing orgone boxes at his summer house in Maine and renting them to people who believed in their medical value.

Reich influenced the sexual revolution through his focus on the orgasm's liberating function and his linkage of authoritarian politics to instinctual repression. He also served as the movement's chief martyr. In 1948 he had his first run-in with the Federal Drug Administration over his medical claims for the orgone accumulators. Thereafter, for the next seven years, he was the target of federal investigations, an FDA injunction, and an indictment for contempt when he refused to comply with an order to cease their manufacture. In 1956 he was tried and convicted. The authorities also destroyed his accumulators and burned his writings, actions that smelled strongly of Nazi tactics. In early 1957 Reich entered Danbury Federal Prison to serve a two-year sentence for defying the FDA. He died in his sleep that fall, a victim, his friends and supporters said, of remorseless persecution by a repressive government.

His teachings were not forgotten. A decade after his death, Tuli Kupferberg, a poet-musician exemplar of the counterculture, would call Reich "one of the beloved (insane) geniuses of our century."[30]

Marcuse, like Reich, was a Freudian, a Marxist, and a refugee from Nazi persecution. During the 1930s he had joined the

Institute for Social Research in Frankfurt am Main, a circle of Marxist social scientists seeking to develop a "critical theory" of society. In 1934, with Hitler's rise to power, the institute, with its endowment intact, fled in a body to New York, where its members, including Marcuse, the psychologist Eric Fromm, political scientist Franz Neumann, the philosopher Max Horkheimer, and the sociologist Theodor Adorno, set about once more applying neo-Marxist concepts to social problems, especially the persistance of class "domination" and the puzzling rise of authoritarian regimes within liberal capitalist societies.

In the post-World War II era, the Frankfurt School no longer had to confront the threat of a triumphant Fascism; Hitler and his minions had been defeated. But there was now a further threat to a truly free society. Like so much of the social thought of the late fifties and early sixties, Marcuse's ideas assumed material abundance; in fact, they were a direct response to the amazing economic performance of Western capitalism after 1945. Clearly, Marx's prediction of the relentless impoverishment of the working class in capitalist countries was false. The purely material post-World War II achievements of bourgeois capitalism were impossible to deny, and in *Eros and Civilization,* published in 1955, Marcuse acknowledged "the high standard of living in the domain of the great corporations. . . ." People have "huge refrigerators filled with frozen food . . . ," they have "innumerable choices, innumerable gadgets. . . ."[31]

But to Marcuse and his colleagues, bourgeois capitalist 1950s' America seemed only marginally less deplorable than the Fascist regimes that Reich had found in Southern and Central Europe in the 1920s and 1930s. They could only defend this position by bringing Freud to the aid of Marx.

Capitalism's very productivity was oppressive, for the flood of goods was accompanied by people's profound detachment from the economy and the work they did. "The alienation of labor is almost complete," Marcuse wrote. "The mechanics of the assembly line, the routine of the office, the ritual of buying and selling are freed from any connection with human potentialities."[32] Here Marcuse, like the French neo-Marxists, was turning capitalism's very virtues against itself. Marcuse's *Eros and Civilization* and his later *One Dimensional Man* (1964) would be major contributions to the New Left's neo-Marxist New Working Class theory.

But the transgressions of bourgeois capitalism went beyond alienation; they included a profound denial of physical pleasure. Marcuse conceded that in the past, when men and women were poor because society as a whole was unproductive, "the performance principle" had to come before "the pleasure principle." Repression of instincts had to be sacrificed on the altar of productivity. But abundance had now been attained and yet repression continued. This "surplus repression" was not inconsistent with a certain amount of eroticism in literature, the media, and even behavior, but it denied the "perversions." Freedom in bourgeois society was accorded only to a narrow "genitality"; all else was rigidly proscribed. Marcuse had no trouble explaining why repression continued: it was for "the specific interest of domination."[33]

Eros and Civilization appealed to the counterculture not only because it sanctioned the struggle for sexual liberation but also because it held out hope that victory was near. It was only after material abundance had been achieved that the reign of "libidinal rationality" could begin. Clearly, that time had come.

Not all the prophets of instinctual fulfillment were Marxists. Norman O. Brown rejected sectarian politics, though he could not avoid becoming identified with the decade's insurgency. In *Life Against Death,* Brown announced that repression flowed primarily from man's fear of death. It was not an essential precondition of civilization as Freud had said. Mankind could permit itself full instinctual expression—"polymorphous perversity," was Brown's term—without fear of social collapse. The work was greeted as a rousing manifesto of sexual liberation.

Paul Goodman, novelist, poet, Gestalt psychologist—though a former Trotskyist—was also primarily apolitical. Goodman was a disciple of Abraham Maslow, father of the "human potential" school of twentieth-century psychology. Maslow saw human individuals as packets of potentials that society must allow them to "actualize." Mental health consisted of overcoming the limitations that a repressive society imposed and of realizing what was within each person. Goodman exalted the natural and the instinctual.

"The childish feelings are important not as a past that must be undone," he wrote in the early fifties, *"but as some of the most beautiful powers of adult life that must be recovered: spontaneity, imagination, directness of awareness and manipulation. . . ."*[34]

Goodman's early writings gave him only a narrow audience. In 1959 he published an article in *Commentary*, then in its brief left-of-center phase, called "Growing Up Absurd" that castigated fifties' America for its failure to find meaningful work for its young. Goodman was describing the very "surplus personnel" that would populate the counterculture, but at this point he had nothing good to say for the society that spawned them. Expanded to a book soon after, the essay made him a cultural celebrity and in due course a counterculture guru.

These were also lesser prophets and popularizers of sexual liberation. During the 1950s Hugh Hefner disseminated his message of sex-is-fun to millions of eager and willing young men through *Playboy*. By 1956 the magazine had become the publishing phenomenon of the decade. At the same time Albert Ellis, a New York psychologist, beat the drums for freer sex through a series of books—*The Folklore of Sex, The American Sexual Tragedy, Sex Without Guilt,* and *The Art and Science of Love*—that urged people to free themselves from their sexual hang-ups. In 1955 Ellis founded his Institute for Rational Living and established branches in New York and California where men and women could learn to shed their inhibitions.

A curious source of sexual-liberation propaganda was Kerista, a utopian organization founded by one John Presmont in 1956. Kerista preached that free love would liberate mankind forever from hate and violence and enable it to achieve its "highest aspirations." Only by "granting each person complete and total freedom" could "the personal development of each human being reach its zenith."[35] By the mid-sixties this lofty statement had transmuted into a number of Kerista communes in New York, Berkeley, and elsewhere, more notable for their squalor than for their Dionysian exaltation. Yet Allen Ginsberg, no less, told reporter John Gruen that Kerista had "sounded a bell that was heard all over the Lower East Side and reverbreated to San Francisco as a possibility for a new society."[36]

Another sextopian organization was the Sexual Freedom League, founded in New York during the early 1960s and transplanted to the Bay Area in mid-decade by Richard Thorne. The league conducted seminars and discussion groups in the San Francisco area on sexual liberation, legalized prostitution, and the cause and cure of venereal disease. But its activities, rather than its teachings, attracted attention. By 1966 the league had become notorious for its nude bathing parties at Pacific beaches near Santa Cruz and its group sex sessions—aka orgies—at private homes where partner swapping and voyeurism were standard practices.

The breakdown of media censorship both measured and amplified the evolving sexual revolution. In 1950 the Hays Office Motion Picture Production Code still prevailed. Movie producers could not show even married couples in a single bed; they could not prolong the length of kisses beyond a second or two or allow open-mouthed kissing; "hell" or "damn" were at the limits of permissible curses. Books too were held to strict canons of "good taste" by local obscenity laws and federal postal and customs regulations. When Norman Mailer published his World War II epic, *The Naked and the Dead,* in 1948, his publishers forced him to convert every realistic Anglo-Saxon "fuck" into the synthetic "fug" so as not to bring down the law on their heads.

Beginning in the early 1960s, the walls of censorship began to crumble. In 1960 the attorney Charles Rembar won a decision in federal court allowing Grove Press to publish D. H. Lawrence's *Lady Chatterley's Lover,* a novel containing sexually explicit passages and forbidden words. The following year he helped win a series of state and local cases lifting the ban on Henry Miller's underground classic, *Tropic of Cancer.* There was little to stem the flood after this, and by mid-decade almost nothing could be banned from print.

The movies too underwent a revolution. By the mid-fifties Hollywood was fighting for its life against television and was hunting for a way to distinguish itself from the family medium. In 1966 the industry authorized an updated version of the Production Code permitting suggestive films if labeled "for mature audiences." In 1968 Jack Valenti, the new head of the Motion Picture Association of America, introduced the G/GP/R/X film-classification system freeing films for adults of any shackles whatsoever. Obscenity had now become an archaic phrase.

The public learned about the emerging sexual revolution through a new underground press that had begun to appear in New York and California. The granddaddy of the new journalism was *The Village Voice*, founded in 1955 by the public relations expert Dan Wolfe, the psychologist Ed Fancher, the English journalist John Wilcock, the novelist Norman Mailer, and a group of left liberals associated with New York's Village Democrats. The *Voice* soon became a major display case for avant-garde opinion in dance, music, literature, and the popular arts, and a forum for political reform and left-wing opinion. In 1958 it was joined by Paul Krassner's *The Realist*, an even more irreverent paper with articles entitled "Computer Calculated Copulation," "I Was an Abortionist for the FBI," and "A Kick in the Inaugural Balls," and text liberally sprinkled with rude Anglo-Saxon words.[37] In 1964 Art Kunkin, a transplanted New York radical, founded the *Los Angeles Free Press*. The *Free Press* at first was closer to the *Voice* than *The Realist*, but the lead article of its first issue covered a police raid on an underground sex-and-violence film by Kenneth Anger, *Scorpio Rising*, foreshadowing its raunchier future.

Bad, worse, worst. In 1962 Ed Sanders, a Missouri boy in New York to attend NYU, began to hang out in the coffee shops and bars of the East Village, the city's new artist-writer-bohemian hub where rents were still cheap. With his wild Zapata moustache and anything-goes attitude, Sanders was a lord of cultural misrule. He quickly discovered the emerging East Village bohemian scene and carried it several steps further. In 1962 he published, out of the Peace Eye bookstore, his first issue of *Fuck You: A Magazine of the Arts*. Sanders proclaimed as his motto I'll Print Anything, and *Fuck You* carried a running editorial extolling "butt-fuckings and group-gropes," along with the more sedate "pacifism, unilateral disarmament, . . . non-violent resistance, . . . anarchy, [and] world federalism. . . ."[38]

The Voice, The Realist, The Free Press, and *Fuck You* were only precursors, however. Not until 1965 did the true underground press emerge. When it did, it would be a major propagator and amplifier of the sexual revolution.

The real pioneer of raunch and revolt was *The Berkeley Barb,* the brainchild of Max Scherr, a bearded, bald, middle-aged, all-purpose radical, who ran the Steppenwolf Bar on Berkeley's San Pablo Avenue, a hangout for local bohemians. Disturbed by the absence of a forum to describe the bubbling Berkeley scene, in August 1965 Scherr founded the *Barb,* its logo a skeletal Don Quixote on a bony horse, his lance tilting at the university campanile.

During the next decade the *Barb* would be the Berkeley rebellion's paper of record. Scherr and his staff covered the doings of the local antiwar movement and the student left. The *Barb* also spotlighted the coffee houses, record stores, pot, acid, and free love of the university's environs and the street pageant along "the Block," the section of Telegraph Avenue between Haste and Dwight just off campus where the rebels clustered. The *Barb* generously publicized the sexual revolution. In its early issues it described the sextopian Keristans and the activities of the Sexual Freedom League at a time when other journals ignored them. Later, the paper's personals would be a bulletin board where the sexually liberated community could exchange information, services, and advice.

New York acquired its own *Barb* in October 1965 when Walter Bowart, an Oklahoma-born painter living in the Soho district, and John Wilcock, a *Village Voice* founder, established the *East Village Other.* The *EVO* was less political than the *Barb.* Bowart and his talented staff were more interested in painting, music, poetry, and life-style than Scherr and his colleagues. The *EVO* was also visually superior to the *Barb.* It featured some of the earliest psychedelic graphics and the earliest adult "comix" published in over-the-counter papers. Another weekly feature of *EVO* was a scantily clad "Slum Goddess," a pretty, "natural"-looking local girl willing to show her naked bosom.

The *EVO,* the *Barb, Fuck You, The Realist,* and the *Free Press* were only a few of the hundreds of underground papers the era stirred to life. The first wave of papers included Detroit's *Fifth*

Estate, East Lansing's *Paper,* and San Francisco's *Oracle.* The last
was the brainchild of Allen Cohen, a former LSD dealer, and was
bankrolled by two San Francisco brothers, Ron and Jay Thelin.
Soon after, there appeared a second wave and then a third,
including Abe Peck's *Chicago Seed,* Mel Lyman's Boston *Avatar,*
Thorne Dreyer's Austin *Rag,* and Jeff Shero's New York *Rat.* By
1968 every college town and every city with the slightest cosmopolitan claim boasted at least one underground paper, most of
them amateurish and puerile, but a few with bite and grasp. As
early as mid-1966 the underground editors decided to organize
an Underground Press Service to pool news, advertising, and
printing costs. A few of the organizers were uneasy with the
"underground" label, but as Wilcock noted: "We all agreed that,
though a little grandiose, it was an appropriate image for a new
Fuck-Censorship press."[39]

The underground press filled a cultural void. Events too alien,
too scandalous, too obnoxious, too threatening to the metropolitan press and its middle-class readers could find a prominent
place in the *EVO,* the *Barb,* or one of the other papers. The
alternate press also helped create a community of attitudes and
feeling. Its coverage of peace marches, campus demonstrations,
and SDS meetings and conventions contributed to the coalescence
of the New Left as a self-conscious entity. Its articles on pot, acid,
rock, and free love contributed even more to what Theodore
Roszak in 1968 would call the "counterculture."

But ideas alone never made a revolution, even a sexual
revolution. If sexual behavior became freer during the 1960s, it
was also because of changing social, biological, and medical
realities.

First, let's not lose sight of a basic fact: sex is fun. Given this, a
rational Bug-eyed Monster from Mars would surely want to know
why sex was ever covert and restricted, not why it was open and
abounding.

We would have to tell him (it?) about cultural and religious
taboos, surely. But we would also have to note the age-old medical
and social consequences of sexual contact. Heterosexual sex
caused pregnancies and babies and all the attending expenses,
commitments, and difficulties. All sex, especially promiscuous

sex, caused disease. Ancient and medieval man contracted various forms of pox, and in early modern times Europeans encountered syphilis. Then in 1943 Sir Alexander Fleming discovered penicillin and venereal infections seemed conquered. In 1960 came "the Pill" and an end of most unwanted pregnancies. As the sixties began, suddenly, for the first time in history, erotic indulgence seemed consequence-free. Today we know it wasn't—and isn't— but during the 1960s a unique window seemed to open that never before existed. Like the assumed end of economic "necessity," the apparent easy cure of sexually transmitted disease and the end of unplanned babies created for a time a sense of limitless social possibility.

Two news items of late 1967 and early 1968 captured these changes. On December 30, 1967, Jane Brody of *The New York Times* reported that recently surveyed college coeds were more likely to enjoy sex on their first experience than their predecessors in the past. If you didn't have to worry about babies and disease, her subjects said, you could really get into it! The following March *BusinessWeek* noted that the birthrate had turned down sharply. At 17.9 per thousand women of childbearing age, it was now lower than it had been at any time since the Great Depression. Recreational sex was in, procreation was out. The postwar baby boom was finally over.

Drugs, sex, Eastern philosophy, liberation, rock music, guerrilla theater, and pop art all merged into one broad stream, conveying, as well as shaping, the new consciousness that Roszak had provided with a name. The citizen of the counterculture domain was in turn called a "hippie."

By 1968 the counterculture had propagated everywhere, but it had already decayed in its two chief centers, San Francisco's Haight-Ashbury and New York's East Village.

The "Haight" was where the hippie was born sometime in the fall of 1966. By mid-decade the district's cheap rents and proximity to Golden Gate Park and San Francisco State College had begun to attract a stream of artists, students, and bohemians. In January 1966 it acquired an anchor, the Psychedelic Shop, run by the Thelin brothers, two young local men who stocked their store with paisley fabrics, incense, dance posters, occult books, and other items in demand among LSD users. The shop at 1535 Haight Street soon became a hangout of young men and women recruited into the LSD culture through the Acid Tests, the Trips Festivals, and the pervasive experimental spirit of the day. Its success soon brought other entrepreneurs eager to capitalize on the growing hippie thing. By mid-year Haight, Page, Clayton, and Ashbury streets were lined with shops and colorful names: Far Fetched Foods, a health-food establishment; In Gear, a mod clothing store; the Blushing Peony, a boutique; and the I/Thou coffee shop. Later there would be the Print Mint, a posters and pictures shop; the Drog [*sic*] Store, a fancy apothecary-cum–ice cream parlor with paisley-topped tables; and many others.

The clientele of these establishments, like hippies in other psychedelias, were young, often teenagers. Many were full-time dropouts from suburban high schools; others were day trippers. They were different from the young radicals. Recruits to SDS and other left student groups—at least at first—were children of leftists who proudly carried their parents' social and political banners. Hippies were largely the children of conservative sub-urbanites, often in the throes of fierce rebellion against their parents. But the social rebels were not "committed" to causes outside their own lives. According to Kenneth Keniston, the Yale psychologist who made the youth culture his special terrain, counterculture youths were "alienated," skeptical of all institu-tions, including political parties, and sought solace in "expressive" personal behavior. They valued "passion and feeling, the search for awareness, the cultivation of responsiveness" and spent their time pursuing "openness to experience, contact with the world, and spontaneity. . . ."[40]

Keniston's sharp distinction between the two populations is overstated. The student left and the counterculture overlapped much more than he allows, especially in the Bay Area. Yet the political left would always be uneasy about the hippies. The Old Leftists denounced them as childish evaders and deniers. When asked by the *Barb* editor his opinion of the "psychedelic revolu-tion," a Trotskyist leader replied: "It is a means of escaping the restlessness imposed by everyday life upon everyone in this society. But it is sterile and infantile because it does not fundamentally transform those restrictions which afflict and affect every one of us."[41] The New Left was less hostile, but still distinctly skeptical. Writing in 1967, SDS's Carl Oglesby warned that at the center of the hippies' "new love ethic" was "an intrinsic capacity for surrender." The new cultural revolutionaries, for all their antibourgeois contempt, were only "suburbanites with beads."[42]

A small incident in the fall of 1965, just as the counterculture began to raise its head, caught the inherent antagonisms between the two realms of antibourgeois protest. The occasion was the Vietnam Day Committee antiwar rally at Berkeley on October 15. Kesey and the Merry Pranksters had been invited to participate and arrived late after the audience of fifteen thousand had been listening for hours to speeches denouncing genocide, the war machine, and the "jackals of history." Amid the duffel coats and blue jeans, the Pranksters' Day-Glo jackets, aviator goggles, and orange-painted World War I helmets were like a visual blast. Kesey used his turn at the rostrum to parody the previous speaker, Paul Jacobs, an old-line Trotskyist, honking his words and waving his arms and making Jacobs seem a homegrown Mussolini. At the same time Kesey managed to suck and blow on a harmonica, while the rank-and-file Pranksters strummed and banged on assorted instruments. The audience was not amused. The listeners sat stony-faced and puzzled. Then Kesey stopped and leaning over the mike delivered his antiwar formula: "There's only one thing to do . . . there's only one thing's gonna do any good at all. . . . And that's everybody just look at it, just look at the war, and turn your backs and say . . . Fuck it. . . ."[43] The man had said the WORD! Shock and dismay. Tom Wolfe, the Thucydides of the Pranksters, is half convinced that the WORD's jolt to the audience's collective system is enough to explain the fiasco later that evening when the protesters were turned back by the Oakland police without reaching their goal.

The economy of the "Hashbury" floated on drugs. However "alienated," many hippies lived on subsidies from home; others panhandled on the streets. But more sold a little "dope," usually marijuana, to other hippies and to the swarms of college students and young professionals who descended on the Haight once it had become the "in" place. The Haight was the West Coast's major trading center for LSD, too. Owsley was the chief supplier of high-grade acid, but there were other brands as well, including trashy, dangerous stuff reputedly manufactured in Italy and attributed to "the mob."

In October 1966 the Haight and all of California psychedelia found itself in crisis. For many months the press had circulated stories of how LSD caused insanity and birth defects and paved the way to still more dangerous drugs. Zonked-out trippers were supposed to be jumping out of windows, drowning themselves, and frying their eyeballs staring into the unfiltered sun. Congress had held hearings, and the federal Food and Drug Administration had clamped down on laboratory experiments with acid and like substances. Then, in early 1966, the California legislature made it a misdemeanor to possess LSD and a felony to sell it after the first week in October.

The citizens of the Haight memorialized the event on October 6 with a Love Pageant Rally at the Panhandle, the long, blockwide eastward extension of Golden Gate Park. It was the first of the many ceremonies that would confirm the emergence of Haight-Ashbury as a community.

The Oracle, which hosted the gathering, had asked people to bring flowers, flutes, drums, feathers, beads, banners, flags, incense, chimes, gongs, cymbals, and "photos of personal saints and gurus and heroes of the underground . . . ,"[44] and the event was a glittering and euphonic spectacle. Hundreds of hippies came to display themselves, hear rock music, and listen to the speeches. Kesey and the Pranksters made an appearance, and the media, print and electronic, were there to report the colorful doings. The focal point of the ceremony was the reading of a "Declaration of Independence" proclaiming "these experiences to be self-evident, that all is equal, that the creation endows us with certain inalienable rights, that among these are: the freedom of the body, the pursuit of joy, and the expansion of consciousness, and that to secure these rights, we the citizens of the earth declare our love and compassion for all conflicting hate-carrying men and women of the world."[45] Everyone agreed the event had been a rousing success.

In the week following the pageant a new force, the Diggers, would intrude into the unfolding Haight scene creating engrossing but painful tensions.

The Diggers took their name from a group of seventeenth-century English social dissenters who, during Cromwell's reign, had demanded division of property among the poor and cooperative economic activities. Seceders from the Mime Troupe, they felt that Ron Davis should replace formal theater with Artaud's "poetry of festivals and crowds." The flowing, turbulent Haight streets, they said, were a much better stage for activist theater than the auditoriums and parks where the Mime Troupe usually performed. The Diggers despised bourgeois capitalist society, but detested equally the political left's dogmatism, rigidities, and lust for power. They also loathed the passive "love ethic" of the hippies. It was spineless and vapid. If any term can describe their ideas and demeanor, it is *anarchism*. The Diggers' motto was Free—free everything: goods, love, behavior, relationships. Their combativeness, antagonism to rules, and recklessness riled almost everyone. Yet they had their partisans. Abbie Hoffman describes them as "slum alley saints" who "lit up the period by spreading the poetry of love and anarchy with broad strokes of artistic genius."[46]

The chief Diggers were Peter Berg, the blond-haired Mime Troupe playwright, and two Mime Troupe actors, Emmett Grogan, a freaky Irish kid from Brooklyn, and his hometown pal, Billy Murcott. The last two were both recent additions to the company and were less respectful of Ron Davis and his mystique than longtime troupers.

During the summer of 1966, posters and signs began to appear mysteriously on the walls of the Mime Troupe studio calling for the company's restructuring. That September Haight inhabitants were bombarded with broadsides signed "George Metevsky,"[47] denouncing hippies for enslavement to the success ethic and attacking the Thelin brothers and other Haight merchants for cashing in on the hippie fad. This assault marked the beginning of chronic war between the anarchists and the Haight merchants. Grogan, Murcott, and their friends were responsible for both attacks but hid their identity behind the Digger label.

For the next year, a stream of cryptic handbills and pamphlets signed "Digger" continued to appear on the streets of Haight-Ashbury announcing events, arguing positions, and advertising the antic ideas of Grogan, Murcott, and company. Many were put out by an organization called the Communications Company, which turned out to be a publishing house run by Beat scene editor and novelist Chester Anderson. They all expressed the anarchists' philosophy and everyone called them the Digger Papers.

The Diggers were soon known by their acts as well as their words. A few days after the Love Pageant, two Diggers handed out a leaflet on Haight Street offering free food in the Panhandle every day and advising people to bring a bowl and spoon. By this time the Haight was beginning to fill up with child refugees from suburbia, many dead broke, and young people flocked to the free feedings. The quality of the provender was unpredictable. The meat was usually fresh, though it was mostly butcher-shop trimmings or chicken wings. The vegetables were often wilted, but in soups that made little difference. The bread was day-old bakery bread. Much of the food was begged; some was just lifted. The victuals were not entirely free. Everyone who wanted food had first to walk through a large wooden frame painted yellow called the "Free Frame of Reference," signifying liberation from materialism. On October 31, at their Full Moon Halloween celebration at the corner of Haight and Masonic, the Diggers passed out six-inch models of the frame with attached strings to be worn around the neck.

The Diggers topped their free-food jape by opening a "free" store in a converted garage on Page Street. There anyone could rummage through boxes and barrels for clothes, pots, dishes, and food. The store expressed Digger contempt for the things the world held dear. At one point, when Paul Krassner came for a visit, someone asked him to give Grogan a ten-dollar bill. Grogan promptly took out a cigarette lighter and burned the bill to ash to the intense pain of the perennially broke *Realist* editor.

The Diggers' exploits begat a flock of imitators. Before the year was out, the Provos, named after attention-getting Dutch anarchist provocateurs, appeared in Berkeley and began to distribute their own free food. In 1967 New York's East Village would acquire its own crazy corps of Diggers.

But it was the January 1967 Be-In in Golden Gate Park that gave the counterculture scene national celebrity.

The Be-In—actually Human Be-In—was conceived jointly soon after the Love Pageant by *Oracle* editors Allen Cohen and Michael Bowen, both missionaries for psychedelia. It would be a gathering of the "tribes," of the men and women of the new age just dawning. The *Oracle* people were acidheads themselves, but they conceived of the event as an occasion to unite the counterculture with the politicos. "Berkeley political activists and the love generation of the Haight-Ashbury," the promoters' press release declared, "will join together . . . to powwow, celebrate, and prophesy the epoch of liberation, love, peace, compassion, and unity of mankind. . . ."[48] Jerry Rubin of the Vietnam Day Committee, recently turned on to LSD, was to be the key link with the left. They also invited the Beat masters Michael McClure, Lawrence Ferlinghetti, and Allen Ginsberg, and the acid high priest Timothy Leary, currently barnstorming the country for his League for Spiritual Discovery and happy to get the free advertising.

As a merger opportunity between the counterculture and the political left, the Be-In was a flop. Among the radicals, only Rubin took it seriously. As an advertisement for psychedelia, however, it was a stupendous success.

January 14 was a warm, dry day; Golden Gate Park was green and sparkling. The ceremonies were scheduled to begin at 1:00 P.M., and all through the morning people in costumes, feathers, and flowers streamed toward the Polo Field. By the time Gary Snyder, the poet, blew on his conch shell to announce the Be-In opening, almost twenty-five thousand people covered the meadow like a human carpet in front of the makeshift stage.

The gathering lasted until five o'clock with its focus ostensibly on the east end of the field where Leary, Rubin, and others sermonized, Lenore Kandel, the poet, read passages from her erotic *Love Book,* and the Jefferson Airplane, the Grateful Dead, Big Brother and the Holding Company, and Quicksilver Messenger Service pounded out their beat. Most of the audience ignored the official proceedings and just grooved. Helen Swick Perry, an older woman who brought the trained eye of a sociologist to the ceremony, was swept up in the mood. "Sights and sounds turned me on, so that I had the sensation of dreaming," she wrote. "The air seemed heady and mystical . . . and I became aware of a phenomenon that still piques me: The dogs did not fight and the children did not cry."[49]

No one went hungry. The Diggers handed out free turkey sandwiches from birds donated by the ubiquitous Owsley. Courtesy of Owsley, too, no one was left unstoned. The Acid King had contributed thousands of capsules containing his latest product, and people circulated through the crowd handing them out like candy. Anyone not on LSD was on pot, so that the whole celebration was filtered through a mind-altering haze that elevated the effect.

The Be-In was a milestone. Ginsberg called it an "epochal event,"[50] and in the Haight it seemed to release energies that the local merchants, now organized as HIP (Haight Independent Proprietors), believed could be put to work to improve the neighborhood. It also made Haight-Ashbury and its culture instantaneously famous. Newspapers, magazines, and the TV media all ran features on the psychedelic community during the late winter and early spring, and an enterprising Hollywood producer was soon marketing a quickie film, *Hallucination Generation,* to exploit the public's fascination. In April the Grey Line Company began to run Haight bus tours for curious squares, advertising them as "the only foreign tours within the United States."[51]

By the late spring it seemed certain that Haight-Ashbury would be buried under a tidal wave of adolescents when school let out. The anticipated migration soon had its own theme song: "San Francisco—Be Sure to Wear Flowers in Your Hair." It did well on the charts and raised the potential for deluge to still higher levels. The HIP merchants, the Diggers, community elders, and the San

Francisco authorities took precautions. The Diggers promised to provide food, information, shelter, and medical services to the expected lemmings. Community leaders organized the Council for the Summer of Love to provide park concerts and other distractions for the arrivals. The San Francisco State College administration expanded its summer Community Works Program to take in the Haight. And everyone issued warnings of big-city dangers. In May the San Francisco Board of Supervisors endorsed the mayor's advice to hippies to stay away from the city. Nothing helped.

At least seventy-five thousand young people descended on the Haight during the summer of 1967. San Francisco's Summer of Love was a spectacle, a festival, a performance, a saga, a tragedy, and a saturnalia. It had everything: love, crime, madness, sex, squalor, drugs, art. It burned the values of the counterculture permanently into the body social and at the same time slowed its forward momentum.

Those who came early enjoyed it more. Acid and pot were plentiful at first, and the police followed a hands-off policy. Then in July some U.S. border guards were shot, and the authorities clamped down on illegal drug traffic from Mexico. The pot well quickly ran dry. What to do? By August many denizens were taking Methedrine, "speed," an amphetamine that produced swift exhilaration followed by a sharp emotional down and then, after long use, hallucinations with a brutal paranoid twist. If not speed, then STP, a fast version of mescaline with a high freak-out potential, or heroin, junk, the big one.

Bad trips were not the only health problems. Speeders injected the stuff and got hepatitis from dirty needles. Free love, even in 1967, carried some risk. Gonorrhea, syphilis, and crabs ran wild through the hippie population. The hordes of flower children created an acute housing crunch. Newcomers were forced to cram into tiny squalid pads where sanitation was abysmal, and people lived and slept cheek by jowl. It was a perfect environment for infectious diseases, and pneumonia, flu, and chicken pox spread quickly from hippie to hippie. Some help for the flower children came from the *Barb*'s "Dr. Hip[ocrates]" medical column written by Dr. Eugene Schoenfeld. More useful was the free medical clinic founded by Dr. David Smith, who had lived in the Haight during his medical internship and felt a responsibility for its denizens. On June 9 the clinic opened its doors at the corner of Haight and Clayton. Thereafter it provided first aid and emergency care for hundreds of patients and also served as a housing bureau for people without shelter.

The Haight was supposed to float on love. It was charged with strife.

Hashbury hippies prated much of love; their symbols were gentle: flowers, butterflies, fairy wands, and the like. Hippie gurus like Ginsberg, *The Oracle*'s Allen Cohen, and the Communications Company's Chet Anderson made stabs at fabricating a mythos of gentleness, communalism, and oneness with nature and the earth. But they often displayed their love, it has been said, "through clenched teeth." Nicholas Von Hoffman, then a radical reporter for *The Washington Post,* who came to observe the Haight during the famous summer, called them "passive-aggressive types suffering from emotional constipation."[52]

The Haight hate took many forms. Many Hashbury hippies did not like "spades." Blacks, they said, were "programmed for hate."[53] And the charge, though insensitive, was not entirely wrong. Poor blacks from the adjacent Fillmore district resented the suburban white kids' poverty act. It seemed phony and insincere. They also found it hard to resist the cornucopia of white chicks and drugs the hippie scene thrust under their noses. The opportunities soon translated into hassles, break-ins, rip-offs, and rapes. Chester Anderson issued a handbill calling blacks the "spiritual fathers" of the hippies through "jazz and grass and rock and roll."[54] His attempt to close the breach didn't work; antagonisms continued. The Hell's Angels served as an informal Haight police force, but their "protection" was often as exploitative as the Mafia's.

Hippies preyed on their own kind, too. Hippie men took advantage of hippie women. Despite all the talk of a "new society," the Haight had its quota of male chauvinists and their female victims. Hippie "chicks" were often pathetic runaways, waifs who found themselves defenseless against the male hustlers who congregated in the Hashbury and preached sexual liberation for their own predatory purposes. A favorite story that circulated during the Summer of Love was of hippie girls drugged comatose and then used as communal sexual resources by all comers. One of the human vultures who spent some time in the Haight during the Summer of Love was Charles Manson, a half-mad ex-con, would-be rock musician, and future mass murderer. The Haight apparently was the school where Manson learned the trick of subjecting female drifters and runaways to his satanic will.

There were also the "burn" artists. Though back in December the Diggers had led a parade through the district to celebrate "the death of money and rebirth of the Haight,"[55] hippies, like everyone else, needed money to live. By late June there were so many kids settled in the Haight that the Diggers could no longer provide free food and closed down their program. The part-timers who made the scene on weekends usually had jobs. Some of the others came with money or were able to extract it from parents at home. The self-supporters panhandled, sold the *Barb, The Oracle,* or the local paper, *The Haight-Ashbury Maverick.* But a large number "dealt" drugs—to one another or to the tourists. The honest dealers sold "righteous" acid or pot, but there were scores of cheats who adulterated, diluted, or misrepresented their wares. They were among the chief villains of the community.

And these were not the only conflicts and tensions. The police and the flower children frequently clashed despite efforts of the Thelin brothers and other HIP merchants to come to an understanding with police chief Tom Cahill and other city authorities. The worst brawl of the summer was an hour-long battle in July that started with a traffic jam at the intersection of Haight and Ashbury. The cops waded in with clubs and arrested nine people; four were badly injured. The Diggers too were a source of discord. They constantly attacked the HIP merchants for exploiting the community and put them on the defensive. They also clashed with the Krishna Consciousness people, who in January 1967 had moved in and set up their temple next door to the Diggers' free-frame headquarters. Though the general public would lump all the fringe groups together in one messy stew, the

Diggers and the Hare Krishnas were very different. The Diggers favored the flesh and plumped for more of it. The Hindu-derived Krishnas renounced the senses. A more important source of disdain: both handed out free food and competed for the hearts and minds of Haight residents.

Despite everything, the Summer of Love was not unrelieved disaster; it was sometimes fun and games. There was pot and poetry and free food on Hippie Hill, a prominent elevation in Golden Gate Park. Hippies glorified American Indians for their primitive naturalness and their victimization by white Americans, and the Hippie Hill gatherings looked like tribal powwows with the celebrants sporting feathers, beads, and headbands. In mid-June thousands of hippies descended on Monterey for four days of nonstop rock featuring Big Brother, Country Joe, the Grateful Dead, Quicksilver, as well as a dozen non–Bay Area groups. Monterey Pop was the first of the big outdoor rock festivals and one of the most peaceful. Later in the summer there were also free rock concerts at Mount Tamalpais in Marin and at the Fillmore.

The Haight was not the only counterculture community in existence by 1967. Hippies found a home in the Telegraph Avenue coffee shops and side streets adjacent to the Berkeley campus. Los Angeles had a large hippie colony located in the Sunset Strip neighborhood. In Seattle hippies congregrated in the University District adjacent to the University of Washington. In Detroit John Sinclair, a massively constructed poet-musician-activist, was the center of a hippie flowering that by 1967 boasted an underground newspaper, *The Fifth Estate,* and a rock band, The Motor City Five (MC-5). Next to the Haight, however, the biggest counterculture community appeared in New York's East Village.

By 1964–65 the East Village was already a self-conscious alternative community with the same mixture as the Haight of drugs, free love, rock music, experimental theater, and young refugees from suburbia seeking a New Jerusalem. Its main drag was St. Mark's Place, and its chief hangouts were the Dom, a converted Ukrainian recreational club, Stanley's on Twelfth

Street, the Psychedelicatessen, and Ed Sanders' Peace Eye bookstore. Besides Sanders, the East Village was home to Paul Krassner and to Allen Ginsberg, who lived in a seedy walk-up on East Fifth Street. In the fall of 1965 Walter Bowart started the *East Village Other* in a local loft.

The first real citizen of the East Village was Abbie Hoffman, who arrived from Worcester, Massachusetts, in 1966 to run a store selling Mississippi-made crafts for SNCC. SNCC soon entered its Black Power phase, and Hoffman, a Jewish stand-up comedian manqué, was forced to look for some other cause.

The East Village had its indigenous counterculture grouplets. The Keristans' City Living Center headquarters was located in a squalid East Village storefront. Preaching love, they exuded suspicion. The Black Mask Revolution (BMR), led by one Ben Morea, professed the anticonsumption theories of the Dadaist French Situationists. Making a fetish of the "spectacle," BMR members dressed in black clothes and snarled a lot. In 1968, under its later, scabrous name, "Up-Against-the Wall Mother-fuckers," Morea and his colleagues would rampage around Manhattan setting fires to the mountainous trash piles that had accumulated during the city's garbage strike, disrupting a performance of the Living Theater at the Fillmore East, and egging on the students at the Columbia SDS uprising. At the more benign end of the counterculture spectrum was the Group Image, a collection of painters, writers, and crafts people living together as a commune.

Yet much of the East Village scene was borrowed from California. New York recognized the psychedelic leadership of the Golden State by commemorating California's delegalization of LSD in October 1966 with a ceremony in Tompkins Square Park. On Easter Sunday, the following March, East Villagers ran their own Be-In in Central Park's Sheep Meadow, a gathering that the *Village Voice*'s Don McNeill called a "surreal and beautifully absurd event."[56] The most momentous import from the Bay Area was Jerry Rubin. Heeding the Mobilization's call to head the fall Pentagon march, he came on his first visit during the summer of 1967 and established instant rapport with Hoffman. Hoffman would later concede that though *he* had a lighter touch, Jerry was better "in getting the cultural revolution incorporated into a broader structure."[57]

The Digger idea came to New York soon after, and during the summer the Diggers established a "free" store on East Tenth Street, stocking it with old clothes from the proceeds of a benefit rock concert.

In August Rubin and Hoffman pulled off a typical Digger caper when they invaded the New York Stock Exchange and showered money from the visitor's gallery onto the trading floor. They had advertised their foray, and when the motley band arrived at the exchange, a guard was there to stop them. "You're hippies," he announced, "and you've come to burn money." Hoffman hotly denied the charge: "I'm Jewish," he replied. Another Digger declared, "I'm Catholic." Confronted by the possibility that he might be charged with religious bigotry, the bemused guard backed down and allowed them in. Once in the balcony, they began to toss money over the railing. In seconds the floor was a mass of lurching, shouting brokers grabbing at the bills as they fluttered down. When the guards finally ejected the Diggers, the traders on the floor booed loudly. The demonstration was not yet over. Outside the building Hoffman told reporters, "No one will ever be a millionaire again." Money was over. "The government owns it and only lets you use it." When someone asked where the Diggers had gotten the cash they had just thrown away, he replied straight-faced: "Catholic charities."[58]

The East Village had its own version of strife. There were fights between hippies and the local Puerto Rican toughs. The older Polish and Ukrainian East Village residents constantly complained about the noise, the dirt, the drugs. The police, under precinct captain Fink, engaged in general hippie bashing. As in the Haight, there were also good times: pageants and free rock at Tompkins Square Park. At times the pot and the acid *did* surely produce ecstasy. Yet on the whole the East Village scene had an angrier, more menacing quality than the Haight. Lewis Yablonsky, a southern California sociologist who visited the East Village during the summer, was appalled by the squalor, the exploitation, and the violence of the scene compared with his own arcadian West Coast.

So many of the hippies were high school and college kids that the Summers of Love would have ended after Labor Day in any case. But the winding-down process was powerfully accelerated by a terrifying and demoralizing series of crimes. In early August two Haight acid dealers, Shob Carter and Superspade, were murdered. Carter had been stabbed twelve times and his right arm cut off at the elbow; Superspade, one of the few black regulars on the Haight scene, had been shot in the heart and the head and thrown over a cliff at Port Reyes along the northern coast. In the East Village two hippie lovers, Linda Rae Fitzpatrick, the daughter of a rich Connecticut executive, and Groovy—James Hutchinson— a poor kid from Rhode Island, were murdered in October. Fitzpatrick had been gang raped. In the wake of the crime, several hundred wayward parents finally got the message and descended on the East Village to recover their misplaced children.

On October 6, the first anniversary of the California anti-LSD law, the Haight elders conducted a Death of Hippie ceremony to announce the end of the hyped-up Summer of Love. The Diggers, the HIP merchants, and the other Haight leaders had never accepted the media image of the hippie. What the papers and the reporters portrayed was a sensationalized caricature, not the real "Free Man" of the new society. Now the imposter would finally be laid to rest.

The funeral ceremony began with a "wake" at All Souls Episcopal Church and ended three days later with a procession of costumed mourners carrying a coffin through the Haight. Spectators threw beads, feathers, posters, buttons—all the supposedly false paraphernalia of the hippie thing—into the open box. At the end they set the coffin on fire. A plume of black smoke marked the end of the Summer of Love.

The counterculture did not end with the fall of 1967. But it did change. With the summer dropouts and tourists gone, the old centers became less congested. They also lost all trace of flower-child gentleness. Andy Warhol, whose loft studio was at the north edge of the East Village, noted that in 1968 the hippie panhandlers had become aggressive and menacing when they asked for "loose change." "Attitudes out on the street," he wrote, "weren't like the summer before when everybody was acting so enchanted."[59]

In 1968 the hippie trip also became national. Haight and East Village summer sojourners carried the seeds to every college town and provincial city in the country. They were also spread by way of the media. The underground press continued to expand, and by 1968 there were three hundred papers, several important ones—Atlanta's *Great Speckled Bird,* New York's *Rat* and *Other Scenes,* and *Old Mole* of Cambridge—organized after the Summer of Love. The sexual revolution acquired its own exclusive journal that year when Al Goldstein published the first issue of *Screw,* the raunchiest, most scabrous sheet of them all.

The pop arts too spread the counterculture style, rhetoric, and values. The movies glamorized the new subculture. *I Love You Alice B. Toklas* told the story of a square Los Angeles lawyer, played by Peter Sellers, who eats some hashish-laced brownies and becomes a beads-and-headband-wearing hippie. *Easy Rider* concerned two young men, Dennis Hopper and Peter Fonda, who get rich selling cocaine and take off on a motorcycle tour of the country with stopovers at a hippie commune and an LSD episode in a New Orleans cemetery. In April 1968 a musical, *Hair,* about a hippie draft evader, opened at New York's Biltmore Theater to rave reviews. *Hair* proclaimed a new Age of Aquarius and celebrated acid, oral sex, peace, and "crystal revelation," all to a blaring rock beat. By 1968 beards, sandals, long hair, pot, had become the badges of millions of middle-class young people, and "like," "man," and "good vibes," an essential part of their daily discourse. The rock scene continued to convey the personal "look," lingo, dress, and habits of the counterculture to the country's young.

The whole hippie phenomenon came to a crescendo at Max Yasgur's six-hundred-acre farm in Woodstock, New York, in August 1969, where Kesey, Hoffman, the Motherfuckers, the

White Panthers, and even SDS Weathermen came together with the Grateful Dead, the Jefferson Airplane, the Who, Jimi Hendrix, Joan Baez, Country Joe, Janis Joplin, and four hundred thousand hippies and semi-hippies in one monumental three-day concert-cum-trip, cum-orgy. The rock historian Geoffrey Stokes would call it "the greatest participatory show on earth."[60] Abbie Hoffman would mythologize the event as a first gathering of the Woodstock Nation," a portent of the new world aborning.

Woodstock notwithstanding, many in the counterculture considered a reformed mass society an illusion after the failure of Haight-Ashbury and the East Village. But there was still the possibility of a new society based on small "intentional communities" or communes, where new forms of human relationships could be tested. The idea had been tried a thousand times in the past by religious brotherhoods, clans of ideologues, and utopians of every sort. Simultaneous with the emergence of the Haight and the East Village, small communitarian experiments had sprung up around Los Angeles, along the north California coast, and in Vermont. These had attracted some of the more purposeful counterculturists. Now they became for some the salvation of preference.

During the Summer of Love, Lou Gottlieb's Morningstar Ranch in Sonoma County had received a spillover of hippies who could not take the hassle of the Haight. These refugees from paradise came to a functioning community on thirty-two acres of apple orchard that Gottlieb, a bearded former member of the Limelighters vocal group, had bought in the Sonoma County woods. Gottlieb had a no-exclusions policy and at first Morningstar welcomed everyone. Some of the newcomers were true seekers of a New Age society in miniature. But others were the casualties of psychedelia, or its sickies, or rough bikers happy to take advantage of Gottlieb's gentle hospitality.

Morningstar flourished modestly until the fall of 1967 as a voluntary, unstructured settlement of tents, gardens, main house, and communal dining room, where everybody shared the chores. The fugitives from Haight ended the Eden. They were unwilling to do the work and the community deteriorated: dishes were dirty, sinks clogged, outhouses stank. In mid-1968, the Sonoma

County authorities cited Gottlieb for health violations and when he refused to comply jailed him for fifteen days and fined him one thousand dollars.

Morningstar was only one of a dozen or so communes that received the post–Summer of Love refugees. Just to the north was Top of the World Ranch with a stricter policy on admittees. In the Los Angeles area there was Strawberry Fields; in the Santa Cruz Mountains near La Honda, Holiday. In the Rockies there was Drop City, a community of geodesic domes constructed ingeniously out of car bodies and other scrap. Near Taos, New Mexico, a whole cluster of communes sprang up where residents grooved on peyote with local Indian shamans. In the East disciples of the conditioning theories of Harvard psychologist B. F. Skinner founded Twin Oaks in the Virginia countryside.

Besides the rural mini-societies, the counterculture diaspora founded a scattering of inner-city communes in low-rent neighborhoods. Each of these sought to preserve the counterculture ideal of a gentle society free of the competitiveness and material striving of conventional American life, and most encouraged sexual experimentation. Few were made up of more than thirty or forty individuals; almost none lasted more than a year or two.

The commune movement was an attempt to preserve the hippie dropout ideal. But in 1968, as the riots, the police busts, and the assassinations piled up, the nation's sense of impending apocalypse built to a crescendo. Other refugees from the counterculture now took the other fork in the road, the one that led to political revolution.

The seeds of the politicization process could be seen well before the new year. The Golden Gate Park Be-In had disappointed its promoters' hope of fusing political and cultural dissent, but it had drawn Jerry Rubin, a skilled veteran of the Berkeley radical wars and the anti-Vietnam movement, into the counterculture. Then, that spring, the call from the Mobe brought Rubin to New York, and the contact with Hoffman and his friends produced a new critical mass. The contingent of wizards, exorcists, and crazies at the Pentagon march was one consequence of the fateful meeting. By this time there were other politicized counterculture elements in New York. The Motherfuckers, for example, the offshoot of Black Mask, sought "a total revolution, cultural as well as social and political. . . ."[61] Berkeley had a number of politicized street-people groups. In Austin, Texas, the site of the state university, the counterculture paper, *The Rag,* was also the center of campus SDS activities and its editor, Jeff Shero, was a former vice-president of SDS. In the spring of 1968, Shero left Austin and *The Rag* to come to New York. There he established *Rat,* as part of "the left-wing love, flower and freedom sect anarchistic division of SDS."[62] The repositioning of part of psychedelia was foreshadowed by an anonymous article in the *Barb* shortly after the Death of Hippie ceremony. Its author pronounced Haight-Ashbury "the last hope; an outpost of humanity in a land of deodorized plastic mannequins. . . ." Its inhabitants, he believed, had been dropouts from the antiwar and civil rights movements. We "lit up our pipes and popped our acid. . . ." We created a new perspective, new forms, a new culture. . . ." But they had failed to change the world. Now the time had come to leave the private realm and return to the public world. The "age of peaceful, lawful protest and dissent is over." The nation was now "living under a tyrannical violent system of oppression" that would stop at nothing, and there was "no alternative but illegal and violent measures."[63]

The debate over "whither" created bitter divisions within the counterculture. At Liberation News Service (LNS), founded in 1967 to provide "movement" stories and reportage for the underground press, the struggle seemed like a performance of absurdist theater.

LNS's creators had been Marshall Bloom, a rich Amherst College kid from Denver, and Ray Mungo, a twenty-one-year-old from a dirty Massachusetts mill town via Boston University. For a year the two worked peacefully at the new agency churning out articles mixing campus protests, university complicity, and the Vietnam War with Wilhelm Reich, Timothy Leary, pot, and personal liberation, all composed on the one electric typewriter in their Washington office. These pieces were then dispatched to LNS's subscribers around the country. Though LNS only charged fifteen dollars a month for subscriptions, and often waived that, it prospered modestly from fees from the expanding underground press eked out with donations. In 1968, with better equipment and a larger staff, it moved its headquarters to New York.

Along the way the LNS staff acquired a contingent of SDS-affiliated Marxists who believed that political revolution, not altered personal life-styles, was the answer to humanity's problems. Mungo described the change as a shift in style and temperament: "We were the crazy people's news service, the forebears of the New Age. And then came this other group who thought they were in this army and had to obey rules and march around."[64] Mungo and Bloom labeled their own group the "Virtuous Caucus"; their adversaries were the "Vulgar Marxists."[65]

In August, as the Vulgar Marxists were all watching a new Beatles movie, *Magical Mystery Tour*, at Fillmore East on the Lower East Side, Bloom, Mungo and their followers loaded LNS's files, furniture, presses, and typewriters onto trucks and carried them off to a farm in Montague, in western Massachusetts, to escape the politicos' growing influence and power. If they had stayed, Mungo later wrote, LNS would have just become "a propaganda outlet for SDS."[66] Outraged, the Marxists charged up to Montague and at midnight burst into the house where the escapees had reestablished themselves. They forced the Virtuous Caucus people into the back bedroom and surrounded them with a ring of inquisitors. Where's the press? Where's the money? Where's the deed? Brandishing baseball bats, an iron rod, and clenched fists, the invaders smashed windows and furniture and knocked Bloom and his colleagues around. Mungo found himself for the first time yearning to see some policemen. After an hour or so of thumps and groans, the Caucus people surrendered their cash and the deed to the Montague farm. But they refused to reveal where the presses were hidden, and the Vulgar Marxists had to leave without them.

For a time there were two LNSes. The Massachusetts division continued to push cultural dissent. The New York group, converted to a "collective," moved even closer to SDS. In June 1969 the entire New York staff decamped for Chicago for the critical SDS national convention, leaving the office with no one to answer the phones. The Massachusetts LNS did not last long. By the end of the year, it had dissolved. In November 1969 Bloom carefully closed the door of the Montague garage and turned on the engine of his green Triumph sportscar. He was found dead the next day. He was twenty-five. LNS–New York survived into the early seventies but then, during the Nixon era, followed the underground press itself into oblivion.

It was the delightful duo, Rubin and Hoffman, who succeeded for a time in forging a single movement out of dissent's feuding halves. Hoffman and Rubin despised the Soviet system. It was "dull, bureaucratic-sterile-puritanical."[67] A revolution like the Soviet Union's in 1917 dealt only with material inequality. There was another side, however: instinctual and cultural repression. Revolution should be fun. "I don't like the concept of a movement built on sacrifice, dedication, responsibility, anger, frustration and guilt . . . ," Hoffman wrote in early 1968.[68] But the Hoffman–Rubin message was a mixed one. On the one hand the cultural revolutionaries should organize, become political. On the other hand they should make a personal revolution. "The revolution is *now*," Rubin shouted. "We create the revolution by *living* it."[69] Yet in the end the idea of a political party, however mischievous and chaotic, won out over the purely personal.

The path to Yippie was short. The idea of the Youth International party (YIP) began shortly after the Pentagon march in October 1967. It came to fruition, as we saw, early on New Year's morning 1968 in Hoffman's apartment on St. Mark's Place as a symptom, apparently, of a psychedelic hangover. The focus at the beginning was narrow: Chicago, where the Democratic National Convention would provide a showcase for politics as theater. There the Yippies would hold a Festival of Life, with lights, music, and action, to show up the "Festival of Death" the Democrats were planning to put on. The goal was political but the means were theatrical. Sheer exhibitionism was one driving force. Hoffman, Rubin, and company were outrageous "tummlers," Jewish clowns, who felt bereft without an audience. In Chicago the audience would number in the millions!

Yet there was a more serious purpose, in a manner of speaking, behind YIP. As Hoffman would explain in July, one of the Yippies' four main objectives was to create "a blending of pot and politics into a potlitical [*sic*] grass leaves movement—a cross-fertilization of the hippie and New Left philosophies."[70] It was a goal that much of the left did not share, and the more the Yippies pushed, the more the Mobe and SDS resisted. In the end, we will see, the Yippies' rhetorical excesses frightened off many would-be protesters, but enough came to create a glorious head-bashing, brick-throwing, window-trashing mess with casualties and arrests in the hundreds. In March 1969 Rubin and Hoffman—along with a group of Resistance and Mobe leaders and Black Panther Bobby Seale—would be indicted for conspiracy to commit riot at Chicago. The trial lasted for five preposterous months with the pompous judge, Julius Hoffman, playing straight man to the Yippie leaders, who turned the courtroom proceedings into a three-ring circus. Most of the defendants were convicted but escaped sentences when the appeals court overturned the verdicts.

The Yippie attempt to combine politics and ecstasy had at least one imitator. In the spring of 1968, the poet-musician-journalist John Sinclair, Michigan's version of Ed Sanders, the East Village's raunchy litterateur, moved his "Trans-Love Energies Commune" to Ann Arbor to escape the unfriendly Detroit police. Soon after, he founded the White Panthers.

A self-described "LSD-crazed maniac,"[71] Sinclair was a living expression of all the most far-out responses of the time. The new group simultaneously emulated the Diggers, the Yippies, and the Black Panthers. The White Panthers endorsed the Black Panthers' "ten point" program: free party leader Huey Newton, release all black prisoners, provide free breakfasts for black children, obtain ghetto self-determination, and accomplish other things. They also demanded "free access" to information, clothes, food, housing, dope, and "bodies." They proclaimed the end of money. Even more than Hoffman and Rubin, Sinclair thrived on shock. He was especially proud of the short version of the White Panther manifesto: "Rock and roll, dope and fucking in the streets," culminating in a "total assault on the culture."[72]

The White Panthers' outrageous rhetoric made them a lightening rod for the authorities, and Sinclair and his friends were constantly hassled by the police. In 1969 "Big John" was sentenced to ten years in jail for possession of two marijuana cigarettes and, despite international protest, served two of these. By the time he was sprung in late 1971, much of the fun was over. The counterculture was dead.

Yippie was the political avatar of the counterculture. It lasted for a year or two at most and then faded away. But there was also a far weightier instance of social rebellion, of "life-style" dissent, in the process of political transubstantiation as the sixties ended. This was women's liberation. It has endured to our own day—and and has changed our world.

Feminism is as old as ancient times; witness Aristophanes' *Lysistrata* and the sex strike of the Athenian women against their war-obsessed husbands. For all we know it goes back to the caveman—and woman. If we remember the cartoons of skin-clad, low-browed males dragging lady Neanderthals by their hair, we can see the motivation. Its modern version seems to derive from the eighteenth-century Enlightenment, that great watershed for most of the social ideas that make our contemporary world turn. One of the earliest attacks on male dominance and female subordination was Mary Wollstonecroft's famous 1792 essay, *A Vindication of the Rights of Woman.*

The powerful reform surge of the early nineteenth century that alerted the liberal American public to the mistreatment of the insane, the dangers of war, the virtues of social cooperation, and the evils of slavery pricked its conscience over the oppression of women, as well. It also "raised the consciousness" of women themselves, to use a modern phrase. The 1848 women's rights convention at Seneca Falls, New York, was convened by female antislavery activists, and its demands for ending sex discrimination in employment and education and the right of women to vote was of a piece with the reform wave that swept the antebellum North. The convention marked the beginning of the modern American women's rights movement.

By 1890 many of the formal and legal disabilities of women had eased. Women could attend colleges and universities; there were women doctors, lawyers, and scientists. The property of a married woman was no longer her husband's. Divorce was freer. Social and economic equality was still a long way off, but increasingly the women's rights movement concentrated on the vote, winning early victories in the Western states and then, in August 1920, achieving the final triumph for formal political equality with the passage of the women's suffrage amendment to the federal Constitution.

During the 1920s and 1930s, a few feminists continued to chop away at the discrimination against women in the job market. A few militants even sought to question the conventional family and the traditional relations between the sexes. But after 1920 the feminist organizations and formal pressure groups went into remission, and the task of expanding women's options and horizons devolved on young, well-educated, urban women who personally challenged the informal taboos prescribing women's proper place and deportment. The twenties' flapper with her short skirt and hair, her dangling cigarette, her mascara and rouge, and her late hours was conquering new social territory for women, creating new liberated zones. Her success can be measured by the volume and intensity of denunciation she provoked among the traditional clergy and the defenders of the social and moral status quo.

World War II, unlike its 1917–18 predecessor, encouraged a return to domesticity. Millions of women had taken jobs to help the war effort and make money. After the long economic drought of the Great Depression, the cash was welcome, but for many women the war seemed only a further delay in getting on with traditional family life. After 1945 the millions of "Rosie the Riveters" married their "GI Joes" and settled down to wifehood and motherhood in the new, expanded suburbias that spread over the land. It is true that by 1960 many more married woman worked than had twenty years earlier. But the surge was not overpowering, and it was not at first accompanied by any change in attitudes. Whether a full-time housewife or a working mother and wife, the typical young woman of 1960 was still convinced that life was good and that the sexual division of labor and roles was mandated by biology and a divine order. During the 1950s the organized women's movement of the previous decades virtually disappeared.

The new decade brought a new spirit. McCarthyism receded and so did the novelty of affluence. Old reformers, fears allayed and confidence restored, once more set about trying to remake the world. A new generation of young men and women, untouched by the dread of economic disaster that had hobbled their elders, appeared on the scene.

The same heady sense of new possibilities that animated the New Left and the counterculture as the sixties began also rejuvenated feminism. In late 1961 President Kennedy, to accommodate Democratic women leaders, established the President's Commission on the Status of Women, with Eleanor Roosevelt as chairperson. Its report in 1963 urged an end to job and legal discrimination and endorsed day-care centers and paid maternity leaves for married working women. But it also acknowledged "the fundamental responsibility" of women to be "mothers and housewives. . . ."[73] However moderate, the president's commission energized the new impulse by creating a network of women—and some men—who considered feminist issues important. Then in 1964 Congress proscribed sex- as well as race-discrimination for jobs in Title VII of the Civil Rights Act and established the Equal Employment Opportunity Commission as its enforcement body. Highly placed on the EEOC were several strong feminists who deplored the commission's conservatism and saw the civil rights movement as the model for women to follow.

The government initiatives coincided with a new burst of feminist feeling touched off by *The Feminine Mystique*, an eloquent book by an outspoken forty-two-year-old Smith College graduate, Betty Friedan. Herself a housewife and mother, though also a magazine writer, Friedan lamented the loss of pre-1945 feminist momentum and denounced the social values that consigned women to domesticity and weakened their self-esteem. Women, she said, "once again are living with their feet bound in the old image of glorified femininity." It was "the same old image . . . that [had] trapped women for centuries."[74] Published in the spring of 1963, the book echoed and reinforced the emerging mood of insurgency among well-educated women and became a runaway best-seller.

In 1966 the new feminists formed the National Organization for Women with Friedan as its first president. NOW from the outset was a moderate organization with a reformist agenda and a traditional leadership hierarchy. Though it attacked the male-chauvinist cultural prejudices of the media, it did not single out men as the collective enemy. Nor did it repudiate traditional family structure, though it would soon demand women's "rights to control their reproductive lives."[75] NOW was a new, updated version of the earlier women's *rights* organizations. Its chief concerns were equal employment and educational opportunities and the child-care centers and maternity leaves needed to facilitate them. These could all be attained within the limits of liberal reform politics; there was no reason to attack society's foundations. NOW's membership was largely middle class, its leadership mostly middle-aged.

As the decade advanced, NOW found itself upstaged by a movement of younger women who unexpectedly attacked on its left flank. Most of these were refugees from the New Left, and they demanded *liberation*.

Women's liberation was the child of two rejections: SNCC's expulsion of its white members, and SDS's refusal to take its women seriously. Yet it was deeply indebted to both. From early SNCC it derived its affinity for the "beloved community," translated into "sisterhood." From the middle-period SDS it acquired its insight that social change began with fighting for one's own liberation, not someone else's. Long after both organizations had abandoned these perspectives, women activitsts continued to embrace them tightly.

Both SNCC and SDS were male-dominated groups. Both had women members, but as the women later recalled, they had been stuck with the scut work—the typing, the coffee making, the telephoning, the cleaning up. Their ideas, when solicited at all, were expropriated by the male "heavies," and all too often they had been expected to serve primarily as bed partners. Women who asserted themselves had been subject to humiliation. When in

1964 Casey Hayden and Mary King, two bright SNCC staffers, presented a position paper on the status of movement women to a SNCC retreat, Stokely Carmichael provoked a big laugh with his remark: "The only position for women in SNCC is prone."[76]

Some movement people would later argue that black men, systematically emasculated by white men, needed all the male chauvinism they could get. But the male SDS heavies had been even worse. Betty Garman, who had belonged to both SDS and SNCC, later said that she had been "allowed to develop and . . . was given much more responsibility in SNCC" than in SDS. "It would have been tougher for me to develop at all in SDS."[77]

In SNCC white women had supplied sorely needed clerical and verbal skills. In SDS women had to compete against a group of uncommonly literate and articulate young men. The early male SDS leaders—Hayden, Booth, Gitlin, Flacks—were an exceptionally aggressive bunch as well. They didn't use their fists. As intellectuals, their tongues were their weapons, and in the verbal arena where SDS operated they were Olympic-scale contenders. In this preliberation era, few women could compete with such oral warriors, and they found themselves relegated to the supply-service and camp-follower roles. Even in the old Communist party, women had been better treated. James Weinstein, an Old Leftist who had helped found *Studies on the Left,* was dismayed to find that at the 1965 SDS national convention "women made peanut butter, waited on tables, cleaned up, got laid."[78]

The 1965 convention was the last time SDS women accepted such subordination. That December, at the SDS National Council meeting in Champaign-Urbana, Illinois, a group of women activists submitted a position paper denouncing SDS's male-chauvinist actions. The men's response was derision—"catcalls, storms of ridicule and verbal abuse." Marlene Dixon remembered shouts of "She just needs a good screw" and "She's a castrating female."[79]

The paper—and the male response—touched off a spontaneous revolt. Even women who had no connection with the rebels found themselves responding enthusiastically to its charges and themes. Many left the main meeting and went off in small groups to various corners of the vast university student union to discuss women's rights and wrongs. For the first time they discovered how angry and frustrated they felt. These passionate and exhilarating discussions were probably the first feminist consciousness-raising sessions of the new era.

Under pressure, SDS adopted a statement pledging to encourage "honest and open" discussion of the inferior position of women within the organization and advising SDS men to reconsider their attitudes toward their female colleagues.[80] The words were the right ones, but the resolution did little to change the way male SDSers thought or conducted themselves. In truth, feminist consciousness was in the process of evolving, and even women were unclear about what they felt. It is not surprising then that most SDS men failed to understand the depth of female discontent or the ways in which they had fallen short of the standards that women wanted.

SDS was spared further discussion of the "women's question" for a year. But outside the SDS orbit, other radical women were coming together in informal clusters to ponder the problems of male-female relationships in modern America and in Western society in general.

Two competing positions quickly emerged within what came to be called "women's liberation." One identified women's plight with the inequality of wealth and power that ran through the whole of Western capitalist society. Most of these "Politicos" were Marxists of some sort and held that women were a part of capitalism's exploited proletariat. Along with blacks and workers they were victims of the capitalists' drive for profit, and like blacks and workers they would be free only when capitalism had been overthrown and replaced by a socialist commonwealth. Women, as consumers and cheap workers, were vital to capitalism's survival. Their defection would be a thrust at its vitals. But women must work with the other oppressed classes—workers and racial minorities—to bring capitalism to its knees. They could not go it alone.

The problem with the Politico position within the liberation movement was that it was both shopworn and insensitive to the emerging mood of rebellion. Many of the new female *enragés* saw

little to distinguish their male colleagues in movement organizations from traditional male oppressors. Given this fact, would
society after the revolution be any different from society before?
Were socialist countries any less male-dominated than capitalist
ones? Besides such rational objections, many of the new feminists
required a closer and more-tangible villain than capitalism—a
theoretical social category, not a flesh and blood adversary. As
more and more radical women considered their status in a
male-dominated society, they concluded that men were the oppressors, all men, whether rich or poor, powerful or weak. Logic
as well as feeling pointed to separatism. Feminists must form their
own groups with their own agendas. They should not remain
submerged in male-dominated organizations.

In time, as feminist intellectuals struggled to develop a larger
theory of society, the concrete enemy became abstract too. *Patriarchy* was the name of the age-old oppressor of women. Patriarchy, not capitalism, was also the primary social exploiter and
ancestor of all oppressor classes. As the oldest form of hierarchy,
it was the prototype of all the others. Sexism, not capitalism—or
even racism—was the evil principle at large in the world. At first
these women simply called themselves "feminists." They would
soon adopt the tag "Radical Feminists" to distinguish themselves
from the Marxist Politicos within the liberation movement.

It took months of groping, of translating feelings into words,
for women liberationists to understand and define themselves and
bring their ideas to the surface. As we look at the small "women's
lib" grouplets forming here and there during 1967, we see the
sharing of experiences and the mutual reinforcement that would
soon create a new and ultimately powerful force for change. The
picture is of a major social movement quickly unfolding before
our eyes.

Chicago, not New York or San Francisco, was the birthplace of
the new liberationist impulse. During the spring of 1967, Heather
Tobis Booth, the wife of the early SDS leader Paul Booth, and
Naomi Weisstein, an experimental psychologist at the University
of Chicago, conducted a seminar on women's concerns as part of
the local "free university" program. These were "counter institutions" that had sprung up at Chicago and at other universities

during the mid-sixties in the wake of the student revolt to provide instruction in subjects the traditional curriculum spurned. The free universities taught everything from "Neo-Colonialism and Revolution in Asia, Africa, and Latin America" to the "Art of Sexual Love" and "The Fundamentals of Astrology."[81] The seminar created a tiny community of women liberationists who continued to meet after the formal course had ended. The New Politics Conference in Chicago that September—the liberal-radical third-party fiasco—became the occasion for the Chicago group to form an ad hoc women's caucus with feminists from other parts of the country and to propose a set of resolutions. Besides equal pay for women and the right to free abortion, the caucus impudently demanded 51 percent of the conference vote. Why not? Blacks had demanded the same thing!

The response was another humiliation. The conference refused to consider any resolutions on women's issues until Jo Freeman and Shulamith Firestone threatened to tie up the sessions with a filibuster. At this point conference chairman William Pepper relented to the extent of allowing debate on a conservative "women for peace" plank. But he denied the militants, waiting anxiously at the rostrum microphones, a hearing on their own proposal—and in a peculiarly dismissive way. As the event was later described in feminist annals, he turned to the formidable Firestone and, patting her on the head, exclaimed: "Move on little girl; we have more important issues to talk about here. . . ."[82] The pat seems too pat, but the account represents a symbolic, if not a literal, truth.

The rebuff at the New Politics Conference added fuel to the angry mood. One of the Chicago women later noted that "rage at what had happened at the convention kept us going for at least three months."[83] In October the Chicagoans issued an address to "the women of the Left" calling on radical women to avoid the early mistake of the civil rights activists in permitting others to influence the course of the movement. Women alone could "define the terms of our struggle." They must go it alone. "It is incumbent on us as women," the document proclaimed, "to organize a movement for women's liberation."[84]

Shortly after this the Chicagoans split into two groups. One, composed of Politicos, took the name Women's Radical Action Project. The other, primarily Radical Feminists, called themselves the Westside Group. Early in 1968 the Westsiders began to publish a three-page newsletter edited by Jo Freeman, a journalist whose feminist passions had been aroused when she experienced discrimination in her field, titled *Voice of the Women's Liberation Movement. Voice* eventually grew into a twenty-five page photo-offset journal. In June 1969, when it ceased publication, it had a circulation of two thousand. In its few months of existence, it reached thousands of readers and helped expand the circle of women radicals and feminist activists committed to the new separatism.

During the early months of 1968, small clusters of women liberationists began to coalesce in cities around the country. In San Francisco the women were New Left dropouts who began to meet for sessions of personal self-examination. Their discussions focused on male oppression and their own sexuality. They came to see, one of their founders reported, that their bodies were not their own; they were controlled by "men, doctors, clothes and cosmetic manufacturers, advertisers, churches and schools—everyone but ourselves. . . ."[85] In New Orleans the impetus came from a group of southern white women formerly active in SNCC and the Southern Student Organizing Committee, a Dixie affiliate of SDS. Boston acquired its first Radical Feminist group when Roxanne Dunbar, a West Coast New Leftist, arrived in June and founded Cell 16. Early in 1969 Cell 16 began to publish *No More Fun and Games*, subtitled *A Journal of Female Liberation*.

Firestone; Pam Allen, a white civil rights activist; Kathie Amatniek, a former TOCSIN peace agitator at Radcliffe College; and Rosalyn Baxandall, the wife of Lee Baxandall, a *Studies on the Left* founder, formed New York Radical Women (NYRW) in the early months of 1968. Shortly after, they were joined by Ann Koedt and Carol Hanisch, two white SNCC workers, Ellen Willis, a pop-music reviewer for *The New Yorker,* and Robin Morgan, a former child actress. Some of these women were Politicos; others Radical Feminists. NYRW mixed activism with introspection. In

January it disrupted the demonstration in Washington of the Jeanette Rankin Brigade, a women's peace group, in order to present its own ceremony celebrating "the burial of traditional womanhood." Amatniek, whose ardent feminism soon induced her to change her name to Kathie Sarachild—to honor her mother rather than her father—delivered a "funeral oration" that defended giving women's issues priority over the Vietnam War. Women's oppression was so closely intertwined with the other injustices in the world, she said, that it could not be postponed until the others were cured. Amatniek's statement was one of the earliest Radical Feminist speeches.

NYRW was also the source of much of the liberationist intellectual arsenal. Its twenty-page mimeographed booklet of June 1968, *Notes From the First Year*, was the first collection of liberationist essays and articles. Many of the pieces were slight, but Ann Koedt's "Myth of the Vaginal Orgasm" would become a classic of liberationist literature and be anthologized a score of times. Later, longer, versions of *Notes* would summarize early liberationist thinking year by year.

NYRW—or at least its Radical Feminist wing—was also the source of consciousness-raising. The practice probably drew from a number of sources. The old Communist left had long used "criticism, self-criticism" sessions to forge a consensus among party members. Mao Tse-tung, Carol Hanisch at one point noted, had used the approach "speak pain to recall pain" to raise political consciousness in Chinese Communist villages.[86] In the South, black congregations had employed "testifying" to express members' religious experiences. Consciousness-raising also resembled group therapy, the precedent probably most familiar to the well-educated women who made up most of the liberationist groups.

Consciousness-raising started as small Thursday evening gatherings in various New York living rooms where NYRW members could discuss common problems and grievances. Participants were encouraged to express their deepest frustrations and angers. In the early months the consciousness-raising sessions were unstructured and open, with no one managing direction or choosing subjects. This openness soon changed. As prescribed in the "Protective Rules for Consciousness Raising" by Redstockings, a 1969 NYRW offshoot, "sisters" had to reach conclusions that gave the views a political context.

Consciousness-raising was a potent device for making the personal political. But Radical Feminists only considered a part of the personal relevant. Not all grievances were equal. Mothers, sisters, daughters, were exempt from attack; it was primarily the buried grievances of a lifetime against men—fathers, brothers, husbands, lovers, employers—that had political value. Vivien Gornick, a feminist journalist, admitted this bias a few years later. CR sessions, she acknowledged encouraged women to look for explanations of their experiences "in terms of the social and cultural dynamic created by sexism. . . ." They were urged to seek the causes of their personal pain primarily in "the cultural fact of . . . patriarchy."[87] A logical extension of the position was the "pro-woman line," which meant, one Redstockings member said, "that we take the woman's side in *everything*."[88]

The feminist perceptions of male oppression were surely valid in part. Women *had* been humiliated, degraded, wronged, manipulated, exploited, abused, belittled, and frustrated by men. It could be argued that women over the centuries had done the same things to men, and at times women had been the victims of other women, not just men. But women *had* been the weaker sex, the *second* and lesser sex, through most of history, and it is easy to understand why intelligent, well-educated middle-class American women, living in a time when all hierarchies, all power elites, all establishments were losing their legitimacy, felt they had to get in their licks. With blacks attacking "The Man," it is not so surprising that women should attack men.

Yet it was difficult for most men, and for many traditional women, not to feel that consciousness-raising exaggerated, blew the valid grievances out of proportion. The antimale response at times seemed so unqualified, so total. "We identify the agents of our oppression as men," proclaimed the Redstockings manifesto. "*All men* receive economic, social, and psychological benefits from male supremacy. *All men* have oppressed women."[89] Ti-Grace Atkinson, a firebrand who split with NOW in the fall of 1968 because it was too moderate and reformist and founded "the

Feminists," declared women's oppression by men as "the source of *all* the corrupt values throughout the world." Men had *"robbed* women of their lives."[90] The antimale urge stigmatized the institution of marriage itself. The Feminists early adopted a rule that no more than one-third of its membership could "be participants in either a formal (with legal contract) or informal (i.e., living with a man) instance of an institution of marriage."[91] At times the attack skirted the fanatic. Men were "an obsolete form of life" so destructive to the environment, wrote Cell 16's Betsy Warrior (her party name), that they should be exterminated on ecological grounds.[92] Atkinson claimed that men "constitute a social disease."[93]

The most extreme onslaught of all came from Valerie Solanis. Solanis was an actress with a deep grievance against men who, in June 1968, pushed her way into Andy Warhol's Union Square studio and pumped him full of bullets. Her motives were unusual: Warhol had refused to return one of her movie scripts and insisted on producing it! Angry and confused, Solanis was also verbally bloodthirsty. SCUM, the Society for Cutting Up Men, the organization she founded in 1968, proclaimed that males were limited creatures governed entirely by their sexual needs. A man would do anything to screw—"swim a river of snot, wade nostril-deep through a mile of vomit, if he thinks there'll be a friendly pussy awaiting him." Men were incapable of anything creative. They had made the world "a shitpile." If anything was to get better, women must seize control of the government. This could be accomplished by "fucking up the system, selectively destroying property, and murder." SCUM would "kill all men who are not in the Men's auxiliary of SCUM." The "few remaining" males could continue to "exist out their puny days dropped out on drugs or strutting around in drag . . . or they can go off to the nearest friendly suicide center where they will be quietly, quickly, and painlessly gassed to death."[94]

Solanis was probably a certifiable lunatic, though the courts tried her as sane and sentenced her to three years in jail for the attack on Warhol. But the antimale frenzy cannot be dismissed solely as dementia. Some of it derived from a half-hidden Lesbian agenda pushed by militants.

The Lesbian theme first comes to the surface in Anne Koedt's "Myth of the Vaginal Orgasm." In this benchmark essay, Koedt attacked the claim of Freudian psychologists that sexual maturity required that women experience vaginal orgasm. The clitoris, she said, was the actual source of orgasm in women. In effect, the Freudians had accused women of sexual and emotional inadequacy because of a colossal ignorance of the female body. But the essay was far more than a technical argument over anatomy. It had wide implications. As the author of the penis-envy concept to explain female personality, Freud seemed a prime source of modern women's notions of inferiority. Since the vaginal orgasm required penetration, it was easy to see it as another assertion of male supremacy. In effect, for a woman to attain emotional maturity, she must, in Freud's view, depend on a man.

Given his time—the turn of the century—and his place—Hapsburg Vienna—Freud's male-supremacist ideas are not surprising. They were also understandably objectionable to feminists. But there was something else. Do away with the vaginal orgasm and you eliminated the sexual indispensability of men, at least in an anatomical sense. Sex could be a solitary occupation with no qualms. More important, it need not be heterosexual. In fact, since women naturally understood the sexual needs of their own kind better than men, Lesbian sex could be superior to straight sex. As Koedt noted, "Lesbian sexuality could make an excellent case, based on anatomical data, for the extinction of the male organ."[95] This scarcely hidden Lesbian message made the Koedt article famous, or infamous, in early liberationist circles.

If men were not needed for pleasure, there still remained reproduction. How could the race continue if heterosexual relations were superseded? At the extreme edge of the women's liberation movement there were minds equal to the challenge. Artifical insemination or, better still, some sort of parthenogenesis as in frogs, might make males totally extraneous. Firestone, for one, talked not only of abolishing the patriarchal family but also of abolishing the need for the patriarch himself by some sort of "artificial reproduction."[96]

Koedt's 1968 essay was a guarded statement of a Lesbian agenda. Of course, most women liberationists and even most

Radical Feminists were straight, but no group within the radical wing of the women's movement had such strong incentive to deplore the reign of patriarchy as Lesbians, and no group labored as actively to advance Radical Feminist interests. Within the Old Left that same sectarian single-mindedness had always worked to the advantage of the Communist party. Within SDS it had given Progressive Labor the edge over its rivals. Now it helped the Lesbians to impose their sensibility disproportionately on the woman's liberation movement. Ti-Grace Atkinson's Feminists went as far as to insist that heterosexuality reduced women to bondage to men. Marriage was nothing more than "legalized rape"[97] and along with the family "must be destroyed."[98]

Straight feminists sometimes fought back, but they were handicapped by the dilemma of an antimale philosophy that made heterosexual relationships problematical. If you believed men were the oppressors, then why not go all the way and give up on them entirely? It would take years before straight feminists could sort out the contradictions in their attitudes toward men.

In early 1968, SDS estimated that there were thirty-five or so small women's liberation groups extant. At this point there could not have been more than a few hundred women actively involved in the radical women's movement, and the general public knew almost nothing of them. In March 1968 *The New York Times*, that gauge of upper-middle-class awareness, carried an article entitled "The Second Feminist Wave" by Martha Lear. It described NOW and its leaders but said nothing of Firestone, Koedt, Amatniek, Dunbar, Morgan, or any of the other liberationists. Then came the September Miss America Pageant in Atlantic City, and women's lib erupted into the American consciousness.

The pageant was a natural target of the liberationists. As they considered the nature of female oppression, they had concluded that the cult of female physical beauty was ultimately a male scheme to keep women distracted, subordinate, and defensive. As a feminist polemic would later phrase it, the ideal women depicted in *Playboy* and in the beauty contests "teach women their role in society, . . . teach them that women are articles of conspicuous consumption in the male market. . . ."[99] It followed that the annual beauty contest ritual in the decaying Jersey Shore resort was a profanation of women, reducing them to pretty things, toys of men. Yet the pageant itself was only one example of enslavement through apparent gallantry. Just as deplorable were the fashions imposed on women, styles that distorted their bodies and hobbled their movements. The three worst offenders were the high-heeled shoe, the corset, and the brassiere.

The two hundred women who descended on Atlantic City in September 1968 to proclaim their disgust were mostly from New York Radical Women. In their call to action, the militants denounced the pageant as a "degrading mindless boob-girlie symbol," "racism with roses," and a "consumer con-game."[100] They intended to conduct a peaceful protest and had negotiated an agreement with Atlantic City Mayor Richard Jackson—concerned over the recent violence at the Democratic presidential convention—to "be orderly and quiet." "We don't want another Chicago," noted one of their leaders, Robin Morgan.[101] The protesters brought with them two key props for their "guerrilla theater": a female puppet with chains dangling from her red, white, and blue bathing suit, and a "freedom ashcan."

Most of the protesters were young, but there were also some gadflies left over from the generation of the 1920s radical Women's Party. One of the oldest was Kathie Amatniek's sixty-five-year-old yellow-hatted grandmother, Martha Berlin, who forgot herself and started to talk to a male reporter until her granddaughter called her back to liberationist rigor.

Barred from the Convention Hall while the audience and judges inside were watching the all-American beauties going through their fatuous paces, the protesters marched up and down the Boardwalk singing a parody version of the pageant theme song, "There She Is, Miss America," in three-part harmony, carrying posters denouncing the sexist performance inside.

Though they would not talk to male reporters, they had no objection whatsoever to being filmed and televised. And they provided great visual copy, ritually shredding a *Playboy* magazine and parading a ram fussily bedecked in yellow and blue ribbons, apparently as a symbolic turnabout. It was all wasted. NBC TV's official version of the Miss America crowning ceremony ignored the protest outside the hall.

The true focus of the ceremonies was the freedom ashcan. Into this receptacle the women tossed a bottle of pink liquid detergent, high-heeled shoes, corsets, eyelash curlers, and at least one bra. Each act of disposal invoked a chant or slogan: "Down with bound feet," for the shoes; "Washing dishes is an atrocity," for the detergent; "No more girdles, no more pain; no more trying to hold the fat in vain," for the corset. There is no record of what the bra chucking called forth. No bra—or anything else, apparently—was ever burned. There had been talk of incinerating the despised objects rather than throwing them out, and at one point Morgan had promised Mayor Jackson that she and her colleagues "wouldn't do anything dangerous, just a symbolic bra-burning."[102] But nothing apparently was incinerated. Yet her remark, the nice alliteration of "bra burner," and the whiff of prewar Nazi book burning, made a spurious brassiere immolation the central ritual in the media account. Radical feminists would protest the "bra burner" label, but the event is inscribed in folk history and will not easily be erased.

The Atlantic City demonstration made the women's liberation movement news. *Life,* the news magazines, and many daily newspapers ran accounts of the event. Much of the coverage was either hostile or derisive. The demonstrators were an ugly bunch of viragos who resented beautiful women out of envy. Or else they were crazies who wanted to deny their womanhood. Who else would burn their bras? The impression the media created may not have been favorable, but it was an impression, and a strong one at that. For the first time the broad public learned that women activists had caught up with blacks and students in the race to challenge mainstream America. The publicity brought new recruits in droves. Morgan later reported that a week before the demonstration no more than 30 women had attended the New York Radical Women's meeting; the week following there were 150.

NYRW's shock tactics were soon duplicated by a new organization calling itself WITCH, supposedly an acronym for "Women's International Terrorist Conspiracy from Hell," but really an attempt to identify with the persecuted women hanged and burned in past centuries as consorts of Satan.

WITCH, a spinoff of NYRW, was founded by Morgan in 1968. WITCH members were Politicos, rather than Radical Feminists, but they were Marxists of a relaxed kind whose jaunty attitudes and cultural focus brought them close to their adversaries. They "identified politically with the confrontation tactics of the male left," Morgan later wrote, "and stylistically with the clownish proto-anarchism of the Yippies."[103] In retrospect, Morgan believed that they were too action-oriented and not clear enough about their long-term goals. At first they seemed primarily concerned with shocking and offending men and square women and making their presence known. They succeeded at both.

WITCH surfaced, literally, when a dozen women dressed as "Shamans, Faerie Queens, Matriarchal Old Sorceresses, and Guerrilla Witches"[104] emerged at noon on Halloween from the subway station at Wall Street in lower Manhattan and danced and gyrated their way to the Federal Reserve Bank "to pit their ancient powers against the evil powers of . . . the Imperialist Phallic Society."[105] The women circled the Federal Hall statue of the country's patriarch, George Washington, and covered it with hex stickers. They then cast a spell on the gold bricks in the bank's vaults to render them worthless. It was the height of the 1968 presidential campaign, and nearby Humphrey and Nixon campaigners heckled the women. They ignored the sexist remarks.

The "coven" then moved on to the New York Stock Exchange where they laid a curse on the market. They later claimed it accounted for the modest Dow Jones decline in the succeeding two days. Visits to the Chase Manhattan Bank, Manufacturers Hanover Trust Company, and Bache and Company were followed by a sortie at dusk to the Lower East Side where they demonstrated against McSorley's men-only saloon, a burlesque house, and a beauty parlor. Their next stop was a discotheque on St. Mark's Place where four male bouncers bodily ejected them. The struggle enabled the WITCHes to try out their newly acquired martial arts, and they managed to land a few blows on their attackers. The final scene was an invasion of a Theater of

Ideas where "the usual group of chic liberals were klatching."[106] The women passed around a "caldron" for contributions and stayed to rap with the audience on theater, ideas, media, women, revolution, and other topics. It was quite a day!

WITCH followed up its Halloween foray with a raid at the January counter-inaugural put on by the left to protest the beginning of Nixon's presidency. The WITCHes were as welcome as a corpse at a wedding. The other women shouted that they were thieves, undignified freaks, and disrupters. Mobe marshals tried to keep them away from the speakers. But they stayed anyway—for the food and drink. In February a WITCH coven burst into the New York Bridal Fair at Madison Square Garden to protest the commercialization of marriage. While the brides-to-be and their doting mothers lined up outside the Garden for the round of fashion shows and entertainment, 150 women picketed, leafleted, and performed guerrilla theater acts as part of their own "unwedding ceremony." Some wore black veils and sang "Here come the slaves,/Off to their graves" to the tune of Wagner's *Lohengrin* "Wedding March."[107] The protesters' targets were the big businesses that got rich on weddings and the assorted rituals of marriage. But as Morgan explained, the main attack was "aimed at the institution of marriage itself, and at the structure of the bourgeois family, which oppresses everyone, and particularly women."[108] Inside the fair itself the women disrupted a question-and-answer session for brides and turned the trousseau fashion show into a shambles by releasing 150 white mice.

WITCH was great copy and the media lapped it up. The *Times* had a full account in its "Food, Fashions, Family, and Furnishings" section.[109] *Life* magazine marked it with an editorial. Most Americans were probably outraged; others clearly were amused. Among dissenters, the reviews were mixed. WITCH apparently touched a sympathetic nerve among some women, and affiliated covens soon sprang up around the country. Radical men approved, hoping, Morgan claimed, that the media attention would bring new female recruits to the left. Yet WITCH came under attack within women's liberation as a trivializing force and an embarrassment to the movement. Its activities soon became the center of cacophonous debates in women's liberation circles.

These attacks and the other stresses of militancy took their emotional toll, and within a year the "mother coven" had disbanded. But before it did, it had adopted consciousness-raising as a key practice, acknowledging thereby the political validity of the personal in women's lives. By the mid-seventies Robin Morgan would abandon Marxism and become one of the most ardent supporters of the Radical Feminist cultural position.

Turning points can go either way, up or down. In 1968 the movement for political and racial change in American life that had stirred into motion a decade earlier began to subside. For the behavioral revolution, 1968 was the start. That was the year that the insurgency of the cultural outsiders—the free lovers, the drug takers, the acid rock listeners, the angry women—decided that they had the right to place their causes on the public agenda. If the civil rights movement, anti-Vietnam War efforts, Great Society liberalism all began to wind down, the crusades for social liberation gathered impetus, forward motion that would carry them successfully through another decade.

One rebel group still in the wings as 1968 began was the homophile community, the nation's gay and Lesbian outsiders. It had already begun to stir, energized by the rhetoric and imperatives of the New Left, civil rights, and especially the cultural liberation movements. But it was still part of a social underground, a half-world, its members anxious to avoid identification or detection. No sector of the nation's outsiders had more to gain from making the personal political than its male homosexuals, and in mid-1969 the community's repressed outrage at its penalization burst forth in New York's Greenwich Village in an incident that launched the gay liberation movement.

In the annals of the homophile community, the battle at the Stonewall Inn, a gay bar on Christopher Street in Greenwich Village, ranks as Pearl Harbor. The establishment operated without a liquor license, reputedly had organized crime connections, and, according to local straights, brought unwelcome blacks and Hispanics into the predominantly white middle-class neighborhood. It was ripe for a raid, and just before midnight on

Friday, June 27, police from the Village's Sixth Precinct entered the bar and arrested the bartender, the bouncer, and several drag queens—men in women's dress. The rest of the patrons, almost two hundred, were let out one by one.

Instead of quietly dispersing in the usual way, the gays gathered outside, and when a cop tried to hustle an angry Lesbian into a patrol car the crowd blew up. Beer cans, bottles, cobblestones, and coins were soon raining on police. The bar burst into flames. Reinforcements saved the trapped cops, but the crowd, swollen by men from the surrounding gay community, rioted far into the night. Thirteen people were arrested.

The next evening the disorders in the Village and adjacent neighborhoods resumed. Gays hurled concrete blocks and garbage at police patrol cars. When the Tactical Patrol Force arrived, they were met by two thousand enraged young men who threw bottles and stones and set fires in trash containers. The rebels had now found a slogan—Gay Power—and used it as a war cry, chanting it on the streets and scrawling it as graffiti all over the sidewalks and walls of the Village.

The newsletter of the New York Mattachine Society, a homosexual rights group formed in the 1950s, called the riot "the hairpin drop heard round the world."[110] It was. In July a group of homophile men and women formed the Gay Liberation Front to fight persecution and discrimination through collective political agitation and protest. By the end of the year, local chapters had sprung up in cities and on campuses across the country. The gay liberation movement transformed the relationships of homosexual men and women to the straight community. By the mid-seventies waves of gay men and women were coming "out of the closet" and declaring their preferences. They were also demanding equal treatment in jobs and housing and even asserting the moral equality of their culture to the straight culture of the majority.

In 1968, or soon after, the country's cultural dissenters shook off their indifference to politics and turned to collective action on the model of the civil rights movement. The late start may have served them well. Long after the political left had torn itself apart, the momentum for cultural change would continue, transforming the values and practices of American society and creating a deep chasm along a fault line of social values.

But in 1968 liberalism still had one more card in its deck, and in Chicago, as the summer drew to a close, the veteran players gathered to try once more to win the pot.

7

Nixon's the One!

RICHARD NIXON flew to Florida on December 28, 1967, to escape the New York winter and to consider whether he should run for president of the United States. Pat Nixon stayed home; she seldom came with him on these trips. Mrs. Nixon did not want her husband to run again, and perhaps this time her absence was as much a political demurrer as a social decision.

Nixon spent the next ten days at a Key Biscayne Hotel villa in the company of Bebe Rebozo, the rich Cuban American businessman who had become his confidant and chum. He could relax with Bebe and talk through his dilemma. Billy Graham, the evangelist, on the mend after a bout of pneumonia, joined them for a few days at Nixon's invitation, and the three, improbably, talked theology along with politics and sports. On New Year's Eve they went to dinner at the Jamaica Inn, sitting at Nixon's favorite table beside an artificial waterfall.

On New Year's Day, as Graham packed to leave, Nixon asked the preacher if he should declare for the presidency. "Dick, I think you should run," Graham replied. "If you don't, you will always wonder whether you should have run or not. You are the best prepared man in the United States to be President."[1]

Nixon returned to New York on the eighth with his mind made up. But he kept his decision to himself until a week later, when Julie, his older daughter, came down from college. On January 15 the family dined together at their Fifth Avenue apartment with Rose Wood, Nixon's longtime secretary. After desert and coffee, he invited Manolo and Fina Sanchez, old family servants, to join the group. He had reached a decision, he announced. Politics was not merely another occupation; it was his whole life, and he could not sit out the presidential race. "I have decided to go," he told his small audience. "I have decided to run again."

The family was enthusiastic. Even Pat said that she would go along with his decision. Fina gave a fervent little speech: "You are the man to lead the country!" she exclaimed. "This was determined before you were born!"[2]

Political realities as well as emotional needs made Richard Nixon a candidate. As 1968 began its jarring course, Nixon was the Republican front-runner, the favorite of the party faithful. In its first issue of the year, *Newsweek* reported that if the Republican nominating convention were held right then, Nixon would receive 561 delegate votes, only 106 fewer than needed for nomination.

At first view, Richard Nixon's credentials as party savior were not impressive. No major political leader had aroused so much sheer distaste in his opponents, in party and out. "Tricky Dick" had been their favorite epithet, but there had been others as well—"Plastic Man," "Man of Paradox," "Virtuoso of Deception"—all capturing some darker part of his personality. In 1956 Adlai Stevenson, the hero of the reform Democrats, described Nixon in terms that anticipated the complex moral disaster we call Watergate. "Nixonland," he declared, was a realm "of slander and scare, a land of sly innuendo, the poison pen, the anonymous phone call, and hustling, pushing, shoving; the land of smash and grab and anything to win."[3]

Many Americans had voted for Richard Nixon for high office—senator, governor, vice-president, president—but few had loved him. He inspired little affection because he seemed himself incapable of love. Pain, anger, resentment, self-pity, hatred—but not love. The Oval Office tapes of the weeks following the 1972 Watergate break-in provide a unique picture of a powerful man in private. The landscape is cold, spiteful, self-absorbed, mean-spirited, and—to everyone's surprise— unfocused and confused. The tapes confirm the jungle world of heartless, brutal calculation and elemental power urges that his critics had long believed infused "Nixonland."

Despite its defects—or because of them—Nixon's personality has intrigued a generation of journalists and scholars. Easterners have sometimes blamed it on geography: he lacked a center because southern California where he was born and raised was all surfaces, without a core. This response is essentially the snobbery of the "Eastern Establishment," of the old money and cultivation that Nixon railed at his whole life; it is also the contempt of writers and intellectuals wooed but not won by Hollywood. Yet there is some truth to it. Even his mother's Quakerism was of a peculiarly southern California sort that had had its grit and character extracted by the warm bath of the Pacific sun.

Nixon was also more than a little shopworn. His road to power had been paved with bad intentions. As a young California congressman in the 1950s, he had made shrewd use of the public's anti-Communist hysteria. His pursuit of Alger Hiss as a prewar spy for the Soviet Union brought him national fame and the Republican nomination for senator from his home state. He had then defeated his opponent, Helen Gahagan Douglas, by calling her the "Pink Lady." He had been Eisenhower's vice-president for two terms, but Ike never really liked him and had never invited him to the family quarters in the White House. In 1952 he had almost dumped Nixon from the ticket following allegations that the young senator had accepted financial favors from a group of California businessmen. Nixon had only survived by a corny TV confessional that exploited Pat's "Republican cloth coat," and his daughters' dog, Checkers.

He had first run for president in 1960, against John Kennedy, and suffered a narrow defeat. In 1962 he staged a comeback by running for governor of California against the incumbent, Pat Brown. He lost again, this time decisively, after a bruising campaign in which he felt the press had savaged him. Bitter at the second defeat in two years, he had allowed his bile to spill over at a press conference the day after the election. Now that "all the members of the press are so delighted that I have lost," he observed, he wanted to make a statement. He had always respected his opponent's integrity and patriotism, but the reporters had never acknowledged *his* fairness or given him the benefit of the doubt. Well, he concluded, "you won't have Nixon to kick around anymore because . . . this is my last press conference."[4]

Nixon's political demise seemed final when soon after, he accepted a partnership in Mudge, Stern, Baldwin, and Todd, a prestigious New York law firm, and moved to Manhattan. He had left his home base behind and relocated in political territory that owed allegiance to Governor Nelson Rockefeller, New York's liberal Republican overlord. There seemed no way that he could ever find the political resources to win major public office again.

But then came the 1964 Goldwater debacle. On November 3, 1964, the GOP suffered the worst electoral catastrophe in its history, exceeding even the mid-depression Alf Landon defeat of 1936. The Goldwater–Miller ticket had carried only five Deep South states, plus Goldwater's own Arizona. In Congress the Republican cohort had been reduced to a nub with only 138 of 435 seats in the House and only 39 of 100 in the Senate. The crash had reverberated through the states. Many more incumbent Democratic governors had been up for reelection, but the Republicans had won only one statehouse and in 1965 would occupy only 17 of the 50. Five hundred Republican state legislators had been swept from their places by the Johnson landslide. As Republican leaders looked over the still-smoking wreckage on November 3, some wondered if the party was not destined to follow the nineteenth-century Whigs into oblivion.

The predictions of doom were of course fatuous. The American two-party system has survived war, depression, and sectional disruption. It is probably as indestructible as the United States itself and was certain to survive Barry Goldwater. The self-healing powers of the major parties are remarkable, but recovery is not spontaneous; it requires solicitous care, and it was here, during the months that followed the debacle, that Richard Nixon had so impressed the party pros.

Nixon was not a Goldwaterite. The consummate pragmatist, he had always maneuvered his way nimbly through the party's ideological minefields and evaded a clear label. Unlike the GOP liberals—Rockefeller, Governor George Romney of Michigan, Governor William Scranton of Pennsylvania, Senator Thomas Kuchel of California, Senator Charles Percy of Illinois—he refused to treat the party's 1964 presidential candidate as a political leper. During the election he campaigned for the Goldwater–Miller ticket and earned the gratitude of the conservatives as well as the nonideological regulars without deeply offending the party left. Two years later he covered thirty thousand miles, making speeches for beleaguered Republican state and national candidates during the off-year elections. The GOP's 1966 comeback in Congress and the states confirmed his reputation as Mr. Republican. In March 1967 investment banker Maurice Stans and a group of younger, second-level Republicans, bankrolled by Elmer Bobst of Warner–Lambert and DeWitt Wallace of the *Reader's Digest,* established the Nixon for President Committee with headquarters in Washington.

While the potential candidate searched his soul in Florida during the 1967 year-end holidays, his friends proceeded. Nixon-for-President headquarters on Pennsylvania Avenue, a few hundred yards from the White House, acquired a staff, a bank of phones, and patriotic bunting. The committee exacted promises of support, financial and moral. Then, on January 31, hours before the filing deadline, Nixon's name was entered in the New Hampshire Republican primary. The next day, in an open letter to New Hampshire voters, he formally announced that his hat was in the ring.

Nixon's late entry had at least one purely strategic motive: George Romney must serve as media lightening rod in the early rounds, sparing Nixon the damage.

The handsome, silver-haired governor of Michigan was the foremost candidate of the party's liberal wing. Rockefeller was the stronger and smarter man, but bruised after disastrous nomination bids in 1960 and 1964, he was reluctant to run and had thrown his support behind Romney. The Michigan governor was also the most vulnerable candidate. A Mormon and former head of American Motors, he had come to politics late and knew little about national issues and less about foreign affairs. His political ideas seemed to come from the Boy Scout Handbook, and to the knowledgeable and cynical men and women of the press he was a figure of fun. One of his critics called him "a certified square so dedicated to good works his entrance into politics is like sending a Salvation Army lass into the chorus at a burlesque house."[5]

Romney worked to correct his deficiencies. In the summer of 1965, he had gone to Vietnam in quest of enlightenment and after the usual one-sided blitz of official briefings in Saigon had returned to make speeches supporting the administration's escalation policies. As the war dragged on, the governor began to have doubts, and in January 1967 he cornered former U.S. Ambassador to Saigon Henry Cabot Lodge in Washington and demanded that he square with him. Lodge admitted that the governor might have been fed some overly optimistic estimates eighteen months before, but pleaded loyalty to the administration as his excuse. Romney felt duped.

For a time the governor kept his own counsel, meanwhile trying to establish some distance between himself and the administration on Vietnam. Then, in September, during an unrehearsed TV interview, he declared that in Saigon in 1965 he had been subjected to "the greatest brainwashing that anybody can get. . . ."[6] The statement was honest and admitted only what many other Americans had experienced. Yet it buried the Michigan governor under an avalanche of derision. The *Chicago Tribune* noted that "to be brainwashed you first must have a brain"[7] The Detroit *News* called the governor incompetent and demanded that he withdraw in favor of Governor Rockefeller of New York.

Romney soon lost his taste for the battle and tried to exit. Rockefeller would not let him. He must continue to bear the liberal Republican banner to the end, the Lord of Pocantico Hills decreed. The Michigan governor soldiered on dutifully, rushing off to Europe and once more to Vietnam to beef up his foreign policy credentials. Nothing helped. He continued to say things that the press ridiculed, and his support dwindled. Just after Christmas a group of Romney aides met secretly at a LaGuardia

Airport conference room in New York to hear the results of a recent Rockefeller-financed poll in New Hampshire. They were devastating: only one in eight New Hampshire Republicans would vote for their candidate. One of the men present said: "I guess the poll shows that New Hampshire Republicans think George Romney is too dumb to be President of the United States."[8]

Still, the Michigan governor slogged on. For the next few weeks he traveled New Hampshire in a campaign bus, turning up at coffee klatches, bowling alleys, and factory gates to pump hands, smile, and murmur friendly words. Slowly his voter acceptability improved, but he could not close the gap on Nixon.

After his January announcement, a confident, relaxed Nixon, smelling easy victory, came to New Hampshire and campaigned hard and effectively. At his kickoff press meeting in Manchester he quipped: "I should make one thing clear at the outset: this is not my last press conference."[9] The goal in New Hampshire was to establish that there was a "new Nixon," a more likable and generous man mellowed by adversity, a statesman tempered by experience. Yet as front-runner, anxious to avoid fumbles, he confined himself to soothing generalities. Meanwhile, his supporters hacked away at Romney's gaffes and his supposed extravagant spending policies as governor. In the third week in February, another poll showed Romney behind six to one. Then the coup de grace. On February 24, at a Republican fund-raiser in Detroit, Rockefeller declared that he would run if drafted. On the twenty-eighth Romney announced that he was withdrawing from the race. On March 12, in the primary, Nixon got 79 percent of the Republican vote; a Rockefeller write-in campaign, well financed but far too late, won 11 percent.

The remainder of the Nixon preconvention campaign went almost as smoothly. Nixon's cheerful to-ing and fro-ing those many months for Republican candidates in 1964 and 1966 had created a reservoir of goodwill among party regulars that translated into scores of delegates for the presidential nominating convention at Miami. After Romney's withdrawal, most of the primaries were pro forma. Nixon's candidacy in Wisconsin in

April was essentially unopposed. In Pennsylvania, later that month, he won an all-write-in primary with over 76 percent of the vote. Indiana and Nebraska in early May were smash victories over barely visible opposition.

In Oregon a real contest developed. Here Nixon confronted the governor of California, Ronald Reagan, the man who in 1966 had beaten Pat Brown, Nixon's 1962 nemesis. At the end of April, Rockefeller had formally entered the presidential race, but it was too late to get his name on the ballot and his friends had to settle again for a write-in effort.

Reagan was to the Republicans what Governor George Wallace of Alabama was to the Democrats. He too had profited politically from the rage against the disruptive changes of the decade. Working-class and middle-class white Californians shared with other conventional Americans the anger at crime, rising welfare costs, ghetto disorders, and "the erosion of traditional values." But California had its own special problem: the radical students. Most traditional Americans—whether in Brooklyn or Berkeley—deplored the student disrupters, but nowhere was the revulsion so strong as in the Golden State, where the student revolt had begun and where it continued with unmatched rancor for the remainder of the decade. Having taxed themselves to establish the best state university system in the nation, many Californians felt betrayed at what seemed the gross ingratitude of the young.

A former liberal whose battles during the late 1940s with the Communists in the Screen Actors' Guild had, he said, driven him to the right, Reagan had won a million more votes for governor in 1966 than Brown as the man who would restore peace to the campuses. In Sacramento he had run a competent and relatively moderate administration. Though frequently stronger on conservative rhetoric than conservative action, he had become the great right hope, heir apparent of Barry Goldwater.

Reagan had promised the California voters that he would serve his full four-year term as governor, but he found it difficult to resist the call of the party's conservatives to challenge Nixon. Much of his support came from Dixie, from that new breed of young Republican lawyers, technicians, and M.B.A.s who had accompanied the rise of the postwar South's spanking new regional offices, shopping malls, and sleek Holiday Inn motels. These people saw Reagan as a country-club version of George Wallace, a man who would preserve the social status quo and show the conservative flag without the crude gibes and fractured grammar of the Alabama redneck.

Reagan did not personally canvass in Oregon. The governor's advisers had read the polls and knew that outside the South their man had only shallow public support. They also had to reckon with his litany of party unity. Yet they believed that he could win if something—a "prairie fire," they phrased it—could be ignited.

The Oregon primary became a battle of TV image making. Reagan's chief weapon was a film biography that ignored his years as an actor and highlighted his recent political triumphs, especially the victory over Brown. As a performer in political film, the former movie star was mediocre.

Nixon too relied on a TV blitz. He was wary of TV. It had, he believed, destroyed him in 1960 when, until the broadcast debates in late September, he had been running ahead of JFK, his inexperienced and untested opponent. And there was substance to his fear. Nixon had little physical grace. His hairline formed a widow's peak; his nose in profile resembled a ski jump. He moved awkwardly. One of his media aides described him "as a funny-looking guy" who appeared "like somebody hung him in a closet overnight. . . ."[10]

But by this time Nixon had been taken over by the political engineers and image manipulators who would help bring him down five years later. In January, at the suggestion of Robert ("Bob") Haldeman, a Seattle advertising executive who had worked for Nixon during his California gubernatorial run, the candidate put himself in the hands of media experts under the overall command of Frank Shakespeare, a former CBS executive. These men recognized that their man posed a problem. But impressed with their own stylish McLuhanesque theories, they believed they could concoct a new persona by creative use of the electronic image. A new Nixon could be spliced into existence.

In Oregon, on the last day of the campaign, they presented their candidate in a format that they would repeat a dozen times before November. For ninety minutes Nixon sat before the cameras in a Portland studio receiving phoned-in questions from Oregon voters. These were screened by an old friend, Bud Wilkinson, the University of Oklahoma football coach, to filter out the hostile ones. Those allowed through, the candidate could field with ease.

In the end, the amateur thespian beat the pro. Nixon took 73 percent of the vote to Reagan's 23 percent. Rockefeller's write-in took a tiny leftover.

That evening a happy Nixon flew out of Portland for Atlanta certain that he would sew up the campaign in the next few days. But one hurdle remained. Southern Republicans still favored Reagan, the true conservative, and to many the sectional reality was expressable in a simple formula: if not Reagan, then Wallace. To win at Miami and then go on to victory in November, Nixon would have to satisfy these men that he was safe on race and on Russia.

On May 31 Nixon conferred for three hours in the Georgia capital with Senator John Tower of Texas, Peter O'Donnell, chairman of the Texas state Republican party, and other southern state leaders. The next day Senator Strom Thurmond of South Carolina, the former Dixiecrat turned Republican, arrived by chartered plane to join the discussions. At these two meetings Nixon sketched the contours of what came to be called his "southern strategy."

Nixon did not sell his political soul. He would refuse as president, he said, to sanction forced busing of school children for the sake of racial balance. On the other hand, he would oppose giving federal funds to any school district that practiced blatant segregation. He would discourage a federal fair housing law, but he would not oppose state laws on the subject. He would avoid as his running mate a "divisive" man, one to his left ideologically. Thurmond, the ranking Republican member of the Senate Armed Services Committee, was most impressed with the candidate's tough anti-communism. As president, Nixon promised, he would endorse a major antiballistics missile system. The candidate left Atlanta with the word of the South's Republican power brokers that as far as they were concerned he was "the one."

There was nothing startling in the assurances Nixon gave the southern barons. Most of what he promised could have been anticipated. Yet the meeting was another turning point in a year full of change. For almost a hundred years, the "solid South" had been surrendered to the Democrats virtually without a fight. Now the South was back on the Republican agenda. In some sense, the meeting marked the return of two-party politics to the whole nation.

After Atlanta it was fairly smooth sailing for Nixon, with only the dithering governor of New York standing in the way.

Nelson Rockefeller was the richest Republican candidate, of course. Grandson of John D. Rockefeller, the founder of Standard Oil and the first American billionaire, he was living proof that looks, family money, and fame do not guarantee unhappiness and personal failure. The secret for eluding disaster apparently is to avoid excess and publicity. The Rockefeller brothers—John D. III, Nelson, Laurance, Winthrop, and David—were sheltered but not smothered. They were not buried in possessions. The children of John D. Rockefeller, Jr., were taught the value of money and made to earn it for themselves. They were rewarded with pennies for killing pesky flies, for shining shoes, for hoeing the garden at the Pocantico Hills family estate on the Hudson River. "I was always so afraid that money would spoil my children," "Junior" later noted, "and I wanted them to know its value and not waste it or throw it away on things that weren't worthwhile."[1]

If Nelson acquired his steady and industrious ways from his father, his political bent may have come from his mother's side of the family. Abby Greene Rockefeller was the daughter of Nelson W. Aldrich, a Republican senator from Rhode Island, one of the most powerful men in Washington during the two decades that bracket the beginning of the twentieth century. Nelson bore his grandfather's name, and it does not require much psychological savvy to see how such a relationship could influence his behavior.

After Dartmouth College, Nelson tried business for a time, and his abounding energies ensured success. Not content with merely adding to the family fortune, during the late 1930s he became a major patron of New York's Museum of Modern Art and a key force in the modern art movement. For the rest of his life, art collecting was his solace and his joy, and he accumulated one of the century's most impressive collections of modern painting and sculpture.

Rockefeller's experience in the oil business of Mexico and Venezuela brought him to Washington as coordinator of the Office of Inter-American Affairs in 1940. After the war, into the mid-fifties, he labored on and off as assistant secretary of state for Latin American affairs, as an expert on government reorganization, as under secretary of the newly organized Department of Health, Education, and Welfare, and finally as the president's special assistant for cold-war strategy.

In 1958 Nelson ran for governor of New York against the incumbent Democrat, Averell Harriman, heir of another great American fortune. The Republican candidate had enormous political assets. He was ruggedly handsome, spoke fluent Spanish, exuded boyish charm, and had the common touch. Despite his wealth, he felt comfortable in the dazzle of New York's ethnic kaleidoscope. His only drawback was an inherited dyslexia that made it difficult for him to read a speech without stumbling. Denouncing his opponent as a tool of Tammany Hall bossism, on November 5, Rocky pulled off a major political upset.

Governor Rockefeller quickly became a baron in the Republican party, some said a robber baron, the label scholars had attached to his paternal grandfather. His looks, his charm, his wealth, his money, and his New York base made him an instant leader of the party's liberal, internationalist wing. In 1960, just two years into elective office, he compelled Richard Nixon to come to his thirty-two room Fifth Avenue apartment to accept major changes in the GOP national platform in exchange for not vetoing his presidential nomination. During his second term, he became an obvious presidential candidate himself, but ruined his chances by a divorce and a remarriage to a younger woman with whom he reputedly had had an affair while she was still married to a microbiologist at the family-endowed Rockefeller Institute. The right-wing victory at the 1964 Republican National Convention owed as much to Rocky's vices as to Goldwater's virtues.

Like most Republican moderates, Rockefeller sat on his hands during the 1964 campaign. After the Goldwater fiasco and his own hairsbreadth reelection as governor in 1966, he announced that he was through with the presidency. But the man of action struggled with new self-doubts over the next two years, producing the spectacle of an actor not knowing whether to play Henry V or Hamlet. When Romney withdrew toward the end of the 1968 New Hampshire primary campaign, Rockefeller refused to step into the breach. Then, two months later, prompted by John Hay Whitney and other exemplars of the Eastern old-money upper class who despised Nixon, he announced he would run. But still his campaign lacked energy and drama.

Then came Robert Kennedy's assassination. Now Rocky could see himself as Bobby's populist successor and his interest soared. Two days later he had prepared a speech offering a choice between "a new leadership and old politics," and soon after, hoping to move the polls sharply in his direction and come to Miami as the candidate who could win in November, he set off on a speech-making tour that resembled in its flesh pressing and hysteria Bobby's campaign swings of a month or two before.

The canvass might have RFK's style, but it did not have his substance. Rocky talked of "the right to learn and the right to work" for everyone, of "making slums of old despair into centers of new hope," of "a floor below which nobody will be allowed to fall."[12] But to the end he remained uneasy with a dove position on Vietnam and waffled to the point of incoherence on what he would do about the war if he had his way. All his speech making and twenty- and thirty-point type ads nudged the polls upward only a few percent and failed to translate into much convention support. He arrived in Miami on August 3 with three hundred or so delegate votes and only a sliver of hope that Reagan and he could pool their strength and stop the Nixon juggernaut from a first-ballot victory.

In 1968 Miami Beach was still a sparkling, world-class play city, a ten-mile strip of palms, white sand, glittering stores, and pastel Casa Blancas, Lucernes, Frontenacs, Deauvilles, Eden Rocs, San Soucis, and Fountainbleaus. Built on an elongated barrier island, it was separated from funky, seething, multiracial Miami proper by Biscayne Bay, a two-and-a-half-mile channel bridged by two narrow causeways. Everyone who wrote of the convention remarked on the city's insulation from American reality. No one should expect a resort to expose hundred-dollar-a-day vacationers to life in the raw. But Miami Beach clearly was a never-never land for a major party convention.

The city was chosen mainly for its convention bid of $850,000. Even the fat-cat Republicans found this enticing. But it also offered security in a year when the atmosphere was charged with social incivility and tumult. Those two slender causeways to the mainland were like stopcocks that could be turned off at the slightest hint of social or political rowdiness in the big city a half mile to the west. After the King and Kennedy assassinations, the city had beefed up its security plans. By the time the delegates arrived, the two-hundred-man Miami Beach police force would be supplemented with hundreds of Miami City highway patrolmen, federal G-Men, and Secret Service agents. On the streets the police kept a low profile for the media; it would not do to look like Nazi Germany. But the convention hall itself was an armed camp, surrounded with blue uniforms and a six-foot-high chain-link fence, with an adjacent detention compound for any unruly demonstrators who might slip through.

And the physical environment was as intimidating as the social. In the hotels and restaurants, the blasting air-conditioning chilled the bones. Outside, the city was a sweatbox, with temperatures never below the high eighties and humidity to match. Norman Mailer, the bard of late sixties' America, said that he could feel the jungle pushing up from beneath the asphalt and cement. Surviving early August in Miami Beach, he wrote in his grossed-out macho way, was like "being obliged to make love to a 300-pound woman who has decided to get on top."[13]

The newspaper humorist Russell Baker would write that the Republican convention had been "planned in advance by six bores and a sadist."[14] Everything seemed to be settled; Nixon had it sewed up and the five thousand delegates and alternates and their families, the six thousand journalists, and the—at times—vast TV audience had little drama to focus attention on.

There was, in truth, some mini-drama at least, but it had been driven away from the convention floor and into the private suites of the candidates and the major state delegations. Would the center hold? The Nixon counters and calculators had toted up for their candidate more than the 667 first-ballot votes needed to win. But erosion, or the threat of erosion, began almost as soon as the delegates arrived. The challengers pushed hard. On Monday evening Rockefeller pulled out the stops with a giant bash for eight thousand delegates, chieftains, spouses, and assorted hangers-on with caviar, shrimp aspic, turkey, pâté, and chocolate éclairs. There were two bands, one for each room, and eight free bars. And the candidate—smiling, virile, hand-pumping.

Monday was also a busy time for the challenger from the right. For several weeks before the convention, Reagan had abandoned his coy-lover approach and had been actively wooing the southern delegates. Arriving in Miami on Thursday, July 31, he had delivered a rousing attack on the law breakers, the student disrupters, and the peace advocates. On Monday he had lunch in his Deauville suite with a group of influential southerners, making his pitch that he was their man. That afternoon Senator William Knowland, the spokesman for the California delegation, emerged from a Deauville caucus room to announce that the delegation "hereby recognizes [that] Governor Reagan in fact is a leading and bona fide candidate for President." The candidate himself acted surprised. "It all came out of a clear blue sky,"[15] he declared modestly. Once again his performance was judged mediocre.

At one point that Monday evening, panic struck Nixon's southern supporters. Some Dixie delegates were still worried that Dick was not sound enough on southern issues and threatened to defect. At ten o'clock, Thurmond and Harry Dent, the South Carolina state Republican chairman, met with Nixon and told him of the danger. He would have to make his views of school desegregation as clear to the rank and file as he had to the leaders in Atlanta in June. He would also have to give reassurances about his running mate. Rumors were flying that Nixon might turn to a northern moderate like Senator Charles Percy of Illinois or

Senator Mark Hatfield of Oregon to balance the ticket. If he did, the South would go for Wallace in November.

The next morning Nixon stopped the hemorrhaging in two back-to-back buns-and-coffee breakfast meetings at his Hilton suite with the southern delegates. He assured the breakfasters that his choice of vice-president would not be made without consultation. No one who did not agree with his views on the issues would be acceptable. Question-and-answer sessions followed in which he repeated his hostility to "forced busing" and to federal open housing laws and declared that his position on Vietnam was peace, but peace through strength. A fan of Theodore Roosevelt, Nixon trotted out TR's favorite foreign policy motto: What we've got to do is walk softly and carry a big stick.[16]

After this, nothing could stop the Nixon express. In Rockefeller's case it was a question of the chickens coming home to roost. Over the years Rocky had made too many enemies in the party, people who disliked his money, his morals, his political methods. In Reagan's case it was realism. In their hearts many delegates thought he was as right as Goldwater, but they had had lean years following their hearts, and this time they meant to follow their heads. Like it or not, Nixon *was* the one!

While the chieftains plotted, bargained, and cajoled, the platform committee plugged away under the gentle instruction of Everett Dirksen, the senior senator from Illinois. Called the "Wizard of Ooze," Dirksen looked like a bloodhound but had the finesse of a fox. Under his deft hand, the document that emerged was an amorphous all-things-to-all-men statement that no one need fear, or seriously regard, one that could accommodate Reagan at one end and Rockefeller at the other without embarrassing either. This time, again, there would be no repetition of 1964.

The convention had already formally opened at 10:00 A.M. on August 5 with Ray Bliss, chairman of the Republican National Committee, calling the handful of inattentive delegates to order. The rest of the day, that evening, and the day following were a blur of welcoming ceremonies and speeches by Goldwater, by

Senator Edward Brooke of Massachusetts, the party's leading black spokesman, and by keynoter Daniel Evans, the young governor of Washington, whose speech, intended to get Republican blood moving, did nothing to break the grip of boredom. On Tuesday Dirksen presented the platform, and his remarks—his usual mixture of oil and ham—momentarily amused the delegates. Just past midnight, on Wednesday morning, the delegates adopted the foggy platform.

Wednesday had been scheduled for the balloting, but the nominating speeches and the mandatory floor demonstrations for favorite sons and real candidates went on interminably. The governor of Maryland, Spiro ("Ted") Agnew, did the honors for Nixon with an address of monumental banality. On Wednesday the Nixon bloc almost came unstuck when members of the Florida delegation threatened to desert to Reagan. The fission was stopped only at the last minute with the help of Thurmond. Meanwhile, across the causeways, the Miami ghetto exploded in violence over a minor racial incident. Despite pleas for calm by Ralph Abernathy, Martin Luther King's successor, and Florida Governor Claude Kirk, both of whom came running from the convention, violence worsened the next day with black mobs dragging white motorists out of their cars and beating them and police spraying tear gas and bullets over a large area of Liberty City. Three Miamians died and hundreds were arrested before the rampage stopped on the eighth, but the causeways served their purposes. Few reverberations had reached the convention hall.

The balloting finally began after 1:00 A.M. on Thursday morning with the time-honored alphabetic roll call. There was some suspense when the list reached Florida, but the center held and Nixon got thirty-two of the state's thirty-four votes. New Jersey was a surprise. The state's liberal senator, Clifford Case, was a favorite-son candidate, trying to hold the line for Rockefeller. But half of his delegation revolted and demanded an individual poll. All forty of the men and women came up one by one to the microphone and declared their preference. Eighteen deserted Case and went for Nixon. The rest of the delegations fell into place, and at 1:50 A.M., Wisconsin pushed Nixon over the top.

The final results were Nixon 692, Rockefeller 277, and Reagan 182, with scattered votes for favorite sons.

By immemorial custom, victorious presidential candidates dictate their running mates to the convention that has just honored them. Nixon would do so too, but within certain constraints.

It seems likely that he had decided weeks before Miami to chose Spiro Agnew, the Maryland governor, as the man who would satisfy the South yet not profoundly offend the North. The strategy at this point was to accept a Wallace sweep in deepest Dixie, but try for the "rimland," the border states from Maryland through Missouri. A Greek American from Baltimore County, Agnew could claim to understand urban and ghetto problems. He had also originally been a Rockefeller liberal who had turned to Nixon only after his hero had played Hamlet once too often. But the beauty of it was that Agnew looked both ways at once. Though a certified moderate, he had fiercely attacked Rap Brown and other black militants, and at the time of Baltimore's post–Martin Luther King upheaval had condemned the city's black leaders for failing to denounce the looters and rioters. The tirade had been widely publicized, and it abruptly changed Agnew's image. "That speech," former Maryland Governor Theodore McKeldin later noted, "made him the darling of the Strom Thurmond set. If he hadn't made it Thurmond would never have heard of him and he wouldn't have become Vice President."[17]

The party liberals, led by Congressman Charles Goodell of New York, briefly resisted, but their attempt to nominate first Mayor John Lindsay of New York City and then Romney quickly broke down when Nixon intervened. At Nixon's request, Lindsay nominated Agnew and the handpicked candidate won the nomination handily.

Nixon gave his acceptance speech to a crammed auditorium of happy Republicans certain that victory was near. He had scratched it out on yellow legal pads at Montauk, Long Island, the week before and then repeatedly polished it until it sounded just right. The address was a mixture of the trite, the shrewd, and the touching. Eisenhower was lying in Walter Reed Hospital following a severe heart attack, and Nixon could not resist invoking the name of the party's hero and most successful recent vote getter. He had spoken to Mrs. Eisenhower, he said, and she had told him that nothing would make the ailing general happier than a Republican victory in November. "Let's win this one for Ike."[18] Republican convention delegates are nothing if not sentimental, and the audience roared its approval.

Once past this opener, however, the speech became an uncanny echo of 1968 America as seen from the nation's heartland. The core was a calculated appeal to the center and an attack on the agents of dissent and disorder. Nixon referred to "the great majority of Americans, the forgotten Americans, the non-shouters, the non-demonstrators" who went about their honest business and decent lives and gave "lift to the American dream. . . ." He attacked the Great Society policy of "pouring billions of dollars into programs that have failed."[19]

Civil rights militants, the left, and many liberals would say that Nixon was sending the same racist signal as Wallace, but that would be too simple. He was not a racist and had once advised Republicans not to go seeking the "fool's gold" of racist votes. He now put in a word for racial justice. "If we are to have respect for law in America, we must have laws that deserve respect."[20] His policies for the ghetto would be "American private enterprise," the "greatest engine of progress ever developed in the history of man." This statement would inspire derision on the left, though it does not seem so evasive and foolish today, and even in 1968 it was not so far from Bobby Kennedy's own ghetto cure-all.

The candidate soon turned to that other heartland anguish, Vietnam. Despite the liberals' suspicions, only the gun freaks and the power crazies liked the war as such. Though Republicans on the whole were surely more reluctant to cut and run than their opponents, even the middle Americans who made up the party's rank and file anguished over the war. The problem was how to end it satisfactorily. Nixon's words were contrivedly ambiguous. He denounced the "four years in Vietnam with no end in sight" and promised "to bring an honorable end" to the struggle. But he proposed nothing new—except his own "new leadership." As a sop to his constituents, he pledged a tough foreign policy line to create a new world respect for America, but also offered to extend "the hand of friendship" to the Russians and even to the Chinese.

The past master of synthetic emotion ended on a note of genuine compassion with touching echoes of his own lower-middle-class childhood in Whittier, California. On this evening of personal triumph, he said, he saw the "face of a child." It was a child that lived in a great city. He was a black child, a white child; a Mexican, Polish, Italian child. It did not matter; he was an American child. That child dreamed the American dream and yet he "awakens to a living nightmare of poverty, neglect, and despair." He fails in school; he ends up on welfare; he dies in Vietnam. To millions of children "in this rich land, this is their prospect of the future."

He also saw another child. This one heard the trains go by at night and dreamed of distant places. This child was aided on his journey through life by a self-sacrificing father who helped him get to college and by a Quaker mother who wept when he went off to war but understood his need to go. He was helped through other important junctures of life by a great teacher, by a remarkable football coach, by a courageous wife and loyal children. And then, "in his chosen profession of politics," by millions "who worked for his success." And tonight "he stands before you— nominated for President of the United States of America."[21]

Can one read these words and not exclaim: What a mixture of the grand and the shoddy is man!

Nixon and Agnew left soon after for a week of strategy sessions in California, stopping at the LBJ Ranch to be briefed on the latest Vietnam developments. The president wanted desperately to keep politics from intruding into his conduct of the war and the negotiations in Paris and brought in Secretary of State Dean Rusk, Richard Helms of the CIA, and Cyrus Vance, a delegate to the Paris talks, to explain to the Republican candidates what was happening. Nixon agreed that any concession by the United States without a quid pro quo from Hanoi would be irresponsible. After the briefing, the Johnsons served lunch—steak, corn on the cob, and Lady Bird's homemade tollhouse cookies. Nixon pronounced the meal "delicious."

A week near San Diego with aides and advisers making campaign plans did not prove restful, and Nixon retreated shortly to Key Biscayne to relax before the rigors of the campaign. The ball was now in the Democrats' court.

Here confusion reigned. Senator Eugene McCarthy was Bobby Kennedy's obvious heir, and in the weeks following the June 5 assassination, blocs of voters, especially blacks and Hispanics, shifted into his camp. Money also poured in, for the first time providing a margin of comfort. On June 18, two weeks after the California primaries, Gene carried a plurality of New York's 123 elected Democratic convention delegates and helped get the Democratic senatorial nomination for the obscure Paul O'Dwyer over the New York regulars' candidate. The presidential polls also looked good. Gene was ahead of Vice-President Hubert Humphrey, his remaining opponent, especially among moderate Republicans and independents.

McCarthy's own account of the events following Bobby's murder depicts him as a political whirlwind, rushing from coast to coast, from North to South, speaking to conventions, caucuses, Democratic meetings, and reform groups, trying to harvest the Kennedy loyalists and to win the uncommitted. The chapter in his book is called "The Great Delegate Hunt."

But the truth is that the rebel candidate, and his candidacy, faded fast. According to Jeremy Larner, his young speech writer, California had exhausted Gene's capacity for political self-seeking, and he had reverted to the complex man of thought who, in his special Thomistic way, preferred to be right than president. "Now in the heat of a lost, hot summer, while millions hoped for him," Larner writes, "Gene McCarthy regressed to his balanced presentation of self, to the sacred ceremony of his personality."[22] Hubert Horatio Humphrey was the inevitable beneficiary.

The Humphrey of 1968 is a tragic figure, a man trapped by loyalty and degraded by the object of that loyalty.

Born in South Dakota in 1911, the vice-president grew up in Doland, a town of six hundred, where his father was a hardworking druggist. Hubert's relationship with his father would be a major formative influence in his life. A former salesman, Hubert senior conferred his gift of gab on his son. No one could be as glib as HHH. Lyndon Johnson would later say that "Hubert has the greatest coordination of mind and tongue of anybody I know."[23] During 1968 the two would not always be in synch.

Hubert senior also taught his son the lesson of loyalty. During the Depression the elder Humphrey moved with his family to Huron, a larger South Dakota town, where he tried again to make a go as a druggist. Hubert, then at the University of Minnesota, had to leave college and help out in the pharmacy to keep the Humphreys from financial disaster. Those five years of bondage to the Huron drugstore were excruciating for the young man, and he paid for his frustrations with periodic fainting spells. Not until 1937, when he returned with his young wife to the university, did the incidents cease.

HHH was a "Prairie Populist" in the mold of William Jennings Bryan, George Norris, Robert La Follette, and other leaders who had swept out of the heartland into national politics as champions of the "common man." His liberalism came originally from his father, a rare Democrat in a Republican sea, a leftover from the farm-belt Bryan tradition. His heritage was powerfully reinforced by the Depression and the New Deal. As a graduate student in political science at Louisiana State University, Hubert junior had written his master's thesis on the political philosophy of the New Deal. The essay was so partisan that his thesis adviser, himself a New Dealer, asked him to tone it down. Later, as mayor of Minneapolis and United States senator from Minnesota, his ideal was activist government that could intervene to help the weak and the hapless. Franklin Roosevelt, or at least the shiny image his disciples created out of the imperfect reality, would remain Humphrey's ideal. These attitudes made him the perfect partner to LBJ, the self-proclaimed perfecter and fulfiller of the incomplete New Deal revolution.

The vice-presidency consigned Humphrey to a worse bondage than the one imposed by Hubert senior thirty years before. This time humiliation was an added ingredient. In 1964 Johnson made Humphrey crawl for the vice-presidential nomination, using him to create some drama in a his own otherwise cut-and-dried coronation ceremony. To the very last minute the president dangled the prize before both Minnesota senators and only gave Humphrey the nod when McCarthy refused to continue the charade.

Before submitting his name to the convention at Atlantic City, LBJ had delivered a stern White House lecture to Humphrey on loyalty. Being vice-president was "like a marriage with no chance of divorce. . . ." *He* had been totally loyal to Kennedy, he reminded Humphrey, and had avoided upstaging his chief. Hubert must do likewise. Eager as a puppy dog to be named, Humphrey had responded solemnly: "You can trust me, Mr. President."[24]

And Humphrey had been loyal—to a fault. For some reason, perhaps to avenge his own uncongenial subordination to John Kennedy, Johnson delighted in degrading his vice-president. Soon after the 1964 convention he had invited Humphrey to the ranch and there had exhibited the uncomfortable-looking vice-presidential candidate to the media perched on a horse, wearing full cowboy regalia. A month after the inauguration, he had denied him the honor of representing the United States at Winston Churchill's funeral in London and had sent Chief Justice Earl Warren instead.

Far worse was Johnson's insistence that the vice-president go along on Vietnam. Humphrey had no difficulty siding with the president on domestic policy; the Great Society was everything that he himself had fought for during the previous twenty-five years. But he had profound misgivings about America's role in Vietnam. In February 1965, just after the Vietcong attack that tripped off Operation Rolling Thunder and the beginning of American escalation, Humphrey, an official member of the National Security Council, had warned against a violent response. He soon learned that the council was meeting without him. Before long the vice-president was also being cut out of other foreign policy roles, even ceremonial ones, although he quickly abandoned any attempt to oppose the president's Vietnam policy and in fact soon talked himself into believing that Johnson was right.

The demeaning process did not end there. For much of the four years that the two men were yoked, Johnson treated his vice-president as a nuisance whose natural extroversion and loquacity were dangerous to himself and to national security. He scolded him for leaks and tried to reduce his public visibility by restricting his official staff and even limiting his use of government planes. Humphrey's speeches had to be submitted to the White House for prior approval and were often butchered. The public, used to the vice-president's extroversion, perceived his dilemma, and as early as the summer of 1965, Tom Lehrer, the topical bard of Harvard, composed one of his witty songs about it:

> Whatever became of Hubert?
> Has anyone heard a thing?
> Once he shone on his own,
> Now he sits alone
> and waits for the phone to ring.[25]

Johnson's sadistic mistreatment of his vice-president continued after his March 1968 renunciation of a second full term. Their first meeting after the withdrawal speech was cool. The president did not urge Humphrey to run in his place; he did not offer to help. The vice-president's main problem, he said, would be money. Johnson was a powerful money-raiser whose persuasive powers could have helped his fellow Democrat immensely. His remark was chilling.

But in fact, money for the nomination race for a time poured in. Scores of rich Democrats feared and hated Bobby, and men like Gardner Cowles of *Look* magazine, motor magnate Henry Ford II, and investment banker John Loeb quickly pledged financial support to Humphrey to deny the New York senator the nomination. Early backing also came from the trade union leaders, people with whom Humphrey had been closely allied ever since his days as mayor of Minneapolis.

The vice-president announced his candidacy on April 27 at a large meeting in Washington's Shoreham Hotel. It was a joyous occasion for Humphrey, the culmination of twenty years of work and hope. The staging was effective, with the network TV cameras coming on just as Senator Fred Harris of Oklahoma brought the audience of two thousand roaring to its feet with his warm-up talk.

Humphrey's prepared speech was statesmanlike, and the audience chanted "We want Hubert" at every pause. Unfortunately, the enthusiasm was too infectious, and the vice-president could not let well enough alone. At the end he ad-libbed: "Here we are, the way politics ought to be in America, the politics of happiness, the politics of purpose, the politics of joy. And that's the way it's going to be, all the way, from here on out."[26]

He paid dearly for his exuberance. Politics did not seem especially joyful to many Americans in late April 1968. Young men were being shipped home from Vietnam in body bags at the rate of two hundred a day; the campuses were in turmoil; the ghettos were exploding like firecrackers. Just three weeks before, Martin Luther King had been gunned down in Memphis. Humphrey's words seemed fatuous. The newspaper editorial writers chided the vice-president for his lack of solemnity in the face of the nation's crisis, and from Indiana came the voice of Robert Kennedy: "It is easy to say this is the politics of happiness —but if you see children starving in the Delta of Mississippi and despair on the Indian reservations, then you know that everybody in America is not satisfied."[27]

Despite the gaffe, during the next few weeks the vice-president picked up hundreds of delegate votes. He had decided that he could not enter the primaries, even those where he was still eligible to appear. It was simply too late, and his two opponents already had the inside track. But in the caucus states, the convention states, where the regular party leaders sat firmly in the saddle, he easily bested his opponents. To these regulars Humphrey was Mr. Democrat, a party man like themselves. His opponents were rebels who had challenged their own president and threatened to damage their party.

During these weeks of May and early June, Humphrey was also helped by the moratorium on Vietnam that accompanied the preliminaries of the Paris peace talks between the United States and the Vietnam enemy. The vice-president could avoid defining his Vietnam position on the plea of not wanting to jeopardize the negotiations.

Bobby's assassination was a shattering blow. As Muriel Humphrey, the candidate's astute wife, would say, "The bullet that killed Bobby Kennedy also wounded Hubert."[28] The murder dried up the vice-president's source of funds. With Bobby gone and McCarthy's campaign stalled, the conservative money men saw little need to pour dollars into the Humphrey coffers. Some of the money would later come back to finance the campaign itself, but much of the anti-Kennedy funds would go to Nixon after August.

More damaging still, the murder in Los Angeles cast a pall over national politics. Millions of men and women who would normally have voted Democratic—the young, the black, the academic—were jolted out of their fragile commitment to traditional politics. It would be hard after the Chicago convention to get them to work for any candidate or even to get them to the polling stations on election day.

The Democratic convention itself made a bad situation worse. The October 1967 Pentagon march had impressed the antiwar movement's left wing with the value of militant tactics. Soon after, radical antiwar leaders began to discuss staging civil disobedience protests at the major 1968 party conventions. In December the National Mobilization had briefly considered the issue of a major demonstration at the August Democratic convention, but the Mobe leaders were divided and the meeting adjourned without a plan.

Undeterred by the organization's indecisiveness, in February, Mobe chieftain David Dellinger authorized former Students for a Democratic Society leaders Tom Hayden and Rennie Davis to open an office on Chicago's South Dearborn Street to plan for the Democratic convention. The two New Left veterans were soon joined by other SDS alumni, Kathy Boudin, Jeff Shero, and John Froines. Soon after setting up shop, Hayden and Davis composed a position paper, "Movement Campaign 1968—an Election Year Offensive," proposing tactics for August and presented it in late

March to a strategy meeting of black militants and left antiwar groups held at Lake Villa, north of Chicago. The plan explicitly eschewed "violence and disruption against the Democratic National Convention"; the approach should be "nonviolent and legal." But its prescription of "massive confrontation with our government," an "attack on the Democratic Convention," and "pinning the delegates in the International Amphitheatre,"[29] made the demurrer seem only a device to appease the antiwar centrists and avoid legal prosecution. The meeting disbanded without a program, but not before a disruptive invasion by long-haired crazies led by Jerry Rubin and Abbie Hoffman who tossed posters in the air inscribed: ABANDON THE CREEPING MEAT-BALL, COME TO CHICAGO.[30]

The Hoffman–Rubin invaders were the Yippies, that fusion of the personal and political born of reefer madness that 1968 New Year's Day in Hoffman's East Village pad. However scary the Hayden–Davis scenario, it was easily outclassed by the unnerving plans of the new insurgents on the scene. The same people who gave the country the Pentagon exorcism ceremony planned to provide something especially picturesque for Chicago, the Festival of Life.

As announced in March by the Youth International Party (YIP), the Festival of Life would be the counter to the Democrats' "Convention of Death." The Yippies would invite every long-haired, pot-smoking, cop-hating, peace freak to come to Chicago for a fiesta of rock concerts, poetry readings, workshops on LSD and draft resistance, films, marches, and light shows, all to be held in a Chicago park as yet unnamed. The key ceremony would be the nomination of a pig ("Pigasus") for president on the campaign pledge: "They nominate a president and he eats the people. We nominate a president and the people eat him."[31] Besides the official agenda, there would be, the handouts from Yippie New York headquarters promised, a wave of chaos-creating convention high jinks. In Chicago, "battalions of super-potent yippie males" would "seduce female convention-goers";[32] phony Yippie-manned taxis would pick up Democratic delegates at their hotels and drop them off miles away in Wisconsin; Yippies would take over the Chicago office of the National Biscuit Company and distribute bread and cookies to the masses; they would stage a mass nude-in at Lake Michigan; they would put LSD in the city water supply. The underground press reported all this, but so did the mainstream media. The reporters knew a good story when they saw it.

Viewed from the sobersides 1980s, much of this seems amusing, even endearing. We know that nobody died, that chaos was not unleashed on the nation. But we must not misjudge intentions. The Yippie Festival of Life was meant to disrupt one of America's most sacred rituals and provoke a violent response. Years later Rubin admitted to Abe Peck, editor of the underground Chicago *Seed*, "We were not just innocent people who were victimized by the police. We came to plan a confrontation. . . ."[33]

The Yippie plan, as intended, sent the public's circuits into overload. Mayor Richard Daley, who had issued his "shoot to kill order" against arsonists at the time of the Martin Luther King riots, reared back in outrage. Nobody was going to make a shambles of *his* convention. Chicago's reputation, and his own, was on the line, and the Democratic National Convention would come off without a hitch, come what may.

The mayor prepared for a major insurrection. The city and the Convention Planning Committee placed all of Chicago's police force on twelve-hour shifts during the convention week, releasing hundreds of uniformed city police, plainclothes detectives, and undercover Red Squad agents for exclusive convention duty. A Chicago Police Department mobile task force of three hundred, equipped with mace, tear gas, gas masks, helmets, nightsticks, and shotguns, would patrol the Loop, the International Amphitheatre, and Lincoln Park in squad cars. In reserve, in case the turmoil got entirely out of hand, would be five thousand national guardsmen and six thousand army regulars equipped with rifles, flamethrowers, and bazookas.

But even radicals and antiwar people had their doubts about the demonstrations. The kids who Hoffman and Rubin were inviting to Chicago were going to get hurt, many said. Daley's cops were going to bloody heads; there would be a massacre. The expectation was reinforced by a "Yip-In" dress rehearsal at New

York's Grand Central Station in March. Cops and five thousand Yippies mixed it up in a wild donnybrook that produced a profusion of cracked bones, bloodied scalps, and misdemeanor arrests.

The reaction soon set in. Abe Peck of the Chicago *Seed* was one of Rubin's friends and at the time of the Lake Villa meeting had agreed to help out at the Chicago end. After Johnson's withdrawal on March 31, Yippie enthusiasm waned. Soon after, following a series of police raids on Chicago hippies and longhairs, Peck began to have second thoughts, too. Robert Kennedy's assassination in June revived Yippie interest, but left Peck unmoved. Fearful of a massacre, in the early August edition of *Seed,* Peck issued a blast against the Festival of Life that ended with the warning: "Don't come to Chicago if you expect a five-day Festival of life, music and love. The word is out. Chicago may host a festival of blood."[34] Even more damaging was the response of *Rolling Stone,* a newly established monthly devoted to the rock music scene. The Yippie leaders were dangerous Pied Pipers who were leading the young astray, wrote editor Jann Wenner. Musicians and rock fans must reject the "new political exploiters."[35]

And generally speaking, they did. The festival turnout was poor. The Rubin–Hoffman Dynamic Duo had announced that a dozen famous rock bands would be there—the Beatles, the Rolling Stones, the Grateful Dead, the Jefferson Airplane, and others. Only one, John Sinclair's Motor City Five (MC-5), showed up. They had promised one hundred thousand hippies and Yippies. Only twenty-five hundred appeared, most from out of town, with a few hundred from the Chicago area. In addition, several hundred Chicago street kids, white and black, delinquent and political, piled on when the action got hot and heavy.

The Mobe did not do much better. On June 29 it formally announced its plans. The Mobe demonstration would "confront" the "warmakers in Chicago" to show that "the politicians do not speak for us." Operating out of thirty small neighborhood centers, it would launch a "little Tet offensive" on "warfare state" targets around the city capped by a march on the convention hall to "vomit" on Humphrey's "politics of joy."[36] This militant scheme, concocted by the Hayden–Davis group and the Dellingerites, dismayed the moderates. The Trotskyists saw no point in provoking the authorities. More serious, thousands of middle-of-the-road peace marchers who might have come to Chicago were frightened off by visions of guerrilla warfare in the streets of the Windy City.

The militants were not solely to blame for the sparse turnout. Daley's refusal to grant parade and outdoor rally permits and requests for sleeping space in six city parks also kept people away. The Mobe leaders got Roger Wilkins of the Justice Department Community Relations Division to intercede on their behalf, but it did no good. Even a lawsuit only extracted permission for one Mobe rally, to take place at Grant Park on the afternoon of Wednesday, August 28, the day of the nominations. The Yippies fared even worse. The mayor refused to comply with any of their requests, and those who came to Chicago faced the prospect of an 11:00 P.M. parks curfew and strict enforcement of the pot laws that promised to cramp their style painfully. By refusing to allow peaceful outlets for dissent, the mayor was probably ensuring violence.

Two other groups that might have swelled the demonstrator rosters during the convention were also sparsely represented. After Robert Kennedy's murder, McCarthy and Allard Lowenstein had organized the Coalition for an Open Convention to bring the insurgent Democrats together. For a time this group considered a program of mass antiwar, antiadministration rallies. Then on August 12 McCarthy told his supporters to stay home and register their opposition by demonstrations in their own communities to avoid "unintended violence."[37] Some obviously ignored his advice. A thousand or so of the people in the thick of the action on the streets, in the parks, or at the entrances to the hotels were young men and women who had fought for Gene, some since New Hampshire. But this was a modest turnout all told.

The organized student New Left also by and large stayed away. By this time SDS had no use for even insurgent electoral politics. On the other hand the convention was an opportunity to increase membership, and SDS brought five hundred recruiters to Chicago to proselytize among the McCarthy kids.

Add the McCarthyites to the Yippies, the SDSers, and the assorted street kids, black and white, and the total figure for the militant protesters was no more than five thousand or so.

Chicago hosted two distinct dramas in late August. The less sensational took place in the smoky convention hotel rooms and on the amphitheatre floor.

Almost no one seriously believed that Humphrey could be stopped. Nixon's nomination at Miami seemed to have all but destroyed whatever faint hope there was to shift the uncommitted or the skeptical to Gene. Rockefeller would have required the McCarthy wit and style; Nixon, the wise money said, was a weak candidate who could be beaten even by the old war-horse, Humphrey.

But the Humphrey forces remained uneasy and insecure. By early July the Paris talks had stalemated and Vietnam once more became a dangerous liability to the Democrats. The vice-president's advisers urged him to announce some new plan to extricate the United States from the Vietnam swamp. His failure to act would prevent a return of the McCarthy supporters to the Democrats and destroy him at the polls. But Humphrey was paralyzed. However badly LBJ had treated him, he had pledged his loyalty and could not now repudiate it. The commitment touched the deepest core of his personality. He could no more defy the wishes of the president than those of his father. There was also expediency. The vice-president feared LBJ's wrath. Johnson still counted with the party regulars, and it remained in his power to deny the vice-president the nomination.

Despite Humphrey's misgivings, his staff prepared a Vietnam statement calling for an immediate cease-fire and a "de-Americanizing" of the fighting. Humphrey showed it to Johnson and then reeled back in dismay. The president said that Humphrey's proposal might cost the life of his two sons-in-law, both servicemen in Vietnam. If Hubert issued the statement, he would use all the powers of the presidency to "destroy" him.[38] There was obviously no way for Humphrey to break out of the prison before securing the nomination.

The Democratic National Convention in Chicago was a disaster. The city of the "big shoulders" was an armed camp and the atmosphere was tense and oppressive. On the night of Thursday, August 22, four days before the official opening, the police shot and killed an American Indian youth dressed like a hippie a few blocks from Lincoln Park. He had, they said, fired a revolver at them.

The tensions erupted again next morning at the Civic Center, when the Yippies tried to conduct their pig-nominating ceremony. Pigasus, a two-hundred-pound porker bought from a local farmer, would run on a platform of garbage, they announced. The authorities were not amused, and while the TV cameras whirred away, the police moved in and arrested Rubin and five other Yippies. In the confusion Pigasus bolted for freedom but was captured after a brief chase and turned over to the Chicago Humane Society.

The Festival of Life preliminaries began in Lincoln Park, between Lake Shore Drive and Old Town, in the late afternoon of Saturday the twenty-fourth with two thousand people listening or dancing to the music of long-haired kids playing bongo drums and guitars. During the entertainment, Yippie marshals at information tables distributed fliers telling people where to go for free food and shelter, and medical aid, if needed. The Yippie leaders were not yet ready for a clash, however. That morning, wearing a karate jacket for its macho effect, Hoffman had gone to the police command center and told the bemused cops that "no one has any plans to fight with the police."[39] During the afternoon the leaders circulated an announcement that the 11:00 P.M. park curfew was to be observed. Most of the Yippies obeyed the deadline and by 11 o'clock only two hundred people remained. The police ejected this group, but after leaving the park some marched through the streets of the adjacent Old Town neighborhood chanting "Peace now! Peace now! Peace now!" and stoning police cars. Eleven were arrested for disorderly conduct. It was the first police-crowd confrontation and the first violent act of a violent week.

Sunday was far worse. The official festival began that afternoon on a depressing note. The turnout at Lincoln Park was disappointing: only a few thousand people were there, many of them tourists, and only a single rock band, Sinclair's MC-5, had showed. One redeeming feature was the presence of Allen Ginsberg, the ur-father of the counterculture. The bearded Ginsberg stood in the middle of a circle of admirers intoning the Buddhist chant "Om, Om" to exert a calming influence.

Hoffman claims that the police started roughing people up during the afternoon. Stew Albert, one of Jerry Rubin's old Berkeley friends, had his scalp split open by a zealous officer. The uniformed police were certainly out in force, and there were others in civvies trying to pass themselves off as spectators or even participants. The Chicago police even infiltrated the Yippie leadership group. During the convention Rubin found himself befriended by a tough biker in a black T-shirt and helmet who offered to be his bodyguard. He accompanied Rubin through the convention week and joined the protesters' battles. His name was Robert Pierson and he was a Chicago cop. There is also some evidence that disguised police *agents provocateurs* helped incite vandalism and violence in the ensuing days. A decade later, in a review of the 1968 Democratic convention, CBS News would claim that "about one demonstrator in six was an undercover agent."[40]

The real trouble began late that afternoon after the tourists left. The police ordered the Yippies to move a flatbed truck decorated with a purple-and-red Yippie flag, brought in for the MC-5's remaining gigs. As the truck began to roll, Yippies, thinking it was leaving the park, tried to stop it. When the police collared a young man for trying to impede the truck and began to lead him away, the crowd blocked the way. Screaming "Kill the Pigs," "Fuck the Pigs," and "Gestapo Pigs," they attacked the police.[41] The fight quickly died down, but tension soon mounted again.

At about nine o'clock a small group of demonstrators surrounded fifteen police at the Lincoln Park field house and began to jeer at them. Police reinforcements arrived and charged the crowd, hitting everyone in reach. Many people were injured. A volunteer from the Northwestern University medical school, acting as a demonstration medic, reported: "When someone would fall, three or four cops would start beating him. One kid was beaten so badly he couldn't get up. He was bleeding profusely from the head."[42]

At 10:30 P.M. a police patrol car began cruising slowly through the crowd, its loudspeakers blaring: "This is a final warning. The park is closed. All persons now in the park . . . are in violation of the law and subject to arrest."[43] Soon after, the police moved in on the thousand or so demonstrators who remained and drove them out of the park. The Yippies fled into the adjacent streets of Old Town, Chicago's Greenwich Village. The cops followed and clubbed indiscriminately everyone with long hair or a Pancho Villa mustache.

While one group of demonstrators returned to the park, a second contingent proceeded along Michigan Avenue toward downtown. As they moved south, they filled the broad avenue from edge to edge, obstructing traffic. The demonstrators were in a destructive mood, and as they marched they tipped over trash cans and smashed car windshields. When they reached the Michigan Avenue Bridge across the Chicago River, they encountered a line of police who ordered them to clear the bridge. They refused and the police charged, driving them back north.

Once more the action shifted to Lincoln Park. A thousand or so Yippies and other militants had returned to the park and confronted several hundred police. A fierce battle erupted as demonstrators refused to yield to the advancing line of Task Force cops and regular police. Tear gas, clubs, flailing nightsticks, screams, curses, thuds, cries of pain, hurtling rocks and bottles— all marked the brawl. In the fracas the police roughed up newsmen from *Newsweek* and the *Philadelphia Bulletin*. The crowd eventually dispersed.

Away from Lincoln Park, Sunday was peaceful. McCarthy arrived at Midway Airport in the afternoon to be greeted by five thousand enthusiastic supporters still hopeful that Gene could somehow make it over the top. Despite a last minute mike failure, contrived, everyone suspected, by the Daley people, he delivered a pep talk that Norman Mailer, on the scene for his

Harper's articles, called mild and diffident, though nice—like his whole campaign. Humphrey arrived at O'Hare later that day, and Mailer contrasted the two receptions. He saw what he wanted to. Half the Humphrey workers were crew-cut types "who could have gone with Ronald Reagan"; the rest were "out of that restaurant where [the] Mafia shakes hands with the union."[44] That same Sunday the Mobe people held workshops around the city to prepare for actions during the next few days.

The convention opened on Monday, August 26, at the International Amphitheatre, built on the site of the reeking old stockyards. The building was ringed with barbed wire and hemmed in with armed guards. Five miles to the northeast, near the lakefront and Grant Park, were the delegates' hotels.

The convention's major decision, choosing a candidate, held little real suspense. McCarthy could count on perhaps 500 delegates, those he had won himself and many of Kennedy's; as convention week began, Humphrey probably had 1,400 to 1,500, more than the 1,312 needed to nominate.

The two sides inhabited different political worlds. To the McCarthy–Kennedy people, politics was essentially an arena where ideas and principles, right and wrong, contended. They had little respect for the party's existing power brokers or the organized interests that made up the Democratic coalition, and often saw their constituency as the voiceless and unorganized. They hoped to remake the democracy in their own egalitarian, antiwar image and were largely indifferent to the bread-and-butter issues that attracted Democratic voters. It is significant that the solid McCarthy Wisconsin delegation had nine professors and not a single farmer. These were amateurs with the amateurs' virtues of disinterestedness and openness to novelty, but also their indifference to practical results.

Their opponents, the regulars, were pragmatists who saw politics as the art of the possible. They represented the party's insiders, its organized elements—unionized labor, farm groups, and the traditional ethnic blocs, not excluding blacks—who were willing to work within regular channels. These were professionals with the professionals' merits of personal loyalty along with realism and practicality, and the professionals' vices of rigidity and, at times, venality. The regulars were willing to accept half a loaf if that could not be avoided. In precise terms the Humphrey contingent at Chicago included the five hundred or so delegates from the South, committed to the vice-president by their hawk positions on Vietnam and their loyalty to LBJ. The rest consisted of the regulars of the remaining big-city machines like the Daley organization, veteran Democratic office holders, and the delegates delivered to the vice-president by his longtime friends in organized labor.

These characterizations do not do justice to the buzzing confusion of the actual convention environment. There were half-breeds of mixed parentage and crossovers who shifted from side to side. The lines should not be drawn too sharply. But the split into pragmatic professionals and issues-oriented amateurs was there, and it lay at the heart of the battle in Chicago.

The media in its own superficial way focused on the smoke-filled-room maneuvering to stop Humphrey. For a time there was talk of a New Politics coalition behind George McGovern, the dovish Senator from South Dakota. There were also New Politics attempts to draft Ted Kennedy. Neither scheme jelled.

The reporters also played up the battle over the Vietnam plank between doves and hawks. And the struggle was bitter. When they cannot win the big prizes, convention minorities demand symbolic victories. But there was more at stake this time than a symbol. Even supporters of Humphrey feared that their candidate's Vietnam stand was a loser: after nomination he could not win in November if he did not break with the Johnson Vietnam policy.

Several weeks before, Chicago Democratic moderates had met in Washington to see if they could contrive a Vietnam plank sufficiently dovish to help the party in November. Such a statement might save Humphrey from himself: he could run as a dove claiming his hands were tied. These maneuvers did not work. The vice-president could still not bring himself to break with the president, and the scheme died. By the time the Democratic Platform Committee began its hearings in Washington on August 19, a big public battle seemed unavoidable.

The doves were scoring points at the hearings when, in the

middle of Secretary of State Dean Rusk's testimony, news arrived that the Soviets had just invaded Czechoslovakia to oust the disobedient Dubcek government. The brutal Soviet suppression of the brief Prague Spring recharged all the cold-war fears of communism and played into the hands of the hawks. "There goes their issue," chortled the hawkish former Senator William Benton of Connecticut.[45] The doves' position was not helped by an inept McCarthy statement that the invasion was "not a major crisis."[46] By the time the platform committee reconvened in Chicago, any chance of the doves winning had disappeared. They would have to settle for a minority plank at best.

The two planks finally submitted to the convention differed on the trigger point for a bombing halt, on whether Vietnam was a "civil war" or pure aggression from the north, and on whether the United States should force the South Vietnamese to accept the Vietcong in a coalition government. From the distance of twenty years, the contrasts do not seem overpowering. But this ignores the psychological realities. To the McCarthy–Kennedy forces, winning on the Vietnam plank was the only recompense left for the months of effort and sacrifice. To Lyndon Johnson, the issue was whether the party would repudiate his whole foreign policy. He had planned to come to Chicago to celebrate his sixtieth birthday, but how could he if he was going to be spurned by the party he headed? The president pulled every wire he could to prevent the peace plank from winning on the convention floor, but in the end he stayed at the ranch. He would be the first incumbent president since 1944 who failed to attend the nominating convention of his party.

The floor debate on the Vietnam plank was stacked against the peace forces. Mayor Daley, who headed the Illinois delegation, sat just below the podium where he could quarterback the plays by signaling with a wave of his hand. The dissidents of the California, New York, and Wisconsin delegations were exiled to Siberia, the outer reaches of the amphitheatre, where they shouted and waved vainly for recognition from the presiding officer at the podium. Rumors had it that Johnson, though physically absent, was the coach of the whole game, calling the signals through a

Hilton Hotel communications center in direct telephone contact with the Ranch.

But there was no conspiracy, no illegitimate use of power behind the scenes. The defeat of the minority peace plank was a foregone conclusion that reflected the underlying reality: the regulars remained in a majority and did not intend to surrender control to their opponents. When introduced on August 28, three days into the convention, the Vietnam plank provoked three hours of debate. The main speakers for the minority plank were three stalwarts of the Kennedy era—Theodore Sorensen, Ken O'Donnell, and Pierre Salinger—who inveighed against the war's distortions of the economy and its social divisiveness. The majority plank supporters—Senator Edmund Muskie of Maine, Governor Warren Hearnes of Missouri, and Congressman Wayne Hays of Ohio—tried to emphasize the similarities between the positions. But Hays gave away their real feelings when he leaped on the antiwar demonstrators as those who would substitute "beards for brains, license for liberty, . . . pot . . . [for] patriotism, sideburns . . . [for] solutions, . . . [and] riots for reason."[47]

The results were conclusive: 1,567 for the majority, 1,041 for the minority. When the tally ended, the delegates from the McCarthy states tied black bands around their arms and, led by folksinger Theodore Bikel, a New York delegate, sang "We Shall Overcome."

While the reporters and the TV analysts fastened on the platform fight, another, more momentous struggle was taking place, one that would profoundly altar the shape of American party politics for twenty years.

The revolution had begun quietly on June 23 in Hartford, when the Connecticut state Democratic convention chose its delegates to Chicago. Of the forty-three men and women selected, only nine were McCarthy supporters, a result the McCarthy leaders considered a gross undercount of their real support among the state's rank-and-file Democrats. That evening the McCarthy people met and established a Commission on the

Selection of Presidential Nominees to deal with such unbalanced outcomes in the future. With a ten-thousand-dollar donation from a small New York publisher, the committee acquired an office in Greenwich Village, a staff of ten young lawyers, and a director, Thomas Alder, a recent associate in Marcus Raskin's left-wing think tank, the Washington-based Institute of Policy Studies.

After the 1967 New Politics convention disaster and the Peace and Freedom party fiasco, Alder had helped Raskin in an abortive scheme to establish a new national party to the left of the Democrats. He had quickly lost faith in the new party and decided to work within the confines of the Democracy, where his views might find some practical expression. As commission director, Alder now collected a group of liberal McCarthy and Kennedy activists and, with Governor Harold Hughes of Iowa, a McCarthy supporter, as titular chairman, set to work on a plan to reform the way the Democrats chose their convention delegates. On August 4, Hughes and Anne Wexler, a McCarthy delegate from Connecticut, announced that the Hughes group would be presenting proposals to the convention's Rules and Credentials committees when their deliberations got under way.

On August 22, with the official convention opening only six days away, the commission issued an eighty-page booklet, *The Democratic Choice*, suggesting new rules for selecting future delegates and for delegation voting procedures. Specifically, the document recommended repeal of the unit rule that allowed a majority of any state's delegates to cast the entire delegation's vote. It also endorsed proportional state representation for the party's various factions and ideological constituencies. There should no longer be any winner-take-all primaries. Finally, it endorsed per diem allowances to all delegates to insure that no group, rich or poor, was excluded from the roll of delegates for economic reasons.

The Rules Committee took the proposals under advisement. At the same time the Credentials Committee began consideration of a clutch of challenges aimed at southern delegations. Despite the 1964 party pledge in Atlantic City of future racial parity, many had turned up in Chicago without a single black member.

There was little in *The Democratic Choice* in itself to shake the political earth. And besides, most of the Hughes commission proposals were voted down by the same regulars' majority that would defeat the minority peace plank. But then the wheels began to turn, and as if by some sort of invisible force, processes were set in motion that transformed the American political scene. As Byron Shafer says, *"The minority report of the Rules Committee, as augmented by developments in the Credentials Committee itself, was to become the 'mandate' . . . for the greatest systematic change in presidential nominating procedures in all of American history."*[48]

What happened was barely noticed at the time. Though the Rules Committee majority refused to accept the minority's recommendations, it did, as a sop, agree to establish a Democratic Rules Commission charged with "studying and evaluating and codifying" past party rules and "investigating the advisability of rules" changes.[49] The Rules Commission would report its findings to the Rules Committee in due course, and the committee in turn would consider them for adoption at the 1972 national convention. This resolution was shortly merged with another directing the commission to focus on democratic group participation in the delegate-selection process. Still another resolution, adopted by the Credentials Committee, would be linked to this proposal. This established a special committee to study the delegate-selection process, to recommend any needed changes to "assure . . . broader citizen participation in the delegate selection process,"[50] and to bring its suggestions to the 1972 convention.

The three complicated resolutions were lost in the glare of lurid events on the Chicago streets and the dramatic McCarthy–Humphrey struggle in the hotels and amphitheatre and were given scant attention by the media. Even the authors of the two major journalistic works on the 1968 election, Theodore White and the astute English team from the *Sunday Times,* Lewis Chester, Godfrey Hodgson, and Bruce Page, barely noticed them, though their accounts enjoyed the luxury of a year's hindsight. Today, it is plain that they were among the most important events of the convention.

Their consequence, however, lay in the future. In the end, the responsibilities charged to what became the Commission on Party

Structure and Delegate Selection fell into the hands of reformers, many belonging to the New Democratic Coalition, a post-1968 extension of the New Politics perspective. These men and women, under the chairmanship of Senator George McGovern, rewrote the party rules to require each state committee to apportion its delegate distribution in accordance with the age, the race, and the gender of the state's population as a whole. The state committees must not merely cease discriminating against blacks, women, and people under thirty; they must actively take "affirmative steps" to ensure a "reasonable relationship" between the delegation's makeup and the demographic characteristics of the state.

The changes were a belated victory for the 1968 New Politics. Incorporated into "Official Guidelines for Delegate Selection of the Commission on Party Structure and Delegate Selection" and accepted by the Democratic National Committee in 1971, these principles shifted control of party conventions from the people who had traditionally made the decisions, the regulars, to the people who had challenged Hubert Humphrey at Chicago, the New Politics circle. No longer would Democratic national conventions be dominated by the mayors, congressmen, county supervisors, union leaders, and state committee chairmen—predominantly white and predominantly male—who had brokered the party ever since the New Deal. They would be run by a rainbow of blacks, Hispanics, women, and young people, who often had little connection with the party except in presidential years. After 1968 the amateur Democrats, rather than the regulars, would nominate their party's presidential candidates.

The change, as Shafer has noted, represents a shift of social elites. Though made in the name of greater grass-roots and minority participation, it changed the party's "collar" from blue to white. The delegates at Miami Beach in '72, New York in '76 and again in '80, and San Francisco in '84, while more ethnically diverse than in the past, were not proletarian. In fact, there were more M.A.'s, Ph.D.'s, and J.D.'s among them than at Chicago in '68—or Miami in '68. Instead of the trade union leaders, the city clerks, and the courthouse lawyers with diplomas from the local commuter law school, there were now the professors, the social workers, the Ivy League J.D.'s. These changes would erode the party's traditional blue-collar constituency and ultimately contribute to the voter shift to the Republicans in 1980 and 1984. If any single thing made Ronald Reagan president in 1980 and confirmed him in office for a second term, it was the obscure rules changes initiated in Chicago in August 1968.

Monday brought an elevation in street violence. It started with the arrest that afternoon of Tom Hayden on charges of disorderly conduct and obstructing the police, the former for supposedly letting air out of a police car tire on Saturday night. In response, Rennie Davis led five hundred protesters carrying Vietcong flags to police headquarters. There they staged a brief demonstration and moved on. At about five o'clock, the Davis group joined other demonstrators in Grant Park, a two-block-wide band of greensward, fountains, band shell, and monuments running north and south with Lake Michigan to the east and the major delegate hotels to the west.

At first the protesters were content to parade around the equestrian statue of "Black Jack" Logan, the mustachioed Civil War general-politician, chanting "Pigs," "Ho–Ho–Ho Chi Minh," and other radical and antiwar standards. A few dozen climbed the statue and covered the figure with their red flags. Police roughly pulled the climbers down and were rewarded by a barrage of rocks, bottles, and curses.

At times, in the accounts of the protesters' misdeeds, their foul tongues seem their most odious offense. The United States attorney, with barely concealed rage, later reported of this clash that "the vilest conceivable language was used by both men and women. . . ."[51] There can be no question that late-sixties' rebels were adept blasphemers. It was a new skill for middle-class kids, and they enjoyed showing their prowess. It was also designed to provoke and it almost always did. On the other hand the opposition's outrage seems contrived. The Chicago police were themselves past masters of the obscene word and gesture and invariably gave as good as they received.

That evening Hayden was released on bail and, disguising his unmistakable pockmarked face with wig, hat, mustache, beard, and dark glasses, continued to direct Mobe activities from the underground.

The evening's events were wilder. At nine o'clock a crowd poured out of Lincoln Park and began to march south on Clark toward the downtown Loop and the convention hotels. Police intervened, roughed up some marchers including several reporters and photographers from *Newsweek* and the *Chicago Sun-Times,* and arrested forty. Back in the park, as the eleven o'clock curfew neared, remaining protesters constructed a long, flag-decorated barricade of picnic tables to hold back the police. At 11:15 P.M. the police announced that the park was closed. They were greeted with shouts of *"Sieg Heil!"* and "Hell no, we won't go!" from the two thousand demonstrators. When a police squad car approached the barricade, the crowd pelted it with stones, smashing the windshield. At 12:30 A.M., after lobbing smoke and tear gas bombs at the picnic tables, the police charged. Witnesses said they were chanting: "Kill! Kill! Kill!"[52] The police cleared the park but forced the swirl of angry demonstrators into the streets, where protesters and innocent bystanders alike were clubbed, gassed, pounded, and cursed. "The scene was so chaotic," wrote the Walker Commission report authors, who reviewed the convention disorders for the U.S. government, "that even residents [of the neighborhood] attempting to assist the police were roughly handled."[53] A doctor returning home that evening observed some "hippies" tipping over trash cans and throwing stones at cars. He reported this to a policeman who shouted at him, "Listen, you god damn mother fucker, get this fucking car out of here," and then battered the man's car with his nightstick.[54]

There was more of the same on Tuesday. That evening, Jerry Rubin, Peace and Freedom party presidential candidate Eldridge Cleaver, and Black Panther leader Bobby Seale addressed the crowd in Lincoln Park with Seale shouting that blacks would lead the post-Chicago revolution and Rubin announcing that whites would "take the same risks as blacks take."[55] Seale also urged blacks to get their "shotguns," their ".357 magnums," their ".45's and everything else" they could get hold of.[56]

As the curfew once again approached, there were some fifteen hundred people still in the park including a contingent of liberal

clergymen who hoped their presence would restrain police violence. It restrained very little. When the demonstrators refused to
disperse, the police sprayed them with tear gas and chased them
out of the park, hitting and macing bystanders and Yippies
indiscriminately, and being barraged in turn with bricks, bottles,
and rocks.

At almost the same time, at the old Chicago Coliseum, the
Mobe was holding an "unbirthday party" for LBJ. Three thousand people attended, and Dellinger, Ginsberg, comedian Dick
Gregory, novelists William Burroughs and Terry Southern,
French playwright Jean Genet, and folksinger Phil Ochs talked,
performed, or both. The party adjourned at about eleven o'clock
and the crowd left the hall to march north to Grant Park, adjacent
to the Hilton, a major delegate hotel where during the day
demonstrators had already clashed with the police. They reached
their destination just as angry people from Lincoln Park began to
arrive, and the combined crowd was soon shouting curses at the
two lines of police that stood between them and the hotel.

At 1:30 A.M. the deputy superintendent of police announced
that if the protesters remained orderly and did not try to cross
Michigan Avenue to the hotel side they could stay in the park
overnight. The crowd cheered and settled down to a community
sing led by folksingers Peter, Paul, and Mary. Exhausted by as
much as seventeen hours of unrelieved duty, the police now took
the opportunity to bring in replacements. Unfortunately, these
were not additional cops, but six hundred of the national guardsmen on standby alert who arrived at the Hilton in full battle gear
including rifles, shotguns, and gas masks.

The protesters were outraged. "You see, you see," a demonstrator screamed. "They did it—not us! It was peaceful until they
came."[57] They had been duped, they felt, and were now in the
power of the soldiers. The crowd taunted and razzed the guardsmen without mercy, and for a time it looked as if there might be a
clash. Violence was averted, however, and eventually, as daylight
broke, the last of the protesters slipped off to bed.

Wednesday, nomination day, was the nadir of the battle of
Chicago. The Mobe knew that the police were under orders to
break up by whatever means necessary any demonstration closer

to the convention than the Hilton, but they and the Yippies intended to march on the amphitheatre in defiance of the authorities.

That afternoon the Mobe held a rally at the blue-painted band shell in Grant Park, the only demonstration for which the protesters at Chicago had a legal permit. The rally, which drew as many as ten thousand people at its height, was a peaceful round of speeches and songs until a youth shinnied up a flagpole to lower an American flag to half-mast. Several police, stationed around the band shell area perimeter, rushed in, pulled him down, and beat him. The crowd replied with a barrage of stones, sticks, cans, and chunks of concrete. Meanwhile, several demonstrators had removed the disputed flag and replaced it with a red one, a gesture that goaded the police to new fury. A flying squad from the perimeter tried to tear down the red banner and run up the Stars and Stripes. Again the demonstrators responded with missiles including cellophane bags of feces. David Dellinger of the Mobe tried to quiet the crowd without success. At this point, believing apparently that they were about to be attacked, a long line of police advanced on the crowd with raised nightsticks. When they reached a line of demonstrator marshals, they began to swing their clubs at everyone in their way, scattering people in all directions.

Surprisingly, this did not end the rally. When the police withdrew, the demonstrators reassembled for their legal rally. It was now late afternoon, and Dellinger appealed to the authorities to relent on their veto of a nonviolent march from Grant Park to the amphitheatre. They would not budge, and as night fell Dellinger announced that the demonstrators would march permit or no.

But how to get out of the park? The police hemmed the protesters in to the south, in the direction of the convention hall, and they were forced to turn north. The marchers, five thousand to six thousand strong, soon encountered a line of cops blocking their movement and sat down while Sidney Peck of the Mobe parleyed with the police.

At about 6:00 or 6:30 P.M., when it became clear that the police would not budge, the Mobe leaders announced that the crowd should disperse and reassemble in front of the Hilton nearby. When the demonstrators tried to cross the Illinois Central tracks separating the park from the Hilton at Balbo Avenue, they were blocked by national guardsmen. As the crowd surged toward them, the guardsmen responded by laying down a blanket of tear gas. Soon hundreds of people were "running, crying, coughing, vomiting, screaming."[58] A breeze off the lake swept much of the gas past the park onto Michigan Avenue, the city's major down-town shopping street, sending pedestrians and bystanders run-ning to find shelter from the acrid fumes. Some of the gas leaked into the air-conditioning system of the Hilton where it brought tears to Hubert Humphrey's eyes.

Shortly after 7:00 P.M., the demonstrators finally found an unblocked route from the park and began to stream out onto Michigan Avenue. There they collided with one of Ralph Abernathy's Poor People's Campaign mule trains that, fortui-tously, was on its way south to the convention hall so Abernathy could speak to the delegates. The protesters tried to slide past the mule train, but were caught in the crush and stopped by another line of police just outside the Hilton.

It was now dark, but TV kleig lights, set up to film the action, illuminated the enormous clot of four thousand Mobe demon-strators, McCarthy kids, reporters, and police in front of the Hilton. The demonstrators knew the news media were present, and some were chanting "The whole world is watching." By this time the police had sent out a 10–1 signal, the emergency call for police officers in trouble. Ten minutes later a busload of heavily armored Chicago police arrived and began to move at a quick walk eastward toward the Hilton a block or so away. On the way they met a group of demonstrators led by Peck trying to leave the scene. Peck shouted through a bullhorn, "We are not violent. . . . We are sitting down."[59] The cops ignored him, sweeping down on the demonstrators like heavy tanks, flailing away with their nightsticks, and spraying mace. Spectators later claimed once again that they were screaming "Kill! Kill! Kill!" The police would describe how they had come under a barrage of missiles and been struck at by stick-wielding demonstrators.

The police fury was indiscriminate. Everyone was fair

game—protesters, reporters, spectators, McCarthy workers, hotel patrons. Many of the crowd were trapped between the charging police and the Hilton. Some escaped into the lobby; others, trying to protect themselves against the rampaging cops, were pushed up against the plate-glass windows of the hotel cocktail lounge. Suddenly the windows shattered and men and women were propelled bodily into the lounge, many badly cut by glass splinters. Police followed them inside and continued to club them. Peck approached the deputy superintendent to stop the mayhem, but the police pounded his head and kidneys and jammed a nightstick between his legs. Bleeding badly, he was dragged several hundred feet to a police van and heaved in.

What the Walker Commission called "a police riot," was over in twenty minutes. It probably assured the Democrats' defeat in November.

A local electricians' strike kept the public from seeing the images live. But by 9:55 P.M. the film taken at the Loop had been processed, and the networks cut away from the speech of Mayor Carl Stokes seconding Humphrey's nomination to broadcast the lurid footage. They repeated their coverage late that evening and again the next day. Millions of Americans saw the ugly pictures in their living rooms.

The mayhem at Balbo and Michigan could not be ignored by the delegates on the amphitheatre floor. Many could see the network tapes on portable TV's, and all but the regulars were horrified. At one point Lowenstein moved that while rights were "being abused on the streets" and people were "being maced and beaten unconscious,"[60] the convention ought to be adjourned. His motion was defeated.

The street action provoked an incident on the convention floor that epitomized the deep split in the party. Senator Abraham Ribicoff of Connecticut was a Kennedy loyalist and a liberal, but he was torn between the McCarthy forces and the regulars of his state. His solution was to support George McGovern. In the midst of his nominating speech, he could not refrain from remarking: "With George McGovern we wouldn't have Gestapo tactics on the streets of Chicago." The hall was stunned, and the TV cameras swiveled to Mayor Daley, sitting close to the stage. Few heard his words, but experts in lip reading would swear that the mayor had shouted: "Fuck you, you Jew son of a bitch, you lousy motherfucker, go home."[61]

And yet the street battle had little effect on the nominations that followed. At eight o'clock the convention hall was a sea of Humphrey signs. The McCarthy people were at a disadvantage: their own placards had been contaminated by a drifting tear-gas cloud that afternoon at the senator's campaign headquarters near the Hilton and were unusable. Security on the floor was tight, most of it directed against the insurgents.

Mayor Joseph Alioto of San Francisco nominated Humphrey with a speech depicting the vice-president as the man to finish the "business of a vital democracy," to "secure justice for all men, freedom for all men, and peace—blessed peace—for all men."[62] Governor Harold Hughes of Iowa nominated McCarthy. The "key issue" was Vietnam. However rich, the country did not have "the resources to finance the machinery of ever-escalating war and, at the same time, to relieve the agony of the cities and repair the deep wounds of poverty and racism in our society."[63] Senator Ribicoff in his nominating speech called George McGovern a man who could "end the division in the hearts of our people."[64]

The balloting finally began at 11:20 P.M. It was anticlimax. Twenty-five minutes later, Pennsylvania put the vice-president over the top with its $103\frac{3}{4}$ votes. The final results: $1760\frac{1}{4}$ for Humphrey, 601 for McCarthy, $146\frac{1}{2}$ for McGovern, and a scattering for others. The next day the newspapers carried a photo showing Humphrey gleefully clapping his hands as the TV screen in his hotel room flashed news of his victory.

That evening, before the tired nominee could get to bed, eight southern governors came to demand their reward for loyal support: the right to name the vice-presidential candidate. Humphrey refused to accept a southerner, however. The next day, at a late afternoon press conference, he announced that he was choosing the Lincolnesque senator from Maine, Edmund Muskie, a Polish Catholic.

The last important event in the amphitheatre was the traditional acceptance speech. A draft prepared by Humphrey's speech writers had been available for several weeks, but after the chaos of the past few days it would not do. Humphrey had won and like all sensible victors was now anxious for party unity, for healing, for rallying round. The new-minted candidate did not want the irate dissidents to stage a walkout during the speech, and he now sat down to revise his talk to deflect their anger.

The vice-president arrived at the convention hall just after Muskie's nomination and strained to give the speech of his life. He acknowledged his "sorrow and distress" at "the troubles and the violence" that had "erupted . . . tragically in the streets of this great city." He invoked the prayer of St. Francis of Assisi: "Where there is hate, let me sow love;/Where there is injury, pardon;/ Where there is doubt, faith;/Where there is despair, hope;/ Where there is darkness, light."[65] He identified the nation's three essential needs: peace in Vietnam, peace at home, unity. He recited a litany of past Democratic glories and succeeded in milking seventy-one bursts of applause and three standing ovations from the delegates. But the speech was not enough. Some of his advisers had urged him to announce his resignation as vice-president and declare himself thereupon free to pursue a new Vietnam policy. But he had refused, and the applause in the amphitheatre could not conceal that he still had nothing new to propose on the all-important issue of war or peace.

That Vietnam would be the most dangerous issue of the campaign was already clear. Minutes after the nomination, Lowenstein and Richard Goodwin, the former RFK aide, announced that the McCarthy supporters would stage a "funeral march" down Michigan Avenue carrying lighted candles. The more pragmatic antiwar folk, meanwhile, gathered at the Drake Hotel to consider Marcus Raskins' scheme to establish a fourth party to the left of the Democrats. The rebels favored Gene as the new party's candidate, but no one believed he would run. Someone suggested nominating Paul Newman, but Newman declined. "My immediate program," the handsome movie star said, "is to get drunk and to stay drunk for the next two weeks."[66] In the end the fourth-party impulse faded away.

On Thursday McCarthy shattered all hope that he might continue his crusade under other auspices. In a farewell talk to his followers, he urged them to continue to push the Vietnam issue and to support candidates who took the right stand in the fall. Later, at Grant Park, he called the demonstrators "the government in exile."[67] That evening he refused the invitation to stand on the platform with Humphrey when he gave his acceptance speech.

A small event put the appropriate period to the Chicago Democratic convention. At four o'clock Friday morning a squad of cops burst into suite 1506A at the Hilton, a McCarthy headquarters staff and reception area, to stop a rain of objects— ashtrays, beer cans, a silver cream pitcher—that national guardsmen complained had been descending on them from the hotel. The police roughed up the people they found, many of them fast asleep, and hustled everyone out to the elevators. Eventually, four people were taken to the hospital for treatment of head injuries. Rudely awakened by the commotion, McCarthy hurried down from his own suite, arriving when most of the action was over. He later wrote that the raid had been "a massive invasion of privacy— action without precedent in the history of American politics."[68]

The Humphrey nomination was badly damaged goods from the outset. The overwhelming emotion of the millions who had seen the shambles at Chicago on their living room screens was disgust. Doves recoiled at the brutal beatings and gassings of the peace forces. Reporters had been roughed up, and the outrage of the media at Mayor Daley and his "minions" poured out in angry phrases—"rigidity," "insensitivity," "repression"—during the first days. Many who blamed Daley also blamed Humphrey, a connection confirmed when the candidate came to the mayor's defense soon after in an interview with Roger Mudd of CBS.

But most Americans held the demonstrators, not the police or Daley, responsible for the chaos. A Harris poll soon after the convention showed that 66 percent of Americans agreed with the statement: "Mayor Daley was right the way he used police against demonstrators." "When the kids met the cops," Richard Scammon and Ben Wattenberg would write in 1970, "they were perceived as challenging the very fabric of the social order."[69] The Daley supporters also blamed the Democrats. They should not have allowed the disgraceful show to take place. From the beginning, the Humphrey nomination was irremediably tainted.

Only a tiny sliver of the public liked what it saw on the Chicago streets. The nation's extreme-left fringe, now far gone in apocalyptic delusion, gloated at Mayor Daley's loss of control. Years later Jerry Rubin told the economist Milton Viorst: "We wanted the tear gas to get so heavy that the reality was tear gas. We wanted to create a situation in which the Chicago police and the Daley administration and the federal government and the United States would self-destruct. We wanted to show that America wasn't a democracy, that the convention wasn't politics. The message of the week was of an America ruled by force. That was a big victory."[70] Even after a decade Rubin could not see that Chicago helped destroy the movement he had labored so hard to promote.

Hubert Humphrey left Chicago with defeat in November staring him in the face. On September 15 the American Independent party, meeting at Dallas, had formally nominated George Wallace. It was predictable that the publicity would produce a temporary Wallace surge. Yet it was startling when Gallup polls on September 20 and 22 showed the voting public splitting Nixon 43 percent, Humphrey 28, Wallace 21. The vice-president was only seven percentage points ahead of the third-party candidate! Could anything be done in the weeks remaining to overcome this enormous handicap?

The Democrats traditionally followed their presidential nominating convention with a giant Labor Day rally in Detroit, the country's biggest union town. Unfortunately, too many United Automobile Workers were sporting Wallace-for-President buttons, and Humphrey settled for the New York Labor Day Parade. The turnout of marchers in Manhattan was impressive, but most New Yorkers had better things to do on Labor Day and only a thin aisle of spectators watched the vice-president and the union men and women as they paraded down Fifth Avenue.

Humphrey returned to his lakeside home at Waverly, Minnesota, soon after and sat down with Senator Fred Harris, Senator Walter Mondale, his longtime aide, Max Kampelman, his former counsel, and Lawrence O'Brien, the veteran Democratic political manager, to put together a campaign strategy. Secretary of Agriculture Orville Freeman, his friend from mayoral days, had written up a complex—and expensive—game plan that he believed would carry Humphrey into the White House. Everyone jumped on the Freeman scheme as impractical and it was immediately scuttled. But it was hard to come up with an alternative, and the Humphrey aides and associates were soon joined in a battle royal over the campaign that mixed equal parts of conflicting perceptions and competing egos.

One immense stumbling block was money. Since the convention, even donors who had remained loyal after Bobby Kennedy's assassination departed, disgusted with the anarchy and mayhem they had seen in Chicago and dismayed by the bad polls. One potential financial resource was the president himself. The Johnson name still had magic for many rich Democrats, and besides he controlled the purse strings of the President's Club treasury, a large pool of dollars that Humphrey had helped raise by countless, painful fund-raising appearances and that LBJ had expected to use himself in '68. But Johnson would not cooperate. Offended by the vice-president's smallest acts of independence, he was behaving at his petty worst. At one point the desperate vice-president told Arthur Krim, LBJ's chief fund-raiser, that he would inform the press that the White House was allied with the Communists and the Republicans in trying to defeat him unless he released some money. In the end Humphrey had to go on a begging mission to Washington. It failed. LBJ promised, Humphrey related, "to work with me closely, to do everything I wanted, and to release the cabinet to help me."[71] But the six hundred thousand dollars in the President's Club fund was never freed for his use.

Yet somehow the Humphrey people managed to scrape up the minimal amount of cash to get started. Ultimately more serious was the candidate's continuing inability to formulate a Vietnam strategy that would break with the past and establish his independence and decisiveness.

Humphrey held his first major rally at John F. Kennedy Plaza in Philadelphia on September 9. It was a chaotic event, thinly attended, with knots of antiwar hecklers who chanted, "Dump the

Hump. Dump the Hump." Things were slow to improve. For the next few weeks, as he moved around the country, Humphrey continued to encounter demands for some new policy to extricate the United States from the Asian quagmire. The vice-president not only failed to oblige, he did not seem to know what was taking place at the Paris peace table or on the battlefronts. At one point, in Houston, he waved a local newspaper headline, TROOPS COME HOME, as proof that Americans would soon be pulling out of Vietnam. He had neglected to read the second paragraph that explained that this was a routine rotation of one marine unit for another without any net change of numbers. The press and the public laughed.

The president could have kept Humphrey informed of the latest turns at the Paris peace talks and in Vietnam, but he feared it would allow the vice-president to set an independent course. Until January 20, *he* was Commander in Chief, not Hubert, he insisted, and he refused to help out. He even slapped the vice-president down. At New Orleans, after the Houston gaffe, Johnson told an American Legion audience pointedly that nobody could predict when American troops would come home. Even Humphrey could not swallow this. The president had "pull[ed] the rug out from under me," he informed friends; the statement was "not an act of friendship."[72]

While the Democrats floundered, the Republicans pulled away fast and smooth from the starting gate. After the strategy conferences in California, Nixon had gone to Key Biscayne and then disappeared on several fishing trips to the Florida keys with his friend Bebe Rebozo. He returned for the second time during the Democratic convention and postponed his plans to leave immediately for New York on the advice of his young aides, Dwight Chapin and Bob Haldeman. Nixon must see for himself what was happening at the Democratic convention, they insisted, and he must not distract attention from the Democrats' self-destruct act by returning to action before the convention adjourned. Nixon complied and along with eighty-nine million other Americans watched with fascination the Wednesday night counterpoint of street riots and politics in Chicago.

The Republican strategy for victory was simple: Nixon must win the great middle, the people who were neither racists nor civil rights activists, who were fed up with Vietnam but did not want to leave in defeat. The strategy was informed by the views of a twenty-seven-year-old lawyer, Kevin Phillips, a Colgate graduate from New York City who had gone to Harvard Law School and then served as administrative assistant to Republican Congressman Paul Fino of the Bronx.

In some ways, Phillips's analysis was nothing more than a theoretical restatement of backlash feelings, though without the truculence of the Wallace rhetoric. A conservative revolution was under way, he believed. After eight years of liberal ascendancy, millions of Americans—white and lower-middle-class—felt despised and rejected. Their discontents were not economic, however; the country was still floating on a wave of prosperity. The issues were social. They concerned law and order, welfare cheating, the disrespect of the young, neighborhood preservation—issues that Wallace had also seized on. A large proportion of the discontented were Catholic ethnics, and Phillips, Irish and from the Bronx, was considered the election campaign's "ethnic specialist." They also included the millions of whites in the newly emerging Sunbelt, the arc of territory from southern Virginia south to the Gulf Coast and then west all the way to southern California. These people were also ethnics in a sense, sharing common cultural values that influenced their political attitudes. So were people from New England, the old Yankees who used to dominate the Grand Old Party.

Phillips, then in the process of writing the book that would appear in 1969 as *The Emerging Republican Majority,* saw all these voters, many former Democrats, as potential Republicans if the party learned how to express their feelings. If the GOP played its cards right, it could win the heartland and usher in a "new American revolution," one that would make it the normal majority party, dethroning the Democrats from the position they had occupied ever since FDR and the Great Depression in the 1930s.

Phillips had a way of stating his case that made him seem callow. "The Democratic party will not carry Oklahoma again for the rest of this century," he told reporter Joe McGinniss.[73] To someone else: "All you've got to do with American politics is work out who doesn't like whom and you've got it."[74] His judgments were also premature. But he had detected a major turning point in the history of American party politics: the nation was on the road to a party realignment that would end the generation-long Democratic liberal reign. If in addition to his charts and his printouts he had known what had taken place on the Democratic convention Credentials and Rules committees in Chicago and what the results would be, he would have considered his thesis proven beyond any reasonable doubt.

Phillips's backlash analysis was applicable only partially as Republican strategy in 1968, whatever its value as astute political analysis. Nixon did not want to out-Wallace Wallace. He knew that raw bigotry was unpalatable to most Americans and that the Deep South was lost to him in any case. He opted in fact for the high road of national unity. He would heal the divisions and bring the country together. In each version of the "the speech," the standard address he delivered extempore at all the whistle-stops and middle-size cities, he talked of a victory that would "be bigger than a party, a victory that will bring to our ranks Democrats, Independents . . . and a team . . . that . . . will unite America. . . ." He told of the "forgotten Americans" who were neither white nor black, who were laborers and managers, who paid their taxes, worked, sent their children to school, went to church. They loved their country and were not "haters."[75]

But there was a subtext to the Republican campaign and it was propagated by Spiro Agnew. Agnew was the GOP's answer to Wallace. With his own staff, plane, and entourage of reporters, he was launched on the political waters in September and charged with the task of containing the loss of backlash voters to the Wallace ticket.

He was soon making headlines as often as Nixon. At a breakfast for Washington news people on September 10, he declared that Humphrey had been "soft on inflation, soft on communism, and soft on law and order over the years." He then modified "soft" with the more graphic "squishy soft." The next day O'Brien declared that Agnew had been "delegated by Mr.

Nixon to travel the low road." But even Republican leaders, men who knew Humphrey from the Senate days, balked at the description. Everett Dirksen announced that he was "not aware of any evidence" that the vice-president was soft on communism.[76]

Agnew apologized for his remarks the next day in Rochester, New York, but he was soon in hot water again. In Chicago on the twelfth, a TV talk-show host asked him about the use of civil disobedience to achieve racial justice. Agnew said that he did not condone it. When the interviewer asked what he thought of those great past advocates of civil disobedience—Jesus, Gandhi, Martin Luther King, and Thoreau—he responded, incorrectly: "The people you have mentioned did not operate in a free society."[77] Another callous Agnew remark soon made the rounds. In mid-October he responded to a question about whether he would campaign in ghetto neighborhoods with the bright observation: "If you've seen one city slum you've seen them all."[78]

Agnew had a talent for the unconscious ethnic slur. In Chicago he called people of Polish origins "Polacks." He later referred to a rotund Japanese American reporter as a "fat Jap."

As the campaign progressed, Agnew zeroed in on the standard Wallaceite targets. He did not aim at the Deep South, where Wallace seemed unassailable, but at the border states and at the pockets of Wallace supporters in the North. At a blue-collar rally in New Jersey, Agnew declared his contempt for "phony intellectuals . . . who don't understand what we mean by patriotism and hard work." He also urged a federal offensive against drugs. In Detroit he attacked SDS and demanded that faculty radicals who supported their tactics be fired from their jobs. In Jacksonville, Florida, he announced that the administration was pouring money into the ghettos largely to buy off militants. Promising the poor better conditions, he insisted, created impossible expectations. These were responsible for "the revolt, the civil disobedience, and the irresponsible dissent sweeping the country."[79] Agnew hammered away at the theme that the Wallace candidacy could only hurt Nixon. A vote for the Alabamian was, in effect, a vote for Humphrey and all his liberal advisers and ideas.

Agnew's campaign hurt more than it helped. Many Americans undoubtedly shared the governor's attitudes, but they also were squeamish about hearing them publicly proclaimed. As early as mid-September, the polls showed that the public preferred Muskie to Agnew by a small margin. The Democrats seized on their advantage and were soon running a TV ad showing an AGNEW FOR VICE-PRESIDENT poster followed by loud laughter. They also played up charges—later proved essentially true—that Agnew had used his positions as county executive and governor to make money out of public contracts and land speculation. By the middle of October, the gap between him and Muskie had widened to a seventeen-point chasm. On the advice of speech writer Patrick Buchanan, Nixon was soon omitting any mention of his running mate.

Nixon's own campaign emphasized television to a surprising degree. Supposedly, TV had killed Nixon in 1960. The critics held that Nixon was wooden, humorless, lupine, uncomfortable on the "tube." What they forgot was that Nixon's masterful Checkers-speech performance in 1952 had saved him from being dumped from the Eisenhower ticket after Democratic revelations of a Nixon "slush fund." In any case, there was all that Republican money to pay for expensive TV time, and the opportunity to overwhelm the poverty-striken Democrats seemed too good to resist.

The centerpiece of the TV blitz was a series of ten regional one-hour telecasts shaped as question-and-answer sessions. The occasions were a little different from the Portland approach during the Oregon primary. Instead of a phone-in telethon, Nixon appeared in the studio before a live audience and a panel. Both were handpicked—the audiences from local Republican party workers; the panels, though they included the mandatory spread of women, blacks, ethnics, blue- and white-collar workers, screened for the right attitudes. The candidate stood on a low platform facing the seven or eight questioners, with the audience behind them, and fielded the queries thrown at him. These were not prepared in advance; to that extent the sessions were spontaneous. But the choice of panelists had eliminated the tough questions indirectly, and Nixon usually sailed through the sessions looking like the "new Nixon."

* * *

Obviously, it was better for the Democrats to have Muskie ahead of Agnew, but of course it was the top of the ticket that counted. That continued to look like a disaster.

For weeks after Chicago, Humphrey remained mired in poverty and bad publicity, with the polls showing overwhelming defeat ahead. The vice-president and his aides tried to squeeze some comfort from Harry Truman's victory-snatched-from-the-jaws-of-defeat campaign of 1948 and tried the same give-'em-hell Harry tack that had worked twenty years before. In Minneapolis Humphrey lambasted Nixon for evasion; in Louisville he heaped sarcastic scorn on his opponent: "The man who campaigns without running, the man who takes it easy and never makes a mistake, . . . who either evades or straddles every issue."[80] But nothing seemed to work. At the end of September a Gallup poll showed him a full fifteen points behind.

By now the candidate was desperate, and at Portland, Oregon, after talking with Muriel, he told his physician and close personal friend, Edgar Berman, that if the polls did not turn up soon he was going to give up, "just . . . take it easy" and slide the last weeks.[81] On September 29, at the Seattle Civic Arena, he ran into the worst heckling he had yet experienced. Two hundred antiwar protesters shouting "Stop the war" interrupted his remarks and those of Senator Warren Magnuson until the police removed them forcefully. Humphrey went on to give a good speech but returned to his hotel room "beat and dejected."[82] He could not sleep and Berman had to give him a tranquilizer.

But a turnaround was imminent. For weeks Humphrey's advisers had been clamoring for a break with the president on Vietnam and preparing drafts of a new Vietnam policy statement. None of these proposed a sharp split with the administration's course, but did promise that after the candidate became president he would order a bombing halt of North Vietnam as a way to facilitate negotiations and the eventual withdrawal of American troops. George Ball and other former Johnson officials had vetted the statement and had then asked Averell Harriman and Cyrus

Vance in Paris if it would undermine their negotiating position
with the North Vietnamese. Harriman objected to any pledge of
an unconditional bombing halt, and Humphrey inserted a
statement that any cessation would depend on Hanoi's accepting
as a precondition the observance of the demilitarized zone, in
effect, a promise not to infiltrate any more troops into the south.
Though warned by O'Brien and his dovish advisers that this
statement was too timid, the vice-president decided to unveil it on
September 30.

The occasion was Salt Lake City and the event was nationally
televised with the last hundred thousand dollars in O'Brien's
coffers. The gist of the speech was in three brief paragraphs at the
beginning. As president, Humphrey said, he would be willing to
"stop the bombing of the north as an acceptable risk for peace";
before taking action he would ask for evidence that the Communists would be willing to restore the demilitarized zone between
North and South Vietnam; if they showed bad faith, he would
order the bombing resumed.[83] The taped thirty-minute talk
concluded with an appeal for funds.

The statement *was* timid. Its distance from the president's
policy was trivial, and the North Vietnamese declared that it
offered nothing new. Yet it turned the campaign around. Its
psychological effects were impressive. Humphrey's biographer
says that the speech lifted a tremendous weight from the vice-
president's mind. On the plane back east, a lighthearted
Humphrey crooned the words of the old peace spiritual: "Ain't
gwine study war no more." When Senator Harris's wife,
LaDonna, remarked that "that's the new party line," he chuckled
appreciatively.[84]

It also had more objective results. On October 5 Americans for
Democratic Action's national board finally endorsed the
Humphrey–Muskie ticket, though declaring itself still "far from
satisfied" by the vice-president's position on Vietnam.[85] The
money logjam eased. In the wake of Salt Lake City, almost three
hundred thousand dollars in contributions, mostly small, poured
in, saving the campaign from imminent bankruptcy. O'Brien
immediately contracted for another big block of TV network
time.

If the shift on Vietnam brought back the liberals, there still remained the blue-collar voters. Well into September, six short weeks before the election, a *New York Times* article claimed that Wallace would receive more electoral votes than Humphrey, leaving the vice-president third in the field. Undoubtedly, some of the Wallace supporters were drawn from Nixon, but many were erstwhile Democrats. How could they be brought back to the party of their fathers?

Wallace himself would obligingly help out. The September American Independent party convention in Dallas had failed to name a vice-presidential candidate, leaving the choice up to the presidential nominee. On October 3, Wallace announced at a press conference in Pittsburgh that his choice had fallen on retired Air Force General Curtis LeMay, a hawk of hawks, who in his recent book, *America in Danger,* had declared that to win the war it might be necessary to destroy "every work of man in North Vietnam," and "bomb" the country "back to the Stone Age."[86]

The proud candidate wasted no time in confirming everybody's worst fears. His first remark at the press conference was that he endorsed nuclear weapons for ending the impasse in Asia. "I don't believe the world would end if we exploded a nuclear weapon," he told the incredulous reporters. He had seen a film on Bikini, the atoll where A-bomb and H-bomb nuclear tests had been held in the 1950s, and they showed very clearly how the flora and the fauna had all returned nicely. Except for the land crabs. They were a little bit "hot" still, but the rats were "bigger, fatter, healthier than they ever were before." At this point a dismayed Wallace tried to break in. "General LeMay hasn't advocated the use of nuclear weapons, not at all," he interjected. "He's against the use of nuclear weapons, and I am too." But the general was not done. When a reporter asked him whether he would use nuclear weapons to "end the war," he replied he "would use anything we could dream up . . . including nuclear weapons, if it was necessary."[87]

After this the Wallace campaign sank like a stone. It was not just that LeMay frightened Americans by his bellicose talk. It was also the growing sense that Wallace was a magnet for disorder. Wherever the governor went he created headlines of hecklers ejected, police called in, clashes between opponents and supporters. Increasingly, the apostle of law and order seemed to be the begetter of chaos. Even more important, the blue-collar working class, especially the white union families, began to return to their traditional political home.

For the first weeks of the campaign, the news from the labor front had all been bad for the Democrats. The industrial heartland showed a vast Wallace surge. In Homestead, Pennsylvania—where the epic struggle of the steelworkers against Andrew Carnegie had taken place during the 1890s—a union official at the U.S. Steel plant talked of 92 percent of the boiler-plant men supporting Wallace. In Flint, Michigan, the site of the famous 1936 sit-down strike, UAW Local 326 endorsed Wallace, while Local 659, representing the enormous Chevrolet plant, refused to endorse any presidential candidate, the first time in years it had not supported the Democrats. Many separate parts of the Wallace message attracted the blue-collar workers, but much of it boiled down to race. As one UAW official noted in mid-September: "The men in the plants want to zap the Negroes by voting for Wallace. It's as simple as that."[88]

Fortunately for Humphrey, the pro-Wallace feeling was partial and thin. The men and women on the shop floor, on the assembly line, at the lathes and drill presses were mostly lifelong Democrats. They believed the party had been captured by its left extremists and had shown too much recent concern for civil rights, for civil liberties, and for peace over strength. But in 1968 many were not yet ready to desert it: wearing the Wallace buttons and applying the Wallace bumper stickers were only ways of blowing off steam. Most of the union leaders despised Wallace. His record as Alabama governor was anti-union. He also posed a challenge to their own influence and jeopardized the precarious racial harmony within union ranks. Besides, how could they abandon a generation-long affiliation with the Democratic party or betray a man whose prolabor record was above reproach? The loyalty to the administration that had held the union leaders in LBJ's camp during the strains of the Vietnam defections now served the vice-president well.

By mid-September, the AFL-CIO Committee on Political Education, had launched a massive campaign to register union members and to get them to vote the Democratic ticket in November. COPE spent over $10 million for the Humphrey–Muskie ticket and marshalled thousands of volunteers to man registration desks, make calls, distribute pamphlets, organize rallies, and hand out leaflets at factory gates.

Through October it churned out a river of pamphlets and handbills denouncing Wallace as an enemy of the northern working man and woman. The Alabama governor, these claimed, had drawn high-paying, unionized factories from the North to his own state by promises of low pay and no unions. Alabama allowed disgraceful child labor and had no minimum wage law. The State Highway Patrol was a union-busting organization. The Heart of Dixie ranked forty-ninth in its aid to dependent children. Alabama wage rates were among the lowest in the country. Some of this was unfair: Wallace was not responsible for his state's low wages, for example. But the monumental propaganda effort awakened surviving blue-collar economic insecurities and succeeded marvelously in submerging the "social issue" under the "pocketbook issue." As the contest approached the wire, white working-class Americans in the North swarmed back to their traditional party allegiance.

The Republicans tried desperately to counter the growing defection by moving closer to Wallace. In the last two weeks, Nixon flailed away at the law-and-order issue. In Cincinnati he quoted Humphrey's remark in 1966 to the effect that if he had been living in a slum, he would be leading a riot himself. The statement, Nixon said, was "adult delinquency . . . not worthy of a Vice-President."[89] At other places he claimed that his opponent had exaggerated the relevance of poverty to crime and that a war on poverty must not preclude a war on crime itself. In a late October tape made at a New York TV studio, the Republican candidate attacked Humphrey's defense of the Democratic attorney general and the party's record on law enforcement. "We need a complete housecleaning in Washington," he declared. "I pledge a new attorney general. I pledge an all-out war against organized crime in this country. I pledge that we shall have policies that will restore freedom from fear on the streets of the cities of America. . . ."[90]

At this same two-hour taping session, Nixon tried to make the suppurating New York City teachers' strike a part of the campaign. It was a wily move, for the strike, though limited to the metropolis in a direct sense, resounded loudly through the nation.

The teachers' strike encapsulated the dilemmas of 1960s American liberalism and exposed the strains that were reversing its fortunes. It pitted two liberal principles—black autonomy and trade union rights—and two liberal constituencies—blacks and Jews—against one another in an encounter that would leave deep scars.

One ingredient in the confrontation was the black separatism that had rejected integration and plumped for Black Power. In the northern ghettos the separatists wanted, among other things, black control of local schools. These, they said, were failing the minority children of the cities. A great majority of these children were reading below grade level and, it seemed clear, would be severely handicapped in the race of life.

In New York City the militants of Harlem, the South Bronx, and Bedford-Stuyvesant, as well as more-moderate groups associated with the distinguished black educator, Professor Kenneth Clark of the City University, demanded that authority over curriculum and personnel be taken from the unresponsive white bureaucracy centralized at Board of Education headquarters at 110 Livingston Street in Brooklyn and dispersed to neighborhood districts. Clark and his colleagues, like the Chicago School sociologists who influenced the federal antipoverty program, emphasized the social drawbacks of powerlessness in the black community and the psychological advantages of autonomy. The militants had a more ideological agenda. Local control would mean more black teachers who could communicate to black children the truth of their own grand heritage and spare them the subtle—and not so subtle—racism of the white faculty. In the militants' often-inflamed rhetoric, these people were engaged in a "genocidal" enterprise to make black children fail.

The separatists were endorsed by some white liberals, including Mayor John Lindsay, and even by some conservatives who privately anticipated a return of racial segregation. Their position was financially backstopped by the Ford Foundation, headed now by McGeorge Bundy, Lyndon Johnson's former national security adviser. In May 1967 the foundation announced that it would contribute $139,000 for three experimental projects in community control—at Intermediate School 201 in Harlem, at Two Bridges on the Lower East Side, and at Ocean Hill–Brownsville, in Brooklyn's "Bed-Stuy." The battle was on.

The experiment turned into a tragedy. Martin Mayer, author of *The Schools*, a major sixties' analysis of contemporary education, would call what happened at Ocean Hill–Brownsville "the worst disaster my native city has experienced in my life time."[91]

Opposed to community control were the mostly white teachers, members of the United Federation of Teachers (UFT) run by Albert Shanker. In New York City the public school teachers were predominantly Jewish women, graduates of the city colleges. They were generally political liberals, but their liberalism was of the old-fashioned kind that favored integration, supported civil liberties, endorsed unions. Marilyn Gittell, one of the players in the events that followed, called them "heirs of middle-class reformism."[92] They found it difficult to understand the new mood of white exclusion that had seized the black community. Many had fought bitterly for union recognition and to replace the Tammany-era political-appointment system, which had formerly excluded them, with civil service merit. They perceived community control as a return to the bad old political-patronage, union-busting days. And they were not entirely wrong. Most separatists no doubt saw community control primarily as a chance to improve education for black children, but others also recognized an opportunity to cut blacks in on the education pork barrel at the expense of the city's licensed teachers. Their case seemed plausible. Almost 50 percent of the New York City school population was black or Puerto Rican, but no more than 8 or 9 percent of the teachers were members of these two groups.

Anti-Semitism made the whole thing worse. Ever since the rise of the Black Power movement in 1965–66, black militants had been uncommonly outspoken in their attacks on Jews. With their collective memory of ancient wrongs and recent horrors still alive, New York's Jews were sensitive to ethnic attacks. Bigotry, however, was not a one-way street. White teachers encountered disorder, crime, drugs, inattention in ghetto classrooms and more than occasionally surrendered to racist responses. The teachers had other failings that if not overtly racist, often seemed so to black parents. Bureaucratic rigidities and the burnout of years of dealing with difficult children had taken its toll. Many had lost whatever enthusiasm they had felt for their calling, and their indifference fueled charges that they were failing the ghetto children and should be replaced. In a word, the circumstances of the experimental schools created the perfect environment for a major social confrontation, and the opportunity was not lost.

In the eye of the storm was the Ford Foundation. The foundation tended to follow the intellectual styles. During its early years, just after World War II, it had devoted its immense resources primarily to higher education and had distributed hundreds of millions to upgrade colleges and universities. During the 1960s it shifted from top-down to bottom-up benevolence. The foundation was a bastion of the Protestant conscience, a center for a latter-day version of that long line of Yankee reformers who, at their best, had transcended their upper-class interests to fight for the oppressed and the discarded. There was an underside of the impulse, however: a tendency to ally the elites with those at the very bottom, at the expense of the middle. In the past, this response was best exemplified by the northern anti-slavery reformers of the early nineteenth century who had made the black slaves of the distant South their special concern and had rebuffed the poor white Irish in their own backyard.

And so it would happen again. By 1967 relations between the union teachers and the militants had deteriorated as a result of attacks on white teachers. Community action groups connected with the antipoverty program had demanded the removal of "racist" teachers and principals. In one school the activists had stuffed teachers' mailboxes with anti-Semitic mail. During its biennial contract negotiation with the Board of Education, the UFT had made matters worse by demanding that teachers be allowed to suspend "disruptive" students from class. At first the community groups had not objected, but over the summer they came to see the teachers' demands as aimed at black children and essentially racist.

The lid blew off with the beginning of the school year in September 1967. The first of the three Ford Foundation experimental projects to leave the starting line was Ocean Hill–Brownsville, where a foundation-sponsored militant planning council calling itself "the People's Board of Education" appointed Rhody McCoy as the district's administrator. McCoy, a black career school official, had long merged his personal frustration at his slow movement through the Board of Ed hierarchy with his sense that racism infused the New York City school system. One of the planning council's first acts was to arrange that August for a community school board election. The election was supposedly open to all parents in the district but few voted, and in the end the planning council managed to pack the community board with its own members. Soon after, the council approved a final plan for the Ocean Hill–Brownsville district that warned that the decentralization scheme represented "the last threads of the community's faith in the school system's purposes and abilities."[93]

McCoy and the teachers soon collided head-on. One of his first acts was to confirm the planning council's choice of Herman Ferguson, a former assistant principal in Queens, as head of Intermediate School 55, a new school in the Ocean Hill–Brownsville district. It was not a wise decision. Ferguson belonged to the Revolutionary Action Movement (RAM), a black extremist organization. Two months before, he and other RAM leaders had been indicted for conspiring to murder Roy Wilkins and Whitney Young, the two black civil rights moderates. When the State Department of Education asked McCoy to withdraw the nomination, he refused, and was supported by C. Herbert Oliver, a militant black minister who headed the newly elected community school board.

During the spring of 1968, McCoy brought the growing antagonisms to a head by dismissing thirteen teachers and six administrators from six district schools on the grounds that they were trying to sabotage the community-control experiment. All but two were white. The UFT retaliated by ordering its members to leave their classes in the Ocean Hill district, promising not to return until the teachers and administrators were reinstated.

The role of the Ford Foundation in the unfolding confrontation was ambiguous. The foundation had breathed life into the plans of the militants, yet it was reluctant to serve as a constant resource. It did, however, establish the Institute for Community Studies, which was headed by Marilyn Gittell, a prodecentralization Queens College professor of education. The institute, funded with close to $1 million, provided legal, financial, administrative, and political advice and assistance to the three experimental districts.

The foundation was also unwilling to endorse unlimited community control of the school districts. In November 1967, after the Ocean Hill–Brownsville project was under way, it issued its formal recommendations for permanent change in the New York City school system. This document, the Bundy Report, urged the formation of thirty to sixty local school districts, loosely federated and loosely coordinated by a central agency, to replace the existing unitary system tightly controlled by 110 Livingston Street. The districts would in turn be governed by local boards, partly elected by parents of school children and partly selected by the mayor. The local boards could choose their own heads, hire and fire teachers, and grant tenure. The citywide system of examinations and licensing would be abolished. These were victories for the community-control people. At the same time, existing teacher tenure rights would be protected and the collective bargaining process between the teachers and the city would remain centralized, positions favored by the UFT. Evenhandedness outrages every partisan. The Bundy Report earned the animus of both conservatives and the militant community-control leaders.

Ford officials might have reservations about community control, but a part of the white establishment—the local chapter of the Urban Coalition—had none. The coalition was a privately financed body of liberal businessmen, clergymen, professionals, and civil rights workers organized in mid-1967 and headed by John Gardner, Johnson's recent secretary of health, education, and welfare. WIth offices in thirty-one cities, it was committed to bringing the black militants within "the system." The coalitions' Educational Task Force attacked the UFT and threw its weight behind McCoy and his allies. It justified its support with the rhetoric of racial idealism. But its critics were skeptical. Here, they said, was a body of upper-class men and women insulated from the insecurities of lower-middle-class life and anxious to protect their own schools and neighborhoods from the pains of integration. Naturally, they were indifferent to the hard-won rights of the UFT teachers. Whether fair or foul, the charges would become a commonplace of the evolving struggle.

As the fall gave way to winter and then spring, the school struggle heated up. The first half of 1968 was a time of agony for the nation. In April Martin Luther King was assassinated and the ghettos exploded. May brought the Columbia student uprising. In June Robert Kennedy was murdered. In August the police and the Yippies rioted in Chicago. These catastrophic events charged the national atmosphere, producing superheated emotions and rhetoric. By the end of the 1968 summer vacation, the teachers and the black community leaders were on a collision course, with the UFT insisting that decentralization could not be achieved if it was at the expense of teachers' rights and the militants convinced that the teachers were uncompromising racists who intended to undermine community control. By Labor Day full-scale war was imminent.

Two days before the opening of classes, McCoy announced that he had hired 350 teachers for Ocean Hill–Brownsville to replace those who had walked out in the spring to protest the firings of the 19 teachers and administrators. He also refused, despite a court order, to reinstate the teachers dismissed in the spring. On September 9 the UFT struck citywide in protest. The strike lasted two days, and then the Board of Education signed a "memorandum of understanding" giving the union most of what it wanted. Livingston Street agreed to extend the protective clauses of its contract with the teachers to all local board districts, agreed to pay the 350 teachers who had walked out in the spring for their time away, and agreed to reinstate them in their jobs, McCoy's new replacements notwithstanding.

The memorandum could not be enforced. When fifteen UFT teachers appeared at their schools in Ocean Hill, they found their entrance blocked by angry crowds shouting curses. Once inside, they were refused assignments and were shunted to an auditorium at I.S. 55 to wait for McCoy to appear. Soon after, fifty black men from the Brooklyn chapter of the Congress of Racial Equality some wearing helmets and carrying sticks, arrived in the auditorium and took seats near the teachers. They began to chant threats and call the teachers "faggots, and pigs, and other names."[94] One man told the frightened teachers that if they came back to the district, they would be carried out in pine boxes. When McCoy arrived he simply dismissed them, and they had to be escorted by the police back to their separate schools where they remained without assignments.

The militants' supporters described the abuse of the teachers as a spontaneous outburst from parents and concerned black citizens angry about their children's inferior education. It was, in part, but it was also more contrived. A McCoy lieutenant later admitted that when the Ocean Hill leaders wanted to intimidate their opponents, they would call in outside black militants, like Robert "Sonny" Carson of Brooklyn CORE, to make trouble.

On September 12 the UFT went on strike again, shutting down the entire city school system, and this time its members stayed out until the end of the month. In this second round the racial and ethnic tensions were even more open than before. Black bystanders called teachers walking picket lines "kikes," and "dirty Jews," and the teachers—the reports said—responded in kind. Black militants circulated anti-Semitic leaflets. One evening a black Ocean Hill–Brownsville teacher, Les Campbell, read an anti-Semitic poem on black militant Julius Lester's WBAI weekly radio program. It concluded with: "Hey there, Jew-boy! I wish you were dead!"[95] The UFT tried to avoid a racial showdown. At a mass rally in front of city hall, Bayard Rustin, the venerable black civil rights leader, stood on the stand with UFT president Albert Shanker to express solidarity. Yet the union also used the racial issue to arouse sympathy, distributing a half million copies of anti-Semitic handbills and flyers handed out by the militants to publicize their racism. One of these attacked the "Middle East murderers of colored people" and the "so-called liberal Jewish friend." The latter was "really our enemy" and was "responsible for the serious educational retardation of our black children."[96]

The teachers returned to work on September 30 following the city's promises that they would be protected at Ocean Hill schools. At Junior High School 271, however, the scabs McCoy had hired barred the door to the UFT teachers and, taking the students with them, walked out. Later there were clashes outside J.H.S. 271 and other district schools. The Board of Education soon after closed J.H.S. 271 and suspended McCoy and most of the district's principals for failing to protect the teachers. But the disorders continued, and on October 14, after the Board announced the reinstatement of the principals without first securing a nonharassment pledge, the UFT went on strike again.

This time the teachers stayed out five weeks, while the city's children hung out on street corners, got under foot, or attended makeshift schools patched together by parents and community leaders. Until now, the white middle class had supported the teachers against McCoy and the Ocean Hill–Brownsville board. But with each passing week, even white parents became resentful of their childrens' wasted education. On the other hand Shanker and UFT picked up support from the city's Central Labor Council, which induced the custodians' union to shut off the school boilers and lock the school doors.

The strike was finally settled on November 19 by an agreement that established a State Supervisory Commission to determine teacher transfers, a state trusteeship for Ocean Hill—in effect, a guarantee of the district's continued autonomy—and a promise of a new overall community-control plan. By this time everyone was exhausted and everyone was angry at someone.

Black anti-Semitism had long been building, but it had been at the periphery of liberal consciousness. Ocean Hill–Brownsville, erupting in the nation's cultural and intellectual capital, could not be ignored, and it would have profound political and ideological effects.

The confrontation of the UFT and Rhody McCoy drove a wedge deep into the liberal community. In New York City, where Jews were the largest bloc of white liberal voters, it split the community into two halves. On one side were the Jews of the outer boroughs—Brooklyn, Queens, the Bronx—still close to their ethnic roots and acutely threatened by the overt anti-Semitism they observed among black militants. Often skilled workers, civil servants, social workers, or schoolteachers themselves, they were also staunch defenders of union rights and saw the Ocean Hill leaders as union busters. On the other side were the assimilated Jews from the brownstones and high-rise apartments of Manhattan's Greenwich Village and Upper East Side, the prosperous lawyers, publishers, brokers, and businessmen who were in some ways Jewish WASPS. These people had little to do with schoolteachers or unions, or, some of their critics said, with Jews as such, either. Like their Gentile counterparts they often felt closer to the black militants than to the petit bourgeois whites of the outer boroughs. Ira Glasser, the New York American Civil Liberties associate director, for example, issued a report blaming the UFT's effort to "undermine local community control"[97] for the chaos that had taken place.

Ocean Hill–Brownsville also divided the nation's intellectual community, nested, to an extraordinary degree, in Manhattan and its academic outriders. Charles Kadushin, in his study of the American intellectual elite, has noted that ". . . the strike was one of those rare occasions in which a set of issues that had once come together as a package was totally unravelled, forcing an entire new set of alignments."[98] Intellectuals with roots in the old social democracy took the side of the teachers out of longtime support for trade unionism. Many of these were Jewish, but they also included Michael Harrington and other Gentile socialists and left liberals. They even included a few black activists like Rustin and A. Philip Randolph, who remembered the epic struggles in the past for union recognition and deplored the overheated rhetoric of Black Power leaders.

Ocean Hill–Brownsville was an especially traumatic blow to the *Commentary* circle of academics, writers, critics, and literati. Though Jewish-affiliated, *Commentary*'s prestige was national in scope. Its editor was Norman Podhoretz, a thirty-eight-year-old former *Wunderkind* who had taken over its management in 1960 and had, during his early years, made it into an outlet for writers like Paul Goodman, Edgar Z. Friedenberg, Dwight Macdonald, Staughton Lynd, and others who had helped create the intellectual base for what became the New Left.

Podhoretz found himself moving to the right as student and civil rights militancy became more pronounced. The Ocean Hill–Brownsville battle helped drive *Commentary* and its circle of contributors over the line. Beginning in early 1969, the journal began to run articles on the renewed anti-Semitism revealed by the strike and other recent events. It soon became a major forum for angry anti–New Left and pro-Vietnam rhetoric.

Commentary's burgeoning conservative mood opened a wide tear in the country's intellectual fabric. Other portions of the intellectual community sided with the Ocean Hill militants. Jason Epstein, editor of *The New York Review of Books*, saw the New York school crisis as a battle between "the excluded class" determined on "improving its position through the education of its children" and the "interest of an established, if largely ineffective, professional group in maintaining prerogatives. . . ."[99] In November, when the battle had heated up, he accused the UFT of counterfeiting anti-Semitic documents and ascribing them to black militants. Epstein's attitudes prompted an angry response among New York's outer-borough Jews. One writer to the *New York Review* told Epstein: "When they come to kill the Jews they will kill you too. You won't escape by buddying up with . . . McCoy."[100]

Epstein's defense of the black militants confirmed the *New York Review*'s fellow traveler, anti-Vietnam New Leftism, a position it retained until well into the 1970s. Thereafter, the partisans of the *Review* and *Commentary* ceased to talk to one another, except to scold. Over the next few years the *Commentary* circle began an intellectual journey that brought them ever further from their original social democratic roots. Ocean Hill–Brownsville would be a giant step toward 1980s' neoconservatism.

The Ocean Hill–Brownsville battle was New York's equivalent of white backlash, and it was easy to see why Nixon would try to use it in the last days of the campaign when he saw his lead slipping. But his scheme to capitalize on the Jewish–black split never came off. He did manage to do a one-minute tape on October 21 extolling "law and order in the classrooms of America" as the only way to assure a better education for the nation's children.[101] But Leonard Garment and Harry Treleaven, his media advisers, vetoed his attempt to intrude into the tangled New York struggle and suppressed it. Yet the war over the New York City schools would help Nixon in the end. As the campaign progressed, Jewish voters, like other traditional Democrats, grew more enthusiastic about Humphrey and in the end gave him thumping majorities as they had all Democratic candidates since the Great Depression. Yet after 1968 they became one of the more conservative blocs within the party, touchy on such issues as affirmative action and other signs of special concern for the party's nonwhite racial minorities.

By late October the race was getting close. Gene McCarthy had taken a Riviera vacation after Chicago, and when he returned, the former first baseman for the Great Soo baseball league had accepted a whimsical assignment from *Life* magazine to cover the world series. Not until mid-October did he break the political surface again, and when he did he refused to endorse Humphrey unless the vice-president accepted the Vietcong as part of a Saigon coalition government, promised to reform the draft drastically, and agreed to reorganize the Democratic party. These were not conditions that Humphrey, struggling to win back the party's center and right, could accept.

But as the days passed, the specter of a Nixon victory had come to haunt McCarthy, and on October 29 he finally endorsed the vice-president. He did not approve of everything Humphrey stood for, he said. On the issues he had raised earlier, the vice-president's position "falls far short of what I think it should be." Yet he was clearly a better choice than Richard Nixon. His endorsement, he announced in his best sackcloth-and-ashes way, was "in no way intended to reinstate" himself personally "in the good graces of the Democratic Party leaders. . . ." Nor should it suggest that he had "forgotten the things that happened both before Chicago and at Chicago."[102] Humphrey was grateful for even this feeble backing and announced that he was "a happy man this morning."[103]

McCarthy's was one of many valuable endorsements during the last two weeks. On October 28 Ralph Abernathy of the Southern Christian Leadership Conference came out for Humphrey. A day later, Coretta King did too. On the last weekend of the campaign, Allard Lowenstein, running for Congress himself from a Long Island district, finally relented, so disillusioning some of his student supporters that a busload of forty, down from Boston to help his campaign, returned home forthwith in disgust. Most important, at long last Lyndon Johnson decided that he was a Democrat after all. On October 26 at Pikeville, Kentucky, at a reservoir dedication, the president denounced the Republicans as enemies of progress and urged a straight Democratic vote "from White House to courthouse." In New York the next day, he attacked Nixon as a "man who distorts history" and catered to special interest groups. Wallace was still worse. His claim to fame "rested on his ability to stand in college doorways defying the law."[104]

Once aroused, Johnson mobilized his vast powers for the party and its candidate. For weeks the negotiations between the United States and the North Vietnamese in Paris had been stalled by the Communist demands for an "unconditional" cessation to the American bombing and the continued exclusion of the South Vietnamese from the peace table. Until these differences were settled, official peace discussions would not begin. The logjam in Paris underscored the futility of the war and the inability of the Democrats to extricate the United States from the morass. Then, on October 11, the North Vietnamese agreed to allow the Saigon regime to participate in return for accepting the Vietcong as separate negotiators and for a no-strings bombing halt. This change produced some movement, but for the next few weeks the agreement to proceed with negotiations was delayed by backing and filling over details such as only diplomats can tolerate.

Knowing that a break in Paris would immeasurably help Humphrey, the president pushed hard to extract a promise from Hanoi to begin official peace talks before the election. He yielded on the Vietcong and also managed to quiet his remaining fears that a bombing halt would jeopardize the American military position in Vietnam. On October 31 he announced that the bombing of North Vietnam would cease the following day, a move that met the last objections of the Hanoi envoys.

We know, of course, that once begun, the negotiations would drag on for almost five years. But no one could foresee such an outcome in late October 1968, and it was hopefully believed that peace talks meant peace, not just talk. Yet one final step still remained: an actual date for the talks to officially begin. The candidate and his aides waited anxiously for some news before election day that Johnson had finally pulled it off.

It never came. The stumbling block was the Saigon government. If Hanoi tilted marginally to the Democrats, Saigon tilted, more emphatically, to the Republicans, believing Nixon likely to be a tougher anti-Communist adversary than Humphrey. The attitudes of South Vietnamese President Nguyen Van Thieu and his colleagues were influenced by Anna Chennault, the Chinese-born widow of General Claire Chennault, the commander of the famous Flying Tiger U.S. Air Corps detachment that had fought the Japanese under the banner of Chiang Kai-shek during World War II. A charter member of the influential anti–Red Chinese China Lobby and a fierce Republican partisan, Anna Chennault worked on Thieu's fears of a Democratic sellout and convinced the Saigon government that delaying its acceptance of the peace talks until after November 5 would help elect the better friend of South Vietnam.

The administration knew of Mme Chennault's intrigues but found Thieu nearly unmovable. Johnson had gone ahead with the bombing-halt announcement, hoping to force the South Vietnamese to yield. Instead, on November 2, with the American election three days away, Thieu summoned his National Assembly and announced that the presence of the Vietcong as a separate negotiating party in Paris was not acceptable and that Saigon would not send delegates to Paris.

Dismayed by the move and convinced that their Republican adversaries had had a hand in the Chennault–Thieu maneuver, Humphrey's advisers urged the vice-president to charge Nixon with sabotaging the peace talks. The vice-president hesitated. Proof of a Chennault–Nixon connection was weak, and he feared that unsubstantiated charges could blow up in the Democrats' face. He did nothing.

It did not seem to matter. By now it appeared that a peace-talk date would not be needed. As October ended the Gallup polls showed Humphrey with 40 percent; the Democrat had pulled to within two percentage points of his opponent.

The last days were the usual frenzy for both candidates. Nixon finished up with a tattoo of brief radio talks on the North Atlantic Treaty Organization, on the draft, on conservation, on labor, on education. On November 3 he appeared on NBC's "Meet the Press" and promised to consult blacks and young people but to avoid "overpromising" anything to anyone. He concluded in Los Angeles with a two-hour telethon phone-in along the lines of the Portland session at the beginning of the campaign: viewers called in questions to 125 telephone operators, and they were relayed to the candidate by football coach Bud Wilkinson. Nixon, sitting in a black swivel chair, responded comfortably and smoothly to queries that had been asked and answered many times before. One new note was the bombing halt, and here the candidate tried to get across the message that peace was still a long way off. His aides and TV advisers thought he had done well. As Roger Ailes, producer of the ten panel shows, left the Burbank studio, he told reporter Joe McGinniss, "Tonight this was the Nixon I met on the [Mike] Douglas show. This was the Nixon I wanted to work for."[105]

Humphrey also ended with a Los Angeles telethon, following a triumphal motorcade through the city's downtown. The Democratic candidate was surrounded by movie stars—Frank Sinatra, Paul Newman, Kirk Douglas, Edward G. Robinson, Burt Lancaster—who took some of the thousands of calls that poured in. Humphrey was more relaxed than Nixon and wandered around the set with a handheld microphone. His message was hope and trust. The cities could be rebuilt; the race problem could be solved.

Wallace too had his campaign capper. He was so far behind now that the money had dried up. His final shot was a half-hour telecast emphasizing the message that there wasn't "a dime's worth of difference" between the two major parties.[106]

*   *   *

The Nixons had already cast absentee ballots, and the Republican candidate did not fly back to New York until election day. As the *Tricia*, the chartered Republican campaign jet, crossed the continent, Americans below were voting by the millions. The mood on the plane was subdued. The race was too close for comfort. Two days before, the *Los Angeles Times* had announced that the gap between Nixon and Humphrey in California had dropped to a single percentage point. The *Tricia* arrived at Newark airport at 6:15 P.M., and by a little after seven o'clock the candidate was ensconced in his Waldorf Towers suite to sweat out the returns.

Humphrey had left Los Angeles the evening before to cast his ballot in person. Landing in Minneapolis in a cold drizzle, he was driven to his Waverly house and after shaving and showering went to the Maryville Township Hall, a white clapboard structure with a single curtained booth. There he dutifully performed the candidate's traditional election-day voting rite, smiling and waving through the fatigue while the photographers' flashed their bulbs. Later that day he went to Democratic headquarters at Minneapolis's Leamington Hotel to await the results.

The first returns of a presidential race are usually meaningless. Some village in rural New Hampshire gives the Republican candidate eight of its twelve votes. Or rich, but Catholic and liberal, Connecticut pours out an early flood of Democratic ballots. That evening the first real signs of a trend came with the early North Carolina and Virginia reports. Nixon was winning, apparently taking the states from both Wallace and Humphrey. The Republican border-state strategy was working.

Then the tide shifted. Toward midnight Humphrey drew ahead in New York, Pennsylvania, and Michigan. Robert McCandless and William Connell, two close aides, predicted victory with either 294 or 340 electoral votes. By 10:20 P.M. the popular totals were a dead draw at 41 percent each for Nixon and Humphrey and Wallace at 18 percent.

The remaining hours were a torture for both candidates with results seesawing repeatedly back and forth. Nixon refused to watch the returns on TV, but sat alone in the living room of the

Waldorf suite receiving reports from aides and making hurried calculations on a yellow legal pad. The Nixon family and guests sat before the flickering screens in another suite.

Through the late evening and early morning, Texas, Ohio, Illinois, and California remained up in the air, but then began to shift into the Republican column. By 2:00 A.M. Humphrey was ready to concede. His friends restrained him, and instead he descended from his suite to the Leamington's Hall of States ballroom, where he gave the would-be celebrators a pep talk and then went to bed. In New York, Nixon finally concluded by three that he was over the top. At 3:15 he returned an earlier call from Agnew and said, "Well, Ted, we've won."[107] At four he awakened Governor Rockefeller and thanked him for the help he had given. Soon after, he gathered his close advisers for a little informal victory celebration, rousing several from sound sleep. The cheerful party consumed beer and sandwiches while reminiscing about the campaign.

The results, when all counted the next day, gave Nixon 301 electoral votes to Humphrey's 191 and Wallace's 46. The solid Nixon electoral majority would spare the country a wrenching state-by-state vote in Congress, unprecedented in this century. But the popular vote was amazingly close. The vice-president had 31,270,000 votes—42.7 percent—to Nixon's 31,785,000—43.4 percent. Wallace got almost 10,000,000 votes, about 13 percent.

The results can be read in different ways. From one perspective, the election suggests continuity. The Democrats had almost regained the ascendancy they had achieved in 1960, the top place that had recently threatened to slip from their grasp. Humphrey had barely missed reassembling the old New Deal coalition of ethnics, Catholics, blacks, and union families that the shocks of the previous four years seemed ready to fragment. In Congress the Democrats had slipped, but by just a sliver; they would retain control of both houses. President Nixon would have to contend with the powerful congressional committee chairmen of the opposition party. By this view, Nixon's victory did not mark a major political change. There had not been a dramatic shift to the Republicans.

Yet political events must be measured by more than the social scientists' statistics. Political changes are also states of mind. And here is where we find the true significance of the Democratic defeat.

The Johnson years had been a time when a political system built for stasis promised to generate major change. For the first time in a generation—only one of four or five occasions in America's history as an independent nation—a majority, albeit tentatively and marginally, favored social change and believed it possible through normal political channels. The tumultuous months since that amazing day in November 1964 when the American people gave change one of its most emphatic mandates had witnessed a severe erosion of the reform coalition. Bit by bit, pieces had sublimed off like the heat shield of a reentering space rocket. But a nub remained on election day 1968 and with Humphrey as president might have revived. Nixon's victory confirmed the end of an era.

It also isolated social reform from the mainstream political process. Humphrey's victory would have kept reform within the boundaries of responsible governance. His defeat turned the party over to its most liberal New Politics element. These were men and women who believed that politics was a forum for enacting virtue, not a mechanism for balancing competing interests and making the system function. Out of office they would pull the party ever farther away from its mainstream working-class and middle-class constituency and make it for a time the vehicle for the nation's liberal ideologues and outsiders. In 1972 they would get the candidate they wanted. But George McGovern's nomination victory at Miami Beach would guarantee the worst Democratic presidential defeat since John W. Davis lost to Calvin Coolidge in 1924. It was a sure formula for permanent minority status and if not for the Republican disgrace following Watergate, would have kept the Democrats out of the White House for a generation or more. Only today, as the Republican begins its third century under the Constitution, does the nation's political landscape seem to be regaining the familiar two-party look of the 1960s.

Epilogue

THE WEEKS following the presidential election were a quiet stretch in an ear-splitting year. In Paris, though the South Vietnamese finally ended their boycott of the peace negotiations, there was little progress toward ending the appalling war. On the Vietnam battlefronts there was skirmishing in the mountains and evidence that the North Vietnamese were violating the neutrality of the demilitarized zone, but no major actions. In late November Charles de Gaulle had his comeuppance when the franc came under attack by the goldbugs threatening its stability. At home the political fires inevitably subsided. It was the transition time between two administrations, and as usual the process was pronounced "orderly" and "smooth."

Yet two of those twenty, eight-column *New York Times* headlines of 1968 appeared at the end of December, during the Christmas season. These would blazon the success of the Apollo 8 mission in orbiting the moon and returning home safely on December 28, three days before the year's end.

The mission had blasted off from Cape Kennedy at dawn on December 21 atop a huge, three-stage Saturn 5 rocket that generated more power than man had ever packed into one engine before. Three men lay strapped into the tiny cone-shaped command module perched 350 feet above the ground—William Anders, a thirty-five year-old air force major; James Lovell, Jr., a navy aviator and test pilot; and Frank Borman, the mission commander, an air force colonel, a man known for his tight self-discipline and total dedication.

Thirty-one hours after blast-off, the crew transmitted the first TV pictures of earth as seen from their speeding craft. Through the fogged-over window it looked like a white blob, though Borman in his radio voice-over described the view as "beautiful, beautiful . . . with a blue background and just huge covers of white clouds."[1]

Earthlings got a better look at their home the following day through a higher-power camera lens when the spacecraft was 214,000 miles out. The *Times* now reported, "It looked like a large misshapen basketball that kept bouncing around and sometimes off the television screens. . . ."[2] Borman added that he and his crewmates could make out the royal blue of the oceans, the dark brown land, and prominent landmarks like Baja California and the mouth of the Mississippi. By this time the service-command module had passed the point where earth's gravity dominated. It was the first time human beings had freed themselves from a cosmic tie that had existed since mankind's birth.

Early on the twenty-fourth, Cape Kennedy time, Apollo 8 passed out of visual and radio communication as it whipped around to the moon's dark side, the face always turned away from earth. The voyagers returned to view twenty tense minutes later. They had successfully fired their rocket while on the dark side and placed themselves in lunar orbit. During the next twenty hours, while the Christian world celebrated the Savior's birth, the astronauts circled the moon ten times broadcasting back to earth their impressions of the gray, jagged lunar landscape and reading aloud a portion of Genesis, the first Christmas sermon from outer space. On Christmas morning they began the return trip and splashed down in the mid-Pacific on December 27. Forty-five minutes later they were lifted safely aboard the carrier *Yorktown*.

TV Guide estimated that nearly a billion people in sixty-four countries had seen some part of the Apollo 8 telecasts. Many more read about the mission and saw the pictures the astronauts brought back. Borman, Lovell, and Anders were *Time* magazine's 1968 Men of the Year.

The Apollo 8 mission would be followed in July 1969 by the successful Apollo 11 moon landing. This landmark in the human adventure would blot out its predecessor. Yet at the time Apollo 8 seemed an event of immense significance. The most memorable impression of the voyage, everyone agreed, was the image of a tiny blue-white-brown earth bobbing against a background of deepest black space.

The color photograph published soon after became another of those indelible images of the 1960s. LBJ, as one of his last acts, sent copies to every head of state, even Ho Chi Minh. Never before had humans seen the entire earth so small and so alone, and it created a spine-tingling sensation of wonder and awe.

The mood lent itself to speculation and philosophizing. Archibald MacLeish, poet, playwright, Librarian of Congress, America's favorite middlebrow intellectual, noted that mankind's sense of self had always depended on its view of the cosmos. In the Middle Ages, when humans saw the earth as the center of the universe, they believed themselves the focus of God's attention. Secure in that high vantage, they had killed and conquered as they pleased. Copernicus and Galileo had moved humanity from the center to the periphery and Newton had made God unnecessary. During the next three to four centuries, mankind had lived in a senseless world where any horror was sanctioned—"worldwide wars, . . . concentration camps, and blasted cities." But now that we had seen the earth from the depths of space, "seen it whole and round and beautiful and small as even Dante . . . had never dreamed of seeing it," we could finally view ourselves as "brothers who know now they are truly brothers."[3]

MacLeish's naive forecast was an echo of early sixties' optimism. It already seemed dated when it appeared. By late 1968 the American public had lost the élan, and also the arrogance, that had infused the moon race from its start seven years before.

Image-making, cold-war rivalry, personal ambition, activism for activism's sake, technocratic hubris, all had moved the young John F. Kennedy when he stood before a special session of Congress in May 1961 and announced that the United States "should commit itself to achieving the goal, before this decade is out, of landing a man on the moon and returning him safely to earth."⁴ But the cynics who belittle the motives of the space race disregard, or have never understood, the thrill and wonder of discovery. It was the American style, especially in the Kennedy– Johnson years, to clothe romantic and humane yearnings in practical and self-serving words for the sake of disguising their awkward idealism.

The public had been moved by the idealism as well as by the anti-Soviet rivalry, and Congress had poured out its billions. By the end of 1968 cynicism had set in. To the ghettos and the campuses the space race had come to seem like a displacement, literally, to another world of resources urgently needed here on terra firma. The space program would continue, yet after the early triumphs of 1968–72—the moon landings of Apollo 11 through 17—space too would cease to be an important part of the mainstream American agenda. Like so much else that had been bound to the prosperity, buoyancy, and optimism of the 1960s, the desire to "go where no man had been before" subsided in the next decade, leaving behind an underfunded and unsafe orbiting facility for military surveillance and commercial communications satellites.

William V. Shannon, a *New York Times* editorial staffer, writing on December 30, would call 1968 "the year that failed to turn."⁵ There had been, he admitted, violence aplenty—on the campuses of Nanterre and Columbia and in the streets of Paris, Chicago, and Berlin. But the year, he wrote, was like 1848, a year when Europe exploded in turmoil, but failed to transform itself. Unlike 1776 and 1789, governments did not fall, constitutions were not permanently rewritten, the downtrodden did not rise, property and wealth were not expropriated.

Shannon set his standards too high. Twelve months seldom provide enough time for an entire society to pivot 180 degrees. Yet by any reasonable measure the changes crammed into 1968 were remarkable. It was the year when the Great Society petered out, when the civil rights movement stopped dead, when the liberal consensus of the sixties came apart, when the Vietnam War leveled off, when the cultural outsiders found their voice. Some one has described 1968 as the worst year of the century. As in everything else, it depends on where you stand.

Notes

Prologue

1. *New York Times*, December 29, 1967.
2. David Burnham, "Urban Riots Foreseen in U.S.," *New York Times*, December 30, 1967.
3. *Newsweek*, January 1, 1968.
4. Committee on Internal Security, House of Representatives, 92nd Cong., 1st sess., *Gun-Barrel Politics: The Black Panther Party, 1966–1972* (Washington, D.C.: Government Printing Office, 1971), p. 17.
5. Irwin Unger, *The Movement: A History of the American New Left, 1959–1972* (New York: Harper & Row, 1974), p. 128.
6. Theodore H. White, *The Making of the President, 1968* (New York: Pocket Books, 1970), p. 493.

1. The Poor Are Always with You

1. Martin Feldstein, "Introduction," in Feldstein (ed.), *The American Economy in Transition* (Chicago: University of Chicago Press, 1980), p. 1.
2. Allen J. Matusow, *The Unraveling of America: A History of Liberalism in the 1960s* (New York: Harper & Row, 1984), p. 33.
3. Richard E. Mooney, "The Financial Crisis," *New York Times*, April 23, 1968.
4. Robert Sobel, *The Last Bull Market: Wall Street in the 1960s* (New York: Norton, 1980), p. 68.
5. *Time*, December 31, 1965, p. 64.
6. Lester Thurow, in Haveman (ed.), *A Decade of Federal Antipoverty Programs: Achievements, Failures, and Lessons* (New York: Academic Press, 1977). p. 118.
7. Frances Fox Piven and Richard A. Cloward, "A Strategy to End Poverty," *Nation*, May 2, 1966, p. 516.

8. Michael Harrington, *The Other America: Poverty in the United States* (New York: Macmillan, 1963), p. 2.

9. James Sundquist, "Origins of the War on Poverty," in Sundquist (ed.), *On Fighting Poverty: Perspectives from Experience* (New York: Basic Books, 1969), p. 7.

10. Lyndon B. Johnson, *The Vantage Point: Perspectives of the Presidency, 1963–1969* (New York: Holt, Rinehart & Winston, 1971), p. 74.

11. *Public Papers of the Presidents of the United States: Lyndon B. Johnson*, vol. 1, p. 114.

12. Adam Yarmolinsky, "The Beginnings of OEO," in Sundquist (ed.), *On Fighting Poverty*, p. 36.

13. Matusow, *op. cit.*, p. 118.

14. *Ibid.*, p. 124.

15. James T. Patterson, *America's Struggle Against Poverty, 1900–1980* (Cambridge, Mass.: Harvard University Press, 1981), p. 140.

16. Theodore H. White, *The Making of the President, 1964* (New York: Atheneum, 1965), p. 39.

17. Doris Kearns, *Lyndon Johnson and the America Dream* (New York: Harper & Row, 1976), p. 216.

18. Johnson, *op. cit.*, p. 219.

19. Eric Goldman, *The Tragedy of Lyndon Johnson* (New York: Knopf, 1969), p. 332.

20. Johnson, *op. cit.*, p. 163.

21. William Bowen, "The U.S. Economy Enters a New Era," *Fortune*, March 1967, p. 114.

22. William C. Crook and Ross Thomas, *Warriors for the Poor: The Story of VISTA, Volunteers in Service to America* (New York: Morrow, 1969), p. 57.

23. Charles Silberman, "The Mixed Up War on Poverty," *Fortune*, August 1965, p. 223.

24. William Selover, "The View from Capitol Hill," in Sundquist (ed.), *On Fighting Poverty*, p. 167.

25. Silberman, *op. cit.*, p. 158.

26. Henry J. Aaron, *Politics and the Professors: The Great Society in Perspective* (Washington, D.C.: Brookings Institution, 1978), p. 22.

27. Jeffrey L. Pressman and Aaron Wildavsky, *Implementation: How Great Expectations in Washington are Dashed in Oakland* (Berkeley: University of California Press, 1973), p. 31.

28. Gregory Farrell, "The View from the City: Community Action in Trenton," in Sundquist (ed.), *On Fighting Poverty*, p. 147.

29. Paul Peterson and J. David Greenstone, "Racial Change and Citizen Participation: The Mobilization of Low Income Communities through Community Action," in Haveman, *A Decade of Federal Antipoverty Programs*, p. 248.

30. Douglas Eldridge, "Militant Group Stirs Controversy," *Newark News*, February 5, 1965.

31. William F. Haddad, "Mr. Shriver and the Savage Politics of Poverty," *Harper's*, December 1965, p. 49.

32. Robert Levine, *The Poor Ye Need Not Have With You: Lessons from the War on Poverty* (Cambridge, Mass.: MIT Press, 1970), p. 54.

33. Selover, *op. cit.*, p. 168.

34. *Ibid.*

35. Matusow, *op. cit.*, pp. 260–61.

36. *Ibid.*, p. 262.

37. *Ibid.*

38. Joan Colebrook, *Innocents of the West: Travels through the Sixties* (New York: Basic Books, 1979), p. 301.

39. *Nation*, May 2, 1966, p. 511.

40. Guida West, *The National Welfare Rights Movement: The Social Protest of Poor Women* (New York: Praeger, 1981), p. 24.

41. Richard Cloward and Frances Fox Piven, "Finessing the Poor," *Nation*, October 7, 1968, p. 102.

42. Tom Wolfe, *Radical Chic & Mau-Mauing the Flak Catchers* (New York: Bantam, 1971), p. 144.

43. David Zarefsky, *President Johnson's War on Poverty: Rhetoric and History* (Tuscaloosa: University of Alabama Press, 1986), p. 62.

44. Sobel, *op. cit.*, p. 199.

45. Lawrence Mayer, "The Troubling Shift in the Trade Winds," *Fortune*, June 1, 1968, p. 77.

46. *Ibid.*, p. 78.

47. Robert Elson, "How the Old Politics Swamped the New Economics," *Fortune*, September 1, 1968, p. 76.

48. *Ibid.,*

49. *Ibid.*, p. 77.

50. *Ibid.*, p. 76.

51. Gordon L. Weil and Ian Davidson, *The Gold War: The Story of the World's Monetary Crisis* (New York: Holt, Rinehart & Winston, 1970), p. 127.

52. *Fortune*, June 1, 1968, p. 114.

53. *New York Times*, March 16, 1968.

54. Lady Bird Johnson, *A White House Diary* (New York: Holt, Rinehart & Winston, 1970), pp, 638–39.

55. Kearns, *op. cit.*, p. 301.

56. Gilbert Burck, "Capitol Hill's 'Show Me' Economist," *Fortune*, February 1968, p. 107.

57. *Ibid.*, p. 204.

58. Elson, *op. cit.*, p. 170.

59. Burck, *op. cit.*, p. 207.

60. *Facts on File, 1968*, p. 43.

61. *Ibid.*, p. 52.

62. *Ibid.*, p. 111.

63. *Ibid.*, p. 93.

64. *New York Times*, January 24, 1968.

65. *Ibid.*, March 13, 1968.

66. *Facts on File, 1968*, p. 160.

67. *New York Times*, March 20, 1968.

68. *Facts on File, 1968*, p. 160.

69. Kearns, *op. cit.*, pp. 300–301.

70. Johnson, *Vantage Point*, p. 454.

71. *Ibid.*, p. 459.

72. *New York Times*, June 22, 1968.

73. *Facts on File, 1968*, pp. 393–94.

74. *Ibid.*, pp. 191–92.

75. Sobel, *op. cit.*, p. 223.

2. No Wider War

1. R. W. Apple, "U.S. Said to Press Sharply for Good Vietnam Reports," *New York Times*, January 1, 1968.

2. George M. Kahin and John W. Lewis, *The United States in Vietnam* (New York: Dell, 1969), p. 49.

3. Marvin Gettleman (ed.), *Vietnam: History, Documents, and Opinions on a Major World Crisis* (Greenwich, Conn.: Fawcett, 1965), pp. 189–92.

4. Michael Maclear, *The Ten Thousand Day War: Vietnam, 1945–1975* (New York: Avon, 1981), p. 24.

5. Stanley Karnow, *Vietnam: A History* (New York: Viking, 1983), p. 214.

6. *Public Papers of the Presidents of the United States: John F. Kennedy*, vol. 1, p. 1.

7. Karnow, *op. cit.*, p. 247.

8. *Ibid.*, p. 253.

9. Townsend Hoopes, *The Limits of Intervention: An Inside Account of How the Johnson Policy of Escalation in Vietnam was Reversed* (New York: David McKay, 1973), p. 8.

10. Doris Kearns, *Lyndon Johnson and the American Dream* (New York: Harper & Row, 1976), p. 330.

11. Hoopes, *op. cit.*, p. 18.

12. Walter Isaacson and Evan Thomas, *The Wise Men: Six Friends and the World They Made* (New York: Simon & Schuster, 1986), p. 643.

13. Karnow, *op. cit.*, p. 323.

14. *Ibid.*, p. 325.

15. *Ibid.*, p. 326.

16. *Ibid.*, p. 325.

17. *Ibid.*, p. 372.

18. Marvin Gettleman, Jane Franklin, Marilyn Young, and H. Bruce Franklin (eds.), *Vietnam and America: A Documented History* (New York: Grove, 1985), p. 250.

19. George C. Herring, *America's Longest War: The United States and Vietnam, 1950–1975* (New York: Knopf, 1986), p. 122.

20. Norman Podhoretz, *Why We Were in Vietnam* (New York: Touchstone, 1983), pp. 70–71.

21. Theodore Draper, *Abuse of Power* (New York: Viking, 1967), p. 67.

22. News conference of June 23, 1964, in *Public Papers of the Presidents of the United States: Lyndon B. Johnson*, vol. 1, p. 804.

23. William Westmoreland, *A Soldier Reports* (New York: Dell, 1980), p. 146.

24. James Pinckney Harrison, *The Endless War: Vietnam's Struggles for Independence* (New York: McGraw-Hill, 1982), p. 253.

25. Kirkpatrick Sale, *SDS* (New York: Vintage, 1974), p. 156.

26. Westmoreland, *op. cit.*, p. 149.

27. *Ibid.*, p. 158.

28. Peter A. Poole, *The United States and Indochina from FDR to Nixon* (Hinsdale, Ill.: Dryden, 1973), p. 146.

29. Neil Sheehan et al., *The Pentagon Papers as Published by the New York Times* (New York: Quadrangle, 1971), p. 453.

30. Isaacson and Thomas, *op. cit.*, p. 650.

31. *Ibid.*, p. 651.

32. *Ibid.*, p. 678.

33. *Ibid.*, p. 680.

34. *Ibid.*

35. Don Oberdorfer, *TET! The Turning Point in the Vietnam War* (New York: Da Capo, 1983), p. 70.

36. Peter Braestrup, *Big Story: How the American Press and Television Reported and Interpreted the Crisis of Tet 1968 in Vietnam and Washington* (New Haven: Yale University Press, 1983), p. 68.

37. Oberdorfer, *op. cit.*, p. 54.

38. *Ibid.*, p. 119.

39. Herbert Y. Schandler, *The Unmaking of a President: Lyndon Johnson and Vietnam* (Princeton, N.J.: Princeton University Press, 1977), p. 75.

40. Oberdorfer, *op. cit.*, p. 34.

41. Braestrup, *op. cit.*, p. 193.

42. Oberdorfer, *op. cit.*, p. 207.

43. Karnow, *op. cit.*, p. 533.

44. Herring, *op. cit.*, p. 190.

45. Braestrup, *op. cit.*, p. 303.

46. Karnow, *op. cit.*, p. 541.

47. Herring, *op. cit.*, p. 215.

48. Seymour Hersh, *My Lai 4: A Report on the Massacre and its Aftermath* (New York: Random House, 1970), p. 9.

49. Joseph Goldstein, Burke Marshall, and Jack Schwartz (eds.), *The My Lai Massacre and its Cover-up: Beyond the Reach of Law?* (New York: Free Press, 1976), p. 99.

50. Hersh, *op. cit.*, p. 41.

51. Goldstein et al., *op. cit.*, p. 97.

52. *Ibid.*, pp. 143–44.

53. Braestrup, *op. cit.*, pp. 132–33.

54. Schandler, *op. cit.*, p. 81.

55. *Ibid.*, p. 85.

56. Oberdorfer, *op. cit.*, p. 248.

57. *Ibid.*, p. 249.

58. *Ibid.*, p. 251.

59. Kathleen J. Turner, *Lyndon Johnson's Dual War: Vietnam and the Press* (Chicago: University of Chicago Press, 1985), pp. 9–10.

60. *Ibid.*, p. 10.

61. *Ibid.* p. 220.

62. Westmoreland, *op. cit.*, p. 461.

63. Lyndon B. Johnson, *The Vantage Point: Perspectives of the Presidency, 1963–1969* (New York: Holt, Rinehart & Winston, 1971), pp. 387–88.

64. Schandler, *op. cit.*, pp. 118–19.

65. Hoopes, *op. cit.*, p. 145.

66. *Ibid.*, p. 152.

67. Karnow, *op. cit.*, p. 552.

68. Schandler, *op. cit.*, p. 145.

69. *Ibid.*, pp. 145–46.

70. *Ibid.*, p. 150.

71. Johnson, *Vantage Point*, p. 400.

72. Neil Sheehan and Hedrick Smith, "Westmoreland Requests 206,000 More Men, Stirring Debate in Administration," *New York Times*, March 10, 1968.

73. Schandler, *op. cit.*, p. 202.

74. Kearns, *op. cit.*, p. 313.

75. Schandler, *op. cit.*, pp. 208–209.

76. *Ibid.*, pp. 215–16.

77. *New York Times*, March 22, 1968.

78. Isaacson and Thomas, *op. cit.*, p. 694.

79. Lady Bird Johnson, *A White House Diary* (New York: Holt, Reinhart & Winston, 1970), p. 641.

80. Isaacson and Thomas, *op. cit.*, p. 699.

81. Willaim A. Williams, Thomas McCormick, Lloyd Gardner, and Walter LeFeber (eds.), *Vietnam in America: A Documentary History* (Garden City, N.Y.: Anchor, 1985), pp. 270–71.

82. Isaacson and Thomas, *op. cit.*, pp. 700–701.

83. Johnson, *Vantage Point,* p. 416.

84. *Ibid.,*

85. Isaacson and Thomas, *op. cit.,* p. 702.

86. Schandler, *op. cit.,* p. 264.

87. Kearns, *op. cit.,* p. 343.

88. Johnson, *Diary,* p. 550.

89. Frank Cormier, *LBJ: The Way He Was* (Garden City, N.Y.: Doubleday, 1977), p. 262.

90. Turner, *op. cit.,* p. 235.

91. Johnson, *Vantage Point,* p. 427.

92. Theodore H. White, *The Making of the President, 1968* (New York: Pocket Books, 1970), p. 147.

93. *Ibid.,* p. 141.

94. *Public Papers of the Presidents of the United States: Lyndon B. Johnson,* vol. 1, pp. 469–70.

95. *Ibid.,* p. 476.

96. *Ibid.,*

97. Schandler, *op. cit.,* p. 288.

98. Johnson, *Vantage Point,* p. 495.

3. We Shall Overcome—Someday

1. August Meier and Elliott Rudwick, *CORE: A Study in the Civil Rights Movement* (Urbana, Ill.: University of Illinois Press, 1975), p. 6.

2. *Ibid.,* p. 13.

3. David J. Garrow, *Bearing the Cross: Martin Luther King, Jr., and the Southern Christian Leadership Conference* (New York: Morrow, 1986), p. 12.

4. *Ibid.,* p. 33.

5. *Ibid.,* p. 35.

6. David Lewis, *King: A Biography* (Urbana, Ill.: University of Illinois Press, 1978), p. 70.

7. Harvard Sitkoff, *The Struggle for Black Equality, 1954–1980* (New York: Hill & Wang, 1981), p. 58.

8. Howell Raines, *My Soul Is Rested: Movement Days in the Deep South Remembered* (New York: Penguin, 1983), p. 76.

9. *Ibid.,* p. 79.

10. Sitkoff, *op. cit.,* p. 93.

11. James Farmer, *Lay Bare the Heart: An Autobiography of the Civil Rights Movement* (New York: Arbor House, 1985), p. 195.

12. Raines, *op. cit.,* p. 109.

13. Juan Williams, *Eyes on the Prize: America's Civil Right Years, 1954–1965* (New York: Viking-Penguin, 1987), p. 169.

14. Lewis, *op. cit.,* p. 151.

15. *Ibid.,* p. 171.

16. Flip Schulke and Penelope McPhee, *King Remembered* (New York: Pocket Books, 1986), p. 118.

17. *Ibid.,* p. 119.

18. Raines, *op. cit.,* p. 148.

19. Schulke and McPhee, *op. cit.,* p. 278.

20. Garrow, *op. cit.,* p. 247.

21. Stephen B. Oates, *Let the Trumpet Sound: The Life of Martin Luther King, Jr.* (New York: New American Library, 1982), p. 228.

22. Garrow, *op. cit.,* p. 252.

23. Sitkoff, *op. cit.*, p. 158.

24. Lewis, *op. cit.*, p. 223.

25. Coretta Scott King (ed.), *The Words of Martin Luther King, Jr.* (New York: Newmarket Press, 1983), pp. 95–98.

26. Schulke and McPhee, *op. cit.*, p. 162.

27. Oates, *op. cit.*, p. 318.

28. Schulke and McPhee, *op. cit.*, p. 194.

29. Lyndon B. Johnson, *The Vantage Point: Perspectives of the Presidency, 1963–1969* (New York: Holt, Reinhart & Winston, 1971), pp. 164–65.

30. Sitkoff, *op. cit.*, p. 194.

31. C. Eric Lincoln, *The Black Muslims in America* (New York: Beacon Press, 1973), p. 79.

32. Alphonso Pinkney, *Red, Black, and Green: Black Nationalism in the United States* (Cambridge, U.K.: Cambridge University Press, 1976), p. 159.

33. *Ibid.*, p. 67.

34. Lincoln, *op. cit.*, p. 210.

35. Clayborne Carson, *In Struggle: SNCC and the Black Awakening of the 1960s* (Cambridge, Mass.: Harvard University Press, 1981), p. 101.

36. Richard Cummings, *The Pied Piper: Allard Lowenstein and the Liberal Dream* (New York: Grove, 1985), p. 244.

37. Carson, *op. cit.*, pp. 127–28.

38. James Baldwin, *The Fire Next Time* (New York: Dial, 1963).

39. Lewis, *op. cit.*, p. 307.

40. Lawrence Lader, *Power on the Left: American Radical Movements Since 1946* (New York: Norton, 1979), p. 208.

41. Meier and Rudwick, *op. cit.*, p. 414.

42. Schulke and McPhee, *op. cit.*, p. 215.

43. Sitkoff, *op. cit.*, p. 213.

44. Oates, *op. cit.*, p. 386.

45. Garrow, *op. cit.*, p. 488.

46. Committee on Internal Security, House of Representatives, 92nd Congress, 1st sess., *Gun-Barrel Politics: The Black Panther Party, 1966–1971* (Washington, D.C.: U.S. Government Printing Office, 1971), pp. 16–17.

47. Eldridge Cleaver, *Soul on Ice* (New York: Dell, 1968), p. 14.

48. Committee on Internal Security, *op. cit.*, p. 24.

49. Alan B. Anderson and George W. Pickering, *Confronting the Color Line: The Broken Promise of the Civil Rights Movement in Chicago* (Athens: University of Georgia Press, 1986), p. 168.

50. *Ibid.*, p. 191.

51. Oates, *op. cit.*, p. 391.

52. *Ibid.*, p. 392.

53. Anderson and Pickering, *op. cit.*, p. 200.

54. *Ibid.*, p. 208.

55. Oates, *op. cit.*, p. 398.

56. *Ibid.*, pp. 398–99.

57. Garrow, *op. cit.*, p. 500.

58. Oates, *op. cit.*, p. 401.

59. Garrow, *op. cit.*, p. 523.

60. Adam Fairclough, "Was Martin Luther King a Marxist?" in C. Eric Lincoln (ed.), *Martin Luther King, Jr.: A Profile* (New York: Hill & Wang, 1984), p. 236.

61. Garrow, *op. cit.*, p. 445.

62. Oates, *op. cit.*, p. 365.

63. Garrow, *op. cit.*, p. 545.

64. Oates, *op. cit.*, p. 418.

65. David Garrow, *The FBI and Martin Luther King, Jr.: From "Solo" to Memphis* (New York: Norton, 1981), p. 168.

66. Oates, *op. cit.,* p. 416; Lewis, *King,* p. 358.

67. Sitkoff, *op. cit.,* p. 217.

68. Carson, *op. cit.,* p. 255.

69. *Ibid.,* p. 268.

70. *Ibid.*

71. *Ibid.*

72. Garrow, *Cross,* p. 581.

73. Oates, *op. cit.,* p. 435.

74. *New York Times,* December 5, 1967.

75. *Ibid.,* December 18, 1967.

76. Oates, *op. cit.,* p. 437.

77. Garrow, *FBI,* p. 186.

78. Jose Yglesias, "Dr. King's March on Washington, Part II," *New York Times Magazine,* March 31, 1968, p. 58.

79. *Ibid.,* p. 31.

80. *Ibid.,* pp. 57–58.

81. Oates, *op. cit.,* p. 442.

82. *Washington Post,* February 8, 1968.

83. Oates, *op. cit.,* p. 449.

84. *New York Times,* March 8, 1968.

85. *Ibid.,* March 5, 1968.

86. *Ibid.,* March 27, 1968.

87. Garrow, *Cross,* pp. 602–603.

88. Oates, *op. cit.,* p. 452.

89. *Ibid.,* p. 457.

90. *U.S. News & World Report,* April 2, 1968, p. 8.

91. *New York Times,* March 30, 1968.

92. *Ibid.*

93. Oates, *op. cit.,* p. 463.

94. Select Committee on Assassinations, U.S. House of Representatives, 95th Cong., 2nd sess., *Findings and Recommendations* (Washington, D.C.: U.S. Government Printing Office, 1979), pp. 358–74.

95. Garrow, *Cross,* p. 621.

96. Charles Fager, *Uncertain Resurrection: The Poor People's Washington Campaign* (Grand Rapids, Mich.: Eerdmans Publishing, 1969), p. 16.

97. Ben W. Gilbert et al., *Ten Blocks from the White House* (New York: Praeger, 1968), p. 15.

98. *Ibid.,* pp. 21–22.

99. *Ibid.,* p. 153.

100. *Ibid.,* p. 161.

101. *Ibid.,* pp. 60–61.

102. *New York Times,* April 9, 1968.

103. Paul Good, "'No Man Can Fill Dr. King's Shoes'—But Abernathy Tries," in August Meier and Elliott Rudwick (eds.), *Black Protest in the Sixties* (Chicago: Quadrangle Books, 1970), p. 288.

104. *Washington Post,* April 29, 1968.

105. *Ibid.,* May 15, 1968.

106. Fager, *op. cit.,* p. 37.

107. *Washington Post,* June 8, 1968.

108. Fager, *op. cit.,* p. 63.

109. *Washington Post,* June 20, 1968.

110. *Ibid.*

111. *Ibid.*

112. Fager, *op. cit.,* p. 95.

113. *Washington Post,* June 23, 1968.

114. *Ibid.,* June 26, 1968.

115. *Ibid.,* June 25, 1968.

116. *Ibid.,* June 26, 1968.

117. Fager, *op. cit.,* p. 124.

118. Meier and Rudwick, *op. cit.,* p. 425.

119. Lader, *op. cit.,* p. 248.

120. *Newsweek,* October 28, 1968.

121. Julius Lester, "From the Other Side of the Tracks," *Guardian,* August 24, 1968.

4. The Left Could Not Hold

1. *New York Times,* June 16, 1968.

2. Kirkpatrick Sale, *SDS* (New York: Vintage, 1974), p. 686.

3. Robert Scheer, "Notes on the New Left," *Root and Branch* (Winter 1963), p. 21.

4. C. Wright Mills, "Letter to the New Left," *New Left Review,* September–October, 1960, pp. 18–23.

5. Sale, *op. cit.,* p. 24.

6. Massimo Teodori (ed.), *The New Left: A Documentary History* (Indianapolis: Bobbs-Merrill, 1969), pp. 163–72.

7. Sale, *op. cit.,* p. 134.

8. Jack Newfield, *A Prophetic Minority* (New York: New American Library, 1966), p. 142.

9. Seymour Lipset and Sheldon Wolin (eds.), *The Berkeley Student Revolt: Facts and Interpretations* (Garden City, N.Y.: Doubleday, 1965), p. 104.

10. Clark Kerr, *The Uses of the University* (Cambridge, Mass.: Harvard University Press, 1963), pp. 87–88.

11. Irwin Unger, *The Movement: A History of the American New Left, 1959–1972* (New York: Harper & Row, 1974), p. 76.

12. Max Heirich, *The Spiral of Conflict: Berkeley, 1964* (New York: Columbia University Press, 1971), p. 148.

13. Lewis Feuer, *The Conflict of Generations: The Character and Significance of Student Movements* (New York: Basic Books, 1969), p. 444.

14. Heirich, *op. cit.,* p. 269.

15. *Ibid.,* pp. 271–72.

16. *Ibid.,* p. 276.

17. *Ibid.,* p. 279.

18. Unger, *op. cit.,* p. 74.

19. *Ibid.,* p. 74.

20. *Ibid.,* p. 78.

21. Larry Spence, "Berkeley: What it Demonstrates," *Studies on the Left,* Winter 1965, pp. 66–67.

22. Wini Breines, *The Great Refusal: Community and Organization in the New Left, 1962–1968* (New York: Praeger, 1982), p. 97.

23. Sale, *op. cit.,* pp. 155–56.

24. *New York Times,* April 18, 1965.

25. Sale, *op. cit.,* p. 211.

26. *Ibid.*, p. 238.

27. *Ibid.*, p. 206.

28. Carl Davidson, "Toward a Student Syndicalist Movement, or University Reform Revisited," in Immanuel Wallerstein and Paul Starr (eds.), *The University Crisis Reader;* vol. 2, *Confrontation and Counterattack* (New York: Vintage, 1971), pp. 98–107.

29. Carl Davidson, "The Multiversity: Crucible of the New Working Class," in Wallerstein and Starr, *The University Crisis Reader;* vol. 1, *The Liberal University Under Attack* (New York: Vintage, 1971), pp. 86–99.

30. *New Left Notes*, February 13, 1967.

31. Greg Calvert, "White America: Radical Consciousness and Social Change," in Teodori, *New Left*, pp. 412–18.

32. John Searle, "A Foolproof Scenario for Student Revolts," *New York Times Magazine*, December 29, 1968, p. 132.

33. *New Left Notes*, February 12, 1968.

34. *Ibid.*, September 25, 1967.

35. *Ibid.*

36. *Ibid.*, May 29, 1967.

37. Sale, *op. cit.*, pp. 398–99.

38. Marvin Garson, "What Happened at Chicago: An Analysis," *Berkeley Barb*, September 15–21, 1967; *New York Times*, September 3, 1967.

39. Richard Blumenthal, "New Politics at Chicago," *Nation*, September, 25, 1967, p. 274.

40. Irwin Unger, "The 'Long March through the Institutions': Movement for a Democratic Society and the New University Conference," in William J. Cooper, Jr., Michael Holt, and John McCardell (eds.), *A Master's Due: Essays in Honor of David Herbert Donald* (Baton Rouge: Louisiana State University Press, 1985), pp. 251–53.

41. *Ibid.*, pp. 252–53.

42. *Ibid.*, pp. 257–58.

43. *New York Review of Books*, December 19, 1968, p. 34.

44. Florence Howe, "What Success at the MLA," MLA File, New University Conference Manuscripts, State Historical Society of Wisconsin, n.d.

45. *Newsweek*, May 31, 1968.

46. Jerry A. Avorn, *Up Against the Ivy Wall: A History of the Columbia Crisis* (New York: Atheneum, 1969), p. 33.

47. *Ibid.*, p. 291.

48. Roger Kahn, *The Battle for Morningside Heights: Why Students Rebel* (New York: Morrow, 1970), p. 104.

49. Archibald Cox, *The Cox Commission Report: Crisis at Columbia* (New York: Vintage, 1968), p. 74.

50. Avorn, *op. cit.*, p. 39.

51. *Ibid.*, p. 40.

52. James Simon Kunen, *The Strawberry Statement: Notes of a College Revolutionary* (New York: Random House, 1969), p. 21.

53. Cox, *op. cit.*, pp. 205–207.

54. Avorn, *op. cit.*, pp. 35–36.

55. *Columbia Spectator*, April 24, 1968.

56. F. W. Dupee, "The Uprising at Columbia," *New York Review of Books*, September 26, 1968, p. 23.

57. Immanuel Wallerstein and Paul Starr (eds.), *Confrontation and Counterattack*, vol. 2 of *The University Crisis Reader* (New York: Vintage, 1971), p. 162.

58. Rusti Eisenberg, "The Strike: A Critical Reappraisal," in Wallerstein and Starr, *Confrontation*, p. 170.

59. Wallerstein and Starr, *op. cit.*, pp. 168–69.

60. Avorn, *op. cit.*, p. 60.

61. *Ibid.*, p. 62.

62. Mark Naison to Paul [Buhle], *Radical America* Manuscripts, State Historical Society of Wisconsin, n.d.

63. *New York Times*, April 27, 1968.

64. Avorn, *op. cit.*, p. 292.

65. *New York Times*, April 29, 1968; Kunen, *op. cit.*, p. 31.

66. Robert Liebert, *Radical and Militant Youth: A Psychoanalytic Inquiry* (New York: Praeger, 1971), p. 94.

67. Cox, *op. cit.*, p. 138.

68. *Ibid.*, p. 119.

69. Diana Trilling, "On the Steps of Low Library: Liberalism and the Revolution of the Young," *Commentary*, November 1968, p. 33.

70. Stephen Spender, *The Year of the Young Rebels* (New York: Random House, 1969), p. 24.

71. *New York Times*, April 30, 1968.

72. Avorn, *op. cit.*, pp. 140–41.

73. Kahn, *op. cit.*, pp. 195–96.

74. Liebert, *op. cit.*, p. 153.

75. *Newsweek*, May 13, 1968.

76. Joanne Grant, *Confrontation on Campus: The Columbia Pattern for the New Protest* (New York: New American Library, 1969), p. 101.

77. Wallerstein and Starr, *op. cit.*, pp. 165–66.

78. Sale, *op. cit.*, p. 443.

79. Avorn, *op. cit.*, p. 260.

80. Tom Hayden, "Two, Three, Many Columbias," *Ramparts*, June 15, 1968, p. 40.

81. Denver Office to Director, June 28, 1968, COINTELPRO, New Left, Scholarly Resources, Inc.

82. Sale, *op. cit.*, pp. 465–66.

83. *New Left Notes*, August 5, 1968.

84. Nancy Zaroulis and Gerald Sullivan, *Who Spoke Up?: American Protest Against the War in Vietnam, 1963–1975* (Garden City, N.Y.: Doubleday, 1984), p. 201.

85. Thomas Powers, *Diana: The Making of a Terrorist* (Boston: Houghton Mifflin, 1971), p. 88.

86. *Ibid.*, p. 87.

87. *New Left Notes*, October 7, 1968.

88. Sale, *op. cit.*, p. 503.

89. *New Left Notes*, December 23, 1968.

90. *New York Times*, December 7, 1968.

91. Dikran Karagueuzian, *Blow it Up! The Black Student Revolt at San Francisco State College and the Emergence of Dr. Hayakawa* (Boston: Gambit, 1971), pp. 101–102.

92. *New York Times*, December 14, 1968.

93. Leo Litwak and Herbert Wilner, *College Days in Earthquake Country: Ordeal at San Francisco State, A Personal Record* (New York: Random House, 1971), p. 124.

94. Wallerstein and Starr, *op. cit.*, p. 440.

95. *Newsweek*, December 16, 1968.

96. *New York Times*, December 3, 1968.

97. Litwak and Wilner, *op. cit.*, p. 187.

98. Todd Gitlin, "Students Club Police Rioters," *East Village Other*, December 13, 1968.

99. Peter Shapiro and Bill Barlow, "San Francisco State: Business as Usual," *Leviathan*, April 1969.

100. *New Left Notes*, December 4, 1968.

101. Cathy Wilkerson, Mike Spiegel, and Les Coleman, "The False Privilege," *New Left Notes,* October 7, 1968.

102. *Radicals in the Professions Newsletter,* November–December 1968.

103. Irwin and Debi Unger interview with Flacks, Santa Barbara, Calif., October 1980.

104. Mike Klonsky, "Toward a Revolutionary Youth Movement," in Wallerstein and Starr, *Confrontation,* pp. 216–21.

105. Wallerstein and Starr, *op. cit.,* pp. 221–26.

106. Carl Davidson, *National Guardian,* January 11, 1969.

107. The most accessible of the Weatherman statements can be found in Harold Jacobs (ed.), *Weatherman* (San Francisco: Ramparts Press, 1970), pp. 51–90.

108. Sale, *op. cit.,* 566–67.

109. *New Left Notes,* June 25, 1969.

110. Milton Viorst, *Fire in the Streets: America in the 1960's* (New York: Simon & Schuster, 1979), p. 487.

111. Andrew Kopkind, "The Real SDS Stands Up," in Jacobs, *Weatherman,* p. 27.

112. *National Guardian,* January 10, 1970.

113. *Ibid.*

5. Good Night, Sweet Prince

1. *New York Times,* January 2, 1968.

2. Eugene McCarthy, *The Year of the People* (Garden City, N.Y.: Doubleday, 1969), pp. 286–89.

3. Lewis Chester, Godfrey Hodgson, and Bruce Page, *An American Melodrama: The Presidential Campaign of 1968* (New York: Viking, 1969), p. 83.

4. Lawrence Wittner, *Rebels Against War: The American Peace Movement, 1933–1983* (Philadelphia: Temple University Press, 1984), p. 244.

5. *New York Review of Books,* September 16, 1965.

6. Robert Pickus, "Political Integrity and Its Critics," *Liberation,* June–July 1965, p. 39.

7. *National Guardian,* May 1, 1965.

8. Fred Halstead, *Out Now!: A Participant's Account of the American Movement Against the Vietnam War* (New York: Monad Press, 1978), p. 270.

9. Roger Rapoport, "Protest, Learning, Heckling Spark a Viet Rally," in Louis Menashe and Ronald Radosh (eds.), *Teach-Ins: U.S.A.* (New York: Praeger, 1967), p. 14.

10. Mark Pilisuk, "The First Teach-In: An Insight into Professional Activism," in Menashe and Radosh, p. 12.

11. Rapoport, in Menashe and Radosh, p. 16.

12. Pilisuk, in Menashe and Radosh, pp. 10–11.

13. Rapoport, in Menashe and Radosh, p. 15.

14. Halstead, *op. cit.,* p. 57.

15. Nancy Zaroulis and Gerald Sullivan, *Who Spoke Up?: American Protest Against the War in Vietnam, 1963–1975* (Garden City, N.Y.: Doubleday, 1984), p. 82.

16. Halstead, *op. cit.,* p. 215.

17. *Ibid.,* p. 255.

18. *Ibid.,* pp. 257–58.

19. *Ibid.,* p. 259.

20. Zaroulis and Sullivan, *op. cit.,* p. 110.

21. *New York Times,* April 13, 1967.

22. Halstead, *op. cit.,* p. 271.

23. *Ibid.,* p. 274.

24. Alice Lynd (ed.), *We Won't Go: Personal Accounts of War Objectors* (Boston: Beacon Press, 1968), p. 225.

25. Zaroulis and Sullivan, *op. cit.*, p. 112.

26. Richard Cummings, *The Pied Piper: Allard Lowenstein and the Liberal Dream* (New York: Grove, 1985), p. 337.

27. Chester, Hodgson, and Page, *op. cit.*, p. 62.

28. Lester and Irene David, *Bobby Kennedy: The Making of a Folk Hero* (New York: Dodd, Mead, 1986), p. 280.

29. Jack Newfield, *Robert Kennedy: A Memoir* (New York: Dutton, 1969), p. 185.

30. *Ibid.*, p. 189.

31. Cummings, *op. cit.*, p. 349.

32. *Ibid.*, p. 353.

33. Theodore H. White, *The Making of the President, 1968* (New York: Pocket Books, 1970), p. 92.

34. Michael Ferber and Staughton Lynd, *The Resistance* (Boston: Beacon Press, 1971), p. 122.

35. Halstead, *op. cit.*, p. 316.

36. Abbie Hoffman, *Soon to Be a Major Motion Picture* (New York: Perigee, 1980), p. 124.

37. Halstead, *op. cit.*, p. 322.

38. Zaroulis and Sullivan, *op. cit.*, p. 139.

39. *Ibid.*

40. *Ibid.* p. 142.

41. *New York Times*, October 26, 1967.

42. Jessica Mitford, *The Trial of Dr. Spock* (New York: Knopf, 1969), pp. 53–55.

43. Zaroulis and Sullivan, *op. cit.*, p. 149.

44. Paul Wieck, "McCarthy in California," *New Republic*, January 27, 1968, p. 15.

45. McCarthy, *op. cit.*, p. 68.

46. Ben Stavis, *We Were the Campaign: New Hampshire to Chicago for McCarthy* (Boston: Beacon Press, 1969), p. 5.

47. White, *op. cit.*, p. 107.

48. Arthur Herzog, *McCarthy for President* (New York: Viking, 1969), p. 97.

49. *Ibid.*, p. 98.

50. *Newsweek*, March 25, 1968.

51. Herzog, *op. cit.*, p. 106.

52. *Newsweek*, March 25, 1968.

53. Newfield, *op. cit.*, p. 228.

54. *Newsweek*, March 25, 1968.

55. Jules Witcover, *85 Days: The Last Campaign of Robert Kennedy* (New York: Putnam's, 1969), pp. 87–88.

56. *Ibid.*, p. 93.

57. *Newsweek*, January 1, 1968.

58. Herbert Parmet, *The Democrats: The Years After FDR* (New York: Oxford University Press, 1976), p. 6.

59. Paul Wieck, "ADA Goes for McCarthy," *New Republic*, February 23, 1968, p. 14.

60. *New York Times*, March 10, 1968.

61. Doris Kearns, *Lyndon Johnson and the American Dream* (New York: Harper & Row, 1976), p. 350.

62. *Atlanta Constitution*, January 2, 1968.

63. Chester, Hodgson, and Page, *op. cit.*, p. 263.

64. *Ibid.*, p. 267.

65. Philip Crass, *The Wallace Factor* (New York: Mason-Charter, 1976), p. 57.

66. Marshall Frady, *Wallace* (New York: World Publishing, 1968), p. 137.

67. *Ibid.*, p. 37.

68. *Ibid.*, p. 14.

69. *Facts on File 1968*, p. 54.

70. *Ibid.*

71. James Silver, "An Ex-Mississippian's Reflections on Wallace," *New Republic*, October 19, 1968, p. 19.

72. Chester, Hodgson, and Page, *op. cit.*, p. 666.

73. Herzog, *op. cit.*, p. 113.

74. Richard M. Scammon and Ben J. Wattenberg, *The Real Majority* (New York: Coward-McCann, 1970), p. 107.

75. Jeremy Larner, *Nobody Knows: Reflections on the McCarthy Campaign of 1968* (New York: Macmillan, 1970), p. 59.

76. Paul Wieck, "The Indiana Trial Run," *New Republic*, May 11, 1968.

77. *Newsweek*, April 8, 1968, p. 36.

78. Hal Higdon, "Indiana: A Test for Bobby Kennedy," *New York Times Magazine*, May 5, 1968, p. 32.

79. *Washington Post*, April 8, 1968.

80. *New York Times*, April 19, 1968.

81. Witcover, *op. cit.*, p. 106.

82. *Ibid.*, p. 116.

83. *New York Times*, April 13, 1968.

84. Witcover, *op. cit.*, p. 110.

85. William Vanden Heuval and Milton Gwirtzman, *On His Own: Robert Kennedy, 1964–1968* (Garden City, N.Y.: Doubleday, 1970), p. 328.

86. White, *op. cit.*, p. 213.

87. David Halberstam, *The Unfinished Odyssey of Robert Kennedy* (New York: Random House, 1969), p. 173.

88. *Ibid.*, p. 177.

89. *Newsweek*, June 10, 1968, p. 26.

90. Witcover, *op. cit.*, p. 217.

91. John H. Davis, *The Kennedys: Dynasty and Disaster, 1848–1984* (New York: McGraw-Hill, 1984), pp. 654–55.

92. Halberstam, *op. cit.*, p. 187.

93. Chester, Hodgson, and Page, *op. cit.*, pp. 302–303.

94. Halberstam, *op. cit.*, pp. 191–92.

95. *New Republic*, June 15, 1968.

96. Larner, *op. cit.*, p. 115.

97. *Ibid.*, p. 247.

98. Herzog, *op. cit.*, p. 188.

99. Stavis, *op. cit.*, p. 125.

100. *Washington Post*, June 6, 1968.

101. *Newsweek*, June 17, 1968.

102. *Washington Post*, June 6, 1968.

103. *Newsweek*, June 17, 1968.

104. Witcover, *op. cit.*, p. 281.

105. *Newsweek*, June 17, 1968.

6. The Personal Is Political

1. Abbie Hoffman, *Soon to Be a Major Motion Picture* (New York: Perigee Books, 1980), p. 137.

2. Milton Viorst, *Fire in the Streets: America in the 1960's* (New York: Simon & Schuster, 1979). p. 431.

3. Robert E. Spiller, Willard Thorp, Thomas Johnson, Henry Seidel Canby, Richard Ludwig (eds.), *Literary History of the United States* (London: Macmillan, 1963), p. 1413.

4. Allen Ginsberg, "Howl," in Thomas Parkinson (ed.), *A Casebook on the Beats* (New York: Crowell, 1961), p. 9.

5. Bruce Cook, *The Beat Generation* (New York: Scribner's, 1971), p. 63.

6. Dennis McNally, *Desolate Angel: Jack Kerouac, the Beat Generation, and America* (New York: Random House, 1979), p. 204.

7. Gerald Nicosia, *Memory Babe: A Critical Biography of Jack Kerouac* (New York: Grove, 1983), p. 556.

8. McNally, *op. cit.*, pp. 107–108.

9. Cook, *op. cit.*, p. 196.

10. Martin A. Lee and Bruce Shlain, *Acid Dreams: The C.I.A. and the Sixties Rebellion* (New York: Grove, 1985), p. xiv.

11. *Ibid.*, p. 13.

12. *Ibid.*, pp. 46–47.

13. *Ibid.*, p. 59.

14. *Ibid.*, p. 73.

15. Timothy Leary, *Flashbacks: An Autobiography* (Los Angeles: Tarcher, 1983), pp. 117–18.

16. *Ibid.*, p. 121.

17. *Ibid.*, p. 160.

18. Timothy Leary, "She Comes in Colors," in Leary, *The Politics of Ecstasy* (New York: Putnam's, 1968), pp. 127–30.

19. Andy Warhol and Pat Hackett, *POPism: The Warhol '60s* (New York: Harper & Row, 1980), p. 184.

20. Art Kleps, *Millbrook* (Oakland, Cal.: Bench Press, 1975), pp. 65–66.

21. *Ibid.*, p. 243.

22. Tom Wolfe, *The Electric Kool-Aid Acid Test* (New York: Bantam, 1969), p. 90.

23. Lee and Shlain, *op. cit.*, p. 147.

24. Charles Perry, *The Haight-Ashbury: A History* (New York: Rolling Stone Press, 1984), pp. 44–45.

25. Wolfe, *op. cit.*, p. 234.

26. Eileen Blumenthal, *Joseph Chaikin: Exploring at the Boundaries of Theater* (Cambridge, U.K.: Cambridge University Press, 1984), p. 14.

27. *Ibid.*, p. 42.

28. R. G. Davis, *The San Francisco Mime Troupe: The First Ten Years* (Palo Alto, Calif.: Ramparts, 1975), p. 70.

29. Myron Sharaf, *Fury on Earth: A Biography of Wilhelm Reich* (New York: St. Martin's, 1983), p. 164.

30. *Berkeley Barb*, August 11–18, 1967.

31. Herbert Marcuse, *Eros and Civilization: A Philosophical Inquiry Into Freud* (Boston: Beacon Press, 1966), p. 100.

32. *Ibid.*, p. 102.

33. *Ibid.*, p. 88.

34. From his book *Gestalt Therapy*, as quoted in Theodore Roszak, *The Making of a Counter Culture: Relfections on the Technocratic Society and Its Youthful Opposition* (New York: Anchor, 1969), p. 198. Italics in original.

35. John Gruen, *The New Bohemia: The Combine Generation* (New York: Grosset & Dunlap, 1966), p. 55.

36. *Ibid.*, p. 52.

37. Robert J. Glessing, *The Underground Press in America* (Bloomington: Indiana University Press, 1970), pp. 16–17.

38. Abe Peck, *Uncovering the Sixties: The Life and Times of the Underground Press* (New York: Pantheon, 1985), p. 15.

39. *Ibid.*, p. 40.

40. Kenneth Keniston, "The Alienated: The Rejection of Conventional Adulthood," in Keniston, *Youth and Dissent: The Rise of a New Opposition* (New York: Harcourt Brace Jovanovich, 1971), p. 178.

41. *Berkeley Barb*, May 12–16, 1967.

42. Carl Oglesby, "The Hippies: Suburbanites With Beads," *Activist*, Fall 1967, p. 12.

43. Wolfe, *op. cit.*, p. 199.

44. Perry, *op. cit.*, p. 96.

45. *Ibid.*

46. Hoffman, *op. cit.*, p. 122.

47. This was a play on the name of the notorious "Mad Bomber," George Metesky, who had terrorized New York in the 1950s.

48. Lee and Shlain, *op. cit.*, p. 160.

49. Helen Swick Perry, *The Human Be-In* (New York: Basic Books, 1970), p. 86.

50. Lee and Shlain, *op. cit.*, p. 162.

51. *Berkeley Barb*, April 21–27, 1967.

52. Nicholas Von Hoffman, *We Are the People Our Parents Warned Us Against: A Close-Up of the Whole Hippie Scene* (Greenwich, Conn.: Fawcett, 1968), p. 39.

53. *Ibid.*, p. 100.

54. Chester Anderson, "Two Page Racial Flap," handbill in New Left Collection, Hoover Institution Library, Stanford, Calif.

55. Perry, *op. cit.*, p. 114.

56. Don McNeill, "The Be-In Was the Beginning," in McNeill, *Moving Through Here* (New York: Knopf, 1970), p. 9.

57. Hoffman, *op. cit.*, p. 128.

58. *East Village Other*, September 1–15, 1967.

59. Warhol and Hackett, *op. cit.*, p. 269.

60. Ed Ward, Geoffrey Stokes, and Ken Tucker, *Rock of Ages: The Rolling Stone History of Rock and Roll* (New York: Rolling Stone Press, 1986), p. 431.

61. *Berkeley Barb*, October 7–13, 1967.

62. Laurence Leamer, *The Paper Revolutionaries: The Rise of the Underground Press* (New York: Simon & Schuster, 1972), p. 65.

63. *Berkeley Barb*, October 27, 1967, in Jesse Kornbluth (ed.), *Notes From the New Underground* (New York: Viking, 1968), pp. 283–85.

64. Peck, *op. cit.*, p. 122.

65. Raymond Mungo, *Famous Long Ago: My Life and Hard Times with Liberation News Service* (Boston: Beacon Press, 1970), p. 155.

66. *Ibid.*, p. 163.

67. Abbie Hoffman, *Revolution for the Hell of It* (New York: Dial, 1968), p. 58.

68. *Ibid.*, p. 61.

69. Jerry Rubin, *Do It!* (New York: Simon & Schuster, 1970), p. 113.

70. Hoffman, *Revolution*, p. 102.

71. John Sinclair, interview conducted by Bret Eynon, transcript in Eynon's possession.

72. *Fifth Estate*, as quoted in *Berkeley Barb*, November 29–December 5, 1968.

73. Judith Hole and Ellen Levine, *The Rebirth of Feminism* (New York: Quadrangle Books, 1971), p. 24.

74. Betty Friedan, *The Feminine Mystique* (New York: Dell, 1970), p. 94.

75. Hole and Levine, *op. cit.*, p. 88.

76. Sara Evans, *Personal Politics: The Roots of Women's Liberation in the Civil Rights Movement and the New Left* (New York: Vintage, 1979), p. 87.

77. *Ibid.*, p. 108.

78. *Ibid.*, p. 160.

79. Hole and Levine, *op. cit.*, p. 112.

80. Evans, *op. cit.*, p. 168.

81. *Catalog of Free University of Seattle*, Spring Session, 1967.

82. Evans, *op. cit.*, p. 199.

83. Hole and Levine, *op. cit.*, p. 114.

84. Evans, *op. cit.*, p. 200.

85. Hole and Levine, *op. cit.*, p. 121.

86. Susan Brownmiller, "'Sisterhood is Powerful': A Member of the Women's Liberation Movement Explains What It's All About," *New York Times Magazine*, March 15, 1970, p. 128.

87. Vivien Gornick, "Consciousness," *New York Times Magazine*, January 10, 1971, pp. 22, 77.

88. Brownmiller, *op. cit.*, p. 130. Emphasis in original.

89. "Redstockings Manifesto," in Robin Morgan (ed.), *Sisterhood is Powerful: An Anthology of Writings from the Women's Liberation Movement* (New York: Vintage, 1970), p. 534.

90. Ti-Grace Atkinson, "Vaginal Orgasm as a Mass Hysterical Response," (mimeographed) (New York: New York Feminists, 1968), p. 3.

91. Cellestine Ware, *Woman Power: The Movement for Women's Liberation* (New York: Tower, 1970), p. 29.

92. Betsy Warrior, "Man As An Obsolete Life Form," in Sookie Stambler (ed.), *Women's Liberation: Blueprint for the Future* (New York: Ace Books, 1970), p. 45.

93. Ti-Grace Atkinson, "Radical Feminism," in Shulamith Firestone and Ann Koedt (eds.), *Notes From the Second Year*, n.d., p. 34.

94. Valerie Solanis, "SCUM Manifesto," in Morgan, *Sisterhood*, pp. 514–19.

95. Anne Koedt, "The Myth of the Vaginal Orgasm," in Judith Clavir Albert and Stewart Edward Albert (eds.), *The Sixties Papers: Documents of a Rebellious Decade* (New York: Praeger, 1984), p. 473.

96. Shulamith Firestone, *The Dialectic of Sex: The Case for Feminist Revolution* (New York: Bantam, 1971), pp. 11–12.

97. Ellen Willis, "Radical Feminism and Feminist Radicalism," in Sohnya Sayres, Anders Stephenson, Stanley Aronowitz, and Frederic Jameson (eds.), *The 60s Without Apology* (Minneapolis: University of Minnesota Press, 1984), p. 103.

98. "The Feminists: A Political Organization to Annihilate Sex Roles," in Anne Koedt, Ellen Levine, and Anita Rapone (eds.), *Radical Feminism* (New York: Quadrangle Books, 1973), p. 370.

99. Una Stannard, "The Mask of Beauty," in Vivien Gornick and Barbara K. Moran, *Women in Sexist Society: Studies in Power and Powerlessness* (New York: New American Library, 1971), pp. 194, 196.

100. "No More Miss America!" in Morgan, *Sisterhood*, p. 522.

101. *New York Times*, September 8, 1968.

102. *Ibid.*

103. Robin Morgan, *Going Too Far: The Personal Chronicle of a Feminist* (New York: Vintage, 1978), p. 72.

104. Robin Morgan, "WITCH Hexes Wall Street," in *Going Too Far*, p. 75.

105. *Ibid.*

106. *Ibid.*, p. 77.

107. *Ibid.*, p. 74.

108. *Ibid.*, p. 81.

109. *New York Times*, Februrary 17, 1969.

110. John D'Emilio, *Sexual Politics, Sexual Communities: The Making of a Homosexual Minority in the United States, 1940–1970* (Chicago: University of Chicago Press, 1983), p. 232.

7. Nixon's the One!

1. Richard Nixon, *Memoirs of Richard Nixon* (New York: Grosset & Dunlap, 1978), pp. 292–93.

2. *Ibid.*, p. 294.

3. Fawn Brodie, *Richard Nixon: The Shaping of His Character* (New York: Norton, 1981), p. 357.

4. Stephen C. Shadegg, *Winning's a Lot More Fun* (London: Macmillan, 1969), p. 20.

5. *Ibid.*, p. 29.

6. *Ibid.*, p. 100.

7. *Ibid.*, p. 101.

8. Theodore H. White, *The Making of the President, 1968* (New York: Pocket Books, 1970), p. 74.

9. Shadegg, *op. cit.*, p. 131.

10. Joe McGinniss, *The Selling of the President, 1968* (New York: Pocket Books, 1970), p. 104.

11. Peter Collier and David Horowitz, *The Rockefellers: An American Dynasty* (New York: Holt, Rinehart & Winston, 1976), pp. 182–83.

12. Norman Mailer, *Miami and the Siege of Chicago: An Informal History of the Republican and Democratic Conventions of 1968* (New York: Signet, 1968), pp. 36–37.

13. *Ibid.*, p. 12.

14. Lewis Chester, Godfrey Hodgson, and Bruce Page, *An American Melodrama: The Presidential Campaign of 1968* (New York: Viking, 1969), p. 434.

15. *Ibid.*, p. 450.

16. *Ibid.*, p. 464.

17. Theo Lippman, Jr., *Spiro Agnew's America* (New York: Norton, 1972), p. 113.

18. White, *op. cit.*, p. 316.

19. Chester Hodgson, and Page, *op. cit.*, p. 497.

20. *Ibid.*

21. Nixon, *Memoirs*, p. 315.

22. Jeremy Larner, *Nobody Knows: Reflections on the McCarthy Campaign of 1968* (New York: Macmillan, 1970), p. 124.

23. Carl Solberg, *Hubert Humphrey: A Biography* (New York: Norton, 1984), p. 12.

24. Hubert H. Humphrey, *Education of a Public Man* (Garden City, N.Y.: Doubleday, 1976), pp. 301–303.

25. Solberg, *op. cit.*, p. 277.

26. *Ibid.*, pp. 332–33.

27. *Ibid.*

28. *Ibid.*, p. 339.

29. Nancy Zaroulis and Gerald Sullivan, *Who Spoke Up?: American Protest Against the War in Vietnam, 1963–1975* (Garden City, N.Y.: Doubleday, 1984), p. 176.

30. Milton Viorst, *Fire in the Streets: America in the 1960's* (New York: Simon & Schuster, 1979), p. 447.

31. Abbie Hoffman, *Soon to Be a Major Motion Picture* (New York: Perigee Books, 1980), p. 144.

32. *Ibid.*, p. 145.

33. Abe Peck, *Uncovering the Sixties: The Life and Times of the Underground Press* (New York: Pantheon, 1985), p. 118.

34. Daniel Walker, *Rights in Conflict: The Walker Report to the National Commission on the Causes and Prevention of Violence* (New York: Bantam, 1968), p. 52.

35. Peck, *op. cit.,* p. 108.

36. *Guardian,* August 24, 1968.

37. Walker, *op. cit.,* p. 54.

38. Solberg, *op. cit.,* p. 348.

39. Hoffman, *op. cit.,* p. 155.

40. Todd Gitlin, *The Whole World Is Watching: Mass Media and the Unmaking of the New Left* (Berkeley: University of California Press, 1980), p. 189.

41. Walker, *op. cit.,* p. 144.

42. *Ibid.,* p. 147.

43. *Ibid.*

44. Mailer, *op. cit.,* p. 101.

45. *Newsweek,* September 2, 1968, p. 24.

46. Chester Hodgson, and Page, *op. cit.,* p. 532.

47. *Ibid.,* p. 580.

48. Byron E. Shafer, *Quiet Revolution: The Struggle for the Democratic Party and the Shaping of Post-Reform Politics* (New York: Russell Sage Foundation, 1983), p. 28. Emphasis in original.

49. *Ibid.,* p. 29.

50. *Ibid.,* p. 32.

51. Walker, *op. cit.,* p. 166.

52. Zaroulis and Sullivan, *op. cit.,* p. 186.

53. Walker, *op. cit.,* p. 182.

54. *Ibid.*

55. Zaroulis and Sullivan, *op. cit.,* p. 187.

56. Walker, *op. cit.,* p. 187.

57. *Ibid.,* p. 211.

58. *Ibid.,* p. 239.

59. Zaroulis and Sullivan, *op. cit.,* p. 194.

60. White, *op. cit.,* p. 376.

61. Zaroulis and Sullivan, *op. cit.,* p. 196.

62. *Chicago Tribune,* August 29, 1968.

63. *Ibid.*

64. *Ibid.*

65. Solberg, *op. cit.,* p. 369.

66. Chester, Hodgson, and Page, *op. cit.,* p. 586.

67. *Ibid.,* p. 588.

68. McCarthy, *op. cit.,* p. 222.

69. Richard Scammon and Ben Wattenberg, *The Real Majority* (New York: Coward-McCann, 1970), p. 162.

70. Viorst, *op. cit.,* p. 459.

71. Solberg, *op. cit.,* p. 375.

72. *Ibid.,* p. 376.

73. McGinniss, *op. cit.,* p. 126.

74. Chester, Hodgson, and Page, *op. cit.,* p. 627.

75. White, *President, 1968,* pp. 403–404.

76. *Facts on File, 1968,* p. 414.

77. Lippman, *op. cit.,* p. 159.

78. *Ibid.,* p. 166.

79. *Ibid.*, p. 162.

80. *Newsweek*, October 7, 1968, p. 29.

81. Solberg, *op. cit.*, p. 381.

82. *Ibid.*

83. *Newsweek*, October 14, 1968, p. 31.

84. Solberg, *op. cit.*, p. 386.

85. *Facts on File, 1968*, p. 437.

86. Chester, Hodgson, and Page, *op. cit.*, p. 695.

87. *Ibid.*, pp. 699–700.

88. *Ibid.*, p. 705.

89. Nixon, *op. cit.*, p. 321.

90. McGinniss, *op. cit.*, pp. 6–7.

91. Martin Mayer, *The Teachers' Strike: New York, 1968* (New York: Perennial Library, 1969), p. 15.

92. Maurice R. Berube and Marilyn Gittell (eds.), *Confrontation at Ocean Hill–Brownsville: The New York School Strikes of 1968* (New York: Praeger, 1969), p. 5.

93. Diane Ravitch, *The Great School Wars: New York City, 1805–1973* (New York: Basic Books, 1974), p. 325.

94. Naomi Levine, *Ocean Hill–Brownsville: A Case History of Schools in Crisis* (New York: Popular Library, 1969), p. 76.

95. Julius Lester, *All Is Well* (New York: Morrow, 1976), pp. 151–52.

96. Berube and Gittell, *op. cit.*, p. 168.

97. *Ibid.*, p. 104.

98. Charles Kadushin, *The American Intellectual Elite* (Boston: Little, Brown, 1974), p. 78.

99. Jason Epstein, "The Brooklyn Dodgers," *New York Review of Books*, October 1968, p. 39.

100. Alexander Bloom, *Prodigal Sons: The New York Intellectuals and Their World* (New York: Oxford University Press, 1986), p. 336.

101. McGinniss, *op. cit.*, p. 16.

102. *Facts On File, 1968*, p. 446.

103. *Ibid.*, p. 447.

104. *Ibid.*, pp. 445–46.

105. McGinniss, *op. cit.*, p. 164.

106. White, *op. cit.*, p. 479.

107. *Ibid.*, p. 489.

Epilogue

1. Courtney G. Brooks, James M. Grimwood, and Lloyd S. Swenson, Jr., *Chariots for Apollo: A History of Manned Lunar Spacecraft* (Washington, D.C.: National Aeronautics and Space Administration, 1979), p. 278.

2. *New York Times*, December 24, 1968.

3. *Ibid.*, December 25, 1968.

4. Walter A. McDougall, *The Heavens and the Earth: A Political History of the Space Age* (New York: Basic Books, 1985), p. 303.

5. William V. Shannon, "The Year That Failed to Turn," *New York Times*, December 30, 1968.

Index